Lecture Notes in Computer Science 14777

The series Lecture Notes in Computer Science (LNCS), including its subseries Lecture Notes in Artificial Intelligence (LNAI) and Lecture Notes in Bioinformatics (LNBI), has established itself as a medium for the publication of new developments in computer science and information technology research, teaching, and education.

LNCS enjoys close cooperation with the computer science R & D community, the series counts many renowned academics among its volume editors and paper authors, and collaborates with prestigious societies. Its mission is to serve this international community by providing an invaluable service, mainly focused on the publication of conference and workshop proceedings and postproceedings. LNCS commenced publication in 1973.

Wei-Ngan Chin · Zhiwu Xu
Editors

Theoretical Aspects of Software Engineering

18th International Symposium, TASE 2024
Guiyang, China, July 29 – August 1, 2024
Proceedings

Editors
Wei-Ngan Chin
National University of Singapore
Singapore, Singapore

Zhiwu Xu
Shenzhen University
Guangdong, China

ISSN 0302-9743 ISSN 1611-3349 (electronic)
Lecture Notes in Computer Science
ISBN 978-3-031-64625-6 ISBN 978-3-031-64626-3 (eBook)
https://doi.org/10.1007/978-3-031-64626-3

This Springer imprint is published by the registered company Springer Nature Switzerland AG
The registered company address is: Gewerbestrasse 11, 6330 Cham, Switzerland

Preface

The International Symposium on Theoretical Aspects of Software Engineering (TASE) gathers together researchers and practitioners interested in new results and innovative advances in software engineering. It records the latest developments in formal and theoretical software engineering methods and techniques. TASE 2024 was the 18th International Symposium on Theoretical Aspects of Software Engineering, a series of symposia started in 2007 with the aim to bring together researchers and developers from academia and industry with an interest in the theoretical aspects of software engineering. In past years, TASE took place in Shanghai (2007), Nanjing (2008), Tianjing (2009), Taipei (2010), Xi'an (2011), Beijing (2012), Birmingham (2013), Changsha (2014), Nanjing (2015), Shanghai (2016), Sophia Antipolis (2017), Guangzhou (2018), Guilin (2019), Hangzhou (2020), Shanghai (2021), Cluj-Napoca (2022), and Bristol (2023).

TASE 2024 was held on July 29 – August 1, 2024 in Guiyang, China. This year we received 76 submissions covering different areas of theoretical software engineering. Each paper was single-blind reviewed by at least three reviewers and the Program Committee accepted 24 regular long papers and 2 short papers, leading to an attractive scientific program. This edition of TASE was enhanced by the presence of 2 keynote speakers, Nobuko Yoshida (University of Oxford, UK) and Zhenjiang Hu (Peking University, China).

TASE 2024 would not have succeeded without the deep investment and involvement of the Program Committee members and the external reviewers who evaluated and selected the best contributions. This event would not exist without the authors and contributors who submitted their proposals. We address our thanks to everyone—reviewers, authors, Program Committee members, and organization committee members—involved in the success of TASE 2024.

The EasyChair system was set up for the management of TASE 2024, supporting submission, review, and volume preparation processes. It proved to be a powerful framework. We thank Springer for the smooth cooperation in the production of this proceedings volume.

TASE 2024 was hosted and sponsored by Guizhou University, China. The local organization committee offered all the facilities to run the event in a lovely and friendly atmosphere. Many thanks to all the local organizers.

Lastly, we wish to express our special thanks to the steering committee members, in particular Shengchao Qin and Huibiao Zhu, for their valuable support.

May 2024

Wei-Ngan Chin
Zhiwu Xu

Organization

General Chairs

Yongbin Qin	Guizhou University, China
Huibiao Zhu	East China Normal University, China

Program Committee Chairs

Wei-Ngan Chin	National University of Singapore, Singapore
Zhiwu Xu	Shenzhen University, China

Program Committee

Yamine Ait Ameur	IRIT/INPT-ENSEEIHT, France
Guangdong Bai	University of Queensland, Australia
Liqian Chen	National University of Defense Technology, China
Yuqi Chen	ShanghaiTech University, China
Wei-Ngan Chin	National University of Singapore, Singapore
Zhe Hou	Griffith University, Australia
Daisuke Kimura	Toho University, Japan
Guoqiang Li	Shanghai Jiao Tong University, China
Yeting Li	Institute of Information Engineering, Chinese Academy of Sciences, China
Jiaxiang Liu	Shenzhen University, China
Yepang Liu	Southern University of Science and Technology, China
Teng Long	China University of Geosciences, China
Frederic Mallet	Université Côte d'Azur, France
Dominique Mery	Université de Lorraine, LORIA, France
Jun Pang	University of Luxembourg, Luxembourg
Yu Pei	Hong Kong Polytechnic University, China
Shengchao Qin	Xidian University, China
Xiaomu Shi	Institute of Software, Chinese Academy of Sciences, China
Yahui Song	National University of Singapore, Singapore

Jingyi Wang	Zhejiang University, China
Cheng Wen	Xidian University, China
Zhilin Wu	Institute of Software, Chinese Academy of Sciences, China
Lili Xiao	Donghua University, China
Hui Xu	Fudan University, China
Zhiwu Xu	Shenzhen University, China
Bai Xue	Institute of Software, Chinese Academy of Sciences, China
Naijun Zhan	Institute of Software, Chinese Academy of Sciences, China
Min Zhang	East China Normal University, China
Hengjun Zhao	Southwest University, China
Lixiao Zheng	Huaqiao University, China
Huibiao Zhu	East China Normal University, China

Additional Reviewers

Ehsan Ahmad
Jialun Cao
Junyong Chen
Florin Craciun
Darius Foo
Jingyang Li
Wenhua Li
Hongming Liu
Ping Lu
Zhi Ma
Stephan Merz
Koji Nakazawa
D. P. Nhat Nguyen
Weike Pan
Yinghui Pan
Adi Prabawa
Huijia Sun
Zeyu Sun
Vincent Trélat
Haijun Wang
Xiong Xu
Bin Zhang
Ye Zheng

DSL Engineering via Lifting Transformation (Invited Abstract)

Zhenjiang Hu

Key Laboratory of High Confidence Software Technologies, School of Computer Science, Peking University, Beijing, China
huzj@pku.edu.cn

Abstract. In the "software defines everything" era of information technology, safe and user-friendly domain-specific languages (DSLs) have gained increasing significance. These DSLs facilitate the direct representation of problems and algorithms tailored to specific professional fields, while empowering domain experts to intuitively craft code using domain-specific terminology and operations. However, developing DSLs tailored for domain experts remains a persistent challenge. Traditional embedded DSL design methodologies provide a rapid prototyping technique for DSL implementation, yet the close integration between the embedded DSL and the host language poses difficulties for domain experts unfamiliar with the host language. In this talk, I introduce a new approach to support rapid DSL implementation and the development of an IDE for the DSL. This approach incorporates an extensible general-purpose core language, a DSL definition technique leveraging syntactic sugars, and crucially, a lifting transformation for generating DSL implementations alongside an IDE optimized for DSL programming. We have devised a system, named Osazone, and employed it to create numerous DSLs, thereby demonstrating the flexibility, efficacy, and practicality of our approach in advancing domain-specific language engineering efforts.

Keywords: Domain Specific Language · Language Engineering · Type Lifting · Semantics Lifting

Contents

Protocol Conformance of Collaborative SPARQL Using Multiparty Session Types

Ari Hernawan and Nobuko Yoshida(✉)

University of Oxford, Oxford, UK
{ari.hernawan,nobuko.yoshida}@cs.ox.ac.uk

Abstract. Decentralised linked data gives users rights over their data while being accessible to other domains. The RDF (Resource Description Framework) and SPARQL have been the standard specifications for managing linked data for several years. Recent research and development introduce scalable, centralised and distributed RDF store engines with the SPARQL. However, writing SPARQL federated queries may grow more complex as the number of domain participants increases, presenting challenges such as source discovery, completeness and performance. This paper presents a SPARQL Query Template (SQT) that applies Multiparty Session Types (MPST) to determine the order of federated queries. We also guarantee protocol conformance between MPST and SPARQL relational algebra.

Keywords: Multiparty session types · SPARQL · Federated Query · Protocol Conformance

1 Introduction

The RDF (Resource Description Framework) and SPARQL 1.1[1] are the two W3C recommended standards for querying and manipulating linked data on the Web. Since SPARQL's introduction in 2008, significant research and technological advancements have supported RDF and SPARQL specifications. Many RDF repositories, such as DBpedia, UniProt (Universal Protein Resource) and Rhea, are publicly available to provide information from diverse domains [1–6]. DBpedia, for example, contains around 900 million triplets as of January 2021[2] and maintains a distributed infrastructure that extracts approximately 5500 triplets per second and 21 billion triples per release. In real-world applications, RDF datasets are often partitioned and built upon distributed environments [7].

There has been rigorous work on handling massive RDF datasets. One way to manage the datasets is by partitioning and distributing them under the same RDF engine or by decentralising them on domain-specific repositories. The latest distributed RDF engine implemented with a custom communication protocol

[1] https://www.w3.org/TR/sparql11-overview/.
[2] https://www.dbpedia.org/resources/latest-core/.

W.-N. Chin and Z. Xu (Eds.): TASE 2024, LNCS 14777, pp. 1–18, 2024.
https://doi.org/10.1007/978-3-031-64626-3_1

has shown superior performance compared to other centralised or MapReduce-based engines [7–16]. In addition, SPARQL 1.1 federated query allows merging data across decentralised repositories and heterogeneous RDF engines. Federated query processors have been improved in many aspects, including querying documents, query planner optimisation and sensitive data access policies [17–23]. A federated query execution framework depends on source selection as it determines which endpoints are relevant to evaluate a given query. The Source selection is a separate step before execution, aiming to reduce the number of requests to the RDF server, optimise resource allocations and minimise network overhead, improving overall query execution time.

Well-specified communication is crucial for distributed RDF engines and federated queries, leading to significant performance increases. For communication-focused programming, a framework of Multiparty Session Types (MPST) provides a typed process that abstracts communication between multiple participants into a global protocol (type) [24]. The theory formalise endpoint projection of the global description in the Web Services Choreography Description Language[3], but it can accommodate other diverse specifications [25]. We aim to integrate this typed theory with SPARQL. This theory matches common issues in the software development process and is essential for a collaborative team of engineers writing SPARQL. A global type (protocol) gives engineers a global view of federated query communication between RDF repositories. The engineers can validate their SPARQL federated query following a global protocol.

We highlight current SPARQL issues as follows. (1) *Source discovery*: Writing a SPARQL query that involves many RDF repositories and complex query joins can be burdensome; and (2) *Performance and completeness*: Query execution time depends on the performance of SPARQL runtime and federated communication cost. More importantly, the query must return a complete result.

This paper introduces a novel SPARQL Query Template (SQT) generator that leverages the benefits of Multiparty Session Types [24,26,27]. The theory notably gives some clarity to complex processes. The SQT generates federated query body syntax that includes the RDF URL source address and guarantees conformance with the projection of a given global type. Moreover, by using a global type to describe communication patterns, we can identify and prevent overhead communications, speed up query execution and ensure the completeness of the results.

In the remainder, Sect. 2 gives preliminaries of RDF, MPST and SPARQL relational algebra through examples. Section 3 illustrates a use case that motivates this work. We explain in detail how SQT produces query templates from a global type. Section 4 explains how local types conform to relational algebra. Section 5 evaluates different network communication costs associated with different implementations. Finally, Sect. 6 discusses current limitations and future works of current work.

[3] https://www.w3.org/2002/ws/chor/.

2 Preliminaries and Examples

This section introduces RDF notations, SPARQL relational algebra and MPST through simple examples.

2.1 RDF and SPARQL

Our basic definitions of RDF and SPARQL follow [28,29]. In addition, we add a representation of RDF graph [16] and conjunctive query [7].

Definition 1 (RDF Triple). *RDF terms* (t) *are consist of IRIs* ($\mathbf{I}$), *literals* ($\mathbf{L}$) *and blank nodes* ($\mathbf{B}$). *These terms form a triple or 3-tuple,* $\langle t_s, t_p, t_o\rangle \in (\mathbf{I} \cup \mathbf{B}) \times (\mathbf{I}) \times (\mathbf{I} \cup \mathbf{B} \cup \mathbf{L})$, *where* s, p *and* o *denote subject, predicate and object of the triple,* $\beta = \{s, p, o\}$.

A set of RDF triples indicates a semantic relationship between terms and can be represented as a directed graph [16]. We can construct and label multiple graphs into a dataset. However, for convenience, this paper focuses on a single graph in a dataset.

Definition 2 (RDF Dataset). *Dataset (D) is a set of triples. The semantic relationship on triples can be described as a directed labelled graph. A graph consists of vertices* (V) *and directed edges* (E), *denoted by* $D = \{V, E\}$. *Vertices* V *denotes a set of resource nodes* $t_s \cup t_o \in V$. *Edges* E *is a set of directed edges connecting the nodes in* V. *To simplify, the directed edge* $t_s \xrightarrow{t_p} t_o$ *is expressed by* $\langle t_s, t_p, t_o\rangle$.

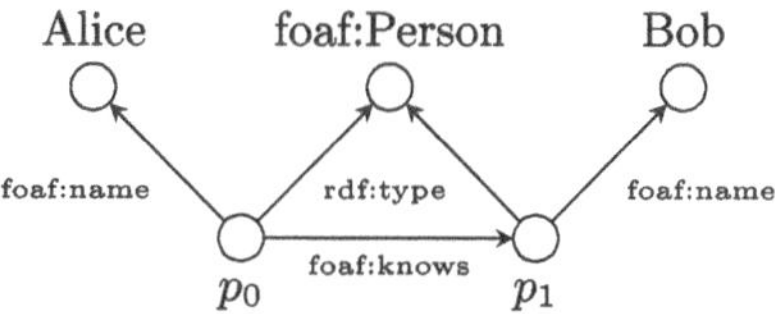

Fig. 1. RDF Dataset

Example 1. To illustrate, we define a dataset carrying a relation between Alice and Bob, presented as vertices and directed edges as shown in Fig. 1.

$$\begin{aligned} D &= \{V, E\} \\ V &= \{\text{Alice}, \text{Bob}, \text{foaf:Person}, p_0, p_1\} \\ E &= \{\langle p_0, \text{foaf:knows}, p_1\rangle, \langle p_0, \text{rdf:type}, \text{foaf:Person}\rangle, \\ &\quad \langle p_1, \text{rdf:type}, \text{foaf:Person}\rangle, \langle p_0, \text{foaf:name}, \text{Alice}\rangle, \langle p_1, \text{foaf:name}, \text{Bob}\rangle\} \end{aligned}$$

Definition 3 (SPARQL Query Template). *The SPARQL Query Template (SQT) syntax is denoted as follows:*

$$\begin{aligned} Q, Q' ::= & \ A && \textit{(triple pattern or atom)} \\ | & \ \mathcal{S}.Q' && \textit{(service federation)} \\ | & \ Q \wedge Q' && \textit{(group of basic graph pattern)} \end{aligned}$$

The SPARQL relational algebra formally defines a query language semantics [7,28,29]. A query's result or solution is a tuple containing variables from queries matched against the RDF dataset. This paper recursively constructs queries from graph patterns, including triple patterns, basic graph patterns and service federation.

Definition 4 (Triple Pattern or Atom). *Triple pattern or atom* (A) *forms* $\langle t_s, t_p, t_o \rangle \in (\mathbf{I} \cup \mathbf{B} \cup \mathbf{V}) \times (\mathbf{I} \cup \mathbf{V}) \times (\mathbf{I} \cup \mathbf{B} \cup \mathbf{L} \cup \mathbf{V})$ *where* $(\mathbf{V})$ *refers to variables. The variables occurring in an atom are denoted by* $vars(A)$*. The triple pattern evaluates RDF triples in* D *by selection function* (σ) *with constant terms* t_k *and by mapping function* (π) *that maps terms* t_j *to the variables* v_i*:*

$$A ::= \pi_{v_i \leftarrow t_j}(\sigma_{t_k}(D)) \qquad (\, j, k \in \beta \quad \text{and} \quad i \in \mathbb{N}\,)$$

$$vars(A) = \{t_\beta | t_\beta \cap \mathbf{V}\} \qquad (\, t_k \in (\mathbf{I} \cup \mathbf{B} \cup \mathbf{L}) \quad \text{and} \quad t_j \in (\mathbf{I} \cup \mathbf{B} \cup \mathbf{L} \cup \mathbf{V})\,)$$

Example 2. A query for finding a person's name on dataset D is defined as:

```
{?x foaf:name ?y}
```

This query translates to the relational operation:

$$\langle x, \text{foaf:name}, y \rangle = \pi_{x,y \leftarrow t_s,t_o}(\sigma_{t_p=\text{foaf:name}}(D))$$

The process begins with searching any triples in a dataset that match the selection's predicate, t_p = foaf:name $\in \mathbf{I}$. Here, we have two variables `?x` and `?y` in subject and object respectively. Subject $t_s \in \mathbf{I} \cup \mathbf{B} \cup \mathbf{V}$ and object $t_o \in \mathbf{I} \cup \mathbf{B} \cup \mathbf{L} \cup \mathbf{V}$ intersect with $\mathbf{V}$ and will be included in $vars(A) = \{t_s, t_o\}$.

Definition 5 (Basic Graph Pattern). *The basic graph pattern is a group of triple patterns. It can be expressed syntactically as a conjunctive query* Q *from finite set atoms, where* $vars(Q)$ *denotes variables occurring in the basic graph pattern.*

$$Q ::= A_1 \wedge \cdots \wedge A_n \qquad \text{and} \qquad vars(Q) = vars(A_1) \cup \cdots \cup vars(A_n)$$

Multiple triple patterns stacked together will construct a basic graph pattern [7]. The basic graph pattern variables are the union of all triple pattern variables. These graph patterns can be evaluated in a local or remote dataset, formalised in Definition 6 [29]. The definition of set variables also applies equally to remote datasets.

Definition 6 (Service Federation). *The SPARQL service ($\mathcal{S}$) is a query evaluation on a remote dataset. Query evaluation Q on remote service $\mathcal{S}$ is denoted as ($\mathcal{S}.Q$) while local query evaluation is denoted as (Q).*

The SPARQL query Q is evaluated over dataset D and then returns solution mapping that represents matched variables on triples in a dataset [29]. The solution mapping function is defined in Definition 7. We assume all variables are bounded and no error returns from the graph pattern.

Definition 7 (Solution Mapping Function). *A solution mapping (π) partially maps variables* $\mathbf{V}$ *from terms* $\mathbf{I} \cup \mathbf{B} \cup \mathbf{L}$. *Suppose* $\{v_i, \ldots, v_n\} \subseteq \mathbf{V}$ *and* $\{x_i, \ldots, x_n\} \subseteq vars(Q)$ *for* $n \in \mathbb{N}$. *Then we denote by* $\{v_i/x_i, \ldots, v_n/x_n\}$ *mapping function* π *such that the solution contains a set of* $dom(\phi) = \{v_i|x_i\}$.

$$\pi_{v_i} = x_i \quad (v_i \in dom(\pi)) \qquad and \qquad \pi_{\emptyset} = \emptyset \quad (dom(\pi) = \emptyset)$$

Example 3. Assume there are two datasets. The local dataset contains triples of persons. The remote dataset contains people's relations with each other. The first graph pattern is evaluated locally and the second pattern is service federation, which is evaluated on a remote dataset as shown in Fig. 2. The local graph pattern finds subject terms with type foaf:Person and map into variable ?x $\in \mathbf{I}$. Then, a service federation pattern finds the person ?y $\in \mathbf{I}$ that is acquainted with ?x. A complete query syntax is presented in Fig. 3.

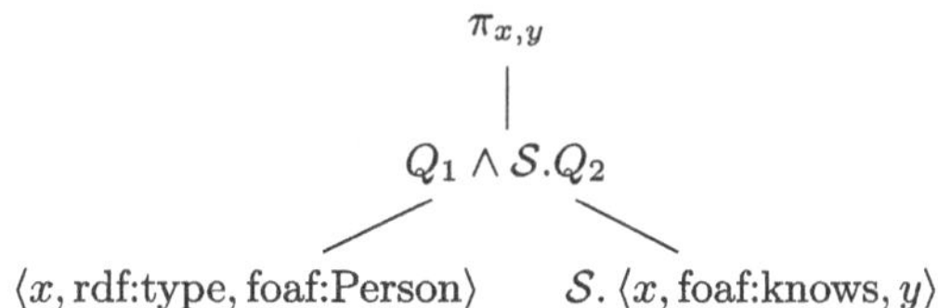

Fig. 2. SPARQL relational algebra

```
SELECT ?x ?y /* return variables */
WHERE {
  ?x rdf:type foaf:Person . /* graph pattern is evaluated on local dataset */
  SERVICE <https://remote>{
    ?x foaf:knows ?y . /* graph pattern is evaluated on remote dataset */
  }
}
```

Fig. 3. SPARQL 1.1 Query

2.2 Multiparty Session Types

Global types (protocol) G provides a blueprint describing communication between participants as a pair of a sender and a receiver [24,26,27]. In Definition 8, *message type* formalises protocol where p sends to q a value with type U Similarly, *branching type* formalises participant p chooses a label l_i from q for some $i \in I$. The *termination type* end denotes communication is finished and no further process.

Definition 8 (Global and Local Types). *The global type G and local type T are denoted as follows:*

$$
\begin{array}{ll}
G ::= \mathbf{end} \mid \mathtt{p} \to \mathtt{q} : [U]; G \mid \mathtt{p} \to \mathtt{q} : \{l_i : G_i\}_{i \in I} & \textit{(termination, message, branching)} \\
T ::= \mathbf{end} \mid \mathtt{q}!\,[U]; T \mid \mathtt{p}?\,[U]; T & \textit{(termination, send, receive)} \\
\quad \mid \mathtt{q} \oplus \{l_i : T_i\}_{i \in I} \mid \mathtt{p} \& \{l_i : T_i\}_{i \in I} & \textit{(internal choice, external choice)}
\end{array}
$$

We require that $\mathtt{p} \neq \mathtt{q}$, $I \neq \emptyset$, *and* $i \neq j$ *whenever* $i \neq j$, *for all* $i, j \in I$.

Local type T defines a process for a single participant following a global type G [24,26,27]. *Termination type* (**end**) denotes the end of a process. *Send type* $\mathtt{q}![U]; T$, sends a message to $\mathtt{q}$ with payload U *Receive type* $\mathtt{p}![U]; T$, waits for a message from $\mathtt{p}$ with payload U *External choice* $\mathtt{p}\&\{l_i : T_i\}_{i \in I}$ waits for selection label l_i from local type to $\mathtt{p}$ to continues. *Internal choice* $\mathtt{q}\oplus\{l_i : T_i\}_{i \in I}$ formalises a label selection l_i at $\mathtt{q}$ and continues.

Definition 9 (Participants). *We define the set of participants of a global type G as follows:*

$$
\begin{aligned}
pt(\mathbf{end}) &= \emptyset \\
pt(\mathtt{p} \to \mathtt{q} : [U]; G) &= \{\mathtt{p}, \mathtt{q}\} \cup pt(G) \\
pt(\mathtt{p} \to \mathtt{q} : \{l_i : G_i\}_{i \in I}; G) &= \{\mathtt{p}, \mathtt{q}\} \cup \textstyle\bigcup_{i \in I} pt(G_i)
\end{aligned}
$$

A set of participants in *message type* is their sender $\mathtt{p}$ and receiver $\mathtt{q}$ which are defined in a global type. Similarly, for *branching type*, a set of participants is the label sender $\mathtt{p}$ and label receiver $\mathtt{q}$. A *branching type* has multiple continuations G_i and the set of participants is a union from all branches. A *termination type* does not have continuation and does not involve any participants.

Definition 10 (Projection). *The projection of a global type G onto a participant $\mathtt{r}$ is defined as follows:*

$$
\begin{aligned}
\mathbf{end} \upharpoonright \mathtt{r} &= \mathbf{end} \\
\mathtt{p} \to \mathtt{q} : [U]; G \upharpoonright \mathtt{r} &= \begin{cases} \mathtt{q}![U]; G \upharpoonright \mathtt{r} & \mathtt{r} = \mathtt{p} \\ \mathtt{p}?[U]; G \upharpoonright \mathtt{r} & \mathtt{r} = \mathtt{q} \\ G \upharpoonright \mathtt{r} & \mathtt{r} \notin \{\mathtt{p}, \mathtt{q}\} \end{cases} \\
\mathtt{p} \to \mathtt{q} : \{l_i : G_i\}_{i \in I}; G \upharpoonright \mathtt{r} &= \begin{cases} \mathtt{q}\oplus\{l_i : G_i \upharpoonright \mathtt{r}\}_{i \in I} & \mathtt{r} = \mathtt{p} \\ \mathtt{p}\&\{l_i : G_i \upharpoonright \mathtt{r}\}_{i \in I} & \mathtt{r} = \mathtt{q} \\ \sqcap_{i \in I} G_i \upharpoonright \mathtt{r} & \mathtt{r} \notin \{\mathtt{p}, \mathtt{q}\} \end{cases}
\end{aligned}
$$

A global type can be projected into a local type of participant $G \upharpoonright \mathtt{r} = T_{\mathtt{r}}$. The *termination type* end does not transform during the projection. The projection of *message type* becomes a *send type* where $\mathtt{r} = \mathtt{p}$, $\mathtt{r}$ is a sender and becomes a *receive type* where $\mathtt{r} = \mathtt{q}$, $\mathtt{r}$ is a receiver. The *branching type* is projected to an *external choice* where $\mathtt{r} = \mathtt{p}$ and into an *internal choice* where $\mathtt{r} = \mathtt{q}$. Projection of *branching type* to the third participant $\mathtt{r}$, neither $\mathtt{p}$ nor $\mathtt{q}$, must specified to have the same continuation for any branch label.

Definition 11 (Global Type Reduction). *Evaluating* $\mathtt{p} \to \mathtt{q}$ *in global type* G *is defined as follows:*

(message reduction)

$$(\mathtt{p} \to \mathtt{q} : [U] ; G) \setminus \mathtt{p} \xrightarrow{U} \mathtt{q} = G$$

(pass message reduction)

$$(\mathtt{r} \to \mathtt{s} : [U] ; G) \setminus \mathtt{p} \xrightarrow{U'} \mathtt{q} = \mathtt{r} \to \mathtt{s} : [U]; (G \setminus \mathtt{p} \xrightarrow{U'} \mathtt{q})$$
$$\textit{if } \{\mathtt{r}, \mathtt{s}\} \cap \{\mathtt{p}, \mathtt{q}\} = \emptyset \textit{ and } \{\mathtt{p}, \mathtt{q}\} \subseteq G$$

(branching reduction)

$$(\mathtt{p} \to \mathtt{q} : \{l_i : G_i\}_{i \in I}) \setminus \mathtt{p} \xrightarrow{l} \mathtt{q} = G_i \qquad \textit{for } l = l_i$$

(pass branching reduction)

$$(\mathtt{r} \to \mathtt{s} : \{l_i : G_i\}_{i \in I}) \setminus \mathtt{p} \xrightarrow{l} \mathtt{q} = \mathtt{r} \to \mathtt{s} : \left\{l_i : G_i \setminus \mathtt{p} \xrightarrow{l} \mathtt{q}\right\}_{i \in I}$$
$$\textit{if } \{\mathtt{r}, \mathtt{s}\} \cap \{\mathtt{p}, \mathtt{q}\} = \emptyset \textit{ and } \forall i \in I : \{\mathtt{p}, \mathtt{q}\} \subseteq G_i$$

Message reduction $\mathtt{p} \xrightarrow{U} \mathtt{q}$ reduces the global type G with *message type* $\mathtt{p} \to \mathtt{q}$: $[U]$ and continues to the next protocol G. *Branching reduction* $\mathtt{p} \xrightarrow{l} \mathtt{q}$ reduces multiple label selection $\mathtt{p} \to \mathtt{q} : \{l_i : G_i\}_{i \in I}$ by choosing one label l_i then continue with G_i. *Pass reduction* applies when participants of reduction $\{\mathtt{p}, \mathtt{q}\}$ do not meet $\{\mathtt{r}, \mathtt{s}\}$ such as reduction $\mathtt{p} \xrightarrow{U} \mathtt{q}$ on $\mathtt{r} \to \mathtt{s}$: $[U]$ or $\mathtt{p} \xrightarrow{l} \mathtt{q}$ on $\mathtt{r} \to \mathtt{s} : \{l_i : G_i\}_{i \in I}$. The reduction continues through the rest of the global type until it meets the same participant.

3 Overview

Many research institutes [1–6] provide open RDF datasets. These datasets are often used towards drug discovery. Researchers use them to work with genomic, metabolomic, molecular structures, reaction pathways and screening drug candidates. The information resides in different domains and locations. Data integration and retrieval are the keys to comprehensive analyses. The SPARQL federated query techniques allow engineers to query remote datasets like a single unified database.

We use UniProt query example number 45[4] to cover all discussions in this paper. The use case describes a query of retrieving drug targets for human enzymes involved in sterol metabolism. The example uses three SPARQL endpoints, Rhea[5], UniProt[6] and Wikidata[7]. The query can be run directly at

[4] https://sparql.uniprot.org/.well-known/sparql-examples/?offset=40.

[5] https://sparql.rhea-db.org/sparql.

[6] https://sparql.uniprot.org/sparql.

[7] https://query.wikidata.org/sparql.

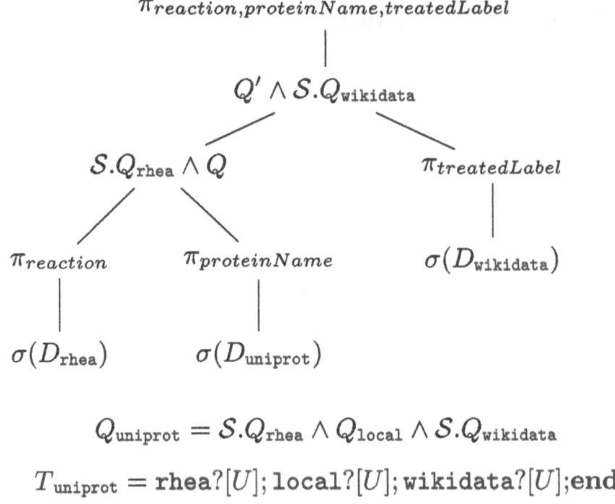

Fig. 4. The relational algebra of retrieving drug targets for human enzymes involved in sterol metabolism

UniProt query editor. Alternatively, it can be executed in Rhea or Wikidata but requires some rewriting at the federated query part. We aim to make it less tiring to write a federated query by modelling this in a global type.

We present a query relational algebra and its local type representation in Fig. 4. The query involves three participants: `rhea`, `uniprot` and `wikidata`. Query $Q_{\texttt{uniprot}}$ is evaluated at `uniprot`. Conjunctive query $Q_{\texttt{uniprot}}$ consists of two service federations and a local graph pattern. The query evaluation follows the sequence: Rhea, UniProt and Wikidata. First, `uniprot` evaluates federated query at `rhea` and retrieves reactions involving some molecules. Then, it joins the result with a local query at `uniprot` to find human enzymes that catalyse reactions. Finally, `uniprot` finds the interaction of enzymes from previous results with drug descriptions in `wikidata`. It is important to note that query $Q_{\texttt{uniprot}}$ and local type $T_{\texttt{uniprot}}$ are specifications for `uniprot` only. Other participants will need a different query algebra and a local type definition. The global type provides a global view and ensures accurate and consistent results across all participants during query execution.

4 Implementation of SQT Workflow

This section explains the workflow used to generate the SPARQL Query Template. The top-down diagram in Fig. 5 shows the process from global type to query template. We define global type G with four participants: `rhea`, `uniprot`, `wikidata` and `local`. The `local` participant physically does not exist. Instead, `local` acts as `rhea`, `uniprot` or `wikidata`.

We begin with building a global type G, in Example 4, using the Scribble script defined in Fig. 6. Suppose a script `Payload() from p to q;` the participant `q` expects a message return from `p`. This is defined as $\texttt{p} \to \texttt{q} : [U]$ where payload Ucontains free tuples of terms t_β. Here, `p` is a participant who owns a dataset and executes query Q either in a local or remote environment.

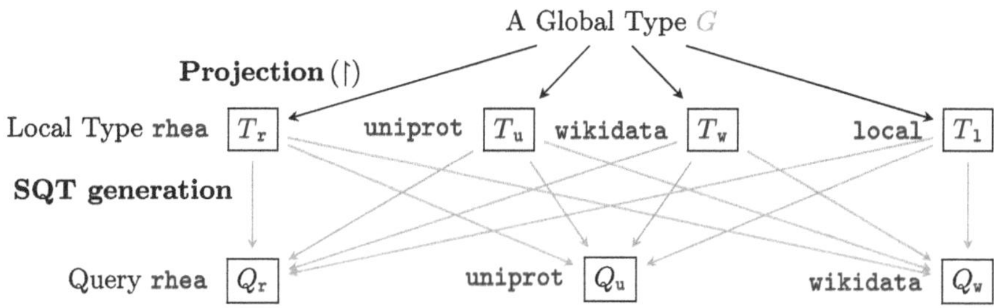

Fig. 5. Top-down view of global type for UniProt query number 45. The `r` stand for `rhea`, `u` for `uniprot`, `w` for `wikidata` and `l` stand for `local`

The global type is implemented in Scribble script in Fig. 6. Lines 4-8 represents $G_{\texttt{rhea}}$ a choice of `local` acts as `rhea`, lines 18-22, $G_{\texttt{uniprot}}$ where `local` as `uniprot` and lines 32-36, $G_{\texttt{wikidata}}$ where `local` as `wikidata`. Implementation of `rhea` evaluates query locally shown in line 10 and federated query in line 11. The definition of global type G is required to be projectable. Otherwise, it cannot produce any local types T and queries Q.

We introduce a *broadcast type* with the global type definition. The *broadcast type* formed as a sequence of *branching type* and uses one label that same as the previously selected branch. In Definition 12, participant $\mathtt{p}$ broadcast a l_i to $\bar{\mathtt{q}}$ is expressed by selecting a label l_i to a finite set number of participant $\bar{\mathtt{q}} = \{\mathtt{q}_1, \mathtt{q}_2, \dots \mathtt{q}_n\}$.

Definition 12 (Broadcast Type). *A broadcast type is sending or selecting the same label to multiple participants. A complete set of global type syntax with broadcast type is given as follows:*

$$G ::= \text{end} \mid \mathtt{p} \to \bar{\mathtt{q}} : [U]; G \quad \textit{(termination, message)}$$
$$\mid \mathtt{p} \to \bar{\mathtt{q}} : \{l_i : G_i\}_{i \in I} \quad \textit{(branching)}$$

$$\mathtt{p} \to \bar{\mathtt{q}} : [U]; G \stackrel{def}{=} \mathtt{p} \to \mathtt{q}_1 : [U]; \mathtt{p} \to \mathtt{q}_1 : [U]; \dots \mathtt{p} \to \mathtt{q}_n : [U]; G \quad \textit{(broadcast message)}$$

$$\mathtt{p} \to \bar{\mathtt{q}} : \{l_i : G_i\}_{i \in I} \stackrel{def}{=} \mathtt{p} \to \mathtt{q}_1 : \{l_i : \mathtt{p} \to \mathtt{q}_2 : \{l_i : \dots \mathtt{p} \to \mathtt{q}_n : \{l_i : G_i\}\}\}_{i \in I} \quad \textit{(broadcast branching)}$$

$$\textit{with } \bar{\mathtt{q}} = \{\mathtt{q}_1, \mathtt{q}_2, \dots, \mathtt{q}_n\} \qquad n \in \mathbb{N}$$

The broadcast reduction evaluates communication between participants of a *broadcast type* in global type G or continues to go through the next types when participants involved in broadcast type differ from the reduction criteria. Reducing *branching type* $\mathtt{p} \xrightarrow{l_i} \mathtt{q}_1$ or $\mathtt{p} \xrightarrow{l_i} \mathtt{q}_2$ in global type G can happen individually in a different order, but a broadcast reduction must reduce all $\bar{\mathtt{q}}$ together.

Definition 13 (Broadcast Reduction). *Evaluating a broadcast type in a global type G is defined as follows:*

(message reduction)

$$(\mathtt{p} \rightarrow \bar{\mathtt{q}} : [U] ; G) \setminus \mathtt{p} \xrightarrow{U} \bar{\mathtt{q}} \cong G$$

(pass message reduction)

$$(\mathtt{r} \rightarrow \bar{\mathtt{s}} : [U] ; G) \setminus \mathtt{p} \xrightarrow{U'} \bar{\mathtt{q}} \cong \mathtt{r} \rightarrow \bar{\mathtt{s}} : [U]; (G \setminus \mathtt{p} \xrightarrow{U'} \bar{\mathtt{q}})$$
$$\textit{if } \{\mathtt{r}, \bar{\mathtt{s}}\} \cap \{\mathtt{p}, \bar{\mathtt{q}}\} = \emptyset \textit{ and } \{\mathtt{p}, \bar{\mathtt{q}}\} \subseteq G$$

(branching reduction)

$$\mathtt{p} \rightarrow \bar{\mathtt{q}} : \{l_i : G_i\}_{i \in I} \setminus \mathtt{p} \xrightarrow{l} \bar{\mathtt{q}} \cong G_i \qquad l = l_i$$

(pass branching reduction)

$$\mathtt{r} \rightarrow \bar{\mathtt{s}} : \{l_i : G_i\}_{i \in I} \setminus \mathtt{p} \xrightarrow{l} \bar{\mathtt{q}} \cong \mathtt{r} \rightarrow \bar{\mathtt{s}} : \left\{ l_i : G_i \setminus \mathtt{p} \xrightarrow{l} \bar{\mathtt{q}} \right\}_{i \in I}$$
$$\textit{if } \{\mathtt{r}, \bar{\mathtt{s}}\} \cap \{\mathtt{p}, \bar{\mathtt{q}}\} = \emptyset \textit{ and } \forall i \in I : \{\mathtt{p}, \bar{\mathtt{q}}\} \subseteq G_i$$

Theorem 1 (Broadcast). *If $G \setminus \mathtt{p} \xrightarrow{l} \bar{\mathtt{q}} \cong G'$ then $G \setminus \mathtt{p} \xrightarrow{l} \mathtt{q}_1 \setminus \mathtt{p} \xrightarrow{l} \mathtt{q}_2 \cdots \setminus \mathtt{p} \xrightarrow{l} \mathtt{q}_n = G'$ where $n \in \mathbb{N}$ and $\bar{\mathtt{q}} = \{\mathtt{q}_1, \mathtt{q}_2, \ldots, \mathtt{q}_n\}$.*

Proof. By induction on n and G.

Example 4. We formalise a global type for UniProt query number 45 as follows:

$$I = \{\mathtt{rhea}, \mathtt{uniprot}, \mathtt{wikidata}\}$$
$$G = \mathtt{local} \rightarrow \mathtt{rhea}\{l_i : \mathtt{local} \rightarrow \mathtt{uniprot}\{l_i : \mathtt{local} \rightarrow \mathtt{wikidata}\{l_i : G_i\}\}\}_{i \in I}$$

$$\begin{aligned} G_{\mathtt{rhea}} &= \mathtt{local} \rightarrow \mathtt{rhea} : [U]; \mathtt{uniprot} \rightarrow \mathtt{rhea} : [U]; \\ &\quad \mathtt{wikidata} \rightarrow \mathtt{rhea} : [U]; \mathrm{end} \\ G_{\mathtt{uniprot}} &= \mathtt{rhea} \rightarrow \mathtt{uniprot} : [U]; \mathtt{local} \rightarrow \mathtt{uniprot} : [U]; \\ &\quad \mathtt{wikidata} \rightarrow \mathtt{uniprot} : [U]; \mathrm{end} \\ G_{\mathtt{wikidata}} &= \mathtt{rhea} \rightarrow \mathtt{wikidata} : [U]; \mathtt{uniprot} \rightarrow \mathtt{wikidata} : [U]; \\ &\quad \mathtt{local} \rightarrow \mathtt{wikidata} : [U]; \mathrm{end} \end{aligned}$$

Below is a global type reduction for `local` by choosing label $l_i = l$:

$$G \setminus \mathtt{local} \xrightarrow{l} \{\mathtt{rhea}, \mathtt{uniprot}, \mathtt{wikidata}\} = G_i$$

Algorithm 1 translates a global type to a query template, following translation on Table 1. The algorithm has two inputs, the projection of global protocol $G \upharpoonright \mathtt{p}$ and target participant $\mathtt{q}$ where a query will be executed. Suppose we use a global type G in Example 4 to build a query template for `uniprot`. This global type G has three branches for different continuations: $G_{\mathtt{rhea}}$, $G_{\mathtt{uniprot}}$ and $G_{\mathtt{wikidata}}$. Initially, we set $\mathtt{p} = \mathtt{uniprot}$ for $G \upharpoonright \mathtt{p}$ and participant $\mathtt{q} = \mathtt{uniprot}$. Next, global type G reduced by selecting a branch for `uniprot`, $\setminus \mathtt{local} \xrightarrow{1} \bar{\mathtt{s}}$ where $l = \mathtt{q}$ and $\bar{\mathtt{s}} = \{\mathtt{rhea}, \mathtt{uniprot}, \mathtt{wikidata}\}$. Selecting label $l_i = l$ continues

```
global protocol FederatedQuery(role Local, role Rhea, role UniProt,role Wikidata){
    choice at Local{
        /* Local tells everyone that it chooses to act as Rhea */
        Rhea() from Local to Rhea;
        choice at Local{
            Rhea() from Local to UniProt;
            choice at Local{
                Rhea() from Local to Wikidata;
                /* Rhea */
                Select(reaction) from Local to Rhea;
                Select(protein,proteinFullName) from UniProt to Rhea;
                Select(chemical,chemicalLabel,treatedLabel) from Wikidata to Rhea;
            }
        }
    }
    or {
        /* Local tells everyone that it chooses to act as UniProt */
        UniProt() from Local to Rhea;
        choice at Local{
            UniProt() from Local to UniProt;
            choice at Local{
                UniProt() from Local to Wikidata;
                /* UniProt */
                Select(reaction) from Rhea to UniProt;
                Select(protein,proteinFullName) from Local to UniProt;
                Select(chemical,chemicalLabel,treatedLabel) from Wikidata to UniProt;
            }
        }
    }
    or {
        /* Local tells everyone that it chooses to act as Wikidata */
        Wikidata() from Local to Rhea;
        choice at Local{
            Wikidata() from Local to UniProt;
            choice at Local{
                Wikidata() from Local to Wikidata;
                /* Wikidata */
                Select(reaction) from Rhea to Wikidata;
                Select(protein,proteinFullName) from UniProt to Wikidata;
                Select(chemical,chemicalLabel,treatedLabel) from Local to Wikidata;
            }
        }
    }
}
```

Fig. 6. Scribble script of global type for UniProt query number 45

with G_i shows the role of `local` which can either become `rhea` following with $G_{\texttt{rhea}}$, `uniprot` with $G_{\texttt{uniprot}}$, or `wikidata` with $G_{\texttt{wikidata}}$.

The Algorithm 1 at line number 2 evaluates $G_i \upharpoonright \texttt{p}$ whether it is an empty (**end**) or continues to be translated. In the case of $\texttt{p} = \texttt{q}$, a *message type* in $G_i \upharpoonright \texttt{p} = \texttt{r}?[U]$ and `r` is a `local` then translates a message type to a query Q. This query will be executed locally at `p`. On the other hand, the message type is translated to service federation $\mathcal{S}_{\texttt{p}}.Q$, when `p` is neither `local` or current target participant `q`. In summary, $G_{\texttt{uniprot}} \upharpoonright \texttt{uniprot}$ translates to a local query in `uniprot` and $G_{\texttt{uniprot}} \upharpoonright \texttt{rhea}$ explains that `uniprot` sends and evaluates a query to `rhea`.

Table 1 only considers a *message type* to be translated directly into a query. The **end** type is translated to nothing and represents the end of a query. However,

Table 1. Translation of local type and SPARQL relational algebra

Local type ($T_{\mathtt{q}} = G \upharpoonright \mathtt{q}$)		**SPARQL algebra** (Q_q)
$[\![\mathbf{end}]\!]$	=	$\emptyset$
$[\![\mathtt{p}?\,[U]\,;G \upharpoonright \mathtt{q}]\!] \quad \mathtt{p} \neq \mathit{Local}$	=	$\mathcal{S}_p.[\![G \upharpoonright \mathtt{p}]\!] \wedge [\![G \upharpoonright \mathtt{q}]\!]$
$[\![\mathtt{p}?\,[U]\,;G \upharpoonright \mathtt{q}]\!] \quad \mathtt{p} = \mathit{Local}$	=	$Q_{\mathtt{q}} \wedge [\![G \upharpoonright \mathtt{q}]\!]$
$[\![\mathtt{p}\,!\,[U]\,;G \upharpoonright \mathtt{q}]\!]$	=	$[\![G \upharpoonright \mathtt{q}]\!]$
$[\![\mathtt{p}\oplus\{l_i : G_i \upharpoonright \mathtt{q}\}_{i\in I}]\!]$	=	$[\![G_i \upharpoonright \mathtt{q}]\!]_{i\in I}$
$[\![\mathtt{p}\&\{l_i : G_i \upharpoonright \mathtt{q}\}_{i\in I}]\!]$	=	$[\![G_i \upharpoonright \mathtt{q}]\!]_{i\in I}$

internal choice and *external choice*, defined in Table 1, do not have a query translation. Instead, it continues to translate the following local types. Although it does not have query translation, it plays an essential part in the reduction process by deciding what is `local` participant role will be.

In a simple federation query where `uniprot` calls federation service to both `rhea` and `wikidata`. Here, `rhea` and `wikidata` send their result directly to `uniprot` and do not expect to receive a result from calling another federation service. Both local types $T_{\mathtt{rhea}}$ and $T_{\mathtt{wikidata}}$ define $\mathtt{rhea}![U]$ which does not translate to any queries. The algorithm continues to read recursively and reduces the local type from all participants until it is finished.

In a nested service federation, each local type for three participants, including `rhea`, `uniprot` and `wikidata` may have called a federation service to other participants. For example, `wikidata` expects a federation service result from `uniprot`, $T_{\mathtt{wikidata}} = \mathtt{uniprot}?[U]$. Meanwhile, `uniprot` is waiting federation service result from `rhea` before it can be sent to `wikidata`, $T_{\mathtt{uniprot}} = \mathtt{rhea}?[U];\mathtt{wikidata}![U]$. The SQT algorithm requires definitions from all participant's local types in order

Algorithm 1. Construct SPARQL Query Template

function $\mathrm{SQT}(G \upharpoonright \mathtt{p}, \mathtt{q})$ ▷ begin with $p = q$ where $\mathtt{p}, \mathtt{q} \in \mathit{pt}(G) \setminus \{\mathtt{local}\}$
  while $(G \setminus \mathtt{local} \xrightarrow{l} \bar{\mathtt{s}}) \upharpoonright \mathtt{p} \neq \mathbf{end}; l = \mathtt{q}$ **do** ▷ $\bar{\mathtt{s}} = \mathit{pt}(G) \setminus \{\mathtt{local}\}$
    if $T_{\mathtt{p}} = \mathtt{r}?[U]$ **then** ▷ $\mathtt{p} \neq \mathtt{r}; \mathtt{r} \in \mathit{pt}(G)$
      if $\mathtt{r} = \mathtt{local}$ **then**
        $Q_{\mathtt{q}} \leftarrow [\![\mathtt{r}?[U]]\!]$ ▷ local query Q
      else
        $\mathcal{S}_{\mathtt{r}}.(Q_{\mathtt{q}}) \leftarrow \mathrm{SQT}(G \upharpoonright \mathtt{r}, \mathtt{q})$ ▷ federated query $\mathcal{S}.Q$
      end if
    end if
    $Q'_{\mathtt{q}} = Q_{\mathtt{q}} \wedge \mathcal{S}_{\mathtt{r}}.Q_{\mathtt{q}} \wedge \cdots \wedge \mathcal{S}_{\mathtt{r}'}.Q_{\mathtt{q}}$ ▷ Conjunctive query
  end while
  return $Q'_{\mathtt{q}}$
end function

to generate a complete query template. The algorithm begins by generating a local query and service federation for target participant q then calling a related local type to generate a query in federated service.

5 Evaluation

We conduct experiments in the docker environment. We build a small-scale environment with three Apache Fuseki containers and a triple dataset to imitate Rhea, UniProt and Wikidata. For statistics `rhea` contains 2051 triples, `uniprot` 129902 triples and `wikidata` 6592 triples. We record the elapsed projection time, constructing SQT and performance differences between variants of federated query communication that follow the current use case.

Example 5. We formalise the general structure of a global protocol (type) for a current evaluation as follows:

$$G \setminus \texttt{local} \xrightarrow{l} \bar{\texttt{q}} = G' \qquad \textit{where} \qquad l \in \textit{pt}(G) \setminus \{\texttt{local}\}$$

We prepare global type G following Example 5. We assign varying numbers of participants to global type G: 10, 30, and 60. Table 2 shows the elapsed time for constructing SQT. The projection column shows the time needed to generate all local types. It shows that increasing the number of participants will result in a longer elapsed time.

We prepared three global types following Example 5 for service federation performance. We define each global type to have three specifications for `rhea`, `uniprot` and `wikidata`. We have nine different test cases in total. Global type G_1 calls two remote service federations from one participant, following Example 4. However, global types G_2 and G_3 call nested service federations. Global type G_2 is given in Example 6.

Example 6. Based on the global type in Example 5, we define $G_{\texttt{uniprot}}$ such that `uniprot` can only call `rhea` service federation through `wikidata`. The complete

Table 2. Construction time for single query

Number of participants in G	Time (second)	
	Projection (total)	SQT (average)
10 participants	0.445	0.321
30 participants	2.720	0.724
60 participants	30.624	1.429

continuation of global type G_i for nested service federation defined as follows:

$$\begin{aligned}
I &= \{\texttt{rhea}, \texttt{uniprot}, \texttt{wikidata}\} \\
G_{\texttt{rhea}} &= \texttt{local} \to \texttt{rhea} : [U]; \texttt{uniprot} \to \texttt{rhea} : [U]; \\
&\quad \texttt{wikidata} \to \texttt{uniprot} : [U]; \text{end} \\
G_{\texttt{uniprot}} &= \texttt{rhea} \to \texttt{wikidata} : [U]; \texttt{wikidata} \to \texttt{uniprot} : [U]; \\
&\quad \texttt{local} \to \texttt{uniprot} : [U]; \texttt{wikidata} \to \texttt{uniprot} : [U]; \text{end} \\
G_{\texttt{wikidata}} &= \texttt{rhea} \to \texttt{wikidata} : [U]; \texttt{uniprot} \to \texttt{rhea} : [U]; \\
&\quad \texttt{local} \to \texttt{wikidata} : [U]; \text{end}
\end{aligned}$$

Table 3. Query elapsed time from different global protocol

Query Template	**Elapsed time** (second)
1. $[\![(G_1 \setminus \texttt{l} \xrightarrow{\texttt{r}} \texttt{r},\texttt{u},\texttt{w}) \upharpoonright \texttt{r}]\!] = Q_{\texttt{r}} \wedge \mathcal{S}_{\texttt{u}}.Q_{\texttt{r}} \wedge \mathcal{S}_{\texttt{w}}.Q_{\texttt{r}}$	23.160
2. $[\![(G_1 \setminus \texttt{l} \xrightarrow{\texttt{u}} \texttt{r},\texttt{u},\texttt{w}) \upharpoonright \texttt{u}]\!] = \mathcal{S}_{\texttt{r}}.Q_{\texttt{u}} \wedge Q_{\texttt{u}} \wedge \mathcal{S}_{\texttt{w}}.Q_{\texttt{u}}$	12.255
3. $[\![(G_1 \setminus \texttt{l} \xrightarrow{\texttt{w}} \texttt{r},\texttt{u},\texttt{w}) \upharpoonright \texttt{w}]\!] = \mathcal{S}_{\texttt{r}}.Q_{\texttt{w}} \wedge \mathcal{S}_{\texttt{u}}.Q_{\texttt{w}} \wedge Q_{\texttt{w}}$	11.334
4. $[\![(G_2 \setminus \texttt{l} \xrightarrow{\texttt{r}} \texttt{r},\texttt{u},\texttt{w}) \upharpoonright \texttt{r}]\!] = Q_{\texttt{r}} \wedge \mathcal{S}_{\texttt{u}}(Q_{\texttt{r}} \wedge \mathcal{S}_{\texttt{w}}.Q_{\texttt{r}})$	24.500
5. $[\![(G_2 \setminus \texttt{l} \xrightarrow{\texttt{u}} \texttt{r},\texttt{u},\texttt{w}) \upharpoonright \texttt{u}]\!] = \mathcal{S}_{\texttt{w}}(\mathcal{S}_{\texttt{r}}.Q_{\texttt{u}}) \wedge Q_{\texttt{u}} \wedge \mathcal{S}_{\texttt{w}}.Q_{\texttt{u}}$	14.824
6. $[\![(G_2 \setminus \texttt{l} \xrightarrow{\texttt{w}} \texttt{r},\texttt{u},\texttt{w}) \upharpoonright \texttt{w}]\!] = \mathcal{S}_{\texttt{r}}(Q_{\texttt{w}} \wedge \mathcal{S}_{\texttt{u}}.Q_{\texttt{w}}) \wedge Q_{\texttt{w}}$	13.076
7. $[\![(G_3 \setminus \texttt{l} \xrightarrow{\texttt{r}} \texttt{r},\texttt{u},\texttt{w}) \upharpoonright \texttt{r}]\!] = Q_{\texttt{r}} \wedge \mathcal{S}_{\texttt{w}}(\mathcal{S}_{\texttt{u}}.Q_{\texttt{r}} \wedge Q_{\texttt{r}})$	23.084
8. $[\![(G_3 \setminus \texttt{l} \xrightarrow{\texttt{u}} \texttt{r},\texttt{u},\texttt{w}) \upharpoonright \texttt{u}]\!] = \mathcal{S}_{\texttt{r}}.Q_{\texttt{u}} \wedge Q_{\texttt{u}} \wedge \mathcal{S}_{\texttt{r}}(\mathcal{S}_{\texttt{w}}.Q_{\texttt{u}})$	19.786
9. $[\![(G_3 \setminus \texttt{l} \xrightarrow{\texttt{w}} \texttt{r},\texttt{u},\texttt{w}) \upharpoonright \texttt{w}]\!] = \mathcal{S}_{\texttt{u}}(\mathcal{S}_{\texttt{r}}.Q_{\texttt{w}} \wedge Q_{\texttt{w}}) \wedge Q_{\texttt{w}}$	4.241

We define a simplified notation in Table 3, `l` for `local`, `r` for `rhea`, `u` for `uniprot` and `w` for `wikidata`. We show federated query elapsed time with different communication sequences. Suppose we take the first case in Table 3 which is generating a query template for `rhea`, $Q'_{\texttt{r}} = Q_{\texttt{r}} \wedge \mathcal{S}_{\texttt{u}}.Q_{\texttt{r}} \wedge \mathcal{S}_{\texttt{w}}.Q_{\texttt{r}}$. Based on Algorithm 1 and an input data $[\![(G_1 \setminus \texttt{l} \xrightarrow{\texttt{r}} \texttt{r},\texttt{u},\texttt{w}) \upharpoonright \texttt{r}]\!]$, global type G_1 is reduced by telling every participant that `local` will acts as `rhea` under reduction of $G_1 \setminus \texttt{local} \xrightarrow{\texttt{rhea}} \{\texttt{rhea}, \texttt{uniprot}, \texttt{wikidata}\}$. This syntactically will produce $G_{\texttt{rhea}}$. Global type is projected to `rhea`, $G_{\texttt{rhea}} \upharpoonright \texttt{rhea} = T_{\texttt{rhea}}$, before being translated into a query with Table 1.

The first query template in Table 3 has an overhead communication exchange between participants, as shown in Fig. 7a and local type definitions. Based on the query execution sequence in Fig. 4, a result from `rhea` must join with `uniprot` to retrieve reactions and related human enzymes. Next, a result must join with `wikidata` to find interactions between those previous enzymes and drug descriptions. Ideally, `uniprot` sends the join result directly to `wikidata` but local type

$T_{\mathtt{u}} = \mathtt{r}![U];\mathbf{end}$ defines a communication that **`uniprot`** can send only to **`rhea`**. The communication **`uniprot`** to **`wikidata`** passes through **`rhea`** first and continues to **`wikidata`** together with federated query $\mathcal{S}_{\mathtt{w}}.Q_{\mathtt{r}}$. Finally, **`wikidata`** sends result back to **`rhea`**. This causes a longer execution time because **`uniprot`** cannot send directly to **`wikidata`** and must pass **`rhea`** first.

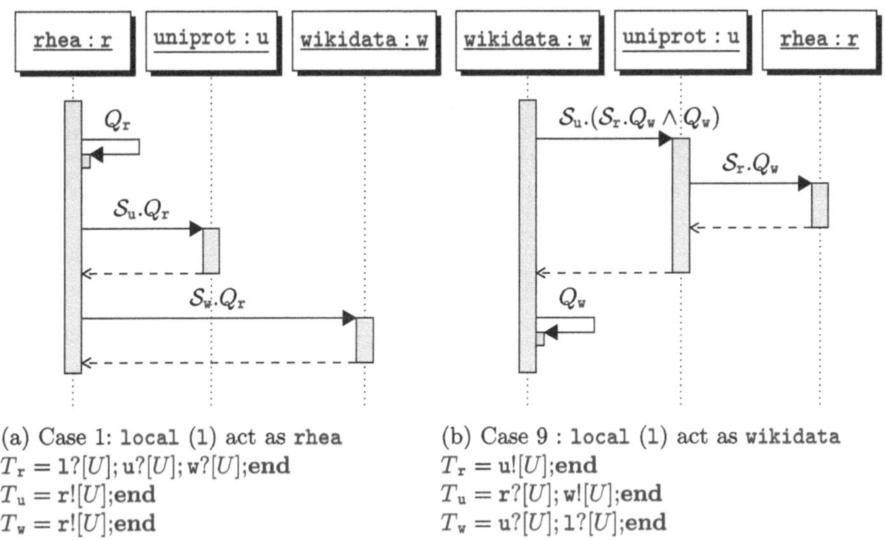

(a) Case 1: `local` (`l`) act as **`rhea`**
$T_{\mathtt{r}} = \mathtt{l}?[U]; \mathtt{u}?[U]; \mathtt{w}?[U];\mathbf{end}$
$T_{\mathtt{u}} = \mathtt{r}![U];\mathbf{end}$
$T_{\mathtt{w}} = \mathtt{r}![U];\mathbf{end}$

(b) Case 9 : `local` (`l`) act as **`wikidata`**
$T_{\mathtt{r}} = \mathtt{u}![U];\mathbf{end}$
$T_{\mathtt{u}} = \mathtt{r}?[U]; \mathtt{w}![U];\mathbf{end}$
$T_{\mathtt{w}} = \mathtt{u}?[U]; \mathtt{l}?[U];\mathbf{end}$

Fig. 7. Federated service implementation between two global protocols

In contrast, case number 9 makes the most efficient communication as shown in Fig. 7b, as the join result is sent directly to the next target participant without an intermediary. According to local type $T_{\mathtt{r}} = \mathtt{u}![U];\mathbf{end}$, **`rhea`** sends directly to **`uniprot`**. Next, **`uniprot`** sends a query result to **`wikidata`** as a final destination, $T_{\mathtt{u}} = \mathtt{r}?[U]; \mathtt{w}![U];\mathbf{end}$.

6 Conclusion

The current SQT (SPARQL Query Template) algorithm is a convenient and faster way of generating queries than writing them manually. The use of global types helps identify RDF sources by checking the interaction between participants. Global types ensure that executing queries on all projections will provide a complete result set. Moreover, the communication sequence described in global types can also be used to check for any overhead communication during a federated query. These benefits can significantly reduce network costs and ultimately make federated queries faster. In addition, we introduce a broadcast reduction for global types and prove its soundness against the original semantics of global types.

Acknowledgements. The first author is funded by the LPDP Indonesian Endowment Fund for Education from the Ministry of Finance of the Republic of Indonesia. This research is funded in part by EPSRC EP/T006544/2, EP/K011715/1, EP/K034413/1, EP/L00058X/1, EP/N027833/2, EP/N028201/1, EP/T014709/2, EP/V000462/1, EP/X015955/1, NCSS/EPSRC VeTSS and Horizon EU TaRDIS 101093006.

References

1. Mendes, P.N., Jakob, M., García-Silva, A., Bizer, C.: DBpedia spotlight: shedding light on the web of documents. In: Proceedings of the 7th International Conference on Semantic Systems, I-Semantics 2011, pp. 1–8. Association for Computing Machinery, New York (2011). https://doi.org/10.1145/2063518.2063519
2. Bateman, A., et al.: UniProt: the universal protein knowledgebase in 2023. Nucleic Acids Res. **51**(D1), D523–D531 (2023)
3. Bansal, P., et al.: Rhea, the reaction knowledgebase in 2022. Nucleic Acids Res. **50**(D1), D693–D700 (2022). https://academic.oup.com/nar/article/50/D1/D693/6424769
4. Aleksander, S.A., et al.: The Gene Ontology knowledgebase in 2023. GENETICS **224**(1) (2023). https://academic.oup.com/genetics/article/doi/10.1093/genetics/iyad031/7068118
5. Bauer-Mehren, A., Bundschus, M., Rautschka, M., Mayer, M.A., Sanz, F., Furlong, L.I.: Gene-disease network analysis reveals functional modules in mendelian, complex and environmental diseases. PLoS ONE **6**(6), e20284 (2011). https://dx.plos.org/10.1371/journal.pone.0020284
6. Mendez, D., et al.: ChEMBL: towards direct deposition of bioassay data. Nucleic Acids Res. **47**(D1), D930–D940 (2019). https://academic.oup.com/nar/article/47/D1/D930/5162468
7. Potter, A., Motik, B., Nenov, Y., Horrocks, I.: Distributed RDF query answering with dynamic data exchange. In: Groth, P., et al. (eds.) ISWC 2016. LNCS, vol. 9981, pp. 480–497. Springer, Cham (2016). https://doi.org/10.1007/978-3-319-46523-4_29
8. Sidirourgos, L., Goncalves, R., Kersten, M., Nes, N., Manegold, S.: Column-store support for RDF data management. Proc. VLDB Endow. **1**(2), 1553–1563 (2008). https://dl.acm.org/doi/10.14778/1454159.1454227
9. Abadi, D.J., Marcus, A., Madden, S.R., Hollenbach, K.: SW-Store: a vertically partitioned DBMS for Semantic Web data management. VLDB J. **18**(2), 385–406 (2009). https://doi.org/10.1007/s00778-008-0125-y
10. Atre, M., Chaoji, V., Zaki, M.J., Hendler, J.A.: Matrix "Bit" loaded. In: Proceedings of the 19th International Conference on World Wide Web, pp. 41–50. ACM, New York (2010). https://dl.acm.org/doi/10.1145/1772690.1772696
11. Neumann, T., Weikum, G.: The RDF-3X engine for scalable management of RDF data. VLDB J. **19**(1), 91–113 (2010). https://doi.org/10.1007/s00778-009-0165-y
12. Rohloff, K., Schantz, R.E.: Clause-iteration with MapReduce to scalably query data graphs in the SHARD graph-store. In: Proceedings of the 4th International Workshop on Data-Intensive Distributed Computing, DIDC 2011, pp. 35–44. ACM (2011)
13. Zhang, X., Chen, L., Tong, Y., Wang, M.: EAGRE: towards scalable I/O efficient SPARQL query evaluation on the cloud. In: Proceedings of the International Conference on Data Engineering, pp. 565–576. IEEE (2013)

14. Hassan, M., Bansal, S.: S3QLRDF: Distributed SPARQL Query Processing Using Apache Spark–A Comparative Performance Study, vol. 41. Springer, Cham (2023). https://doi.org/10.1007/s10619-023-07422-4
15. Zeng, K., Yang, J., Wang, H., Shao, B., Wang, Z.: A distributed graph engine for web scale RDF data. Proc. VLDB Endow. **6**(4), 265–276 (2013)
16. Gurajada, S., Seufert, S., Miliaraki, I., Theobald, M.: TriAD: a distributed shared-nothing RDF engine based on asynchronous message passing. In: Proceedings of the ACM SIGMOD International Conference on Management of Data, pp. 289–300 (2014)
17. Daga, E., Asprino, L., Mulholland, P., Gangemi, A.: Facade-X: an opinionated approach to SPARQL anything. In: Alam, M., Groth, P., de Boer, V., Pellegrini, T., Pandit, H.J. (eds.) Further with Knowledge Graphs, vol. 53, pp. 58–73. IOS Press (2021). http://oro.open.ac.uk/78973/
18. Hernawan, A., Sunarwidhi, A., Prasedya, E., Widyastuti, S.: A generalization SPARQL federated query: an initial step towards machine-readable web of data for halal food products. In: IOP Conference Series: Earth and Environmental Science, vol. 913, no. 1, p. 012040 (2021). https://iopscience.iop.org/article/10.1088/1755-1315/913/1/012040
19. Quilitz, B., Leser, U.: Querying distributed RDF data sources with SPARQL. In: Bechhofer, S., Hauswirth, M., Hoffmann, J., Koubarakis, M. (eds.) ESWC 2008. LNCS, vol. 5021, pp. 524–538. Springer, Heidelberg (2008). https://doi.org/10.1007/978-3-540-68234-9_39
20. Schwarte, A., Haase, P., Hose, K., Schenkel, R., Schmidt, M.: FedX: a federation layer for distributed query processing on linked open data. In: Antoniou, G., et al. (eds.) ESWC 2011. LNCS, vol. 6644, pp. 481–486. Springer, Heidelberg (2011). https://doi.org/10.1007/978-3-642-21064-8_39
21. Khan, Y., et al.: SAFE: SPARQL federation over RDF data cubes with access control. J. Biomed. Semant. **8**(1), 5 (2017). http://jbiomedsem.biomedcentral.com/articles/10.1186/s13326-017-0112-6
22. Görlitz, O., Staab, S.: SPLENDID: SPARQL endpoint federation exploiting VOID descriptions. In: Proceedings of the Second International Conference on Consuming Linked Data, COLD 2011, vol. 782, pp. 13–24. CEUR-WS.org, Aachen (2011)
23. Troumpoukis, A., et al.: Developing a benchmark suite for semantic web data from existing workflows. In: Fundulaki, I., Krithara, A., Ngomo, A.N., Rentoumi, V. (eds.) Proceedings of the Workshop on Benchmarking Linked Data (BLINK 2016) co-located with the 15th International Semantic Web Conference (ISWC), Kobe, Japan, 18 October 2016. CEUR Workshop Proceedings, vol. 1700. CEUR-WS.org (2016). https://ceur-ws.org/Vol-1700/paper-04.pdf
24. Honda, K., Yoshida, N., Carbone, M.: Multiparty asynchronous session types. J. ACM **63**(1), 1–67 (2016)
25. Yoshida, N.: Programming language implementations with multiparty session types. In: de Boer, F.S., Damiani, F., Hähnle, R., Johnsen, E.B., Kamburjan, E. (eds.) Active Object Languages: Current Research Trends. Lecture Notes in Computer Science, vol. 14360, pp. 147–165. Springer, Cham (2024). https://doi.org/10.1007/978-3-031-51060-1_6
26. Coppo, M., Dezani-Ciancaglini, M., Padovani, L., Yoshida, N.: A gentle introduction to multiparty asynchronous session types. In: Bernardo, M., Johnsen, E. (eds.) SFM 2015. LNCS, vol. 9104, pp. 146–178. Springer, Cham (2015). https://doi.org/10.1007/978-3-319-18941-3_4

27. Yoshida, N., Gheri, L.: A very gentle introduction to multiparty session types. In: Hung, D.V., D'Souza, M. (eds.) ICDCIT 2020. LNCS, vol. 11969, pp. 73–93. Springer, Cham (2020). https://doi.org/10.1007/978-3-030-36987-3_5
28. Cyganiak, R.: A relational algebra for SPARQL. HP (2005). http://www.hpl.hp.com/techreports/2005/HPL-2005-170.pdf
29. Salas, J., Hogan, A.: Semantics and canonicalisation of SPARQL 1.1. Semant. Web **13**(5), 829–893 (2022)

Composition Machines: Programming Self-organising Software Models for the Emergence of Sequential Program Spaces

Damian Arellanes(✉)

Lancaster University, Lancaster LA1 4WA, UK
damian.arellanes@lancaster.ac.uk

Abstract. We are entering a new era in which software systems are becoming more and more complex and larger. So, the composition of such systems is becoming infeasible by manual means. To address this challenge, self-organising software models represent a promising direction since they allow the (bottom-up) emergence of complex computational structures from simple rules. In this paper, we propose an abstract machine, called the composition machine, which allows the definition and the execution of such models. Unlike typical abstract machines, our proposal does not compute individual programs but enables the emergence of multiple programs at once. We particularly present the machine's semantics and demonstrate its operation with well-known rules from the realm of Boolean logic and elementary cellular automata.

Keywords: Automatic Software Composition · Self-Organising Software Models · Emergent Software · Applied Category Theory

1 Introduction

Building programs that build programs is a long-standing challenge which has been considered the holy grail of Computer Science since the inception of Artificial Intelligence [15,23,31]. As software systems are becoming increasingly large and complex (e.g., Cyber-Physical Systems [6]), this challenge needs to be seriously considered for avoiding the infeasibility of manual composition of complex software at scale.

As a first step towards this challenge, we have introduced the notion of *composition by self-organisation* in which complex software models are not explicitly programmed, but emerge from simple rules in a decentralised manner [4]. In this paper, we propose a discrete-time abstract machine that fits into such a paradigm, called the *composition machine*, for the definition and the execution of *self-organising software models*. In this context, a software model is not a single program performing a specific functionality, but a space of programs evolving through well-defined, deterministic self-organisation rules. Thus, the goal of the

W.-N. Chin and Z. Xu (Eds.): TASE 2024, LNCS 14777, pp. 19–37, 2024.
https://doi.org/10.1007/978-3-031-64626-3_2

composition machine is not the computation of a fixed functionality, but the time-dependent emergence of multiple programs at once. Multiple programs are encapsulated in spaces which are self-similar computational structures rooted in Category Theory. We adopt this formalism for leveraging the large corpus of existing theorems in categorical settings, particularly those related to composition properties.

The rest of the paper is structured as follows. Section 2 sets the context of the paper and discusses related work. Section 3 introduces preliminaries for the formal definition of the proposed machine. Section 4 presents the semantics of composition and program spaces. Section 5 describes the semantics of the composition machine. Section 6 presents an example in which complex program spaces emerge from simple rules. Finally, Sect. 7 presents future directions and final remarks.

2 Related Work

The work we propose in this paper is motivated by the problem of automated software composition, an active research problem that falls under the umbrella of program synthesis [15]. Program synthesis is a field that has aimed at providing methods, techniques and tools to automatically generate individual programs without explicitly coding them, usually from high-level specifications. Diverse algorithmic techniques to achieve this task have been proposed over time such as inductive program synthesis [38], stochastic search [2] and constraint solving [19]. Unlike most of the work done in program synthesis, our intent is not to offer efficient algorithms to synthesize individual programs, but to provide an actual abstract machine able to automatically produce a space of sequential programs at every step of its discrete-time operation process. Our abstract machine is implementation-independent and serves to capture the very essence of program emergence from simple rules. Accordingly, it just requires an initial configuration, a set of simple operation rules and a fixed number of elementary programs (from which complex sequential programs emerge over time).

Likewise, our work is related to automatic component composition (or what we call *synthesis-in-the-large*) [22] which consists on automatically finding optimal component-based configurations (or software architectures) that better satisfy specific (functional or non-functional) requirements such as reliability, response time or even end-user specifications. A vast number of approaches have been proposed over time to tackle this problem, ranging from AI planning [26] to evolutionary algorithms [18,30], especially for the realm of service-oriented computing. Apart from purely algorithmic solutions, self-adaptive component models [10,13,14,17,34] have also been proposed to enable structural manipulation of individual composite components under uncertain, dynamically changing environments. Unfortunately, dynamically changing a composite requires *ad hoc* algorithmic mechanisms that lie beyond component model semantics, e.g., a feedback control loop or an assembly-perception-learning framework. Some self-adaptive component models provide semantic constructs to dynamically switch between a small number of hardcoded composite variants [13,14]. These variants are not generated automatically but need to be manually coded by some designer. We are aware of only one component model [7] offering algebraic operators for semantically defining explicit spaces of sequential composites. Although individual composites are not created manually, the spaces that contain them are. To algorithmically collapse spaces into individual composites, such a model has been endowed with a MAPE-K controller [5] which, again, is "semantically intrusive" as it does not form part of the model semantics. In contrast to existing self-adaptive component models, the abstract machine we propose in this paper does not require any "intrusive entities" since the synthesis process is entirely governed by the operational semantics of the machine *per se*.

Like our abstract machine, self-assembly models of computation [37] are not intrusive in the sense they offer well-founded semantic constructs for the emergence of complex structures from simple rules. Algorithmic tile-based self-assembly [12] is the most representative example in this class of models of computation. Computing via self-assembly has its roots in the core principles of Cellular Automata (CAs). Generally speaking, CAs are discrete dynamical systems that exhibit complex global behaviour from a set of locally interacting components [36]. Network automata [8,28,32,35] form a particular class of CAs, whose aim is to encode fixed transition rules for the evolution of a graph configuration. In this way, complex graph structures can emerge over time and halting occurs when a certain (stable) configuration pattern oscillates *ad infinitum*.

Although they have some similarities, our abstract machine and CA-related approaches differ in their core underlying semantics and purpose. While a CA is just a collection of cells that form some pattern via well-defined rules, our machine defines a collection of cells that categorically represent some sequential computation each. So, the global state of our machine is equivalent to a *space of programs* that exist at some point in time. More precisely, the global state is a category that defines all the possible sequential compositions at a certain instant. So, unlike a CA, the purpose of our machine is not the computation of a single program but the emergence of entire spaces each containing a single or multiple sequential programs.

Kolmogorov machines [16] and storage modification machines [29] are also related to our work as they allow the dynamic evolution of connected graphs. However, like CAs, they only operate over time-varying graphs which can represent a single program each. Graph rewriting [25] also yields a model for computing over individual directed acyclic graphs via rule-based graph transformations. Their focus is on the computation of individual programs, not on the emergence of program spaces.

3 Preliminaries

This section presents preliminaries in terms of *Category Theory* and *Quiver Theory* for the formal specification of the proposed machine. Our intention is not to provide a deeper analysis, but just to present the most important definitions and theorems for our purposes. For a deeper treatment of categorical foundations and quivers, we refer the reader to [9,11,24].

3.1 Category Theory

A category consists of a collection of objects, a collection of morphisms between objects, an identity morphism for each object and a way to compose morphisms. There are two laws that composition must satisfy: *associativity* and *unity*. Associativity yields the same composite no matter how composition operands are grouped, and unity leaves unchanged a non-identity morphism when it is composed with an identity morphism. To better understand the semantics of a category, let us describe an example:

Definition 1 (Category of Sets). *$\mathscr{S}$ is the category where:*

- *$\mathscr{S}_0$ is a collection of sets, called objects,*
- *$\mathscr{S}_1$ is a collection of functions between sets, called morphisms,*
- *dom: $\mathscr{S}_1 \to \mathscr{S}_0$ is a collection morphism that takes each function $f \in \mathscr{S}_1$ to its domain $dom(f) \in \mathscr{S}_0$,*
- *cod: $\mathscr{S}_1 \to \mathscr{S}_0$ is a collection morphism that takes each function $f \in \mathscr{S}_1$ to its codomain $cod(f) \in \mathscr{S}_0$,*
- *there is an identity function $1_X \colon X \to X$ for each set $X \in \mathscr{S}_0$ such that $1_X \in \mathscr{S}_1$,*
- *there is a composite function $g \circ f \in \mathscr{S}_1$ for every pair $(f, g) \in \mathscr{S}_1 \times \mathscr{S}_1$ satisfying $cod(f) = dom(g)$,*
- composition is associative*: $\forall (f, g, h) \in \mathscr{S}_1 \times \mathscr{S}_1 \times \mathscr{S}_1, (h \circ g) \circ f = h \circ (g \circ f) \iff cod(f) = dom(g) \wedge cod(g) = dom(h)$, and*
- composition satisfies unity*: $\forall (f \colon X \to Y) \in \mathscr{S}_1, 1_Y \circ f = f = f \circ 1_X$.*

Remark 1. We say that a category is *small* if and only if it is internal in $\mathscr{S}$.

To avoid set-theoretic issues related to the Russell-Zermelo paradox [27], Category Theory defines a category of categories, *Cat*, where objects are small categories and morphisms are functors. A functor is a structure-preserving mapping between two categories, which assigns the objects of one category to the objects of another one. It also assigns the morphisms of one category to the morphisms of the other. Functors preserve both identity morphisms and composition of morphisms.

Definition 2 (Functor). *A functor $F \colon \mathscr{D} \to \mathscr{E}$ assigns each object $a \in \mathscr{D}_0$ to an object $F(a) \in \mathscr{E}_0$ and each morphism $f \in \mathscr{D}_1$ to a morphism $F(f) \in \mathscr{E}_1$ such that:*

- *$F(1_a) = 1_{F(a)}$ for each object $a \in \mathscr{D}_0$, and*
- *$F(g \circ f) = F(g) \circ F(f)$ for all composable morphisms $f, g \in \mathscr{D}_1$.*

Definition 3 (Natural Transformation). *Let $F, G \colon \mathscr{D} \to \mathscr{E}$ be two functors each from the category $\mathscr{D}$ to the category $\mathscr{E}$. A natural transformation $\eta \colon F \to G$ is a morphism between F and G, which satisfies the following:*

- *for every object* $a \in \mathscr{D}_0$*, there is a morphism* $\eta_a\colon F(a) \to G(a)$ *between objects of* $\mathscr{E}$*, and*
- *for every morphism* $(f\colon a \to b) \in \mathscr{D}_1$*, we have* $\eta_b \circ F(f) = G(f) \circ \eta_a$*.*

3.2 Quiver Foundations

The underlying structure of a category is typically represented as a *quiver* which is a directed multigraph with loops allowed. The term quiver is used among category theorists to avoid confusions derived from the multiple meanings of the word *graph*. The formal definition of a quiver is presented below, along with other related formalisms. Whenever convenient, we treat a function as a set of relations.

Notation 1 (Walking Quiver Category) *Let* $\mathscr{Q}$ *be the walking quiver category consisting of a collection* $\mathscr{Q}_0$ *of vertices, a collection* $\mathscr{Q}_1$ *of arrows, a source morphism* $s\colon \mathscr{Q}_1 \to \mathscr{Q}_0$ *and a target morphism* $\tau\colon \mathscr{Q}_1 \to \mathscr{Q}_0$*.*

Definition 4 (Quiver). *A* quiver Q *is a functor* $\mathscr{Q} \to \mathscr{S}$*. Intuitively, it is a quadruple* (Q_0, Q_1, s, τ) *where* Q_0 *is a set of vertices,* Q_1 *is a set of arrows,* $s\colon Q_1 \to Q_0$ *is a source function and* $\tau\colon Q_1 \to Q_0$ *is a target function. If an arrow* $\alpha \in Q_1$ *has source vertex* $x \in Q_0$ *and target vertex* $y \in Q_0$*, we say that* α *is directed from* x *to* y*. This is denoted* $\alpha\colon x \to y$ *with* $x = s(\alpha)$ *and* $y = \tau(\alpha)$*. We call* Q *finite if and only if the sets* Q_0 *and* Q_1 *are both finite.*

Definition 5 (Subquiver). *We say that* $Q' = (Q'_0, Q'_1, s', \tau')$ *is a* subquiver *of* $Q = (Q_0, Q_1, s, \tau)$*, written* $Q' \subseteq Q$*, if and only if* $Q'_0 \subseteq Q_0$*,* $Q'_1 \subseteq Q_1$*,* $s' = s|_{Q'_1}$ *and* $\tau' = \tau|_{Q'_1}$*.*

Definition 6 (Non-Trivial Path). *A* non-trivial path $\rho = (\alpha_n, \alpha_{n-1}, \ldots, \alpha_1)$ *in a quiver* Q *is a finite sequence of arrows such that* $n \geq 1$ *is the length of* ρ*,* $\alpha_i \in Q_1$ *for all* $i \in \mathbb{N} \cap [1, n]$ *and* $\tau(\alpha_j) = s(\alpha_{j+1})$ *for all* $j \in \mathbb{N} \cap [1, n-1]$*. The source vertex of* ρ *is denoted by* $s(\rho)$ *and the target vertex by* $\tau(\rho)$ *so that* $s(\rho) = s(\alpha_1)$ *and* $\tau(\rho) = \tau(\alpha_n)$ *(clearly an abuse of notation but convenient). By convention, all paths are read from right to left as in function composition, and the same arrow can occur more than once in* ρ*.*

Definition 7 (Trivial Path). *A* trivial path ρ_x *in a quiver* Q *is just a vertex* $x \in Q_0$*. Its length is* 0 *and there are as many trivial paths as there are vertices in* Q_0*.*

Definition 8 (Path Concatenation). *Let* ρ_1 *and* ρ_2 *be two paths. We say that* $\rho_2 * \rho_1$ *is a new path, called a path concatenation, if and only if* $\tau(\rho_1) = s(\rho_2)$*. Unambiguously, the source of* $\rho_2 * \rho_1$ *is denoted by* $s(\rho_2 * \rho_1)$ *and its target by* $\tau(\rho_2 * \rho_1)$ *such that* $s(\rho_2 * \rho_1) = s(\rho_1)$ *and* $\tau(\rho_2 * \rho_1) = \tau(\rho_2)$*.*

Definition 9 (Set of Paths). *By convention,* Q_m *is the set of paths of length* $m \geq 0$ *in a quiver* Q*, and* $Q_* = \bigcup_{m \in \mathbb{N}} Q_m$ *is the set of all the possible paths in* Q*.*

Theorem 1 ([11]). *Given a quiver Q, Q_* is finite if and only if Q is finite and has no oriented cycles.*

Definition 10 (Path Category). *The* path category $P(Q)$ *on a quiver Q consists of:*

- *a collection $P(Q)_0$ whose objects are the vertices in Q_0,*
- *a collection $P(Q)_1$ whose morphisms are the paths in Q_*,*
- *a collection morphism $s\colon P(Q)_1 \to P(Q)_0$ that maps each path $\rho \in P(Q)_1$ to its source vertex $s(\rho) \in P(Q)_0$,*
- *a collection morphism $\tau\colon P(Q)_1 \to P(Q)_0$ that maps each path $\rho \in P(Q)_1$ to its target vertex $\tau(\rho) \in P(Q)_0$,*
- *a trivial path $1_x \in P(Q)_1$ for every vertex $x \in P(Q)_0$, called the identity of x, and*
- *a path concatenation $\rho_2 * \rho_1 \in P(Q)_1$ for every pair $(\rho_1, \rho_2) \in P(Q)_1 \times P(Q)_1$ satisfying $\tau(\rho_1) = s(\rho_2)$.*

Remark 2. The category $P(Q)$ is sound because:

- *composition is associative*: $\forall(\rho_1, \rho_2, \rho_3) \in P(Q)_1 \times P(Q)_1 \times P(Q)_1, (\rho_3 * \rho_2) * \rho_1 = \rho_3 * (\rho_2 * \rho_1) \iff \tau(\rho_1) = s(\rho_2) \wedge \tau(\rho_2) = s(\rho_3)$, and
- *composition satisfies unity*: $\forall \rho \in P(Q)_1, 1_{\tau(\rho)} * \rho = \rho = \rho * 1_{s(\rho)}$.

Remark 3. Given a path category $P(Q)$, the composition of two morphisms in $P(Q)_1$ is defined by the concatenation of two paths in Q_*, and an identity path $1_x \in P(Q)_1$ corresponds to a trivial path $\rho_x \in Q_0$. Also, every path $\rho \in Q_1$ is mapped to its one morphism in $P(Q)_1$.

Theorem 2 ([9]). *Let $\mathscr{S}^{\mathscr{Q}}$ be the category where objects are functors $Q\colon \mathscr{Q} \to \mathscr{S}$ (i.e., quivers) and morphisms are natural transformations between such functors. Then, there is a functor $P\colon \mathscr{S}^{\mathscr{Q}} \to Cat$ that sends each quiver Q to its corresponding path category $P(Q)$, by taking each vertex $x \in Q_0$ to an object $P(x) \in P(Q)_0$ and each path $\rho \in Q_*$ to a morphism $P(\rho) \in P(Q)_1$.*

4 Semantics of Composition and Program Spaces

In this section, we present the semantics of composition and program spaces for the rest of the paper. For this, we introduce the notion of a *computon* which is the fundamental unit of computation in our proposal.[1] Informally, a computon is a sequential program that produces exactly one output value for a given input value via some finite computation. A value is an element of some set referred to as data type.[2] Formally:

[1] The word *computon* derives from the Latin root for computation (*computus*) and the Greek suffix *-on*. In Physics, this suffix is traditionally used to designate subatomic particle names.

[2] Examples of data types include the set of integers and the set of real numbers [21,33]. A detailed overview of data types is out of the scope of this paper. This is because the definition of type systems depends on the application domain.

Definition 11 (Data Type). *A data type d is a set of values equipped with at least one* k-ary *operation $d^k \rightarrow d$ that can be performed on those values.*

Definition 12 (Computon). *A* computon *$f\colon d_1 \rightarrow d_2$ is a function from an input data type d_1 to an output data type d_2. We say that it is an identity computon if $d_1 = d_2$ and $\forall v \in d_1, f(v) = v$. Otherwise, f is a non-identity computon.*

Definition 13 (Composite Computon). *A* composite computon *$f_2 \circ f_1$ is a higher-order function given by the composition of computons f_1 and f_2 where $cod(f_1) = dom(f_2)$.*

Definition 14 (Computon Category). *A* computon category *$\mathscr{C}$ consists of:*

- *a collection $\mathscr{C}_0$ of data types,*
- *a collection $\mathscr{C}_1$ of computons,*
- *a morphism $in\colon \mathscr{C}_1 \rightarrow \mathscr{C}_0$ that takes each computon $f \in \mathscr{C}_1$ to an input data type $d \in \mathscr{C}_0$,*
- *a morphism $out\colon \mathscr{C}_1 \rightarrow \mathscr{C}_0$ that takes each computon $f \in \mathscr{C}_1$ to an output data type $d \in \mathscr{C}_0$,*
- *a composite computon $f_2 \circ f_1 \in \mathscr{C}_1$ for every pair $(f_1, f_2) \in \mathscr{C}_1 \times \mathscr{C}_1$ satisfying $out(f_1) = in(f_2)$, and*
- *an identity computon $1_d \in \mathscr{C}_1$ for every data type $d \in \mathscr{C}_0$,*

such that composition of computons*:*

- is associative*: $\forall (f_3, f_2, f_1) \in \mathscr{C}_1 \times \mathscr{C}_1 \times \mathscr{C}_1, (f_3 \circ f_2) \circ f_1 = f_3 \circ (f_2 \circ f_1) \iff out(f_1) = in(f_2) \ \wedge \ out(f_2) = in(f_3)$, and*
- satisfies unity*: $\forall (f\colon d_1 \rightarrow d_2) \in \mathscr{C}_1$, $1_{d_2} \circ f = f = f \circ 1_{d_1}$.*

Definition 15 (Program Space). *Given a subcategory $\mathscr{C}'$ of a computon category $\mathscr{C}$, let $R\colon \mathscr{C}' \rightarrow \mathscr{S}$ be an injective functor which takes each data type $d \in \mathscr{C}'_0$ to its underlying set $R(d) \in \mathscr{S}_0$ and each computon $f \in \mathscr{C}'_1$ to a function $R(f) \in \mathscr{S}_1$. A* program space *is the subcategory $R(\mathscr{C}')$ of $\mathscr{S}$, where $R(\mathscr{C}')$ denotes the image of $\mathscr{C}'$ under R.*

Intuitively, a program space $R(\mathscr{C}')$ on a computon category $\mathscr{C}'$ is a quadruple $(R(\mathscr{C}')_0, R(\mathscr{C}')_1, in, out)$ where $R(\mathscr{C}')_0$ is a set of data types, $R(\mathscr{C}')_1$ is a set of computons, $in\colon R(\mathscr{C}')_1 \rightarrow R(\mathscr{C}')_0$ is an input function and $out\colon R(\mathscr{C}')_1 \rightarrow R(\mathscr{C}')_0$ is an output function.

Definition 16 (Transformer). *A* transformer *$T\colon P(Q) \rightarrow \mathscr{C}$ is a functor for presenting the path category on a quiver Q in a computon category $\mathscr{C}$. It takes the collection $P(Q)_0$ of vertices to a collection $\mathscr{C}_0$ of data types and the collection $P(Q)_1$ of paths to a collection $\mathscr{C}_1$ where each $f \in F$ is a computon from a data type $d_1 \in D$ to a data type $d_2 \in D$ such that:*

- *there is an identity computon $1_{T(x)} \in \mathscr{C}_1$ for each vertex $x \in P(Q)_0$ where $T(x) \in \mathscr{C}_0$, and*
- *there is a composite computon $T(\rho_n * \cdots * \rho_1) \in \mathscr{C}_1$ for every path concatenation $\rho_n * \ldots * \rho_1 \in P(Q)_1$ such that $T(\rho_n * \cdots * \rho_1) = T(\rho_n) \circ \cdots \circ T(\rho_1)$ with $T(\rho_1), \ldots, T(\rho_n) \in \mathscr{C}_1$.*

Notation 2 *$(T \circ P)(Q)$ denotes a computon category generated from the path category on a quiver Q. Its collection of data types is denoted by $(T \circ P)(Q)_0$ and its collection of computons by $(T \circ P)(Q)_1$.*

Definition 17. *From Definitions 15 and 16, we can specify a composite functor $R \circ T \colon P(Q) \to \mathscr{S}$ for transforming the path category on a quiver Q into its corresponding program space $(R \circ T \circ P)(Q)$. For short, we refer $(R \circ T \circ P)(Q)$ to as the program space on Q.*

Example 1. This example is a walkthrough for the construction of the program space $(R \circ T \circ P)(Q)$ on the quiver $Q = (Q_0, Q_1, s, \tau)$. This quiver is illustrated in Fig. 1 and is defined as follows:

- $Q_0 = \{x_i \mid i \in \mathbb{N} \cap [1, 8]\}$,
- $Q_1 = \{\alpha_i \mid i \in \mathbb{N} \cap [1, 6]\}$,
- $s = \{(\alpha_1, x_1), (\alpha_2, x_2), (\alpha_3, x_3), (\alpha_4, x_1), (\alpha_5, x_6), (\alpha_6, x_7)\}$, and
- $\tau = \{(\alpha_1, x_2), (\alpha_2, x_3), (\alpha_3, x_4), (\alpha_4, x_5), (\alpha_5, x_7), (\alpha_6, x_8)\}$.

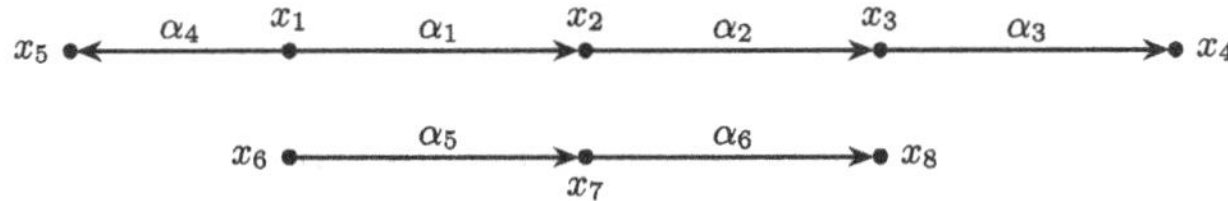

Fig. 1. Graphical representation of the quiver Q described in Example 1.

Once the quiver Q has been defined, we can transform it into a computon category as follows. Let $D = \{d_i \mid i \in \mathbb{N} \cap [1, 8]\}$ be a set of data types and $F = \{f_j \mid j \in \mathbb{N} \cap [1, 6]\}$ be a set of computons with $f_1 \colon d_1 \to d_2$, $f_2 \colon d_2 \to d_3$, $f_3 \colon d_3 \to d_4$, $f_4 \colon d_1 \to d_5$, $f_5 \colon d_6 \to d_7$ and $f_6 \colon d_7 \to d_8$. According to Definition 16, we can specify a transformer T to present $P(Q)$ in a computon category $(T \circ P)(Q)$. We accomplish this by mapping each vertex $P(x_i) \in P(Q)_0$ to a data type $d_i \in D$ for all $i \in \mathbb{N} \cap [1, 8]$ and each path $P(\alpha_j) \in P(Q)_1$ of length one to a computon $f_j \in F$ for all $j \in \mathbb{N} \cap [1, 6]$. Particularly, composite computons correspond to path concatenations, and identity computons are trivial paths. This construction is formally defined as follows:

- $\forall i \in \mathbb{N} \cap [1, 8], x_i \in Q_0 \implies T(P(x_i)) \in (T \circ P)(Q)_0$ such that $P(x_i) \in P(Q)_0$ and $T(P(x_i)) = d_i \in D$,
- $\forall i \in \mathbb{N} \cap [1, 8], x_i \in Q_0 \implies T(1_{P(x_i)}) \colon T(P(x_i)) \to T(P(x_i))$ such that $1_{P(x_i)} \in P(Q)_1$, $T(1_{P(x_i)}) \in (T \circ P)(Q)_1$, $P(x_i) \in P(Q)_0$, $T(P(x_i)) \in (T \circ P)(Q)_0$ and $T(P(x_i)) = d_i \in D$,
- $\forall i \in \mathbb{N} \cap [1, 6], \alpha_i \in Q_1 \implies T(P(\alpha_i)) \in (T \circ P)(Q)_1$ such that $P(\alpha_i) \in P(Q)_1$ and $T(P(\alpha_i)) = f_i \in F$, and
- $\forall (\rho_n * \cdots * \rho_1) \in P(Q)_1, [T(\rho_n) \circ \cdots \circ T(\rho_1)] \in (T \circ P)(Q)_1$.

Finally, the resulting computon category $(T \circ P)(Q)$ can be presented in $\mathscr{S}$ via the functor R (see Definition 15). Intuitively, this is the program space $(R \circ T \circ P)(Q) = ((R \circ T \circ P)(Q)_0, (R \circ T \circ P)(Q)_1, in, out)$ where:

- $(R \circ T \circ P)(Q)_0 = D$,
- $(R \circ T \circ P)(Q)_1 = F \cup \{f_2 \circ f_1, f_3 \circ f_2, f_3 \circ f_2 \circ f_1, f_6 \circ f_5, 1_{d_1}, 1_{d_2}, 1_{d_3}, 1_{d_4}, 1_{d_5}, 1_{d_6}, 1_{d_7}, 1_{d_8}\}$ such that $f_2 \circ f_1 \colon d_1 \to d_3$, $f_3 \circ f_2 \colon d_2 \to d_4$, $f_3 \circ f_2 \circ f_1 \colon d_1 \to d_4$, $f_6 \circ f_5 \colon d_6 \to d_8$ and $1_{d_i} : d_i \to d_i$ for all $i \in \mathbb{N} \cap [1, 8]$,
- $in = \{(f_1, d_1), (f_2, d_2), (f_3, d_3), (f_4, d_1), (f_5, d_6), (f_6, d_7), (f_2 \circ f_1, d_1), (f_3 \circ f_2, d_2), (f_3 \circ f_2 \circ f_1, d_1), (f_6 \circ f_5, d_6), (1_{d_1}, d_1), (1_{d_2}, d_2), (1_{d_3}, d_3), (1_{d_4}, d_4), (1_{d_5}, d_5), (1_{d_6}, d_6), (1_{d_7}, d_7), (1_{d_8}, d_8)\}$, and
- $out = \{(f_1, d_2), (f_2, d_3), (f_3, d_4), (f_4, d_5), (f_5, d_7), (f_6, d_8), (f_2 \circ f_1, d_3), (f_3 \circ f_2, d_4), (f_3 \circ f_2 \circ f_1, d_4), (f_6 \circ f_5, d_8), (1_{d_1}, d_1), (1_{d_2}, d_2), (1_{d_3}, d_3), (1_{d_4}, d_4), (1_{d_5}, d_5), (1_{d_6}, d_6), (1_{d_7}, d_7), (1_{d_8}, d_8)\}$.

The program space $(R \circ T \circ P)(Q)$ is illustrated in Fig. 2. Although we omit identity computons for clarity, the above definition reveals that the identities are elements of the set $(R \circ T \circ P)(Q)_1$. Without loss of generality, hereafter we do not show identity computons when depicting program spaces.

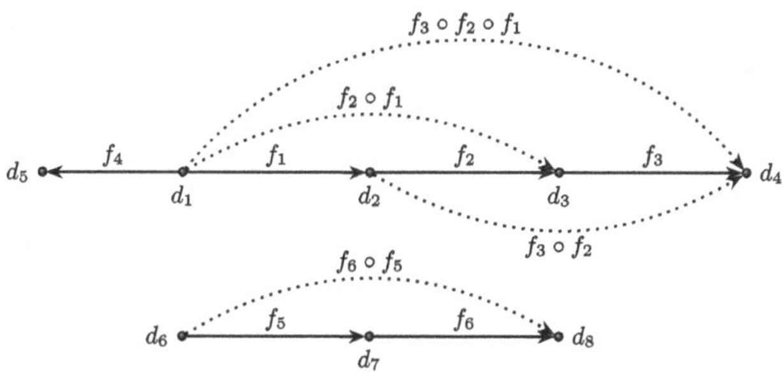

Fig. 2. Graphical representation of the program space $(R \circ T \circ P)(Q)$ described in Example 1.

5 Composition Machines

We propose the notion of composition machines for the emergence of sequential program spaces. These machines allow the definition and the execution of self-organising software models [4], and represent a shift from the computation of single programs to the emergence of program spaces.

Definition 18 (Composition Machine). *A composition machine M is a septuple $(D, F, Q, \mu, S, N, \delta)$ where:*

- *D is a non-empty finite set of data types,*
- *F is a non-empty finite set of computons such that $\forall f, g \in F, cod(f) = cod(g) \iff f = g$ and $\forall f \in F, dom(f) \neq cod(f)$,*
- *Q is an acyclic quiver where each vertex $x \in Q_0$ represents a data type $d \in D$ and each arrow $\alpha \in Q_1$ (called an organism) represents a computon $f \in F$ such that $\forall \alpha_1, \alpha_2 \in Q_1, \tau(\alpha_1) = \tau(\alpha_2) \iff \alpha_1 = \alpha_2$ and $\forall \alpha \in Q_1, s(\alpha) \neq \tau(\alpha)$,*

- *μ consists of a pair of bijective functions, $\mu_0 : Q_0 \to D$ and $\mu_1 : Q_1 \to F$, for mapping vertices to data types and organisms to computons, respectively, such that $\mu_1(\alpha) = f \iff \mu_0(s(\alpha)) = dom(f) \wedge \mu_0(\tau(\alpha)) = cod(f)$,*
- *$S = \{0, 1\}$ is the set of possible organism states,*
- *$N = \{N_1, N_2, N_3, N_4\}$ is a non-empty finite collection of neighbourhoods:*
  - *$N_1 \subseteq Q_1$ is a set where each element $(\alpha) \in N_1$ is the unary neighbourhood of an isolated organism $\alpha \in Q_1$ that has has no neighbours to the right and no neighbours to the left, i.e., $\forall(\alpha) \in N_1, \nexists \alpha_0 \in Q_1, \tau(\alpha_0) = s(\alpha) \vee \tau(\alpha) = s(\alpha_0)$.*
  - *$N_2 \subseteq Q_1 \times Q_1$ is a set where each element $(\alpha_1, \alpha_2) \in N_2$ is the binary neighbourhood of an organism $\alpha_1 \in Q_1$ that has only one neighbour to the right, i.e., $\forall(\alpha_1, \alpha_2) \in N_2, (\nexists \alpha_0 \in Q_1, \tau(\alpha_0) = s(\alpha_1)) \wedge \tau(\alpha_1) = s(\alpha_2)$.*
  - *$N_3 \subseteq Q_1 \times Q_1$ is a set where each element $(\alpha_1, \alpha_2) \in N_3$ is the binary neighbourhood of an organism $\alpha_2 \in Q_1$ that has only one neighbour to the left, i.e., $\forall(\alpha_1, \alpha_2) \in N_3, (\nexists \alpha_0 \in Q_1, \tau(\alpha_2) = s(\alpha_0)) \wedge \tau(\alpha_1) = s(\alpha_2)$.*
  - *$N_4 \subseteq Q_1 \times Q_1 \times Q_1$ is a set where each element $(\alpha_1, \alpha_2, \alpha_3) \in N_4$ is the ternary neighbourhood of an organism $\alpha_2 \in Q_1$ which has exactly one neighbour to the right and exactly one neighbour to the left, i.e., $\forall(\alpha_1, \alpha_2, \alpha_3) \in N_4, \tau(\alpha_1) = s(\alpha_2) \wedge \tau(\alpha_2) = s(\alpha_3)$.*
- *δ consists of four local state transition functions:*
  - *$\delta_1 : S \to S$ for every $\alpha \in Q_1$ with a neighbourhood $(\alpha) \in N_1$,*
  - *$\delta_2 : S^2 \to S$ for every $\alpha_1 \in Q_1$ with a neighbourhood $(\alpha_1, \alpha_2) \in N_2$,*
  - *$\delta_3 : S^2 \to S$ for every $\alpha_2 \in Q_1$ with a neighbourhood $(\alpha_1, \alpha_2) \in N_3$, and*
  - *$\delta_4 : S^3 \to S$ for every $\alpha_2 \in Q_1$ with a neighbourhood $(\alpha_1, \alpha_2, \alpha_3) \in N_4$.*

Intuitively, a composition machine $M = (D, F, Q, \mu, S, N, \delta)$ consists of $|F|$ *organisms* operating in discrete time.[3] Each organism represents a computon $f \in F$ and has at most three neighbours (including itself). We say that two different organisms $\alpha_1 \in Q_1$ and $\alpha_2 \in Q_1$ are neighbours if there is a non-trivial path (α_1, α_2) or a non-trivial path (α_2, α_1). Equivalently, two different organisms are neighbours if the computons they represent are composable (see Definition 13).

At each time step $t \in \mathbb{N}$, an organism $\alpha \in Q_1$ is in a state $c(\alpha)^t \in S$. If $c(\alpha)^t = 1$, we say that α is alive; otherwise, we say that α is dead (see Fig. 3).

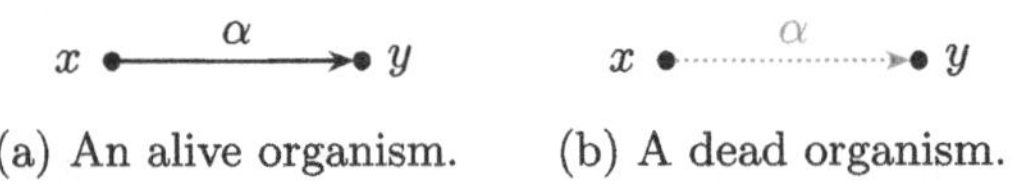

(a) An alive organism. (b) A dead organism.

Fig. 3. At time t, an organism α is (a) alive if $c(\alpha)^t = 1$ or (b) dead if $c(\alpha)^t = 0$.

The configuration of M at t is then a function $c : Q_1 \to S$ that assigns a state to each organism $\alpha \in Q_1$. Intuitively, it is a snapshot of all the states in the system of organisms at some moment in time. Initially, at $t = 0$, M is in the

[3] As the function μ_1 is bijective (see Definition 18), we have that $|F| = |Q_1|$.

so-called *initial configuration* and, in subsequent steps, the states of its organisms are updated in parallel according to four δ functions.

A δ function is a local update rule that defines the next state of an organism based on the current state of n neighbours. More concretely, if the neighbours of an organism have states $c(\alpha_1)^t, c(\alpha_2)^t, \ldots, c(\alpha_n)^t$ at t, then the state of that organism at $t+1$ is given by $\delta_i(c(\alpha_1)^t, c(\alpha_2)^t, \ldots, c(\alpha_n)^t)$ such that $i \in \mathbb{N} \cap [1, 4]$ and $n \in \mathbb{N} \cap [1, 3]$. Particularly, $n = 1$ for unary neighbourhoods, $n = 2$ for binary neighbourhoods and $n = 3$ for ternary neighbourhoods.

Moreover, as an organism can be alive or dead, there are 2^1, 2^2 and 2^3 possible patterns for unary, binary and ternary neighbourhoods, respectively (see Fig. 4). So, $|dom(\delta_1)| = |S| = 2$, $|dom(\delta_2)| = |dom(\delta_3)| = |S|^2 = 4$ and $|dom(\delta_4)| = |S|^3 = 8$. Accordingly, there are $2^2 \times 2^4 \times 2^4 \times 2^8 = 2^{18}$ possible rules for a composition machine.

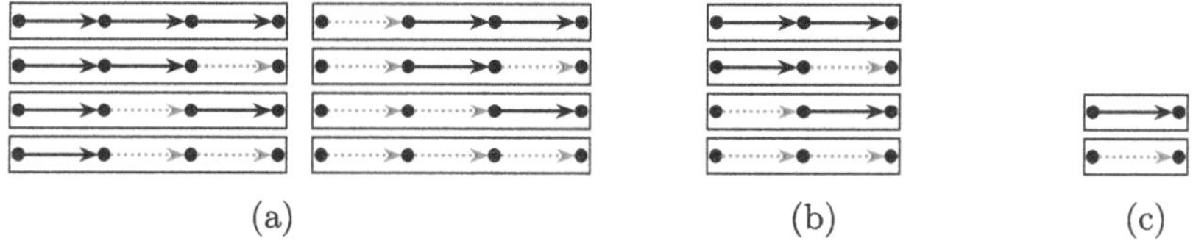

Fig. 4. Possible patterns for (a) ternary neighbourhoods, (b) binary neighbourhoods and (c) unary neighbourhoods.

To explain how rules can be defined, let us consider a simple transition function for organisms that have only one neighbour to the right:

$$\delta_2(c(\alpha_1)^t, c(\alpha_2)^t) = c(\alpha_1)^t \oplus c(\alpha_2)^t \tag{1}$$

where $\oplus$ is the exclusive-or (XOR) operator defined in Boolean algebra.

Without loss of generality, let us assume $(\alpha_1, \alpha_2) \in N_2$ is the binary neighbourhood of some organism α_1. If both organisms are alive at time t, then the next state of α_1 would be given by $c(\alpha_1)^{t+1} = \delta_2(1, 1) = 0$, as shown in Fig. 5.

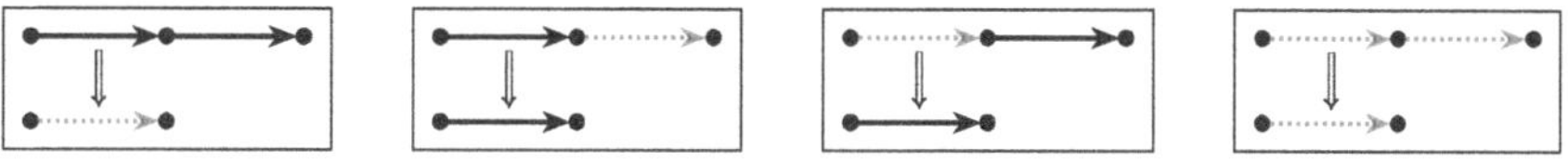

Fig. 5. An example of a local transition rule for an organism that has only one neighbour to the right. This rule is equivalent to an XOR operation and corresponds to the δ_2 function described in Eq. 1.

Figure 5 shows an example of a local transition rule for the binary neighbourhood N_2 in some machine M. In a similar fashion, we can define rules for the other neighbourhoods to independently transform organisms' states. These transformations occur by simultaneously applying the appropriate rule for each $\alpha \in Q_1$, leading to a time evolution of the global configuration of M. Particularly, evolving a configuration c into another one is given by a global transition function $G\colon S^{Q_1} \rightarrow S^{Q_1}$.[4] So, the time evolution of M results from the repeated application of G, i.e., $c \mapsto G(c) \mapsto (G \circ G)(c) \mapsto (G \circ G \circ G)(c) \mapsto \ldots$

As c is the initial configuration, we can deduce that the machine's orbit $orb(c)$ is equal to $c, G(c), (G \circ G)(c), (G \circ G \circ G)(c), \ldots$[5] In this case, time refers to the number of applications of G. Particularly, the configuration c exists at time $t = 0$, the configuration $G(c)$ is present at time $t = 1$, the configuration $(G \circ G)(c)$ appears at time $t = 2$, and so on. Indeed, the time evolution of a composition machine is similar to that of a synchronous cellular automaton [1,20,36]. The difference lies in their underlying semantics.

In a composition machine M, each organism $\alpha \in Q_1$ is causally related to some computon $f \in F$ via μ_1. Furthermore, the global state of M at t is semantically equivalent to a category which defines all the possible sequential compositions at that moment in time. So, the machine's purpose is not the computation of a single program but the emergence of a whole program space. More formally, a program space in M at t is generated from the path category $P(\overrightarrow{Q}^t)$, where $\overrightarrow{Q}^t$ is referred to as the *alive quiver* at t.

Definition 19 (Alive Quiver). *Let $M = (D, F, Q, \mu, S, N, \delta)$ be a composition machine and c be a machine configuration at t. The* alive quiver *$\overrightarrow{Q}^t \subseteq Q$ is a quadruple $(\overrightarrow{Q}_0, \overrightarrow{Q}_1, \overrightarrow{s}, \overrightarrow{\tau})$ where $\overrightarrow{Q}_0 = \{x \in Q_0 \mid \exists \alpha \in Q_1, c(\alpha)^t = 1 \ \wedge \ s(\alpha) = x \ \vee \ \tau(\alpha) = x\}$, $\overrightarrow{Q}_1 = \{\alpha \in Q_1 \mid c(\alpha)^t = 1\}$, $\overrightarrow{s} = \{(\alpha, s(\alpha)) \in Q_1 \times Q_0 \mid c(\alpha)^t = 1\}$, and $\overrightarrow{\tau} = \{(\alpha, \tau(\alpha)) \in Q_1 \times Q_0 \mid c(\alpha)^t = 1\}$.*

The path category on an alive quiver $\overrightarrow{Q}^t$ generates the space $(R \circ T \circ P)(\overrightarrow{Q}^t)$ of all possible sequential computons at time t. As per Definition 17, this space is produced through a computon category $(T \circ P)(\overrightarrow{Q}^t)$ which we refer to as the *alive category* at t.

Definition 20 (Alive Category). *Given a composition machine $M = (D, F, Q, \mu, S, N, \delta)$ and some alive quiver $\overrightarrow{Q}^t = (\overrightarrow{Q}_0, \overrightarrow{Q}_1, \overrightarrow{s}, \overrightarrow{\tau})$, the* alive category *$(T \circ P)(\overrightarrow{Q}^t)$ generated from $P(\overrightarrow{Q}^t)$ consists of:*

- *a collection $(T \circ P)(\overrightarrow{Q}^t)_0$ of data types such that $\forall x \in P(\overrightarrow{Q}^t)_0, \exists! d \in (T \circ P)(\overrightarrow{Q}^t)_0, d = \mu_0(x)$, and*
- *a collection $(T \circ P)(\overrightarrow{Q}^t)_1$ of computons where:*
  - *$\forall x \in P(\overrightarrow{Q}^t)_0, \exists! 1_d \in (T \circ P)(\overrightarrow{Q}^t)_1, d = \mu_0(x)$, and*
  - *$\forall (\alpha_n, \ldots, \alpha_1) \in P(\overrightarrow{Q}^t)_1, \exists! (f_n \circ \cdots \circ f_1) \in (T \circ P)(\overrightarrow{Q}^t)_1, f_1 = \mu_1(\alpha_1) \wedge \cdots \wedge f_n = \mu_1(\alpha_n)$ with $n \geq 1$.*

---

[4] S^{Q_1} is the set of all the possible configurations in a given machine, i.e., the set of all the functions from Q_1 to S.

[5] An orbit is a finite/infinite sequence of configurations of some composition machine.

Theorem 3. *Given a composition machine* $M = (D, F, Q, \mu, S, N, \delta)$, $(R \circ T \circ P)(Q)$ *is the maximal program space defining all the possible sequential programs that can exist in* M *at any moment in time.*

Proof. Let $M = (D, F, Q, \mu, S, N, \delta)$ be a composition machine and $\overrightarrow{Q}^t$ be some alive quiver at time t. By Definition 19, we know that $\overrightarrow{Q}^t \subseteq Q$. Then, it trivially follows that $\overrightarrow{Q}^t = Q$ is the largest subset and, therefore, the maximal alive quiver that can be formed at any moment in time. By Definition 17, we construct the maximal program space $(R \circ T \circ P)(Q)$ as required.

A sequence of different program spaces can emerge periodically as a consequence of an intermittent configuration pattern appearing in the system of organisms. If a unique configuration pattern is repeated *ad infinitum* after time t in a machine M, then we say that M halts at t (see Definitions 21 and 22).

Definition 21 (Configuration Pattern). *A configuration pattern of period* $k \geq 1$ *is a finite orbit* $orb(c_1) = c_1, c_2, \ldots, c_k$ *where* c_i *and* c_{i+1} *are different configurations for all* $i \in \mathbb{N} \cap [1, k-1]$.

Definition 22 (Composition Machine Halting). *A composition machine* M *halts at time* t *if and only if* $c_1, c_2, \ldots, c_k$ *is a unique pattern appearing every* k *time steps after* t. *Equivalently,* M *halts when a unique finite sequence of distinct program spaces emerges every* k *time steps after* t.

6 Example

We now present an example to demonstrate how (complex) sequential program spaces emerge from simple rules. For this, we consider the composition machine $M = (D, F, Q, \mu, S, N, \delta)$ where:

- $D = \{d_i \mid i \in \mathbb{N} \cap [1, 13]\}$,
- $F = \{f_i \colon d_i \to d_{i+1} \mid i \in \mathbb{N} \cap [1, 6] \ \wedge \ d_i, d_{i+1} \in D\} \cup \{f_7 \colon d_8 \to d_9 \mid d_8, d_9 \in D\} \cup \{f_i \colon d_{i+2} \to d_{i+3} \mid i \in \mathbb{N} \cap [8, 10] \ \wedge \ d_{i+2}, d_{i+3} \in D\}$,
- $Q = (Q_0, Q_1, s, \tau)$ where:
  - $Q_0 = \{x_i \mid i \in \mathbb{N} \cap [1, 13]\}$,
  - $Q_1 = \{\alpha_i \mid i \in \mathbb{N} \cap [1, 10]\}$,
  - $s = \{(\alpha_i, x_i) \mid i \in \mathbb{N} \cap [1, 6]\} \cup \{(\alpha_7, x_8)\} \cup \{(\alpha_i, x_{i+2}) \mid i \in \mathbb{N} \cap [8, 10]\}$,
  - $\tau = \{(\alpha_i, x_{i+1}) \mid i \in \mathbb{N} \cap [1, 6]\} \cup \{(\alpha_7, x_9)\} \cup \{(\alpha_i, x_{i+3}) \mid i \in \mathbb{N} \cap [8, 10]\}$,
- $\mu_0 = \{(x_i, d_i) \in Q_0 \times D \mid i \in \mathbb{N} \cap [1, 13]\}$,
- $\mu_1 = \{(\alpha_i, f_i) \in Q_1 \times F \mid i \in \mathbb{N} \cap [1, 10]\}$,
- $S = \{0, 1\}$,
- $N = \{N_1, N_2, N_3, N_4\}$ with $N_1 = \{(\alpha_7)\}$, $N_2 = \{(\alpha_1, \alpha_2), (\alpha_8, \alpha_9)\}$, $N_3 = \{(\alpha_5, \alpha_6), (\alpha_9, \alpha_{10})\}$ and $N_4 = \{(\alpha_1, \alpha_2, \alpha_3), (\alpha_2, \alpha_3, \alpha_4), (\alpha_3, \alpha_4, \alpha_5), (\alpha_4, \alpha_5, \alpha_6), (\alpha_8, \alpha_9, \alpha_{10})\}$,
- δ_1 is the NOT function, δ_2 and δ_3 are XOR operations, and δ_4 corresponds to *Rule 54* from elementary cellular automata. In its Boolean form, Rule 54 is equivalent to a function defined by $(p, q, r) \mapsto q \oplus (p \vee r)$ where $(p, q, r) \in \{0, 1\} \times \{0, 1\} \times \{0, 1\}$ and $q \oplus (p \vee r) \in \{0, 1\}$ (cf. [36]).

Figure 6 illustrates the quiver Q and the maximal program space in M, viz. $(R \circ T \circ P)(Q)$. According to Theorem 3, this space is the most complex that our example machine can construct when all the organisms are alive. For simplicity, we do not show the identity computons looping over each data type, and we do not draw labels on composites to improve readability.

To arise familiarity, all the local transition functions of M are based on existing ones. Particularly, isolated organisms evolve through a NOT operation. Organisms with a binary neighbourhood change their states via the XOR operator. And organisms with a ternary neighbourhood evolve according to *Rule 54*. Thus, the orbit of M is given by the synchronous application of the rules illustrated in Fig. 7, starting from the initial configuration $c = \{(\alpha_1, 1), (\alpha_2, 1), (\alpha_3, 0), (\alpha_4, 1), (\alpha_5, 1), (\alpha_6, 0), (\alpha_7, 1), (\alpha_8, 0), (\alpha_9, 0), (\alpha_{10}, 1)\}$. This initial configuration and its corresponding program space $(R \circ T \circ P)(\overrightarrow{Q}^0)$ are illustrated in $t = 0$ of Fig. 8.

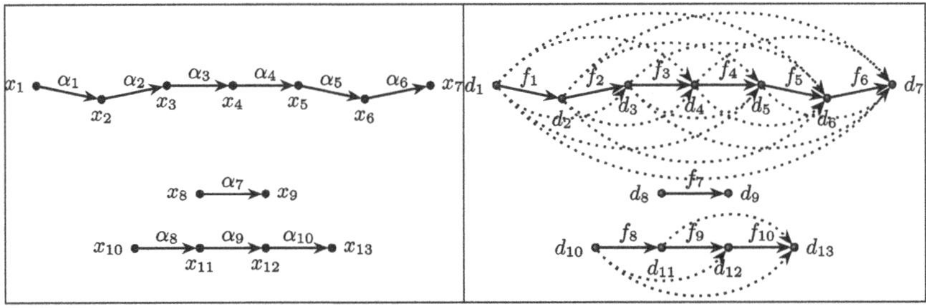

Fig. 6. The quiver Q and the corresponding maximal program space in M.

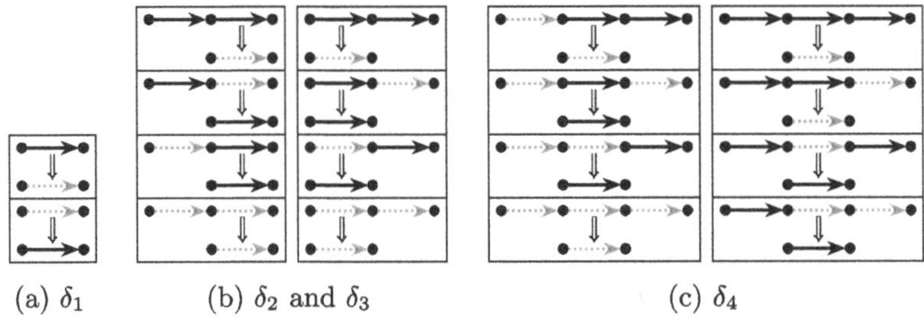

Fig. 7. Unary neighbourhoods are associated with the NOT operator, binary neighbourhoods with the XOR operator and ternary ones with *Rule 54*.

More precisely, Fig. 8 shows the orbit of M from $t = 0$ to $t = 2$, where it is clear that the isolated organism α_7 alternates its state via the NOT rule. Accordingly, the computon f_7 emerges at even time steps and disappears at odd ones. This figure also shows that there are two, one and ten composite computons in $(R \circ T \circ P)(\overrightarrow{Q}^0)_1$, $(R \circ T \circ P)(\overrightarrow{Q}^1)_1$ and $(R \circ T \circ P)(\overrightarrow{Q}^2)_1$, respectively. For example, $f_{10} \circ f_9$ is present in $(R \circ T \circ P)(\overrightarrow{Q}^1)_1$ because $c(\alpha_9)^1 = 1$, $c(\alpha_{10})^1 = 1$, $\mu_1(\alpha_9) = f_9$ and $\mu_1(\alpha_{10}) = f_{10}$. Supposing f_9 is a program of type $\mathbb{Z} \to \mathbb{R}$ that multiplies an integer by 0.5 and f_{10} is a program of type $\mathbb{R} \to \mathit{String}$ that converts a real number into its equivalent string representation, then $f_{10} \circ f_9 \colon \mathbb{Z} \to \mathit{String}$ defines a (composite) sequential program that takes an integer z and returns the string representation of $z \times 0.5$. This composite program is not created manually by some coder, but it is automatically generated by M at time $t = 1$. As the notion of a composition machine is implementation-agnostic, in this paper we do not deal with concrete data types or concrete computons. The example we consider is rather abstract with the aim of preserving generality.

In our example, organisms with a binary neighbourhood evolve via the XOR rule. So, they are alive in the next time step if only one neighbour is alive in the current time step. For example, α_6 becomes alive at $t = 1$ because its left neighbour α_5 is alive at $t = 0$. But α_1 is dead at $t = 1$ since $c(\alpha_1)^0 = c(\alpha_2)^0 = 1$. Consequently, we have $f_6 \in (R \circ T \circ P)(\overrightarrow{Q}^1)_1$ and $f_1 \notin (R \circ T \circ P)(\overrightarrow{Q}^1)_1$. More concretely, the application of the XOR rule on binary neighbourhoods from $t = 0$ to $t = 1$ results in the following state transitions:

$$
\begin{aligned}
c(\alpha_1)^1 &= \delta_2(c(\alpha_1)^0, c(\alpha_2)^0) = 1 \oplus 1 = 0 \\
c(\alpha_8)^1 &= \delta_2(c(\alpha_8)^0, c(\alpha_9)^0) = 0 \oplus 0 = 0 \\
c(\alpha_6)^1 &= \delta_3(c(\alpha_5)^0, c(\alpha_6)^0) = 1 \oplus 0 = 1 \\
c(\alpha_{10})^1 &= \delta_3(c(\alpha_9)^0, c(\alpha_{10})^0) = 0 \oplus 1 = 1
\end{aligned}
$$

Organisms with a ternary neighbourhood evolve according to *Rule 54*. For instance, the organism α_9 becomes alive at $t = 1$ since $c(\alpha_8)^0 = c(\alpha_9)^0 = 0$ and $c(\alpha_{10})^0 = 1$; thus, making available the computon $f_9 \in (R \circ T \circ P)(\overrightarrow{Q}^1)_1$. As the organism α_{10} is also alive at that moment in time, the composite computon $f_{10} \circ f_9 \in (R \circ T \circ P)(\overrightarrow{Q}^1)_1$ emerges. In general, the application of *Rule 54* on ternary neighbourhoods from $t = 0$ to $t = 1$ results in the following transitions:

$$
\begin{aligned}
c(\alpha_2)^1 &= \delta_4(c(\alpha_1)^0, c(\alpha_2)^0, c(\alpha_3)^0) = \delta_4(1, 1, 0) = 0 \\
c(\alpha_3)^1 &= \delta_4(c(\alpha_2)^0, c(\alpha_3)^0, c(\alpha_4)^0) = \delta_4(1, 0, 1) = 1 \\
c(\alpha_4)^1 &= \delta_4(c(\alpha_3)^0, c(\alpha_4)^0, c(\alpha_5)^0) = \delta_4(0, 1, 1) = 0 \\
c(\alpha_5)^1 &= \delta_4(c(\alpha_4)^0, c(\alpha_5)^0, c(\alpha_6)^0) = \delta_4(1, 1, 0) = 0 \\
c(\alpha_9)^1 &= \delta_4(c(\alpha_8)^0, c(\alpha_9)^0, c(\alpha_{10})^0) = \delta_4(0, 0, 1) = 1
\end{aligned}
$$

To further investigate the emergence of program spaces, we implemented our composition machine M.[6] After executing this example over 10000 time steps, we

[6] Our tool is available at https://github.com/damianarellanes/compositionmachine.

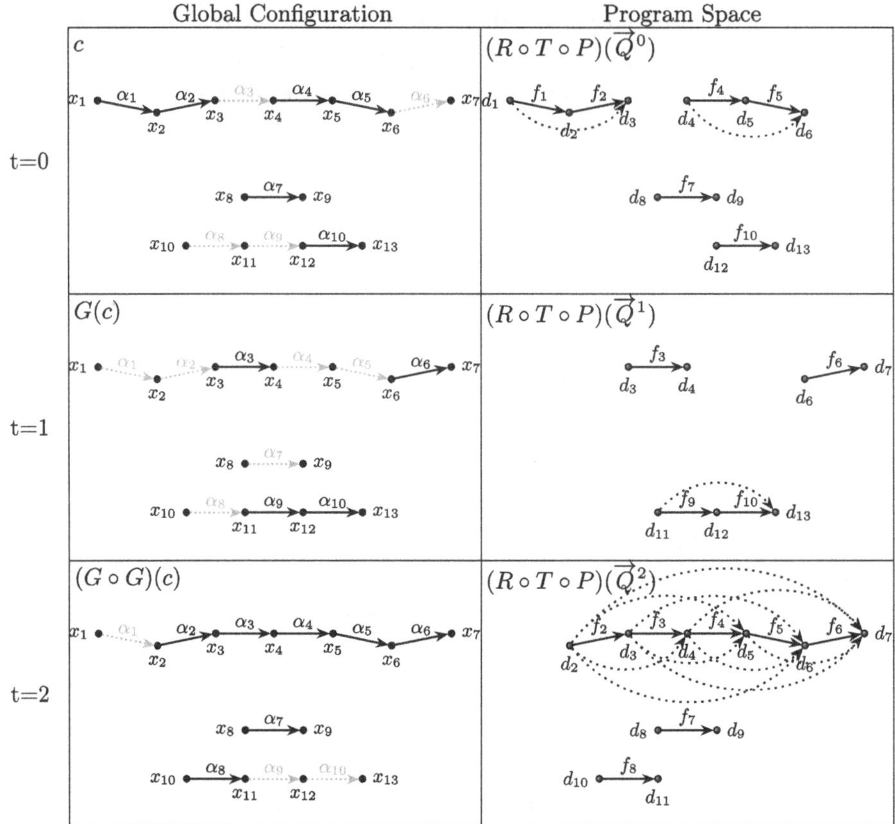

Fig. 8. Orbit of M over three time steps via the rules described in Fig. 7.

found that the most complex program space is formed at $t = 2$, i.e., when all the organisms in the path $(\alpha_6, \ldots, \alpha_2)$ become alive. Accordingly, $f_6 \circ f_5 \circ f_4 \circ f_3 \circ f_2 \in (R \circ T \circ P)(\overrightarrow{Q}^2)_1$ is the most complex composite computon (i.e., the largest sequential program) in our example. With our tool, we also found that there is a repeating pattern every four time steps, starting from $t = 5$, meaning that the compositions formed before $t = 5$ are unique and, after that, there are only four different program spaces. Such a repeating pattern indicates that M halts at $t = 4$. Although we do not show it due to space constraints, the pattern is depicted in [3]. In [3], we additionally present a more complex example.

7 Conclusions

In this paper, we introduced the notion of composition machines for the emergence of sequential program spaces via self-organisation rules. A composition machine evolves a quiver in discrete-time and its global state is semantically equivalent to a category that defines a space of all the possible compositions of computons at some instant. To demonstrate its operation, we presented an example in which complex sequential program spaces emerge from simple rules.

As it is not trivial to engineer emergence, we plan to investigate novel mechanisms for defining rules that match contextual intention or high-level specifications. Also, we plan to study alternative neighbourhoods to allow the evolution of cyclic quivers and, thus, the emergence of infinite categories. In this vein, we would like to explore different program space patterns through the synchronous application of varied local transition rules. In any case, Category Theory will be the *de facto* reasoning framework. We believe that Category Theory will play a fundamental role in the understanding of self-organisation and, in particular, in the study of self-organising software models. This is because such a theory follows an emergentist view rather than a reductionist one. So, the main focus of Category Theory is not to study isolated abstract objects but the relevant interactions between them and their composition. It is indeed a formal framework to reasoning about compositionality and self-organisation.

This paper brings together these worlds in the form of an implementation-independent abstract machine that allows the definition and the execution of self-organising software models. The aim of this machine is not to compute single programs, but to build programs (i.e., composite computons) from other programs (i.e., predefined computons) via self-organisation rules. Under this umbrella, we envision that in the future, instead of manually coding them, complex software models could grow from simple rules (just as biological organisms do).

References

1. Acerbi, L., Dennunzio, A., Formenti, E.: Conservation of some dynamical properties for operations on cellular automata. Theor. Comput. Sci. **410**(38), 3685–3693 (2009)
2. Alur, R., et al.: Syntax-guided synthesis. In: Formal Methods in Computer-Aided Design, pp. 1–8 (2013)
3. Arellanes, D.: Composition machines: programming self-organising software models for the emergence of sequential program spaces. Technical report. arXiv:2108.05402v1, arXiv (2021)
4. Arellanes, D.: Self-organizing software models for the Internet of Things: complex software structures that emerge without a central controller. IEEE Syst. Man Cybern. Mag. **7**(3), 4–9 (2021). https://doi.org/10.1109/MSMC.2021.3062822
5. Arellanes, D., Lau, K.K.: Workflow variability for autonomic IoT systems. In: International Conference on Autonomic Computing (ICAC), pp. 24–30. IEEE (2019)
6. Arellanes, D., Lau, K.K.: Evaluating IoT service composition mechanisms for the scalability of IoT systems. Futur. Gener. Comput. Syst. **108**, 827–848 (2020)
7. Arellanes, D., Lau, K.K., Sakellariou, R.: Decentralized data flows for the functional scalability of service-oriented IoT systems. Comput. J. **66**(6), 1477–1506 (2023)
8. Arrighi, P., Dowek, G.: Causal graph dynamics. Inf. Comput. **223**, 78–93 (2013)
9. Awodey, S.: Category Theory, 2nd edn. Oxford University Press, New York (2010)

10. Bruneton, E., Coupaye, T., Leclercq, M., Quéma, V., Stefani, J.B.: The FRACTAL component model and its support in Java. Softw. Pract. Experience **36**(11–12), 1257–1284 (2006)
11. Derksen, H., Weyman, J.: An Introduction to Quiver Representations. Graduate Studies in Mathematics, vol. 184. American Mathematical Society, Providence (2017)
12. Doty, D.: Theory of algorithmic self-assembly. Commun. ACM **55**(12), 78–88 (2012)
13. Filho, R.R., Porter, B.: Defining emergent software using continuous self-assembly, perception, and learning. ACM Trans. Auton. Adaptive Syst. **12**(3), 16:1–16:25 (2017)
14. Floch, J., Hallsteinsen, S., Stav, E., Eliassen, F., Lund, K., Gjorven, E.: Using architecture models for runtime adaptability. IEEE Softw. **23**(2), 62–70 (2006)
15. Gulwani, S., Polozov, O., Singh, R.: Program Synthesis, Foundations and Trends in Programming Languages, vol. 4. Now Publishers, Hanover (2017)
16. Gurevich, Y.: On Kolmogorov machines and related issues. In: Current Trends in Theoretical Computer Science. World Scientific Series in Computer Science, vol. 40, pp. 225–234. World Scientific (1993)
17. Hirsch, D., Kramer, J., Magee, J., Uchitel, S.: Modes for software architectures. In: Gruhn, V., Oquendo, F. (eds.) EWSA 2006. LNCS, vol. 4344, pp. 113–126. Springer, Heidelberg (2006). https://doi.org/10.1007/11966104_9
18. Iovino, M., Styrud, J., Falco, P., Smith, C.: Learning behavior trees with genetic programming in unpredictable environments. In: IEEE International Conference on Robotics and Automation (ICRA), pp. 4591–4597 (2021)
19. Jha, S., Gulwani, S., Seshia, S.A., Tiwari, A.: Oracle-guided component-based program synthesis. In: ACM/IEEE International Conference on Software Engineering (ICSE), pp. 215–224. ACM (2010)
20. Kari, J.: Theory of cellular automata: a survey. Theor. Comput. Sci. **334**(1–3), 3–33 (2005)
21. Lehmann, D.J., Smyth, M.B.: Algebraic specification of data types: a synthetic approach. Math. Syst. Theory **14**(1), 97–139 (1981)
22. Mohr, F.: Automated Software and Service Composition: A Survey and Evaluating Review. SpringerBriefs in Computer Science, Springer, Cham (2016)
23. Neumann, J.V.: Theory of Self-reproducing Automata. University of Illinois Press, Urbana (1966)
24. Pierce, B.C.: Basic Category Theory for Computer Scientists. Foundations of Computing, MIT Press, Cambridge (1991)
25. Plump, D.: Term graph rewriting. In: Handbook of Graph Grammars and Computing by Graph Transformation, pp. 3–61. World Scientific (1999)
26. Rao, J., Su, X.: A survey of automated web service composition methods. In: Cardoso, J., Sheth, A. (eds.) SWSWPC 2004. LNCS, vol. 3387, pp. 43–54. Springer, Heidelberg (2005). https://doi.org/10.1007/978-3-540-30581-1_5
27. Russell, B.: The Principles of Mathematics, vol. 1. Cambridge University Press, Cambridge (1903)
28. Sayama, H.: Generative network automata: a generalized framework for modeling complex dynamical systems with autonomously varying topologies. In: IEEE Symposium on Artificial Life, pp. 214–221 (2007)
29. Schönhage, A.: Storage modification machines. SIAM J. Comput. **9**(3), 490–508 (1980)

30. da Silva, A.S., Ma, H., Mei, Y., Zhang, M.: A survey of evolutionary computation for web service composition: a technical perspective. IEEE Trans. Emerg. Top. Comput. Intell. **4**(4), 538–554 (2020)
31. Simon, H.A.: Whether software engineering needs to be artificially intelligent. IEEE Trans. Softw. Eng. **SE-12**(7), 726–732 (1986)
32. Smith, D.M.D., Onnela, J.P., Lee, C.F., Fricker, M.D., Johnson, N.F.: Network automata: coupling structure and function in dynamic networks. Adv. Complex Syst. **14**(03), 317–339 (2011)
33. Spivak, D.I.: Functorial data migration. Inf. Comput. **217**, 31–51 (2012)
34. Töpfer, M., Abdullah, M., Bureš, T., Hnětynka, P., Kruliš, M.: Machine-learning abstractions for component-based self-optimizing systems. Int. J. Softw. Tools Technol. Transfer **25**(5), 717–731 (2023)
35. Waldegrave, R., Stepney, S., Trefzer, M.A.: Developmental Graph Cellular Automata. MIT Press, Cambridge (2023)
36. Wolfram, S.: A New Kind of Science, 1st edn. Wolfram Media, Champaign (2002)
37. Woods, D.: Intrinsic universality and the computational power of self-assembly. Philos. Trans. R. Soc. A: Math. Phys. Eng. Sci. **373**(2046), 1–13 (2015)
38. Yoon, Y., Lee, W., Yi, K.: Inductive program synthesis via iterative forward-backward abstract interpretation. Proc. ACM Program. Lang. **7**(174), 1657–1681 (2023)

Slicing Assisted Program Verification: An Empirical Study

Wenjian Chai[1,2], Rongjie Yan[1,2(✉)], Wenhui Zhang[1,2], and Jian Zhang[1,2(✉)]

[1] Key Laboratory of System Software (CAS) and State Key Laboratory of Computer Science, ISCAS, Beijing, China
{chaiwj,yrj,zwh,zj}@ios.ac.cn

[2] University of Chinese Academy of Sciences, Beijing, China

Abstract. Simplifying programs before verification aims to reduce program complexity thus saving the verification effort. In the paper, we investigate the impacts of applying program slicing before verification. We consider various techniques and verifiers for the workflow and adopt benchmarks from the software verification community to evaluate the strengths and issues in adopting slicing techniques for program simplification. The evaluation considers reachability as the property to be verified and checks the consistency of verification results, the improvement of verification efficiency, and the advantages of different toolchains when verifying reachability. The investigation shows that most programs keep consistent verification results after slicing and verifying programs with much code unrelated to the properties becomes faster when slicing is applied before verification. However, it is surprising that verification time for some programs can be significantly longer after slicing. We have investigated the reasons for such phenomenon concerning the features of these programs, and provide insightful conclusions obtained from using the slicing+verification approach.

Keywords: Slicing · Program verification · Reachability

1 Introduction

Formal verification aims at proving the correctness of programs (systems) rigorously, often using methods based on formal logic and discrete mathematics. In some sense, it is an exhaustive analysis of a program/system with respect to its specified requirements. Thus formal verification is usually quite expensive, in terms of execution time and memory as well as human efforts.

Currently, automated formal verification techniques and tools have not yet been applied routinely to non-trivial software systems. To make them more scalable and practical, we can combine them with other techniques. For example, a simple idea is to simplify the system first, and then verify it. In fact, several researchers have proposed to combine model checking with slicing [18,20,21]. Typically, these approaches convert a large program into an abstract model,

W.-N. Chin and Z. Xu (Eds.): TASE 2024, LNCS 14777, pp. 38–57, 2024.
https://doi.org/10.1007/978-3-031-64626-3_3

then apply slicing to obtain a smaller model, and finally adopt some model checker to verify the model.

Although the above approaches have been applied in several case studies successfully, it is not so clear whether we can use similar ideas as the solution for a broader class of programs. In this paper, we report our experiences with the slicing-enhanced verification approach, using industry-strength tools and well-known benchmarks (a large set of C programs).

There are several issues that we would like to investigate. Program slicing is to analyze and extract the subset of a program's source code or bytecode, which directly influences a specific variable or output at a particular point in the program's execution. Formal verification is to explore all the possibilities and show the absence of property violations. The first doubt is whether slicing will remove any elements concerned in verification. The second issue is whether program slicing can reduce the cost of verification. Nowadays, there are various verification techniques, such as abstraction interpretation [11], bounded model checking [6], CEGAR [10], and symbolic execution [31], to improve the scalability of verifiers. Will the benefit of program slicing be shadowed by the above techniques? The third issue is what types of programs are suitable for the slicing+verification approach. Obviously, for small programs, we can obtain little benefit with slicing. Another case is for programs whose slicing effort is much higher than the verification effort.

To answer these questions, we conduct extensive experiments with various tools and programs from the competition on software verification. Meanwhile, we investigate experimental results to provide comprehensive explanations.

The contributions of this work are multi-fold:

- We propose various ways to combine different slicing and verification tools to compare the pains and gains of slicing-assisted verification.
- We adopt a large number of benchmarks with various types of C programs to find the types of programs that are suitable for the combined approach.
- We provide detailed discussions on the investigation, which can be the guidance before utilizing the combination of slicing and verification.

The remainder of this paper is organized as follows. Section 2 explains basic concepts as well as necessary notations. Section 3 discusses the related work. We provide the research questions and the experimental setting in Sect. 4. Section 5 presents the experimental results and the associated analysis. Section 6 provides the discussion and finally, Sect. 7 concludes.

2 Preliminaries

In this section, we introduce the definition of program slicing and the concepts of Program/System Dependence Graph applied in current slicing techniques.

2.1 Program Slicing

The general purpose of program slicing [29] is to preserve all the statements that influence the slicing criterion and to remove other irrelevant statements from the source program. A slicing criterion denoted by $[p, v]$ usually consists of a program point p, such as a statement s, and a variable v whose value at p users are interested in. The idea is feasible for a set of points P and a set of variables V.

We can regard a program as a fine-grained *Control Flow Graph* (CFG) $G_C = \langle N_C, E_C \rangle$, where N_C, the set of nodes, is the set of statements in the program and $E_C \subseteq N_C \times N_C$, the set of directed edges, shows the control flow of the statements. When a slicing criterion $[p, v]$ is determined, the slice of the program is N'_C, a subset of N_C that influences the value of variable v at p. And the sliced program is a graph $G'_C = \langle N'_C, E'_C \rangle$, where E'_C keeps the control flow of the source program after the statements $N_C \setminus N'_C$ are removed. To be precise, for statements $s, t \in N'_C$, $(s, t) \in E'_C$ if and only if there is a directed path from s to t in G_C and other nodes in this path all belong to $N_C \setminus N'_C$.

2.2 Program/System Dependence Graph

Program Dependence Graph (PDG) [22] $G_P = \langle N_P, E_P \rangle$ shows the dependencies among statements of a program. The set of nodes N_P is the same as N_C and the set of edges E_P indicates control dependencies and data dependencies among program statements. Control dependencies represent that one statement can affect whether another statement will be executed, while data dependencies are the commonly understood *def-use* relationship, i.e., one statement refers to the data of another statement.

System Dependence Graph (SDG) [16] $G_S = \langle N_S, E_S \rangle$ shows the dependencies among statements of a program with the consideration of inter-procedural calls. The set of nodes N_S is $N_C \cup N_I$, where the nodes in N_I represent assignments to arguments and reception of return values during function calls. The set of edges E_S is $E_P \cup E_I$, where the edges in E_I indicate the dependencies about the statements in N_I.

When programs contain only assignments, `if-then-else`, `while-do` and output statements, and all variables are constants or scalars without pointers, slicing based on PDG/SDG can ensure that if a program P halts on some input I, then the sliced program P_S halts on I and simulates P's behaviors, i.e., the sequence of values at each program point of P_S is the same as that at the corresponding point of P [15,24].

3 Related Work

Earlier works extract the required program slice through data flow analysis on CFGs, by calculating the def-use chains among program statements [29]. The dependencies in programs are also used to compute the slice with higher efficiency and program slicing could be simply transformed into a graph-reachability problem with PDG [22]. SDGs extended from PDGs can handle inter-procedural calls during slicing [16].

There are many slicing tools for Java programs, e.g., Slicer4J [3], JavaSlicer [13], Indus [23] and JavaBST [1]. We consider slicing tools for C programs in this study. However, there are a very small number of static program slicing tools for C programs that support function calls, pointers, and arrays. Indeed, due to the rich semantics and complex data structures of C language, it is hard to cover all kinds of dependencies in C programs and find all the dependencies in a variety of source programs. The well-known static analysis tool, CodeSurfer [26], is commercial and inaccessible. Another open-source tool that can provide source-code analysis of C software, Frama-C [12], has a plug-in called Slicing. It supports static inter-procedural program slicing with SDGs and diverse slicing criteria, including backward slicing based on the calls of some functions. Moreover, it can cut unreachable branches based on the semantic analysis during slicing, which cannot be realized by extracting dependencies.

Some slicing tools utilize LLVM Intermediate Representation (IR) as their target language, obtained by translating C source code through compilation. The features of IR language, such as the compact instruction set, the benefit of Static Single Assignment (SSA) form, and the extensible infrastructure, facilitate the dependency analysis for program slicing. The SDG-based inter-procedural static slicing tool, llvm-slicing [32], applies the symbolic slicing technique to avoid re-analysis and improve efficiency. The slicing criterion is of the form *variable@function*. After slicing, the results are the instructions with the original locations in the C programs, which are not executable. Another inter-procedural static slicing tool, llvm-slicer [7], can output executable sliced IR programs with flexible slicing criteria.

Various efforts exist to combine slicing and verification for various models, programs, and systems. Millett et al. [20] extended program slicing to PROMELA language and obtained significant time reduction with verifier SPIN for three protocols. Vasudevan et al. [27] used conditioned slicing for Hardware Description Languages and the speedup was great in verifying nine safety properties of the Verilog implementation of the USB 2.0 protocol. Yi et al. [30] proposed the slicing execution technique and applied it to verify the handshake protocol in openssl-0.9.6c, demonstrating its practicability and efficacy. Wang et al. [28] introduced a program slicing algorithm to their tool CodeAuditor for vulnerability detection and achieved efficiency improvement in verifying five assertions in the *minicom* program. Odenbrett et al. [21] proposed a slicing algorithm for AADL Specifications that reduced the state space of the case study in verifying CTL* properties. Sabouri and Sirjani [25] applied three slicing techniques to reduce Rebeca models based on a property and gained obvious state space reduction and efficiency improvement when verifying nine benchmarks. Matsubara et al. [18] implemented a slicing technique based on Variable Dependence Graph (VDG) and took 35% less time to verify the case study with SPIN. However, the applicability of the idea to combine verification and slicing techniques for a broad class of programs remains to be studied.

A verification tool called Symbiotic [8] employs the tool llvm-slicer to simplify source programs before verification [9]. Recently, Kumar et al. [17] also investigated the time variations of debugging and validity of 50 programs before and after slicing with KLEE, DIVINE, and Frama-C.

In this paper, we consider various combinations of available tools with more benchmarks (compared with the work in [17]) and provide a thorough analysis on the consistency of results, and the variations in verification time concerning the scale and the types of programs and the portion of removed code. As Chalupa and Strejček have discussed the influence of non-termination (in)sensitive slicing on program verification, we apply the default parameter in llvm-slicer and mainly investigate the causes for inconsistent verification results and unexpected time variations before and after program slicing.

4 Experimental Evaluation

We first outline the research questions that the experimental evaluation is designed to investigate and then explain the settings of the experimentation.

4.1 Research Questions

C programs usually involve various data structures such as pointers and arrays. A general question is whether the slicing techniques support precise analysis of such programs. To investigate the savings by adopting slicing for program simplification and verification, we ignore C programs beyond the abilities of either slicing or verification techniques. We focus on reachability properties which can be expressed as slicing criteria, and consider the following research questions.
RQ1: Does program slicing maintain the verification results? In which cases are the verification results inconsistent before and after program slicing?
RQ2: Does program slicing improve the verification performance? Is there a clear relationship between the amount of code removed by program slicing and the savings during verification?
RQ3: What types of programs are suitable for adopting program slicing before verification?

To answer **RQ1**, we compare the verification results before and after slicing, and the ground-truths. To answer **RQ2**, we ignore the cases with inconsistent results and compare the time consumption before and after slicing, as well as the portion of removed code. To answer **RQ3**, we further investigate the features of programs, to find the direct impacts on program simplification for verification.

4.2 Experimental Setup

Adopted Tools and Benchmarks. We adopt various publicly available tools for program slicing and verification, respectively. Currently, there are both slicing and verification tools for C programs and the compiled programs. We select two slicing techniques and three verifiers, which are listed in Table 1.

With these tools, we employ the following three ways in the experimentation.

Table 1. The tools used in the experiments and their input and output

types	tools	input	output
slicing	Frama-C	C program	sliced C program
	llvm-slicer	LLVM IR program	sliced IR program
verification	UAutomizer [14]	C program	verification logs and result
	GDart-LLVM[a]	C and LLVM IR program	
	Gazer-Theta [2]		
decompilation	llvm2c [19]	LLVM IR program	C program

[a] https://github.com/tudo-aqua/gdart-llvm

- Apply slicing tools for a given C program, and then verify the sliced C program with the corresponding verifiers.
- Compile source C programs into LLVM IR programs with Clang, and adopt slicing tools to obtain sliced IR programs. Then decompile the sliced IR programs into C programs for verification.
- Verify the sliced LLVM IR programs directly.

Both slicing tools employ SDGs as the basis for slicing programs. In addition, Frama-C also relies on semantic extraction in slicing. However, Frama-C has limited support for pointers and arrays. On the contrary, llvm-slicer can deal with pointers and arrays for the lower complexity when processing them in LLVM IR instructions. As llvm2c does not support the transformation for LLVM IR programs with vector instructions, and Frama-C requires manual efforts to deal with pointers and arrays, the set of benchmarks with verifiers for C programs is limited.

Verifier GDart-LLVM adopts dynamic symbolic execution in verification. It only considers one category of the benchmarks in SV-COMP 2023 [5]. Verifier Gazer-Theta provides various parameters with different verification techniques: Gazer-Theta (BMC) extracts path constraints with bounded model checking; Gazer-Theta (EXP) adopts CEGAR-based algorithms with the abstract domain of explicit values; and Gazer-Theta (PRE) adopts Cartesian predicates [4] in the abstract domain. Therefore, we consider the following six toolchains shown in Table 2 to carry out the study. We adopt benchmarks in SV-COMP 2023 in the experimentation. Due to the limitations of Frama-C, llvm2c, and GDart-LLVM, we choose 49 C programs without arrays or pointers as the benchmarks for the first three toolchains. For the rest, we consider 3207 programs (including the mentioned 49 programs) verified by Gazer-Theta in SV-COMP 2023.

Among 49 programs, Frama-C cannot analyze a function in a program named recHanoi03-1.c. Therefore, we only consider 48 programs for the first toolchain in Table 2. For the larger set of benchmarks that can be verified by Gazer-Theta, some of them (among 3207 programs) cannot be sliced. The detail is as follows: 1) one cannot be compiled; 2) 287 programs cannot be sliced by llvm-slicer (286 crash in the slicing process and one runs out of memory); 3) four programs reach the time limit (the same as required in SV-COMP 2023) during slicing. For the rest 2915 programs, Table 3 shows their scale and respective slicing time, and the slicing cost is positively associated with the scale of programs. For programs of similar scale, code with numerous interdependent variables requires more time for slicing, such as the nine programs in the first row; in contrast, the slicing cost of code with fewer variables and data dependencies is relatively low, such as the six programs in the second row.

Table 2. Six toolchains with corresponding tools and benchmarks

No	toolchains	benchmarks
1	Frama-C+UAutomizer	48 C programs
2	llvm-slicer+llvm2c+UAutomizer	49 C programs
3	llvm-slicer+GDart-LLVM	
4	llvm-slicer+Gazer-Theta (BMC)	2915 C programs
5	llvm-slicer+Gazer-Theta (EXP)	
6	llvm-slicer+Gazer-Theta (PRE)	

Table 3. The scale and the slicing time (by llvm-slicer) of the rest 2915 programs

lines of code	total	slicing time			
		≤1 s	1–10 s	10–100 s	>100 s
≤5k	2662	2369	284	9	0
5–50k	249	6	61	182	0
>50k	4	0	0	1	3

Parameters. The reachability considered in SV-COMP 2023 is that a program will never call the function named *reach_error* in any finite execution. The property in linear temporal logic is

$$G \quad \neg \quad call(reach\_error())$$

Consequently, we can select all calls of the *reach_error* function as the slicing criterion. The command line parameters for the two slicing tools are as follows:

Frame-C : *-slice-calls reach_error*
llvm-slicer : *-c __assert_fail*

The latter is reasonable because the *reach_error* function will call the *assert* function with parameter 0 and then trigger assertion failure, i.e., call the *__assert_fail* function after compilation. The change ensures that the *reach_error* function is not empty after slicing and the output of llvm-slicer is a valid IR program.

For the toolchains with LLVM IR programs, we compile the source C programs with Clang versions required by the verifiers and parameters extracted from the source code or explained in the documents. If not specified, we use the latest version of Clang that tools in the toolchain can support with default parameters.

Table 4. Parameters from C to LLVM IR

toolchains	Clang version	parameters
llvm-slicer+llvm2c+UAutomizer	14	default
llvm-slicer+GDart-LLVM	14	default
llvm-slicer+Gazer-Theta	9	-g, -O1 and -Xclang -disable-llvm-passes

We apply UAutomizer and GDart-LLVM in the same way as described in the documents or mentioned in the scripts. For Gazer-Theta, it applies three techniques successively, until one of them obtains a definite result, or the three have been executed. To investigate the impacts of program slicing on individual verification techniques, we consider applying the three techniques separately (Table 4).

Notations. The verification results include CORRECT (C), WRONG (W), UNKNOWN (U), ERROR (E), and TIMEOUT (T). The first three indicate that verification terminates normally within the time limit (the same as required in SV-COMP 2023). CORRECT and WRONG mean that the result obtained by the verification tool is the same as and opposite to the expected result, respectively. UNKNOWN means that the verifier does not obtain a definitive result. ERROR shows that the verifier crashes within the time limit. TIMEOUT shows that verification cannot stop within the time limit.

The types of inconsistency before and after slicing, such as from UNKNOWN to WRONG (U2W) and ERROR to CORRECT (E2C), indicate potential problems or benefits introduced by program slicing.

To answer **RQ2**, we consider the time consumption in slicing together with that in verification. We present the comparison with obvious increases or decreases in time consumption, including the cases from CORRECT to TIMEOUT and TIMEOUT to CORRECT.

To answer **RQ3**, we focus on the last three toolchains with diverse types of C programs. We divide them into various groups according to the categories listed in SV-COMP.

5 Experimental Results

This section shows the results and findings of our experiments to answer the research questions raised in Sect. 4.

5.1 RQ1: Result Consistency

To provide a comparison with various slicing and verification techniques, we first consider the 49 programs. Table 5 shows that almost all of these programs obtain consistent verification results after slicing when the toolchains are applied.

Table 5. Inconsistent results among the 49 programs

toolchains	total	inconsistency	programs and types
Frama-C+UAutomizer	48	0	
llvm-slicer+llvm2c+UAutomizer	49	1	soft_float_3a.c.cil.c, T2W[a]
llvm-slicer+GDart-LLVM		0	
llvm-slicer+Gazer-Theta (BMC)		1	gcd_4.c, C2U
llvm-slicer+Gazer-Theta (EXP)		1	s3_clnt_3.BV.c.cil-2a.c, C2U
llvm-slicer+Gazer-Theta (PRE)		2	s3_clnt_3.BV.c.cil-1a.c, T2U s3_clnt_3.BV.c.cil-2a.c, C2U

[a] TIMEOUT to WRONG, similar abbreviations for other types of inconsistency

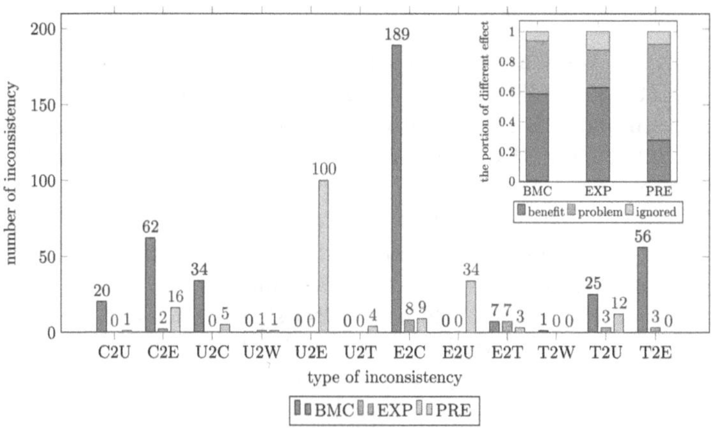

Fig. 1. For the rest 2866 (2915-49) programs of the benchmarks, the cases that verification results are inconsistent when applying llvm-slicer+Gazer-Theta

For soft_float_3a.c.cil.c and gcd_4.c, the preprocessing step before verification leads to the inconsistency. UAutomizer finds a wrong counterexample when verifying the sliced program of soft_float_3a.c.cil.c. The reason is that the `unsigned long long` type is changed to the `unsigned long` type during decompilation in the 64-bit desktop. The bit lengths of the two types are different in the 32-bit system which is required by the rules of SV-COMP, causing UAutomizer to obtain an unexpected number. For Gazer-Theta, the frontend requires compilation with the argument -g (debug information) and uses these important debug instructions to construct models. However, lifetime records of certain variables for function inlining and later error position lifting are removed from IR programs of gcd_4.c during slicing, as the records are not involved in the slicing criterion. Consequently, the control flow automaton of the sliced IR program generated by the verifier is quite different from that of the original IR program, leading to an UNKNOWN result.

For programs s3_clnt_3.BV.c.cil-1a.c and s3_clnt_3.BV.c.cil-2a.c, we can obtain correct results with Gazer-Theta (BMC). But for the case of the other two options, the verifier stops exploration when it finds a potential error trace. However, the trace may not reach an error position, leading to an UNKNOWN result.

For the rest 2866 programs, we obtain 394 inconsistent results with the fourth chain. For the other two chains, the inconsistent results are 24 and 185, respectively. The numbers and types of inconsistency with three techniques are shown in Fig. 1. We consider U2C, E2C, E2U, E2T of inconsistency as **benefits** obtained from slicing, and C2U, C2E, U2W, U2E, T2W, T2E as **problems**. Cases with U2T and T2U are ignored. The portions of different effects for the inconsistency with three toolchains are shown in the top right corner of Fig. 1.

Table 6. Time variations for the 49 programs

toolchains	total	significant reduction	significant increase
Frama-C+UAutomizer	38	20	0
llvm-slicer+llvm2c+UAutomizer	36	10	14
llvm-slicer+GDart-LLVM	24	2	0
llvm-slicer+Gazer-Theta (BMC)	7	1	1
llvm-slicer+Gazer-Theta (EXP)	1	1	0
llvm-slicer+Gazer-Theta (PRE)	0	0	0

In Fig. 1, the portion of E2C from Gazer-Theta (BMC) is larger than the other parts, demonstrating the benefit of slicing for program verification. There are some corner instructions that the verifier can not handle, leading to verification failure at the frontend. When these instructions are removed during slicing, verification can be carried out smoothly. Moreover, as some irrelevant variables and statements are filtered in sliced programs, it is possible to obtain more accurate constraints or tighter over-approximations in sliced programs.

However, when looking into the details of a program whose verification results change from TIMEOUT or UNKNOWN to WRONG, we find problems in the slicing process. In program fragtest_simple.c, a loop body contains an `if` statement that decides whether to call the *reach_error* function. The tool llvm-slicer fails to keep the `if` and `break` statements that jump out of this loop. Consequently, this loop of the sliced program never terminates, and the condition to call the *reach_error* function will mistakenly be satisfied.

5.2 RQ2: Efficiency Improvement

To answer this question, we focus on programs satisfying the following requirements.

- We can obtain the verification results from source and sliced programs. And the results are both CORRECT, or CORRECT before slicing and TIMEOUT after slicing, or TIMEOUT before slicing and CORRECT after slicing.
- The verification time for source programs is more than one second.

Comparison with Six Toolchains. For the 49 programs, we consider the cases with an increase or decrease of at least 10% after slicing. The comparison of time variations is shown in Table 6.

More than half of programs sliced by Frama-C need much less time to be verified. The semantic analysis of Frama-C plays a key role. For example, Fig. 2(a) shows a program to calculate the greatest common divisor g of two variables x and y. The precondition of the assertion $y \geq g$ is $y > 0$. If we assume $y > 0$ when the program calls function *gcd_test*, the condition of the `if` statement in line 25 will never be satisfied. The `if` branch is removed during semantic slicing. Consequently, the verification of the sliced program takes only 120 s while verifying the source program reaches the time limit of 960 s. Moreover, for some simple programs, the analysis of Frama-C can decide whether the function is reachable. For example, in Fig. 2(b), Frama-C predicts that variable y must be an odd integer and the assertion is always true under any inputs. After slicing, there is only an empty *main* function, and the result that the *reach_error* function is unreachable becomes obvious.

For the second toolchain, the gains in program slicing are not obvious. The reason is that decompilation from LLVM IR to C introduces more code, and the structures of the programs become more complex. For example, many `goto` statements will be added based on the basic blocks in the LLVM framework. In every function, each of its arguments will be assigned to a new variable. An `if` statement with complex logical condition will be divided into multiple nested `if` statements. Consequently, it takes more time for UAutomizer to annotate Hoare Logic and the verifier may need more iterations to obtain the correct verification results.

Moreover, the types of variables can also cause trouble. LLVM does not make distinctions between signed and unsigned `char/integer/long long`, and both signed and unsigned types will be lowered to `i8/i32/i64`. In sliced C programs generated by llvm2c, signed variables will be defined as unsigned and used after being cast to signed ones. In such cases, it becomes more difficult to generate loop invariants or path constraints, and the satisfiability analysis of complex formulas will take more time.

```
signed char gcd_test(signed char a, signed char b) {
    ...
    if (b < (signed char)0) b = -b;
    ...
  }
...
int main() {
    ...
    g = gcd_test(x, y)
    if (y > (signed char)0) {
        __VERIFIER_assert(y >= g);
    }
    ...
}
```

(a) Code snippet from gcd_2.c

```
int main() {
    unsigned int y;
    y = 1U;
    while(1) {
        y = y +2U*__VERIFIER_nondet_uint();
        __VERIFIER_assert (y!=0U);
        }
    return 0;
}
```

(b) Code snippet from jain_1-1.c

```
int main() {
    unsigned int i, n = __VERIFIER_nondet_uint(), sn = 0;
    for(i = 0; i <= n; i++) {
        sn = sn + i;
    }
    __VERIFIER_assert(sn == (n * (n + 1)) / 2 || sn == 0);
}
```

(c) Code snippet from sum02-1.c

Fig. 2. Code snippets for case study

However, the mismatched types of variables sometimes improve the efficiency of verification. For example, when 64-bit variables are changed to 32-bit variables, as mentioned in Sect. 5.1, the state space is reduced. Another feature in the sliced programs is the gain from the compilers. For example, compilers will calculate some constants during compilation, such as 1 << 24 to 16777216, and these constants remain in sliced C programs after decompilation. Such a feature simplifies the verification process with Hoare Logic.

For GDart-LLVM, we notice that the verification result of a client changes from TIMEOUT to CORRECT. The slicing tool removes more than 1/3 of instructions in its IR program and the sliced program was verified successfully within 60% of the time limit. But for most cases, code removed by llvm-slicer is not significant. As the semantics of programs are not changed, the verification cost is almost the same.

Table 7. Time variations for 2866 programs with llvm-slicer+Gazer-Theta

toolchains	total	significant reduction	significant increase
llvm-slicer+Gazer-Theta (BMC)	348	116	126
llvm-slicer+Gazer-Theta (EXP)	127	118	5
llvm-slicer+Gazer-Theta (PRE)	154	43	31

Comparison with Gazer-Theta. Gazer-Theta either obtains the correct results within one second or cannot obtain the correct results for almost all of the 49 programs. The numbers of considered programs in Table 6 are less than other toolchains. Therefore, we compare the time changes for verifying the rest 2866 programs with Gazer-Theta and present the results in Table 7.

For the toolchain with Gazer-Theta (BMC), the number of cases with time increase after slicing is more than we expected. Gazer-Theta (BMC) can verify some large programs with more than 5000 lines of code. However, slicing those programs with llvm-slicer needs half or even more time for verification. When only a small portion of code is removed after slicing and the time consumption in verification remains the same or reduces slightly, the total cost for slicing and verification increases. If we do not consider the slicing cost, the numbers of programs with significant time decreases and increases are 137 and 78, respectively. We further compare the verification processes before and after slicing. After slicing, the size of the models is smaller, and the potential error traces become shorter. Even though, the cost of the solver for path constraints decides the total verification cost.

For Gazer-Theta (EXP), the cost for most of the programs decreases. As irrelevant variables and corresponding instructions are removed during slicing, the processes of abstraction and refinement are simplified, thus reducing the time consumption.

For Gazer-Theta (PRE), time reduction with sliced programs is not obvious. As it adopts predicate abstraction in the verification process, the simplification may result in extracting inadequate predicates. Therefore, more iterations are necessary to obtain a result, leading to an increase in verification time.

Comparison Between Reduced Code and Reduced Time. In Fig. 3, we represent the relation between program size with the number of lines of source code, the ratio of removed IR instructions to the original IR program, and the ratio of verification cost after slicing to that before slicing. If the ratio of verification cost is 100%, the verification time before and after slicing is the same. To ease the observation, the color of the dots changes gradually from dark blue to red to indicate a time increase.

We observe that for programs with almost the same size and a similar ratio of removed code, the changes in verification time differ or even vary dramatically. From the experimentation, we cannot ascertain a clear correlation between the ratio of removed instructions and the decrease in verification time.

5.3 RQ3: Program Types

We reorganize the verification results based on different categories of the benchmarks to answer this question. Table 8 shows the numbers of inconsistent results from every category for the last three toolchains. We focus on the groups with the highest number of inconsistent results and then extract features that cause the inconsistency.

When applying Gazer-Theta (BMC), the verification results of 162 programs from the category `loops` change from CORRECT or TIMEOUT to UNKNOWN

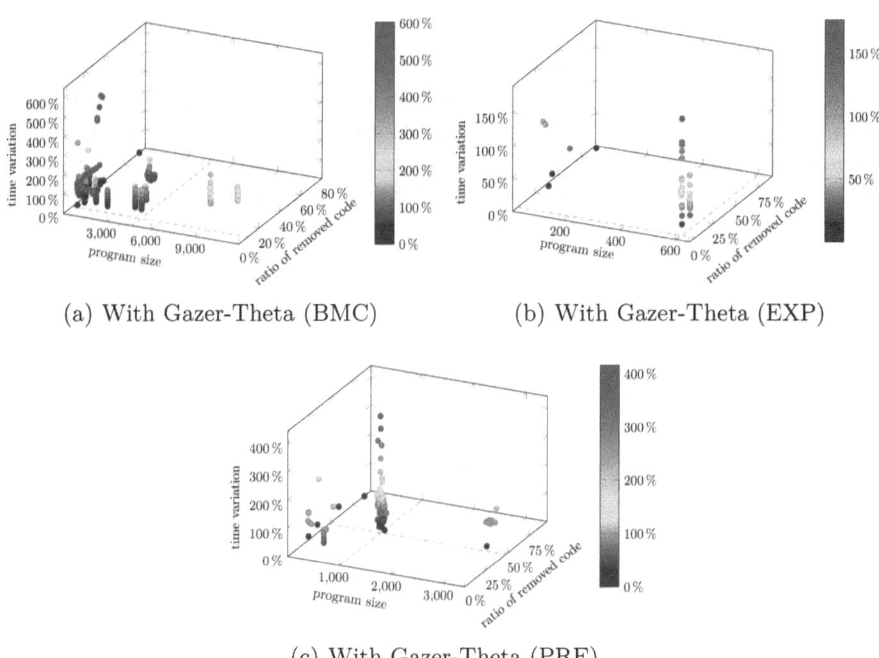

(a) With Gazer-Theta (BMC)

(b) With Gazer-Theta (EXP)

(c) With Gazer-Theta (PRE)

Fig. 3. The relation between the size of programs, the ratio of removed instructions, and the ratio of time variations

Table 8. Inconsistency in different categories with llvm-slicer+Gazer-Theta

category	total	llvm-slicer+Gazer-Theta		
		BMC	EXP	PRE
bitvectors	49	1	1	2
controlflow	22	1	1	1
eca	972	0	0	0
floats	433	6	4	4
loops	699	175	18	169
productlines	597	212	0	10
recursive	59	0	1	1
xcsp	114	0	0	0

or ERROR. For Gazer-Theta (PRE), the results of 157 programs from `loops` change from other results to UNKNOWN or ERROR. Gazer-Theta regards the loops as procedures and inlines them as common functions. With assertions in the `while` loops, the sliced programs without necessary debugging information are prone to cause failure or make mistakes in the modeling process.

For category `productlines`, around 1/3 of the code can be removed during slicing. Consequently, Gazer-Theta (BMC) can generate more accurate constraints, and 212 programs are verified to be UNKNOWN or ERROR before slicing but obtain correct results after slicing. However, these programs are mainly composed of control flow statements, and the over-approximation of abstract interpretation in processing these control flows leads to the loss of accuracy. Hence, Gazer-Theta (EXP) and (PRE) still can not obtain more correct results with the sliced code.

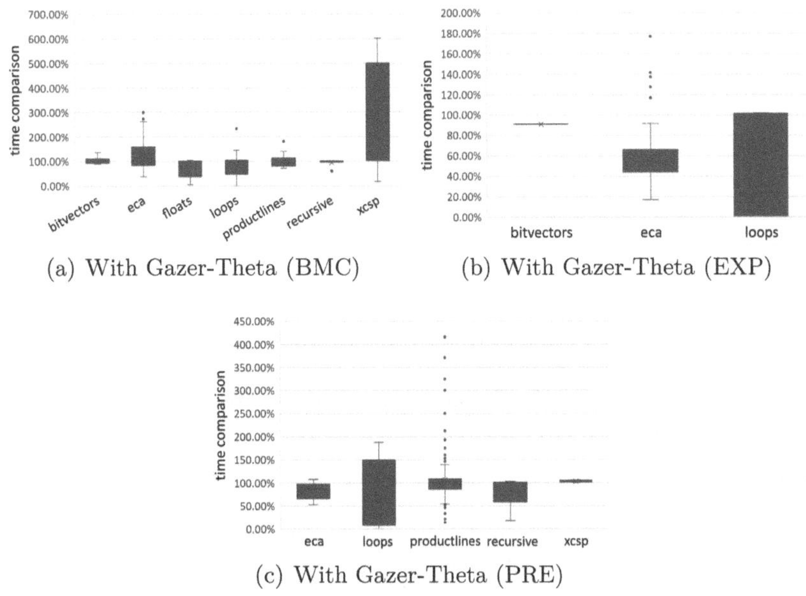

Fig. 4. The changes of verification time from different categories when employing llvm-slicer+Gazer-Theta

We also draw box plots, shown in Fig. 4, to illustrate the changes in verification time based on different categories of the benchmarks. The change of time is also represented by the ratio of verification time after slicing to that before slicing. We focus on the groups that as a whole need significantly more or less time on verification after slicing.

The programs in `eca` contain hundreds or thousands of `if` statements and only several variables related to the conditions. For functions that call the *reach_error* function, the values returned from different branches are removed during slicing, and simplification in the abstraction and refinement processes leads to time reduction for Gazer-Theta (EXP) and (PRE). However, this simplification has little impact on Gazer-Theta (BMC), because path constraints are not affected after slicing. Meanwhile, the increased cost of slicing for large-scale programs also leads to an increase in the verification time for sliced programs.

Two programs in `floats` category use dramatically less time to be verified by Gazer-Theta (BMC). However, the slicing tool adopting the non-termination insensitive technique considers that the `if` and `break` statements of one loop are not related to the reachability of the error location, and the loop body is executed only once in the sliced program. Therefore, the verifier luckily obtains correct results in a short time.

In `loops` category, some programs involve a mass of operations not related to the property to be verified, such as considerable irrelevant memory read and write. Once such code is removed, the verification cost is reduced.

The programs in `xcsp` can be directly transformed into SMT problems. Such programs contain an error location at the end and a lot of assumptions on the ranges and relations of variables that can hardly be removed during slicing. Moreover, the cost of slicing for those programs is high, leading to a sharp increase in verification time for sliced programs.

From the experimental results, we conclude that if a program contains a lot of code not related to the goal of verification, program slicing can improve the performance of the verifiers. However, extracting incorrect dependencies and removing additional information required by verifiers may lead to inconsistent verification results.

6 Discussion

6.1 Programs Features

When a program's objective is straightforward and the property under verification is close to the functionality of the program, slicing can hardly remove any part even with semantic reasoning. Figure 2(c) shows a program in SV-COMP to calculate the sum sn from 0 to a variable n. It will call the *reach_error* function when sn is not $n * (n + 1)/2$ or 0 (when n is less than 0). All statements in the main function have direct or indirect dependencies with this condition. Therefore, the whole main function will be preserved after slicing. For this program, though some debug information is removed from the compiled IR program during slicing of llvm-slicer, the semantics remain the same.

6.2 Various Verification Technique

Although we have only applied three verification tools in the experiments, they utilize different verification techniques, such as bounded model checking and abstract refinement.

With the bounded model checking technique, the verification tool usually searches for error paths incrementally with an upper bound, during which the verifier extracts path constraints and adopts SAT/SMT solvers to check the feasibility. When the simplification fails to reduce the number and lengths of error paths, such as the programs in `eca` discussed in Sect. 5.3, slicing can hardly improve verification performance with this technique.

Abstract refinement simulates the program semantics through the repetitive abstraction and refinement processes. The verification tool can adopt various abstract domains, initialization and refinement strategies, over-approximation and under-approximation methods, and solutions to validate potential error traces. Therefore, more efforts are required to identify which methods can enhance verification performance with the sliced program.

Indeed, the efficacy of program slicing in the context of verification is influenced by a multitude of factors beyond the slicing process itself. To obtain obvious gains in verification, we may have to choose specific slicing strategies after understanding the verification techniques adopted in the verifiers.

6.3 Limitations of Tools/Toolchains

The experimentation with the first three toolchains might be inadequate due to the limitations in handling arrays and pointers. Anyway, the semantic reasoning in slicing is important to reduce state space and keep consistent results.

Slicing large-scale programs can be notably resource-intensive, often requiring substantial memory and extensive time for storing PDGs/SDGs and analyzing dependencies within these graphs. The five largest programs in the original benchmarks, ranging from 18 MB to 81 MB, are exactly the five ones that run out of memory or exceed the time limit when sliced by llvm-slicer, although none of them can be correctly verified by Gazer-Theta within the time limit.

Some engineering issues bring additional overheads to the slicing goal when various toolchains are employed. Code reorganization from sliced statements to a sliced program in Frama-C, and decompilation from sliced LLVM IR to C may complicate the original code, such as multiple branches, unnecessary type casts, and additional value selections and jump statements, which possibly cause the analysis and verification to be more complex and laborious. We apply llvm-slicer+llvm2c+Gazer-Theta to the 49 C programs to evaluate the adverse effect introduced by decompilation, compared with the last three toolchains in Table 2. Seven programs, taking more than one second to obtain correct verification results with the fourth toolchain, are verified at a reduced performance when decompilation is employed. One program nearly doubles its original verification cost due to the solver in Gazer-Theta (BMC) grappling with substantial type casting operations. Meanwhile, the verification cost for the remaining programs increases slightly, by less than 10%. Moreover, when we employ llvm-slicer+llvm2c+GDart-LLVM, the verification results of 10 programs become wrong, compared with those obtained without decompilation. Decompilation by llvm2c introduces inline assembly code to these programs, and GDart-LLVM cannot handle the corresponding instructions, thus failing to conduct sound verification.

7 Conclusions and Future Work

In this paper, we have investigated the feasibility of adopting program slicing to simplify C programs and save the verification effort. We have chosen the latest tools for slicing and verification and benchmarks from the software verification community, and tried various combinations to make a detailed comparison and analysis. With extensive experiments, we can reach the following conclusions: 1) the features and limitations of slicing tools and verifiers restrict the generalizability of the solution; 2) semantic-based slicing is more efficient in program simplification, whose performance also relies on the types of the programs; 3) due to the limited precision in the static analysis, or ignoring the concerns of certain verifiers, slicing may lead to inconsistency before and after slicing; 4) semantic simplification, not the scale of programs or the portion of reduced code, is the main indicator for performance improvement.

In this paper, we consider reachability properties, which can cover most assertions but are hard to indicate some potential problems of programs concerned by developers, such as unsafe behaviors about the memory, data races in concurrent programs, overflows, and non-terminating states. The properties to check these problems may need defining new slicing criteria and adjusting the slicing techniques, which will be the future directions.

The benchmarks are selected from SV-COMP. We did not apply the combination to real-world C projects, for the difficulty in understanding the purposes and functions and then inserting reasonable and suitable properties. Therefore, we will also investigate the methods of automatic generation of properties.

Acknowledgments. This work is partly funded by the Major Project of ISCAS (ISCAS-ZD-202302) and supported by the National Natural Science Foundation of China (NSFC) under grant number 62132020. We would like to thank Yingzhou Zhang, Jun Yan and Xutong Ma https://orcid.org/0009-0009-1510-1668 for their discussion and advice on this paper, and the anonymous reviewers for their constructive opinions and suggestions on this research.

References

1. Abdallah, M., Alokush, B., Alrefaee, M., Salah, M., Bader, R., Awad, K.: JavaBST: Java backward slicing tool. In: ICIT, pp. 614–618. IEEE (2017)
2. Ádám, Z., Sallai, G., Hajdu, Á.: Gazer-Theta: LLVM-based verifier portfolio with BMC/CEGAR (competition contribution). In: TACAS 2021. LNCS, vol. 12652, pp. 433–437. Springer, Cham (2021). https://doi.org/10.1007/978-3-030-72013-1_27
3. Ahmed, K., Lis, M., Rubin, J.: Slicer4J: a dynamic slicer for Java. In: ESEC/FSE, pp. 1570–1574 (2021)
4. Ball, T., Podelski, A., Rajamani, S.K.: Boolean and cartesian abstraction for model checking C programs. In: Margaria, T., Yi, W. (eds.) TACAS 2001. LNCS, vol. 2031, pp. 268–283. Springer, Heidelberg (2001). https://doi.org/10.1007/3-540-45319-9_19
5. Beyer, D.: Competition on software verification and witness validation: SV-COMP 2023. In: Sankaranarayanan, S., Sharygina, N. (eds.) TACAS 2023. LNCS, vol. 13994, pp. 495–522. Springer, Cham (2023). https://doi.org/10.1007/978-3-031-30820-8_29
6. Biere, A., Cimatti, A., Clarke, E.M., Strichman, O., Zhu, Y.: Bounded model checking. Handb. Satisfiability **185**(99), 457–481 (2009)

7. Chalupa, M.: DG: a program analysis library. Softw. Impacts **6**, 100038 (2020)
8. Chalupa, M., Jašek, T., Novák, J., Řechtáčková, A., Šoková, V., Strejček, J.: Symbiotic 8: beyond symbolic execution. In: TACAS 2021. LNCS, vol. 12652, pp. 453–457. Springer, Cham (2021). https://doi.org/10.1007/978-3-030-72013-1_31
9. Chalupa, M., Strejček, J.: Evaluation of program slicing in software verification. In: Ahrendt, W., Tapia Tarifa, S.L. (eds.) IFM 2019. LNCS, vol. 11918, pp. 101–119. Springer, Cham (2019). https://doi.org/10.1007/978-3-030-34968-4_6
10. Clarke, E., Grumberg, O., Jha, S., Lu, Y., Veith, H.: Counterexample-guided abstraction refinement. In: Emerson, E.A., Sistla, A.P. (eds.) CAV 2000. LNCS, vol. 1855, pp. 154–169. Springer, Heidelberg (2000). https://doi.org/10.1007/10722167_15
11. Cousot, P., Cousot, R.: Abstract interpretation: a unified lattice model for static analysis of programs by construction or approximation of fixpoints. In: POPL, pp. 238–252 (1977)
12. Cuoq, P., Kirchner, F., Kosmatov, N., Prevosto, V., Signoles, J., Yakobowski, B.: Frama-C: a software analysis perspective. In: Eleftherakis, G., Hinchey, M., Holcombe, M. (eds.) SEFM 2012. LNCS, vol. 7504, pp. 233–247. Springer, Heidelberg (2012). https://doi.org/10.1007/978-3-642-33826-7_16
13. Galindo, C., Perez, S., Silva, J.: A program slicer for Java (tool paper). In: Schlingloff, B.H., Chai, M. (eds.) SEFM 2022. LNCS, vol. 13550, pp. 146–151. Springer, Cham (2022). https://doi.org/10.1007/978-3-031-17108-6_9
14. Heizmann, M., Hoenicke, J., Podelski, A.: Refinement of trace abstraction. In: Palsberg, J., Su, Z. (eds.) SAS 2009. LNCS, vol. 5673, pp. 69–85. Springer, Heidelberg (2009). https://doi.org/10.1007/978-3-642-03237-0_7
15. Horwitz, S., Reps, T.: The use of program dependence graphs in software engineering. In: ICSE, pp. 392–411 (1992)
16. Horwitz, S., Reps, T., Binkley, D.: Interprocedural slicing using dependence graphs. ACM Trans. Program. Lang. Syst. **12**(1), 26–60 (1990)
17. Kumar, N., Neema, S., Das, M., Mohan, B.R.: Program slicing analysis with KLEE, DIVINE and Frama-C. In: ICAC, pp. 1–5. IEEE (2021)
18. Matsubara, M., Sakurai, K., Narisawa, F., Enshoiwa, M., Yamane, Y., Yamanaka, H.: Model checking with program slicing based on variable dependence graphs. In: FTSCS, pp. 56–68 (2012)
19. Mihalkovič, B.V.: Improved translation of LLVM IR code to C
20. Millett, L.I., Teitelbaum, T.: Issues in slicing PROMELA and its applications to model checking, protocol understanding, and simulation. Int. J. Softw. Tools Technol. Transf. **2**, 343–349 (2000)
21. Odenbrett, M., Nguyen, V.Y., Noll, T.: Slicing AADL specifications for model checking. In: NFM (2010)
22. Ottenstein, K.J., Ottenstein, L.M.: The program dependence graph in a software development environment. ACM Sigplan Notices **19**(5), 177–184 (1984)
23. Ranganath, V.P.: Indus-Java program slicer (2006)
24. Reps, T., Yang, W.: The semantics of program slicing and program integration. In: Díaz, J., Orejas, F. (eds.) TAPSOFT 1989. LNCS, vol. 352, pp. 360–374. Springer, Heidelberg (1989). https://doi.org/10.1007/3-540-50940-2_47
25. Sabouri, H., Sirjani, M.: Slicing-based reductions for Rebeca. Electron. Notes Theor. Comput. Sci. **260**, 209–224 (2010)
26. Teitelbaum, T.: Codesurfer. ACM SIGSOFT Softw. Eng. Notes **25**(1), 99 (2000)
27. Vasudevan, S., Emerson, E.A., Abraham, J.A.: Efficient model checking of hardware using conditioned slicing. Electron. Notes Theor. Comput. Sci. **128**(6), 279–294 (2005)

28. Wang, L., Zhang, Q., Zhao, P.: Automated detection of code vulnerabilities based on program analysis and model checking. In: SCAM, pp. 165–173. IEEE (2008)
29. Weiser, M.: Program slicing. IEEE Trans. Softw. Eng. **4**, 352–357 (1984)
30. Yi, X., Wang, J., Yang, X.: Slicing execution for model checking C programs. Int. J. Softw. Eng. Knowl. Eng. **16**(05), 747–768 (2006)
31. Zhang, J.: Constraint solving and symbolic execution. In: Meyer, B., Woodcock, J. (eds.) VSTTE 2005. LNCS, vol. 4171, pp. 539–544. Springer, Heidelberg (2008). https://doi.org/10.1007/978-3-540-69149-5_59
32. Zhang, Y.Z.: SymPas: symbolic program slicing. J. Comput. Sci. Technol. **36**, 397–418 (2021)

An Approach to Improving Reliability of Parallel Graph Computation

Jin Cui[1(✉)] and Zhenhua Duan[2(✉)]

[1] Xi'an Shiyou University, Xi'an 710065, People's Republic of China
cuijin_xd@126.com
[2] ICTT and ISN Laboratory, Xidian University, Xi'an 710071
, People's Republic of China
zhhduan@mail.xidian.edu.cn

Abstract. The distributed programming framework for parallel graph computation has been proposed to process and analyze large scale graph data. However, how to model and verify properties of parallel graph computation deserves our attention and studying so as to improve the reliability of big data processing. In this paper, we propose an approach based on runtime verification at code level to verify properties of the parallel graph computation process. With this approach, the parallel computation framework Pregel for graph data processing is modeled in MSVL (Modeling, Simulation and Verification Language), a property to be verified is specified by a PPTL (Propositional Projection Temporal Logic) formula, then a compiler MCII is employed to verify whether a property is satisfied. Case studies of the shortest path problem and PageRank algorithm are conducted to demonstrate our approach.

Keywords: Runtime verification at code level · Parallel graph computation · MSVL · Reliability

1 Introduction

Parallel computation frameworks Pregel [1] and Hama [2] for clusters of computers have been designed to process large scale graph data in social networks, transportation networks, and transmission routes of infectious diseases. In the process of parallel graph computation, each vertex is assigned a processor to perform computation, and messages are passed along edges between vertices. As these computing platforms become indispensable, their reliability and security deserves our attention and studying. There may be bugs in processing graph data. These vulnerabilities or malicious attackers could change intermediate or output results, leading to accidents or even disasters.

Formal verification uses strict mathematical methods to prove whether a system satisfies desired properties or not. It has been introduced to verify different

This research is supported by NSFC No. 62272359, and Special Scientific Research Project No. 21JK0844 of Education Department of Shaanxi Province.

W.-N. Chin and Z. Xu (Eds.): TASE 2024, LNCS 14777, pp. 58–72, 2024.
https://doi.org/10.1007/978-3-031-64626-3_4

big data computing processes such as Hadoop MapReduce, Spark, Amazon S3 and so on [3–6]. Runtime verification is a lightweight formal method and pursues to check whether a certain execution trace satisfies a given property by monitoring the execution of a system. At the price of a limited execution coverage, runtime verification can give precise information on the runtime behaviour of the monitored system. A runtime verification process typically consists of three stages: generating monitors from properties, generating the relevant events to be fed to the monitor from a system, and analyzing the system execution by the monitor. The system to be analyzed and the properties to be verified are usually in different formalism, extracting information from a running system and sending them to monitors may generate a large runtime overhead [7,8]. This paper employs a novel runtime verification approach based on dynamic execution of MSVL programs to model and verify the parallel graph computation process.

MSVL (Modeling, Simulation and Verification Language) is a parallel temporal logic programming language, programs in MSVL can be both executed and verified. In this paper, we propose an approach for verification based on MSVL and runtime verification at code level. With this approach, the parallel graph computation is modeled as a program M in MSVL, and the property to be verified is represented by a PPTL (Propositional Projection Temporal Logic) formula ϕ. And $\neg\phi$ is transformed to another MSVL program M'. Whether M satisfies ϕ can be judged by executing the program $M \wedge M'$. If the execution result of $M \wedge M'$ is $false$, it indicates that M satisfies ϕ; otherwise, a counterexample of M violating ϕ can be found. In fact, we can use the existing compiler MCII [9,10] to execute the MSVL program $M \wedge M'$, so that a verification result can be obtained.

The contributions of this paper are as follows: we employ runtime verification approach at code level to verify safety and correctness of graph computation in distributed environment; we formalize the parallel graph computation with MSVL language, a formal model for parallel graph computation is obtained, the data safety and functional correctness are verified using the MSVL compiler; to demonstrate our approach to verifying graph computation in MSVL, two case studies are given in detail. This paper is the first application of MSVL runtime verification technique to graph parallel computation.

The remainder of this paper is organized as follows. In the next section, we briefly introduce Pregel computation, basic concepts of MSVL language and runtime verification approach. Section 3 presents our approach for modeling and verifying Pregel computation. In Sect. 4, we conduct two case studies shortest path problem and PageRank algorithm to show how to verify safety and correctness of Pregel computation with our approach. Section 5 is a summary of the paper.

2 Preliminaries

2.1 Pregel Computation

Pregel computation is designed based on the BSP (Bulk Synchronous Parallel) computing model [11], which involves a large number of processors connected through networks. Each processor has a local memory and is assigned various computing threads. A computation process composed of several threads of BSP includes a series of global supersteps. A global superstep is an iteration in the computation, as shown in Fig. 1. It includes local computing, communication, and barrier synchronization. Local computing refers to the fact that each processor involved in the computation has its own task, which reads data and process it in local memory. Further, tasks of different processors are independent and asynchronous. Communication refers to the exchange of data among processors. Synchronization means that when one processor finishes its task, it will wait for the completion of tasks of other processors to start the next superstep.

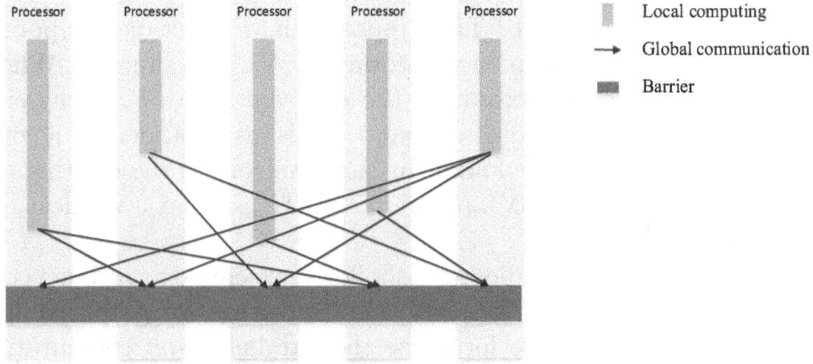

Fig. 1. A structure of a global superstep

In order to model Pregel computation, usually a directed graph is employed to represent the data to be processed, and it is also the basis for parallel graph computation since a vertex is assigned a processor to perform computation. With this model, each vertex is uniquely identified with an identifier. Each vertex is also associated with a mutable user-defined value. A directed edge has a mutable user-defined value as well.

Initially, in superstep 0, all vertices in a graph are in active state, and these vertices perform the computation task. When a vertex does not need to perform computation, its state is set to inactive and it will be waked up by a message sent to it in any following supersteps. When all vertices in the graph becomes inactive, the iterative process terminates.

2.2 MSVL Language

Modeling, Simulation and Verification Language (MSVL) [4,12] is an executable subset of Projection Temporal Logic (PTL) [13]. The following is a brief introduction to the syntax and semantics of MSVL. For more details, please refer to [13]. With MSVL, expressions can be treated as terms and statements as formulas in PTL. The arithmetic expression e and boolean expression b are inductively defined by the following grammar.

$$e ::= c \mid v \mid \bigcirc e \mid \ominus e \mid f(e_1, \ldots, e_m)$$
$$b ::= true \mid false \mid e_1 = e_2 \mid e_1 < e_2 \mid \neg b \mid b_1 \wedge b_2$$

where c is a constant, v a variable; $\bigcirc e$ and $\ominus e$ denote e at the next and previous state over an interval, respectively. The arithmetic operation $e_1\, op\, e_2$ ($op ::= + \mid - \mid * \mid /$) is regarded as function $f(e_1, e_2)$. Boolean expressions are composed of boolean constants $true$, $false$, relational operations on arithmetic expressions, and logical operations on boolean expressions.

With MSVL, variables are of types such as integer, float, char, and string as well as pointer, array, and struct [14]. In addition, MSVL also supports function calls of C library functions [15].

Table 1. The syntax and semantics of MSVL statements

Statements	*Syntax*	*Model semantics*
Termination	$empty$	$\stackrel{\text{def}}{=} \varepsilon$
Assignment	$v <== e$	$\stackrel{\text{def}}{=} v = e \wedge p_v$
Unit assignment	$v := e$	$\stackrel{\text{def}}{=} \bigcirc v = e \wedge \bigcirc p_v \wedge \mathsf{skip}$
State frame	$lbf(v)$	$\stackrel{\text{def}}{=} \neg p_v \rightarrow \exists e : \ominus v = e \wedge v = e)$
Interval frame	$frame(v)$	$\stackrel{\text{def}}{=} \Box(more \rightarrow \bigcirc lbf(v))$
Next	$next\ \phi$	$\stackrel{\text{def}}{=} \bigcirc\phi$
Always	$alw\ \phi$	$\stackrel{\text{def}}{=} \Box\phi$
Conjunction	$\phi_1\ and\ \phi_2$	$\stackrel{\text{def}}{=} \phi_1 \wedge \phi_2$
Selection	$\phi_1\ or\ \phi_2$	$\stackrel{\text{def}}{=} \phi_1 \vee \phi_2$
Sequential	$\phi_1 ; \phi_2$	$\stackrel{\text{def}}{=} \phi_1 ; \phi_2$
Parallel	$\phi_1 \| \phi_2$	$\stackrel{\text{def}}{=} \phi_1 \wedge (\phi_2 ; true) \vee (\phi_1 ; true) \wedge \phi_2 \vee \phi_1 \wedge \phi_2$
Local	$local\ v$: ϕ	$\stackrel{\text{def}}{=} \exists v : \phi$
Conditional	$if\ (b)\ then\ \{\phi_1\}\ else\ \{\phi_2\}$	$\stackrel{\text{def}}{=} (b \wedge \phi_1) \vee (\neg b \wedge \phi_2)$
While	$while(b)\{\phi\}$	$\stackrel{\text{def}}{=} (b \wedge \phi)^* \wedge \Box(\varepsilon \rightarrow \neg b) \vee \Box(more \wedge \phi)$
Projection	$(\phi_1, \ldots, \phi_m)\ \mathsf{prj}\ \phi$	$\stackrel{\text{def}}{=} (\phi_1, \ldots, \phi_m)\ \mathsf{prj}\ \phi$
Await	$await(b)$	$\stackrel{\text{def}}{=} frame(V_b) \wedge halt(b)$

The syntax of the statements of MSVL are defined in Table 1. A brief explanation of the statements in Table 1 is given as follows: *empty* means the current interval is terminating; $v <== e$ means assigning the value of e to v at the current state while $v := e$ means assigning the value of e to v at the next state and the interval length is one. In the assignment statements, atomic proposition p_v is used to identify an appearance of assignment to v. Using p_v, $lbf(v)$ can be used to inherit the value of framed variable v at a state; $next\ \phi$ means ϕ is executed from the next state; *alw* ϕ means that ϕ is executed at all the future states including the current one over an interval; ϕ_1 and ϕ_2 means that ϕ_1 and ϕ_2 are executed concurrently, and share the same interval; ϕ_1 or ϕ_2 means ϕ_1 or ϕ_2 is executed; ϕ_1 ; ϕ_2 means that ϕ_2 is executed after ϕ_1 finishes; $\phi_1 \parallel \phi_2$ means that ϕ_1 and ϕ_2 are executed in parallel, while they are not required to terminate at the same time; and *local* $v{:}\phi$ enables ϕ to use local variable v; the meanings of conditional and while constructs are the same as in programming languages C and Java; *await*(b) waits until the condition b becomes true, at which point it terminates; $(\phi_1, \ldots, \phi_m)$ prj ϕ means that ϕ is executed in parallel with $\phi_1 ; \phi_2 ; \ldots ; \phi_m$ over an interval obtained by taking the endpoints of the intervals over which $\phi_1, \ldots, \phi_m$ are sequentially executed.

2.3 Runtime Verification at Code Level

Model checking verifies whether a system satisfies the desired property by traversing the state space of the model and searching a counter-example. However, it suffers from state explosion problem, especially for large scale program verification. Recently, a diversion approach called runtime verification at code level is proposed to fight the state explosion problem. The principle of runtime verification is based on model checking. To do so, it checks whether a property is satisfied by executing the program in parallel with a monitor program representing the negative of the property. If a successful execution path is found, it indicates that the property is violated, otherwise, we cannot determine whether the program is error free. The existing widely used runtime verification tools are RiTHM, T2 and Ultimate LTLAutomizer [16–18].

3 An Approach for Verifying Pregel Computation

In this section, we propose an innovative approach for verifying parallel graph computation. With this approach, MSVL programs and runtime verification are combined to verify safety and correctness of parallel graph computation. To do so, the parallel graph computation is modeled as a MSVL program M; a property to be verified is specified by a PPTL formula ϕ; and then $\neg\phi$ is transformed into a MSVL program M'; thus a new MSVL program M *and* M' is executed by means of compiler MCII [9]. As a result, if a successful execution path is found, it indicates that the property is violated; otherwise, we cannot determine whether the program is error free. In fact, our approach facilitates runtime verification since we convert execution of programs and checking property into a unique execution of a MSVL program. An outline of our approach is shown in Fig. 2.

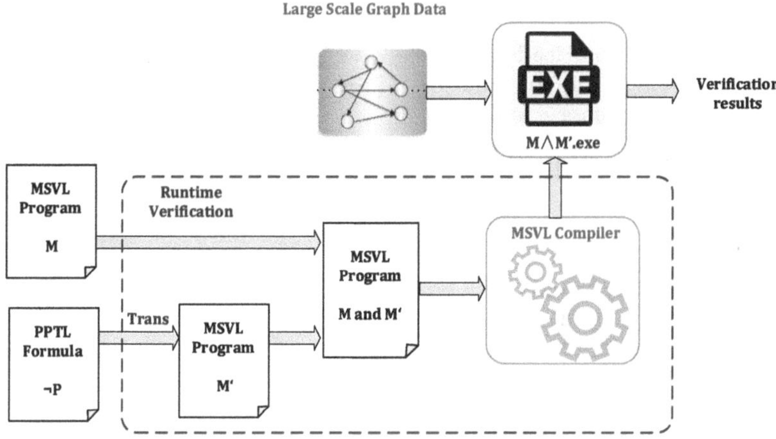

Fig. 2. An outline of runtime verification with MSVL

3.1 Modeling the Parallel Graph Computation

Modeling the Graph Structure. We use the cross list to represent the graph structure, define *struct GraphNode* to represent a vertex, and *struct Arc* to represent a directed edge of a graph in Fig. 3. In *GraphNode*, the member variable $ndName$ represents the ID of a vertex, and *data* the associated value of a vertex. The type of *data* can also be others except for integer. The member variable *isActive* is used to record whether a vertex is in the active state, and the member variable $isFsh$ indicates whether the execution of *Compute()* completes. The lists $firstIn$ and $firstOut$ of *Arc* type record all incoming and outgoing edges of a vertex, respectively.

In *struct Arc*, variables $ndTail$ and $ndHead$ represent the tail vertex and head vertex of an edge, respectively. The variable msg records a message associated with an edge. Note that an edge points from the tail vertex to the head vertex. Thus an edge is both in lists of the outgoing edges of its tail vertex and incoming edges of its head vertex. To record the next outgoing edge of a tail vertex $ndTail$, an edge contains pointers $tailNext$ of *Arc* type. Similarly, to record the next ingoing edge of a head vertex $ndHead$, an edge contains pointers $headNext$ of *Arc* type. Thus all incoming and outgoing edges of a vertex can be quickly found. Based on definitions of vertices and edges above, a graph with N vertices can be defined as $GraphNodeG[N]$:

Suppose that array $data[N]$ records the values associated with each vertex and two-dimensional array $matrix[N][N]$ stores the adjacency relation of a graph. It means that if there is a directed edge from vertex i to vertex j, $matrix[i][j] = 1$; otherwise, $matrix[i][j] = 0$. To create graph G is to initialize member variables $ndName$, $data$, outgoing edges list $firstIn$, incoming edges list $firstOut$ of each $GraphNode$ instance, as well as the member variables of each outgoing and incoming edge according to arrays $data$ and $matrix$. We define the function $initialize()$ to initialize the graph G. Based on the graph G created by

```
struct Arc{
        int  ndHead and
        int  ndTail and
        int  msg  and
        Arc *headNext  and
        Arc *tailNext
};

struct GraphNode{
    int ndName and
    int data and
    int isActive and
    int isFsh and
    int nOut and
    Arc *firstIn and
    Arc *firstOut
};

GraphNode G[N];
```

Fig. 3. Basic data structures for modeling a graph

this process, we can perform subsequent operations in the graph computations process.

Message Passing Mechanism. A message is sent through the outgoing edge of a vertex. With the cross list structure defined above, a vertex sending a message is represented by mutating the value of variable *msg* of all the outgoing edges of the vertex with the computation result of the current superstep. We define function *send_msg*() to implement the process in which a vertex sends out a message. Similarly, a vertex receiving a message is expressed by reading the values of variable *msg* of all its ingoing edges.

Modeling the Pregel Computation Process. We define function *mCompute*() in MSVL to represent the computation executed in a processor. It may involve the following operations: reading variable *ndName* of a vertex, getting the number of supersteps of the current computation, reading and mutating the value of a vertex, traversing the outgoing edges of a vertex, setting the vertex state to inactive and so on.

With the graph structure, as well as functions defined above, we define the MSVL model M for the parallel graph computation in Fig. 4.

The global variable *noStep* records the number of supersteps and $noStep = 0$ initially. Function *initalize*() initializes the graph data to be processed, and function *mCompute*() defines the operations to be performed in a superstep according to the data processing requirements. Next, messages are sent out to

```
frame(G,matrix,data,noStep,N)
and
GraphNode G[N] and
int noStep<==0 and
int N<==5 and skip;
initialize(G,matrix,data,N);
while( G[0].isActvie or G[1].isActive or ...
          or G[N-1].isActive)
{
   (mCompute(&G[0]) ||...||mCompute(&G[N-1]) );
   (send_msg(&G[0],...)||...||send_msg(&G[N-1],...));
    noStep:=noStep+1
}
```

Fig. 4. MSVL model M for the graph computation in Pregel

other vertices (if needed) when computation on vertices is completed. The definition of *mCompute*() depends on the specific computational requirements. In the following section, we give two case studies the shortest paths problem and PageRank algorithm.

3.2 Converting a Property into a MSVL Program

In order to verify a property ϕ with MSVL program M based on runtime verification, we need to convert $\neg\phi$ into another MSVL program M'. To do so, we first construct an LNFG (Labelled Normal Form Graph) G for $\neg\phi$; then we traverse vertices and edges of G to generate various pathes of G; these pathes can be used to generate a MSVL program M'. The details of the transformation can be found in [10]. We can use the existing tool *P2M* [10] to transform $\neg\phi$ to a MSVL program M' automatically.

3.3 Runtime Verification with MSVL

The verification process is conducted as follows:

(1) The Pregel parallel graph computation is modeled as a MSVL program M in a similar way as shown in Subsect. 3.1.
(2) The property to be verified is described by a PPTL formula ϕ.
(3) We convert $\neg\phi$ into a MSVL program M' in the same way as given in Subsect. 3.2.
(4) A new MSVL program M *and* M' is generated and executed by means of compiler MCII.

If there exists a successful path in the execution result, then a counterexample is found which indicates that M violates property ϕ. Otherwise, we cannot determine whether M satisfies property ϕ.

Please note that the runtime verification approach is incomplete. It means that during the verification process, if a successful path is found, we confirm the counterexample is also found. However, if the execution is failed, we have no conclusion whether the program satisfies the property. To take over this problem, we need to take advantage of tools KLEE and Z3 [19,20] to generate more arguments of the program so that more paths of the program can be executed.

4 Case Studies

This section takes the shortest path problem and PageRank algorithm as examples to demonstrate the effectiveness of the runtime verification approach presented in the previous section. The properties to be verified are the correctness of computation, data consistency and so on.

4.1 Case Study A: The Shortest Paths Problem

The shortest paths problem is well-known in graph theory and arise in a wide variety of applications, with several important variants. The single source shortest paths problem requires finding a shortest path between a single source vertex and every other vertex in a graph.

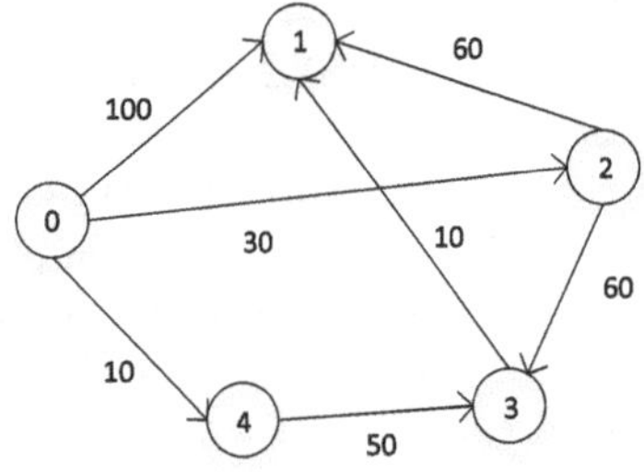

Fig. 5. A graph instance for determining the shortest paths

Using Pregel, the values of all vertices are initialized to infinity. In superstep S, each vertex receives a message from its neighbor, the message contains the shortest potential distance from the source vertex to the neighbor, which have been updated since the end of the previous superstep $S-1$ by the neighbor vertex. In each superstep S, for any vertex v in the graph, after receiving the message sent to it by the neighbor vertex in the previous superstep $S-1$, if the minimum value of the value contained in all the messages is less than the current value of the vertex, then the vertex v will update its own association value. The message is then sent along the outgoing edge to the other neighbor vertices. This process continues until no more vertex updates occur in the graph

```
function mCompute(GraphNode *gnode, int noStep)
{frame(mindist,arcp,arcp1) and(
  if(gnode->isActive=1 or gnode->hasMsg=1)
  then{
    if(gnode.ndName=0)
    then{gnode->mindist:=0}
    else{gnode->mindist:=999};
    if(gnode->hasMsg=1)
    then{Arc *arcp<==gnode->firstIn and skip;
        while(NULL!=arcp)
        {gnode->mindist:=min(gnode->mindist,arcp->msg);
        arcp:=arcp->headNext}  };
     gnode->isActive:=0
          }     )
};
function  send_msg(GraphNode *gnode)
{frame(arcp1) and (
if(gnode->mindist < gnode->data)
then{gnode->data:=gnode->mindist;
         Arc *arcp1<==gnode->firstOut and skip;
        while(NULL!=arcp1)
        {arcp1->msg:=gnode->mindist+ arcp1->weight;
        G[arcp1->ndHead].hasMsg:=1;
        arcp1:=arcp1->tailNext}
   } )
};
```

Fig. 6. Basic functions of the single source shortest paths algorithm for Pregel

and the program terminates. In this case, the associated value of all vertices in the graph is the shortest distance from the source vertex to itself.

Functions *mCompute*() and *send_msg*() for determining the shortest paths are defined in Fig. 6. We take the graph in Fig. 5 as an input and denote the MSVL program instance as *M_ShortestPath*, we verify two properties P_1 and P_2 defined in Table 2 for *M_ShortestPath* using the compiler MCII. P_1 means the out degree of each vertex is always be $2, 2, 1, 1, 3$ respectively in the computation process, and P_2 means that the length of shortest path for each vertex will be $0, 70, 30, 60, 10$ respectively. By compiling and executing programs $M\_ShortestPath \wedge \neg P_1$ and $M\_ShortestPath \wedge \neg P_1$ with compiler MCII, we obtain that P_1 and P_2 are both valid to *M_ShortestPath*.

4.2 Case Study B: PageRank Algorithm

PageRank algorithm was originally proposed to calculate the importance of Internet pages of Google search engine by Page and Brin in 1990 [21,22]. By using PageRank algorithm on a collection of large amount of pages with the link

Table 2. Definitions of properties in the shortest path algorithm

$P_1 \overset{\text{def}}{=} som(p0\ and\ p1\ and\ p2\ and\ p3\ and\ p4)$	
define $p0 : G[0].data = 0;$	define $p1 : G[1].data = 70;$
define $p2 : G[2].data = 30;$	define $p3 : G[3].data = 60;$
define $p4 : G[4].data = 10;$	
$P_2 \overset{\text{def}}{=} alw(p0\ and\ p1\ and\ p2\ and\ p3\ and\ p4)$	
define $p0 : G[0].nOut = 2;$	define $p1 : G[1].nOut = 2;$
define $p2 : G[2].nOut = 1;$	define $p3 : G[3].nOut = 1;$
define $p4 : G[4].nOut = 3;$	

relationship known, the rank values indicating the importance of pages can be obtained, and pages with higher rank values may be at the top of the list of internet searches. The link relationship among pages can be conveniently expressed as a connected digraph, where a page is represented as a vertex, the linked in and out relationship among pages are represented by ingoing and outgoing edges. The graph is extremely large for real Web pages. Figure 7 shows only a small fragment of the link relationship instance of Web pages, and we can see that page v_1 contains external links to pages v_2 and v_4, page v_5 is the source link of pages v_1, v_2 and v_3 in this graph.

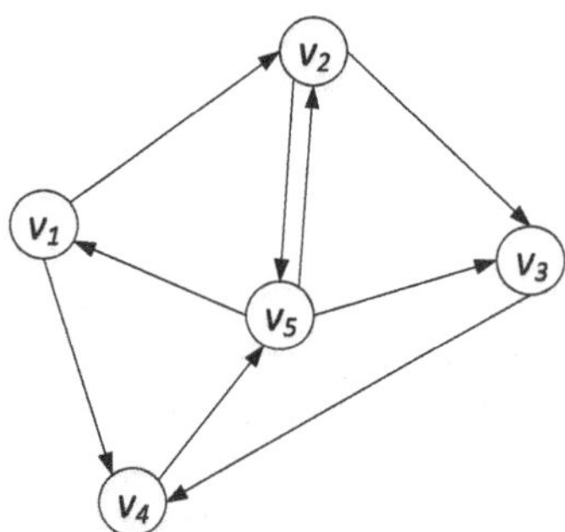

Fig. 7. A fragment instance of link relationship in Web pages

To calculate the PageRank value PR of a page, the basic formula of the PageRank algorithm is as follows [21,22]:

$$PR = \beta \sum_{i=1}^{n} \frac{PR_i}{N_i} + (1-\beta)\frac{1}{N}$$

where n is the number of pages, N_i is the out degrees of the ith source link, PR_i represents the PageRank value of the ith source link, and β is a constant ranged over interval $(0, 1]$. The formula indicates that to calculate the PR value of a page, we need to have the PR values of all its source links first.

Functions *mCompute*() and *send_msg*() of the PageRank algorithm for Pregel are defined in Fig. 8.

```
function mCompute(GraphNode *gnode, int noStep)
{frame(sum,arcp,n) and(
 float sum<==0 and
 Arc *arcp<==gnode->firstIn and skip;
 if(noStep>0)
 then
 { while(NULL!=arcp)
   {sum:=summ+arcp->msg;
        arcp:=arcp->headNext
   };
   gnode->data:=sum
  }  )
};
function send_msg(GraphNode *gnode, int noStep)
{frame(arcp,n) and (
 int n<==gnode->nOut and
 Arc *arcp<==gnode->firstOut  and skip;
 if(noStep<30)
 then{
   while(NULL!=arcp)
   {search_send(&G[arcp->ndHead],arcp->ndHead,
                         arcp->ndTail, gnode->data/n);
    arcp := arcp->tailNext
   }
 }
 else{gnode->isActive<==0 and  skip};
 gnode->isFsh:=1
 ) };
```

Fig. 8. Basic functions of the PageRank algorithm for Pregel

We demonstrate the verification process of Pregel computation by means of compiler MCII with MSVL program *mprg_pr*5*n*. It is an instance of Pregel computation model M defined in Sect. 3. We have defined functions *mCompute*() and *send_msg*() for PageRank algorithm. The input is the directed graph shown in Fig. 7, the number of iterations is set to 30, and β is set to 1.

In the iterative process of calculating the PR value for each page, the initial value of each page should be set to $1/N$ in the algorithm, namely $1/5$ for the program *mprg_pr*5*n*. After several rounds of iteration, the PR value of each page will eventually tend to a stable value. The PR value indicates the probability of a page being visited by surfers, and the page link graph is a strong connection graph. Thus in the computation process, the PR value of each page needs to be greater than 0 and less than 1. The property to be verified is specified in PPTL formula P_1 defined in Table 3.

Table 3. Definitions of properties in PageRank algorithm

$P_1 \stackrel{\text{def}}{=} alw(p \rightarrow (\ p0\ and\ q0\ and\ p1\ and\ q1\ and$ $p2\ and\ q2\ and\ p3\ and\ q3\ and\ p4\ and\ q4))$	
define $p : noStep > 0;$	
define $p0 : G[0].data < 1.0;$	define $q0 : G[0].data > 0;$
define $p1 : G[1].data < 1.0;$	define $q1 : G[1].data > 0;$
define $p2 : G[2].data < 1.0;$	define $q2 : G[2].data > 0;$
define $p3 : G[3].data < 1.0;$	define $q3 : G[3].data > 0;$
define $p4 : G[4].data < 1.0;$	define $q4 : G[4].data > 0;$
$P_2 \stackrel{\text{def}}{=} alw(p0\ and\ p1\ and\ p2\ and\ p3\ and\ p4)$	
define $p0 : G[0].nOut = 2;$	define $p1 : G[1].nOut = 2;$
define $p2 : G[2].nOut = 1;$	define $p3 : G[3].nOut = 1;$
define $p4 : G[4].nOut = 3;$	

Data safety means that during the computation process, some data cannot be modified, for example, the out degree of each vertex should satisfy the property specified by PPTL formula P_2 defined in Table 3

By verifying property P_1 in program $mprg\_pr5n$ with MCII compiler, a counterexample is found, by analyzing the state sequence of the counterexample, we found that in $mprg\_pr5n$, there exists a mistake when initialize variables $G[0].data$, $G[1].data$, $G[2].data$, $G[3].data$, and $G[4].data$. They are wrongly initialized with 2.0, which should be 0.2 actually. We revise the mistake in $mprg\_pr5n$, and denote the program repaired as $mprg\_pr5n'$. By compiling and executing $mprg\_pr5n' \wedge M_1'$ (M_1' is the MSVL program obtained by converting $\neg P_1$ via the tool $P2M$) with compiler MCII, the output indicates that $mprg\_pr5n'$ satisfies property P_1. Using MCII, and repeating the similar interactive procedure for verifying property P_2 in the program $mprg\_pr5n'$, it shows P_2 is also valid to $mprg\_pr5n'$.

Although there is no counterexample found for both of the two properties in $mprg\_pr5n'$, the verification results just show that the properties are only satisfied on the path which is run in compiler MCII. The runtime verification at code level is based on the idea of unified model checking. Because the approach detects only one path of the model at a time, it avoids the problem of state space explosion. However, this method is incomplete. If a counterexample is found, it indicates that there exists defects in the program; otherwise, we know nothing about whether the model satisfies the property unless all paths of the model are searched.

5 Conclusion

In this paper, an approach to improving reliability of parallel graph computation for large scale graph data in the distributed environment is proposed. With this approach, we use MSVL language to implement the Pregel computation framework. Parallel constructs in MSVL are employed to realize the parallel in each computation iteration, and with the cross list structure denoting the graph data, message passing among connected vertices is conveniently expressed. With the formal model of parallel graph computation in MSVL, runtime verification at code level is employed to verify safety and correctness of the parallel computation process. We take the shortest path problem and PageRank algorithm as case studies to show the verification process. Properties are verified automatically with the help of the compiler MCII. In the future, we will study how to verify more properties such as data security of the parallel graph computation as well as other big data computation model with our approach. In order to take over the incompleteness of runtime verification, we also need to study how to generate more arguments of the program so that more execution paths of the program can be covered. In this way, the effectiveness of the runtime verification can be improved.

References

1. Malewicz, G., et al.: Pregel: a system for large-scale graph processing. In: Proceedings of the 2010 ACM SIGMOD International Conference on Management of Data, pp. 135–146 (2010)
2. http://hama.apache.org/index.html
3. Chiang, D.-L., et al.: Modeling and analysis of Hadoop mapreduce systems for big data using petri nets. Appl. Artif. Intell. **35**(1), 80–104 (2021)
4. Zhang, N., Wang, M., Duan, Z., Tian, C.: Verifying properties of mapreduce-based big data processing. IEEE Trans. Reliab. **71**(1), 321–338 (2022)
5. Fan, K., Wang, M.: DAG-based formal modeling of with MSVL. Information **14**(12), 658 (2023)
6. Bornholt, J., et al.: Using lightweight formal methods to validate a key-value storage node in Amazon S3. In: Proceedings of the ACM SIGOPS 28th Symposium on Operating Systems Principles, pp. 836–850 (2021)
7. Chalupa, M., Henzinger, T.A.: Bubaak: runtime monitoring of program verifiers. In: Sankaranarayanan, S., Sharygina, N. (eds.) TACAS 2023. LNCS, vol. 13994, pp. 535–540. Springer, Cham (2023). https://doi.org/10.1007/978-3-031-30820-8_32
8. Chai, M., Wang, H., Tang, T., Liu, H.: Runtime verification of train control systems with parameterized modal live sequence charts. J. Syst. Softw. **177**, 110962 (2021)
9. Yang, K., Duan, Z., et al.: A compiler for MSVL and its applications. Theor. Comput. Sci. **749**, 2–16 (2018)
10. Wang, M., Tian, C., et al.: Verifying full regular temporal properties of programs via dynamic program execution. IEEE Trans. Reliab. (2018)
11. Valiant, L.G.: A bridging model for parallel computation. Commun. ACM **33**(8), 103–111 (1990)
12. Wang, M., Tian, C., Zhang, N., Duan, Z., Yao, C.: Translating XD-C programs to MSVL programs. Theor. Comput. Sci. **809**, 430–465 (2020)

13. Duan, Z.: Temporal Logic and Temporal Logic Programming. Science Press (2005)
14. Wang, X., Tian, C., Duan, Z., Zhao, L.: MSVL: a typed language for temporal logic programming. Front. Comput. Sci. **11**, 762–785 (2017)
15. Zhang, N., Duan, Z., Tian, C.: A mechanism of function calls in MSVL. Theor. Comput. Sci. **654**, 11–25 (2016)
16. Navabpour, S., et al.: RiTHM: a tool for enabling time-triggered runtime verification for C programs. In: Proceedings of the 2013 9th Joint Meeting on Foundations of Software Engineering, pp. 603–606 (2013)
17. Brockschmidt, M., Cook, B., Ishtiaq, S., Khlaaf, H., Piterman, N.: T2: temporal property verification. In: Chechik, M., Raskin, J.-F. (eds.) TACAS 2016. LNCS, vol. 9636, pp. 387–393. Springer, Heidelberg (2016). https://doi.org/10.1007/978-3-662-49674-9_22
18. Dietsch, D., Heizmann, M., Langenfeld, V., Podelski, A.: Fairness modulo theory: a new approach to LTL software model checking. In: Kroening, D., Păsăreanu, C.S. (eds.) CAV 2015. LNCS, vol. 9206, pp. 49–66. Springer, Cham (2015). https://doi.org/10.1007/978-3-319-21690-4_4
19. Cadar, C., et al.: KLEE: unassisted and automatic generation of high-coverage tests for complex systems programs. In: OSDI, vol. 8, pp. 209–224 (2008)
20. de Moura, L., Bjørner, N.: Z3: an efficient SMT solver. In: Ramakrishnan, C.R., Rehof, J. (eds.) TACAS 2008. LNCS, vol. 4963, pp. 337–340. Springer, Heidelberg (2008). https://doi.org/10.1007/978-3-540-78800-3_24
21. Brin, S., Page, L.: The anatomy of a large-scale hypertextual web search engine. Comput. Netw. ISDN Syst. **30**(1–7), 107–117 (1998)
22. Tortosa, L., Vicent, J.F., Yeghikyan, G.: An algorithm for ranking the nodes of multiplex networks with data based on the pagerank concept. Appl. Math. Comput. **392**, 125676 (2021)

Safe and Infinite Resource Scheduling Using Energy Timed Automata

Pieter J. L. Cuijpers[1,2], Jonas Hansen[3(✉)], and Kim G. Larsen[3]

[1] Technische Universiteit Eindhoven, Eindhoven, The Netherlands
p.j.l.cuijpers@tue.nl
[2] Radboud Universiteit, Nijmegen, The Netherlands
[3] Aalborg Universitet, Aalborg, Denmark
{jonash,kgl}@cs.aau.dk

Abstract. We study the existence of infinite and safe schedules for resource-aware timed systems, in the setting of multiple continuous resources. Specifically, we explore the multi-variable extension of Energy Timed Automata, where variables are constrained by polyhedra in $\mathbb{R}^n$. We ask the question of whether there exist infinite runs satisfying such boundary constraints and show how schedules can be synthesized by characterising these runs as limit sets using quantifier elimination for linear real arithmetic.

Additionally, we show that this existential problem is decidable under the assumption that limit sets are linear, we relate this to an earlier decidability result for single-variable Energy Timed Automata that are flat and segmented, and show constructively that there exist flat and segmented multi-variable Energy Timed Automata that give rise to non-linear limit sets.

Keywords: Energy Timed Automata · Infinite Constrained Runs · Quantifier Elimination · Multiple Continuous Variables

1 Introduction

Resource scheduling is a broad topic that, among others, encapsulates a plethora of safety problems. For cyber-physical systems, a typical problem is the construction of infinite schedules that satisfy given non-functional requirements, such as timing and energy constraints [7,17]. As an example, think of load balancing in a smart grid or the management of oil pressure in a hydraulic system. A key characteristic of these systems is that resources are both produced and consumed over time, and that capacity for storage is limited. Automatic generation of such schedules can, for example, serve as a basis for synthesising system controllers.

The development of a sufficiently expressive formalism for modeling cyber-physical systems, as well as associated procedures for verifying safety properties, has been an active area of research in the past decades [9]. In particular, two important and interconnected questions are still being explored; "Is it possible to

W.-N. Chin and Z. Xu (Eds.): TASE 2024, LNCS 14777, pp. 73–90, 2024.
https://doi.org/10.1007/978-3-031-64626-3_5

behave badly, and if so, how?" (reachability), and "Is bad behaviour guaranteed to never occur?" (safety). Formally, both problems are verified by exploring a system's state space, which may be infinite. The notion of bad behaviour is captured by identifying certain states as undesirable. Reachability analysis asks whether such states lie on some path that follows from the semantic rules. Safety asks whether every path that follows from these rules is void of such states, or, in a control-theoretic sense, whether it is always possible to pick a path continuation that avoids them. In the field of formal methods, there is an ever ongoing pursuit to refine and expand the frontier of decidable formalisms for verifying correctness properties, in particular, reachability and safety [9].

It is well known that Hybrid Automata (HA) [1] are capable of modelling general cyber-physical systems that exhibit both continuous and discrete dynamics. As an example, consider the simple mono cell battery depicted in Fig. 1, modelled as an HA. We assume that it is rated for the maximum capacity of $k = 1000$ mAh and interpret time as seconds. The model defines three distinct modes; **Charging**, **Idling** and **Discharging**. Variable *charge* captures the amount of charge currently stored. The battery is limited to charge a maximum of 7.2 A for up to two seconds, with a one second required rest between charges, the timing of which is captured by variables *delay* and *rest* respectively. Whenever discharging, the battery provides the fixed amount of 3.6 A. In the model we use the unit mAh exclusively, e.g., discharging by 3.6 A per second is the same as removing 1 mAh of charge from the battery per second ($mAh = A \cdot hrs \cdot 1000$). The model also captures battery degradation, captured by variable *soh*, which characterises its state of health, i.e., its maximum capacity expressed in percentage of its initial capacity. The specific degradation ratio is captured by the constant $z = 10^{-3}$. Longer charges decreases its state of health faster than shorter charges, which is captured by the differential equation $soh' = -delay \cdot z$. Storage capacity is limited by its state of health, which is imposed by the invariant $charge \leq k \cdot soh$ in mode **C**. Finally, when charging, change in *charge* is proportional to its state of charge (*soc*), i.e., the amount of charge stored as a percentage of its maximum capacity, captured by the differential equation $charge' = 2 - 2 \cdot (\frac{charge}{k \cdot soh})$, where $soc = \frac{charge}{k \cdot soh}$. This simply means that charging will become slower (approaching 0 A) the closer we get to a full battery.

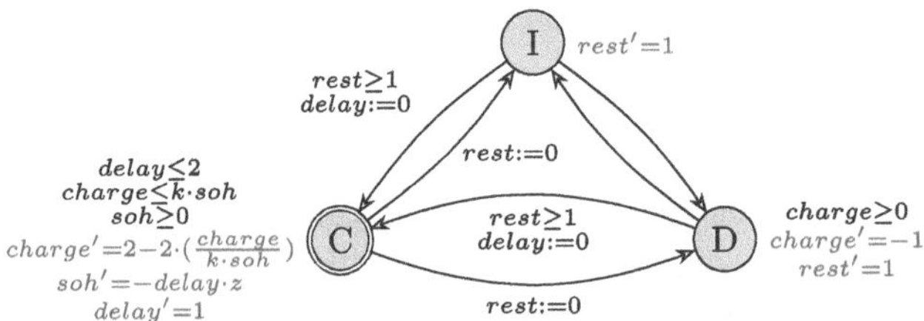

Fig. 1. An HA model of a mono-cell battery, defined over variables; *rest*, *delay*, *charge* and *soh* with discrete modes I, C and D. Omitted rates are assumed to be 0.

Now, there are numerous safety questions we could ask: "Given some behaviour of discharge, i.e., a duty cycle (maybe modelled as a separate HA) is it possible to fulfil it without running out of power?", "Is it possible to fulfil a sequence of duty cycles without degrading the battery more than 50%?", or even, ignoring degradation completely, i.e., $z = 0$, "Does there exist behaviour that fulfils some infinite sequence of duty cycles, that is, does the battery have sufficient capacity to allow this?". In this paper we are interested in that last flavour of safety problems, whether infinite behaviour is possible given some initial conditions and boundary constraints on certain variables.

Sadly however, it is well known that reachability and safety are undecidable for this class of models in general [19]. For the special case of Timed Automata (TA) [2], a sub-class of HA where continuous dynamics are limited to real variables (clocks), that evolve with constant rate 1 (their first derivative), both problems are decidable [13]. However, a TA model of our battery would only be able to capture the timing constraints, with **rest** and **delay** being clocks. TAs are not expressive enough to capture the behaviour of stored charge. Weighted [3] (a.k.a. Priced [12]) Timed Automata (WTA), extend TAs by considering one or more continuous variables that evolve in a positive piece-wise constant manner in addition to the clocks. WTAs allow for the modeling of cost accumulation as evolution of variables, but contrary to HA, their behavior is not affected by them. This is why continuous variables in WTAs are usually referred to as observers. Modelling our battery using a WTA would allow us to capture the behaviour of either charging or discharging, but not both simultaneously. It has been shown that cost optimal reachability [5] and cost optimal safety are decidable for WTAs [6], even in the multi-observer setting [14].

For scheduling problems that involve balancing real variables, we need to consider both production and consumption simultaneously, as in Fig. 1. This can be approached by allowing both positive and negative evolution of variables. As such, variables directly model accumulators. This connects back to the control-theoretic sense of safety, by characterising desirable states using boundary constraints on said accumulators. This approach is taken in, e.g., Resource Timed Automata [10] and Energy Timed Automata (ETA) [4]. As shown in [18], this approach brings us close to the frontier of decidability.

In [4] the formalism of ETA is presented as a general framework for constrained WTAs with both positive and negative rates. Notably, here we are no longer considering observers, as the discrete behaviour of ETAs depend on the evolution of continuous variables, which we therefore call resources.

Consider the mono-cell battery depicted in Fig. 2, modelled as an ETA. Like the model depicted in Fig. 1, we assume the rated maximum capacity of the battery is 1000 mAh. Note, *soh* is not considered in this model. Runs of ETAs are subject to constraints on their resources. Here, variable *charge* is constrained by the interval $[0, 1000]$.

With ETAs, we have a sufficiently expressive framework for modelling accumulators where it is possible to ask the kind of question we initially pursued, that is, "Does there exists an infinite run that never runs out of power, given some

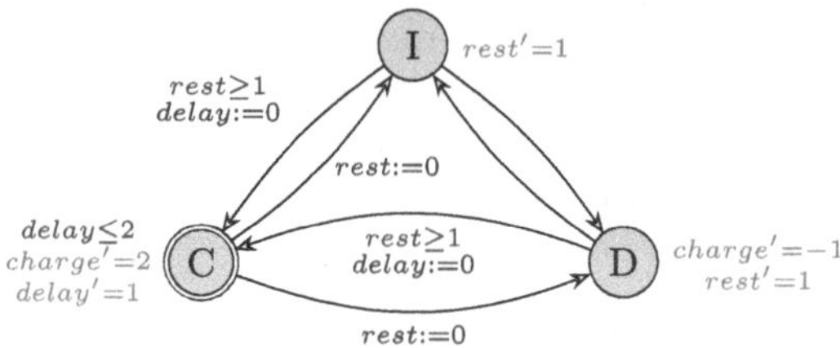

Fig. 2. An ETA model of a mono-cell battery, defined over resource *charge*, constrained by $charge \in [0, 1000]$. It imposes the same timing constraints as the model depicted in Fig. 1.

boundary constraints on the battery itself?". As shown in [4], using quantifier elimination for linear real arithmetic [15] it is possible to compute the greatest limit set of valuations that allow for infinite behaviour under given boundary constraints, in the single resource setting. Furthermore, ascertaining whether a desired set of valuations is reachable given some initial conditions, is computable as well, thanks to certain topological properties.

In this paper, we further refine this result by considering its multi-variable extension, hence broadening the class of models for which we can ascertain the existence of infinite behaviour. We show that in the multi-resource setting, by assuming linearity, limit sets of permissive resource valuations that allow for infinite behaviour, can be characterised as first-order formulas. We prove that in general, such limit sets can be non-linear, which is not the case if only a single resource is considered. Finally, we show how safe and infinite schedules can be synthesised using this assumption.

The remainder of this paper is structured as follows; In Sect. 2 we formally introduce ETAs and safety. In Sect. 3, the analysis method and the theoretical foundation is introduced. In Sect. 4, fixed points of valuation limit sets are characterised. Finally, in Sect. 5 we conclude our findings and discuss future research directions.

2 Energy Timed Automata

We now formally introduce the modelling language of ETA, together with constrained safety. We start with some preliminaries on clocks and resources.

Clocks are defined in the usual way, as real-valued variables. Let X be a finite set of m clocks. We define the set of clock constraints (guards) over X, denoted $\mathcal{C}(\mathrm{X})$, by the abstract syntax: $g ::== x \leq c \mid x \geq c \mid g \wedge g$, where $x \in \mathrm{X}$, and $c \in \mathbb{Q}_{\geq 0}$. For convenience we use $x == c$ to denote the constraint $x \leq c \wedge x \geq c$.

We write $\varsigma : \mathrm{X} \to \mathbb{R}_{\geq 0}$ for valuations of clocks. Let ς be a clock valuation and $g \in \mathcal{C}(\mathrm{X})$ a clock constraint. The evaluation of ς in g, denoted $\varsigma \models g$, is defined inductively on the structure of g: $\varsigma \models x \leq c \iff \varsigma(x) \leq c$, $\varsigma \models x \geq c \iff \varsigma(x) \geq c$, $\varsigma \models g_1 \wedge g_2 \iff \varsigma \models g_1 \wedge \varsigma \models g_2$, where $g_1, g_2 \in \mathcal{C}(\mathrm{X})$ and $x \in \mathrm{X}$. Additionally, we define the following algebra over valuations. Let

$x \in \mathrm{X}$ be a clock, $S \subseteq \mathrm{X}$ a set of clocks and $t \in \mathbb{R}_{\geq 0}$, then: $(\varsigma_1 + \varsigma_2)(x) = \varsigma_1(x) + \varsigma_2(x)$, $(\varsigma + t)(x) = \varsigma(x) + t$, $\mathbf{0}(x) = 0$, and $\varsigma[S \to 0](x) = \begin{cases} 0, & x \in S \\ \varsigma(x), & x \notin S \end{cases}$.

By V, we denote a finite set of n real-valued resources and write $\sigma : \mathrm{V} \to \mathbb{R}$ for valuations of V. Additionally, we define the following algebra. Let $v \in \mathrm{V}$ be a resource, then: $(\sigma_1 + \sigma_2)(v) = \sigma_1(v) + \sigma_2(v)$, $(\sigma + k)(v) = \sigma(v) + k$, where $k \in \mathbb{R}$.

For convenience, valuations are interpreted as vectors; resources as $\vec{\sigma} \in \mathbb{R}^n$, where $\vec{\sigma} = [\sigma(v_1)\ \sigma(v_2)\ \cdots\ \sigma(v_n)]^T$ and clocks as $\vec{\varsigma} \in \mathbb{R}^m_{\geq 0}$, where $\vec{\varsigma} = [\varsigma(x_1)\ \varsigma(x_2)\ \cdots\ \varsigma(x_m)]^T$ together with the standard vector arithmetic over the fields $\mathbb{R}^n$ and $\mathbb{R}^m$.

We define constraints on resources as (topologically) compact n-dimensional polyhedra, that is, closed and bounded sets in the metric space over $\mathbb{R}^n$ and Euclidean distance, whose convex hull can be defined by the conjunction of finitely many linear inequalities with rational coefficients. By P we denote the set of all resource constraints.

Definition 1 (Energy Timed Automata). *ETAs are defined as tuples:* $\mathrm{H} = \langle \mathrm{S}, \mathrm{s_0}, \mathrm{X}, \mathrm{Inv}, \mathrm{V}, \rho, \mathrm{T} \rangle$, *where* S *is a finite set of modes,* $\mathrm{s_0} \in \mathrm{S}$ *is the initial mode,* X *is a finite set of* m *clocks,* $\mathrm{Inv} : \mathrm{S} \to \mathcal{C}(\mathrm{X})$ *assigns clock invariants to modes,* V *is a finite set of* n *resources,* $\rho : \mathrm{S} \to \mathbb{Q}^n$ *assigns rates (first derivative in time) to resources in each mode, and* $\mathrm{T} \subseteq \mathrm{S} \times \mathcal{C}(\mathrm{X}) \times \mathbb{Q}^n \times 2^{\mathrm{X}} \times \mathrm{S}$ *is a finite set of transitions, defined by their start and end modes, clock guards, discrete resource updates and the set of clocks to reset.*

In depictions, we use double perimeters to designate initial modes, Lagrange's notation to denote rates, e.g., $v' = 3$, and assume that any omitted discrete updates are zero. In addition, for $c \in \mathbb{Q}$, we use the following notation in updates: $v \mathrel{+}= c$ for $v = v + c$ and $v \mathrel{-}= c$ for $v = v - c$. An example ETA is shown in Fig. 3.

We define the states of an ETA $\langle \mathrm{S}, \mathrm{s_0}, \mathrm{X}, \mathrm{Inv}, \mathrm{V}, \rho, \mathrm{T} \rangle$ as tuples $(p, \vec{\varsigma}, \vec{\sigma}) \in \mathrm{S} \times \mathbb{R}^m_{\geq 0} \times \mathbb{R}^n$, where p is a mode, $\vec{\varsigma}$ is a clock valuation and $\vec{\sigma}$ is a resource valuation. For some $k \in \mathbb{N}$, let $\mathcal{T} = (t_i)_{0 \leq i \leq k}$ be a sequence of transitions where $t_i = (s_i, g_i, \vec{c}_i, R_i, s_{i+1}) \in \mathrm{T}$, here s_i and s_{i+1} are modes and g_i is a clock guard that whenever satisfied enables t_i, thereby allowing for the transition to mode s_{i+1} from s_i. Runs of ETAs are defined as sequences of states visited when alternately following an enabled transition and letting time elapse in a mode.

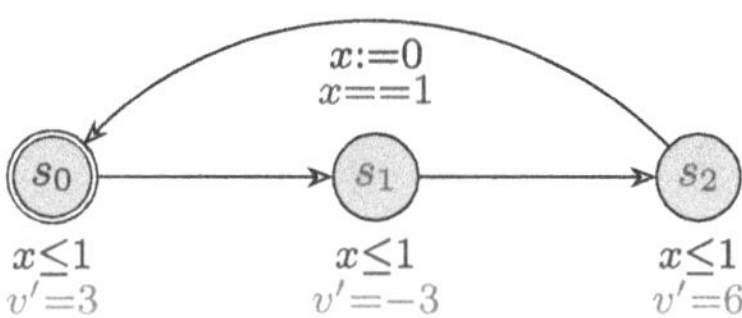

Fig. 3. An ETA defined over clock x, resource v and the modes s_0, s_1 and s_2, with initial mode s_0. Invariantly, clock x must be lower than or equal to 1 in all modes and is reset on the last transition from s_2 to s_0.

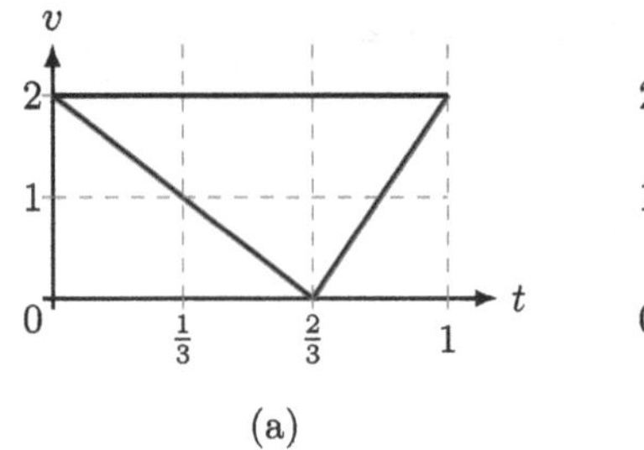

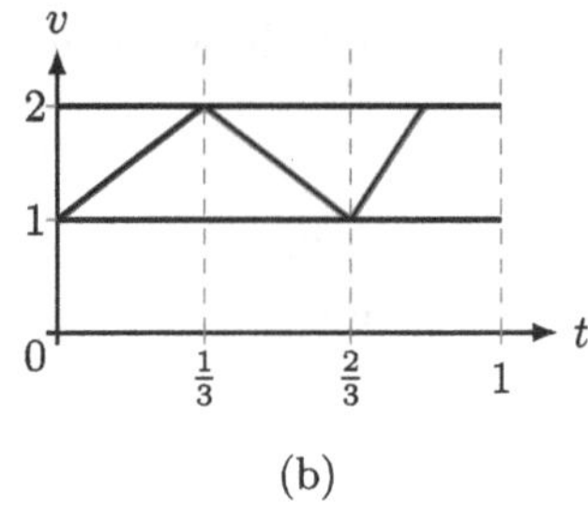

Fig. 4. Two distinct runs of the ETA depicted in Fig. 3. Here, the value of resource v is depicted as a function of time. Colours indicate in which mode delays are spent during a given run; s_0, s_1, or s_2. Initial conditions are: $v = 2$ for a), and $v = 1$ for b), with $\mathrm{E} = \{r \in \mathbb{R} \mid 0 \leq r \leq 2\}$ in a) and $\mathrm{E} = \{r \in \mathbb{R} \mid 1 \leq r \leq 2\}$ in b).

Definition 2 (Finite Runs). *Let* $\mathrm{H} = \langle \mathrm{S}, \mathrm{s_0}, \mathrm{X}, \mathrm{Inv}, \mathrm{V}, \rho, \mathrm{T}\rangle$ *be an ETA and* $\mathrm{E} \in \mathrm{P}$ *a constraint. Given a sequence of transitions* $\mathcal{T} = (s_i, g_i, \vec{c}_i, R_i, s_{i+1})_{0 \leq i \leq k}$, *a finite run of* H *in* $\mathcal{T}$, *is given by a sequence of states* $\tau = (p_i, \vec{\varsigma}_i, \vec{\sigma}_i)_{0 \leq i \leq 2k}$ *for which there exists a sequence of delays* $(d_i)_{0 \leq i < k}$ *s.t., for all* $0 \leq i < k$, *the following holds:* $p_{2i} = p_{2i+1} = s_i$ *and* $p_{2k} = s_k$; $\vec{\varsigma}_{2i+1} = \vec{\varsigma}_{2i} + d_i$ *and* $\vec{\varsigma}_{2i+2} = \vec{\varsigma}_{2i+1}[R_i \rightarrow 0]$; $\vec{\varsigma}_{2i} \models \mathrm{Inv}(s_i)$ *and* $\vec{\varsigma}_{2i+1} \models \mathrm{Inv}(s_i) \wedge g_i$; $\vec{\sigma}_{2i+1} = \vec{\sigma}_{2i} + d_i \cdot \rho(s_i)$ *and* $\vec{\sigma}_{2i+2} = \vec{\sigma}_{2i+1} + \vec{c}_i$.

Furthermore, all resource valuations must satisfy constraint E, i.e., $\forall_{0 \leq i \leq k} : \vec{\sigma}_i \in \mathrm{E}$.

Figure 4 depicts two example runs. We use the suffix $\circ$ to denote legal concatenations of runs (in the sense of Def. 2), e.g., based on the run depicted in Fig. 4a, let $\tau = ((s_0, x = 0, v = 2), (s_0, x = 0, v = 2), (s_1, x = 0, v = 2), (s_1, x = \frac{2}{3}, v = 0), (s_2, x = \frac{2}{3}, v = 0), (s_2, x = 1, v = 2))$. By $\tau \circ \tau$ we denote the two time unit run which repeats the behaviour depicted in Fig. 4b.

Definition 3 (Infinite Runs). *Let* $\tau = (p_i, \vec{\varsigma}_i, \vec{\sigma}_i)_{i \in \mathrm{N}}$ *be an infinite sequence of states. We call* τ *an infinite run if every finite prefix of* τ *is a finite run.*

2.1 Constrained Safety

Observe that all runs are defined over some resource constraint. Therefore safety in terms of ETAs is actually a question about the existence of infinite runs. There are two central questions we could explore: "Are all finite runs a prefix of some infinite run?" (the Universal Problem), or, "Does there exists an infinite run?" (the Existential Problem). For the sake of brevity our focus is on the latter.

Definition 4 (Existential Problem). *Let* $\langle \mathrm{S}, \mathrm{s_0}, \mathrm{X}, \mathrm{Inv}, \mathrm{V}, \rho, \mathrm{T}\rangle$ *be an ETA and* $\mathrm{E} \in \mathrm{P}$ *a constraint. The existential problem asks whether there exists an infinite run* $\tau = (p_i, \vec{\varsigma}_i, \vec{\sigma}_i)_{i \in \mathrm{N}}$ *with initial state* $(p_0, \vec{\varsigma}_0, \vec{\sigma}_0) = (\mathrm{s_0}, \vec{0}, \vec{\sigma}_0)$, *where* $\vec{\sigma}_0 \in \mathbb{Q}^n$, *s.t.,* $\forall_{i \in \mathrm{N}} : \vec{\sigma}_i \in \mathrm{E}$.

Looking at Fig. 4a, observe that the existential problem is satisfied and witnessed by the infinite concatenation of the depicted run, while the run depicted in Fig. 4b does not witness a finite prefix to an infinite run, since a deadlock occurs in mode s_2, that is, time cannot progress, without violating E.

Various related decidability results have been shown in the literature. If we consider one clock and one resource without discrete updates, like the example in Fig. 3, the existential problem is shown to be decidable in [8]. Generally, the existential problem is undecidable, even when only considering two clocks and one resource or one clock and two resources [18]. In [8] it is also shown that allowing discrete updates of resources pertains decidability for lower-bounded safety, at least in the single clock and resource setting. As it turns out, when considering one resource with discrete updates, the existential problem is decidable for ETAs under the restrictions of segmentation and flatness [4].

2.2 Flat and Segmented ETAs

Segmentation requires ETAs to be dividable into distinct linear segments, in which all clocks are reset on the last transition in each segment. We refer to such ETAs as Segmented ETA (SETA), which are made up of a finite number of segments, each of which is defined by an Energy Timed Path (ETP).

Definition 5 (Energy Timed Path). *Let* $\mathrm{H} = \langle \mathrm{S}, \mathrm{s}_0, \mathrm{X}, \mathrm{Inv}, \mathrm{V}, \rho, \mathrm{T} \rangle$ *be an ETA, where* S *is ordered:* $\mathrm{S} = (s_j)_{0 \leq j \leq z}$ *for some* $z \in \mathbb{N}$, *s.t.,* $\mathrm{s}_0 = s_0$. *We say that* H *is an ETP if* T *satisfies the following:* $\mathrm{T} = \{(s_j, g_j, \vec{c}_j, R_j, s_{j+1}) \mid s_j, s_{j+1} \in \mathrm{S}\}$, *and* $R_{z-1} = \mathrm{X}$.

We use $s_\top$ to denote the last mode in the ordering $s_\top = s_z$ and $\bar{\mathrm{S}}$ to denote S except for the initial and last mode, thus $\bar{\mathrm{S}} = \mathrm{S} \setminus \{s_0, s_\top\}$. So ETPs essentially define ETAs where the set of modes is ordered, with a single transition between each mode and its neighbors in this ordering, in addition to resetting all clocks on its last transition. By $\mathcal{L}$ we denote the set of all ETPs. An example ETP is shown in Fig. 5a.

Definition 6 (Segmented ETA). *SETAs are defined as tuples* $\langle \mathrm{M}, \mathrm{L}, \delta \rangle$ *where* (M, L) *is a finite graph with nodes* M *called macro-modes and edges* L *called*

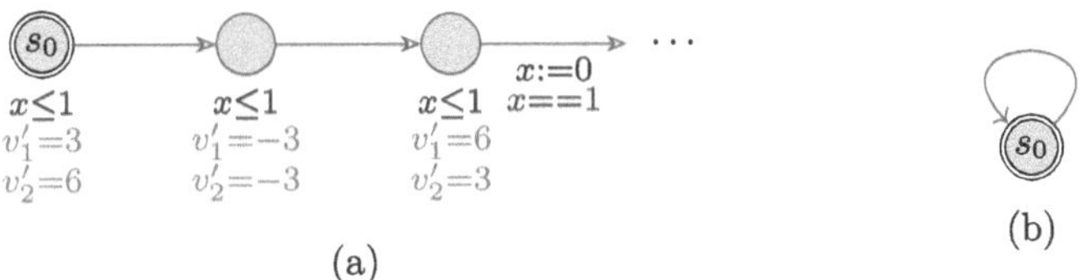

Fig. 5. (a) An ETP defined over clock x and resources v_1 and v_2. Notice how clock x is reset on the last transition. Note, the last mode omitted. (b) A single loop SETA with its macro-transition having assigned the ETP shown in (a) with colours indicating how (a) is interpreted in (b).

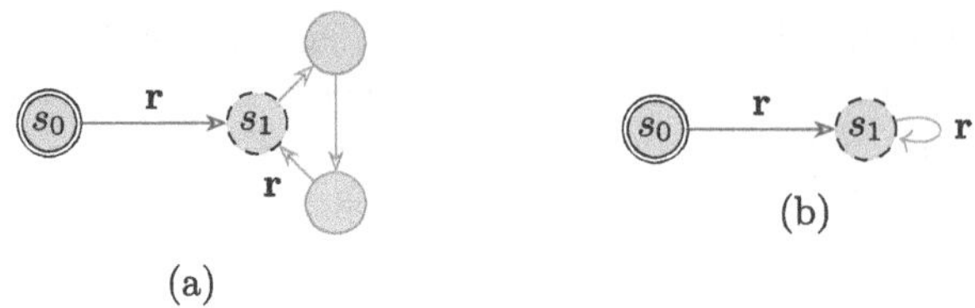

Fig. 6. An SETA interpreted as an ETA a) respectively, a finite graph (Def. 6) b). Since segmentation affects the structure, we have omitted actual rates, updates and resets, except for the indicator **r** which denotes where all clocks are reset. The colours indicate which underlying ETP a macro- transition or mode is related to, dashed perimeters denote shared macro-modes.

macro-transitions, with $\delta : \mathrm{L} \rightarrow \mathcal{L}$ *assigning an ETP* $\langle \mathrm{S}, \mathrm{s}_0, \mathrm{X}, \mathrm{Inv}, \mathrm{V}, \rho, \mathrm{T} \rangle$ *to each macro-transition* $(m, m') \in \mathrm{L}$ *s.t.* $\mathrm{s}_0 = m$ *and* $s_\top = m'$*. For all macro-transitions* $l, l' \in \mathrm{L}$ *with* $\delta(l) = \langle \mathrm{S}, \mathrm{s}_0, \mathrm{X}, \mathrm{Inv}, \mathrm{V}, \rho, \mathrm{T} \rangle$*, and* $\delta(l') = \langle \mathrm{S}', \mathrm{s}_0', \mathrm{X}', \mathrm{Inv}', \mathrm{V}', \rho', \mathrm{T}' \rangle$ *we have:* $\bar{\mathrm{S}} \cap \bar{\mathrm{S}}' = \emptyset$*. finally, for all macro-transitions* $\delta(l) = \langle \mathrm{S}, \mathrm{s}_0, \mathrm{X}, \mathrm{Inv}, \mathrm{V}, \rho, \mathrm{T} \rangle$*, we have:* $\forall s \in \bar{\mathrm{S}} : s \notin \mathrm{M}$.

So SETAs are finite graphs with transitions being labelled by ETPs, s.t., all such ETPs have disjoint mode-spaces, except for their initial and final modes, them being (possibly distinct) macro-modes. An example SETA is shown in Fig. 6.

Definition 7 (Flat SETA). *Let* H *be a SETA defined over macro-modes* S*, we say that* H *is flat if for all modes* $s \in \mathrm{S}$*, there is at most one non-empty path (in the graph sense) from* s *to itself.*

Note, in general, composition schemes (synchronised, additive, etc.) are not closed under flatness, hence why we do not address it in the remainder of this paper. Structurally, flatness prohibits nested loops, e.g., the SETA shown in Fig. 6b is flat.

3 Infinite Runs in Flat SETAs

We now dive into the characteristics of infinite runs in Flat SETAs. Recall that macro-transitions of SETAs are defined by ETPs. A single ETP will only allow for an infinite run if it can delay indefinitely in one of its modes, which is a trivial case. Therefore, in the remainder we assume that all ETPs have at least one upper bounded invariant, i.e., a clock constraint on the form $x \leq c$, for some clock x, that prevents such an infinite delay. For convenience, lets also assume that no contradictions arise from any invariant or guard.

In order to ascertain the existence of infinite runs and to find witnessing schedules, we start by establishing a method for characterising finite runs.

3.1 Binary Resource Relations

Given an ETP, to characterise all finite runs, the goal is to find all valuation pairs $(\vec{v}, \vec{w}) \in \mathbb{R}^n \times \mathbb{R}^n$ for which there exist a finite run of the ETP with initial state $(\mathrm{s}_0, \vec{\mathbf{0}}, \vec{v})$ and final state $(\mathrm{s}_z, \vec{\mathbf{0}}, \vec{w})$, i.e., a complete run from s_0 to s_z.

Definition 8 (Binary Resource Relation). *Let* $\mathrm{H} = \langle \mathrm{S}, \mathrm{s_0}, \mathrm{X}, \mathrm{Inv}, \mathrm{V}, \rho, \mathrm{T}\rangle$ *be an ETP, and let* $\mathrm{E} \in \mathrm{P}$ *be a constraint. Recall that transitions are defined as tuples* $(s_j, g_j, \vec{c}_j, R_j, s_{j+1}) \in \mathrm{T}$ *for some* $0 \leq j \leq z$ *with* $z \in \mathbb{N}$*. We define the binary resource relation* $R_H^E \subseteq \mathbb{R}^n \times \mathbb{R}^n$ *as the following first-order formula, which is quantified over delays:* $\vec{v} R_H^E \vec{w} = \exists (d_j)_{0 \leq j < z} : \phi_t \wedge \phi_r \wedge \vec{v} \in \mathrm{E} \wedge \vec{w} \in \mathrm{E} \wedge \vec{w} = \vec{v} + \sum_{j=0}^{z-1} (d_j \cdot \rho(s_j) + \vec{c}_j)$*. Where* ϕ_t *characterises timing constraints:* $\phi_t = \bigwedge_{j=0}^{z-1} d_j \in [L_j(prev(j)), U_j(prev(j))]$*, using the following functions:*

$$L_j(\vec{\varsigma}) = min_{d \in \mathbb{R}_{\geq 0}} ((\vec{\varsigma} + d \models \mathrm{Inv}(s_j) \wedge g_j) \wedge (\vec{\varsigma} + d)[R_j \rightarrow 0] \models \mathrm{Inv}(s_{j+1}))$$

$$U_j(\vec{\varsigma}) = max_{d \in \mathbb{R}_{\geq 0}} ((\vec{\varsigma} + d \models \mathrm{Inv}(s_j) \wedge g_j) \wedge (\vec{\varsigma} + d)[R_j \rightarrow 0] \models \mathrm{Inv}(s_{j+1}))$$

$$prev(j) = \begin{cases} (prev(j-1) + d_{j-1})[R_{j-1} \rightarrow 0], & j > 0 \\ \vec{0}, & j = 0 \end{cases}$$

Resource constraints are characterised by ϕ_r*:*

$$\phi_r = (\vec{v} + \rho(\mathrm{s_0}) \cdot d_0) \in \mathrm{E} \ \wedge \bigwedge_{k=0}^{z-1} \left(\vec{v} + \sum_{j=0}^{k} (\rho(s_j) \cdot d_j + \vec{c}_j) \right) \in \mathrm{E} \ \wedge$$
$$\bigwedge_{k=1}^{z-2} \left(\vec{v} + \sum_{j=0}^{k} (\rho(s_j) \cdot d_j + \vec{c}_j) + (\rho(s_{j+1}) \cdot d_{j+1}) \right) \in \mathrm{E}$$

Functions L_i and U_i define the smallest, respectively, the largest feasible delay in a given mode starting with valuation $\vec{\varsigma}$, and *prev* characterises feasible clock valuations in a given mode, dependent on the delays made in previous modes. The intuition of Def. 8 is best understood using an example, consider the following.

Example 1. Consider the ETP depicted in Fig. 5a*, referred to as* H*, subject to a rectangular resource constraint in the* $\mathbb{R}^2$ *plane:* $\mathrm{E} = \{\vec{v} \in \mathbb{R}^2 \mid v_1 \leq 5 \wedge v_1 \geq 2 \wedge v_2 \leq 5 \wedge v_2 \geq 2\}$*. The binary resource relation* R_H^E *is given by:*

$$\begin{aligned} \vec{v} R_H^E \vec{w} \iff & \exists_{d_0, d_1, d_2} : d_0 \in [0,1] \wedge d_1 \in [0, 1 - d_0] \wedge d_2 == 1 - d_0 - d_1 \wedge \\ & [v_1 + 3d_0, v_2 + 6d_0]^T \in \mathrm{E} \wedge \\ & [v_1 + 3d_0 - 3d_1, v_2 + 6d_0 - 3d_1]^T \in \mathrm{E} \ \wedge \vec{v} \in \mathrm{E} \wedge \vec{w} \in \mathrm{E} \wedge \\ & w_1 == v_1 + 3d_0 - 3d_1 + 6d_2 \ \wedge \ w_2 == v_2 + 6d_0 - 3d_1 + 3d_2 \end{aligned}$$

So resource relations are defined by existentially quantified systems of linear inequalities over the reals. Such a system can be simplified since the theory of linear real arithmetic is decidable and has quantifier elimination (QE), that is, there exists a formula void of quantified variables, for which a valid assignment to the remaining variables constitutes a solution to the original system.

A standard algorithm for eliminating variables from systems of linear inequalities is Fourier-Motzkin Elimination (FME), which works as follows. Let $F(x, Y) = \bigwedge_{1 \leq i \leq m} x \leq \phi_i(Y) \wedge \bigwedge_{1 \leq j \leq n} x \geq \psi_j(Y)$ be a system of linear inequalities defined over variables $\{x\} \cup Y$. FME eliminates x by characterising all value

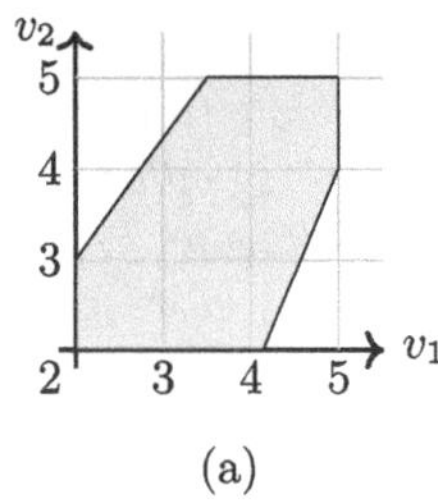

(a)

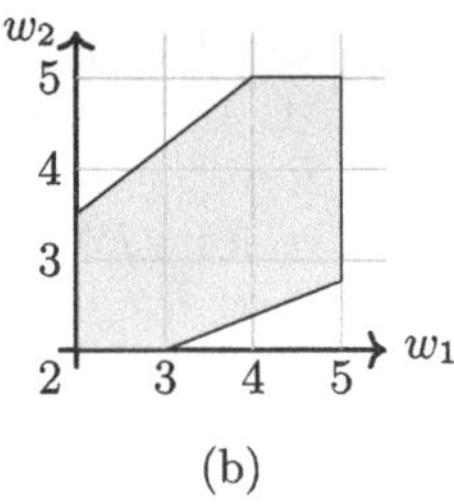

(b)

Fig. 7. The set of all start- (a), respectively, end-valuations (b) for which there exist a complete run of the ETP depicted in Fig. 5a.

assignments of Y which constitute a solution of F: $\{Y \mid \exists x : F(x, Y)\} = \{Y \mid \forall_{1 \leq i \leq m} : \forall_{1 \leq j \leq n} : \psi_j(Y) \leq \phi_i(Y)\}$.

Using the fact that the formula $\exists x : F(x, Y) \vee F'(x, Y)$ is equivalent to $\exists x : F(x, Y) \vee \exists x : F'(x, Y)$, we can eliminate variables from linear systems in disjunctive normal form as well. Since universal and existential quantifiers are dual, we can use FME to eliminate universally quantified variables as well. Consider the following example.

Example 2. By applying FME to the system shown in Ex. 1*, we obtain a four dimensional solution in terms of v_1, v_2, w_1 and w_2. We can further eliminate $\vec{w}$ or $\vec{v}$ to obtain solutions in terms of $\vec{v}$ or $\vec{w}$ as shown in Fig.* 7*.*

Lemma 1. *Let* H *be an ETP and* E $\in$ P *a constraint, we find that R_H^E is topologically convex and compact.*

Proof. Because only weak clock guards/invariants are allowed in H, and since resource constraints are compact by definition, using Heine-Borel's theorem, $R_H^E \subseteq \mathrm{P}$ must be compact since it is closed and bounded (topologically). Since constraints are convex and H is flat, R_H^E is convex as well. □

3.2 Resource Functions

Binary resource relations can be used to describe macro-transitions of SETAs. We now develop a method for analysing simple cycles.

For each binary resource relation we define two functions, which capture feasible sets of start and end valuations, for a given initial set of valuations.

Definition 9 (Resource Functions). *Let R_H^E be a binary resource relation. We define resource functions $\mathcal{R}, \mathcal{R}^* : \mathbb{R}^n \to \mathbb{R}^n$ to be: $\mathcal{R}(X) = \{\vec{w} \in \mathrm{E} \mid \exists \vec{v} \in X : \vec{v} R_H^E \vec{w}\}$, and $\mathcal{R}^*(X) = \{\vec{v} \in \mathrm{E} \mid \exists \vec{w} \in X : \vec{v} R_H^E \vec{w}\}$*

So $\mathcal{R}$ gives us all end valuations that are reachable, by a complete run, from a given set of start valuations and dually for $\mathcal{R}^*$. Note that the two functions form a Galois connection, in that they are monotone: for any $X, Y \in \mathbb{R}^n$ we find $X \subseteq Y$ implies $\mathcal{R}(X) \subseteq \mathcal{R}(Y)$ (analogously for $\mathcal{R}^*$), and adjoint, for any

$X, Y \subseteq \mathbb{R}^n$ we find $\mathcal{R}(\mathrm{X}) \subseteq Y$ iff $X \subseteq \mathcal{R}^*(\mathrm{Y})$. Furthermore, using Heine-Borel's theorem and Lemma 1, both $\mathcal{R}(X)$ and $\mathcal{R}^*(X)$ are convex and compact if X is. We use the notation $\mathcal{R}^k(X)$, respectively, $(\mathcal{R}^*)^k(X)$ for $k \in \mathbb{N}$ to denote k sequential applications of a resource function.

Using their monotonicity, by induction, we find that they both form decreasing sequences in the subset ordering.

Lemma 2. *For all compact sets $X \in \mathbb{R}^n$, both $\mathcal{R}$ and $\mathcal{R}^*$ form decreasing sequences in the subset ordering: $\mathcal{R}(X) \subseteq X \implies \forall_{k\in\mathbb{N}} : \mathcal{R}^{k+1}(X) \subseteq \mathcal{R}^k(X)$, and $\mathcal{R}^*(X) \subseteq X \implies \forall_{k\in\mathbb{N}} : (\mathcal{R}^*)^{k+1}(X) \subseteq (\mathcal{R}^*)^k(X)$.*

Particularly, this holds for $\mathcal{R}(\mathrm{E})$ and $\mathcal{R}^*(\mathrm{E})$, meaning that sequential applications of either functions starting from E will result in a decreasing chain of compact sets $(X_i)_{i\in\mathbb{N}}$ with $X_i \subseteq \mathbb{R}^n$ and $X_i \supseteq X_{i+1}$. Since all sets are compact, using Cantor's Intersection Theorem we know that if all sets X_i are non-empty, then so is their limit $\bigcap_{i\in\mathbb{N}} X_i$.

Furthermore, we find that $\mathcal{R}^*$ (and $\mathcal{R}$) distributes over the intersection of a decreasing sequence of compact sets:

Theorem 1. *Let $(X_i)_{i\in\mathbb{N}}$ be a decreasing chain of compact sets, with $X_i \supseteq X_{i+1}$. the following holds: $\mathcal{R}^*\left(\bigcap_{i\in\mathbb{N}} X_i\right) = \bigcap_{i\in\mathbb{N}} \mathcal{R}^*(X_i)$*

Proof. In both directions, we use Lemma 2.

The left to right implication is straightforward. For any $\vec{v} \in \mathcal{R}^*\left(\bigcap_{i\in\mathbb{N}} X_i\right)$ there exists a $\vec{w} \in \bigcap_{i\in\mathbb{N}} X_i$ with $\vec{v}R\vec{w}$. This implies $\vec{w} \in X_i$ for all $i \in \mathbb{N}$ hence $\vec{v} \in \mathcal{R}^*(X_i)$ for all i, therefore $\vec{v} \in \bigcap_{i\in\mathbb{N}} \mathcal{R}^*(X_i)$.

For the right to left implication, assume $\vec{v} \in \bigcap_{i\in\mathbb{N}} \mathcal{R}^*(X_i)$. Then for every i there exists a $\vec{w}_i \in X_i$ with $\vec{v}R\vec{w}_i$. This means that the set $\mathcal{R}(\{\vec{v}\}) \cap X_i$ is non-empty. Furthermore, as singletons are compact, so are $\mathcal{R}(\{\vec{v}\})$ and the intersection $\mathcal{R}(\{\vec{v}\}) \cap X_i$. Using Cantor's intersection theorem, we find that $\bigcap_{i\in\mathbb{N}} \mathcal{R}(\{\vec{v}\}) \cap X_i = \mathcal{R}(\{\vec{v}\}) \cap \bigcap_{i\in\mathbb{N}} X_i$ is non-empty. Hence there exists a $\vec{w}$ with $\vec{v}R\vec{w}$ and $\vec{w} \in \bigcap_{i\in\mathbb{N}} X_i$, and in particular $\vec{v} \in \mathcal{R}^*\left(\bigcap_{i\in\mathbb{N}} X_i\right)$. □

3.3 Post Fixed Points of Resource Functions

The last step in our analysis of simple loops is to characterise sets of permissive start valuations that allow for infinitely many iterations of such a loop. By Lemma 2, we know that $\forall_{j\in\mathbb{N}} : (\mathcal{R}^*)^j(\mathrm{E})$ forms a decreasing chain of compact sets. Hence, by Theorem 1, the greatest fixed point of $\mathcal{R}^*$, denoted $\nu\mathcal{R}^*$, exists and is compact: $\nu\mathcal{R}^* = \bigcap_{i\in\mathbb{N}} (\mathcal{R}^*)^i(\mathrm{E})$. Furthermore, $\nu\mathcal{R}^*$ is convex, since all sets in the chain are convex.

So $\nu\mathcal{R}^*$ defines the largest post fixed point of $\mathcal{R}^*$. That is, it defines the greatest subset $\mathrm{E}' \subseteq \mathrm{E}$, s.t., starting from any valuation $\vec{v} \in \mathrm{E}'$, it is possible to iterate the ETP defined by R, infinitely many times.

To obtain post fixed points of $\mathcal{R}^*$ we can simplify Eq. 1 using QE.

$$\forall_{\vec{v}\in X} : \exists_{\vec{w}\in X} : \vec{v}R^E_H\vec{w} \wedge X \subseteq \mathrm{E} \tag{1}$$

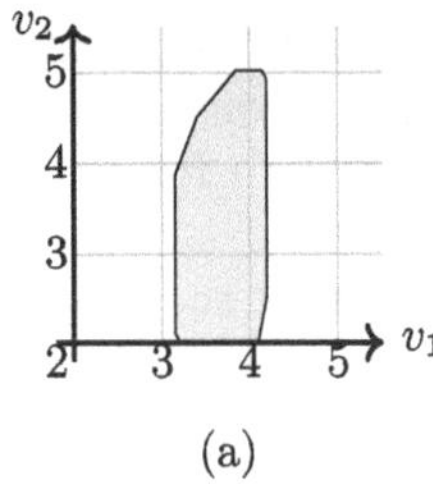

(a)

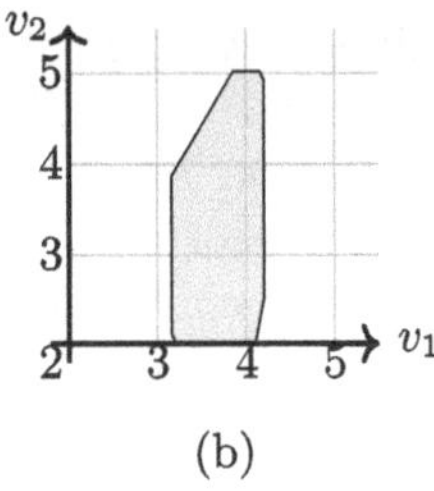

(b)

Fig. 8. Two distinct post fixed points of the simple loop depicted in Fig. 5b.

where X is a formula that characterises a compact and convex set in $\mathbb{R}^n$. Eliminating $\vec{v}$ and $\vec{w}$ results in a formula that characterises a post fixed point of $\mathcal{R}^*$ in the free variables of X.

Now, if X is a linear system, then FME can be applied to Eq. 1. Indeed this results in a post fixed point of $\mathcal{R}^*$ described by a linear system as well. Naturally, the characteristics of such a fixed point depends on the formula we substitute for X.

Returning to the ETP shown in Ex. 1, assuming that the ETP is now assigned to a loop, as is shown in Fig. 5b, we can compute post fixed points of that loop, as seen in the following example.

Example 3. If X is described by an axis-aligned rectangle with four free variables $\mathrm{X} = \{\vec{x} \in \mathbb{R}^2 \mid a_1 \leq x_1 \leq b_1 \wedge a_2 \leq x_2 \leq b_2\}$*, by applying FME to Eq.* 1 *we obtain a post fixed point of $\mathcal{R}^*$ described by those four variables. To obtain the same fixed point in terms of start valuations $\vec{v} \in X$ we relate to it the formula $a_1 \leq v_1 \leq b_1 \wedge a_2 \leq v_2 \leq b_2$, followed by eliminating a_1, b_1, a_2 and b_2, the result of which is shown in Fig. 8a. If we relate an additional inequality, say: $x_1 + x_2 \leq b_1$, to X, and follow the same procedure, we obtain another distinct post fixed point, as shown in Fig. 8b.*

3.4 Putting It All Together

So far we have seen how macro-transitions and simple loops of SETAs can be described by resource relations and post fixed points of resource functions. Using this, we will now see how infinite runs of flat SETAs can be characterised and in turn how schedules in terms of permissive delays can be synthesised.

Notice how resource relations are closed under relational composition. Hence, we can describe a resource relation for a given SETA path by such a composition. If a simple cycle occurs at the end of a path, like in Fig. 6b, we can check whether the path permits an infinite run of the simple loop, by first computing a post fixed point of the cycle's corresponding $\mathcal{R}^*$ function expressed in terms of start and end valuations. This is followed by relating this fixed point to the resource relation of the path, interpreting the path's end as the fixed point's start. Hence, by simplifying this relational composition we obtain a set of resource valuations that allow for an infinite run of the cycle starting from the path. If this is empty, we then conclude that any infinite run of the overall SETA should skip this loop completely.

Now, if the post fixed point in question is the greatest, i.e., $\nu\mathcal{R}^*$ and the previously mentioned valuation set is empty, then it is guaranteed that no infinite run exists for such a path and cycle, as was shown in [4] for the single resource case, here lifted to multiple resources.

Theorem 2. *Let* H *be an ETP,* $\mathrm{E} \in \mathrm{P}$ *a constraint and* $D \subseteq \mathrm{E}$ *a compact set. Either* $D \cap \nu\mathcal{R}^* \neq \emptyset$*, or* $\mathcal{R}^k(D) = \emptyset$ *for some* $k \in \mathbb{N}$.

Proof. Assuming $D \cap \nu\mathcal{R}^* \neq \emptyset$, we have: $D \cap \nu\mathcal{R}^* = D \cap \bigcap_{n\in\mathbb{N}}(\mathcal{R}^*)^n(\mathrm{E}) = D \cap \bigcap_{n\in\mathbb{N}} \mathcal{R}^*(\mathcal{R}^n(\mathrm{E})) = \bigcap_{n\in\mathbb{N}} (D \cap \mathcal{R}^*(\mathcal{R}^n(\mathrm{E})))$. Since, by Lemma 2, $((\mathcal{R}^*)^n(\mathrm{E}))_{n\in\mathbb{N}}$ forms a decreasing sequence, so does $(D \cap \mathcal{R}^*(\mathcal{R}^n(\mathrm{E})))_{n\in\mathbb{N}}$. By assumption, we have $\bigcap_{n\in\mathbb{N}}(D \cap \mathcal{R}^*(\mathcal{R}^n(\mathrm{E})) = \emptyset$. Using Cantor's Intersection theorem we have: $D \cap (\mathcal{R}^*(\mathcal{R}^n(\mathrm{E}))) = \emptyset$ for some $n \in \mathbb{N}$, since D is compact.

Assuming $\mathcal{R}^n(D) \neq \emptyset$, we have $\vec{w} \in \mathcal{R}^n(D)$ and $\vec{v} \in D$, for some valuations, s.t., $\vec{v} R_{\mathrm{H}}^{\mathrm{E}} \vec{w}$. Hence $\vec{v} \in (\mathcal{R}^*)^n(\mathrm{E})$, therefore $D \cap (\mathcal{R}^*)^n(\mathrm{E}) \neq \emptyset$, so $\mathcal{R}^n(D)$ must be empty. □

So either a given resource valuation intersects with $\nu\mathcal{R}^*$ or it will lead to the empty set by applying $\mathcal{R}^*$ finitely many times.

Of course this is not necessarily the case for arbitrary post fixed points. The key takeaway here is that the existential problem is decidable if the greatest post fixed point can be described by a linear system, since FME is then applicable and because only finitely many cycles occur in flat SETAs, hence, only finitely many computations are necessary. To obtain schedules, in terms of permissive delays in each mode, we can relate any post fixed point to the original resource relation of a given path in the SETA. Using FME we can then simplify it, resulting in a formula describing all delays that permits infinite behaviour in the that path.

4 Non-linear Limit Sets

We have seen how infinite behaviour can be characterised by post fixed points of resource functions. These can be computed by assuming their characteristics to be linear, captured by some formula X. Substituting X into Eq. 1 and then simplifying it results in a post fixed point of $\mathcal{R}^*$. However, depending on what formula is substituted for X, it is not guaranteed to be the greatest post fixed point. In fact, so far we have no guarantees that $\nu\mathcal{R}^*$ can even be described by a linear system. If this is not the case, then $\nu\mathcal{R}^*$ cannot be obtained by simplifying Eq. 1 using FME.

Recall that $\nu\mathcal{R}^*$ is convex and compact. For the single resource case, we therefore know that $\nu\mathcal{R}^*$ is defined by a closed line segment. This is because any compact one-dimensional system of linear inequalities, can be defined by the intersection of two half-spaces, as was utilised in [4].

4.1 Expressiveness of ETPs

Before we fully dive into the characteristics of $\nu\mathcal{R}^*$ in the multi-resource setting, it is helpful to understand the expressiveness of ETPs in general by developing a number of syntactic constructions, referred to as gadgets. To avoid needlessly complicated formulas, in the remainder of this section, unless otherwise stated, we assume constraint E takes on the form of an n-dimensional hypercube $E = \{\vec{v} \in \mathbb{R}^n \mid \forall 0 \leq i \leq n : v_i \in [0, u]\}$, where $u \in \mathbb{Q}$.

Recall that runs cannot violate E. Hence, in each mode we are implicitly testing all resources against the closed line segment $[0, u]$. This fact can be used to test the value of a resource against its boundary values, see Fig. 9a and 9b. Semantically, Fig. 9a characterizes the run $((s_0, y = 0, v = \alpha), (s_0, y = \frac{u-\alpha}{c}, v = u), (s_1, y = 0, v = 0), (s_2, y = 0, v = u))$ and Fig. 9b characterises the run $((s_0, y = 0, v = \alpha), (s_0, y = \frac{\alpha}{c}, v = 0), (s_1, y = 0, v = u), (s_2, y = 0, v = 0))$. Only resource valuations σ for which u can be subtracted from, respectively, added to v, is $\sigma(v) = u$, respectively, $\sigma(v) = 0$. Hence, we know the value of v whenever any of these transitions are enabled. Notice how the gadget shown in Fig. 9b is essentially **resetting** v.

A useful consequence of testing against boundary values is the ability to make copies of resources, say $\sigma(v) = k$. This is done by first resetting our copy/copies, say v^c, followed by simultaneously decreasing target v using rate $-c$ and increasing the copies by c, for some $c \in \mathbb{Q}_{>0}$, see Fig. 9c. This gadget characterises the run $\tau \circ ((s_1, y = 0, \{v = \alpha, v^c = 0\}), (s_1, y = \frac{\alpha}{c}, \{v = 0, v^c = \alpha\}), (s_2, y = 0, \{v = u, v^c = \alpha\}), (s_3, y = 0, \{v = 0, v^c = \alpha\}))$, where τ is a run that resets v^c using the gadget shown in Fig. 9b. Since the second transition only becomes enabled whenever v is 0, it means that for all valuations σ in mode s_2, we have $\sigma(v^c) = k$. Notice how we destroy the information in v whenever we make copies of it.

Using copies we can now begin to define more advanced behaviour, in particular, linear transformations. Say that we would like to encode the following: $\sigma_{end}(v) = \sigma_{start}(v) \cdot c$, where $c \in \mathbb{Q}$ is some rational. That is, the final valuation of v is proportional to its initial valuation. This is accomplished by first copying v into v^c and then simultaneously increasing v by c and deceasing v^c by -1, see Fig. 9d. This gadget characterises the run $\tau \circ ((s_1, y = 0, \{v = 0, v^c = \alpha\}), (s_1, y = \alpha, \{v = \alpha \cdot c, v^c = 0\}), (s_2, y = 0, \{v = \alpha \cdot c, v^c = u\}), (s_3, y =$

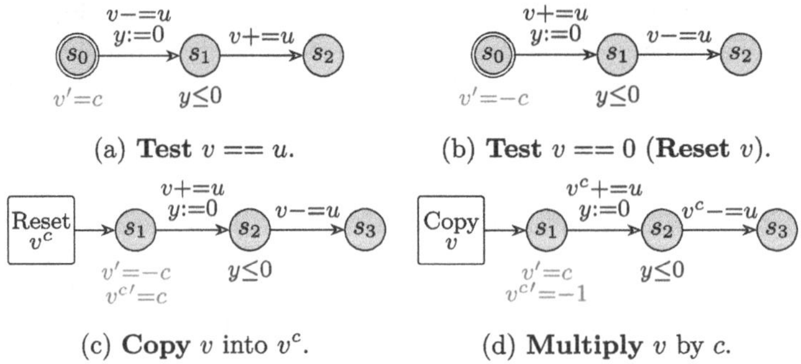

Fig. 9. Four gadgets where $c \in \mathbb{Q}_{>0}$ is some positive rational, clock y is used to ensure urgency in certain modes and squares denote gadgets. In (a) we **test** for $v == u$. In (b) we **test** for $v == 0$. In (c) we **Copy** v into v^c, i.e., $v^c = v$. In (d) we **Multiply** v by c, i.e., $v = v \cdot c$.

$0, \{v = \alpha \cdot c, v^c = 0\}))$, where τ is a run that copies v into v^c using the gadget shown in Fig. 9c. Because v^c is a copy of v, all we are doing here is multiplying the original value of v by c.

4.2 $\nu\mathcal{R}^*$ with Multiple Resources

We have seen how ETPs defined over multiple resources are capable of encoding linear transformations between resource valuations using the gadgets shown in Fig. 9d and Fig. 9c. This gives us an inclination to study the specifics of $\nu\mathcal{R}^*$ when the binary relation R is defined by a linear transformation $T : \mathbb{R}^n \to \mathbb{R}^n$.

We will now show that there exists ETPs for which the greatest post fixed point is non-linear, using a rotation transformation as an example. For simplicity we focus on the $\mathbb{R}^2$ plane. Consider the following linear transformation:

$$T_\Theta(\begin{bmatrix} v_1 \\ v_2 \\ v_3 \end{bmatrix}) = \begin{bmatrix} 1 & 0 & u \\ 0 & 1 & u \\ 0 & 0 & 1 \end{bmatrix} \begin{bmatrix} \cos\Theta & \sin\Theta & 0 \\ -\sin\Theta & \cos\Theta & 0 \\ 0 & 0 & 1 \end{bmatrix} \begin{bmatrix} 1 & 0 & -u \\ 0 & 1 & -u \\ 0 & 0 & 1 \end{bmatrix} \begin{bmatrix} v_1 \\ v_2 \\ v_3 \end{bmatrix} \tag{2}$$

This transformation describes the clockwise rotation of vectors in the $\mathbb{R}^2$ plane at each distinct point in the third dimension through Θ about (u, u). It uses the standard method for rotating vectors about points distinct from origin: $T(\vec{v}) = LAL^{-1}$, where A is a rotation matrix and L is a transformation. In the remainder, we limit ourselves to vectors where $v_3 = 1$, since the third dimension is purely mechanical. Now, consider the constraint $E = \{\vec{v} \in \mathbb{R}^3 \mid v_1, v_2, v_3 \in [0, 2u], u \in \mathbb{Q}_{\geq 0}\}$. That is, all resources are constrained by a closed line segment with median u. We combine Eq. 2 and E to define the following binary resource relation: $\vec{v} R_\Theta \vec{w} \iff \vec{w} = T_\Theta(\vec{v}) \land \vec{v}, \vec{w} \in$ E. Hence $R_\Theta \subseteq \mathbb{R}^3 \times \mathbb{R}^3$ is parametrized by rotation angle Θ. We can now say something about the characteristics of $\nu\mathcal{R}^*_\Theta$.

Theorem 3. *If the rotation angle Θ is irrational, then the greatest post fixed point $\nu\mathcal{R}^*_\Theta$ of $\mathcal{R}^*_\Theta$ forms a disk*[1] *in $\mathbb{R}^2$ at $v_3 = 1$.*

Proof. Recall that the fixed point is given by: $\nu\mathcal{R}^*_\Theta = \bigcap_{i \in \mathbb{N}} (\mathcal{R}^*_\Theta)^i(\text{E})$. By definition, the set $\mathcal{R}^*_\Theta(D)$, where $D \subseteq \mathbb{R}^3$ is a compact set, defines the rotation of D through Θ about (u, u) intersected with E. Hence, $\nu\mathcal{R}^*_\Theta$ is characterised by the infinite application of rotation transformation T_Θ. However, since Θ is irrational, for any $m \in \mathbb{N}$, the rotation $T^m_\Theta(\vec{v})$ is unique, i.e., the infinite application of T_Θ determines a circle. As E defines a square in the $\mathbb{R}^2$ plane at $v_3 = 1$, with side length $2u$ and diagonals intersecting in (u, u), $\nu\mathcal{R}^*_\Theta$ defines a disk of radius u centered at (u, u): $\nu\mathcal{R}^*_\Theta = \{[v_1, v_2, 1]^T \in \mathbb{R}^3 \mid (v_1 - u)^2 + (v_2 - u)^2 \leq u^2\}$. □

So for irrational rotations, $\nu\mathcal{R}^*_\Theta$ cannot be characterised by finitely many linear inequalities. Consider Niven's theorem [16], which states the following:

Theorem 4 (Niven's theorem). *The only rational values of Θ in the interval $0° \leq \Theta \leq 90°$ for which the sine of Θ is rational, are:* $\sin 0° = 0$, $\sin 30° = 1/2$, $\sin 90° = 1$.

[1] Region bounded by a circle.

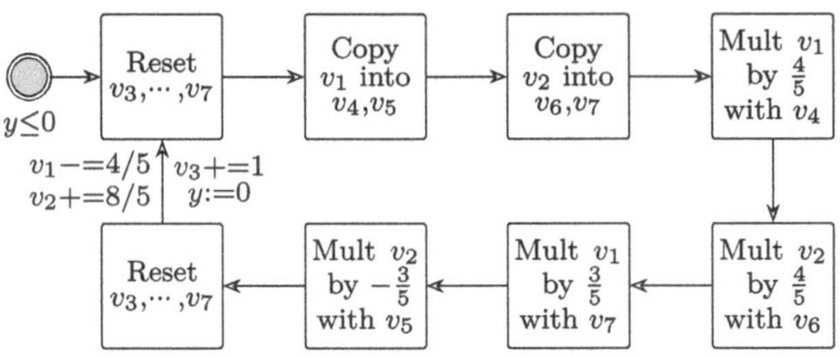

Fig. 10. An SETA modeled using the gadgets shown in Fig. 9b, 9c and 9d. Note, it is flat and segmented with clock y being reset at the end of each loop.

Hence it is quite easy to find an instance of T_Θ that defines an irrational rotation. Consider the simple right triangle defined by $\sin\Theta = 3/5$, $\cos\Theta = 4/5$ and $\tan\Theta = 1$. Using Niven's theorem, Θ must be irrational. T_Θ is shown in Eq. 3:

$$T_\Theta(\begin{bmatrix} v_1 \\ v_2 \\ 1 \end{bmatrix}) = \begin{bmatrix} \frac{4}{5}v_1 + \frac{3}{5}v_2 - \frac{2}{5}u \\ -\frac{3}{5}v_1 + \frac{4}{5}v_2 + \frac{4}{5}u \\ 1 \end{bmatrix} \tag{3}$$

We are now show that some ETPs define non-linear $\nu\mathcal{R}^*$.

Theorem 5. *There exist ETPs for which the greatest post fixed point of $\mathcal{R}^*$ is non-linear.*

Proof. Let $E = \{\vec{v} \in \mathbb{R}^7 \mid \forall i \leq 7 : v_i \in [0, 4]\}$ be a constraint. Consider the flat and segmented SETA defined over clock y shown in Fig. 10. By H we denote the ETP assigned to the loop in this SETA.

Ignoring the time spent on resetting resources, notice how only three distinct delays are possible in all modes; 0, $d_1 = \sigma_{init}(v_1)$, or $d_2 = \sigma_{init}(v_2)$ time units. Disregarding delays that are always 0 or duplicates, the binary resource relation $\vec{v}R^E_H\vec{w}$ (after applying FME) is given by:

$$\vec{v}R^E_H\vec{w} \iff \bigwedge_{i\leq 7}(v_i \in [0,4] \wedge w_i \in [0,4]) \wedge \bigwedge_{i\in[4,7]} w_i == 0 \wedge w_3 == 1 \wedge$$
$$w_1 == \frac{4}{5}v_1 + \frac{3}{5}v_2 - \frac{4}{5} \;\wedge\; w_2 == -\frac{3}{5}v_1 + \frac{4}{5}v_2 + \frac{8}{5}$$

Since $w_4, \cdots, w_7 = 0$, this corresponds exactly to the system described by Eq. 3 with $u = 2$. By Eq. 2 we know that this system describes a rotation transformation. By Niven's theorem we know that its rotation angle is irrational. Hence, by theorem 3, the greatest fixed point $\nu\mathcal{R}^*$ is described by a disk in $\mathbb{R}^2$ at $v_3 = 1$. □

5 Conclusion

We have shown how resource-aware timed systems can be modelled using ETAs by modelling accumulators as real-valued variables, called resources. For these models, ascertaining the existence of infinite behaviour that adhere to some resource constraints turns out to be possible when valuation limits are linear. Under the restriction that ETAs are flat and segmented (referred to as SETAs), infinite runs can be characterised in terms of valuation limit sets by employing quantifier elimination for linear real arithmetic. The conditions of flatness and segmentation help to ensure that such limit sets are convex and compact. Convexity, in turn, ensures that all finite runs of such systems can be described by systems of linear inequalities, while compactness ensures that limit sets of cycles exists and are non-empty if all iterations of such cycle are non-empty as well. Finally, flatness ensures that only finitely many cycles exists, therefore only finitely many limit sets need to be computed, each describing a set of initial valuations that permit infinite behaviour.

Synthesising safe schedules for SETAs in terms of permissive delays, is accomplished by relating a given valuation set to the original model, followed by simplifying this linear system using QE with respect to delays. Contrary to state-of-the-art approximation methods and semi-decidable procedures, our method is exact, produces real solutions, and will always terminate. However, the method is also incomplete; we show that limit sets of flat SETAs can be non-linear, in which case, a linear characterisation may not yield a solution, even if it exists.

Whether the existential problem is decidable for ETAs defined over multiple resources, is yet to be determined. Since we have identified sufficient conditions for which the existential problem is decidable it could be beneficial to explore known sub-languages to determine whether they are a fit for these criteria.

Ensuring tool support is also an important future direction. Currently, a tool chain has been made in Mathematica [11] employing the library of Mjollnir [15] as its engine for performing FME. To properly solidify the usefulness of the method, an appropriate case study must be studied, using such a tool chain.

References

1. Alur, R., Courcoubetis, C., Henzinger, T.A., Ho, P.-H.: Hybrid automata: an algorithmic approach to the specification and verification of hybrid systems. In: Grossman, R.L., Nerode, A., Ravn, A.P., Rischel, H. (eds.) HS 1991-1992. LNCS, vol. 736, pp. 209–229. Springer, Heidelberg (1993). https://doi.org/10.1007/3-540-57318-6_30
2. Alur, R., Dill, D.: Automata for modeling real-time systems. In: Paterson, M.S. (ed.) ICALP 1990. LNCS, vol. 443, pp. 322–335. Springer, Heidelberg (1990). https://doi.org/10.1007/bfb0032042
3. Alur, R., La Torre, S., Pappas, G.J.: Optimal paths in weighted timed automata. In: Di Benedetto, M.D., Sangiovanni-Vincentelli, A. (eds.) HSCC 2001. LNCS, vol. 2034, pp. 49–62. Springer, Heidelberg (2001). https://doi.org/10.1007/3-540-45351-2_8
4. Bacci, G., Bouyer, P., Fahrenberg, U., Larsen, K.G., Markey, N., Reynier, P.-A.: Optimal and robust controller synthesis. In: Havelund, K., Peleska, J., Roscoe, B., de Vink, E. (eds.) FM 2018. LNCS, vol. 10951, pp. 203–221. Springer, Cham (2018). https://doi.org/10.1007/978-3-319-95582-7_12

5. Behrmann, G., et al.: Minimum-cost reachability for priced time automata. In: Di Benedetto, M.D., Sangiovanni-Vincentelli, A. (eds.) HSCC 2001. LNCS, vol. 2034, pp. 147–161. Springer, Heidelberg (2001). https://doi.org/10.1007/3-540-45351-2_15
6. Behrmann, G., Larsen, K.G., Rasmussen, J.I.: Priced timed automata: algorithms and applications. In: de Boer, F.S., Bonsangue, M.M., Graf, S., de Roever, W.-P. (eds.) FMCO 2004. LNCS, vol. 3657, pp. 162–182. Springer, Heidelberg (2005). https://doi.org/10.1007/11561163_8
7. Bisgaard, M., Gerhardt, D., Hermanns, H., Krčál, J., Nies, G., Stenger, M.: Battery-aware scheduling in low orbit: the GomX–3 case. In: Fitzgerald, J., Heitmeyer, C., Gnesi, S., Philippou, A. (eds.) FM 2016. LNCS, vol. 9995, pp. 559–576. Springer, Cham (2016). https://doi.org/10.1007/978-3-319-48989-6_34
8. Bouyer, P., Fahrenberg, U., Larsen, K.G., Markey, N.: Timed automata with observers under energy constraints. In: Proceedings of the 13th ACM International Conference on Hybrid Systems: Computation and Control, HSCC 2010, pp. 61–70. Association for Computing Machinery, New York (2010). https://doi.org/10.1145/1755952.1755963
9. Clarke, E.M., Henzinger, T.A., Veith, H., Bloem, R.: Handbook of Model Checking, 1st edn. Springer, Cham (2018). https://doi.org/10.1007/978-3-319-10575-8
10. Hansen, J., Larsen, K.G., Cuijpers, P.J.: Balancing flexible production and consumption of energy using resource timed automata. In: 2022 11th Mediterranean Conference on Embedded Computing (MECO), pp. 1–6 (2022). https://doi.org/10.1109/MECO55406.2022.9797191
11. Inc., W.R.: Mathematica, Version 14.0, Champaign, IL (2024). https://www.wolfram.com/mathematica
12. Larsen, K., et al.: As cheap as possible: effcient cost-optimal reachability for priced timed automata. In: Berry, G., Comon, H., Finkel, A. (eds.) CAV 2001. LNCS, vol. 2102, pp. 493–505. Springer, Heidelberg (2001). https://doi.org/10.1007/3-540-44585-4_47
13. Larsen, K.G., Pettersson, P., Yi, W.: Uppaal in a nutshell. Int. J. Softw. Tools Technol. Transf. **1**(1), 134–152 (1997). https://doi.org/10.1007/s100090050010
14. Larsen, K.G., Rasmussen, J.I.: Optimal reachability for multi-priced timed automata. Theoret. Comput. Sci. **390**(2), 197–213 (2008)
15. Monniaux, D.: Quantifier elimination by lazy model enumeration. In: Touili, T., Cook, B., Jackson, P. (eds.) CAV 2010. LNCS, vol. 6174, pp. 585–599. Springer, Heidelberg (2010). https://doi.org/10.1007/978-3-642-14295-6_51
16. Niven, I.: Certain Algebraic Numbers, Irrational Numbers. Mathematical Association of America, 1 edn., vol. 11, pp. 28–41 (1985). http://www.jstor.org/stable/10.4169/j.ctt5hh8zn.6. 16 Dec 2023
17. Phan, A.-D., Hansen, M.R., Madsen, J.: EHRA: specification and analysis of energy-harvesting wireless sensor networks. In: Iida, S., Meseguer, J., Ogata, K. (eds.) Specification, Algebra, and Software. LNCS, vol. 8373, pp. 520–540. Springer, Heidelberg (2014). https://doi.org/10.1007/978-3-642-54624-2_26
18. Quaas, K.: On the interval-bound problem for weighted timed automata. In: Dediu, A.-H., Inenaga, S., Martín-Vide, C. (eds.) LATA 2011. LNCS, vol. 6638, pp. 452–464. Springer, Heidelberg (2011). https://doi.org/10.1007/978-3-642-21254-3_36
19. Ratschan, S.: Safety verification of non-linear hybrid systems is quasi-semidecidable. In: Kratochvíl, J., Li, A., Fiala, J., Kolman, P. (eds.) Theory and Applications of Models of Computation, pp. 397–408. Springer, Berlin Heidelberg, Berlin, Heidelberg (2010)

Intrathread Method Orders Based Adaptive Testing of Concurrent Objects

Yibo Dai[1,2], Peng Wu[1,2(✉)], Shecheng Cui[1,3], and Linhai Ma[4]

[1] Key Laboratory of System Software (Chinese Academy of Sciences) and State Key Laboratory of Computer Science, Institute of Software, Chinese Academy of Sciences, Beijing, China
{daiyb,wp,cuisc}@ios.ac.cn
[2] University of Chinese Academy of Sciences, Beijing, China
[3] Hangzhou Institute for Advanced Study, University of Chinese Academy of Sciences, Hangzhou, China
[4] Department of Computer Science, University of Miami, Coral Gables, USA
l.ma@miami.edu

Abstract. Concurrent data structures or classes are designed to provide secure access and simultaneous updates by multiple threads to shared objects in a concurrent environment, with the goal of enhancing parallelism and throughput. However, testing concurrent data structures poses significant challenges due to the potential explosions of concurrent test spaces, the variety of programming vulnerabilities, and the inherent nondeterminism of concurrent test executions. In this paper, we propose an Intrathread Method Orders based Adaptive Concurrency Testing (IMOACT) framework for testing concurrent data structures. IMOACT can capture diverse behaviors of interthread method pairs through characterizing concurrent execution contexts with intrathread method orders. Moreover, IMOACT can adaptively optimize concurrent test executions by generating scheduling sequences based on key scheduling points visited so far, streamlining test generation and execution organically across multiple tests. Experimental case studies with typical C/C++ concurrent data structures demonstrate that IMOACT outperforms baseline approaches. On average, IMOACT promotes the effectiveness of detecting concurrency bugs by 65%, and achieves a speedup of 2.43× compared to the underlying state-of-the-art concurrency testing approach.

Keywords: concurrent data structures · concurrent object testing · concurrency bug detection · data race · intrathread method order

1 Introduction

Concurrent data structures or classes are meant to facilitate safe accesses and updates by parallel threads within a concurrent environment. These structures aim to achieve high concurrency performances, leveraging the advantages of

W.-N. Chin and Z. Xu (Eds.): TASE 2024, LNCS 14777, pp. 91–108, 2024.
https://doi.org/10.1007/978-3-031-64626-3_6

the underlying multi-threading or multi-core architectures. These concurrency supports foster enhanced parallelism and throughput. Typical concurrent data structures include concurrent queues, concurrent stacks, concurrent hash tables, concurrent linked lists, and so on. In contrast to their sequential counterparts, concurrent data structures necessitate carefully designed synchronization and mutual exclusion mechanisms to ensure consistent sharing and accurate operations on objects shared among multiple threads, such as spinlocks, read-write locks, atomic primitives, and condition variables [27]. These algorithms play a pivotal role in guaranteeing object consistency, integrity, and thread safety along concurrent accesses.

However, concurrent data structures are as vulnerable to programming vulnerabilities as concurrent programs. Testing concurrent data structures poses a more intricate challenge than testing concurrent programs, due to their inherent inability to run independently [1,2]. A test case for a concurrent data structure involves a multi-threaded program that concurrently accesses a shared object, which is an instance of the concurrent data structure under test. Evidently, the test case space is infinite in general. A fundamental inquiry then arises about how to automatically generate valid multi-threaded test cases (i.e., concurrent programs) for testing concurrent data structures systematically. The challenge is further exacerbated by the nondeterministic executions of a concurrent program, which lead to an exponential explosion of possible thread interleavings.

Existing methodologies of testing concurrent data structures, mostly targeting Java concurrent objects, focus on exploring interleaving pairs of method calls that access shared objects simultaneously from parallel threads. CovCon [8], a coverage-guided testing approach, quantifies the covering frequencies of these interthread method pairs in concurrent executions and directs test generation towards those covered infrequently or not covered at all. AutoConTest [9] intends to achieve a high interleaving coverage to expose concurrency bugs. MAPTest [10] establishes a memory-access pattern (MAP) coverage criterion for thread-safety testing. Moreover, adaptive testing approaches proposed in [3] generate concurrent test cases for C/C++ concurrent objects based on syntactic (static) and/or interleaving pairs based (dynamic) diversity metrics. However, these methodologies face a notable deficiency in addressing variant behaviors of interthread method pairs under distinct concurrent contexts; while by executing standalone concurrent test cases independently, these methodologies may encounter duplicate interleavings pairs inevitably.

In this introduction we present an Intrathread Method Orders based Adaptive Concurrency Testing (IMOACT) framework to address the issues related to test generation and execution for concurrent data structures. IMOACT adopts a novel strategy to capture the diverse behaviors of interthread method pairs by characterizing the diverse concurrent contexts with intrathread method orders. Through evaluating intrathread method order diversity per thread among a pool of random candidates, IMOACT opts for a follow-up test case that extends the ongoing concurrent context most diversely. IMOACT then tailors the test execution for a targeted exploration of interleaving scenarios by generating scheduling sequences adaptively based on the key scheduling points visited so far. This eliminates the need to systematically execute the concurrent test case from scratch, hence avoiding exploring duplicate interleavings pairs. Therefore, IMOACT streamlines concurrent test generation and execution organically across multiple test cases, and thus can adaptively probe potential thread interleavings across shared objects in a more effective and efficient way.

We implement IMOACT upon a state-of-the-art concurrency testing engine Period [7]. This implementation is then evaluated on 13 typical C/C++ concurrent data structures in comparison with baseline approaches, including Period with randomized tests and the recent C/C++ concurrent object testing approach S-ATG [3]. Experimental results demonstrate that IMOACT outperforms the baseline approaches by detecting on average 65% more concurrency bugs. Compared to the original scheduling sequence generation method in Period, the key scheduling point based generation method in IMOACT can detect the concurrency bugs with an average speedup of 2.43×. We further investigate the correlation between the step size of an intrathread method order and its concurrency bug detection capability in IMOACT. Our observation suggests that the larger step size of an intrathread method order can lead to the more in-depth detection of concurrency bugs in most concurrent data structures. This confirms the motivation and advantage of intrathread method orders in exposing concurrency bugs hidden within complex concurrent contexts.

The main contributions of this work can be summarized as follows:

- We propose a novel adaptive test generation approach for concurrent data structures, which characterizes the diversity of concurrent contexts through intrathread method orders.
- We propose an optimization approach for scheduling sequence generation, which is based on key scheduling points and enables adaptive test executions for concurrent data structures.
- We implement the above test generation and execution approaches in IMOACT. The empirical case studies show that IMOACT is cost-effective in revealing hidden concurrency bugs in concurrent data structures.

The rest of this paper is organized as follows. In Sect. 2, we define the notion of intrathread method order. In Sect. 3, we present the details of the IMOACT framework. The experimental evaluation is reported and discussed in Sect. 4. We review the related work in Sect. 5 and then conclude the paper in Sect. 6.

2 Intrathread Method Order

Testing concurrent objects mostly concerns about exploring pairs of method calls that run in parallel from different threads [8]. However, such an interthread method pair may exhibit variant behaviors under distinct concurrent execution histories. Consider the example class XY defined in Fig. 1, where a conditional data race is highlighted in red between Line 11 in method updateXorY() and Line 19 in method updateY(). Merely executing this method pair concurrently may not be sufficient to trigger the concurrency error, because this requires a call to method switchFlag() immediately before a call to method updateY() within a same thread. Note that calling method switchFlag() before method updateXorY() within a same thread still cannot trigger that data race, because the effect of method switchFlag() switching flag from 0 to 1 is overwritten by resetting it to 0 at Line 7 in method updateXorY(). Thus, for the concurrent threads depicted in Fig. 2, a concurrent execution of thread0 and thread1 may trigger the concurrency error, but a concurrent execution of thread0 and thread2 may not. This discrepancy is attributed to the distinct concurrent contexts established in each thread before the target interthread method pair.

```
1  class XY {
2  static:
3      int x, y, flag;
4  public:
5      XY();
6      void updateXorY() {
7          flag = 0;
8          if(flag == 0){
9              x = 3;
10         } else {
11             y = 3;
12         }
13     }
14     void switchFlag() {
15         flag = 0;
16         flag = 1;
17     }
18     void updateY() {
19         y = 1;
20     }
21 }
```

Fig. 1. An example class

```
XY var0;
void *thread0(void* arg) {
    var0.updataXorY();
}
void *thread1(void* arg) {
    var0.switchFlag();
    var0.updateY();
}
void *thread2(void* arg) {
    var0.updateY();
}
```

Fig. 2. Concurrent threads

Definition 1 (Intrathread Method Order). *An intrathread method order indicates the order of method calls within a single thread, and can be represented by an indicator matrix* $M_{iz} \in 2^{\{0,\ldots,m-1\}\times\{0,\ldots,m-1\}}$ *for thread* i*, where*

- $z \geq 0$ *is the step size of the intrathread method order, i.e., the distance between two method calls,*
- m *is the number of public methods (excluding constructors and destructors) of a concurrent data structure or class,*
- *for methods* $0 \leq a, b < m$, $M_{iz}(a, b) = 1$ *if and only if there exists a call of method* b *after* z *step from a call of method* a *within thread* i.

For the concurrent threads depicted in Fig. 2, the intrathread method order indicator $M_{10}(1,2) = 1$ for thread1, while $M_{20}(1,2) = 0$ for thread2, where method indexes 1 and 2 refer to methods switchFlag() and updateY(), respectively. Thus, the concurrent context necessary for triggering the concurrency error shown in Fig. 1 can be exactly characterized through the intrathread method orders

$$M_{00} = \begin{pmatrix} 0\,0\,0 \\ 0\,0\,0 \\ 0\,0\,0 \end{pmatrix} \qquad M_{10} = \begin{pmatrix} 0\,0\,0 \\ 0\,0\,1 \\ 0\,0\,0 \end{pmatrix}.$$

3 Our Approach IMOACT

The workflow of our approach IMOACT is shown in Fig. 3. It mainly consists of two stages: adaptive test case generation, and test case execution with adaptive scheduling sequences. The first stage is to generate concurrent test cases adaptively driven by their intrathread method order diversity. A follow-up test case is then selected from a set of randomly constructed candidates that extends the previous one with the most diverse concurrent context. The second stage is to execute the test case under adaptively generated scheduling sequences, eliminating redundant explorations of duplicate thread interleavings. Thus, IMOACT constitutes a practical solution for systematically testing concurrent objects from both perspectives of test generation and execution. The overall testing algorithm of IMOACT is shown in Algorithm 1.

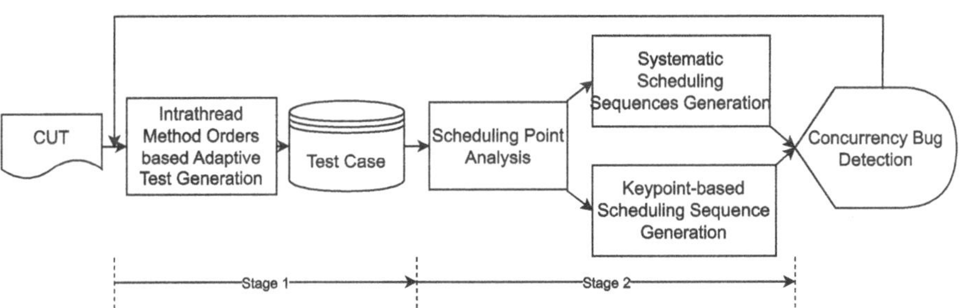

Fig. 3. Overview of IMOACT

3.1 Intrathread Method Orders Based Adaptive Test Generation

IMOACT aims to achieve high diversity of concurrent test cases in terms of intrathread method orders. Given a concurrent data structure or class, it intends to explore any potential concurrent context of each interthread method pair, characterized through intrathread method orders per thread.

At Lines 1–3 in Algorithm IMOACT, the following parameters are initialized: the number m of public methods other than constructors and destructors of a given concurrent data structure, the maximum step size k of an intrathread method order, the initial concurrent test case t. At Lines 4–6, the following global variables are initialized: the set R of concurrency bugs found, initialized as empty; the termination counter *stop*, initialized as 0; and the set KSP of key scheduling points visited, initialized as empty. The algorithm terminates if no new concurrency bugs are found for consecutive $N > 0$ times, or the intrathread method order M_{iz}^{t} is saturated for each thread i and each step size $0 \leq z < k$. The loop between Lines 7 and 17 iteratively generates an optimal test extension tc^{*} with the most diverse intrathread method orders (Line 8), which is then appended to test case t (Line 9) to synthesize a follow-up test case for concurrency testing at Line 10.

Algorithm 1: IMOACT

1 $m \leftarrow$ number of public methods other than constructors and destructors;
2 $k \leftarrow$ maximum step size;
3 $t \leftarrow$ initial test case;
4 $R \leftarrow \emptyset$;
5 $stop \leftarrow 0$;
6 $KSP \leftarrow \emptyset$;
7 **while** $stop < N$ *and* M_{iz}^{t} *is not saturated for each thread* i *and* $0 \leq z < k$ **do**
8     $tc^{*} \leftarrow$ `GetTestExt(`t`)`;
9     $t \leftarrow t \# tc^{*}$;
10     $R' \leftarrow$ `RunTestExt(`t`)` ;
11   **if** $R' - R = \emptyset$ **then**
12         $stop = stop + 1$;
13   **else**
14         $R \leftarrow R \cup R'$;
15         $stop = 0$;
16   **end**
17 **end**
18 **Function** `GetTestExt(`t`)`:
19   Generate a candidate set TC of random method sequences;
20   **return** $tc^{*} \in TC$ *such that for any* $tc \in TC$, $\Delta(tc, t) \leq \Delta(tc^{*}, t)$
21 **end**

The optimal extension tc^{*} is determined from a fixed number of random candidates by calling function `GetTestExt()`, of which the definition is shown between Lines 18 and 21. An extension is a n-tuple $tc = (tc_0, \ldots, tc_{n-1})$, where n is the number of threads in test case t and each tc_i with $0 \leq i < n$ is a method sequence for extending thread i. Let M_{iz}^{tc} denote the intrathread method order of step size $0 \leq z < k$ for thread i extended with tc_i. At Line 19, a set TC of candidate extensions is randomly constructed. Then, for each $tc \in TC$, the diversity between the current test case t and the candidate follow-up test case $t\#tc$, denoted $\Delta(tc, t)$, is defined as follows.

$$\Delta(tc,t)=\sum_{i=0}^{n-1}\sum_{z=0}^{k-1}\sum_{x=0}^{m-1}\sum_{y=0}^{m-1}\mathbb{1}_{M_{iz}^{tc}(x,y)-M_{iz}^{t}(x,y)=1}$$

where $\mathbb{1}_{(\cdot)}$ is the indicator function. $M_{iz}^{tc}(x,y)-M_{iz}^{t}(x,y)=1$ indicates that the ordered method pair (x,y) (i.e., method y is z step from method x) is covered in $t\#tc$ but not in t, that is, $M_{iz}^{tc}(x,y)-M_{iz}^{t}(x,y)=1$ if and only if $M_{iz}^{tc}(x,y)=1$ and $M_{iz}^{t}(x,y)=0$. At Line 20, the extension tc^* that takes the most number of uncovered ordered pairs into account, capturing the most diverse concurrent context for concurrency testing.

The extended test case t is executed by calling function `RunTestExt()`, which returns a set R' of concurrency bugs found in this run (Line 10). The detail of this function will be discussed later in the next subsection. If there are no new concurrency bugs found, i.e., $R'-R=\emptyset$, counter *stop* is incremented (Line 12); otherwise, concurrency bug set R is expanded with R' and counter *stop* is reset to 0 (Lines 14–15).

If counter *stop* reaches the pre-specified upper bound N, IMOACT terminates because no new concurrency bugs have been found in consecutive N tests. This suggests the search for concurrency bugs may reach a saturation. Alternatively, IMOACT terminates when test case t reaches a saturation in its intrathread method orders, i.e., $M_{iz}^{t}(a,b)=1$ for all thread $0\leq i<n$, step size $0\leq z<k$ and methods $0\leq a,b<m$. This indicates all the ordered method pairs up to the step size k have been covered by each thread for establishing complex concurrent contexts.

3.2 Key Scheduling Point Based Scheduling

A testing approach for a standalone concurrent program is often less efficient in testing a concurrent data structure, because it has to run various concurrent tests, which however may repeatedly visit the same thread interleavings across a shared instance of the concurrent data structure under test.

Take a state-of-the-art concurrency testing approach, Period [7], for example. It mainly comprises a schedule generator and a periodical executor. Given a concurrent program under test, the schedule generator systematically generates dynamic key point slices (DKPSs) as scheduling sequences. The key points within the target program, initially identified through static analysis, encompass instructions crucial to observable program behaviors, e.g., accessing shared memory locations or synchronization primitives; then the target program is instrumented with scheduling points before these key points. Scheduling sequences are generated based on the number of scheduling points within each thread, denoted np_i for thread i with $0\leq i<n$.

Definition 2 (Scheduling Sequence). *A scheduling sequence or or dynamic key point slice (DKPS), as in [7]), can be represented as a sequence*

$$\pi=\{T_{i_0}\times K_{i_0}\}\cdot\cdots\cdot\{T_{i_{q-1}}\times K_{i_{q-1}}\}$$

of q periods for n threads with $q>0$ and $n>1$ such that,

– *for each period* $\{T_{i_j} \times K_{i_j}\}$ *with* $0 \leq j < q$, $0 \leq i_j < n$ *and* $K_{i_j} \geq 1$*;*
– *for each period* $\{T_{i_j} \times K_{i_j}\}$ *with* $0 \leq j < q-1$, $i_{j+1} \neq i_j$*;*
– *for each thread* $0 \leq \iota < n$ *and all* $i_j = \iota$ *with* $0 \leq j < q$, $\sum_{i_j=\iota} K_{i_j} = np_\iota$*.*

Specifically, a scheduling sequence π *is pairwise if each thread* $0 \leq \iota < n$*, there exists a pair of periods* $\{T_\iota \times K\}$ *and* $\{T_\iota \times K'\}$ *in* π *such that* $K + K' = np_\iota$*. For simplicity,* $\{T_{i_j} \times K_{i_j}\}$ *is abbreviated as* $\{T_{i_j}\}$ *if* $K_{i_j} = 1$*.*

Given a scheduling sequence π, in each period $\{T_{i_j} \times K_{i_j}\}$ with $0 \leq j < q$, the slice of thread i_j with sequentially K_{i_j} key points is to be executed in the program order without any overlapping with the other threads, and then thread i_{j+1} with $i_{j+1} \neq i_j$ is scheduled in the next period if $0 \leq j < q-1$. Typically, as in Period, scheduling sequences can be constructed using the Pigeonhole principle, i.e., distributing the key points of each thread to these periods. Such a distribution of the key points results in a unique DKPS for each thread. Subsequently, the periodical executor runs the instrumented target program sequentially, adhering to the generated scheduling sequences, and detects concurrency bugs through dynamic analysis. However, various concurrent programs accessing a shared instance of a concurrent data structure under test may highly probably expose redundant thread interleavings between the public methods of the concurrent data structure. This undermines dramatically the effectiveness and efficiency of detecting heisenbugs in concurrent data structures.

Function `RunTestExt()` in IMOACT optimizes the executions of a series of concurrent test cases with key scheduling points based scheduling sequence generation. The algorithm of this function is shown in Algorithm 2. Without loss of generality, pairwise scheduling sequences with $2n$ periods are exploited so that each thread may get overlapped with any other thread at any of its scheduling points. If a new concurrency bug is detected under a scheduling sequence π, the number k_{n-1} of scheduling points in the first period of thread $n-1$ is kept as a *key scheduling point* and added into the set KSP of key scheduling points (Line 23). This suggests that it is rather possible to detect a concurrency bug across the $k_n - 1$-th key point in thread $n-1$, which may happen either before or after certain key point in another thread.

In the loop between Lines 5 and 14, tuples $(k_0, \ldots, k_{n-1})$ are enumerated and kept in set S as scheduling constraints such that for each thread i, its first k_i key points with $0 < k_i < np_i$ are to be assigned in the program order to its first period, while the rest of its key points is assigned to its second period. At Line 16, the pairwise scheduling sequences satisfying each constraint $s \in S$ are built and exploited for executing test case t by calling function `ScheduledConcurrencyTest()`. In order to reduce the redundancy in exploring thread interleavings already induced by the previous test cases, only the following two groups of constraints are kept in set S: for each $s = (k_0, \ldots, k_{n-1})$ with $0 < k_i < np_i$ for each thread i,

– if $k_{n-1} \geq np^l_{n-1}$, then $s \in S$ (Line 12). This is because the current test case t extends the previous one, and the number np_{n-1} of scheduling points in thread $n-1$ of t is no less than the number np^l_{n-1} of scheduling points

Algorithm 2: RunTestExt(t)

1 Let np^l_{n-1} be the number of scheduling points in thread $n-1$ of the previous test case;
2 Let np_i be the number of scheduling points in each thread i of test case t ;
3 $R^t \leftarrow R$;
4 $S \leftarrow \emptyset$;
5 **for** *each* $(k_0, \ldots, k_{n-1})$ *with* $0 < k_i < np_i$ *for each thread* i **do**
6   **if** $k_{n-1} < np^l_{n-1}$ **then**
7   **if** $k_{n-1} \in KSP$ **then**
8             $S \leftarrow S \cup \{(k_0, \ldots, k_{n-1} - 1)\}$;
9             $S \leftarrow S \cup \{(k_0, \ldots, k_{n-1})\}$;
10   **end**
11   **else**
12         $S \leftarrow S \cup \{(k_0, \ldots, k_{n-1})\}$;
13   **end**
14 **end**
15 **for** *each* $s = (k_0, \ldots, k_{n-1}) \in S$ **do**
16   `ScheduledConcurrencyTest(`$k_0, \ldots, k_{n-1}$`);`
17 **end**
18 **return** R^t;
19 **Function** `ScheduledConcurrencyTest(`$k_0, \ldots, k_{n-1}$`):`
20   **for** *each pairwise DKPS* π *with periods* $\{T_i \times k_i\}$ *and* $\{T_i \times (np_i - k_i)\}$ *for each thread* i **do**
21   Let R_π be the result returned by running t under DKPS π;
22   **if** $R_\pi - R^t \neq \emptyset$ **then**
23             $KSP \leftarrow KSP \cup \{k_{n-1}\}$;
24   **end**
25         $R^t \leftarrow R^t \cup R_\pi$;
26   **end**
27 **end**

in thread $n-1$ of the previous test case. Thus, the new scheduling points introduced in the current test case t need to be prospected for concurrency bug detection.

- If $k_{n-1} < np^l_{n-1}$ but $k_{n-1} \in KSP$, then $s \in S$ (Line 9) and $s' = (k_0, \ldots, k_{n-1} - 1) \in S$ (Line 8). This is to revisit only the key scheduling points found before, which may heuristically contribute to detecting more concurrency bugs, while ignoring previous scheduling points that have not yet caught a concurrency bug. Enforcing s and s' is to trigger interleaving scenarios where the $k_n - 1$-th key point in thread $n-1$ happens before or after certain key point in another thread.

Take the concurrent threads shown in Fig. 2 for example. It can be seen that `thread0` has the following key points: writing `flag` at Line 7, reading `flag` at Line 8, and writing `x` at Line 9; while `thread1` has the following key points: writing `flag` at Lines 15 and 16, and writing `y` at Line 19. Table 1 shows some scheduling

Table 1. DKPSs for the concurrent threads shown in Fig. 2

	DKPSs		DKPSs
π_1	$\{T_0\} \cdot \{T_1\} \cdot \{T_0 \times 2\} \cdot \{T_1 \times 2\}$	π_3	$\{T_0 \times 2\} \cdot \{T_1\} \cdot \{T_0\} \cdot \{T_1 \times 2\}$
π_2	$\{T_0\} \cdot \{T_1 \times 2\} \cdot \{T_0 \times 2\} \cdot \{T_1\}$	π_4	$\{T_0 \times 2\} \cdot \{T_1 \times 2\} \cdot \{T_0\} \cdot \{T_1\}$

Table 2. Key scheduling points based scheduling sequence generation

	DKPSs
π_5	$\{T_0\} \cdot \{T_1\} \cdot \{T_0 \times 4\} \cdot \{T_1 \times 5\}$
π_6	$\{T_0\} \cdot \{T_1 \times 2\} \cdot \{T_0 \times 4\} \cdot \{T_1 \times 4\}$
π_7	~~$\{T_0\} \cdot \{T_1 \times 3\} \cdot \{T_0 \times 4\} \cdot \{T_1 \times 3\}$~~
π_8	$\{T_0\} \cdot \{T_1 \times 4\} \cdot \{T_0 \times 4\} \cdot \{T_1 \times 2\}$
π_9	$\{T_0\} \cdot \{T_1 \times 5\} \cdot \{T_0 \times 4\} \cdot \{T_1\}$

sequences of 4 periods for 2 threads. It can be seen that scheduling sequence π_1 leads to an interleaving execution of Lines 7, 15, 8, 9, 16, 19, which can expose the following data race:

(writing flag at Line 16) after (reading flag at Line 8)

while scheduling sequence π_2 leads to an interleaving execution of Lines 7,15,16,8,9,19, which can expose the following data race:

(reading flag at Line 8) after (writing flag at Line 16)

Thus, this pair of data races between Lines 8 and 16 can be both detected through calling `ScheduledConcurrencyTest(1, 1)` and `ScheduledConcurrencyTest(1, 2)`. Scheduling sequence π_4 can expose the following data race, while π_3 cannot.

(writing y at Line 19) after (writing y at Line 11)

This concurrency bug occurs because thread0 switches to the else-branch under scheduling sequence π_4. Thus, the interleaving scenarios triggered by calling `ScheduledConcurrencyTest(2, 1)` and `ScheduledConcurrencyTest(2, 2)` can guide test execution toward exploring distinct branches in each thread for concurrency bug detection.

Suppose the previous 2-threaded test case visited $np_1^l = 4$ scheduling points in its thread 1 with $KSP = \{2\}$, and a current test case extends the previous one with two more scheduling points in its thread 1, i.e., $np_1 = 6$. Table 2 lists the scheduling sequences with $k_0 = 1$ derived for test execution, except the one with a delete line (π_7). Scheduling sequences π_8 (with $k_1 = 4$) and π_9 (with $k_1 = 5$) are resulted for the case $k_1 \geq np_1^l$, while π_5 (with $k_1 = 1$) and π_6 (with $k_1 = 2$) are resulted for the case $k_1 < np_1^l$ but $k_1 + 1 \in KSP$ and $k_1 \in KSP$, respectively. Scheduling sequence π_7 (with $k_1 = 3$) is dropped so as to reduce the redundancy in visiting the previous scheduling points, which have not yet contributed to any concurrency bugs.

4 Experiments

We implement the above test generation and execution algorithms of IMOACT for C/C++ concurrent data structures, using Period as the underlying testing engine, which is built upon LLVM [11] and SVF [12]. The implementation is then evaluated empirically to address the following research questions (RQs) regarding its effectiveness and efficiency in detecting concurrency bugs in concurrent data structures.

(RQ1) Does the key scheduling points based scheduling sequence generation in IMOACT improve the testing efficiency in comparison with Period itself?
(RQ2) Is IMOACT more effective than the state-of-the-art baseline approaches?
(RQ3) How does the maximum step size parameter k affect the testing effectiveness of IMOACT?

The following 13 open-source concurrent classes are utilized for the evaluation, abbreviated as classes $C_1, \ldots, C13$, respectively.

- *UnboundedDequeue* (C_1) and *BoundedDequeue* (C_2) [27] are unbounded and bounded concurrent queue classes, respectively, consisting of an array with top and bottom fields.
- *WorkStealQueue* (C_3) [7] assigns tasks to multiple worker threads, each maintaining its own queue of tasks. When a thread completes a task, it can try to "steal" tasks from the queues of other threads, in order to keep the workload of each thread balanced.
- *BoundedBuffer* (C_4) [7] is an array for coordinating data transfer between producer and consumer threads.
- *SkipList* (C_5) [28] is a multi-threaded implementation of a skiplist class.
- *LockfreeList* (C_6) [27] is a typical lock-free concurrent list class based on the compare-and-swap (CAS) instruction.
- *OptimisticList* (C_7) and *LazyList*(C_8) are lock-based concurrent list classes using optimistic synchronization [13] and lazy synchronization [14], respectively.
- *RingQueue* (C_9) [29] is a concurrent ring queue class with lock-free methods.
- *LockFreeQueue* (C_{10}) is a lock-free concurrent queue class based on the CAS instruction, and *MSQueue* (C_{11}) is a lock-free concurrent queue class using the Michael and Scott algorithm [15].
- *BackoffStack* (C_{12}) is a concurrent stack class based on a backoff algorithm [16].
- *LockBasedHashTable* (C_{13}) implements a concurrent hash table class with striped locks [30].

As suggested in literature such as [26], most concurrency bugs can be manifested with no more than two threads. Our early experiments also show that a concurrent test case with two threads, one of which even contains just one method call, are able to locate certain concurrency bugs in a concurrent data structure. Thus, we consider 2-threaded test cases ($n = 2$) in this evaluation.

For IMOACT, the maximum step size k is set to 2 by default, the maximum length of a candidate extension is set to 4, the iteration upper bound N is set to 4, and the number q of periods in DKPSs is set to 4 (as set for Period herein and in [7]). All the experiments are conducted on a machine with 40-core Intel Xeon Gold 5215 @2.50 GHz and 512G memory, running 64-bit Ubuntu 22.04. Each experimented is repeated 5 times for average statistics.

4.1 RQ1 - Efficiency with Key Scheduling Points Based Schedules

To address RQ1, we evaluate our key scheduling points based scheduling sequence (*ksp-based schedule*) in IMOACT and the original systematic scheduling sequence (*raw schedule*) generation in Period using the same test cases. The experimental results are reported in Table 3, where column Time shows the average time (in minute) spent on test execution, column Schedules shows the average number of schedules that have triggered concurrency bugs, and column Bugs shows the average number of concurrency bugs detected. The last two columns report the average speedup of IMOACT in test time consumption and the average reduction of IMOACT in the number of schedules required.

Table 3. Testing Efficiency (time in minute)

Class	*ksp*-based schedules			raw schedules			Speedup	Reduction
	Time	Schedules	Bugs	Time	Schedules	Bugs		
C_1	16.60	5577.60	11.00	36.40	9477.40	11.00	**2.19**	**41.15%**
C_2	13.00	3229.80	8.80	30.20	7356.80	8.80	**2.32**	**56.10%**
C_3	33.00	7899.60	23.20	70.20	16459.60	23.80	**2.12**	**52.01%**
C_4	18.20	1261.60	15.20	25.00	1821.20	15.60	**1.37**	**30.73%**
C_5	117.20	9219.80	14.40	271.60	17395.20	14.20	**2.31**	**47.00%**
C_6	105.20	8802.20	19.20	309.50	22539.20	19.20	**2.94**	**60.95%**
C_7	77.40	10068.40	22.40	188.00	21690.00	22.40	**2.42**	**53.58%**
C_8	102.40	10597.40	22.00	255.80	24446.80	22.00	**2.49**	**56.65%**
C_9	13.80	2973.80	18.20	25.00	5220.20	18.40	**1.81**	**43.03%**
Average	55.20	6625.57	17.16	134.63	14045.15	17.26	**2.43**	**52.83%**

It can be seen that the key scheduling points based scheduling sequence generation in IMOACT can, on average, significantly accelerate concurrent tests by 2.43x and substantially reduce the number of necessary scheduling sequences by 52.83%, without sacrificing its testing effectiveness for concurrency bug detection.

Figure 4 illustrates how the number of detected concurrency bugs changes over test time under the two schedule generation approaches, as well as the area under each curve (auc). It can be seen that IMOACT, with the key scheduling points based scheduling sequences, often identifies more concurrency bugs than Period itself within the same test time budgets. The key scheduling points based

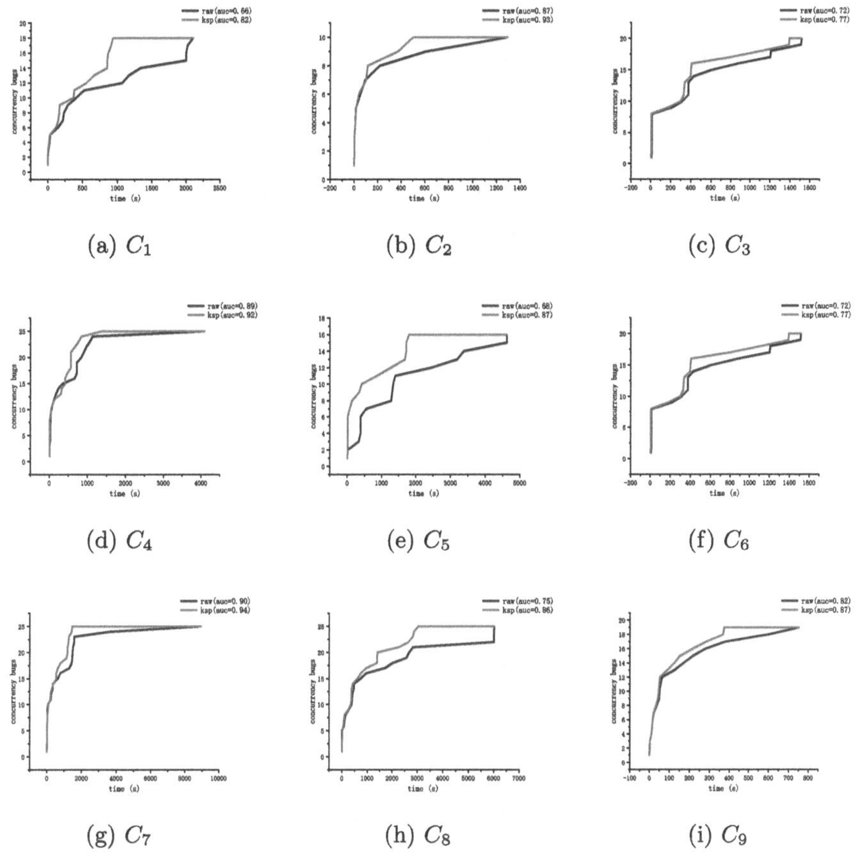

(a) C_1 (b) C_2 (c) C_3

(d) C_4 (e) C_5 (f) C_6

(g) C_7 (h) C_8 (i) C_9

Fig. 4. Concurrency bugs found over time

scheduling sequence generation in IMOACT raises the values of auc by 3.81% - 27.86% for these concurrent classes, indicating the significant effect of key scheduling points on improving testing efficiency.

4.2 RQ2 - Concurrency Bug Detection Capabilities

For RQ2, two state-of-the-art baseline approaches are evaluated in comparison with IMOACT, including Period with randomized tests (Period-Random) and the recent C/C++ concurrent object testing approach S-ATG [3]. The size of each concurrent class is shown in lines of code (Column LoC) in Table 4. The experimental results are reported in this table, where each of the last three columns shows the average number of concurrency bugs detected in each class by each approach. It can be seen that IMOACT detects considerably more concurrency bugs on all the classes except C_7, for which S-ATG may detect slightly more concurrency bugs than IMOACT. On average, IMOACT detects 65.05% and 13.86% more concurrency bugs than S-ATG and Period-Random, respectively. This demonstrates the advantage of intrathread method orders based test generation of IMOACT over the Levenshtein distance based test generation of S-ATG and random test generation for concurrency bug detection.

Table 4. Testing Effectiveness for Concurrency Bug Detection

Class	LoC	IMOACT	S-ATG	Period-Random
C_1	202	**19.40**	12.20	11.20
C_2	113	**12.00**	7.60	9.60
C_3	385	**27.60**	12.20	21.20
C_4	410	**20.50**	8.0	20.00
C_5	502	**17.00**	4.80	14.80
C_6	363	**22.80**	17.80	21.00
C_7	225	32.20	**33.00**	30.40
C_8	224	**31.60**	14.40	27.40
C_9	141	**23.00**	9.00	21.20
C_{10}	132	**4.00**	4.00	4.00
C_{11}	183	**5.00**	5.00	5.00
C_{12}	135	**3.00**	3.00	3.00
C_{13}	571	**3.00**	3.00	3.00
Average		**17.00**	10.30	14.93

4.3 RQ3 - Maximum Step Size

To address RQ3, we evaluate the total number of test cases generated and executed by IMOACT in a complete testing of a concurrent data structure under different settings of maximum step size k. Figure 5 shows the average results for each group of the concurrent classes with the same number npf of public methods. It can be seen that as the maximum step size and the number of public methods increase, the number of test cases required in IMOACT also increases accordingly to explore more and diverse concurrent contexts.

5 Related Work

Concurrent Program Testing. There are mainly three categories of testing approaches for concurrent programs: stress testing, systematic testing and active testing.

Stress testing involves repeated executions of test cases. However, it tends to perform meaningless tests with less chance to explore a wide range of thread interleaving scenarios. PCT [4] and its parallelized variation PPCT [17] use thread priorities, which can be configured dynamically through the underlying operating system or runtime environment, to schedule thread context switches as precisely as possible, showcasing the effectiveness of randomized scheduling.

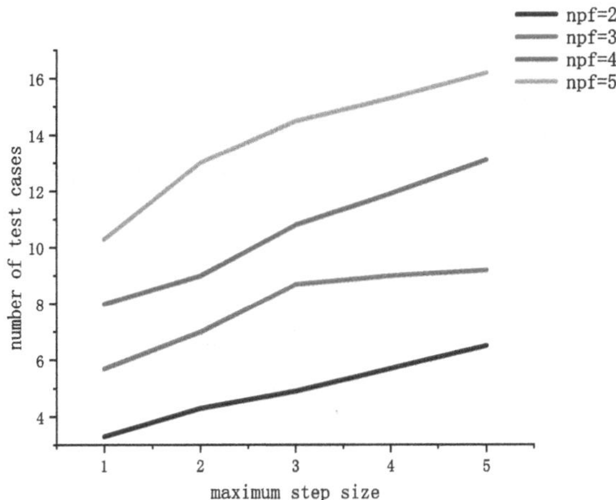

Fig. 5. Different values of k

Systematic testing aims to run all possible thread interleavings for a gvien test case through systematic control of thread scheduling, hence requiring effective ways to tackle the inherent scalability issue. Dynamic partial order reduction (DPOR) [5] relies on facilities such as persistent sets to identify equivalent thread interleavings. CHESS [18,19] searches possible thread interleavings in a bounded preemptive context. In [20], ordering constraints are dynamically learned over shared object accesses and favors highly risky interleavings for test executions. ARS [21] adaptively explores the search space to lessen the burden of detecting concurrency bugs. Recently, Period [7] models an execution of a concurrent program as a periodical execution and systematically explores the interleaving space with a given number of periods.

Active testing first predicts suspicious interleaving with respect to certain types of concurrency bugs, e.g., data races and memory-related bugs, and then enforces the potential buggy interleavings actively for text execution. RAProducer [22] identifies contention- or error-related locks and shared variables from executions of given Proof-of-Concept (PoC) samples, which can help narrow down the search space for data contentions and buggy thread interleavings significantly. ToccRACE [23] proposes a partial order model with the notion of fix-point event, which can not only predict data races in case of no control-flow changes, but also soundly infer witness traces with potential control-flow changes. SeqCheck [24] checks whether a sequence of events can occur in a specific order, which may lead to a potential concurrency bug.

Concurrent Object Testing. There are also mainly three categories of testing approaches for concurrent data structures: random testing, coverage guided testing and adaptive testing. Most of these testing approaches target Java concurrent objects, such as ConTeGe, BC-ConTest, CovCon, AutoConTest, and MAPTest.

ConTeGe [25] is a random testing approach for thread safety of concurrent classes. BC-ConTest [6] combines the advantages of the bug-driven and coverage-guided strategies for concurrent test generation. CovCon [8], a coverage-guided approach, measures how often pairs of methods are executed concurrently and focuses on pairs of methods that have been covered infrequently or not at all. AutoConTest [9] proposes a context-sensitive interleaving coverage metric to capture execution contexts of shared memory accesses, and synthesizes concurrent tests from these sequential accesses for promoting the interleaving coverage. MAPTest [10] introduces a memory-access pattern (MAP) coverage criterion for thread safety testing. Only the adaptive testing algorithms proposed in [3] targets C/C++ concurrent objects, generating concurrent test cases adaptively from perspectives of static and dynamic diversity. S-ATG in [3] is close to our work in concurrent test generation, but as shown in our experiments, the static Levenshtein distance based diversity metric exhibits less correlation with buggy thread interleavings.

6 Conclusion

In this paper, we present the concept of intrathread method order to relate test case diversity with concurrent contexts covered by test cases. We then propose the intrathread method orders based adaptive concurrency testing approach IMOACT for concurrent data structures. It is implemented specifically for C/C++ concurrent objects, for which Period is adopted as the underlying test execution engine. Moreover, we optimize the systematic scheduling sequence generation in Period with the key scheduling points based scheduling sequence generation, to reduce the deficiency of applying Period for testing concurrent data structure. IMOACT functions as an organic synergy of concurrent test generation and execution for concurrent object testing by systematically exploring thread interleavings across shared objects in an on-the-fly manner. The experimental results obtained from 13 open-source concurrent classes highlight the effectiveness of intrathread method orders in guiding the generation of diverse test cases, and the efficiency of the key scheduling points based scheduling sequences for concurrent test execution. IMOACT outperforms the state-of-the-art baseline approaches by detecting more concurrency bugs with substantially fewer schedules and less time consumption. As future work, it would be interesting to investigate the application of IMOACT for concurrency testing on weak memory models.

Acknowledgment. We thank the anonymous referees for their valuable and insightful comments. This work is partially supported by the National Key R&D Program of China under Grant No. 2022YFA1005100, 2022YFA1005101, and 2022YFA1005104, and the Major Project of ISCAS under the Grant No. ISCAS-ZD-202302.

References

1. Bianchi, F.A., Margara, A., Pezzè, M.: A survey of recent trends in testing concurrent software systems. IEEE Trans. Softw. Eng. **44**(8), 747–783 (2017)
2. Huang, J., Zhang, C.: Debugging concurrent software: advances and challenges. J. Comput. Sci. Technol. **31**, 861–868 (2016)
3. Ma, L., Wu, P., Chen, T.Y.: Diversity driven adaptive test generation for concurrent data structures. Inf. Softw. Technol. **103**, 162–173 (2018)
4. Burckhardt, S., Kothari, P., Musuvathi, M., Nagarakatte, S.: A randomized scheduler with probabilistic guarantees of finding bugs. ACM SIGARCH Comput. Archit. News **38**(1), 167–178 (2010)
5. Flanagan, C., Godefroid, P.: Dynamic partial-order reduction for model checking software. ACM Sigplan Not. **40**(1), 110–121 (2005)
6. Bo, L., Jiang, S., Qian, J., Wang, R., Wang, X.: Efficient test case generation for thread-safe classes. IEEE Access **7**, 26984–26995 (2019)
7. Wen, C., He, M., Wu, B., Xu, Z., Qin, S.: Controlled concurrency testing via periodical scheduling. In: Proceedings of the 44th International Conference on Software Engineering, pp. 474–486 (2022)
8. Choudhary, A., Lu, S., Pradel, M.: Efficient detection of thread safety violations via coverage-guided generation of concurrent tests. In: 2017 IEEE/ACM 39th International Conference on Software Engineering (ICSE), pp. 266–277 (2017)
9. Terragni, V., Cheung, S. C.: Coverage-driven test code generation for concurrent classes. In: Proceedings of the 38th International Conference on Software Engineering, pp. 1121–1132 (2016)
10. Wang, Z., Zhao, Y., Liu, S., Sun, J., Chen, X., Lin, H.: Map-coverage: a novel coverage criterion for testing thread-safe classes. In: 2019 34th IEEE/ACM International Conference on Automated Software Engineering (ASE), pp. 722–734 (2019)
11. Lattner, C., Adve, V.: LLVM: a compilation framework for lifelong program analysis & transformation. In: International Symposium on Code Generation and Optimization, pp. 75-86 (2004)
12. Sui, Y., Xue, J.: SVF: interprocedural static value-flow analysis in LLVM. In: Proceedings of the 25th International Conference on Compiler Construction, pp. 265–266 (2016)
13. Herlihy, M., Lev, Y., Luchangco, V., Shavit, N.: A simple optimistic skiplist algorithm. In: Prencipe, G., Zaks, S. (eds.) SIROCCO 2007. LNCS, vol. 4474, pp. 124–138. Springer, Heidelberg (2007). https://doi.org/10.1007/978-3-540-72951-8_11
14. Heller, S., Herlihy, M., Luchangco, V., Moir, M., Scherer, W.N., Shavit, N.: A lazy concurrent list-based set algorithm. In: Anderson, J.H., Prencipe, G., Wattenhofer, R. (eds.) OPODIS 2005. LNCS, vol. 3974, pp. 3–16. Springer, Heidelberg (2006). https://doi.org/10.1007/11795490_3
15. Michael, M.M., Scott, M.L.: Simple, fast, and practical non-blocking and blocking concurrent queue algorithms. In: Proceedings of the Fifteenth Annual ACM Symposium on Principles of Distributed Computing, pp. 267–275 (1996)
16. Hendler, D., Shavit, N., Yerushalmi, L.: A scalable lock-free stack algorithm. In: Proceedings of the Sixteenth Annual ACM Symposium on Parallelism in Algorithms and Architectures, pp. 206-215 (2004)
17. Nagarakatte, S., Burckhardt, S., Martin, M.M., Musuvathi, M.: Multicore acceleration of priority-based schedulers for concurrency bug detection. In: Proceedings of the 33rd ACM SIGPLAN Conference on Programming Language Design and Implementation, pp. 543–554 (2012)

18. Emmi, M., Qadeer, S., Rakamarić, Z.: Delay-bounded scheduling. In: Proceedings of the 38th Annual ACM SIGPLAN-SIGACT Symposium on Principles of Programming Languages, pp. 411–422 (2011)
19. Musuvathi, M., Qadeer, S., Ball, T., Basler, G., Nainar, P.A., Neamtiu, I.: Finding and reproducing heisenbugs in concurrent programs. In: OSDI (2008)
20. Wang, C., Said, M., Gupta, A.: Coverage guided systematic concurrency testing. In: Proceedings of the 33rd International Conference on Software Engineering, pp. 221–230 (2011)
21. Wang, Z., Zhang, D., Liu, S., Sun, J., Zhao, Y.: Adaptive randomized scheduling for concurrency bug detection. In: 2019 24th International Conference on Engineering of Complex Computer Systems (ICECCS), pp. 124–133 (2019)
22. Yuan, M., Lee, Y., Zhang, C., Li, Y., Cai, Y., Zhao, B.: RAProducer: efficiently diagnose and reproduce data race bugs for binaries via trace analysis. In: Proceedings of the 30th ACM SIGSOFT International Symposium on Software Testing and Analysis, pp. 593–606 (2021)
23. Zhu, S., Guo, Y., Zhang, L., Cai, Y.: Tolerate control-flow changes for sound data race prediction. In: 2023 IEEE/ACM 45th International Conference on Software Engineering (ICSE), pp. 1342–1354 (2023)
24. Cai, Y., Yun, H., Wang, J., Qiao, L., Palsberg, J.: Sound and efficient concurrency bug prediction. In: Proceedings of the 29th ACM Joint Meeting on European Software Engineering Conference and Symposium on the Foundations of Software Engineering, pp. 255–267 (2021)
25. Pradel, M., Gross, T. R.: Fully automatic and precise detection of thread safety violations. In: Proceedings of the 33rd ACM SIGPLAN Conference on Programming Language Design and Implementation, pp. 521–530 (2012)
26. Lu, S., Park, S., Seo, E., et al.: Learning from mistakes: a comprehensive study on real world concurrency bug characteristics. In: Proceedings of the 13th International Conference on Architectural Support for Programming Languages and Operating Systems, pp. 329–339 (2008)
27. Herlihy, M., Shavit, N., Luchangco, V., Spear, M.: The Art of Multiprocessor Programming. Newnes (2020)
28. SkipList. https://github.com/shreyas-gopalakrishna/Concurrent-Skip-list. Accessed 11 Jan 2021
29. Ring_Queue. https://github.com/dodng/fast_ring_queue. Accessed 12 Sept 2018
30. Hashmap. https://github.com/kumagi/hashmap. Accessed 29 Mar 2011

An Abstract Interpretation-Based Data Leakage Static Analysis

Filip Drobnjaković[1], Pavle Subotić[1], and Caterina Urban[2](✉)

[1] Microsoft, Beograd, Serbia
[2] Inria & ENS | PSL, Paris, France
caterina.urban@inria.fr

Abstract. Data leakage is a well-known problem in machine learning which occurs when the training and testing datasets are not independent. This phenomenon leads to overly optimistic accuracy estimates at training time, followed by a significant drop in performance when models are deployed in the real world. This can be dangerous, notably when models are used for risk prediction in high-stakes applications.

In this paper, we propose an abstract interpretation-based static analysis to prove the absence of data leakage. We implemented it in the NBLyzer framework and we demonstrate its performance and precision on 2111 Jupyter notebooks from the Kaggle competition platform.

1 Introduction

As artificial intelligence (AI) continues its unprecedented impact on society, ensuring machine learning (ML) models are accurate is crucial. To this end, ML models need to be correctly trained and tested. This iterative task is typically performed within data science notebook environments [9,19]. A notable bug that can be introduced during this process is known as a *data leakage* [18]. Data leakages have been identified as a pervasive problem by the data science community [10,11,17]. In a number of recent cases data leakages crippled the performance of real-world risk prediction systems with dangerous consequences in high-stakes applications such as child welfare [1] and healthcare [24].

Data leakages arise when dependent data is used to train and test a model. This can come in the form of overlapping data sets or, more insidiously, by library transformations that create indirect data dependencies.

Example 1 (Motivating Example). Consider the following excerpt of a data science notebook (based on *569.ipynb* from our benchmarks, and written in the small language that we introduce in Sect. 3.3):

```
data = read("data.csv")
X_norm = normalize(X)
X_train = X_norm.select[[⌊0.025 * R_X_norm⌋ + 1, ..., R_X_norm]][]
X_test = X_norm.select[[0, ..., ⌊0.025 * R_X_norm⌋]][]
train(X_train)
test(X_test)
```


W.-N. Chin and Z. Xu (Eds.): TASE 2024, LNCS 14777, pp. 109–126, 2024.
https://doi.org/10.1007/978-3-031-64626-3_7

Line 1 reads data from a CSV file and line 2 normalizes it. Line 3 and 4 split the data into training and testing segments (we write R_x for the number of data rows stored in x). Finally, line 5 trains a ML model, and line 6 tests its accuracy.

In this case, a data leakage is introduced because line 2 performs a normalization, *before* line 3 and 4 split into train and test data. This implicitly uses the mean over the entire dataset to perform the data transformation and, as a result, the train and test data are implicitly dependent on each other. In our experimental evaluation (cf. Sect. 5) we found that this is a common pattern for introducing a data leakage in several real-world notebooks. In the following, we say that the data resulting from the normalization done in line 2 is *tainted*.

Mainstream methods rely on detecting data leakages retroactively [11,18]. Given a suspicious result, e.g., an overly accurate model, data analysis methods are used to identify data dependencies. However, a reasonable result may avoid suspicion from a data scientist until the model is already deployed. This is a natural use case for *static analysis* to detect data leakages at development time.

In this paper, we propose a static analysis for proving the absence of data leakage in data-manipulating programs: it tracks the origin of data used for training and testing and verifies that they originate from *disjoint* and *untainted* data sources. In Example 1 our analysis identifies a data leakage since `X_train` and `X_test` originate from previously normalized data (despite being disjoint).

Our static analysis (cf. Sect. 4) is designed within the abstract interpretation framework [5]: it is derived through successive abstractions from the (sound and complete, but not computable) collecting program semantics (cf. Sect. 3). This formal development allows us to formally justify the soundness of the analysis (cf. Theorem 3), and to exactly pinpoint where it can lose precision (e.g., modeling data joins, cf. Sect. 4.2) to guide the design of more precise abstractions, if necessary in the future (in our evaluation we found the current analysis to be sufficiently precise, cf. Sect. 5). Moreover, it allows a clear comparisons with other related static analyses, e.g., information flow and taint analyses (cf. Sect. 6). Finally, this design principle allowed us to identify and overcome issues and shortcomings of previous data leakage analysis attempts [20,21].

We implemented our analysis in the NBLyzer [21] framework. We evaluate its performance on 2111 Jupyter notebooks from the Kaggle competition platform, and demonstrate that our approach scales to the performance constraints of interactive data science notebook environments while detecting 25 real data leakages with a precision of 93%. Notably, we are able to detect 60% more data leakages compared to the ad-hoc analysis previously implemented in NBLyzer.

2 Background

2.1 Data Frame-Manipulating Programs

We consider programs manipulating data frames, that is, tabular data structures with columns labeled by non-empty unique names. Let $\mathbb{V}$ be a set of (heterogeneous atomic) values (i.e., such as numerical or string values). We can formalize a data frame as a possibly empty $(r \times c)$-matrix of values, where $r \in \mathbb{N}$ and $c \in \mathbb{N}$ denote the number of matrix rows and columns, respectively. The first row of non-empty data frames contains the labels of the data frame columns. Let $\mathbb{D} \stackrel{\text{def}}{=} \bigcup_{r \in \mathbb{N}} \bigcup_{c \in \mathbb{N}} \mathbb{V}^{r \times c}$ be the set of all possible data frame. Given a data frame $D \in \mathbb{D}$, we use R_D and C_D to denote the number of its rows and columns, respectively, and write $\mathsf{hdr}(D)$ for the set of labels of its columns. We also write $D[r]$ for the specific row indexed with $r \in R_D$ in D.

2.2 Trace Semantics

The *semantics* of a data frame-manipulating program is a mathematical characterization of its behavior when executed for all possible input data. We model the operational semantics of a program in a language-independent way as a *transition system* $\langle \Sigma, \tau \rangle$, where Σ is a (potentially infinite) set of program states and the transition relation $\tau \subseteq \Sigma \times \Sigma$ describes the possible transitions between states. The set of *final states* of the program is $\Omega \stackrel{\text{def}}{=} \{s \in \Sigma \mid \forall s' \in \Sigma \colon \langle s, s' \rangle \notin \tau\}$.

In the following, let $\Sigma^{+\infty} \stackrel{\text{def}}{=} \Sigma^{+} \cup \Sigma^{\omega}$ be the set of all non-empty finite or infinite sequences of program states. A *trace* is a non-empty sequence of program states that respects the transition relation τ, that is, $\langle s, s' \rangle \in \tau$ for each pair of consecutive states $s, s' \in \Sigma$ in the sequence. The *trace semantics* $\Upsilon \in \mathcal{P}(\Sigma^{+\infty})$ generated by a transition system $\langle \Sigma, \tau \rangle$ is the union of all finite traces that are terminating with a final state in Ω, and all infinite traces [2]:

$$\begin{aligned} \Upsilon \stackrel{\text{def}}{=} & \bigcup_{n \in \mathbb{N}^{+}} \{s_0 \dots s_{n-1} \in \Sigma^{n} \mid \forall i < n-1 \colon \langle s_i, s_{i+1} \rangle \in \tau, s_{n-1} \in \Omega\} \\ & \cup \ \{s_0 \dots \in \Sigma^{\omega} \mid \forall i \in \mathbb{N} \colon \langle s_i, s_{i+1} \rangle \in \tau\} \end{aligned} \tag{1}$$

In the rest of the paper, we write $[\![P]\!]$ for the trace semantics of a program P.

3 Concrete Data Leakage Semantics

The trace semantics fully describes the behavior of a program. However, reasoning about a particular property of a program is facilitated by the design of a semantics that abstracts away from irrelevant details about program executions. In this section, we define our property of interest—absence of data leakage—and use abstract interpretation to systematically derive, by abstraction of the trace semantics, a semantics that precisely captures this property.

3.1 (Absence of) Data Leakage

We use an extensional definition of a *property* as the set of elements having such a property [5,6]. This allows checking property satisfaction by set inclusion (see below) also across abstractions (cf. Theorems 1 and 2). Semantic properties of programs are properties of their semantics. Thus, properties of programs with trace semantics in $\mathcal{P}(\Sigma^{+\infty})$ are sets of sets of traces in $\mathcal{P}(\mathcal{P}(\Sigma^{+\infty}))$. The set of program properties forms a complete boolean lattice $\langle \mathcal{P}(\mathcal{P}(\Sigma^{+\infty})), \subseteq, \cup, \cap, \emptyset, \mathcal{P}(\Sigma^{+\infty})\rangle$ for subset inclusion (i.e., logical implication). The strongest property is the standard *collecting semantics* $\Lambda \in \mathcal{P}(\mathcal{P}(\Sigma^{+\infty}))$: $\Lambda \overset{\text{def}}{=} \{\Upsilon\}$, i.e., the property of "being the program with trace semantics Υ". Let $(\!|P|\!)$ denote the collecting semantics of a program P. Then, a program P satisfies a given property $\mathcal{H} \in \mathcal{P}(\mathcal{P}(\Sigma^{+\infty}))$ if and only if its collecting semantics is a subset of $\mathcal{H}$: $P \models \mathcal{H} \Leftrightarrow (\!|P|\!) \subseteq \mathcal{H}$. In this paper, we consider the property of *absence of data leakage*, which requires data used for training and data used for testing a machine learning model to be *independent*.

Example 2 ((In)dependent Data Frame Variables). Let us consider a program P with a single input data frame variable reading data frames with four rows and one single column with values in $\{3, 9\}$, i.e., data frames in $\bigcup_{r \in \{1,2,3,4\}} \{3, 9\}^r$ (cf. Sect. 2.1). Imagine that P first performs min-max normalization (i.e., rescaling all data frame values to be in the $[0, 1]$ range) and then splits the data frame in half to use the first two rows for training and the last two rows for testing. The table below shows all possible train and test data resulting from all possible input data of this program:

input data	3	3	3	3	9	9	9	9	3	3	3	3	9	9	9	9	1
	3	3	9	9	3	3	9	9	3	3	9	9	3	3	9	9	2
	3	9	3	9	3	9	3	9	3	9	3	9	3	9	3	9	3
	3	3	3	3	3	3	3	3	9	9	9	9	9	9	9	9	4
	↓	↓	↓	↓	↓	↓	↓	↓	↓	↓	↓	↓	↓	↓	↓	↓	
train data	0	0	0	0	1	1	1	1	0	0	0	0	1	1	1	0	1
	0	0	1	1	0	0	1	1	0	0	1	1	0	0	1	0	2
test data	0	1	0	1	0	1	0	1	0	1	0	1	0	1	0	0	1
	0	0	0	0	0	0	0	0	1	1	1	1	1	1	1	0	2
												σ				σ'	

In this case, train and test data are *not* independent: if we consider, for instance, the execution σ with input data frame value "3|9|9|9" we can change the value of its first row (i.e., $r = 1$ in Eq. 2) from $\bar{v} = 3$ to $\bar{v} = 9$ (while leaving all other rows unchanged) to obtain an execution σ' resulting in a difference in *both* train and test data (i.e., $\sigma(\mathrm{U}_P^{\mathrm{train}}) \neq \sigma'(\mathrm{U}_P^{\mathrm{train}})$ and $\sigma(\mathrm{U}_P^{\mathrm{test}}) \neq \sigma'(\mathrm{U}_P^{\mathrm{test}})$ in Eq. 2, with train data differing at line 2 and test data differing at both lines 1 and 2).

Instead, the table below shows all possible resulting train and test data if the normalization is performed *after* the split into train and test data:

input data	3	3	3	3	9	9	9	9	3	3	3	3	9	9	9	9	1
	3	3	9	9	3	3	9	9	3	3	9	9	3	3	9	9	2
	3	9	3	9	3	9	3	9	3	9	3	9	3	9	3	9	3
	3	3	3	3	3	3	3	3	9	9	9	9	9	9	9	9	4
	↓	↓	↓	↓	↓	↓	↓	↓	↓	↓	↓	↓	↓	↓	↓	↓	
train data	0	0	0	0	1	1	0	0	0	0	0	0	1	1	0	0	1
	0	0	1	1	0	0	0	0	0	0	1	1	0	0	0	0	2
test data	0	1	0	1	0	1	0	1	0	0	0	0	0	0	0	0	1
	0	0	0	0	0	0	0	0	1	0	1	0	1	0	1	0	2

Here train and test data remain independent as modifying any input data row r in any execution yields another execution that may result in a difference in either train and test data *but never both*. Equivalently, all possible values of *either* train and test data are possible independently of the choice of the value of the row r.

More formally, let $\mathbb{X}$ be the set of all the (data frame) variables of a (data frame-manipulating) program P. We denote with $\mathrm{I}_P \subseteq \mathbb{X}$ the set of its *input* or source data frame variables, i.e., data frame variables whose value is directly read from the input, and use $\mathrm{U}_P \subseteq \mathbb{X}$ to denote the set of its *used* data frame variables, i.e., data frame variables used for training or testing a ML model. We write $\mathrm{U}_P^{\text{train}} \subseteq \mathrm{U}_P$ and $\mathrm{U}_P^{\text{test}} \subseteq \mathrm{U}_P$ for the variables used for training and testing, respectively. For simplicity, we can assume that programs are in static single-assignment form so that data frame variables are assigned exactly once: data is read from the input, transformed and normalized, and ultimately used for training and testing. Given a trace $\sigma \in [\![P]\!]$, we write $\sigma(i)$ and $\sigma(o)$ to denote the value of the data frame variables $i \in \mathrm{I}_P$ and $o \in \mathrm{U}_P$ in σ. We can now define when used data frame variables are independent in a program with trace semantics $[\![P]\!]$:

$$
\begin{aligned}
&\textsc{ind}([\![P]\!]) \stackrel{\text{def}}{=} \forall \sigma \in [\![P]\!], i \in \mathrm{I}_P, r \in R_i \colon \textsc{unch}(\sigma, i, r, \mathrm{U}_P^{\text{test}}) \lor \textsc{unch}(\sigma, i, r, \mathrm{U}_P^{\text{train}}) \\
&\textsc{unch}(\sigma, i, r, U) \stackrel{\text{def}}{=} \forall \bar{v} \in \mathbb{V}^{C_i} \colon \sigma(i)[r] \neq \bar{v} \Rightarrow (\exists \sigma' \in [\![P]\!] \colon \\
&\qquad \sigma'(i)[r] = \bar{v} \land \sigma(i) \stackrel{\bar{r}}{=} \sigma'(i) \land \sigma(\mathrm{I}_P \setminus \{i\}) = \sigma'(\mathrm{I}_P \setminus \{i\}) \land \sigma(U) = \sigma'(U))
\end{aligned}
\tag{2}
$$

where R_i and C_i stand for $R_{\sigma(i)}$ (i.e., number of rows of the data frame value of $i \in \mathrm{I}_P$) and $C_{\sigma(i)}$ (i.e., number of columns of the data frame value of $i \in \mathrm{I}_P$), respectively, $\sigma(i) \stackrel{\bar{r}}{=} \sigma'(i)$ stands for $\forall r' \in R_i \colon r' \neq r \Rightarrow \sigma(i)[r'] = \sigma'(i)[r']$ (i.e., the data frame value of $i \in \mathrm{I}_P$ remains unchanged for any row $r' \neq r$), and $\sigma(X) = \sigma'(X)$ stands for $\forall x \in X \colon \sigma(x) = \sigma'(x)$. The definition requires that changing the value of a data source $i \in \mathrm{I}_P$ can modify data frame variables used for training ($\mathrm{U}_P^{\text{train}}$) or testing ($\mathrm{U}_P^{\text{test}}$), *but not both*: the value of data frame variables used for either training or testing in a trace σ remains the same independently of all possible values $\bar{v} \in \mathbb{V}^{C_i}$ of any portion (e.g., any row $r \in R_i$) of any input data frame variable $i \in \mathrm{I}_P$ in σ. Note that this definition quantifies over changes in data frame rows since the split into train and test data happens across rows (e.g., using `train_test_split` in Pandas), but takes into account all possible column values in each row ($\bar{v} \in \mathbb{V}^{C_i}$). It also implicitly takes into account implicit flows of information by considering traces in $[\![P]\!]$. In particular, in terms of secure information flow, notably non-interference, this definition says that *we cannot simultaneously observe different values* in $\mathrm{U}_P^{\mathrm{train}}$ and $\mathrm{U}_P^{\mathrm{test}}$, regardless of the values of the input data frame variables. Here we weaken non-interference to consider either $\mathrm{U}_P^{\mathrm{train}}$ or $\mathrm{U}_P^{\mathrm{test}}$ as low outputs (depending on which row of the input data frame variables is modified), instead of fixing the choice beforehand. Note also that UNCH quantifies over all possible values $\bar{v} \in \mathbb{V}^{C_i}$ of the changed row i rather than quantifying over traces to allow non-determinism, i.e., not all traces that only differ at row $r \in R_i$ of data frame variable $i \in \mathrm{I}_P$ need to agree on the values of the used variables $U \subseteq U_P$ but all values of U that are feasible from a value of r of i need to be feasible for *all* possible values of r of i. In terms of input data (non-)usage [23], this definition says that training and testing *do not use* the same (portions of the) input data sources. Here we generalize the notion of data usage proposed by Urban and Müller [23] to multi-dimensional variables and allow multiple values for all outcomes but one (variables used for either training or testing) for each variation in the values of the input variables.

The absence of data leakage property can now be formally defined as the set $\mathcal{I} \stackrel{\text{def}}{=} \{[\![P]\!] \in \mathcal{P}(\Sigma^{+\infty}) \mid \mathrm{IND}([\![P]\!])\}$ of programs (semantics) that use independent data for training and testing ML models. Thus $P \models \mathcal{I} \Leftrightarrow (\!|P|\!) \subseteq \mathcal{I}$.

In the rest of this section, we derive, by abstraction of the collecting semantics Λ, a *sound* and *complete* semantics $\dot{\Lambda}_I$ that contains only and exactly the information needed to reason about (the absence of) data leakage. A further abstraction in the next section, loses completeness but yields a *sound* and *computable* over-approximation of $\dot{\Lambda}_I$ that allows designing a static analysis to effectively detect data leakage in data frame-manipulating programs.

3.2 Dependency Semantics

From the definition of absence of data leakage, we observe that for reasoning about data leakage we essentially need to track the flow of information between (portions of) input data sources and data used for training or testing. Thus we can abstract the collecting semantics into a set of dependencies between (rows of) input data frame variables and used data frame variables.

We define the following Galois connection:

$$\langle \mathcal{P}(\mathcal{P}(\Sigma^{+\infty})), \subseteq \rangle \underset{\alpha_{I \rightsquigarrow U}}{\overset{\gamma_{I \rightsquigarrow U}}{\leftrightarrows}} \langle \mathcal{P}((\mathbb{X} \times \mathbb{N}) \times (\mathbb{X} \times \mathbb{N})), \supseteq \rangle \tag{3}$$

between sets of sets of traces and sets of relations (i.e., dependencies) between data frame variables indexed at some row. The abstraction and concretization function are parameterized by a set $I \subseteq \mathbb{X}$ of input variables and a set $U \subseteq \mathbb{X}$ of used variables of interest. In particular, the dependency abstraction $\alpha_{I \rightsquigarrow U} : \mathcal{P}(\mathcal{P}(\Sigma^{+\infty})) \rightarrow \mathcal{P}((\mathbb{X} \times \mathbb{N}) \times (\mathbb{X} \times \mathbb{N}))$ is:

$$\alpha_{I \rightsquigarrow U}(S) \stackrel{\text{def}}{=} \left\{ i[r] \rightsquigarrow o[r'] \;\middle|\; \begin{array}{c} i \in I, r \in \mathbb{N}, o \in U, r' \in \mathbb{N}, (\forall T \in S\colon \\ \exists \sigma \in T, \bar{v} \in \mathbb{V}^{C_i}\colon \forall \sigma' \in T\colon \sigma(i) \stackrel{\bar{r}}{=} \sigma'(i) \wedge \\ \sigma(I \setminus \{i\}) = \sigma'(I \setminus \{i\}) \wedge \sigma(o)[r'] = \sigma'(o)[r'] \\ \Rightarrow \sigma'(i)[r] \neq \bar{v}) \end{array} \right\}$$

where we write $i[r] \rightsquigarrow o[r']$ for a dependency $\langle\langle i, r\rangle, \langle o, r'\rangle\rangle$ between a data frame variable $i \in I$ at the row indexed by $r \in \mathbb{N}$ and a data frame variable $o \in U$ at the row indexed by $r' \in \mathbb{N}$. In particular, $\alpha_{\rightsquigarrow}$ extracts a dependency $i[r] \rightsquigarrow o[r']$ when (in all sets of traces T in the semantic property S) there is a value $\bar{v} \in \mathbb{V}^{C_i}$ for row r of data frame variable i that changes the value at row r' of data frame variable o, that is, there is a value for row r' of data frame variable o that cannot be reached if the value for row r of i is changed to $\bar{v}$ (and all else remains the same, i.e., $\sigma(i) \stackrel{\bar{r}}{=} \sigma'(i) \wedge \sigma(I \setminus \{i\}) = \sigma'(I \setminus \{i\})$).

Note that our dependency abstraction generalizes that of Cousot [3] to non-deterministic programs and multi-dimensional data frame variables, thus tracking dependencies between portions of data frames. As in [3], this is an abstraction of semantic properties thus the dependencies must hold for all semantics having the semantic property: more semantics have a semantic property, fewer dependencies will hold for all semantics. Therefore, sets of dependencies are ordered by superset inclusion $\supseteq$ (cf. Eq. 3).

Example 3 (Dependencies Between Data Frame Variables). Let us consider again the program P from Example 2. Let i denote the input data frame of the program and let o_{train} and o_{test} denote the data frames used for training and testing. In this case, for instance, we have $i[1] \rightsquigarrow o_{\text{train}}[2]$ because, taking execution σ, changing only the value of $i[1]$ from 3 to 9 yields execution σ' which changes the value of $o_{\text{train}}[2]$, i.e., all other executions either differ at other rows of i or differ at least in the value of $o_{\text{train}}[2]$ (such as σ'). In fact, the set of dependencies for the whole set of executions of the program shows that o_{train} and o_{test} depend on *all* rows of the input data frame variable i.

Instead, performing normalization *after* splitting into train/test data yields $\{i[1] \rightsquigarrow o_{\text{train}}[j], i[2] \rightsquigarrow o_{\text{train}}[j], i[3] \rightsquigarrow o_{\text{test}}[j], i[4] \rightsquigarrow o_{\text{test}}[j]\}$, $j \in \{1, 2\}$, where o_{train} and o_{test} depend on disjoint subsets of rows of the input data frame i.

It is easy to see that the abstraction function $\alpha_{\text{I}_P \rightsquigarrow \text{U}_P}$ is a complete join morphism. Thus, $\gamma_{\text{I}_P \rightsquigarrow \text{U}_P}(D) \stackrel{\text{def}}{=} \bigcup \{S \mid \alpha_{\text{I}_P \rightsquigarrow \text{U}_P}(S) \supseteq D\}$.

We can now define the *dependency semantics* $\Lambda_{I \rightsquigarrow U} \in \mathcal{P}((\mathbb{X} \times \mathbb{N}) \times (\mathbb{X} \times \mathbb{N}))$ by abstraction of the collecting semantics Λ: $\Lambda_{I \rightsquigarrow U} \stackrel{\text{def}}{=} \alpha_{I \rightsquigarrow U}(\Lambda)$. In the rest of the paper, we write $(\!|P|\!)_{\rightsquigarrow}$ to denote the dependency semantics of a program P, leaving the sets of data frame variables of interest I and U implicitly set to I_P and U_P, respectively. The dependency semantics remains sound and complete:

Theorem 1. $P \models \mathcal{I} \Leftrightarrow (\!|P|\!)_{\rightsquigarrow} \supseteq \alpha_{\text{I}_P \rightsquigarrow \text{U}_P}(\mathcal{I})$.

3.3 Data Leakage Semantics

As hinted by Example 3, we observe that for detecting data leakage (resp. verifying absence of data leakage), we care in particular about which rows of input data frame variables the used data frame variables depend on. In case of data leakage (resp. absence of data leakage), data frame variables used for different purposes will depend on *overlapping* (resp. *disjoint*) sets of rows of input data frame variables. Thus, we further abstract the dependency semantics $\Lambda_{\rightsquigarrow^+}$ pointwise [7] into a map for each data frame variable associating with each data frame row index the set of (input) variables (indexed at some row) from which it depends on.

Formally, we define the following Galois connection:

$$\langle \mathcal{P}\left((\mathbb{X} \times \mathbb{N}) \times (\mathbb{X} \times \mathbb{N})\right), \supseteq\rangle \xleftrightarrow[\dot{\alpha}]{\dot{\gamma}} \langle \mathbb{X} \to (\mathbb{N} \to \mathcal{P}\left(\mathbb{X} \times \mathbb{N}\right)), \dot{\supseteq}\rangle \tag{4}$$

where the abstraction $\dot{\alpha}\colon \mathcal{P}\left((\mathbb{X} \times \mathbb{N}) \times (\mathbb{X} \times \mathbb{N})\right) \to (\mathbb{X} \to (\mathbb{N} \to \mathcal{P}\left(\mathbb{X} \times \mathbb{N}\right)))$ is:

$$\dot{\alpha}(D) \stackrel{\text{def}}{=} \lambda x \in \mathbb{X}\colon (\lambda r \in \mathbb{N}\colon \{i[r'] \mid i \in \mathbb{X}, r' \in \mathbb{N}, i[r'] \rightsquigarrow x[r] \in D\}) \tag{5}$$

Example 4 (Data Leakage Semantics). Let us consider again the last dependencies in Example 3: $\{i[1] \rightsquigarrow o_{\text{train}}[j], i[2] \rightsquigarrow o_{\text{train}}[j], i[3] \rightsquigarrow o_{\text{test}}[j], i[4] \rightsquigarrow o_{\text{test}}[j]\}$, $j \in \{1, 2\}$. Its abstraction following Eq. 5 is the following map:

$$\lambda x\colon \begin{cases} \lambda r\colon \begin{cases} \{i[1], i[2]\} & r = 1 \\ \{i[1], i[2]\} & r = 2 \end{cases} & x = o_{\text{train}} \\ \lambda r\colon \begin{cases} \{i[3], i[4]\} & r = 1 \\ \{i[3], i[4]\} & r = 2 \end{cases} & x = o_{\text{test}} \end{cases}$$

Instead, the abstraction of the set of dependencies resulting from performing normalization *before* splitting into train and test data is the following map:

$$\lambda x\colon \begin{cases} \lambda r\colon \begin{cases} \{i[1], i[2], i[3], i[4]\} & r = 1 \\ \{i[1], i[2], i[3], i[4]\} & r = 2 \end{cases} & x = o_{\text{train}} \\ \lambda r\colon \begin{cases} \{i[1], i[2], i[3], i[4]\} & r = 1 \\ \{i[1], i[2], i[3], i[4]\} & r = 2 \end{cases} & x = o_{\text{test}} \end{cases}$$

The abstraction function $\dot{\alpha}$ is another complete join morphism so it uniquely determines the concretization function: $\dot{\gamma}(m) \stackrel{\text{def}}{=} \bigcap \{D \mid \dot{\alpha}(D) \dot{\supseteq} m\}$.

We finally derive our *data leakage semantics* $\dot{\Lambda} \in \mathbb{X} \to (\mathbb{N} \to \mathcal{P}\left(\mathbb{X} \times \mathbb{N}\right))$ by abstraction of the dependency semantics $\Lambda_{\rightsquigarrow}$: $\dot{\Lambda} \stackrel{\text{def}}{=} \dot{\alpha}(\Lambda_{\rightsquigarrow})$. In the following, we write $(\!|\dot{P}|\!)$ for the data leakage semantics of a program P. The abstraction $\dot{\alpha}$ does not lose any information, so we still have both soundness and completeness:

Theorem 2. $P \models \mathcal{I} \Leftrightarrow (\!|\dot{P}|\!) \dot{\supseteq} \dot{\alpha}(\alpha_{\mathrm{I}_P \rightsquigarrow \mathrm{U}_P}(\mathcal{I}))$.

We can now equivalently verify absence of data leakage by checking that data frames used for different purposes depend on disjoint (rows of) input data:

Lemma 1. *$P \models \mathcal{I} \Leftrightarrow \forall o_1 \in \mathrm{U}_P^{\text{train}}, o_2 \in \mathrm{U}_P^{\text{test}}\colon (\!|\dot{P}|\!)o_1 \cap (\!|\dot{P}|\!)o_2 = \emptyset$ where, with a slightly abuse of notation, $(\!|\dot{P}|\!)o$ stands for $\bigcup_{r \in \mathrm{dom}((\!|\dot{P}|\!)o)} (\!|\dot{P}|\!)o(r)$, i.e., the union of all sets $(\!|\dot{P}|\!)o(r)$ of rows of input data frame variables in the range of $(\!|\dot{P}|\!)o$ the data leakage semantics $(\!|\dot{P}|\!)$ for the used data frame variable o.*

Example 5 (Continued from Example 4). The first map in Example 4 satisfies Lemma 1 since the set $\{i[1], i[2]\}$ of input data frame rows on which o_{train} depends is *disjoint* from the set $\{i[3], i[4]\}$ of input data frame rows on which o_{test} depends. Thus, performing min-max normalization *after* splitting into train and test data does not create data leakage.

This is not the case for the second map in Example 4 where the sets of input data frame rows from which o_{train} and o_{test} depend are identical, indicating data leakage when normalization is done *before* the split into train and test data.

Small Data Frame-Manipulating Language. The formal treatment so far is language independent. In the rest of this section, we give a constructive definition of our data leakage semantics $\dot{\Lambda}_I$ for a small data frame-manipulating language which we then use to illustrate our data leakage analysis in the next section. (Note that the actual implementation of the analysis handles more advanced constructs such as branches, loops, and procedures calls, cf. [8, Appendix D]).

We consider a simple sequential language without procedures nor references. The only variable data type is the set $\mathbb{D}$ of data frames. Programs in the language are sequences of statements, which belong to either of the following classes:

1. **source:** $y = \mathrm{read}(name)$ — $name \in \mathbb{W}$
2. **select:** $y = x.\mathrm{select}[\bar{r}][C]$ — $\bar{r} \in \mathbb{N}^{k \leq R_x}, C \subseteq \mathsf{hdr}(x)$
3. **merge:** $y = op(x_1, x_2)$ — $x_1, x_2 \in \mathbb{X}, op \in \{\mathrm{concat}, \mathrm{join}\}$
4. **function:** $y = f(x)$ — $x \in \mathbb{X}, f \in \{\mathrm{normalize}, \mathrm{other}\}$
5. **use:** $f(X)$ — $X \subseteq \mathbb{X}, f \in \{\mathrm{train}, \mathrm{test}\}$

where $name \in \mathbb{W}$ is a (string) data file name; we write R_x and $\mathsf{hdr}(x)$ for the number of rows and set of labels of the columns of the data frame (value) stored into the variable x. The *source* statement (representing library functions such as `read_csv`, `read_excel`, etc., in Python pandas) reads data from an input file and stores it into a variable y. The *select* statement (loosely corresponding to library functions such as `iloc`, `loc`, etc., in Python pandas) returns a subset data frame y of x, based on an array of row indexes $\bar{r}$ and a set of column labels C. The selection parameters $\bar{r}$ and C are optional: when missing the selection includes all rows or columns of the given data frame. The *merge* statements are binary merge operations between data frames (the *concat* and *join* operations roughly match the default Python pandas `concat` and `merge` library functions, respectively). The *function* statements modify a data frame x either by normalizing it (with the *normalize* function) or by applying some *other* function. The *normalize* function produces a *tainted* data frame y (representing normalization functions such as standardization or scaling in Python Sklearn). We assume that any *other* function does not produce tainted data frames. Finally, *use* statements employs data frames for either training ($f = \mathrm{train}$) or testing ($f = \mathrm{test}$) a ML model.

Constructive Data Leakage Semantics. We can now instantiate the definition of our data leakage semantics $\dot{\Lambda}_I$ with our small data frame-manipulating language. Given a program $P \equiv S_1, \ldots, S_n$ written in our small language (where $S_1, \ldots, S_n$ are statements), the set of input data frame variables I_P is given (with a slight abuse of notation, for simplicity) by the set of data files read by *source* statements, i.e., $\mathrm{I}_P \stackrel{\text{def}}{=} i[\![P]\!] = i[\![S_n]\!] \circ \cdots \circ i[\![S_1]\!]\emptyset$, where $i[\![y = \text{read}(name)]\!]I \stackrel{\text{def}}{=} I \cup \{name\}$ and $i[\![S]\!]I \stackrel{\text{def}}{=} I$ for any other statement S in P. Similarly, we define the set of used variables $\mathrm{U}_P \stackrel{\text{def}}{=} u[\![P]\!] = u[\![S_n]\!] \circ \cdots \circ u[\![S_1]\!]\emptyset$, where $u[\![f(X)]\!]U \stackrel{\text{def}}{=} U \cup X$ and $u[\![S]\!]U \stackrel{\text{def}}{=} U$ for any other statement S, and analogously for $\mathrm{U}_P^{\text{train}} \subseteq \mathrm{U}_P$ (when $f = \text{train}$) and $\mathrm{U}_P^{\text{test}} \subseteq \mathrm{U}_P$ (when $f = \text{test}$).

Our constructive data leakage semantics is $(\!|\dot{P}|\!) \stackrel{\text{def}}{=} s[\![S_n]\!] \circ \cdots \circ s[\![S_1]\!]\dot{\emptyset}$ where $\dot{\emptyset}$ is the totally undefined function and the semantic function $s[\![S]\!]$ for each statement S in P is defined as follows:

$$
\begin{aligned}
s[\![y = \text{read}(name)]\!]m &\stackrel{\text{def}}{=} m\left[y \mapsto \lambda r \in R_{\text{read}()} \colon \{name[r]\}\right] \\
s[\![y = x.\text{select}[\bar{r}][C]]\!]m &\stackrel{\text{def}}{=} m\left[y \mapsto \lambda r \in R_{x.\text{select}[\bar{r}][C]} \colon m(x)(\bar{r}[r])\right] \\
s[\![y = \text{concat}(x_1, x_2)]\!]m &\stackrel{\text{def}}{=} \\
& m\left[y \mapsto \lambda r \in R_{\text{concat}(x_1,x_2)} \colon \begin{cases} m(x_1)r & r \leq |\text{dom}(m(x_1))| \\ m(x_2)(r - |\text{dom}(m(x_1))|) & r > |\text{dom}(m(x_1))| \end{cases}\right] \\
s[\![y = \text{join}(x_1, x_2)]\!]m &\stackrel{\text{def}}{=} m\left[y \mapsto \lambda r \in R_{\text{join}(x_1,x_2)} \colon m(x_1)\overleftarrow{r} \cup m(x_2)\overrightarrow{r}\right] \\
s[\![y = \text{normalize}(x)]\!]m &\stackrel{\text{def}}{=} m\left[y \mapsto \lambda r \in R_{\text{normalize}(x)} \colon \bigcup_{r' \in \text{dom}(m(x))} m(x)r'\right] \\
s[\![y = \text{other}(x)]\!]m &\stackrel{\text{def}}{=} m\left[y \mapsto \lambda r \in R_{\text{other}(x)} \colon m(x)r\right] \\
s[\![\text{use}(x)]\!]m &\stackrel{\text{def}}{=} m
\end{aligned}
$$

The semantics of the *source* statement maps each row r of a read data frame y to (the set containing) the corresponding row in the read data file ($name[r]$). The semantics of the *select* statement maps each row r of the resulting data frame y to the set of data sources ($m(x)$) of the corresponding row ($\bar{r}[r]$) in the original data frame. The *concat* operation between two data frames x_1 and x_2 yields a data frame with all rows of x_1 followed by all rows of x_2. Thus, the semantics of *concat* statements accordingly maps each row r of the resulting data frame y to the set of data sources of the corresponding row in x_1 (if $r \leq |\text{dom}(m(x_1))|$, that is, r falls within the size of x_1) or x_2 (if $r > |\text{dom}(m(x_1))|$). Instead, the *join* operation combines two data frames x_1 and x_2 based on a(n index) column and yields a data frame containing only the rows that have a matching value in both x_1 and x_2. Thus, the semantics of *join* statements maps each row r of the resulting data frame y to the union of the sets of data sources of the corresponding rows ($\overleftarrow{r}$ and $\overrightarrow{r}$) in x_1 and x_2. We consider only one type of join operation (inner join) for simplicity, but other types (outer, left, or right join) can be similarly defined. The normalize function is a tainting function so the semantics for the *normalize* function introduces dependencies for each row r in the normalized data frame y with the data sources $(m(x))$ of each row r' of the data frame before normalization. Instead, the semantics of *other* (non-tainting) functions maintains the same dependencies $(m(x)r)$ for each row r of the modified data frame y. Finally, *use* statements do not modify any dependency so the semantics of *use* statements leaves the dependencies map unchanged.

4 Data Leakage Analysis

In this section, we abstract our concrete data leakage semantics to obtain a sound data leakage static analysis. In essence, our analysis keeps track of (an over-approximation of) the data source cells each data frame variable depends on (to detect potential explicit data source overlaps). Plus, it tracks whether data source cells are tainted, i.e., modified by a library function in such a way that could introduce data leakage (by implicit indirect data source overlaps).

4.1 Data Sources Abstract Domain

Data Frame Abstract Domain. We over-approximate data sources by means of a parametric data frame abstract domain $\mathbb{L}(\mathbb{C}, \mathbb{R})$, where the parameter abstract domains $\mathbb{C}$ and $\mathbb{R}$ track data sources columns and rows, respectively. We illustrate below two simple instances of these domains.

Column Abstraction. We propose an instance of $\mathbb{C}$ that over-approximates the set of column labels in a data frame. As, in practice, data frame labels are pretty much always strings, the elements of $\mathbb{C}$ belong to a complete lattice $\langle \mathcal{C}, \sqsubseteq_C, \sqcup_C, \sqcap_C, \bot_C, \top_C \rangle$ where $\mathcal{C} \stackrel{\text{def}}{=} \mathcal{P}(\mathbb{W}) \cup \{\top_C\}$; $\mathbb{W}$ is the set of all possible strings of characters in a chosen alphabet and $\top_C$ represents a lack of information on which columns a data frame *may* have (abstracting any data frame). Elements in $\mathcal{C}$ are ordered by set inclusion extended with $\top_C$ being the largest element: $C_1 \sqsubseteq_C C_2 \stackrel{\text{def}}{\Leftrightarrow} C_2 = \top_C \vee (C_1 \neq \top_C \wedge C_1 \subseteq C_2)$. Similarly, join $\sqcup_C$ and meet $\sqcap_C$ are set inclusion and set intersection, respectively, extended to account for $\top_C$:

$$C_1 \sqcup_C C_2 \stackrel{\text{def}}{=} \begin{cases} \top_C & C_1 = \top_C \vee C_2 = \top_2 \\ C_1 \cup C_2 & \text{otherwise} \end{cases} \qquad C_1 \sqcap_C C_2 \stackrel{\text{def}}{=} \begin{cases} C_1 & C_2 = \top_C \\ C_2 & C_1 = \top_C \\ C_1 \cap C_2 & \text{otherwise} \end{cases}$$

Finally, the bottom $\bot_C$ is the empty set $\emptyset$ (abstracting an empty data frame).

Row Abstraction. Unlike columns, data frame rows are not named. Moreover, data frames typically have a large number of rows and often ranges or rows are added to or removed from data frames. Thus, the abstract domain of intervals [4] *over the natural numbers* is a suitable instance of $\mathbb{R}$. The elements of $\mathbb{R}$ belong to the complete lattice $\langle \mathcal{R}, \sqsubseteq_R, \sqcup_R, \sqcap_R, \bot_R, \top_R \rangle$ with the set $\mathcal{R}$

defined as $\mathcal{R} \stackrel{\text{def}}{=} \{[l,u] \mid l \in \mathbb{N}, u \in \mathbb{N} \cup \{\infty\}, l \leq u\} \cup \{\bot_R\}$. The top element $\top_R$ is $[0,\infty]$. Intervals in $\mathbb{R}$ abstract (sets of) row indexes: the concretization function $\gamma_R \colon \mathcal{R} \to \mathcal{P}(\mathbb{N})$ is such that $\gamma_R(\bot_R) \stackrel{\text{def}}{=} \emptyset$ and $\gamma_R([l,u]) \stackrel{\text{def}}{=} \{r \in \mathbb{N} \mid l \leq r \leq u\}$. The interval domain partial order ($\sqsubseteq_R$) and operators for join ($\sqcup_R$) and meet ($\sqcap_R$) are defined as usual (e.g., see Miné's PhD thesis [15] for reference).

In addition, we associate with each interval $R \in \mathcal{R}$ another interval $\mathsf{idx}(R)$ of indices: $\mathsf{idx}(\bot_R) \stackrel{\text{def}}{=} \bot_R$ and $\mathsf{idx}([l,u]) \stackrel{\text{def}}{=} [0, u-l]$; this essentially establishes a map $\phi_R \colon \mathbb{N} \to \mathbb{N}$ between elements of $\gamma_R(R)$ (ordered by $\leq$) and elements of $\gamma_R(\mathsf{idx}(R))$ (also ordered by $\leq$). In the following, given an interval $R \in \mathcal{R}$ and an interval of indices $[i,j] \in \mathcal{R}$ (such that $[i,j] \sqsubseteq_R R$), we slightly abuse notation and write $\phi_R^{-1}([i,j])$ for the sub-interval of R between the indices i and j, i.e., we have that $\gamma_R(\phi_R^{-1}([i,j])) \stackrel{\text{def}}{=} \{r \in \gamma(R) \mid \phi^{-1}(i) \leq r \leq \phi^{-1}(j)\}$. We need this operation to soundly abstract consecutive row selections (cf. Sect. 4).

Example 6 (Row Abstraction). Let us consider the interval $[10,14] \in \mathcal{R}$ with index $\mathsf{idx}(R) = [0,4]$. We have an isomorphism ϕ_R between $\{10,11,12,13,14\}$ and $\{0,1,2,3,4\}$. Let us consider now the interval of indices $[1,3]$. We then have $\phi_R^{-1}([1,3]) = [11,13]$ (since $\phi_R^{-1}(1) = 11$ and $\phi_R^{-1}(3) = 13$).

Data Frame Abstraction. The elements of the data frame abstract domain $\mathbb{L}(\mathbb{C},\mathbb{R})$ belong to a partial order $\langle \mathcal{L}, \sqsubseteq_L \rangle$ where $\mathcal{L} \stackrel{\text{def}}{=} \mathbb{W} \times \mathcal{C} \times \mathcal{R}$ contains triples of a data file name $file \in \mathbb{W}$, a column over-approximation $C \in \mathcal{C}$, and a row over-approximation $R \in \mathcal{R}$. In the following, we write file_R^C for the abstract data frame $\langle \text{file}, C, R \rangle \in \mathcal{L}$. The partial order $\sqsubseteq_L$ compares abstract data frames derived from the same data files: $X_R^C \sqsubseteq_L Y_{R'}^{C'} \stackrel{\text{def}}{\Leftrightarrow} X = Y \wedge C \sqsubseteq_C C' \wedge R \sqsubseteq R'$.

We also define a predicate for whether abstract data frames overlap:

$$\text{overlap}(X_R^C, Y_{R'}^{C'}) \stackrel{\text{def}}{\Leftrightarrow} X = Y \wedge C \sqcap_C C' \neq \emptyset \wedge R \sqcap R' \neq \bot_R \tag{6}$$

and partial join ($\sqcup_L$) and meet ($\sqcap_L$) over data frames from the same data files:

$$X_{R_1}^{C_1} \sqcup_L X_{R_2}^{C_2} \stackrel{\text{def}}{=} X_{R_1 \sqcup_R R_2}^{C_1 \sqcup_C C_2} \qquad X_{R_1}^{C_1} \sqcap_L X_{R_2}^{C_2} \stackrel{\text{def}}{=} X_{R_1 \sqcap_R R_2}^{C_1 \sqcap_C C_2}$$

Finally, we define a constraining operator $\downarrow_R^C$ that restricts an abstract data frame to given column and row over-approximations: $X_R^C \downarrow_{R'}^{C'} \stackrel{\text{def}}{=} X_{\phi^{-1}(\mathsf{idx}(R) \sqcap_R R')}^{C \sqcap_C C'}$. Note that here the definition makes use of $\mathsf{idx}(R)$ and $\phi^{-1}([i,j])$ to compute the correct row over-approximation.

Example 7 (Abstract Data Frames). Let $\text{file}_{[10,14]}^{\{id,city\}}$ abstract a data frame with columns $\{id, city\}$ and rows $\{10,11,12,13,14\}$ derived from a data source *file*. The abstract data frame $\text{file}_{[12,15]}^{\{country\}}$ does not overlap with it, while $\text{file}_{[12,15]}^{\{id\}}$ does. Joining $\text{file}_{[10,14]}^{\{id,city\}}$ with $\text{file}_{[12,15]}^{\{country\}}$ yields $\text{file}_{[10,15]}^{\{id,city,country\}}$. Instead, the meet with $file_{[12,15]}^{\{id\}}$ yields $\text{file}_{[12,14]}^{\{id\}}$. Finally, the constraining $\text{file}_{[10,15]}^{\{id,city,country\}} \downarrow_{[1,2]}^{\{city\}}$ results in $\text{file}_{[11,12]}^{\{city\}}$ (since $\phi_{[10,15]}^{-1}(1) = 11$ and $\phi_{[10,15]}^{-1}(2) = 12$).

In the rest of this section, for brevity, we simply write $\mathbb{L}$ instead of $\mathbb{L}(\mathbb{C}, \mathbb{R})$.

Data Frame Set Abstract Domain. Data frame variables may depend on multiple data sources. We thus lift our abstract domain $\mathbb{L}$ to an abstract domain $\mathbb{S}(\mathbb{L})$ of sets of abstract data frames. The elements of $\mathbb{S}(\mathbb{L})$ belong to a lattice $\langle \mathcal{S}, \sqsubseteq_S, \sqcup_S, \sqcap_S \rangle$ with $\mathcal{S} \stackrel{\text{def}}{=} \mathcal{P}(\mathcal{L})$. Sets of abstract data frames in $\mathcal{S}$ are maintained in a *canonical form* such that no abstract data frames in a set can be overlapping (cf. Eq. 6). The partial order $\sqsubseteq_S$ between canonical sets relies on the partial order between abstract data frames: $S_1 \sqsubseteq_S S_2 \stackrel{\text{def}}{\Leftrightarrow} \forall L_1 \in S_1 \exists L_2 \in S_2 \colon L_1 \sqsubseteq_L L_2$.

The join ($\sqcup_S$) and meet ($\sqcap_S$) operators perform a set union and set intersection, respectively, followed by a reduction to make the result canonical:

$$S_1 \sqcup_S S_2 \stackrel{\text{def}}{=} \text{REDUCE}^{\sqcup_L}(S_1 \cup S_2) \qquad S_1 \sqcap_S S_2 \stackrel{\text{def}}{=} \text{REDUCE}^{\sqcap_L}(S_1 \cap S_2)$$

where $\text{REDUCE}^{op}(S) \stackrel{\text{def}}{=} \{L_1 op L_2 \mid L_1, L_2 \in S, \text{overlap}(L_1, L_2)\} \cup \{L_1 \in S \mid \forall L_2 \in S \setminus \{L_1\} : \neg\text{overlap}(L_1, L_2)\}$

Finally, we lift $\downarrow_R^C$ by element-wise application: $S \downarrow_R^C \stackrel{\text{def}}{=} \{L \downarrow_R^C \mid L \in S\}$.

Example 8 (Abstract Data Frame Sets). Let us consider the join of two abstract data frame sets $S_1 = \left\{\text{file1}_{[1,10]}^{\{id\}}, \text{file2}_{[0,100]}^{\{name\}}\right\}$ and $S_2 = \left\{\text{file1}_{[9,12]}^{\{id\}}, \text{file3}_{[0,100]}^{\{zip\}}\right\}$ Before reduction, we obtain $\left\{\text{file1}_{[1,10]}^{\{id\}}, \text{file1}_{[9,12]}^{\{id\}}, \text{file2}_{[0,100]}^{\{name\}}, \text{file3}_{[0,100]}^{\{zip\}}\right\}$. The reduction operation makes the set canonical: $\left\{\text{file1}_{[1,12]}^{\{id\}}, \text{file2}_{[0,100]}^{\{name\}}, \text{file3}_{[0,100]}^{\{zip\}}\right\}$.

In the following, for brevity, we omit $\mathbb{L}$ and simply write $\mathbb{S}$ instead of $\mathbb{S}(\mathbb{L})$.

Data Frame Sources Abstract Domain. We can now define the domain $\mathbb{X} \to \mathbb{A}(\mathbb{S})$ that we use for our data leakage analysis. Elements in this abstract domain are maps from data frame variables in $\mathbb{X}$ to elements of a data frame sources abstract domain $\mathbb{A}(\mathbb{S})$, which over-approximates the (input) data frame variables (indexed at some row) from which a data frame variable depends on.

In particular, elements in $\mathbb{A}(\mathbb{S})$ belong to a lattice $\langle \mathcal{A}, \sqsubseteq_A, \sqcup_A, \sqcap_A, \bot_A \rangle$ where $\mathcal{A} \stackrel{\text{def}}{=} \mathcal{S} \times \mathbb{B}$ contains pairs $\langle S, B \rangle$ of a data frame set abstraction in $S \in \mathcal{S}$ and a boolean flag in $B \in \mathbb{B} \stackrel{\text{def}}{=} \{\text{UNTANINTED}, \text{MAYBE-TAINTED}\}$. In the following, given an abstract element $m \in \mathbb{X} \to \mathcal{A}$ of $\mathbb{X} \to \mathbb{A}(\mathbb{S})$ and a data frame variable $x \in \mathbb{X}$, we write $m_s(x) \in \mathcal{S}$ and $m_b(x) \in \mathbb{B}$ for the first and second component of the pair $m(x) \in \mathcal{A}$, respectively.

The abstract domain operators apply component operators pairwise: $\sqsubseteq_A \stackrel{\text{def}}{=} \sqsubseteq_S \times \leq$, $\sqcup_A \stackrel{\text{def}}{=} \sqcup_S \times \vee$, $\sqcap_A \stackrel{\text{def}}{=} \sqcap_S \times \wedge$, where $\leq$ in $\mathbb{B}$ is such that $\text{UNTAINTED} \leq \text{MAYBE-TAINTED}$. The bottom element $\bot_A$ is $\langle \emptyset, \text{UNTAINTED} \rangle$.

Finally, we define the concretization $\gamma \colon (\mathbb{X} \to (\mathbb{N} \to \mathcal{A})) \to (\mathbb{X} \to (\mathbb{N} \to \mathcal{P}(\mathbb{X} \times \mathbb{N})))$: $\gamma(m) \stackrel{\text{def}}{=} \lambda x \in \mathbb{X} \colon (\lambda r \in \mathbb{N} \colon \gamma_A(m(x)))$, where $\gamma_A \colon \mathcal{A} \to \mathcal{P}(\mathbb{X} \times \mathbb{N})$

is $\gamma_A(\langle S, B\rangle) \stackrel{\text{def}}{=} \{X[r] \mid X^C_R \in S, r \in \gamma_R(R)\}$ (with $\gamma_R\colon \mathcal{R} \to \mathcal{P}(\mathbb{N})$ being the concretization function for row abstractions, cf. Sect. 4.1). Note that, γ_A does not use $B \in \mathbb{B}$ nor $C \in \mathcal{C}$. These are devices uniquely needed by our abstract semantics (that we define below) to track (and approximate the concrete actual) dependencies across program statements.

4.2 Abstract Data Leakage Semantics

Our data leakage analysis is given by $(\!|\dot{P}|\!)^\natural \stackrel{\text{def}}{=} a[\![S_n]\!] \circ \cdots \circ a[\![S_1]\!]\dot{\bot}_A$ where $\dot{\bot}_A$ maps all data frame variables to $\bot_A$ and the abstract semantic function $a[\![S]\!]$ for each statement in P is defined as follows:

$$
\begin{aligned}
a[\![y = \text{read}(name)]\!]m &\stackrel{\text{def}}{=} m\left[y \mapsto \langle\left\{name^{\top_C}_{[0,\infty]}\right\}, \text{FALSE}\rangle\right] \\
a[\![y = x.\text{select}[\bar{r}][C]]\!]m &\stackrel{\text{def}}{=} m\left[y \mapsto \begin{cases} \langle m_s(x) \downarrow^C_{[\min(\bar{r}),\max(\bar{r})]}, m_b(x)\rangle & \neg m_b(x) \\ \langle m_s(x), m_b(x)\rangle & \text{otherwise} \end{cases}\right] \\
a[\![y = \text{op}(x_1, x_2)]\!]m &\stackrel{\text{def}}{=} m\left[y \mapsto \langle m_s(x_1) \sqcup_S m_s(x_2), m_b(x_1) \vee m_b(x_2)\rangle\right] \\
a[\![y = \text{normalize}(x)]\!]m &\stackrel{\text{def}}{=} m\left[y \mapsto \langle m_s(x), \text{TRUE}\rangle\right] \\
a[\![y = \text{other}(x)]\!]m &\stackrel{\text{def}}{=} m\left[y \mapsto \langle m_s(x), m_b(x)\rangle\right] \\
a[\![\text{use}(x)]\!]m &\stackrel{\text{def}}{=} m
\end{aligned}
$$

The abstract semantics of the *source* statement simply maps a read data frame variable y to the untainted abstract data frame set containing the abstraction of the read data file ($name^{\top_C}_{[0,\infty]}$). The abstract semantics of the *select* statement maps the resulting data frame variable y to the abstract data frame set $m_s(x)$ associated with the original data frame variable x; in order to soundly propagate (abstract) dependencies, $m_s(x)$ is constrained by $\downarrow^C_{[\min(\bar{r}),\max(\bar{r})]}$ (cf. Sect. 4.1) only if $m_s(x)$ is untainted. The abstract semantics of *merge* statements merges the abstract data frame sets $m_s(x_1)$ and $m_s(x_2)$ and taint flags $m_b(x_1)$ and $m_b(x_2)$ associated with the given data frame variables x_1 and x_2. Note that such semantics is a sound but rather imprecise abstraction, in particular, for the *join* operation. More precise abstractions can be easily defined, at the cost of also abstracting data frame contents. The abstract semantics of *function* statements maps the resulting data frame variable y to the abstract data frame set $m_s(x)$ associated with the original data frame variable x; the *normalize* function sets the taint flag to TRUE, while *other* functions leave the taint flag $m_b(x)$ unchanged. Note that, unlike the analysis sketched by Subotić et al. [21], we do not perform any renaming or resetting of the data source mapping (cf. Sect. 4.2 in [21]) but we keep tracking dependencies with respect to the input data frame variables. Finally, the abstract semantics of *use* statements leave the abstract dependencies map unchanged.

The abstract data leakage semantics $(\!|\dot{P}|\!)^\natural$ is *sound*:

Theorem 3. $P \models \mathcal{I} \Leftarrow \gamma((\!|\dot{P}|\!)^\natural) \mathrel{\dot{\supseteq}} \dot{\alpha}(\alpha_{\rightsquigarrow^+}(\mathcal{I}))$

Similarly, we have the sound but not complete counterpart of Lemma 1 for practically checking absence of data leakage:

Lemma 2.

$$
\begin{aligned}
P \models \mathcal{I} \Leftarrow & \forall o_1 \in \mathrm{U}_P^{\text{train}}, o_2 \in \mathrm{U}_P^{\text{test}}: \\
& \bigcup_{r_1 \in \operatorname{dom}(\gamma((\dot{P})^\natural) o_1)} \gamma((\dot{P})^\natural) o_1(r_1) \;\cap \bigcup_{r_2 \in \operatorname{dom}(\gamma((\dot{P})^\natural) o_2)} \gamma((\dot{P})^\natural) o_2(r_2) = \emptyset \\
\Leftrightarrow & \forall o_1 \in \mathrm{U}_P^{\text{train}}, o_2 \in \mathrm{U}_P^{\text{test}}: \forall X_R^C \in (\dot{P})_s^\natural o_1, Y_{R'}^{C'} \in (\dot{P})_s^\natural o_2: \\
& \neg \text{overlap}(X_R^C, Y_{R'}^{C'}) \wedge \left(X = Y \Rightarrow \neg (\dot{P})_b^\natural o_1 \wedge \neg (\dot{P})_b^\natural o_2\right)
\end{aligned}
$$

Specifically, Lemma 2 allows us to verify absence of data leakage by checking that any pair of abstract data frames sources X_R^C and $Y_{R'}^{C'}$ for data respectively used for training (i.e., o_1) and testing (i.e., o_2) are disjoint (i.e., $\neg\text{overlap}(X_R^C, Y_{R'}^{C'})$, cf. Eq. 6) and untainted (i.e., $\neg(\dot{P})_b^\natural o_1 \wedge \neg(\dot{P})_b^\natural o_2$ if $X = Y$, that is, if they originate from the same data file).

Example 9. (Motivating Example (Continued)). The data leakage analysis of our motivating example (cf. Example 1) is the following:

$$a[\![\texttt{data = read("data.csv")}]\!]\dot{\bot}_A = \left(m_1 \stackrel{\text{def}}{=} \lambda x : \begin{cases} \langle \{\text{data.csv}_{[0,\infty]}^{\top_C}\}, \text{FALSE} \rangle & x = data \\ \text{undefined} & \text{otherwise} \end{cases} \right)$$

$$a[\![\texttt{X = data.select[][\{"X\_1", "X\_2", "y"\}]}]\!] m_1 =$$

$$\left(m_2 \stackrel{\text{def}}{=} m_1 \left[X \mapsto \left\langle \left\{ \text{data.csv}_{[0,\infty]}^{\{``X\_1", ``X\_2", ``y"\}} \right\}, \text{FALSE} \right\rangle \right] \right)$$

$$a[\![\texttt{X\_norm = normalize(X)}]\!] m_2 = \left(m_3 \stackrel{\text{def}}{=} m_2 \left[X\_norm \mapsto \left\langle \left\{ \text{data.csv}_{[0,\infty]}^{\{``X\_1", ``X\_2", ``y"\}} \right\}, \text{TRUE} \right\rangle \right] \right)$$

$$a[\![\texttt{X\_train = X\_norm.select[[}\lfloor 0.025 * R_{\texttt{X\_norm}} \rfloor \texttt{ + 1, ..., } R_{\texttt{X\_norm}}\texttt{]][]}]\!] m_3 =$$

$$\left(m_4 \stackrel{\text{def}}{=} m_3 \left[X\_train \mapsto \left\langle \left\{ \text{data.csv}_{[\lfloor 0.025 * R_{X\_norm} \rfloor + 1, R_{X\_norm}]}^{\{``X\_1", ``X\_2", ``y"\}} \right\}, \text{TRUE} \right\rangle \right] \right)$$

$$a[\![\texttt{X\_test = X\_norm.select[[0, ..., }\lfloor 0.025 * R_{\texttt{X\_norm}} \rfloor\texttt{]][]}]\!] m_4 =$$

$$\left(m_5 \stackrel{\text{def}}{=} m_4 \left[X\_test \mapsto \left\langle \left\{ \text{data.csv}_{[0, \lfloor 0.025 * R_{X\_norm} \rfloor]}^{\{``X\_1", ``X\_2", ``y"\}} \right\}, \text{TRUE} \right\rangle \right] \right)$$

$$a[\![\texttt{test(X\_test)}]\!](a[\![\texttt{train(X\_train)}]\!] m_5) = m_5$$

At the end of the analysis, $X\_train \in \mathrm{U}^{\text{train}}$ and $X\_test \in \mathrm{U}^{\text{test}}$ depend on disjoint but *tainted* abstract data frames derived from the same input file *data.csv*. Thus, the absence of data leakage check from Lemma 2 (rightfully) fails.

5 Experimental Evaluation

We implemented our static analysis into the open source NBLyzer [21] framework for data science notebooks. NBlyzer performs the analysis starting on an individual code cell (*intra-cell analysis*) and, based on the resulting abstract state, it proceeds to analyze *valid* successor code cells (*inter-cell analysis*). Whether a code cell is a valid successor or not, is specified by an analysis-dependent *cell propagation condition*. We refer to the original NBLyzer paper [21] and to the extended version of this paper [8] for further details.

We evaluated[1] our analysis against the data leakage analysis previously implemented in NBLyzer [21], using the same benchmarks. These are notebooks written to succeed in non-trivial real data science tasks and can be assumed to closely represent code written by non-novice data scientists.

Table 1. Alarms raised by the previous [21] vs our analysis.

Analysis	TP		FP
	Taint	Overlap	
[21]	10	0	2
Ours	**10**	**15**	**2**

We summarize the results in Table 1. For each reported alarm, we engaged 4 data scientists at Microsoft to determine true (TP) and false positives (FP). We further classified the true positives as due to a normalization taint (Taint) or overlapping data frames (Overlap). Our analysis found 10 Taint data leakages in 5 notebooks, and 15 Overlap data leakage in 11 notebooks, i.e., a 1.2% bug rate, which adheres to true positive bug rates reported for null pointers in industrial settings (e.g., see [12]). The previous analysis only found 10 Taint leakages in 5 notebooks. It could not Overlap data leakages because it cannot reason at the granularity of partial data frames. The cost for our more precise analysis is a mere 7% slowdown. Both analyses reported 2 false positives, due to different objects having the same function name (e.g., `LabelEncoder` and `StandardScaler` both having the function `fit_transform`). This issue can be solved by introducing object sensitive type tracking in our analysis. We leave it for future work.

The full experimental evaluation is described in [8, Appendix E].

6 Related Work

Related Abstract Interpretation Frameworks and Static Analyses. As mentioned in Sect. 3, our framework generalizes the notion of data usage proposed by Urban and Müller [23] and the definition of dependency abstraction used by Cousot [3]. In particular, among other things, the generalization involves reasoning about dependencies (and thus data usage relationships) between multi-dimensional variables. In [23], Urban and Müller show that information flow analyses can be used for reasoning about data usage, albeit with a loss in precision unless one repeats the information flow analysis by setting each time a different input variable as high security variable (cf. Sect. 8 in [23]). In virtue of the generalization mentioned above, the same consideration applies to our work, i.e., information flow analyses can be used to reason about data leakage, but with an even higher cost to avoid a precision loss (the analysis needs to be repeated each time for different portions of the input data sources). Analogously, in [3], Cousot shows that information flow, slicing, non-interference, dye,

[1] Experiments done on a Ryzen 9 6900HS with 24GB DDR5 running Ubuntu 22.04.

and taint analyses are all further abstractions of his proposed framework (cf. Sect. 7 in [3]). As such, they are also further (and thus less precise) abstractions of our proposed framework. In particular, a taint analysis will only be able to detect a subset of the data leakage bugs that our analysis can find, i.e., those solely originating from library transformations but not those originating from (partially) overlapping data. Vice versa, our proposed analysis could also be used as a more fine-grained information flow or taint analysis.

Static Analysis for Data Science. Static analysis for data science is an emerging area in the program analysis community [22]. Some notable static analyses for data science scripts include an analysis for ensuring correct shape dimensions in TensorFlow programs [13], an analysis for constraining inputs based on program constraints [23], and a provenance analysis [16]. In addition, static analyses have been proposed for data science notebooks [14,21]. NBLyzer [21] contains an ad-hoc data leakage analysis that detects Taint data leakages [21]. An extension to handle Overlap data leakages was sketched in [20] (but no analysis precision results were reported). However, both these analysis are not formalized nor formally proven sound[2]. In contrast, we introduce a sound data leakage analysis that has a rigorous semantic underpinning.

7 Conclusion

We have presented an approach for detecting data leakages statically. We provide a formal and rigorous derivation from the standard program collecting semantics, via successive abstraction to a final sound and computable static analysis definition. We implement our analysis in the NBLyzer framework and demonstrate clear improvements upon previous ad-hoc data leakage analyses.

Acknowledgements. We thank our colleagues at Microsoft Azure Data Labs and Microsoft Development Centre Serbia for all their feedback and support.

References

1. Chouldechova, A., Prado, D.B., Fialko, O., Vaithianathan, R.: A case study of algorithm-assisted decision making in child maltreatment hotline screening decisions. In: FAT, pp. 134–148 (2018)
2. Cousot, P.: Constructive design of a hierarchy of semantics of a transition system by abstract interpretation. Electron. Notes Theor. Comput. Sci. **277**(1–2), 47–103 (2002)
3. Cousot, P.: Abstract semantic dependency. In: Chang, B.-Y.E. (ed.) SAS 2019. LNCS, vol. 11822, pp. 389–410. Springer, Cham (2019). https://doi.org/10.1007/978-3-030-32304-2_19
4. Cousot, P., Cousot, R.: Static determination of dynamic properties of programs. In: Second International Symposium on Programming, pp. 106–130 (1976)

[2] We found a number of soundness issues in [20] when working on our formalization.

5. Cousot, P., Cousot, R.: Abstract interpretation: a unified lattice model for static analysis of programs by construction or approximation of fixpoints. In: POPL, pp. 238–252 (1977)
6. Cousot, P., Cousot, R.: Systematic design of program analysis frameworks. In: POPL, pp. 269–282 (1979)
7. Cousot, P., Cousot, R.: Higher order abstract interpretation (and application to comportment analysis generalizing strictness, termination, projection, and PER analysis. In: ICCL, pp. 95–112 (1994)
8. Drobnjaković, F., Subotić, P., Urban, C.: An abstract interpretation-based data leakage static analysis. CoRR abs/2211.16073 (2022). https://arxiv.org/abs/2211.16073
9. Guzharina, A.: We downloaded 10m Jupyter notebooks from GitHub - this is what we learned (2020). https://blog.jetbrains.com/datalore/2020/12/17/we-downloaded-10-000-000-jupyter-notebooks-from-github-this-is-what-we-learned/. Accessed 22 Jan 2022
10. Kapoor, S., Narayanan, A.: Leakage and the reproducibility crisis in machine-learning-based science. Patterns **4**(9), 100804 (2023)
11. Kaufman, S., Rosset, S., Perlich, C., Stitelman, O.: Leakage in data mining: formulation, detection, and avoidance. ACM Trans. Knowl. Discov. Data **6**(4) (2012)
12. Kharkar, A., Moghaddam, R.Z., Jin, M., Liu, X., Shi, X., Clement, C., Sundaresan, N.: Learning to reduce false positives in analytic bug detectors. In: ICSE, p. 1307-1316 (2022)
13. Lagouvardos, S., Dolby, J., Grech, N., Antoniadis, A., Smaragdakis, Y.: Static analysis of shape in TensorFlow programs. In: ECOOP, pp. 15:1–15:29 (2020)
14. Macke, S., Gong, H., Lee, D.J.L., Head, A., Xin, D., Parameswaran, A.G.: Fine-grained lineage for safer notebook interactions. CoRR abs/2012.06981 (2020). https://arxiv.org/abs/2012.06981
15. Miné, A.: Weakly relational numerical abstract domains. Ph.D. thesis, École Polytechnique, Palaiseau, France (2004). https://tel.archives-ouvertes.fr/tel-00136630
16. Namaki, M.H., et al.: Vamsa: automated provenance tracking in data science scripts. In: KDD, pp. 1542–1551 (2020)
17. Nisbet, R., Miner, G., Yale, K.: Handbook of Statistical Analysis and Data Mining Applications, 2nd edn. Academic Press, Boston (2018). https://doi.org/10.1016/C2012-0-06451-4
18. Papadimitriou, P., Garcia-Molina, H.: A model for data leakage detection. In: ICDE, pp. 1307–1310 (2009)
19. Perkel, J.: Why Jupyter is data scientists' computational notebook of choice. Nature **563**, 145–146 (2018)
20. Subotić, P., Bojanić, U., Stojić, M.: Statically detecting data leakages in data science code. In: SOAP, pp. 16–22 (2022)
21. Subotić, P., Milikić, L., Stojić, M.: A static analysis framework for data science notebooks. In: ICSE, pp. 13–22 (2022)
22. Urban, C.: Static analysis of data science software. In: SAS, pp. 17–23 (2019)
23. Urban, C., Müller, P.: An abstract interpretation framework for input data usage. In: Ahmed, A. (ed.) ESOP 2018. LNCS, vol. 10801, pp. 683–710. Springer, Cham (2018). https://doi.org/10.1007/978-3-319-89884-1_24
24. Wong, A., et al.: External validation of a widely implemented proprietary sepsis prediction model in hospitalized patients. JAMA Intern. Med. (2021)

On the Decidability of Disassembling Binaries

Daniel Engel[1(✉)], Freek Verbeek[1,2], and Binoy Ravindran[2]

[1] Open University, 6419 AT Heerlen, The Netherlands
{daniel.engel,freek.verbeek}@ou.nl
[2] Virginia Tech, Blacksburg, VA 24061, USA
binoy@vt.edu

Abstract. The general consensus is that disassembly of binaries is undecidable. The cause lies in distinguishing instructions from data, and resolving indirections. Furthermore, binaries can behave in "weird" ways which have no counterpart in assembly languages, e.g., instructions may overlap, or use other instructions as data. Yet, the general consensus is that, for a large part of production binaries, disassembly works sufficiently well for the use cases at hand. This paper aims to address the question: for which binaries is disassembly decidable? For which binaries can disassembly become decidable if an external oracle, e.g., provides the set of instruction addresses, or resolves indirections? We present a set of five theorems on decidability of disassembly; each theorem corresponding to a use case. All five theorems are accompanied by a proof of correctness based on bisimilarity between the input binary and the output assembly program, and have been formalized in the Isabelle/HOL theorem prover.

Keywords: Disassembly · Formal Methods · Decidability

1 Introduction

Disassembling is the process of retrieving an *assembly program* for a given *binary*. It is a well-known fact in the decompilation community that it is not possible to create an algorithm which, for every binary, performs disassembling in such a way that the semantics of the assembly program is equivalent to the semantics of the original binary [8,15,18,23,28,32]. The bytes in a binary do not indicate whether they encode instructions (i.e., the program text) or raw data. In order to decide this, one must know which bytes are reachable as the start of an instruction and which are unreachable by any execution of the program, which is an *undecidable* problem [24].

Matters are complicated by the ability of binaries to behave "weirdly" [6]. They may read their program text as raw data, modify its instructions to dynamically change the control flow, execute raw data as instructions or jump into the middle of an instruction. Most assembly languages do not allow such behavior: there is a clear distinction between the program text and data, instructions may

W.-N. Chin and Z. Xu (Eds.): TASE 2024, LNCS 14777, pp. 127–145, 2024.
https://doi.org/10.1007/978-3-031-64626-3_8

not overlap and self-modification is usually not allowed. This may even make it impossible to disassemble weird binaries to well-formed assembly code to begin with.

This paper addresses the question *in which scenarios is disassembling decidable?* A scenario is characterized by *assumptions* about the input binary, *oracles* that provide information over the binary and *requirements* for the output assembly program. The assumptions may allow or exclude binaries that modify themselves, use text as data and vice-versa, jump into the middle of instructions, etc. These assumptions might be statically or dynamically verified, or be enforced at compile time. The oracles may solve hard problems such as reachability analysis or indirection resolution. They too could be created by a static or dynamic analysis tool, or be created as an additional compilation artifact. The requirements enable different *use cases* in which disassembling is needed. For example, in order to symbolically execute an assembly program, one needs a Control Flow Graph (CFG), while recompiling into a binary requires a byte-consistent assembly output.

In this work, we identify five scenarios for which we prove sound disassembling to be decidable: 1. *Debugging*, for which the distinction between text and data is unimportant, 2. *Verification*, for which an overapproximation of all reachable addresses is needed, 3. *Traversing*, for which an overapproximative CFG is needed, 4. *In Situ Patching*, for which the encoding of instructions may not influence the behavior of other instructions, and 5. *Decompilation* for which entire program sections need to be relocatable.

The contribution of this paper is a set of five theorems on decidability of disassembly; one for each scenario. The theorems have been formally proven correct in the Isabelle/HOL theorem prover [20]. The motivation behind these theorems is twofold:

- Binaries are known to be opaque. Current research focuses on extending the binary format with metadata that makes the binary analysis more tractable. The DWARF format[1] provides debugging information, but is, in itself, not enough to recover, e.g., a CFG. This paper aims to provide a formal answer to the question: what metadata (i.e., oracles) should an extended binary format at least contain to make it amenable for the aforementioned use cases?
- We argue that our effort effectively formalizes several properties that capture the intuition of "normal" behavior for binaries (in contrast to their possible "weird" behaviors). Lifting a binary to a semantically equivalent Intermediate Representation (IR) requires that the binary behavior is expressible in that IR. Self-modification, as a single example, generally is not. We thus formalize negations of "weird" behaviors such as the aforementioned ones, and prove that these properties allow lifting to IRs.

In the following section, we present an overview of these five scenarios together with the proofs that their respective disassembling is decidable. We also contribute a meta theorem that allows combination of different scenarios.

[1] https://dwarfstd.org.

Section 2 discusses the related work on decidability of disassembly. The overview of Sect. 3 is presented in more mathematical rigor in Sect. 4. In Sect. 5, we discuss the implications of the assumptions and oracles over the binaries, and the limitations of our model of assembly programs. Section 6 provides a conclusion and possible future work.

2 Related Work

The general consensus in related work is that disassembly is undecidable [1,8–10, 15,27,32]. Cifuentes phrases the intuition as follows: " Given a binary program, the separation of data from code, even in programs that do not allow such practices as self-modifying code, is equivalent to the halting problem, since it is unknown in general whether a particular instruction will be executed or not (e.g. consider the code following a loop).» [9]. This observation has triggered research into incorporating heuristics into disassembly algorithms [21], or in applying machine learning to disassemble binaries [14,22,31]. These techniques aim to be precise but acknowledge they can never be provably sound. Wartell et al. explicitly state that " fully correct x86 disassembly is provably undecidable: Bytes are code if and only if they are reachable at runtime - a decision that reduces to the halting problem" [31].

Yet, one can take a binary, overapproximate the set of reachable instruction addresses by taking the entire address space of the binary, and run a per-instruction disassembler on each address. Assuming trust in a per-single-instruction disassembler, the result is sound and recompilable to a byte-equivalent binary [26], and the process is clearly decidable. Thus: disassembly *is* decidable. This observation has triggered research into disrupting a static disassembler through obfuscation [11,17] to provide protection against intellectual property theft in case of closed-source software.

The reconciliation between these two contradictory statements is that both are true, depending on the definition of "disassembly". If "disassembly" is defined as lifting a binary to a representation with solely the requirement that the IR is executable, then the above argument for decidability holds. This is exactly what we formalize as Theorem 1 in Fig. 1 (which is discussed in the next section). However, if "disassembly" is defined as lifting to an IR with more requirements (which is often implicitly done in literature), it becomes undecidable and oracles are needed. For example, disassembly to a representation that can be recompiled without fixing the location of the text- and datasections in memory, is undecidable as it requires resolving indirections (this is the argument by Cifuentes quoted above). This is exactly the statement made in Theorem 5 in Fig. 1.

To the best of our knowledge, there is no existing work that aims to formalize how decidability of disassembly depends on the definition of "disassembly", on its requirements and use cases, and on the assumptions made over the binaries.

3 Overview

This section provides a semi-formal overview over the theorems proven in this paper. We formally define the meaning of a *decidability theorem* for disassembling, and informally present and discuss different properties for both binary and assembly programs, which are used as the assumptions and requirements. This combines into a set of decidability theorems as shown in Fig. 1.

We model both binaries and assembly programs to abstract over all kinds of real-world architectures. Binaries are partial maps from addresses to bytes. Assembly programs consist of two partial maps, one from addresses to bytes (the *program data*) and one from addresses to instructions (the *program text*). Both mark sections of the program to be executable, readable or writable.

The semantics for both are given as unlabeled transitions systems. Programs are executed in an environment Γ which contains the offset at which the program is loaded into memory, and the addresses and semantics of external symbols. The semantics for a binary β in environment Γ are denoted $TS(\Gamma;\beta)$, and are defined as straightforwardly as possible. The initial states have their instruction pointer (`RIP`) set to the entry point of the binary β and all of its bytes are loaded into memory. Transitions are given by fetching the bytes at the current `RIP`, decoding them as an instruction and executing it. The semantics for an assembly program, denoted by $TS(\Gamma;\alpha)$, are defined similarly, with the difference that the instructions are fetched directly from α's program text, not from memory. Note that the binary semantics allow self-modification while the assembly semantics do not.

3.1 Theorems

A *disassembler* is a computable function that takes as input an binary and a (possibly empty) set of oracles, and produces an assembly program as output. *Assumptions* are predicates over binary programs, *requirements* are predicates over assembly programs. *Oracles* can be used by the disassembler function to retrieve information about the binary program. We use the standard notion of *bisimilarity* [3] (notation $\simeq$) as the correctness relation between the assembly and binary semantics.

Definition 1 (Sound Disassembler). *Given assumptions $\mathcal{A}$, requirements $\mathcal{R}$ and oracles $\mathcal{O}$, a disassembler d is* sound *iff, for every binary β for which the assumptions hold, the resulting assembly program α fulfills the requirements and the semantics are bisimilar.*

$$sound(d,\mathcal{A},\mathcal{O},\mathcal{R}) := \forall\beta,\Gamma\cdot\mathcal{A}(\beta) \implies (\mathcal{R}(\alpha)\wedge TS(\beta;\Gamma)\simeq TS(\alpha;\Gamma))$$
$$\textbf{\textit{where}}\ \alpha = d(\beta,\mathcal{O})$$

Definition 2 (Decidability Theorem). *Disassembling from a set of binaries fulfilling assumptions $\mathcal{A}$ to a set of assembly programs fulfilling requirements $\mathcal{R}$ using oracles $\mathcal{O}$ is* decidable *iff a sound disassembler exists. We use the notation $\mathcal{A}\overset{\mathcal{O}}{\longmapsto}\mathcal{R}$ to denote this decidability.*

$$\mathcal{A} \overset{\mathcal{O}}{\longmapsto} \mathcal{R} := \exists d \cdot sound(d, \mathcal{A}, \mathcal{O}, \mathcal{R})$$

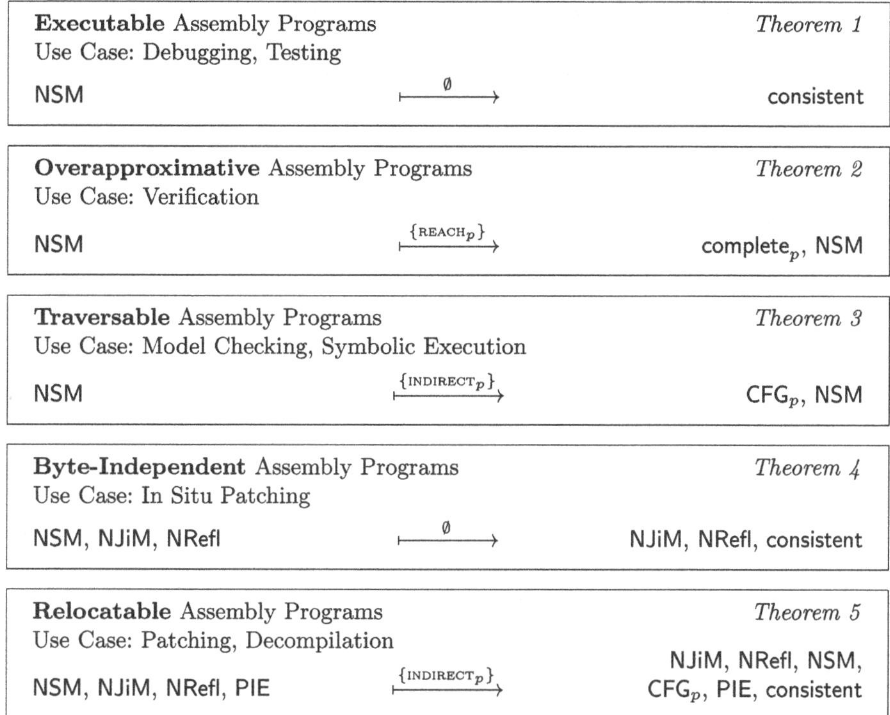

Fig. 1. Overview of the five decidability theorems. The set of properties on the left are the assumptions made over the input binary, the set of properties on the right are the requirements over the output assembly program guaranteed by the disassembler, the set of oracles on the arrow are the oracles needed for the scenario.

Executable Assembly Programs can be used to *interactively debug* the binary. In a debugging scenario, the user is only interested in the instructions that are executed and not in semantic properties such as the distinction between instructions and data, the overlapping of instructions with each other and with data, or the entire CFG of the program. For this, the assembly program is only required to be *byte-consistent*, meaning that any overlapping instructions or any instructions overlapping with data must agree on their byte encoding. The only assumption on the binary is that it is *non self-modifying (*NSM*)* since our assembly semantics do not capture self-modifying behavior. Byte-consistency does not need to be assumed on binaries since all binaries are byte-consistent. Intuitively, the disassembler can decode the bytes at every address in the binary, regardless of whether or not they are reachable, as both text and as data, as this distinction is not important for debugging.

Overapproximative Assembly Programs can be used to verify safety properties such as absence of buffer overflows or probing functions return normally. In order to do so soundly, a verification tool needs a *complete* set of all instructions that may be reachable. A disassembler thus requires some oracle that provides a set containing at least all reachable addresses of the binary. The precision of the verification increases with a more precise (smaller) reachability oracle. In order for the oracle to correctly model all reachable instructions, the assembly program and thus the binary are assumed to be NSM.

Traversable Assembly Programs extend overapproximative assembly programs by enabling static traversal of the program in order to perform model checking techniques [5,16], abstract interpretation [4,19] or symbolic execution [12,25]. In order to traverse the program, it is not enough to know which instructions are reachable, but rather which instructions can be directly reached from which other instructions. In the realm of low-level programs, the construction of CFGs is even more difficult than for high-level programs since indirect jumps are ubiquitous. Examples for indirect jumps include jump instructions to dynamically computed addresses such as `jmp rax`, calls to callbacks such as `call rdi` or even simple return statements `ret`, as they need to load the return address from the stack to indirectly jump to it. A disassembler creating traversable programs may use an *indirection oracle* to build the CFG.

Byte-Independent Assembly Programs have semantics that do not depend on the encoding of instructions. This allows for *in situ patching* where individual instructions are changed without affecting the semantics of unchanged instructions [13]. The three properties that guarantee that the encoding does not influence the behavior are: 1. NSM so that the program cannot change individual bytes in an instruction, 2. *non reflexive (*NRefl*)* so that the program cannot read the encoding of instructions as raw bytes, and 3. *no jumps in the middle (*NJiM*)* so that the partial encoding of instructions cannot be interpreted as new instructions. In addition to these properties, the assembly program needs to be able to be assembled into a binary again, requiring it to be byte-consistent.

Relocatable Assembly Programs extend the use case of in situ patching by making entire program sections relocatable. On the one hand, this is needed for *full scale patching* for which new instructions may be introduced, requiring later instructions to be moved to other addresses. On the other hand, this is needed by further *decompilation* steps such as symbolization, for which sections need to be moved from constant offsets to arbitrary, more abstract program points. In addition to the byte-independence properties consistent, NSM, NRefl and NJiM, relocatable programs also need to be position independent executables (PIEs). Position independence means that the offset at which the program is loaded into memory does not affect the program behavior, thus parts of the program can be relocated to arbitrary offsets.

The properties used in Fig. 1 are *semantic* properties, i.e., they are formulated as properties over the transition systems provided by $TS(\Gamma;\beta)$ and $TS(\Gamma;\alpha)$. As example, NSM is defined as "if an address is a reachable instruction address, then there exists no execution that writes to that address". Such a property can be hard to verify. However, several properties have a *syntactic* counterpart that enforces the semantical property by construction. For example, NSM can be enforced if the executable address space does not overlap with the writable address space (denoted with $X\overline{\wedge}W$). For binaries that enforce the desired semantical properties syntactically, there is no need to verify whether the binary satisfies the assumptions. The syntactic version implies its semantic counterpart.

Table 1 presents an overview of the properties used in Fig. 1, all of which are formally defined in Sect. 4.

Table 1. Overview of the properties used as assumptions and requirements. The first two columns are the semantic and syntactic version of the property, most syntactic properties are only defined for assembly programs.

Semantic	Syntactic	Description	Definitions
	consistent†	The overlapping bytes of different instructions and data match	Definition 5
NSM‡	$X\overline{\wedge}W$	The program does not change its text at runtime	Definitions 10, 6
NRefl	$X\overline{\wedge}R$	The program does not read its instructions as data	Definitions 11, 7
NJiM	mosaic	The control flow does not lead into the middle of an instruction	Definitions 12, 8
PIE		The semantics do not depend on the offset where the program is loaded into memory	Definition 13
complete$_p$		All reachable addresses are known, there are at most p addresses	Definition 14
CFG$_p$		The complete control flow is known, there are at most p edges	Definition 15

†: Always true for binaries; ‡: Always true for assembly programs.

3.2 Meta Theorem

The theorems presented in Sect. 3.1 represent individual scenarios in which disassembling a binary can be used to enable certain use cases while guaranteeing preservation of the semantics. In addition to these five theorems, we show that the requirements and assumptions used in these theorems can be combined to create new scenarios.

In order to show that the combination of the five theorems is possible, we first need to define the *merge* function for disassemblers. Merging is done by applying both disassemblers to the input binary and oracles, and keeping the parts both resulting assembly program agree on. In particular, for the text and data, at every address, the instruction or byte both assembly programs have at that address is kept in the result. The different program sections are joined, meaning each address of the merged assembly program is only marked as executable/writable/readable iff it is in both original assembly programs. The entry address can be arbitrarily chosen from the original assembly programs. If the disassemblers are sound then the entry addresses of both original assembly programs must be equal.

Definition 3 (Merging of disassemblers). *The* merge *function is a higher order function taking two disassemblers d_1, d_2 as an input and returning a disassembler that combines the outputs of d_1 and d_2.*

$$
\begin{aligned}
merge(d_1, d_2)(\beta, \mathcal{O}) :=& \langle text', data', X_1 \cap X_2, W_1 \cap W_2, R_1 \cap R_2, E_1 \rangle \\
\textbf{\textit{where}}\ & \langle text_1, data_1, X_1, W_1, R_1, E_1 \rangle := d_1(\beta, \mathcal{O}) \\
& \langle text_2, data_2, X_2, W_2, R_2, E_2 \rangle := d_2(\beta, \mathcal{O}) \\
& text'(a) := \begin{cases} i & \text{if } text_1(a) = text_2(a) = i \\ \emptyset & \text{otherwise} \end{cases} \\
& data'(a) := \begin{cases} b & \text{if } data_1(a) = data_2(a) = b \\ \emptyset & \text{otherwise} \end{cases}
\end{aligned}
$$

Theorem M (Combination of Scenarios). *For any two sound disassemblers d_1 and d_2 presented in Fig. 1, the merged disassembler is sound:*

$$
\begin{aligned}
&sound(d_1, \mathcal{A}_1, \mathcal{O}_1, \mathcal{R}_1) \wedge sound(d_2, \mathcal{A}_2, \mathcal{O}_2, \mathcal{R}_2) \\
&\qquad \Longrightarrow sound(merge(d_1, d_2), \mathcal{A}_1 \wedge \mathcal{A}_2, \mathcal{O}_1 \cup \mathcal{O}_2, \mathcal{R}_1 \wedge \mathcal{R}_2)
\end{aligned}
$$

In particular, this means:

$$
\mathcal{A}_1 \xmapsto{\mathcal{O}_1} \mathcal{R}_1 \wedge \mathcal{A}_2 \xmapsto{\mathcal{O}_2} \mathcal{R}_2 \Longrightarrow (\mathcal{A}_1 \wedge \mathcal{A}_2) \xmapsto{(\mathcal{O}_1 \cup \mathcal{O}_2)} (\mathcal{R}_1 \wedge \mathcal{R}_2)
$$

Proof. Given the input binaries β_1, β_2, the assumptions, requirements and oracles $\mathcal{A}_1, \mathcal{A}_2, \mathcal{R}_1, \mathcal{R}_2, \mathcal{O}_1, \mathcal{O}_2$, and the sound disassemblers d_1, d_2, let the resulting programs $\alpha_1 = d_1(\beta_1, \mathcal{O}_1), \alpha_2 = d_2(\beta_2, \mathcal{O}_2)$ and $\alpha' = merge(d_1, d_2)(\beta, \mathcal{O}_1 \cup \mathcal{O}_2)$. By soundness of the the disassemblers, we have for all Γ, $TS(\alpha_1; \Gamma) \simeq TS(\alpha_2; \Gamma)$. This is implies that α_1 and α_2 must agree on all reachable instructions and on all bytes that are loaded or stored. Since merging keeps all instructions and data both programs agree upon and since they are bisimilar, the resulting program α' must also be bisimilar to α_1 and α_2.

We need to show that that all properties are preserved in α' as long as they are fulfilled by either α_1 or α_2. consistent is preserved as α' only contains the bytes α_1 and α_2 agree upon. The semantic properties NSM, NRefl and NJiM are preserved by bisimilarity of the transition systems $TS(\alpha_1; \Gamma)$, $TS(\alpha_2; \Gamma)$ and $TS(\alpha'; \Gamma)$. Merging does not introduce any new instructions, as only the ones α_1 and α_2 agree on are kept, so no new instruction can read, write or overlap with other instructions. Preservation of PIE follows directly from bisimilarity.

From $\mathsf{complete}_p(\alpha_1)$ and $\mathsf{complete}_q(\alpha_2)$, we have $\mathsf{complete}_r(\alpha')$, for some r where $r \leq min(p, q)$. The set of reachable addresses in α' must have at most as many bytes as the smaller one from α_1 and α_2 since only the bytes both agree on are kept. This set contains at least all reachable addresses as α' is bisimilar to α_1 and α_2. The same reasoning holds for CFG_p.

4 Formalization

This section provides more mathematical rigor for the definitions used in Sect. 3. Our model of the low-level languages runs on an abstract machine with an *infinite address space.* We use α for assembly programs, β for binaries, π for programs that can be either of the two, ω for oracles, ψ for abstract machine states and Γ for execution contexts. We use $\psi[a]$ for a memory read or write in state ψ at address a.

We first present the syntax and syntactic properties of assembly programs and binaries. Both assembly programs and binaries contain partial mappings from addresses to some form of data. Binaries only contain raw bytes as they serve the dual purpose as instructions (summarized in Table 2) to be decoded, and as data. Assembly programs make a distinction between these two forms of information. Additionally, both assembly and binaries contain indications for e*X*ecutable, *R*eadable and *W*ritable sections and an *E*ntry address.

Definition 4 (Programs). *Assembly programs and binaries are tuples containing the program text and data, or the raw bytes representing them, a set for each the executable, readable and writable addresses and an entry address.*

$$\begin{aligned} Asm := \langle\ & text : Addr \rightharpoonup Instr, \\ & data : Addr \rightharpoonup Byte, \\ & X : \{Addr\}, W : \{Addr\}, \\ & R : \{Addr\}, E : Addr\ \rangle \end{aligned}$$

$$\begin{aligned} Bin := \langle\ & \text{-- no text mapping} \\ & bytes : Addr \rightharpoonup Byte, \\ & X : \{Addr\}, W : \{Addr\}, \\ & R : \{Addr\}, E : Addr\ \rangle \end{aligned}$$

Both types of programs are subject to *well-formedness* conditions to ensure their semantics are well-defined. For all assembly programs α and binaries β, we have:

$$\begin{aligned} & reachable(\alpha) \subseteq dom(text(\alpha)) \land \\ & dom(data(\alpha) \subseteq W(\alpha) \cup R(\alpha)) \land \\ & dom(text(\alpha) \subseteq X(\alpha)) \end{aligned}$$

$$\begin{aligned} & reachable(\beta) \subseteq dom(fetch(\beta)) \land \\ & dom(bytes(\beta)) \subseteq (W \cup R \cup X)(\beta)) \end{aligned}$$

The syntactic properties over both types of programs can be easily checked, and overapproximate the semantic properties used in Fig. 1. *Byte-consistency* describes that the bytes of overlapping instructions and data in assembly programs must agree with another, ensuring the assembly program can be assembled into a binary. For binaries, there is no distinction between text and data and there can only ever be at most one byte at an address. Thus, binaries always fulfill this property. A *mosaic* assembly program does not have any overlapping instructions, as such, it does not allow for any jumps into the middle of instructions. The properties $X\bar{\wedge}W$ and $X\bar{\wedge}R$ ensure that the text-sections of a program do not overlap with the data sections. In turn, programs fulfilling these properties cannot, by construction, modify themselves, or read the encoding of their own instructions.

Definition 5 (Byte-Consistency). *An assembly program* α *is* byte-consistent *iff, for every address a, the bytes of overlapping instructions agree with another and with the data bytes at a. Let text−bytes be the function that returns the set of bytes corresponding to the decoding of all instructions that are at a given address.*

$$\begin{aligned} \mathit{byte-consistent}(\alpha) := \; & (\forall a \cdot \mathit{data}(a) = b \Longrightarrow b \in \mathit{text-bytes}(\alpha, a)) \\ & \wedge (\forall a \cdot |\mathit{text-bytes}(\alpha, a)| \leq 1) \end{aligned}$$

Definition 6 (No Execute Where Write). *The property* $X\bar{\wedge}W$ *describes that no address is both in an executable and a writable section.*

$$X\bar{\wedge}W(\pi) := X(\pi) \cap W(\pi) = \emptyset$$

Definition 7 (No Execute Where Read). *The property* $X\bar{\wedge}R$ *describes that no address is both in an executable and a readable section.*

$$X\bar{\wedge}R(\pi) := X(\pi) \cap R(\pi) = \emptyset$$

Definition 8 (Mosaic). *An assembly program* α *is* mosaic *iff no two instruction in the program text overlap.*

$$\mathsf{mosaic}(\alpha) := \forall (a_1, a_2 \in \mathit{dom}(\mathit{text}(\alpha))) \cdot \neg (a_1 \leq a_2 < a_1 + |\mathit{text}(\alpha, a_1)|)$$

Programs have no a priori knowledge of where they are loaded into memory or the behavior of dynamically linked (external) symbols. This information is captured in the *execution context* Γ.

The semantics for both binary and assembly programs are given as unlabeled transition systems. We write $TS(\alpha; \Gamma)$ and $TS(\beta; \Gamma)$ for the transition system describing the execution of the assembly program α or the binary β. The initial states have all bytes of the program loaded into memory at the loading offset of Γ. Transitions between states are given 1. for binaries by fetching bytes at `RIP` from memory and decoding them as instructions, 2. for assembly programs by fetching the instruction at `RIP` from the program text, and then executing them according to Table 2. Addresses within the domain of the *bytes* for a binary or *data* for an assembly program can only be read if they are elements of the R set, and only be written if they are elements of the W set. Similarly, addresses can only be fetched as instructions if they are within in X set.

Table 2. Generic instruction set used for the binary and assembly languages. Real-world instructions can be built from one or multiple instructions above. For example, `add RAX, 42` can be modeled by `const` ρ_{tmp}, 42 `; apply` (+), `rax`, `rax`, ρ_{tmp}.

Opcode	Arguments	Behavior
`halt`	$\emptyset$	Stops program execution
`const`	$(\rho : Reg)(v : \mathbb{Z})$	Writes the constant v into register ρ
`load`	$(\rho_d, \rho_s : Reg)$	Reads address a from register ρ_s, reads value v from memory at a, writes v into register ρ_d
`store`	$(\rho_d, \rho_s : Reg)$	Reads address a from register ρ_d, reads value v from register ρ_s, write v into memory at a
`cond`	$(\rho_c, \rho_d, \rho_s : Reg)$	Reads value c from register ρ_c, if $c \neq 0$: Reads value v from register ρ_s, writes v into register ρ_d
`size`	$(\rho_d, \rho_s : Reg)$	Reads value v from register ρ_s, writes the number of bytes needed to represent v into register ρ_d
`symb`	$(\rho : Reg)(s : Sym)$	Queries the execution context for the address a of the symbol s, writes a into register ρ_d
`apply`	$(f)(\rho_d, \rho_1, \rho_2 : Reg)$	Reads values v_1, v_2 from registers ρ_1, ρ_2, writes $f(v_1, v_2)$ into register ρ_d

Definition 9 (Execution Context). *The* execution context *is a tuple containing the load address, the location and the semantics of external symbols.*

$$\begin{aligned} Ctx := \langle\ & load{-}addr : Addr,\ \ externs : Sym \to Addr, \\ & extern{-}sem : Addr \rightharpoonup State \times State\ \rangle \end{aligned}$$

The semantic properties define constraints over states reachable from the entry point of a program. All of them use the notations $reachable_n(ts, \psi)$ and $reachable(ts, \psi)$ indicating that state ψ is reachable within n steps or any number of steps in the transition system ts. A binary is *non self-modifying* if no memory write occurs within the boundaries of its executable sections. For assembly programs, the instructions are not fetched from memory, thus they do not have a notion of self-modification. Similarly, a program is *non reflexive* if no memory read occurs within its executable sections. The property *no jump-in-the-middle* captures that no two states are reachable for which the current instructions overlap with another. A program is *position independent* if its semantics do not depend on the execution context's loading offset.

Definition 10 (No Self-Modification). *A binary is* non self-modifying (NSM) *iff no memory writes occurs within the executable sections.*

$$\begin{aligned} \mathsf{NSM}(\beta) := \forall \Gamma, \alpha, \psi_1, \psi_2, n \cdot & \\ & reachable_n(TS(\beta; \Gamma), \psi_1) \implies \\ & reachable_{(n+1)}(TS(\beta; \Gamma), \psi_2) \implies \\ & \psi_1[a] \neq \psi_2[a] \implies a \notin dom(X(\beta)) \end{aligned}$$

Definition 11 (No Reflexivity). *A binary or assembly program is* nonreflexive (NRefl) *iff the encoding of any instruction other than the current one does not influence the behavior of the current instruction.*

$$\begin{aligned}\mathsf{NRefl}(\pi) := \forall \Gamma, \pi', \psi_1, \psi_2, \psi_2' \cdot \\ &\mathit{reachable}_n(\mathit{TS}(\pi;\Gamma), \psi_1) \wedge \mathit{reachable}_n(\mathit{TS}(\pi';\Gamma), \psi_1) \implies \\ &\mathit{reachable}_{(n+1)}(\mathit{TS}(\pi;\Gamma), \psi_2) \wedge \mathit{reachable}_{(n+1)}(\mathit{TS}(\pi';\Gamma), \psi_2') \implies \\ &\mathit{fetch}(\pi, \mathit{RIP}(\pi)) = \mathit{fetch}(\pi', \mathit{RIP}(\pi')) \implies \psi_2 = \psi_2'\end{aligned}$$

Definition 12 (No Jump-In-The-Middle). *A binary or assembly program fulfills the no* jumps in the middle (NJiM) *property iff there are no two instructions reachable which overlap with another.*

$$\begin{aligned}\mathsf{NJiM}(\pi) := \forall \Gamma, (\psi_1, \psi_2 \in \mathit{reachable}(\mathit{TS}(\pi;\Gamma)) \cdot \\ &\neg(\mathit{RIP}(\psi_1) \leq \mathit{RIP}(\psi_2) < \mathit{RIP}(\psi_1) + |\mathit{fetch}(\pi, \psi_1, \mathit{RIP}(\psi_1))|)\end{aligned}$$

Definition 13 (Position Independent Executable). *A binary or assembly program is a* position independent executable (PIE) *iff the offset at which it is loaded into memory does not influence the semantics of the program.*

$$\mathsf{PIE}(\pi) := \forall \Gamma, a_1, a_2 \cdot \ \mathit{TS}(\pi; \Gamma(\mathit{load{-}addr} := a_1)) = \mathit{TS}(\pi; \Gamma(\mathit{load{-}addr} := a_2))$$

Finally, a binary or assembly program is $\mathsf{complete}_p$ if all reachable addresses are known in a set of cardinality p. The set containing these addresses is the *reachability oracle* REACH_p. Here, p serves as a *precision metric*, the smaller p is, the greater the precision of the oracle. Without the precision metric, generating the oracle would become trivial as one can overapproximate the set of reachable addresses by all addresses. Similarly, the program has a known CFG_p if all pairs of successively reachable addresses are known in a set of cardinality p, the corresponding oracle is the *indirection oracle* INDIRECT_p. Again, p serves as the precision metric counting the edges in the CFG. One could trivially overapproximate this oracle by considering all addresses reachable from all other addresses.

Definition 14 (Complete). *An assembly program or binary π is* $\mathsf{complete}_p$ *iff there exists a set containing at least all reachable addresses.*

$$\mathsf{complete}_p(\pi) := \exists \omega \cdot |\omega| \leq p \wedge \forall \Gamma \cdot \mathit{reachable}(\mathit{TS}(\pi;\Gamma)) \subseteq \omega$$

Definition 15 (Known Control Flow). *A binary or assembly program π has a known control flow (CFG_p) iff for all reachable addresses the immediately next reachable addresses are known and the resulting CFG contains p edges.*

$$\begin{aligned}\mathsf{CFG}_p(\pi) := \exists \omega \cdot |\omega| \leq p \wedge \forall \Gamma, \psi_1, \psi_2, n \cdot \\ &\mathit{reachable}_n(\mathit{TS}(\pi;\Gamma), \psi_1) \implies \\ &\mathit{reachable}_{(n+1)}(\mathit{TS}(\pi;\Gamma), \psi_2) \implies \\ &\langle \psi_1, \psi_2 \rangle \in \omega\end{aligned}$$

5 Discussion

The formalization of binary and assembly languages presented in Sects. 3 and 4 make certain assumptions over the semantics of assembly languages, the availability of oracles for the translations, and properties of the input binaries.

5.1 Self-modification

Our model of assembly languages contains *static* program text. Instructions are fetched directly from an unchangeable assembly program instead of being *dynamically* loaded from memory, which stands in contrast to what binaries do. There do exist formalizations of self-modifying assembly programs such as [2,7,29], but for the purposes of this paper, non-self-modifying assembly programs are better suited.

Static Program Text is what one usually wants from a disassembler, as it allows the program text to be analyzed easier. The disadvantage is that the runtime semantics between a binary, which always has a dynamic program text, and the assembly program can differ, even when they *initially* contain the same instructions. Figure 2 shows an example program where a memory write alters the dynamic text of the binary by changing the last instruction while the static text of the assembly program remains unaltered.

```
self_modification_bin:
  ; Overwrites the next instruction
  mov BYTE [RIP], 0xC3

  ; Changes to a ret (0xC3)
  nop
```

```
self_modification_asm:
  ; Does not influence the text
  mov BYTE [RIP], 0xC3
  ; Remains a nop in the text
  ; Changes to a 0xC3 in memory
  nop
```

Fig. 2. Difference in semantics between a binary (left) and an assembly program (right). Both write 0xC3 into memory where the next address will be. For the binary, this changes the program text since instructions are fetched from memory. For the assembly program, the memory does not influence the program text.

Dynamic Program Text models the semantics of both the binary and the assembly program in the same way. Programs such as the one in Fig. 2 behave the same for binaries and assembly programs with a dynamic program text. The disadvantage of a dynamic assembly program text is that the lines between text and data are necessarily blurred. Figure 3 shows two example assembly programs with different instructions but the same binary encoding. Under dynamic semantics, where instructions are loaded from memory, these two programs behave the same. For this work, this would make disassembling always trivial as one would never need to resolve the starting addresses of any instructions, as any binary with the correct encoding would be considered bisimilar.

```
push RBP       ; 55
mov  RBP, RSP  ; 48 89 E5
call printf    ; E8 00 00 00 00
add  RAX, 5    ; 48 83 C0 05
```

```
.bytes 0x894855  ; 55 48 89
in  EAX, 0xe8    ; E5 E8
add [RAX], AL    ; 00 00
add [RAX], AL    ; 00 00
add RAX,0x5      ; 48 83 C0 05
```

Fig. 3. Self-Modifying semantics for assembly programs allow even incorrect disassemblers to be considered correct. The original program (left) and the incorrectly disassembled (right) program will have the same behavior under self-modifying semantics. Both contain exactly the same bytes, so fetching instructions from memory will result in the same execution traces. At the same time, both program have instructions with completely different semantics.

5.2 The Oracles

Figure 1 makes use of an oracle to overapproximate all reachable addresses (REACH_p) and an oracle to overapproximate the CFG (INDIRECT_p). Neither of these is available in any current debugging format like DWARF. We discuss whether – and how – these oracles can be obtained either at compile-time (when source code is available), or from a stripped binary (when source is not available).

Both can be implemented trivially by overapproximation of the actual address space and CFG if one considers all addresses to be reachable from all other addresses. However, such an overapproximation would be practically unusable for any real use cases and generating them with a high precision proves to be a difficult problem.

From Source Code. At the source code level, one might expect the information to generate the oracles to be present. For example, the instruction selection phase of a compiler emits all intended instructions and the linker assigns them their final addresses. Based on this information, the compiler might create a reachability oracle by emitting all these addresses as an additional artifact.

However, this only captures the *intended* instruction addresses, reachable from well-behaved source-level code. At runtime, unexpected behaviors like stack overflows may cause the program to set its `RIP` to an unintended address. In this case, the oracle is no longer a sound overapproximation of all reachable addresses.

For the indirection oracle, the intended addresses are not fully known, not even at compile time. Indirections are ubiquitous in binaries as they are used for the jump tables in control flow constructs like `switch` statements, implement the mechanism used in `return` statements, and model the invocation of callbacks. While jump tables might be fully known at compile time, it is not possible to know all possible targets of `return` statements as this would require a full call graph. Moreover, note that even at the source level unresolved indirections may exist due to, e.g., callbacks.

Still, these artifacts can prove valuable in security analyses and binary hardening, even if they only capture the intention of the compiler. If the set of intended addresses is known, one can analyze the program to see if any address outside this set is reachable, uncovering a vulnerability rooted in low-level behavior not present in the source code. Similarly, one can harden the binary by adding a check before indirect jumps to abort the program if any unintended address is reached.

From Binary Code. At the binary level, the information needed to create the oracles must be recovered directly from the binary itself. In practice, the two oracles conflate, i.e., in order to get the set of reachable instruction addresses one must recover an overapproximative CFG. Deriving an overapproximative CFG requires establishing binary-level invariants that statically bound the values that certain state parts may have at run-time, in order to resolve indirections. This is known hard problem [30].

Real-world disassemblers try to uncover this information by one of two approaches: 1. Linear Sweep, or 2. Recursive Traversal. Tools such as *objdump* start at an entry address and linearly sweep through the section they try to disassemble. The instruction at the current address is decoded and the address is incremented by the instruction's size. For simple binaries, this approach works well, but as soon as text and data are mixed in unexpected ways, a linear sweep will fail to distinguish them. More sophisticated tools such as the disassemblers used in Ghidra, IDA-Pro or Binary Ninja, aim to decode all reachable instructions by following the binary's control flow. In contrast to a linear sweep, this is able to distinguish text from data even when they are mixed but will still fail for indirect jumps for which all possible successor edges in the CFG need to be recognized.

Figure 4 shows an example program where both linear sweep and recursive traversal will fail to produce the full and correct assembly code corresponding to the binary. Both linear sweep and recursive traversal are able to decode the instructions before a jump occurs (address `4000`). The byte following that instruction (address `4002`) is intended to be a raw data byte, but if one linearly decodes all instruction in the snippet, it will be decoded as an incorrect instruction. If one instead follows the CFG to address `4003`, the instructions of the original program can be decoded. However, even recursively traversing the CFG fails after the last instruction (address `4006`) since it is impossible to know all possible values of `rax`.

```
4000: jmp $+1                          | 4000: EB FF
4002: .byte 00                         | 4002: 00
4003: sub RAX, RBX                     | 4003: 48 29 D8
4006: jmp RAX                          | 4006: FF E0
```

```
; Linear sweep decodes the first       | ; CFG traversal can resolve all 3
; instruction                          | ; instructions correctly
4000: jmp $+1                          | 4000: JMP jmp $+1
; But it will continue to              | 4002: .byte 00
; disassemble after it                 | 4003: sub RAX, RBX
; 4002: 00 48 29                       | ; But it will not be able to continue
; 4005: D8 FF E0                       | ; correctly after an indirect jump
4002: add [RAX+0x29],CL                | ; to an unknown location
4005: fdivr st,st(7)                   | 4006: jmp RAX
```

Fig. 4. An example program which cannot be correctly disassembled without the usage of the indirection oracle. The top left shows the original assembly code, top right shows the assembled result. The bottom left shows the result of linearly sweeping through the program. The first instruction is decoded correctly, but continuing to disassemble directly after it results in incorrect instructions. The bottom right shows the result of traversing the CFG. This results in the correct instructions being decoded on the snipped, but without further information, the indirect jump at the end means that the traversal cannot continue.

6 Conclusion

Generally, it is not possible to disassemble every binary into an equivalent assembly program. We provide a formalization for general binary and assembly languages and show that in certain scenarios, they can be correctly translated to each other. The key in showing that these translations are possible is to lift restrictions on the assembly language which are useful for writing assembly code by hand but are not always needed when doing disassembling.

In order to perform the disassembling correctly, oracles to enumerate the address space or resolve indirections may be needed. Generating these oracles itself can be an undecidable problem. Future work may see these oracles be implemented at compile time by leveraging information that is already known.

In this paper, we only examine the first step of many in a decompilation chain: converting a raw binary to an assembly program in which instructions are referenced by addresses. Further steps of de- and recompilation require the assembly program to be in a *symbolized* format, meaning that instructions can be referenced by abstract program labels. This requires a thorough *pointer analysis*, which could be a third oracle. In contrast to the assembly language presented in this work, one does not only need to distinguish between instructions and data, but also between addresses pointing to instructions and addresses pointing to data. Similar to the resolution of indirections, a sound and complete pointer analysis is not possible in the general case. But one may ask the question "In which scenarios can data- and text-pointers be told apart?". Future work may see an extension of the Isabelle code-base presented here with a third language:

symbolized assembly; and theorems describing the conversion between assembly and symbolized assembly.

Acknowledgements. We would like to thank the anonymous reviewers for their insightful comments and suggestions, which helped to greatly improve the paper. This work is supported by the Defense Advanced Research Projects Agency (DARPA) and Naval Information Warfare Center Pacific (NIWC Pacific) under Contract No. N66001-21-C-4028, and by DARPA under Agreement No. HR00112090028.

References

1. An, X., Verbeek, F., Ravindran, B.: DSV: disassembly soundness validation without assuming a ground truth. In: Deshmukh, J.V., Havelund, K., Perez, I. (eds.) NFM 2022. LNCS, vol. 13260, pp. 636–655. Springer, Cham (2022). https://doi.org/10.1007/978-3-031-06773-0_34
2. Anckaert, B., Madou, M., De Bosschere, K.: A model for self-modifying code, vol. 4437, pp. 232–248 (2006). https://doi.org/10.1007/978-3-540-74124-4_16
3. Baier, C., Katoen, J.: Principles of Model Checking. MIT Press, Cambridge (2008)
4. Balakrishnan, G., Gruian, R., Reps, T., Teitelbaum, T.: CodeSurfer/x86—a platform for analyzing x86 executables. In: Bodik, R. (ed.) CC 2005. LNCS, vol. 3443, pp. 250–254. Springer, Heidelberg (2005). https://doi.org/10.1007/978-3-540-31985-6_19
5. Balakrishnan, G., et al.: Model checking x86 executables with CodeSurfer/x86 and WPDS++. In: Etessami, K., Rajamani, S.K. (eds.) CAV 2005. LNCS, vol. 3576, pp. 158–163. Springer, Heidelberg (2005). https://doi.org/10.1007/11513988_17
6. Bangert, J., et al.: The {Page-Fault} weird machine: lessons in instruction-less computation. In: 7th USENIX Workshop on Offensive Technologies (2013)
7. Bonfante, G., Marion, J.Y., Reynaud-Plantey, D.: A computability perspective on self-modifying programs. In: Seventh IEEE International Conference on Software Engineering and Formal Methods, pp. 231–239 (2009). https://doi.org/10.1109/SEFM.2009.25
8. Bonfante, G., et al.: CoDisasm: medium scale concatic disassembly of self-modifying binaries with overlapping instructions. In: 22nd ACM SIGSAC Conference on Computer and Communications Security, pp. 745–756. Association for Computing Machinery (2015). https://doi.org/10.1145/2810103.2813627
9. Cifuentes, C.: Reverse compilation techniques. Queensland University of Technology, Brisbane (1994)
10. Cohen, F.: Computer viruses: theory and experiments. Comput. Secur. **6**(1), 22–35 (1987)
11. Collberg, C., Thomborson, C.: Watermarking, tamper-proofing, and obfuscation - tools for software protection. IEEE Trans. Software Eng. **28**(8), 735–746 (2002). https://doi.org/10.1109/TSE.2002.1027797
12. David, R., et al.: BINSEC/SE: a dynamic symbolic execution toolkit for binary-level analysis. In: IEEE 23rd International Conference on Software Analysis, Evolution, and Reengineering, vol. 1, pp. 653–656. IEEE (2016). https://doi.org/10.1109/SANER.2016.43
13. Duck, G.J., Gao, X., Roychoudhury, A.: Binary rewriting without control flow recovery. In: 41st ACM SIGPLAN Conference on Programming Language Design and Implementation, pp. 151–163 (2020). https://doi.org/10.1145/3385412.3385972

14. He, J., et al.: Debin: predicting debug information in stripped binaries. In: 2018 ACM SIGSAC Conference on Computer and Communications Security, pp. 1667–1680 (2018). https://doi.org/10.1145/3243734.3243866
15. Kargén, U., et al.: desync-cc: a research tool for automatically applying disassembly desynchronization during compilation. Sci. Comput. Program. **228**, 102954 (2023). https://doi.org/10.1016/j.scico.2023.102954
16. Kinder, J., Katzenbeisser, S., Schallhart, C., Veith, H.: Detecting malicious code by model checking. In: Julisch, K., Kruegel, C. (eds.) DIMVA 2005. LNCS, vol. 3548, pp. 174–187. Springer, Heidelberg (2005). https://doi.org/10.1007/11506881_11
17. Linn, C., Debray, S.: Obfuscation of executable code to improve resistance to static disassembly. In: 10th ACM Conference on Computer and Communications Security, pp. 290–299 (2003). https://doi.org/10.1145/948109.948149
18. Liu, Z., Wang, S.: How far we have come: testing decompilation correctness of c decompilers. In: 29th ACM SIGSOFT International Symposium on Software Testing and Analysis, pp. 475–487. Association for Computing Machinery (2020). https://doi.org/10.1145/3395363.3397370
19. Navas, J.A., Schachte, P., Søndergaard, H., Stuckey, P.J.: Signedness-agnostic program analysis: precise integer bounds for low-level code. In: Jhala, R., Igarashi, A. (eds.) APLAS 2012. LNCS, vol. 7705, pp. 115–130. Springer, Heidelberg (2012). https://doi.org/10.1007/978-3-642-35182-2_9
20. Nipkow, T., Paulson, L.C., Wenzel, M.: Isabelle/HOL: A Proof Assistant for Higher-Order Logic, vol. 2283. Springer, Heidelberg (2002). https://doi.org/10.1007/3-540-45949-9
21. Pang, C., et al.: SoK: all you ever wanted to know about x86/x64 binary disassembly but were afraid to ask. In: 2021 IEEE Symposium on Security and Privacy, pp. 833–851. IEEE (2021). https://doi.org/10.1109/SP40001.2021.00012
22. Pei, K., et al.: XDA: accurate, robust disassembly with transfer learning. arXiv preprint arXiv:2010.00770 (2020). https://doi.org/10.48550/arXiv.2010.00770
23. Priyadarshan, S., Nguyen, H., Sekar, R.: Accurate disassembly of complex binaries without use of compiler metadata. In: 28th ACM International Conference on Architectural Support for Programming Languages and Operating Systems, vol. 4, p. 1–18. Association for Computing Machinery (2024). https://doi.org/10.1145/3623278.3624766
24. Rice, H.G.: Classes of recursively enumerable sets and their decision problems. Trans. Am. Math. Soc. **74**(2), 358–366 (1953). http://www.jstor.org/stable/1990888
25. Saxena, P., et al.: Loop-extended symbolic execution on binary programs. In: 18th International Symposium on Software Testing and Analysis, pp. 225–236 (2009). https://doi.org/10.1145/1572272.1572299
26. Schulte, E., et al.: Evolving exact decompilation. In: Workshop on Binary Analysis Research (2018). https://doi.org/10.14722/bar.2018.23008
27. Schwarz, B., Debray, S., Andrews, G.: Disassembly of executable code revisited. In: 2002 Proceedings of the Ninth Working Conference on Reverse Engineering, pp. 45–54. IEEE (2002). https://doi.org/10.1109/WCRE.2002.1173063
28. Selçuk, A.A., Orhan, F., Batur, B.: Undecidable problems in malware analysis. In: 2017 12th International Conference for Internet Technology and Secured Transactions, pp. 494–497 (2017). https://doi.org/10.23919/ICITST.2017.8356458
29. Touili, T., Ye, X.: LTL model checking of self modifying code. Formal Methods Syst. Des. **60**(2), 195–227 (2022). https://doi.org/10.1007/s10703-022-00394-8

30. Verbeek, F., et al.: Formally verified lifting of c-compiled x86-64 binaries. In: Jhala, R., Dillig, I. (eds.) PLDI 2022: 43rd ACM SIGPLAN International Conference on Programming Language Design and Implementation, pp. 934–949. ACM (2022). https://doi.org/10.1145/3519939.3523702
31. Wartell, R., Zhou, Y., Hamlen, K.W., Kantarcioglu, M., Thuraisingham, B.: Differentiating code from data in x86 binaries. In: Gunopulos, D., Hofmann, T., Malerba, D., Vazirgiannis, M. (eds.) ECML PKDD 2011. LNCS (LNAI), vol. 6913, pp. 522–536. Springer, Heidelberg (2011). https://doi.org/10.1007/978-3-642-23808-6_34
32. Wartell, R., Zhou, Y., Hamlen, K.W., Kantarcioglu, M.: Shingled graph disassembly: finding the undecideable path. In: Tseng, V.S., Ho, T.B., Zhou, Z.-H., Chen, A.L.P., Kao, H.-Y. (eds.) PAKDD 2014. LNCS (LNAI), vol. 8443, pp. 273–285. Springer, Cham (2014). https://doi.org/10.1007/978-3-319-06608-0_23

Finding Deep-Hidden Bugs in Android Apps via Functional Semantics Guided Exploration

Siyi Gu[1], Xiaoqiang Liu[1](✉), Hui Guo[1], Bochun Cao[1], Baiyan Li[1], Lizhi Cai[2], and Hu Yun[2]

[1] School of Computer Science and Technology, Donghua University, Shanghai, China
liuxq@dhu.edu.cn

[2] Shanghai Key Laboratory of Computer Software Evaluating and Testing, Shanghai, China

Abstract. As Android apps get more complicated, current automated testing techniques are not sufficient for discovering deep-hidden bugs. The deep-hidden bugs are triggered by sequential Data Manipulation Functions(DMFs), which often represents functional semantics (Create, Read, Update, Delete and Search). The Data Manipulation Function Sequence (DMFSQ) is composed of DMFs. Testing by DMFSQs can closely mirror real user interactions, and provide a more in-depth evaluation of the app's functions. Therefore, to find the deep-hidden bugs, we propose a novel functional semantics guided exploration strategy based on DMFs and DMFSQs. Our idea is that we can (1) extract DMFs from the apps, and (2) use functional semantics of DMFs in the execution trace to guide the test exploration. To achieve this idea, we conducted a study on the GUI of various apps' DMFs to identify accurate and universal GUI patterns as the extraction rule. With the rule, an algorithm is developed to extract DMFs from apps while detecting regular bugs during depth-first test exploration. Based on extracted DMFs, we design a exploration strategy based on Q-learning, a classic reinforcement learning algorithm for detecting deep-hidden bugs. We have implemented our idea as an automated testing tool DmsDroid. DmsDroid can not only discover regular bugs, but also generate meaningful DMFSQs to detect deep-hidden bugs. The evaluation results of DmsDroid on 16 real-world apps shows that DmsDroid outperforms the state-of-practice Android testing techniques in terms of code coverage and bug detection. So far, 7 of our reported bugs have been confirmed.

Keywords: deep-hidden bugs · data manipulations function · Android app testing · reinforcement learning

1 Introduction

As the number of Android apps continue to increase, the complexity of these apps also rises [38]. Consequently, discovering deep-hidden bugs has become increasingly challenging. Specifically, even if performing all single executable

W.-N. Chin and Z. Xu (Eds.): TASE 2024, LNCS 14777, pp. 146–164, 2024.
https://doi.org/10.1007/978-3-031-64626-3_9

UI events in the app also cannot completely guarantee that this app is bug-free. One obvious phenomenon is that the app can successfully execute a single function, but the diverse combinations of multiple functions could crash it. Thus, a mature testing tool should not only test each individual function, but also needs to consider the relationship between functions to find deep-hidden bugs in the series of operations.

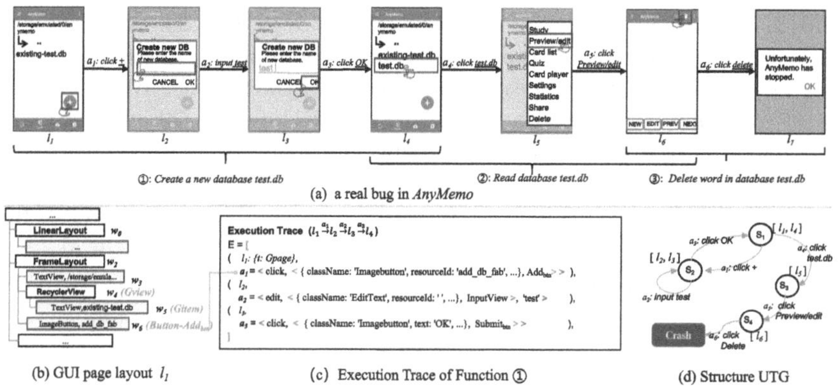

Fig. 1. *AnyMemo.* (a) is the scenario that a real bug triggered by continuous function execution. (b) shows the GUI page layouts l_1 and l_4. (c) is the execution tarce of function ①. (d) is the structure UTG of (a).

An Illustrative Example. Figure 1.a shows a real bug triggered by the combination of multiple functions in AnyMemo. AnyMemo is a vocabulary memorization app with over 100K downloads on Google Play. The user executes 3 functions continuously. ① Creates a database test.db (see $l_1 \sim l_4$). The user clicks the button +, enters the text test and clicks the button OK. ② Read the database test.db (see $l_4 \sim l_6$). The user selects this database test.db in the file list and clicks Preview/edit operation to view the vocabularies in test.db. ③ Delete the vocabularies in test.db (see $l_6 \sim l_7$). The user clicks the button delete to remove the vocabularies. However, because the newly created test.db is an empty database and there is no vocabulary, the app crashes when performing the function ③.

This bug is triggered when three individual data manipulation functions (DMFs) are executed sequentially. We call such an execution sequence (e.g., ①→②→③) as data manipulation functions sequence(DMFSQ). A DMFSQ contains a series of functional semantics (Create, View, Update, Delete, Search), closely mirroring the actions of real users. From the example, we infer that deep-hidden bugs often lurk within DMFSQs. By automating the generation and execution of DMFSQs, the hidden bugs can be detected in the overall functional flow of the app. However, detecting such deep-hidden bugs by DMFSQs is non-trivial due to two major reasons. First, the User Interface (UI) characteristic of apps is diverse, it is difficult to identify different kinds of DMFs for each app under test (AUT). Second, the combinations of DMFs are varied, which meaning that the functional semantics contained in DMFSQs are complex and diverse. For example, triggering the bug in Fig. 1.a required a specific execution order of DMFSQ of ①→②→③.

Limitations of Existing Testing Techniques. Many techniques have been employed for automated testing in Android apps. However, existing techniques have two major limitations in detecting these bugs triggered by combinations of DMFs. First, the majority of existing techniques [6,9,11,23,24] are designed to respond to single GUI operation or individual function. Thus, these techniques struggle to generate meaningful test cases containing diverse combinations of multiple DMFs. Second, some testing techniques [29,36] can extract short sequences of events and combine them in a way of cross-enumeration to find bugs. However, owing to the lack of prior knowledge before testing, they may lead to an exponential increase in testing workload as the number of function points grows. Therefore, these techniques may not be so efficient at testing the bugs triggered by function combinations.

Our Approach. To this end, we propose a functional semantics guided exploration strategy to efficiently find these deep-hidden bugs. Our idea is that, we should (1) extract the DMFs automatically during the first testing exploration, and (2) further utilize these DMFs to effectively guide the testing exploration toward finding the deep-hidden bugs. Inspired by reinforcement learning-based techniques [4,30,31,35,37], we design a functional semantics guided exploration strategy based on Q-learning. The reward function in the strategy considers the current operation's relevance to DMFs, the variety of explored DMFs, and the functional semantics of explored DMFSQs during the exploration. Based on this strategy, the Q-learning agent can explore more meaningful DMFSQs, which contains different DMFs in effective orders.

At the same time, in order to find the DMFs in various kinds of app as completely as possible, the co-authors conducted an Empirical Study, summarizing patterns in the DMF GUI of 81 apps. We identify universal GUI change patterns of DMFs as extraction rules. This study serves as the foundation for the real-time automated extraction algorithm of DMFs. The extraction algorithm extracts DMFs simultaneously with depth-first test exploration, which can detect regular bugs. With the extracted DMFs, we further explore the app via functional semantics guided strategy to detect the bugs triggered by DMFSQs.

Contributions. Overall, our contributions can be summarized as follows:

- We surveyed the GUI of 81 apps, formulated a set of DMF extraction rules.
- We designed a real-time DMF extraction algorithm to extract DMFs simultaneously while finding regular bugs with depth-first exploration.
- We proposed a functional semantics guided exploration strategy based on Q-learning to effectively explore more DMFSQs to find deep-hidden bugs.

Our approach DmsDroid and the data used in the experiments can be found on GitHub[1]. The evaluation on 16 real-world apps shows DmsDroid can discover more bugs in some complex cases.

[1] https://github.com/TestingDMS/DMSDroid.

2 Background

2.1 DMFs in Apps

Data manipulation functionalities (DMFs) perform the common CRUDS operations (create, read, update, delete, search) to handle app-specific data [33]. Users generally perform Data Manipulation Functions (DMFs) through the graphical user interface (GUI) in apps. GUI [16] is a fundamental component of Android apps, providing an easy-to-use and intuitive interface that enables users to communicate with the app. The GUI typically consists of a set of page layouts (see $l_1 \sim l_6$ in Fig. 1.a), and represent the actions that users can perform on that interface (see $a_1 \sim a_6$ in Fig. 1.a). The layout-action pair (l, a) can be combined to form an execution trace $[(l_1, a_1), ...(l_i, a_i), ...(l_n, a_n)]$. In Fig. 1.a, three layout-action pairs are executed continuously $[(l_1, a_1), (l_2, a_2), (l_3, a_3)]$ and achieve the functional semantics *Create a new database*. Therefore, ① is a DMF, similarly, ② and ③ are as well. The functions ①→②→③ formed a DMFSQ.

2.2 Q-Learning for Android Testing

Q-learning [37] is a widely-used model-free reinforcement learning (RL) algorithm. At time t, the agent first observes the environment to obtain the current state ($s_t \in S$) and an immediate reward ($r_t \in R$). The agent then selects an action ($a_t \in A$) based on these variables. This action causes a transition in the environment from the current state (s_t) to the next state ($s_{t+1} \in S$) and generates the subsequent reward ($r_{t+1} \in R$). The process repeats for each interaction until a specified time limit is reached. Equation (1) shows the Bellman equation for updating the action value function. where α is the learning rate, γ is the discount factor, and $max_a Q(s_{t+1}, a)$ is the maximum expectation of the next state s_{t+1} award.

$$Q(s_t, a_t) = Q(s_t, a_t) + \alpha(r + \gamma max_a Q(s_{t+1}, a) - Q(s_t, a_t)) \tag{1}$$

The Q-values of future state-action pairs, $Q(s_{t+1}, a)$, influence previous pairs $Q(s_t, a)$. With ample exploration, the Q-table values converge to their true values. Therefore, the Q-table can accurately guide the agent to maximize cumulative rewards by selecting the highest-valued actions. There are also many testing tools [15,20,30] that choose to conduct testing exploration based on Q-learning. Inspired by this, we choose Q-learning algorithm to guide the test exploration with functional semantic guidance.

3 Empirical Study

In order to summarize general and accurate GUI pattern, we did an empirical study on DMF's GUI in this section. From a batch of different apps, we describe how to analyze the GUI of the app and elaborate the specific process of defining DMF extraction rules.

3.1 App Collection

To conduct a comprehensive analysis and research on the GUI of DMFs, we analyzed the GUI of DMFs using open-source apps from GitHub and F-Droid, and popular apps from Google Play. To ensure rule universality, we studied 10 app categories, collecting 81 apps in total: 61 open-source and 20 closed-source. Figure 2 shows the statistics of these apps. The information includes the number of stars on GitHub, the number of commits on GitHub, the app rating and the number of downloads on Google Play Store, and the categories of these apps. These data shows that our study population is (1) well-maintained (containing an average of thousands of commits), (2) popular (90% of downloads exceed 1000K and ratings exceed 4.0), and (3) diverse (covering 10 categories).

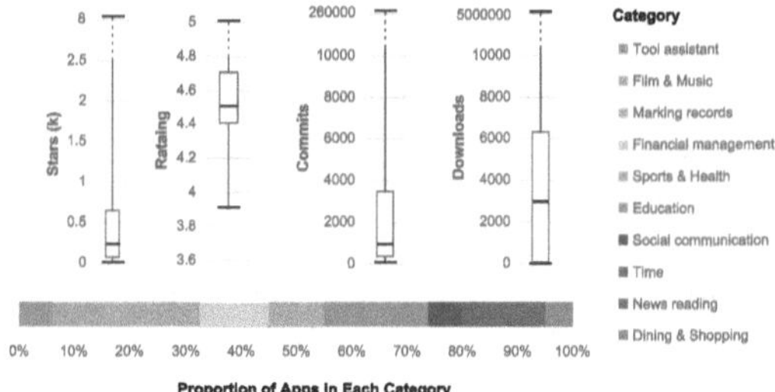

Fig. 2. Statistics of Apps in Each Category

3.2 Identify GUI Patterns of DMFs

Actions represent the user's interactions with the widgets, which can be clicking buttons on the screen, entering text, etc. The action $a = <t, w, d>$ is a tuple, where $a.t$ denotes the action's type (e.g., click, edit), $a.w$ denotes the current widget w, and $a.d$ denotes the optional data of a (e.g., the text inputted by edit).

Layouts define the arrangement and structure of the widgets within the GUI. The layout $l = <t, W>$ is a tuple. $l.W$ is the set of widgets on layout l. If there is a widget $w.c$=`Gview`, we infer that $l.t$=`Gpage`. Figure 1.b shows the details of l_1. l_1 contains widgets $w_0 \sim w_6$. The category of w_4 is `Gview`, so l_1 can be expressed as $l_1 = <$`Gpage`, $\{w_0 ..., w_6\}>$.

Execution trace E consists of consecutively executed layout-action pairs, i.e., E=$[(l_1, a_1), ...(l_i, a_i), ...(l_n, a_n)]$. The page layout after perform E is also the key for us to judge whether it is a complete DMF. Therefore, we define l_{end} to denote the ending page layout of execution trace E. If a GUI view with a certain data d appears in l_{end}, it represents as $d \rightarrowtail l_{end}$. Since DMF is an execution trace with specific functional semantics, we define a DMF as a 3-tuple $\sigma = <t, E, d>$, where $\sigma.t$ denotes the operation type (*Create*, *Read*, *Update*, *Delete* or *Search*). $\sigma.E$ denotes the execution trace of σ, and $\sigma.d$ denotes the optional data of σ. The DMF collection that stores σ as $\Sigma = \{\sigma_1, ..., \sigma_i, ..., \sigma_n\}$. When E satisfies DMF extraction rule, E will be extracted as a DMF σ and stored in Σ.

Based on the formal definition of various GUI elements, we spend a total of 20 person-days investigating the GUI patterns of DMFs in all 81 apps.

3.3 Rule Definition for Extracting DMFs

The DMF extraction rule is designed to identify DMFs by analyzing the GUI of each (l, a) pair and evaluating l_{end} to ascertain the data presence or absence (we refer to PBFDROID to formulate post-conditions). Based on the GUI pattern, we design the DMF extraction rule, which is shown in Table 1.

DMF extraction rule R is structured as a dictionary <*key, value*>. *Key* represents the semantics of DMF. *Value* include the GUI requirement of (l, a) and the post-condition l_{end}. In a specific DMF, there is a set of key layout-action pairs. The GUI-pattern of each key layout-action pair (l, a) can be expressed as *R.key.step*. *R.key.end* denotes the GUI requirement of l_{end}. For instance, R.create.1 denotes the first key (l, a) GUI requirement, i.e., $l.t = Gview$, $a.t = click$, $w.c = add_btn$ in the Create DMF. *R.create.end* is $d \rightarrowtail l_{end}$. Note that the post-condition of *Search* is empty due to the lack of clear restrictions on input characters. For a given search keyword, it may either be found or not found.

Table 1. Semantic extraction rule R

DMF Type	(l, a) in E	l_{end}
Create	① $l.t{=}Gview, a.t{=}click, w.t{=}add_{btn}$	$d \rightarrowtail End(E)$
	② $a.t{=}edit, a.w.t{=}inputview$; $d{=}a.d$	
	③ $a.t{=}click, a.w.t{=}submit_{btn}$	
Read	① $a.t{=}click, a.w.t{=}Gitem$ $d{=}w.v.text$ or $w.v.description$	$d \rightarrowtail End(E)$
Delete	① $a.t{=}click, w.t{=}delete_{btn}$	$\neg d \rightarrowtail End(E)$
	② $a.t{=}click, a.w.t{=}submit_{btn}$	
Update	① $a.t{=}click, a.w.t{=}modify_{btn}$	$(\neg d \rightarrowtail End(E))$ $\wedge$ $(d' \rightarrowtail End(E))$
	② $a.t{=}edit, a.w.t{=}inputview$; $d{=}a.w.v.text, d'{=}a.d$	
	③ $a.t{=}click, a.w.t{=}submit_{btn}$	
Search	① $a.t{=}click, a.w.t{=}search_{btn}$	-
	② $l.t{=}Gview, a.t{=}edit, a.w.t{=}inputview$; $d{=}a.d$	

In the Empirical Study, we establish the theoretical basis for the GUI extraction process for DMF. By collecting apps, defining GUI elements with formal languages, and summarizing the GUI change rules of DMFs, the tool is able to deeply understand the association patterns of GUI elements in DMF.

4 Approach

This section presents the technical details of DMSDROID. Figure 3 depicts the overview of our two-stage automated testing approach. (1) $Stage_1$: Automatically extract DMFs according to semantic extraction rules during depth-first test exploration, for detecting regular bugs; (2) $Stage_2$: Explore AUT with functional semantic guidance and generate DMFSQs as meaningful test cases by the extracted DMFs, for detecting deep-hidden bugs.

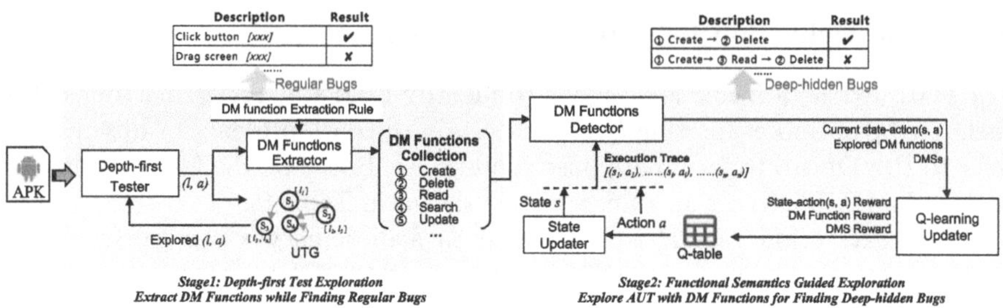

Fig. 3. Workflow of DMSDROID

4.1 DMF Extraction While Depth-First Exploration

Depth-first exploration is a systematic test exploration method used by many tools [9,13,22,36]. Through depth-first exploration, the regular problems in the apps can be discovered. Figure 1.d shows the structure UI Transition Graph (UTG) of the execution trace in Fig. 1.a. During depth-first exploration, DMSDROID generates the structure UTG of the app to avoid operations from being executed repeatedly. At the same time, the paths in the app can be fully traversed, which makes DMF fully extracted. We record and compare pairs of page layout and action (l, a) in real-time while the depth-first test exploration. Based on this idea, we design the real-time DMF extraction algorithm (Algorithm 1).

Before all, we initialize E, *step*, *type*, and data d (line 1). In dynamic exploration, we record executed operation in G (line 3). We analyze the current page's layout and actions and select an action from the actions (line 5, 6). If the layout-action pair has not been executed before, we execute this layout-action pair and continue exploration via recursive depth-first calls (line 7–11). The real-time extraction function *FunctionEventExtraction* receives the layout-action pair (l_t, a_t) as input (line 14). It first checks if the exploration is targeting a specific DMF. If (l, a) matches the initial requirement for a function type in the rule, it sets *type*, *step*, and records (l, a) in E (lines 15–18). In second condition, it verifies if the execution trace is complete and satisfies the criteria (line 19). If so, it creates a tuple σ with E, *type*, and data d, storing it in Σ, and then resets E, *type*, and *step* (lines 20, 21). In the third condition, during trace exploration but before reaching the end, if l doesn't cause a loop in E, it infers the target requirement $rule_{target}$ (line 22). If (l, a) satisfies $rule_{target}$, incrementing *step* by 1 (lines 23–26). Data d is also obtained at specific steps according to functional extraction rules R (lines 27,28).

Example 1. In Fig. 1.a, the user creates a new database *test* (①). First, the user clicks the + button (a_2) on page l_1, where $l_1.t = Gview$, $a_1.t = click$, and $a_1.w.c = add_{btn}$, satisfying the first step of DMF *Create*. We change *step* as $step = 1$, and record the execution trace as $E = [(l_1, a_2)]$. The subsequent layout-action pair needs to meet the requirements of $R.create.2$, i.e., $a.t = edit, w.c = inputview$. Fortunately, the second layout-action pair (l_2, a_2)

Algorithm 1: Real-time function extraction algorithm

```
E ← List(), step ← 0, type ← ⊥, d ← ⊥ // initialize execution trace, step, type, data
Function DepthFirstExploration(app)
    G ← ∅ // save executed operations
    if ¬isTimeOver() then
        l_t, actions_t ← getPageDetails()
        a_t ← selectRandomNotExecutedAction(actions_t, G)
        if (l_t,a_t) ∉ G then
            execute(l_t, a_t)
            FunctionEventExtraction(l_t, a_t)
            DepthFirstExploration(app)
            G ← G ∪ (l_t, a_t)
        SwitchBackTo(l_t)
    return G
Function FunctionEventExtraction(l, a)
    if curStep = 0 then
        if satisfyGUIPatternInRule((l, a), (any(R.type_s.0) ∈ R)) then
            type ← type_s, step ← 1
            E.append(l, a)
    else if isFinalStep(step, type) ∧ satisfyEnd(d, l_end, R.type.end) then
        σ ← (type, E, d), Σ.append(σ)
        Init(E, type, step, d)
    else if notLoop(seq, s) then
        rule_target ← getTargetStepRule(R, type, step)
        E.append(l, a)
        if satisfyGUIPatternInRule((l, a), rule_target) then
            step ← step + 1
            if shouldGetData(rule_target) then
                d ← GetData(rule_target)
```

satisfies the second step *R.create*.2, i.e., $step = 2$, $E = [(l_1, a_1), (l_2, a_2)]$. Meanwhile, according to the rule, we obtain the data $d = test$. The next layout-action pair (l_3, a_3) satisfies *R.create*.3, leading us to increase *step* and record execution trace $E = [(l_1, a_1), (l_2, a_2), (l_3, a_3)]$. As $step = 3$, which is the final step, we check $d \rightarrowtail l_{end}$ to confirm that the execution trace complies with the DMF *Create*, and then set $\sigma = [t, E, d]$, storing it in Σ.

4.2 Functional Semantics Guided Q-Leaning Exploration

Reinforcement learning provides a method for systematically exploring app functions [4,19,30,35]. In order to discover more deep-hidden bugs, it is necessary to consider the functional semantics to guide subsequent exploration. DmsDroid uses Q-learning to explore the app guided by the functional semantics.

Formulating Android Testing as MDP. An Android GUI testing problem is mathematically formalized as an MDP, $<S,A,P,R>$. The definition of S, A, and R in Android GUI testing significantly impacts the effectiveness and efficiency of the testing process. We do not definite P, because Q-learning does not assume to know the transition probability function [34]. We employ the following formulations:

S: States. S represents the set of all possible Android GUI states during exploration. We refer to the abstraction of state in Q-TESTING [30], and use the C-Lv4 standard in GUICC [10] to define the state of each layout.

A: Actions. *A* represents the set of all possible actions of the certain state. Similar to previous work [4,30,35], DMSDROID infers executable actions in the current state by analyzing the dumped widget hierarchy.

$$selectAction(s) = \begin{cases} argmax_a Q(s,a) & 1-\epsilon \\ random\ UI\ event & \frac{1}{2}\epsilon \\ random\ system\ event & \frac{1}{2}\epsilon \end{cases} \tag{2}$$

Equation (2) describes the ϵ *-greedy* policy that is utilized by DMSDROID to select the next action. The ϵ value is set to 0.2 in DMSDROID. DMSDROID selects the event with the highest Q-value in the Q-table with a probability of 0.8. For random UI events and system-level events, it has a probability of 0.1 to select.

R: Reward. The reward in GUI testing is a numerical value assigned to a specific state or state-action pair. To explore the apps more effectively, we take the exploration of DMF and DMFSQs as important considerations.

Reward Function. DMSDROID aims to effectively guide the test agent in exploring DMFs and discovering deep-hidden bugs. The functional reward r_{fun} is defined by (3). Based on the DMFs extracted in the depth-first testing exploration, we calculate the functional semantics reward from three aspects. First, we use $h(s,a)$ to calculate whether the current operation matches any key step of the function extraction rule. If it matchs, rewards 1, otherwise rewards 0. Then we use the sliding window algorithm to obtain the part of the DMFs E_{fun} in the entire execution trace E. We calculate the proportion of explored DMFs in the execution trace, i.e., $\frac{|E_{fun}|}{|E|}$. Finally, we set a semantic sequence Seq_{bug} to calculate the proportion of DMFSQs that are valid and promising to trigger bugs, which is recorded as $\frac{g(E_{fun},Seq_{bug})}{|E_{fun}|}$.

$$r_{fun} = h(s,a) + \frac{|E_{fun}|}{|E|} + \frac{g(E_{fun},Seq_{bug})}{|E_{fun}|} \tag{3}$$

Furthermore, solely depending on rewards linked to functional semantics could result in explorers getting stuck in exploration errors characterized by sparse rewards. Hence, drawing from prior research, we introduced the r_{basic} (4) parameter to mitigate this risk. $f(s,a,E)$ is used to calculate the frequency of occurrence of (s,a) in the current execution trace E.

$$r_{basic} = -f(s,a,E) \tag{4}$$

The final reward function can be expressed as $r_{fun} + r_{basic}$.

Functional Semantics Guided Exploration. We employ Q-learning algorithm to achieve a functional semantics guided exploration strategy. The function *FunctionalGuidedExploration* in Algorithm 2 describes the detail of functional

Algorithm 2: Functional Semantics Guided Exploration

1 **Function** *FunctionGuidedExploration(Σ, app)*
2 $Q \leftarrow$ **InitQTable(Σ)** `// initialize Q-table`
3 $C \leftarrow \varnothing$ `// save executed DMFs`
4 $E \leftarrow$ **List()** `// save the execution trace`
5 **while** $\neg isTimeOver()$ **do**
6 $s_t, actions_t \leftarrow getPageDetails()$
7 **foreach** $action_t \in actions_t$ **do**
8 **if** $action_t \notin Q$ **then**
9 $setQvalue(Q, s_t, action_t, Q_{init})$
10 $a_t \leftarrow selectAction(Q, s_t)$
11 $s_{t+1} \leftarrow executeAction(app, a_t)$
12 $E.append(s_t, a_t)$
13 $E_{fun} \leftarrow getCurFn(seq)$ `// Get current DMF using a sliding window`
14 $r_{fun}, r_{basic} \leftarrow getReward(s_t, a_t, E, E_{fun}, C)$
15 $Q(s_t, a_t) \leftarrow Q(s_t, a_t) + \alpha(r_{fun} + r_{basic} + \gamma \max_a Q(s_{t+1}, a) - Q(s_t, a_t))$
16 **if** $E_{fun} \neq null \wedge intent \notin C$ **then** `// new DMF`
17 $C \leftarrow C \cup E_{fun}$
18 **return** Q

semantics guided exploration strategy. First, DmsDroid assign an inital value of the Q-table based on the extracted DMFs' collection Σ (line 2). DmsDroid get the detail of GUI page, including state s_t and find out all the executable actions $actions_t$ (line 5). Q-table records the value of each action or assign an initial value if it is executed for the first time (line 8, 9). Then DmsDroid employs (2) to select an action a_t. DmsDroid executes a_t and saves the exploring state and action into E (line 10–12). Then DmsDroid obtain the part of the DMF E_{fun} in the entire execution trace E (line 13). Based on s_t, a_t and E_{fun}, DmsDroid calculates the functional reward r_{fun} by (3) and the basic reward by (4) (line 14, 15). After extensive experimentation, γ is set to 0.9 in DmsDroid to strengthen the impact of unexplored functions. The $Q_{max}(s_{t+1}, a_{t+1})$ will be relatively higher for unexplored DMFs. Benefiting from the propagation property of Q-value, the change of reward can guide the agent in DmsDroid to explore more meaningful test cases (line 16). For subsequent guided exploration, when the agent discovers new DMFs, it store them in the set C (line 16–17).

DmsDroid extracts valuable insights by calculating the explored DMFs and potential error-triggering DMFSQs. The Q-learning agent can explore different cases that contain multiple DMFs and various execution orders of DMFs. Additionally, it employs a frequency penalty to optimize action exploration, thereby enhancing learning and system stability with each iteration.

5 Evaluation

In our experimental evaluation, we seek to answer three questions:

RQ1: **Functions Extraction.** How efficiently does DmsDroid extract DMFs from the apps, as measured by concrete metrics?

RQ2: **Testing Efficiency.** How does the testing coverage and bug detection performance of DmsDroid compare to other popular testing tools?
RQ3: **DMFs Usefulness.** How effective are the DMFs and DMFSQs in improving the testing effectiveness?

5.1 Experiment Setup

Tool Implementation. DmsDroid reuses and extends the testing techniques: DroidBot [22] is the foundation for our tool for generating UTG. Android Debug Bridge(ADB) [2] for sending UI events, and Logcat [3] for recording the execution of DMFs and monitoring runtime exceptions.

Table 2. Testing Results of 16 open-source apps

Target APP		% Coverage							# Crashes						
App Name	**ELOC**	**M**	**Q**	**Cb**	**Pb**	**Dm**	**Dm$^{\alpha}$**	**Dm$^{\beta}$**	**M**	**Q**	**Cb**	**Pb**	**Dm**	**Dm$^{\alpha}$**	**Dm$^{\beta}$**
BookCatalogue	75241	12	38	42	32	36	32	34	1	2	2	3	1	2	3
Amaze	60325	27	34	40	30	40	23	28	1	4	3	0	3	3	2
K9Mail	93455	18	15	26	21	27	22	25	1	1	1	0	2	2	1
AnyMemo	30661	31	55	64	45	48	55	35	1	0	1	1	3	2	1
BudgetWatch	9863	43	45	63	40	57	59	46	1	1	0	2	1	1	2
CatimaLoyalty	11547	34	22	61	48	66	50	55	1	0	2	1	1	0	0
Uhabits	10296	35	40	38	45	42	30	42	2	0	0	1	1	3	2
Runnerup	40001	28	24	38	36	35	30	44	0	2	0	0	0	0	0
TrackandGraph	16991	19	43	18	40	45	47	52	0	0	1	0	2	0	2
PhonographPlus	43261	14	20	14	26	30	34	44	0	0	0	1	2	1	1
GrowTracker	15339	22	32	45	31	50	34	36	1	1	1	1	2	1	2
Notally	1559	37	45	56	36	54	60	58	0	0	1	0	1	0	0
OmniNotes	28462	22	21	29	30	44	37	23	2	0	1	0	2	2	1
Activitydiary	9254	39	71	55	54	67	53	73	0	1	0	2	0	0	0
Markor	25674	21	-	-	46	45	43	37	1	-	-	2	1	1	1
Antennapod	117753	15	28	19	23	30	24	21	0	0	0	1	0	0	1
Average/Sum	-	26.06	35.53	40.53	36.43	44.75	39.56	40.81	12	12	13	15	22	18	19

[1] Column **M**, **Q**, **Cb**, **Pb** and **Dm** denote Monkey, Q-testing, ComboDroid and DmsDroid.
[2] Markor failed during testing with Q-testing and ComboDroid, resulting in empty data.

App Subjects. The first column of Table 2 lists the 16 evaluation subjects, selected according to the following rules. First, we selected the five large apps evaluated in existing work (with ELOC greater than 50,000): BookCatelogue, AmazeFileManager, AntennaPod, Markor and K9-mail. Second, we selected six apps with at least 5K Downloads evaluated in the existing work: Budget Watch, Runnerup, AnyMemo, Uhabits, OmniNotes and Catima. Additionally, we randomly selected three popular open-source apps from GitHub (at least 100 stars by 2023): ActivityDiary, PhonographPlus, Track&Graph, and GrowTracker.

Execution Environment. All the 16 open-source apps ran on Android emulators (Marshmallow version, Android 7.0) deployed on a 64-bit Ubuntu physical machine with Intel(R) Core(TM) i5-12490F CPU and 32 GB RAM. For each emulator, we allocated 2 GB RAM and stored different types of external files in SDCard for ensuring file access of apps.

Bug and Coverage Metrics. We measure the thoroughness of testing using two metrics. The first is bytecode instruction coverage collected by JaCoCo [17], as a higher code coverage strongly correlates to a better exercise of an app's functions. Second, we study whether the techniques can manifest previously bugs by examining the Android system's logs. For bugs, we refer to the definition of fault in stoat [32]. Bugs are identified by crash or exception lines in stack traces (exceptions without AUT package name keywords are excluded). We review the bug log, remove duplicates, exclude non-app errors (e.g., network errors).

Evaluation Setup of RQ1. To evaluate the extraction ability of DMFs in each app, we manually organized all relevant DMFs in the AUTs. The co-authors analyze the GUIs of the DMFs in each app and collect them as a basis for evaluation. To ensure the completeness and accuracy, each author first collects the DMFs in AUTs and then discussed, adjusted and merged all the DMFs collected by each individual. In total, we collected 133 DMFs for 16 apps.The functions which are collected manually are regarded as correctly extracted.

We employ three evaluation metrics to evaluate the performance of DMFs extraction. Precision is the proportion of DMFs that are correctly extracted among all extracted functions. Recall is the proportion of DMFs that are correctly extracted among all DMFs. F1-score is the harmonic mean of precision and recall, which combine both of the two metrics above. For all metrics, a higher value represents better performance. In order to prevent the inaccuracy, we extracted DMFs 5 times for 16 apps, and each extraction took 1 h.

Evaluation Setup of RQ2. In this part of evaluation, DmsDroid is compared with Monkey , Q-testing, PbfDroid and ComboDroid.

Monkey is a widely-used state-of-practice testing tool based on random events. Q-testing is a state-of-art testing tool that bases on Q-learning. Q-testing employs a curiosity-driven exploration strategy to select events. ComboDroid is a model-based tool employing the idea of combining short sequences to generate meaningful and extensive test cases. PbfDroid is a property-based tool with a focus on combining DMFs to detect bugs in the apps. It collects DMFs manually and explores pages related to DMFs.

According to previous work, the testing time of each tool is set to two hours for full exploration, and each tool tested 5 times. We set 200 milliseconds event interval for Monkey. Q-testing is a closed-source testing tool, so we adopted the default configuration. For ComboDroid, the 2-h testing time includes the time obtaining use cases and enmuerating use cases combos. PbfDroid is a semi-automated functional bug testing tool. The authors manually collected DMFs in advance according to the user manual and set PbfDroid to execute events with a maximum time of 2 h. We allocated 1 h for DmsDroid to extract the DMFs and 1 h for functional semantics guided exploration.

Evaluation Setup of RQ3. DmsDroid extracts the DMFs and use the functional semantics to guided the exploration, which aims to find more deep-hidden bugs. Thus, we implemented two versions of DmsDroid as the baselines to evaluate the effectiveness of these strategies.

- DmsDroid$^{\alpha}$: This baseline comparison aims to evaluate the effectiveness of the functional semantics guided exploration. Specifically, for the workflow in Fig. 3, DmsDroid$^{\alpha}$ only runs $Stage_1$ (Depth-first Exploration) but without $Stage_2$ (Functional Semantics Guided Exploration). In the second hour of testing, DmsDroid$^{\alpha}$ will no longer give rewards. If DmsDroid outperforms DmsDroid$^{\alpha}$, functional semantics guided exploration is proven beneficial.
- DmsDroid$^{\beta}$: This baseline comparison aims to evaluate the necessity of extracting DMFs, the effectiveness of the reward function based on DMFs and DMFSQs. Specifically, for the workflow in Fig. 3, DmsDroid$^{\beta}$ only runs $Stage_2$ (Functional semantics guided exploration) and limits the functional reward to only $h(s, a)$. If DmsDroid outperforms DmsDroid$^{\beta}$, it proves the necessity of DMF extraction and the effectiveness of the reward function based on DMFs and DMFSQs.

5.2 Experimental Results

Answer to RQ1: Figure 4 shows the effectiveness of DmsDroid in extracting DMFs. The horizontal axis marks metrics, and vertical axis corresponds to the values. DmsDroid was able to extract 87.72% DMFs (recall values range from 0.577 to 1.0), indicating that the extraction strategy is effective.

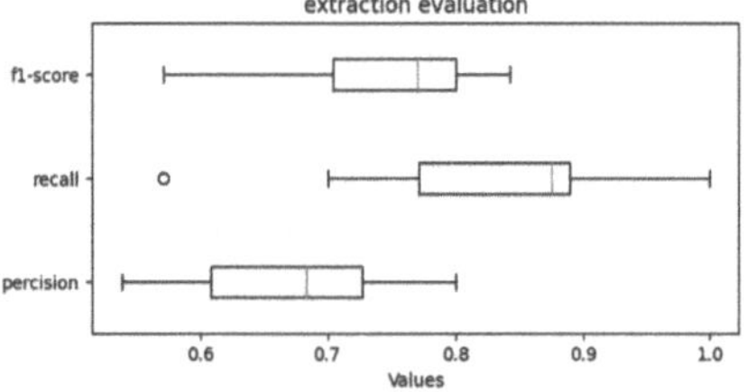

Fig. 4. DMF extraction evaluation Result

However, DmsDroid does not extract DMFs accurately enough (prediction values range from 0.535 to 0.809). We speculate that there are three reasons. First, some developers name DMF-related buttons without clear semantics during the development process. In GrowTracker, the *Navigate up* button submits new plant data. DmsDroid has no way to recognize such a submit button, resulting in missing some DMFs. Second, there are many useless extracted event sequences, most of them belong to the wrongly extracted *Read* DMF, whose pattern is relatively simple. Thirdly, during the automatic extraction of DMF, the explored actions are not explored again, leading to miss some DMFs.

Overall, the result of extraction experiment is reasonable. The recall rate shows that the most of confirmed DMFs can be executed. DmsDroid can do subsequent functional semantics guide exploration based on the extracted DMFs.

In summary, DmsDroid *can extract DMFs in real time within one hour of exploration, and its integrity is guaranteed.*

Answer to RQ2: Table 2 shows the achieved code coverage and revealed bugs of five testing tools (Monkey, Q-testing, ComboDroid, PbfDroid and DmsDroid) and the gray cell denotes which tool covers the highest coverage or discovers the most bugs. The last line in Table 2 gives the overall average result of 16 apps. For coverage, DmsDroid achieves 44.75% on average and much

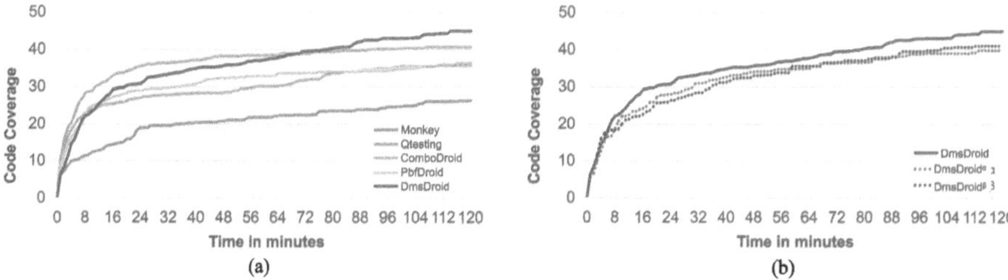

Fig. 5. The achieved code coverage over execution time. (a) shows the coverage changes of DmsDroid compared with other testing tools; (b) shows the coverage changes of DmsDroid compared with its two versions (DmsDroid$^{\alpha}$ and DmsDroid$^{\beta}$).

higher than Monkey (26.06%), Q-testing (35.53%), ComboDroid (40.53%) and PbfDroid(36.43%). For bugs, DmsDroid detects 22 bugs, which is 1.8 times Monkey and Q-testing (12), 1.7 times ComboDroid (13) and 1.46 times PbfDroid(15). Note that the bug detection efficacy of PbfDroid in this paper is limited as the bug definition here excludes functional bugs.

Figure 5.a depict the average instruction coverage over execution time. Monkey has a relatively slower coverage growth due to its random strategy. Before the 13th minute, DmsDroid does not perform as well as others. This situation is because (1) Q-testing is driven by curiosity exploration; (2) PbfDroid uses DMF extracted manually in advance for combination; (3) ComboDroid fully combines a large number of event sequences with dataflow. However, since PbfDroid relies heavily on manual DMF collection, it miss simple operational bugs, resulting in subsequent slow coverage growth. After the 71th minute, the code coverage of DmsDroid gradually exceeds that of ComboDroid. Because in the second stage, DmsDroid adopts the exploration strategy of reinforcement learning, to effectively combine the DMFs generated in $Stage_1$.

To prove the authenticity of the bugs discovered by DmsDroid, we have reported these bugs to developers. So far, 7 reported bugs have been confirmed, shown in Table 3. For the bugs triggered by DMFs, Monkey and Q-testing is hard to detect, because they are more concerned with the single execution event, rather than the complete execution of the functions. ComboDroid, PbfDroid and DmsDroid could detect the most deep-hidden bugs triggered by DMFs. However, ComboDroid and PbfDroid use a cross-enumeration method to combine these sequences, which takes longer to detect deep-hidden problems.

In summary, DmsDroid *achieves the highest code coverage and reveals the most bugs on 16 target apps when comparing to other testing tools.*

Answer to RQ3. Table 2 shows the testing effectiveness of DmsDroid$^{\alpha}$ and DmsDroid$^{\beta}$. For the achieved code coverage, DmsDroid achieve 44.75% code coverage higher than DmsDroid$^{\alpha}$ (39.56%) and DmsDroid$^{\beta}$ (40.81%). For bugs, DmsDroid detects 20 bugs, more than DmsDroid$^{\alpha}$(15) and DmsDroid$^{\beta}$(16).

Table 3. Confirmed bugs by testing tools

ID	App Name	Discovered by	status	Functional semantics	Cause
1	GrowTracker	All	confirmed	Create, Update	IndexoutOfboundExceptions
2	Anymemo	Dm, Cb, Pb	waiting	Create, Read, Delete	NullPointerExceptions
3	K9mail	Dm	fixed	Create	SettingsImportExportException
4	Uhabits	Dm,Q,M	fixed	–	ClassNotFoundException
5	PhonographPlus	Dm, Pb	fixed	Create, Read,Update	IllegalArgumentException
6	Track&graph	All	confirmed	–	ConcurrentModificationException
7	Amaze	Dm	confirmed	Create	StringIndexOutOfBoundsException
8	Amaze	Dm,Q,Cb,Pb	fixed	Create,Delete(Update)	NullPointerException

[1] **All** denotes that all tools dircovered this bug. **M**, **Q**, **Cb**, **Pb** and **Dm** denote MONKEY, Q-TESTING, COMBODROID, PBFDROID and DMSDROID, respectively.

Figure 5.b shows the achieved code coverage over execution time for DMSDROID, DMSDROID$^{\alpha}$ and DMSDROID$^{\beta}$. The coverage changes of DMSDROID is better than DMSDROID$^{\alpha}$ and DMSDROID$^{\beta}$, which proves the usefulness of DMFs. The coverage changes of DMSDROID$^{\beta}$ and DMSDROID$^{\alpha}$ are similar. DMSDROID$^{\alpha}$ use depth-first strategy to fully explore the paths in AUT, while DMSDROID$^{\beta}$ uses the exploration strategy of reinforcement learning to perform more operations related to DMFs. Since DMSDROID$^{\beta}$ will briefly fall into the sparse reward problem of reinforcement learning when not enough events are clicked, the code coverage is lower than DMSDROID$^{\alpha}$ before 59th minutes. After breaking away from sparse rewards, the code coverage of DMSDROID$^{\beta}$ gradually surpassed DMSDROID$^{\alpha}$.

When the 2-hour test ends, the coverage and bug detection effect of DMSDROID$^{\alpha}$ is relatively worse than that of DMSDROID$^{\beta}$. Because DMSDROID$^{\alpha}$ only uses depth-first exploration to traverse the AUT, while DMSDROID$^{\beta}$ uses reinforcement learning to enable the tester to continuously learn to adjust events, and generate test cases with DMFs to improve testing efficiency.

In summary, DMSDROID *can generate meaningful DMFSQs for testing. Both the extraction of DMFs and the use of DMFSQs for exploration are essential.*

6 Related Work

Recently, there has been a surge of interest in the realm of automated testing for Android apps. The work related to the paper is as follows:

Generic Automated Testing Tools for Android Apps. A variety of automated GUI testing tools have been developed for ensuring the reliability and quality of Android apps. Random testing tools [1,8,18,25] utilize stochastic methods to explore the app's behavior and generating random sequences of events. Model-based testing tools [7,10,11,13,24,32] leverage formal models of the app to systematically generate test cases. Search-based testing tools [5,12,22,26,27] efficiently find bugs by searching through lots of possible test inputs.

Reinforcement Learning-based Testing Tools. The reinforcement learning based testing tools [4,19–21,30,31,35] dynamically adapt the test strategy based on feedback from the app's execution, optimizing the testing process over time. Q-TESTING [30] designs a curiosity-driven exploration strategy to explore previously unvisited GUI pages. ARES [31] and DQT [21] uses deep reinforcement learning for black-box testing of apps. ICCDROID [15] designs an ICC-guided exploration strategy to systematically test intents in the app.

Testing Tools Related with Functional Semantics. The testing exploration strategies of some tools [14,28,33] are related to functional semantics. SQDROID [14] designs a dynamic semantic reward function to understand the business logic of apps to find deep bugs. PBFDROID [33] finds DMFs in the app and detects the bugs by randomly interleaving the functions. AUGUSTO [28] tests one CRUD operation independently, and does not consider their combinations.

The testing tools do not explicitly account for DMF execution. Our approach find the app crashes guided by the functional semantics in DMFs. To ensure the efficiency of bug detection, we use Q-learning to guide testing exploration.

7 Conclusion

In this paper, we propose a novel approach to find deep-hidden bugs triggered by data manipulation functions (DMFs). After surveying app GUIs, we defined an extraction rule and designed a real-time algorithm to extract DMFs while detecting regular bugs. To detect deep-hidden bugs, we design the Q-learning based functional semantics guided exploration strategy by extracted DMFs. The realization of our idea, DMSDROID, has detected 1.4 to 1.8 times more bugs in 16 apps, outperforming other tools. We have reported previously unreported bugs to the developers, with 75% of them being related to DMFs. So far, 7 reported bugs have been confirmed and 4 of which have already been fixed. In our future work, we will enhance DMSDROID's performance and explore ways to generate bug reports with functional semantics during testing to assist developers to reproduce deep-hidden bugs.

References

1. Ui/application exerciser monkey (2022). https://developer.android.com/studio/test/monkey
2. Android debug bridge (2023). https://developer.android.com/studio/command-line/adb
3. Logcat command-line tool (2023). https://developer.android.com/studio/command-line/logcat
4. Adamo, D., Khan, M.K., Koppula, S., Bryce, R.: Reinforcement learning for android GUI testing. In: Proceedings of the 9th ACM SIGSOFT International Workshop on Automating TEST Case Design, Selection, and Evaluation, pp. 2–8 (2018)

5. Amalfitano, D., Amatucci, N., Fasolino, A.R., Tramontana, P.: Agrippin: a novel search based testing technique for android applications. In: Proceedings of the 3rd International Workshop on Software Development Lifecycle for Mobile, pp. 5–12 (2015)
6. Amalfitano, D., Fasolino, A.R., Tramontana, P., De Carmine, S., Memon, A.M.: Using GUI ripping for automated testing of android applications. In: Proceedings of the 27th IEEE/ACM International Conference on Automated Software Engineering, pp. 258–261 (2012)
7. Amalfitano, D., Fasolino, A.R., Tramontana, P., Ta, B.D., Memon, A.M.: Mobiguitar: automated model-based testing of mobile apps. IEEE Softw. **32**(5), 53–59 (2015). https://doi.org/10.1109/MS.2014.55
8. Arcuri, A., Briand, L.: A hitchhiker's guide to statistical tests for assessing randomized algorithms in software engineering. Softw. Test. Verif. Reliab. **24**(3), 219–250 (2014)
9. Azim, T., Neamtiu, I.: Targeted and depth-first exploration for systematic testing of android apps. In: Proceedings of the 2013 ACM SIGPLAN International Conference on Object Oriented Programming Systems Languages & Applications, pp. 641–660 (2013)
10. Baek, Y.M., Bae, D.H.: Automated model-based android GUI testing using multi-level GUI comparison criteria. In: Proceedings of the 31st IEEE/ACM International Conference on Automated Software Engineering, pp. 238–249 (2016)
11. Cai, T., Zhang, Z., Yang, P.: Fastbot: a multi-agent model-based test generation system Beijing Bytedance network technology co., ltd. In: Proceedings of the IEEE/ACM 1st International Conference on Automation of Software Test, pp. 93–96 (2020)
12. Dong, Z., Böhme, M., Cojocaru, L., Roychoudhury, A.: Time-travel testing of android apps. In: Proceedings of the ACM/IEEE 42nd International Conference on Software Engineering, pp. 481–492 (2020)
13. Gu, T., et al.: Practical GUI testing of android applications via model abstraction and refinement. In: 2019 IEEE/ACM 41st International Conference on Software Engineering (ICSE), pp. 269–280. IEEE (2019)
14. Guo, H., Liu, X., Li, B., Cai, L., Hu, Y., Cao, J.: Sqdroid: a semantic-driven testing for android apps via q-learning. In: 2021 IEEE 21st International Conference on Software Quality, Reliability and Security (QRS), pp. 301–310. IEEE (2021)
15. Guo, H., Su, T., Liu, X., Gu, S., Sun, J.: Effectively finding ICC-related bugs in android apps via reinforcement learning. In: 34th IEEE International Symposium on Software Reliability Engineering (ISSRE) (2023)
16. Hu, C., Neamtiu, I.: Automating GUI testing for android applications. In: Proceedings of the 6th International Workshop on Automation of Software Test, pp. 77–83 (2011)
17. KG, M.G..C., Contributors: Jacoco - java code coverage library (2019). https://www.jacoco.org/jacoco/trunk/index.html. Accessed 7 Aug 2019
18. Kong, P., Li, L., Gao, J., Liu, K., Bissyandé, T.F., Klein, J.: Automated testing of android apps: a systematic literature review. IEEE Trans. Reliab. **68**(1), 45–66 (2018)
19. Koroglu, Y., Sen, A.: Reinforcement learning-driven test generation for android GUI applications using formal specifications. arXiv preprint arXiv:1911.05403 (2019)
20. Koroglu, Y., et al.: QBE: qlearning-based exploration of android applications. In: 2018 IEEE 11th International Conference on Software Testing, Verification and Validation (ICST), pp. 105–115. IEEE (2018)

21. Lan, Y., et al.: Deeply reinforcing android GUI testing with deep reinforcement learning. In: Proceedings of the 46th IEEE/ACM International Conference on Software Engineering, pp. 1–13 (2024)
22. Li, Y., Yang, Z., Guo, Y., Chen, X.: Droidbot: a lightweight UI-guided test input generator for android. In: 2017 IEEE/ACM 39th International Conference on Software Engineering Companion (ICSE-C), pp. 23–26. IEEE (2017)
23. Li, Y., Yang, Z., Guo, Y., Chen, X.: Humanoid: a deep learning-based approach to automated black-box android app testing. In: 2019 34th IEEE/ACM International Conference on Automated Software Engineering (ASE), pp. 1070–1073. IEEE (2019)
24. Lv, Z., Peng, C., Zhang, Z., Su, T., Liu, K., Yang, P.: Fastbot2: reusable automated model-based GUI testing for android enhanced by reinforcement learning. In: Proceedings of the 37th IEEE/ACM International Conference on Automated Software Engineering, pp. 1–5 (2022)
25. Machiry, A., Tahiliani, R., Naik, M.: Dynodroid: an input generation system for android apps. In: Proceedings of the 2013 9th Joint Meeting on Foundations of Software Engineering, pp. 224–234 (2013)
26. Mahmood, R., Mirzaei, N., Malek, S.: Evodroid: segmented evolutionary testing of android apps. In: Proceedings of the 22nd ACM SIGSOFT International Symposium on Foundations of Software Engineering, pp. 599–609 (2014)
27. Mao, K., Harman, M., Jia, Y.: Sapienz: multi-objective automated testing for android applications. In: Proceedings of the 25th International Symposium on Software Testing and Analysis, pp. 94–105 (2016)
28. Mariani, L., Pezzè, M., Zuddas, D.: Augusto: exploiting popular functionalities for the generation of semantic GUI tests with oracles. In: Proceedings of the 40th International Conference on Software Engineering, pp. 280–290 (2018)
29. Nguyen, C.D., Marchetto, A., Tonella, P.: Combining model-based and combinatorial testing for effective test case generation. In: Proceedings of the 2012 International Symposium on Software Testing and Analysis, pp. 100–110 (2012)
30. Pan, M., Huang, A., Wang, G., Zhang, T., Li, X.: Reinforcement learning based curiosity-driven testing of android applications. In: Proceedings of the 29th ACM SIGSOFT International Symposium on Software Testing and Analysis, pp. 153–164 (2020)
31. Romdhana, A., Merlo, A., Ceccato, M., Tonella, P.: Deep reinforcement learning for black-box testing of android apps. ACM Trans. Softw. Eng. Methodol. (TOSEM) **31**(4), 1–29 (2022)
32. Su, T., et al.: Guided, stochastic model-based GUI testing of android apps. In: Proceedings of the 2017 11th Joint Meeting on Foundations of Software Engineering, pp. 245–256 (2017)
33. Sun, J., Su, T., Jiang, J., Wang, J., Pu, G., Su, Z.: Property-based fuzzing for finding data manipulation errors in android apps. In: Proceedings of the 31st ACM Joint European Software Engineering Conference and Symposium on the Foundations of Software Engineering (ESEC/FSE '23). ACM (2023)
34. Sutton, R.S., Barto, A.G.: Reinforcement Learning: An Introduction. MIT Press, Cambridge (2018)
35. Vuong, T.A.T., Takada, S.: A reinforcement learning based approach to automated testing of android applications. In: Proceedings of the 9th ACM SIGSOFT International Workshop on Automating TEST Case Design, Selection, and Evaluation, pp. 31–37 (2018)

36. Wang, J., Jiang, Y., Xu, C., Cao, C., Ma, X., Lu, J.: Combodroid: generating high-quality test inputs for android apps via use case combinations. In: Proceedings of the ACM/IEEE 42nd International Conference on Software Engineering, pp. 469–480 (2020)
37. Watkins, C.J., Dayan, P.: Q-learning. Mach. Learn. **8**, 279–292 (1992)
38. Zhang, J., Sagar, S., Shihab, E.: The evolution of mobile apps: an exploratory study. In: Proceedings of the 2013 International Workshop on Software Development Lifecycle for Mobile, pp. 1–8 (2013)

Detecting Vulnerabilities via Explicitly Leveraging Vulnerability Features on Program Slices

Haoyu Guo, Xiaodong Zhang(✉), Zhiwei Zhang, and Yulong Shen

Xidian University, Xi'an, Shan Xi 710071, China
ghy@stu.xidian.edu.cn, {zhangxiaodong,zwzhang}@xidian.edu.cn, ylshen@mail.xidian.edu.cn

Abstract. As the size and complexity of software continue to increase, detecting software vulnerabilities becomes increasingly challenging. Traditional static and dynamic analysis methods often suffer from poor accuracy or little reliance on expert knowledge. In recent years, deep learning has emerged as a promising direction in this field due to its ability to automatically learn the subtle features in the massive software data. However, existing deep learning-based vulnerability detection methods have the following limitations: 1) They struggle with processing long source code sequences effectively, leading to sub-optimal feature representation. 2) Although they can find similar vulnerability features across different vulnerable programs, they often fail to explicitly leverage these vulnerability features, resulting in slightly inferior performance of model detection. In this paper, we propose a vulnerability detection method called DV-LVF, based on explicitly leveraging vulnerability features on program slices, to effectively detect vulnerabilities at both function and statement levels. Specifically, we introduce Gated Recurrent Unit (GRU) statement embedding technique combined with program slicing to enhance program feature representation. We introduce a vulnerability dictionary (vulDict), which can explicitly summarize and exploit these vulnerability features, to improve the performance of model detection. Our evaluation on real-world software shows that DV-LVF outperforms the state-of-the-art in both function-level and statement-level detection.

Keywords: Vulnerability detection · Vulnerability features · Deep learning

1 Introduction

In recent years, the global software market has been continuously expanding. According to Gartner data, global information technology spending is projected to reach $4.7 trillion by 2023. Concurrently, the number and complexity of software vulnerabilities are also increasing gradually. According to data from the

W.-N. Chin and Z. Xu (Eds.): TASE 2024, LNCS 14777, pp. 165–185, 2024.
https://doi.org/10.1007/978-3-031-64626-3_10

national vulnerability database, as of December 2023, the number of newly added vulnerabilities reached as high as 30,947, an increase of 14.59% compared to 2022, bringing the total number of vulnerabilities to 222,998. This marks the highest number of vulnerabilities ever reported within a year. These data clearly demonstrate the current urgent situation of software vulnerability attacks: the number of vulnerabilities is growing rapidly, the attack speed continues to increase, and the impact is gradually escalating. Threat parties are more focused on sensitive assets, and the destructive index continues to rise. In view of this situation, efficient and accurate detection of software vulnerabilities has become especially necessary.

Existing vulnerability detection methods can be categorized into static analysis-based, dynamic analysis-based and deep learning-based methods. Static analysis method is to analyze the program source code from the syntactic or semantic level to deduce its syntactic or semantic properties, e.g. [1–3]. However, these methods are prone to actual unreachable situations, and it takes a lot of time to judge the feasibility of abstract paths, so it can easily lead to a high false alarm rate. The dynamic analysis method is to obtain and analyze the runtime information by determining the semantic properties of its runtime, e.g. [4–6]. Dynamic analysis only focuses on obtaining the actual feasible path and reachable status of the program, thereby ensuring that the analysis results have no false positives. However, due to the inability to cover all possible execution paths during program execution, this often leads to a higher rate of missed vulnerabilities. Additionally, both static analysis and dynamic analysis methods are constrained by expert knowledge and have certain limitations [7]. More importantly, the most crucial issue is that when faced with the large-scale software vulnerabilities of today, their detection effectiveness is not ideal [17].

In order to solve the limitations of traditional methods, researchers have proposed a series of new approaches utilizing deep learning techniques, e.g., Recurrent Neural Network (RNN)-based [7–10,18,22,26,27,35,36], Graph Neural Network (GNN)-based [11,12,33,34,37], as well as Transformer-based [13–15,31,32,38]. These methods mainly relys on the unique advantages of deep learning, which does not require manual feature extraction, thereby significantly reducing the consumption of manual resources. These studies have fully confirmed the effectiveness of deep learning in the field of vulnerability detection, and achieved high detection accuracy on experimental data sets, far exceeding traditional vulnerability detection methods. However, existing methods based on deep learning still have some limitations: 1) The program source code features they extract are not ideal, mainly because they mostly employ direct truncation operations, resulting in the loss of some features. For example, methods based on Transformer typically truncate at 512 tokens, which only fully covers 86% of the function code in the dataset. 2) Most of the models proposed in these studies have slightly inferior detection performance because existing methods lack the extraction and utilization of vulnerability features. These challenges indeed impede the further development of deep learning methods.

In this work, we propose a vulnerability detection method called DV-LVF, which is based on explicitly leveraging vulnerability features on program slices to effectively detect vulnerabilities at both the function and statement levels. In DV-LVF, we introduce a technique called GRU statement embedding, combined with program slicing technology, to obtain **a more comprehensive representation of program features**, addressing the issue of feature loss in the preprocessing stage. To further enhance the model's performance, we propose a method for explicitly utilizing vulnerability features for detection, thereby **increasing the model's sensitivity and detection capability for vulnerabilities**. Specifically, we introduce the concept of vulDict, which extracts vulnerability features from program slice vectors and constructs them using clustering algorithms. During training and inference, we embed source code into elements of vulDict to identify the most similar cluster centers. Finally, through a composite classifier, we achieve detection at both the function and statement levels to improve the model's detection performance. Additionally, we introduce the concept of top-k statement prediction, which identifies the k statements most likely to contain vulnerabilities in the vulnerable function to **accurately locate vulnerable statements**.

Experimental results show that our method can handle up to 3000 tokens, 6 times the 512 tokens set in the pre-trained model [28,29], and can fully represent 99% of the data in the dataset. Furthermore, our method outperforms the state-of-the-art in terms of F1 scores at both function-level prediction and statement-level prediction. For top-k statement-level prediction, when $k = 5$, the accuracy has reached 99.11%, that is, there is a 99.11% probability that there will be a vulnerable statement in these three statements. The overall results verify the effectiveness of DV-LVF. Our code is available at: https://github.com/1272383808/DV-LVF.

The key contributions of this work are as follows.

1. We propose a novel vulnerability detection method, called DV-LVF, to effectively detect vulnerabilities at both function and statement levels.
2. In the preprocessing stage, we propose a GRU statement embedding method, combined with program slicing technology [22], to achieve a complete feature representation of the function source code.
3. We introduced vulDict, which is constructed by extracting vulnerability feature information. During both training and inference stages, we match vulDict with the code under inspection to detect vulnerabilities more effectively.
4. We conduct a comprehensive evaluation on high-quality C/C++ vulnerability datasets, and the experimental results shows our method outperforms the state-of-the-art.

This paper is organized as follows: Sect. 2 reviews related works. Section 3 introduces the specific process of DV-LVF implementation. Section 4 introduces the design of the experiment and the data sets used. Section 5 shows the experimental results and verifies the effectiveness of DV-LVF, which is then followed by a conclusion in Sect. 6.

2 Background and Related Work

2.1 Program Slicing Technique

Program slicing is a critical program analysis technique that extracts the necessary code segments from complex program code [21]. In DV-LVF, program slicing reduces detection granularity, simplifies complexity, and improves detection accuracy. Additionally, it enhances the expression of vulnerability features. In this paper, we adopt the program slicing generation method proposed by Li et al., as it has been verified to effectively extract relevant code fragments. This method summarizes four code features prone to vulnerabilities, including Library/API Function Call, Array Usage, Pointer Usage, and Arithmetic Expression. We utilize the Joern [23] tool for program slicing, with specific steps including generating the Abstract Syntax Tree (AST) of the source code and identifying vulnerability key points, followed by performing forward and backward slicing using Program Dependency Graphs (PDGs) to extract relevant code lines. Finally, we connect the forward and backward slices, remove duplicate lines, and form the final program slice. Figure 1 shows the program slice constructed for the *strncpy* key point.

```
1 void fun(){
2       char *data;
3       char *firstBuffer = (char *)alloca(50*sizeof(char));
4       char *secondBuffer = (char *)alloca(100*sizeof(char));
5       if(GLOBAL_CONSTANT_FIVE == 5){
6           data = firstBuffer;
7           data[0] = '\0';  // null terminated
8       }
9       char source[100];
10      memset(source, 'F', 100-1);  // fill with 'F'
11      source[100-1] = '\0';  // null terminated
12      strncpy(data, source, 100-1);
13      data[100-1] = '\0';
14      printf("%s\n", data);
15 }
```

```
1  void fun(){
2  char *data;
3  char *firstBuffer = (char *)alloca(50*sizeof(char));
5  if(GLOBAL_CONSTANT_FIVE == 5){
6  data = dataBadBuffer;
7  data[0] = '\0';
9  char source[100];
10 memset(source, 'F', 100-1);
11 source[100-1] = '\0';
12 strncpy(data, source, 100-1);
13 data[100-1] = '\0';
14 printf("%s\n", data);
```

Fig. 1. A simple function source code along with the program slice constructed from the vulnerability key point *strncpy*.

2.2 Related Work

With the advancement of deep learning technology, researchers have proposed various vulnerability detection methods based on deep learning. These methods include ICVH [36], SyseVR [22], mVulPreter [35], Vuldeepecker [7], μVulDeePecker [8], FS-VDT [9] and Vuldeelocator [10] based on RNN, LineVul [31], VELVET [32], VulD-Transformer [15], and other pre-trained models [13,14] based on Transformer [25], as well as FUNDED [11], GGNN [12], ReGVD [33], Devign [34], and VulTeller [37] based on GNN, and LineVD [38] combining Transformer and GNN. While RNN-based methods have been proven to outperform dynamic and static analysis tools in vulnerability detection, they have limitations in capturing long-term dependencies, which may lead to the loss of early sequence information and thus affect detection performance. In contrast, Transformer-based methods overcome the limitation of long-term dependency relations through attention mechanisms, enabling better capture of long-distance dependencies and further improving vulnerability detection performance. However, current methods typically rely on implicit learning of vulnerability features to detect vulnerabilities, lacking in the extraction and utilization of vulnerability features, thus limiting further improvement in model performance. Methods based on GNNs typically employ subgraph prediction to refine the granularity of detection, aiming to identify statements relevant to vulnerabilities. However, subgraphs still encompass multiple lines of code, thus remaining a coarse-grained form of detection.

Additionally, token sequence length is an important factor affecting performance [16]. Due to the difficulty of handling long sequences, SyseVR [22] and mVulPreter [35] proposed a method to extract program slices to address this issue. Their motivation is that not every line of code is equally important for vulnerability prediction. Therefore, they only consider program slices extracted from vulnerability key points for vulnerability detection, omitting the rest. This approach shortens the granularity of detection to some extent, considers more code features, and improves detection performance. However, as software scale and complexity increase, this approach still cannot fully represent the entire code.

3 Approach

The architecture of DV-LVF is illustrated in Fig. 2. First, in the preprocessing stage, we introduce GRU statement embedding method combined with program slicing to enhance program feature representation. Second, we introduce vulDict, which is obtained by clustering vulnerable code, to extract vulnerability patterns in vulnerable codes. Third, during the model training and inference stages, source code embedding is matched with elements from vulDict and processed through the CodeT5 pre-trained model and classifier. This enables DV-LVF to predict potential vulnerabilities at both function and statement levels. Next, we will introduce the components of DV-LVF and their rationality.

3.1 GRU Statement Embedding

To overcome the limitations of poor feature performance caused by long source code sequences, we propose a GRU statement embedding method [18], denoted as GRU_{stmt}, as shown in Fig. 3. This method takes advantage of the features of the GRU network and uses the number of tokens r of each code statement as the time step to aggregate the information of the entire statement. In the token sequence, each token has an impact on the network state, and the hidden state of the last time step is the synthesis of these impacts, thereby capturing the state and key information of the entire code statement. Combined with program

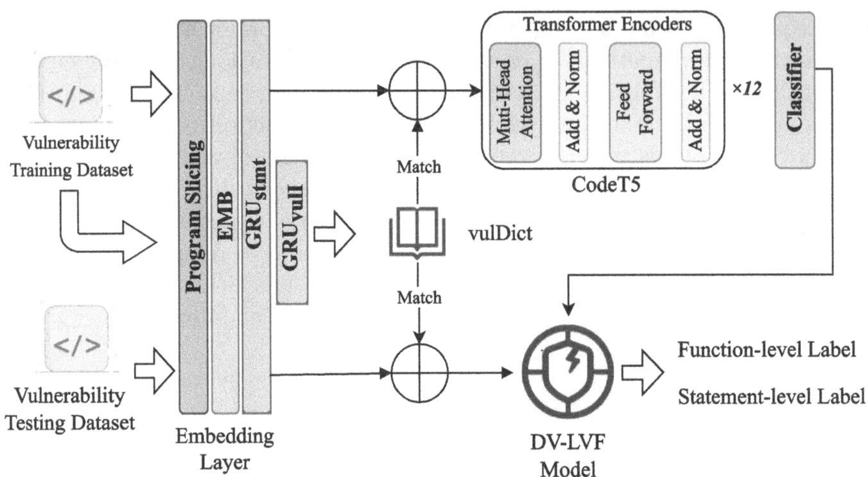

Fig. 2. Overview of DV-LVF structure

slicing technology proposed by Li et al. [22], the overall features performance of the source code can be improved.

Specifically, the function source code is sliced to obtain several program slices, one of which is represented as $S = [x_1, x_2, \ldots, x_n]$, where each x_i represents the i-th line of the slice, and there are n lines in total. Then, we use the Byte Pair Encoding (BPE) tokenizer [19] to segment x_i and obtain the token sequence $x_i = [t_1, t_2, \ldots, t_r], i \in \{1, 2, \ldots, n\}$, where r is the maximum number of tokens in the code statement. Subsequently, the vocabulary embedding layer $EMB \in \mathbb{R}^{v \times d}$ is used to obtain the token embedding of each token t_j, where v is the vocabulary size of the tokenizer and d is the embedding dimension. In this way, the token embedding matrix of each slice S can be expressed as $S' \in \mathbb{R}^{n \times r \times d}$. Embed S' into $\overline{S} \in \mathbb{R}^{n \times 1 \times d}$ to obtain the statement of slice S using GRU_{stmt}, as shown in Eq. 1.

$$\overline{S} = GRU_{stmt}(S'),\ S' \in \mathbb{R}^{n \times r \times d},\ \overline{S} \in \mathbb{R}^{n \times 1 \times d} \tag{1}$$

3.2 Constructing VulDict

Existing deep learning-based vulnerability detection methods have demonstrated that learning vulnerability features from datasets can accurately capture vulnerabilities [22,31]. However, in practical scenarios, common vulnerabilities often appear in different forms and locations, for example, the same type of vulnerability may exhibit different vulnerability features due to different coding styles. These methods typically rely on the default learning approach of deep learning for detection tasks and do not consider similar vulnerability features in vulnerability code. To overcome this limitation, we introduce the concept of vulDict (as defined in 4). VulDict clusters these vulnerability codes into a certain number

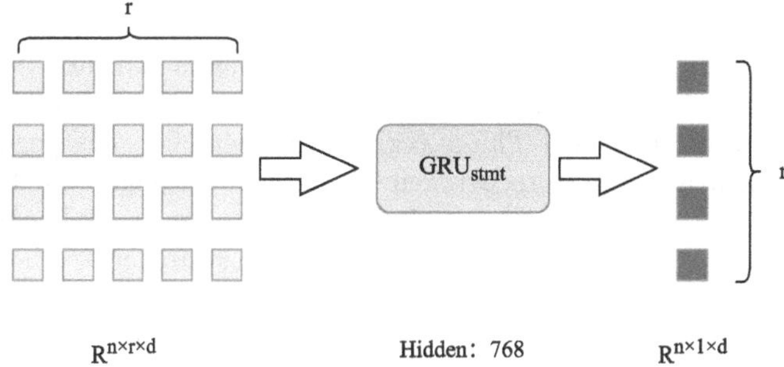

Fig. 3. GRU statement embedding method flowchart

of cluster centers (as defined in 3) to depict these similar vulnerability features. According to Definition 1, this paper considers the vulI of a program slice to be the collection of all vulnerability statements in that program slice.

Definition 1. *Vulnerability Instance (vulI) is the collection of all statements with vulnerabilities in the real vulnerable program slice.*

Definition 2. *Vulnerability Set (vulSet) is the set of vulI in all vulnerability program slices in the used vulnerability data set after certain vector transformations.*

Definition 3. *Vulnerability Center (vulCenter) is the center of a cluster obtained by applying a clustering algorithm in vulSet. Each vulCenter represents a class of similar vulI.*

Definition 4. *Vulnerability Dictionary (vulDict) is a collection that contains all vulCenter and can represent all vulI.*

The construction process of vulDict is shown in the Fig. 4, which specifically includes the following steps:

Step 1, Constructing the Program Slices. We utilize the Big-Vul dataset [20], which is currently one of the largest C/C++ function vulnerability datasets capable of extracting vulnerability labels at the statement level. We process these vulnerable functions using the program slicing technique introduced in Sect. 2.1, augmenting them with corresponding statement labels. Finally, by examining whether the statement labels contain vulnerability tags, we ascertain the presence of vulnerabilities in the program slice, thereby obtaining the desired program slice.

Step 2, Constructing vulSet. We filter out the program slices containing vulnerabilities from the generated program slices. Each program slice is represented as $S = [x_1, x_2, \ldots, x_n]$, where n is the specified Maximum number of statements per program slice. S contains several statements with and without vulnerabilities. Subsequently, the vulnerability statements in these program slices are extracted, and vulI in S is represented as $V = [y_1, y_2, \ldots, y_m]$, where m is each specified program The maximum number of vulnerable statements in a slice. Next, we use the BPE tokenizer [19] to tokenize each statement and obtain the token sequence $[t_1, t_2, \ldots, t_r]$, where r is each The maximum number of tokens per statement. Then, each token is mapped to a token ID in the vocabulary. In this step, if the number of tokens in a statement is less than r, the special token <pad> will be used to fill it; if the number of vulnerable statements is less than m, r× <pad> will be used to fill it. For sequences that are too long, truncation is performed. Next, use the embedding layer $EMB \in \mathbb{R}^{v \times d}$ to map each token t to a 768-dimensional vector, then the token embedding matrix of each vulI can Expressed as $V' \in \mathbb{R}^{m \times r \times d}$. Then, the GRU statement embedding method is used to summarize each statement of V' to obtain $\overline{V} \in \mathbb{R}^{m \times 1 \times d}$.

In order to facilitate the construction of vulSet, we use GRU_{vulI} to further summarize the statement embedding $\overline{V}$ of each vulI, and obtain the hidden state V_h (see formula 2). Then remove the first dimension of V_h, map it to the plane vector $P \in \mathbb{R}^{1 \times d}$ and add it to $vulSet \in \mathbb{R}^{a \times d}$, where a is the total number of vulnerability slices extracted. The GRU_{vulI} structure here has the same idea as GRU_{stmt}.

$$V_h = GRU_{vulI}(\overline{V}),\ \overline{V} \in \mathbb{R}^{m \times 1 \times d},\ V_h \in \mathbb{R}^{1 \times 1 \times d} \tag{2}$$

Step 3, Constructing vulDict. As shown in the Fig. 4, the red square represents the vulnerable statement and the green square represents the non-vulnerable statement. For the vulSet $\in \mathbb{R}^{a \times d}$ constructed in the Step two, it may contain many repeated or similar vulIs. In addition, due to the large size of vulSet, a large amount of computing resources are required for matching in the subsequent training and inference stages, because we need to match each program slice with the elements in the vulSet, and the vulI extracted from the training set in this article has 33647 indivual. In order to overcome this problem, we use the K-means clustering algorithm [24] to streamline and summarize vulSet, and obtain vulDict (see definition 4), expressed as $D = [c_1, c_2, \ldots, c_q]$, where each c_i is the center vector of vulDict, called vulCenter (see definition 3), and q is the number of elements in vulDict. Intuitively, vulDict integrates vulIs with similar features, where each vulCenter can represent a group or type of similar vulIs, providing more representative features for subsequent vulnerability detection and analysis.

3.3 Model Training

During the training of DV-LVF, we employed a Transformer model, which demonstrates superior performance in handling long sequences. Its attention mechanism effectively learns the relationships between every two tokens in the input sequence, thereby capturing the connections between tokens more effectively. Consequently, to better integrate vulDict, we concatenate the embedded input code with the vulCenter in vulDict that is most similar to it, enabling comprehensive learning of the relationship between code embedding and vulnerability centers. Specifically, our method includes two tasks: slice-level label

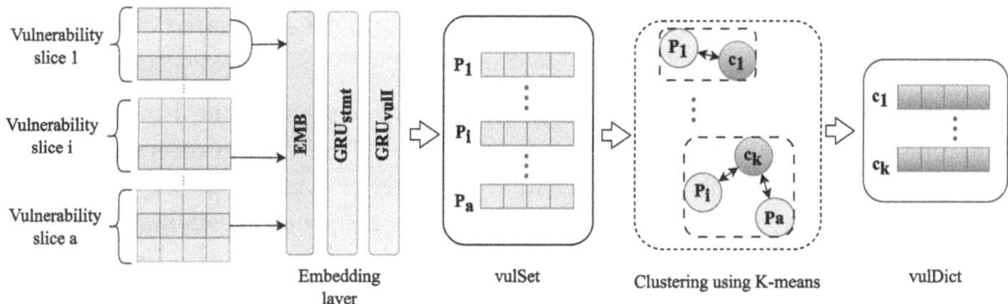

Fig. 4. Construction Process of vulDict Flowchart (Color figure online)

prediction and statement-level label prediction. Next, we will introduce in detail how to use vulDict and model training information. The overall process is shown in Fig. 5.

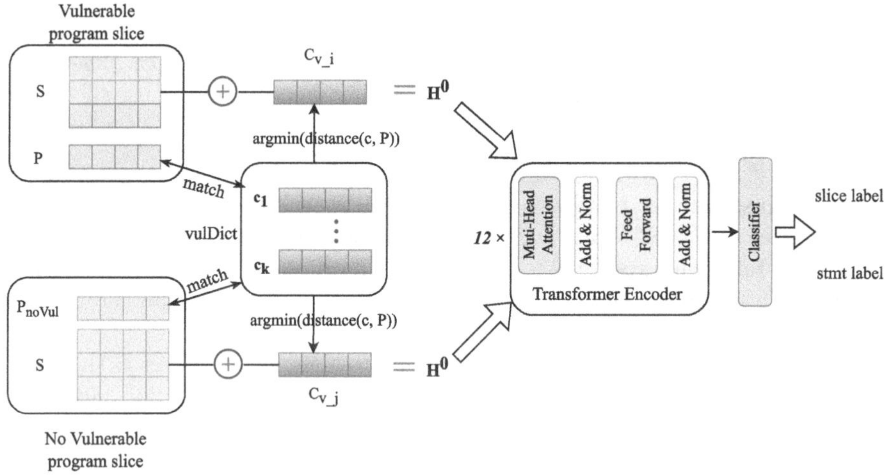

Fig. 5. Overall process diagram of DV-LVF training phase

Step 1, Data Preprocessing. First, we need to build program slices. The input to the model includes program slices that contain vulnerabilities and program slices that do not contain vulnerabilities. We performed a series of processes on these slices, including BPE word segmentation [19], vocabulary embedding, and GRU_{stmt} to obtain vector representations of program slices $\overline{S} \in \mathbb{R}^{n \times d}$. At the same time, for the vulI in the program slice containing the vulnerability, we use GRU_{stmt} and GRU_{vulI} to process to obtain the plane vector of vulI $P \in \mathbb{R}^{1 \times d}$. For program slices that do not contain vulnerabilities, we use a special embedding matrix $V_{noVul} \in \mathbb{R}^{m \times r \times d}$ instead, where the tokens are filled with <pad> . Similarly, use GRU_{stmt} and GRU_{vulI} to summarize V_{noVul} as a plane vector $P_{noVul} \in \mathbb{R}^{1\times d}$.

Step 2, Combining vulDict for Training. We calculate the Euclidean distance between the plane vector P corresponding to each program slice and the cluster center in vulDict, and determine the cluster center $c_p \in \mathbb{R}^{1\times d}$ closest to P through the formula 3. Finally, We splice the program slicing statement embedding $S \in \mathbb{R}^{n\times d}$ with the matching $c_p \in \mathbb{R}^{1\times d}$ to get H^0, as the input of the model, see formula 4. The training labels are program slice labels and corresponding statement labels.

$$c_p = argmin(distance(c_j, P)), j \in [1, 2, \dots, q] \tag{3}$$

$$H^0 = S \oplus c_p, H^0 \in \mathbb{R}^{(n+1)\times d} \tag{4}$$

In order to speed up the training process and improve the generalization ability of the model, we chose to fine-tune based on the CodeT5 [28] pre-trained model. The pre-trained model consists of 12 layers of Transformer encoders. The self-attention mechanism in each encoder unit can effectively capture the correlation between each element in the input sequence and learn the importance weight of each element to other elements, and is not limited by distance. Therefore, the model's input H^0 can learn the relationship between program slices and vulCenter. H^0 serves as the input of the first encoder, and the input of subsequent encoders is the output of the previous layer encoder.

Step 3, Classifier and Subsequent Stages. We select the output of the last layer encoder $H^{12} \in \mathbb{R}^{n\times d}$ as the input of the classifier, where n is the maximum number of statements specified for each slice. The classifier structure is shown in Fig. 6, which is divided into two tasks: slice-level label prediction and statement-level label prediction.

For statement-level label prediction, the classifier first processes the input H^{12} through a dropout layer, a fully connected layer, an activation layer, and a dropout layer again. Subsequently, a fully connected layer maps the second dimension features to n scalar values for final statement-level label prediction. For slice-level label prediction, we use the GRU network [18] to summarize H^{12}, obtain the hidden layer state of the last time step and compress it, and obtain $H_{slice} \in \mathbb{R}^d$. Then after the same processing as above, it is finally mapped to a scalar value for slice-level label prediction.

After being processed by the CodeT5 pre-training model and classifier, we use the cross-entropy loss function to calculate the slice-level loss (slice_loss) and statement-level loss (stmt_loss) respectively. These two loss values are calculated through the formula 5 are combined, where α and β are two parameters that control the composition of the loss to comprehensively evaluate the model's performance on slice-level and statement-level tasks. Next, the backpropagation algorithm is used to transfer gradient information, and the model parameters are adjusted through the AdamW optimizer to minimize the loss. The entire process is designed to gradually adjust model weights to improve performance and generalization capabilities.

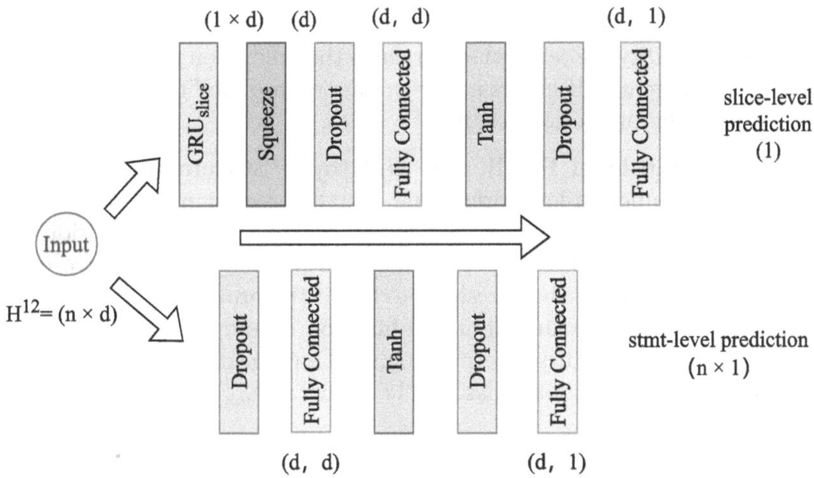

Fig. 6. DV-LVF classifier structure

$$loss = \alpha * slice\_loss + \beta * stmt\_loss \tag{5}$$

3.4 Model Inference

In the previous article, we used program slicing technology to reduce the detection granularity of the vulnerability detection task, but in the inference stage, only using slice-level information is obviously not enough for the complete function. Therefore, a function is used as the basic unit of DV-LVF detection. The specific process is as follows:

Step 1, Data Preprocessing. First, remove the annotation information of the function F to be detected, and then use program slicing technology to cut F into several program slices, assuming the number is z, and save the line number of the statement in each slice corresponding to the function F. Next, a series of processing is performed on the obtained program slices, including BPE word segmentation [19], vocabulary mapping, unifying the number of statements to n, and vocabulary embedding. For program slices with less than n statements, -1 is used to indicate the line number supplement to keep the number consistent. Finally, GRU_{stmt} is used to obtain the vector form for model input, which is expressed as $S_i, i \in [1, z]$.

Step 2, Model Inference. At this stage, we use vulDict to match vulnerability features, splice each S_i with each vulCenter in vulDict, and then input it into the model. The final output is the prediction result of S_i matching this vulCenter. After all vulCenter combinations are completed, each program slice S_i will obtain q slice-level prediction probabilities and statement-level prediction probabilities.

For the slice-level prediction probability, we select the maximum value among the q probabilities. In a sense, the vulI in the slice S_i matches the cluster of vulCenter corresponding to the maximum probability. For the statement-level prediction probability, we select the average of the prediction probabilities of each statement in different vulCenters as the prediction probability of this statement. Finally, we get the prediction results of z slices.

Step 3, Function-level Prediction and top-k Statement-level Prediction. The first is function-level prediction. For the prediction results obtained on z slices, we take the maximum probability of the z slice-level prediction results as the function-level prediction probability, and predict whether there is a vulnerability in F by setting the threshold to 0.5, if the probability is less than 0.5, it means that there is no vulnerability in function F, and the subsequent process will not be executed. Intuitively speaking, if the program slice of function F is vulnerable, then the function must also be vulnerable.

Definition 5. *top-k statement-level prediction, based on statement-level detection, selects the k statements with the highest probability ranking as the statements most likely to contain vulnerabilities.*

The second is top-k statement level prediction. According to the definition 5 and the original line number corresponding to each slice statement saved in Step One, we map the predicted probability of the statement in each slice to the original statement of the function F, and select each the maximum prediction probability in a statement represents the prediction probability of this statement, and a threshold of 0.5 is used to predict whether there is a vulnerability in this statement, thereby obtaining statement-level predictions of function F. Finally, the k statements with the highest prediction probability are selected to obtain the k statements most likely to have vulnerabilities.

4 Experimental Design

In this section, we will present the motivation for our three research questions, and our studied dataset.

4.1 Research Questions

The key goal of this paper is to evaluate DV-LVF and compare it with multiple baseline approaches. Below, we present the motivation for the following three research questions.

(RQ1) What are the hyperparameters of DV-LVF that achieve the best results? In the previous section, several key parameters of the DV-LVF method were mentioned, including the maximum number of statements in program slices n, the maximum number of vulnerable statements m, the maximum number of tokens in statements r, the influence of α and β in Eq. 5 on the composition of the loss, the number of elements in vulDict, and some conventional training parameters. Therefore, we set this RQ to investigate the optimal parameter settings for achieving the best performance of DV-LVF.

(RQ2) How well does DV-LVF perform in detecting function-level and statement-level vulnerabilities compared to the state-of-the-art? Recently, researchers have proposed numerous deep learning-based vulnerability detection methods, including those implemented with RNN [22,35,36], Transformer [31,32], GNN [33,34,37], as well as combinations of Transformer and GNN [38], and methods based on LLMs implementation [29,30]. We set this RQ to investigate the performance comparison between DV-LVF and these baseline methods in function-level and statement-level detection.

(RQ3) What are the benefits of key components in DV-LVF for vulnerability detection? DV-LVF involves two key components: GRU_{stmt} and vulDict. However, the specific contributions of these components in DV-LVF are not well understood. Therefore, we have set up this RQ to conduct ablation experiments to explore the necessity of GRU_{stmt} and vulDict for DV-LVF.

4.2 Experimental Dataset

To verify the effectiveness of DV-LVF, we utilize the open source vulnerability data set Big-Vul [20]. The dataset contains 188,000 C/C++ functions, and covers 91 CWE types, making it one of the largest vulnerability datasets with statement-level labels. We divide the data set into training set, validation set and test set. For the functions of the training set and validation set, we adopted program slicing processing to achieve appropriate detection granularity. We mark the vulnerability feature as "1" and the non-vulnerability feature as "0". The final number of functions and slices is shown in Table 1.

Table 1. Dataset partitioning

Type	Train(func)	Valid(func)	Test(func)	Train(slice)	Valid(slice)
vul	9,459	1,182	1,182	33,647	5,159
no-vul	202,478	25,309	25,309	386,545	26,348
Total	211,937	26,491	26,491	420,192	31,507

5 Experimental Results

(RQ1) What are the hyper-parameters of DV-LVF that achieve the best results?
To answer this RQ, we employed statistical and controlled variable methods. Firstly, regarding parameters related to program slicing, we conducted statistical analysis on the training dataset to determine the appropriate parameters for representing more tokens effectively. Secondly, for the α and β proportions in Eq. 5 and the number of elements in vulDict, we employed controlled variable

methods. Keeping other conditions constant, we evaluated different parameter values using Precision, Recall, F1-Score, and Accuracy metrics to assess the model's performance at the function level, statement level, and top-k statement level, thereby identifying the optimal parameter values.

For the key parameters of program slicing. Based on the statistics of experimental data, we stipulate that each program slice contains n = 120 statements, each statement contains r = 25 tokens, and each program slice contains m = 10 vulnerable statements. Here n = 120 already covers 99% of the program slices, and r = 25 can also cover 99% of the statements. Therefore, each program slice can represent up to 120 * 25 = 3000 tokens, which is 6 times the 512 tokens set in the pre-training model, helping to learn more complete feature information.

For α and β in Formula 5, they respectively represent the weight ratios of slice-level loss (slice_loss) and statement-level loss (stmt_loss) during model training. We compared different combinations of α and β. Tables 2 and 3 demonstrate, under other conditions being constant, the performance on function-level prediction, statement-level prediction, and top-k statement prediction on the test set with different α and β ratios, where bold indicates the best-performing results. Experimental results indicate that with $\alpha : \beta = 3 : 7$, DV-LVF achieves the optimal F1 scores for function-level prediction, statement-level prediction, and top-k (k > 3) statement prediction, demonstrating the best performance.

Table 2. The comparison results of different ratios of α and β on function-level and statement-level detection performance on the test set

$\alpha : \beta$	Func-Level				Stmt-Level			
	Acc	Prec	Rec	F1	Acc	Prec	Rec	F1
5:5	98.21	87.99	93.87	90.79	99.14	78.24	80.18	79.20
3:7	**98.59**	**91.19**	94.14	**92.64**	**99.27**	**83.06**	**81.82**	**81.93**
7:3	98.38	88.79	**94.74**	91.67	99.22	81.67	80.13	80.87

Intuitively, DV-LVF is a model that focuses on statement-level detection. Therefore, when statement-level loss has a greater proportion in the overall loss, the model's performance tends to be superior. This is also consistent with the experimental results. Ultimately, this study selected $\alpha : \beta = 3 : 7$ as the parameter for subsequent experiments.

For the number of vulCenters q in vulDict, we conducted experiments to explore the impact of different numbers of clusters q on the performance of DV-LVF. Tables 4 presents the performance of function-level prediction and statement-level prediction on the test set under consistent conditions, with bold indicating the best-performing results. Experimental results indicate that with a cluster number of q=150, DV-LVF achieves the optimal F1 score on the test set, demonstrating the best performance.

Table 3. The comparison results of different ratios of α and β on the accuracy of top-k statement predictions on the test set.

$\alpha : \beta$	k = 1(%)	k = 2(%)	k = 3(%)	k = 5(%)	k = 7(%)	k = 10(%)
5:5	94.77	95.92	96.94	98.21	98.72	98.98
3:7	95.68	97.20	**98.22**	**99.11**	**99.49**	**99.75**
7:3	**96.09**	**97.35**	98.11	98.61	98.99	99.12

Table 4. The comparison results of different q values on function-level and statement-level detection performance on the test set

clusters	Func-Level				Stmt-Level			
	Acc	Prec	Rec	F1	Acc	Prec	Rec	F1
50	98.56	90.88	94.14	92.48	99.22	80.98	80.89	80.93
100	98.33	88.48	94.62	91.45	99.21	80.12	81.84	80.98
125	98.57	90.61	94.62	92.57	99.20	82.55	77.50	79.94
150	**98.59**	**91.19**	94.14	**92.64**	**99.27**	**83.06**	81.82	**81.93**
200	98.31	87.69	**95.45**	91.41	99.15	79.95	77.96	78.94
250	98.34	88.40	94.86	91.52	99.21	79.52	**82.83**	81.14

We conducted experiments on a Windows machine equipped with an Intel i7-10700 processor, 32 GB of RAM, and an NVIDIA GeForce RTX 3060 with 12 GB of VRAM. We utilized the CodeT5 [28] pre-trained model to implement DV-LVF. Finally, we have determined all the parameter information for DV-LVF. Please refer to Table 5 for details.

Table 5. DV-LVF model hyperparameters

Param	batch	epochs	lr	n	r	m	q
Value	8	50	1e−4	120	25	10	150

(RQ2) How well does DV-LVF perform in detecting function-level and statement-level vulnerabilities compared to the state-of-the-art? To answer this RQ, we trained DV-LVF using the aforementioned parameter settings and compared it with baseline methods on the vulnerability detection task, including predictions at both function and statement levels. Some of the baseline methods were generated based on the code provided by the original authors, while others were generated using the best metric data provided by the baseline methods on the same dataset. For example, SyseVR and Devign both stem from comparative experiments set up in mVulPreter. Additionally, baseline methods based on LLMs are similar to the token embedding method used in the second ablation experiment of RQ3, with the difference lying in the specific LLMs used. We evaluated each method using metrics including Accuracy, Precision, Recall, and F1-score. Finally, we further demonstrated the superiority of DV-LVF through top-k statement predictions.

Baseline methods for function-level vulnerability detection tasks include vulnerability detection methods based on LLMs CodeBERT [29] and CodeGPT [30]; vulnerability detection methods implemented based on Transformer such as LineVul [31] and VELVET [32], as well as those based on graph neural networks like ReGVD [33] and Devign [34]; and methods based on RNN such as SyseVR [22], mVulPreter [35], and ICVH [36].

Table 6. Performance comparison between DV-LVF and baseline methods on function-level detection

Method	Accuracy(%)	Precision(%)	Recall(%)	F1-score(%)
DV-LVF	98.59	91.19	**94.14**	**92.64**
LineVul [31]	98.61	**97.00**	86.00	91.00
VELVET [32]	**98.88**	93.37	80.86	86.67
CodeBERT [29]	98.15	92.15	82.89	87.28
CodeGPT [30]	98.75	91.25	84.81	87.91
ReGVD [33]	97.12	77.92	50.24	61.09
Devign [34]	96.90	72.29	50.24	59.28
SyseVR [22]	94.83	49.65	53.97	51.92
mVulPreter [35]	96.01	51.78	67.34	58.54
ICVH [36]	96.56	77.44	33.25	46.53

Table 6 presents the performance comparison of DV-LVF with baseline methods in function-level vulnerability detection tasks. Observing the results, it is evident that compared to baseline methods, DV-LVF demonstrates improvements ranging from 4.37% to 46.11% in F1 scores and from 11.25% to 60.89% in recall rates. In terms of accuracy, there is only a 0.29% difference compared to the best-performing baseline method, and the precision is only 2% lower than the best-performing baseline method. F1 score, as a metric that considers both precision and recall, is crucial for evaluating the performance of classification models. Therefore, DV-LVF exhibits excellent performance in function-level vulnerability detection, demonstrating its potential for practical applications.

Baseline methods for statement-level vulnerability detection tasks include methods implemented based on LLMs CodeBERT [29] and CodeGPT [30]; Transformer-based implementations such as VELVET [32]; graph neural network-based approaches like VulTeller [37]; a combination of Transformer and graph neural networks in LineVD [38]; and RNN-based implementation ICVH [36].

Table 7. Performance comparison between DV-LVF and baseline methods in statement-level detection

Method	Accuracy(%)	Precision(%)	Recall(%)	F1-score(%)
DV-LVF	**99.27**	**83.06**	**81.82**	**81.93**
CodeBERT [29]	96.89	19.29	63.54	29.60
CodeGPT [30]	98.23	32.54	67.34	43.88
VulTeller [37]	98.50	38.90	55.60	45.80
VELVET [32]	98.50	38.19	73.50	50.26
LineVD [38]	95.19	27.10	53.30	36.00
ICVH [36]	97.77	21.31	43.17	28.53

Table 7 presents the performance comparison of DV-LVF with baseline methods in statement-level vulnerability detection. Observing the results, it is evident that compared to baseline methods, DV-LVF demonstrates improvements ranging from 0.77% to 4.08% in accuracy, from 44.16% to 63.77% in precision, from 8.32% to 38.65% in recall, and from 31.67% to 53.4% in F1 score. It can be seen that DV-LVF outperforms baseline methods in statement-level vulnerability detection tasks. This is mainly due to DV-LVF being the first to extract and utilize statement-level labels from source functions, allowing for a finer-grained learning of statement-level features, thus providing a clear advantage in the final statement predictions.

Finally, building upon the statement-level predictions of DV-LVF, we introduced the concept of top-k statement-level prediction. Specifically, for functions predicted to have vulnerabilities, DV-LVF extracts the top-k statements with the highest probabilities within that function, which are considered the most likely to contain vulnerabilities. We believe that if there are vulnerable statements among these k statements, it can be regarded as successfully locating the vulnerabilities. Table 8 describes the accuracy of DV-LVF in top-k statement-level prediction. It can be observed that at k = 5, the accuracy has already reached 99%, indicating that DV-LVF can accurately predict the location of vulnerable statements.

Table 8. The accuracy of DV-LVF prediction at the top-k statement level

k value	1	2	3	5	7	10
Accuracy(%)	95.68	97.20	98.22	**99.11**	99.49	99.75

(RQ3) What are the benefits of key components in DV-LVF for vulnerability detection?

To answer this RQ, we conducted ablation experiments. Specifically, we compared the cases of using and not using vulDict, as well as compared GRU statement embedding with regular token embeddings, to validate the effectiveness of components in DV-LVF.

Table 9. Performance comparison of DV-LVF and method without vulDict matching on function-level and statement-level detection

Method	Func-Level				Stmt-Level			
	Acc	Prec	Rec	F1	Acc	Prec	Rec	F1
DV-LVF	**98.59**	**91.19**	**94.14**	**92.64**	**99.27**	**83.06**	**81.82**	**81.93**
No vulDict	94.81	45.91	86.48	59.98	98.06	29.11	58.53	38.88

Table 9 presents the performance comparison between DV-LVF and No vulDict in function-level and statement-level detection. "No vulDict" indicates that only the classifier is utilized during both training and inference phases. The experimental results indicate that in function-level prediction, compared to DV-LVF, No vulDict experiences a decrease of 45.28% in precision and 32.66% in F1 score. In statement-level prediction, precision, recall, and F1 score decrease by 53.95%, 23.29%, and 43.05% respectively. This underscores the importance of constructing vulDict and utilizing it for vulnerability matching in DV-LVF to achieve high-performance levels.

Table 10. Performance comparison of GRU statement embedding and token embedding in DV-LVF on function-level and statement-level detection

Method	Func-Level				Stmt-Level			
	Acc	Prec	Rec	F1	Acc	Prec	Rec	F1
DV-LVF	**98.59**	91.19	**94.14**	**92.64**	**99.27**	**83.06**	**81.82**	**81.93**
TokenEmbs	98.15	**92.15**	82.89	87.28	98.23	32.54	67.34	43.88

Table 10 shows the performance of GRU statement embeddings and regular token embeddings in function-level and statement-level detection within DV-LVF. Regular token embeddings refer to using simple averaging instead of GRU statement embeddings to obtain embedding vectors for each statement. The experimental results show that in function-level prediction, compared to the GRU statement embeddings method, the regular token embeddings method experiences a decrease of 11.25% in recall and 5.36% in F1 score. In statement-level prediction, precision, recall, and F1 score decrease by 50.52%, 14.48%, and 38.05% respectively. This also emphasizes that GRU statement embeddings in DV-LVF can comprehensively consider token information, extracting more complete features than token embeddings, thereby achieving better performance.

Through the analysis of the experimental results in RQ2 and RQ3, we found that DV-LVF achieved good performance in statement-level prediction. This is mainly attributed to two factors: firstly, vulDict, which plays a crucial role in our approach, is responsible for collecting and utilizing vulnerability feature information from the code, thus enabling more effective detection of vulnerable statements during the inference phase. Secondly, GRU statement embeddings, which retain token features at each time step, allow for a more effective summarization of statement information.

6 Conclusion

In this work, we propose a novel vulnerability detection method called DV-LVF, which detects vulnerabilities by extracting and utilizing common vulnerability features present in the vulnerability code. Specifically, we propose GRU statement embedding method, combined with program slicing techniques, to obtain a more comprehensive feature representation. Additionally, we introduce the concept of vulDict, which quantifies features in vulnerability code and constructs them using clustering algorithms. During training and inference, identify the vulCenter that is most similar to the source code embedding, and combine this vulCenter with the source code embedding for the model input. Finally, function-level and statement-level predictions are obtained through a composite classifier. We conduct comprehensive evaluations on high-quality C/C++ vulnerability datasets, demonstrating the outstanding performance of DV-LVF in function-level and statement-level detection. Finally, through ablation experiments, we validate the utility of key components in DV-LVF.

References

1. Li, Z., et al.: Vulpecker: an automated vulnerability detection system based on code similarity analysis. In: Proceedings of the 32nd Annual Conference on Computer Security Applications (2016)
2. Kim, S., et al.: Vuddy: a scalable approach for vulnerable code clone discovery. In: 2017 IEEE Symposium on Security and Privacy (SP). IEEE (2017)
3. Wheeler, D.A.: Flawfinder (2016). https://www.dwheeler.com/flawfinder/. Accessed 20 May 2018
4. Sutton, M., Greene, A., Amini, P.: Fuzzing: Brute Force Vulnerability Discovery. Pearson Education, London (2007)
5. Newsome, J., Song, D.X.: Dynamic taint analysis for automatic detection, analysis, and signaturegeneration of exploits on commodity software. In: NDSS, vol. 5 (2005)
6. Zaazaa, O., El Bakkali, H.: Dynamic vulnerability detection approaches and tools: state of the art. In: 2020 Fourth International Conference On Intelligent Computing in Data Sciences (ICDS). IEEE (2020)
7. Li, Z., et al.: Vuldeepecker: a deep learning-based system for vulnerability detection. arXiv preprint arXiv:1801.01681 (2018)
8. Zou, D., et al. : μ VulDeePecker: a deep learning-based system for multiclass vulnerability detection. IEEE Trans. Dependable Secure Comput. **18**(5), 2224–2236 (2019)

9. Russell, R., et al.: Automated vulnerability detection in source code using deep representation learning. In: 2018 17th IEEE International Conference on Machine Learning and Applications (ICMLA). IEEE (2018)
10. Li, Z., et al.: VR: a deep learning-based fine-grained vulnerability detector. IEEE Trans. Dependable Secure Comput. **19**(4), 2821–2837 (2021)
11. Wang, H., et al.: Combining graph-based learning with automated data collection for code vulnerability detection. IEEE Trans. Inf. Forensics Secur. **16**, 1943–1958 (2020)
12. Zhuang, Y., et al.: Software vulnerability detection via deep learning over disaggregated code graph representation. arXiv preprint arXiv:2109.03341 (2021)
13. Thapa, C., et al.: Transformer-based language models for software vulnerability detection. In: Proceedings of the 38th Annual Computer Security Applications Conference (2022)
14. Purba, M.D., et al.: Software vulnerability detection using large language models. In: 2023 IEEE 34th International Symposium on Software Reliability Engineering Workshops (ISSREW). IEEE (2023)
15. Zhang, X., et al.: VulD-Transformer: source code vulnerability detection via transformer. In: Proceedings of the 14th Asia-Pacific Symposium on Internetware (2023)
16. Chakraborty, S., et al.: Deep learning based vulnerability detection: are we there yet? In: ACM/IEEE International Conference on Software Engineering (2022)
17. Zeng, P., et al.: Software vulnerability analysis and discovery using deep learning techniques: a survey. IEEE Access **8**, 197158–197172 (2020)
18. Chung, J., et al.: Empirical evaluation of gated recurrent neural networks on sequence modeling. arXiv preprint arXiv:1412.3555 (2014)
19. Sennrich, R., Haddow, B., Birch, A.: Neural machine translation of rare words with subword units. arXiv preprint arXiv:1508.07909 (2015)
20. Fan, J., et al.: AC/C++ code vulnerability dataset with code changes and CVE summaries. In: Proceedings of the 17th International Conference on Mining Software Repositories (2020)
21. Weiser, M.: Program slicing. IEEE Trans. Softw. Eng. **4**, 352–357 (1984)
22. Li, Z., et al.: SySeVR: a framework for using deep learning to detect software vulnerabilities. IEEE Trans. Dependable Secure Comput. **19**(04), 2244–2258 (2022)
23. Joern[EB/OL]. https://github.com/octopus-platform/joern/
24. Lloyd, S.: Least squares quantization in PCM. IEEE Trans. Inf. Theory **28**(2), 129–137 (1982)
25. Vaswani, A., et al.: Attention is all you need. Adv. Neural Inf. Process. Syst. **30** (2017)
26. Zaremba, W., Sutskever, I., Vinyals, O.: Recurrent neural network regularization. arXiv preprint arXiv:1409.2329 (2014)
27. Shi, X., et al.: Convolutional LSTM network: a machine learning approach for precipitation nowcasting. Adv. Neural Inf. Process. Syst. **28** (2015)
28. Wang, Y., et al.: Codet5: identifier-aware unified pre-trained encoder-decoder models for code understanding and generation. arXiv preprint arXiv:2109.00859 (2021)
29. Feng, Z., et al.: CodeBERT: a pre-trained model for programming and natural languages. arXiv preprint arXiv:2002.08155 (2020)
30. Lu, S., et al.: Codexglue: a machine learning benchmark dataset for code understanding and generation. arXiv preprint arXiv:2102.04664 (2021)
31. Fu, M., Tantithamthavorn, C.: Linevul: a transformer-based line-level vulnerability prediction. In: Proceedings of the 19th International Conference on Mining Software Repositories (2022)

32. Ding, Y., et al.: VELVET: a novel ensemble learning approach to automatically locate vulnerable statements. In: 2022 IEEE International Conference on Software Analysis, Evolution and Reengineering (SANER). IEEE (2022)
33. Nguyen, V.-A., et al.: ReGVD: revisiting graph neural networks for vulnerability detection. In: Proceedings of the ACM/IEEE 44th International Conference on Software Engineering: Companion Proceedings (2022)
34. Zhou, Y., et al.: Devign: effective vulnerability identification by learning comprehensive program semantics via graph neural networks. Adv. Neural Inf. Process. Syst. **32** (2019)
35. Zou, D., et al.: mVulPreter: a multi-granularity vulnerability detection system with interpretations. IEEE Trans. Dependable Secure Comput. (2022)
36. Nguyen, V., et al.: Information-theoretic source code vulnerability highlighting. In: 2021 International Joint Conference on Neural Networks (IJCNN). IEEE (2021)
37. Zhang, J., et al.: Learning to locate and describe vulnerabilities. In: 2023 38th IEEE/ACM International Conference on Automated Software Engineering (ASE). IEEE (2023)
38. Hin, D., et al.: LineVD: statement-level vulnerability detection using graph neural networks. In: Proceedings of the 19th International Conference on Mining Software Repositories (2022)

Fuzzing for Stateful Protocol Implementations: Are We There Yet?

Kunpeng Jian[1,2,3,4], Yanyan Zou[1,2,3,4], Yeting Li[1,2,3,4(✉)], Jialun Cao[5], Menghao Li[1,2,3,4], Jian Sun[1,2,3,4], Jingyi Shi[1,2,3,4], and Wei Huo[1,2,3,4(✉)]

[1] Institute of Information Engineering, Chinese Academy of Sciences, Beijing, China
{jiankunpeng,zouyanyan,liyeting,limenghao,sunjian, shijingyi,huowei}@iie.ac.cn

[2] School of Cyber Security, University of Chinese Academy of Sciences, Beijing, China

[3] Key Laboratory of Network Assessment Technology, Chinese Academy of Sciences, Beijing, China

[4] Beijing Key Laboratory of Network Security and Protection Technology, Beijing, China

[5] Hong Kong University of Science and Technology, Hong Kong, China
jcaoap@cse.ust.hk

Abstract. Stateful protocols, such as FTP, SIP, and RTSP, play a significant role in computer systems. However, their implementation is prone to security vulnerabilities, which have drawn attention from both industry and academia. Various fuzzing techniques, including the AFLNet fuzzer, have been proposed to test stateful protocol implementations. However, the effectiveness of these existing techniques has not been systematically evaluated, and the understanding of their strengths and weaknesses is limited. To fill this gap, we conducted a comprehensive study to explore the performance of state-of-the-art fuzzing techniques on stateful protocols. In particular, we systematically investigated six state-of-the-art fuzzers on 13 widely used programs using identical seed inputs. Our empirical study revealed the following key findings: (i) State coverage guidance effectively navigates through complex states, although with limitations in directly improving code coverage; (ii) Sequence mutation is pivotal yet requires refinement for effectiveness; (iii) Replacement of asynchronous network socket with synchronous shared memory not only improves test throughput but also improve test efficiency. Finally, based on our findings, we further pinpointed the further research in the broad area of stateful protocol fuzzing.

Keywords: Stateful protocols fuzzing · Bug revealing · Empirical study

W.-N. Chin and Z. Xu (Eds.): TASE 2024, LNCS 14777, pp. 186–204, 2024.
https://doi.org/10.1007/978-3-031-64626-3_11

1 Introduction

As an essential part of the computer system, stateful protocol implementations are ubiquitous, and their security has attracted increasing attention. These implementations can interact with each other over the Internet, allowing malicious attackers to exploit computer systems that contain programs without physical access. For example, the infamous *EternalBlue* [10] exploit utilized a vulnerability in a stateful protocol called SMB to infiltrate Windows systems, leading to the global WannaCry ransomware cyberattack.

With the security of stateful protocol implementations increasingly important, fuzzing is now extensively applied to test stateful protocol implementations to find security bugs, which has become the de facto standard technique for discovering software bugs. Stateful protocol fuzzing can be mainly divided into two main paradigms: template-based [1,7–9,25] and mutation-based [2–5,16,17,20,23,27–29] techniques. For template-based techniques, they require predefined templates about stateful protocols, so their effectiveness is affected by the quality of these templates. Moreover, for complicated stateful protocols, composing adequate and high-quality templates is labor-intensive and impractical for developers and even experts. To this end, the latest research proposed mutation-based techniques to overcome the defects of template-based techniques. These mutation-based techniques can directly test stateful protocol programs without manual templates, thereby reducing user requirements.

Despite the noticeable progress, the effectiveness of existing techniques has not been systematically studied and compared without bias. In addition, little is known about their advantages and disadvantages, let alone the reasons behind them. Moreover, are existing techniques complementary to each other, and whether the integration of them can enhance their effectiveness? Therefore, a comprehensive empirical study is urgently needed to explore and evaluate the effectiveness of state-of-the-art (SOTA) stateful protocol fuzzing techniques.

To fill this gap, this paper conducts a systematic empirical study for stateful protocol fuzzing including six SOTA fuzzers on a most comprehensive benchmark, *i.e.*, ProFuzzBench [24], including programs with 1k to 143k lines of code (LoC). We evaluate these fuzzing techniques from four aspects: (i) code coverage (§ 4.1), (ii) state machine coverage (§ 4.2), (iii) bug revealing capability (§ 4.3) and (iv) test throughput (§ 4.4). This investigation yields several insightful findings, summarized as follows:

- **State coverage guidance effectively navigates through complex states, although with limitations in directly improving code coverage.** Our findings indicate that while state coverage guidance excels in enabling the fuzzer to explore deeper states (see Finding 5), it does not inherently improve code coverage (see Finding 1). This insight underscores the importance of leveraging state coverage as a complementary metric to traditional code coverage, thereby enriching the strategy for uncovering bugs hidden within the nuanced stateful behaviors of network programs (see Finding 6).

- **Sequence mutation are pivotal yet require refinement for effectiveness.** The effectiveness of sequence mutation in improving code and state machine coverage is recognized; however, the current methods' simplicity and randomness highlight a pressing need for optimization. Refining these methods is essential for elevating the precision and effectiveness of fuzzing efforts, suggesting a valuable direction for future research to improve fuzzer capabilities in covering code with complex condition and complex state transitions (see Findings 2 and 3).
- **Replacement of asynchronous network socket with synchronous shared memory not only improves test throughput but also improves test efficiency.** The replacement of asynchronous network socket with synchronous shared memory is identified as a critical factor in improving test throughput (see Finding 8). This replacement is not only essential for enhancing the efficiency of fuzzing processes but also for addressing the unique challenges posed by testing stateful network programs, ensuring a more controlled and effective testing environment (see Finding 4). This adjustment aligns with the necessity of optimizing test infrastructure to support the intricate requirements of stateful protocol fuzzing.

These findings help us (i) understand the effectiveness of existing techniques, including their advantages and disadvantages; (ii) understand the reasons behind their advantages and disadvantages of existing techniques; (iii) provide a series of guidelines for stateful protocol fuzzing in the future.

In summary, this paper makes three major contributions:

- To the best of our knowledge, we conducted the first comprehensive empirical study of stateful protocol fuzzing by evaluating from four aspects: code coverage, state machine coverage, bug revealing, and test throughput.
- We quantitatively and qualitatively analyzed the advantages and disadvantages of current research. Our findings reveal a nuanced landscape of stateful protocol fuzzing, highlighting the significant impact of state coverage guidance for deep state exploration, the critical need for refined sequence mutation techniques, and the efficiency gains from replacing asynchronous network sockets with synchronous shared memory. These insights underscore the complexity of achieving optimal fuzzing results and the potential for methodological and technical advancements.
- On the basis of our empirical results and findings, we point out the limitation of existing work and the directions that can be improved.

The complete evaluation result is available online. For further details, please refer to our website [15].

2 Background

2.1 Terminologies of Stateful Protocol

A *stateful protocol* is a set of transition rules that requires the receiver and sender to maintain session *states* during the interaction (*i.e.*, sending and receiving various types of *messages*). In general, a stateful protocol consists of two components, namely, the message format, and the protocol state machine. *Message formats* specify the syntax rules that the protocol message content must follow, including the definition of keywords, delimiters, fields, and the relationships between fields. *Protocol state machines* describe the temporal logic that the protocol follows when processing different messages. A stateful protocol usually contains multiple *states* and types of *messages*, representing different states or functions of the protocol. For example, Fig. 1 shows the state machine of Protocol SIP (Session Initialization Protocol). The state machine consists of six states (*e.g.*, `Idle`, `Invited`) and nine types of messages (*e.g.*, *Invite*, *Session modify*), which are represented by circular nodes and lines in the figure, respectively.

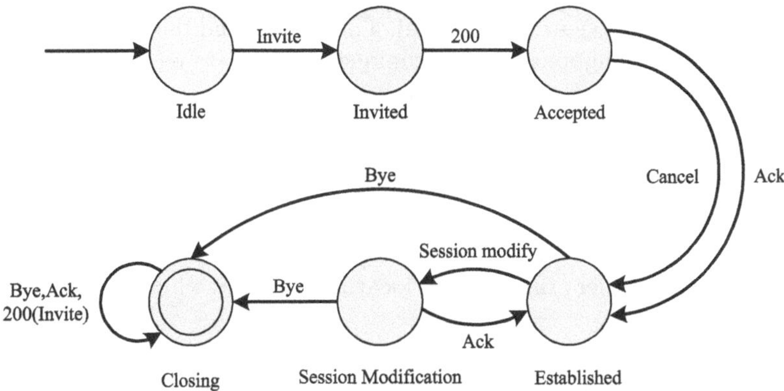

Fig. 1. An Illustration of State Machine of SIP Protocol. Circular nodes denote the states, arrow lines represent the transition rules, and texts over lines denote the messages.

A state is *covered* if it is reached by following the defined transition rules from the initial state. Take Fig. 1 as an example, to cover the state `Session Modification`, its predecessor state `Established` should be first reached, followed by the execution of the message *Session modify*. In this way, the state `Session Modification` is thus considered to be covered. The transitions between the states are governed by the rules defined by the protocol. Similarly, a *transition is covered* if the transition rule is executed.

2.2 General Workflow of Stateful Protocol Fuzzers

We summarize the general workflow of the state-of-the-art fuzzing techniques in Fig. 2. The upper part (in green) of the figure shows the workflow of the *mutation-based fuzzing approaches* [11]. These approaches mainly adopt *message mutation* and use the *code coverage* (*e.g.*, line coverage, branch coverage) as guidance. Particularly, a seed (*i.e.*, message) is selected from the seed queue and mutated before being executed during a test run. If the mutant triggers a crash, it is saved for further analysis; otherwise, a code coverage analysis is performed to determine its effectiveness in terms of covering new code. Depending on the results of the analysis, the mutant may be added to the seed queue for further mutation or discarded.

For stateful protocol testing, boosting code coverage does not necessarily lead to more adequate testing. As illustrated in Fig. 1, the message sequences `Ack->Session modify` and `Ack->Session modify->Ack` achieve identical code coverage, yet they differ in state transitions (*i.e.*, the former includes two state transitions, whereas the latter involves three transitions). Therefore, *stateful protocol fuzzing approaches* [2–5,16,17,20,23,27–29] are proposed to complement the traditional mutation-based fuzzing approaches. As shown in the Fig. 2's lower part (in blue), these approaches adopt *sequence mutation* (*e.g.*, deleting, inserting, or repeating messages in a test case). Then, they send the mutated test case. To improve test throughput, some techniques (*e.g.*, state recovery, the method of replacing the asynchronous network socket by synchronous share memory) are proposed. Any non-crash mutants are evaluated by a state machine coverage analysis in terms of covering the new states. Also, it is noteworthy that there are two main ways for obtaining state machine coverage to guide the mutation, *i.e.*, response-based [27] and variable-based [23] state coverage guidance. The first method parses the replied response messages to infer the protocol states, while the second method infers the state by locating variables which contain protocol states.

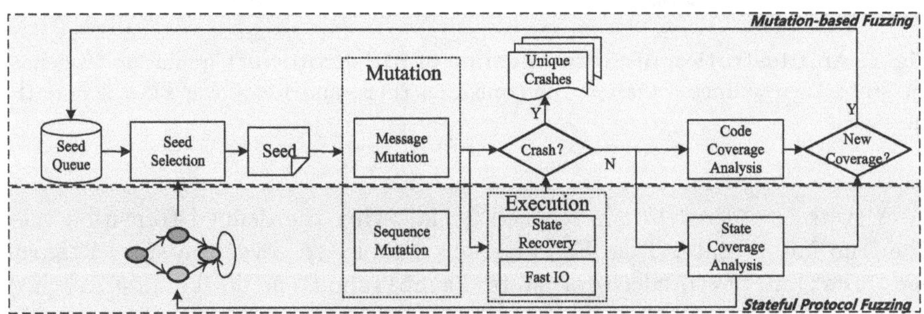

Fig. 2. General Workflow of Stateful Protocol Fuzzing Approaches.

3 Study Design

The experiments are conducted on Ubuntu 20.04 TLS with Intel Xeno Gold 6242R and 128 GB Memory. To reduce the randomness inherent in fuzzing, each method was executed ten times. In the following, we will introduce the study design in terms of benchmarks, fuzzing techniques, and research questions.

Benchmarks. To facilitate the replication and verification of our experiments, we use a widely-used benchmark, ProFuzzBench [24], for evaluation. For better displaying, the statistics are listed in the online website. In particular, the benchmark consists of 13 stateful protocol programs. The scale of each program ranges from 1,128 to 143,727 LoC. These programs implement ten prevalent network protocols, *i.e.*, (1) FTP (including Bftpd, LightFTP, ProFTPD, and Pure-FTPd), (2) DICOM (including Dcmtk), (3) DNS (including Dnsmasq), (4) SMTP (including Exim), (5) DAAP (including Forked-daapd), (6) SIP (including Kamailio), (7) RTSP (including Live555), (8) SSH (including OpenSSH), (9) TLS (including OpenSSL), (10) DTLS (including TinyDTLS). All the listed network protocols, except DNS and SMTP, are stateful protocols.

Fuzzing Techniques. We select six representative and SOTA netwrok protocol fuzzers from both academia and industry [29] as our study subjects, *i.e.*, AFLNet [27], AFLNetLegion [17], StateAFL [23], SnapFuzz [2], Nyx-Net [29] and AFLNWE [12]. These include the first four fuzzers, which support state coverage guidance, and the first five fuzzers, which facilitate sequence mutation. The fifth fuzzer Nyx-Net is distinguished by its state recovery capabilities and its novel approach of substituting asynchronous network sockets with synchronous shared memory. The first five fuzzers comprehensively demonstrate the general fuzzing workflow mentioned in §2.2. The last fuzzer AFLNWE [12], which is based on the classic fuzzer AFL, adds support for network protocols.

Note that SnapFuzz [2] was only able to successfully launched on five programs (*i.e.*, LightFTP, Dnsmasq, Live555, TinyDTLS and Dcmtk) in our benchmark and crashed on the rest. Our investigation traced the crash to its implementation of binary rewriting during the network socket hooking.

Research Questions(RQs). Our study aims to answer the following:

RQ1: What is the Code Coverage of Existing Approaches? Code coverage is considered an indicator of test adequacy. We show the branch coverage achieved by each approach.

RQ2: What is the State Machine Coverage of Existing Approaches? State machine coverage is also a critical coverage criterion for testing stateful protocols, apart from code coverage.

RQ3: Are Existing Approaches Capable of Bug Revealing? Since the ultimate goal of boosting test adequacy is to reveal bugs in the program, we hereby evaluate the bug-revealing capability of existing works.

RQ4: How Effective are Stateful Protocol Fuzzers' Techniques in Test Throughput? Test throughput affects the efficiency of test case generation. The higher the test throughput, the faster the test case could be generated.

4 Evaluation Results and Findings

4.1 RQ1. Effectiveness of Code Coverage

Code coverage (*e.g.*, line coverage, branch coverage) could reflect the test adequacy. The more adequate a testing approach is, the more likely it is to reveal bugs in the program under test. To answer RQ1, we apply the subjects against the benchmark and calculate the branch coverage. Table 1 shows the evaluation results on branch coverage. The highest branch coverage for each benchmark is highlighted in bold.[1]

From Table 1, it is clear that Nyx-Net outperforms other approaches in all programs, followed by AFLNet. On the other hand, StateAFL falls behind the average against most benchmarks, especially against LightFTP and Kamailio benchmarks. Surprisingly, among the five programs supported by SnapFuzz, only the result for Dnsmasq outperforms AFLNet, despite SnapFuzz being an enhanced version of AFLNet in terms of efficiency. AFLNWE demonstrates the worst branch coverage across most benchmarks.

Table 1. The Evaluation Results on Branch Coverage. The symbol "–" denotes that the fuzzers are unable to perform testing on the corresponding benchmark. The column "#Branches" represents the total number of branches. The row "Average" shows the average coverage ratio over all the benchmarks. Nyx-Net's data in Forked-daapd is taken from [29] because Nyx-Net fails to perform testing on Forked-Daapd during our evaluation.

Benchmark	#Branches	Nyx-Net	AFLNet	StateAFL	AFLNetLegion	SnapFuzz	AFLNWE
Bftpd	1,356	**35.77%**	35.10%	32.23%	34.44%	–	33.33%
LightFTP	809	**47.59%**	43.63%	32.88%	41.90%	40.05%	20.64%
ProFTPD	23,532	**23.22%**	21.52%	21.58%	21.21%	–	20.95%
Pure-FTPD	3,601	**37.21%**	27.69%	25.47%	31.35%	–	13.69%
Dnsmasq	11,997	**9.81%**	6.91%	6.80%	8.73%	8.48%	6.74%
Exim	27,554	**16.30%**	15.95%	15.66%	16.15%	–	3.99%
Forked-Daapd	15,139	**16.66%**	16.01%	15.71%	15.21%	–	13.17%
Live555	13,693	**22.01%**	21.97%	21.59%	21.47%	19.46%	18.63%
OpenSSH	17,090	**21.69%**	21.11%	20.60%	20.06%	–	20.84%
OpenSSL	91,595	**11.89%**	11.07%	10.34%	10.58%	–	8.26%
TinyDTLS	1,703	**34.12%**	31.36%	28.60%	27.36%	23.84%	18.73%
Dcmtk	48,558	**6.52%**	6.42%	6.34%	6.38%	6.39%	6.24%
Kamailio	200,466	**5.57%**	4.27%	3.66%	4.46%	–	3.79%
Average	–	**22.18%**	20.23%	18.57%	19.95%	19.64%	14.54%

Taking a closer look, we observed that two major reasons may be attributed to the unsatisfactory results. Fuzzers represented by AFLNet, which adopts state coverage guidance, have more branch coverage compared to AFLNWE, which does not adopt state coverage guidance. But compared to Nyx-Net, which does not adopt state coverage guidance but has high test throughput, AFLNet has less

[1] To address randomness of fuzzing, we also employ the Mann-Whitney U test [21] and put the data on the online website [15].

branch coverage. This indicates that state coverage guidance can improve code coverage. However, stateful protocol programs are often complex, and increasing code coverage requires generating message sequences that satisfy complex conditions. State coverage guidance can only passively schedule seeds and cannot generate message sequences that meet complex conditions. Therefore, state coverage guidance can only make fuzzers achieve converging code coverage faster. It cannot raise the upper bound of code coverage. High test throughput without state coverage guidance can also make the fuzzer achieve a similar level of improvement in code coverage.

Finding 1: State coverage guidance can improve code coverage compared to fuzzers without it, ★ but high test throughput without state coverage guidance can also make fuzzer achieve a similar level improvement of code coverage.

To evaluate the impact of sequence mutation, we modify the Nyx-Net and AFLNet with sequence mutation disabled. Table 2 shows their evaluation results in Nyx-Net-NS and AFLNet-NS columns respectively. After disabling the sequence mutation, Nyx-Net performs a decrease of over 5% in branch coverage on 7 benchmarks. Meanwhile, AFLNet only performs a decrease of over 5% in branch coverage on 2 benchmarks.

Table 2. The Evaluation Results on Branch Coverage with Disabling Sequence Mutation. The columns "Nyx-Net-NS" and "AFLNet-NS" show the number of covered branches when the sequence mutation is disabled. The symbol "–" denotes that the fuzzers are unable to perform testing on the corresponding benchmark. The blue-box and orange-box highlight the results where the branch coverage increases or decreases over 5% with sequence mutation disabled, respectively. The data in the brackets are the reduction or increase ratio.

Benchmark	Nyx-Net	Nyx-Net-NS	AFLNet	AFLNet-NS
Bftpd	485	486 (+0.21%)	476	477 (+0.21%)
LightFTP	385	352 (-8.57%)	353	352 (-0.28%)
ProFTPD	5,464	5,239 (-4.12%)	5,063	4,954 (-2.15%)
Pure-FTPD	1,340	1,278 (-4.63%)	997	1,121 (+12.44%)
Dnsmasq	1,177	1,121 (-4.76%)	829	838 (+1.09%)
Exim	4,490	3,842 (-14.43%)	4,396	4,420 (+0.55%)
Forked-Daapd	2,522	–	2,423	2,419 (-0.17%)
Live555	3,014	2,659 (-11.78%)	3,009	2,784 (-7.48%)
OpenSSH	3,707	3,472 (-6.34%)	3,608	3,603 (-0.14%)
OpenSSL	10,888	9,854 (-9.5%)	10,140	10,135 (-0.05%)
TinyDTLS	581	310 (-46.64%)	534	498 (-6.74%)
Dcmtk	3,168	3,118 (-1.58%)	3,119	3,112 (-0.22%)
Kamailio	11,159	9,497 (-14.89%)	8,557	9,099 (+6.33%)

From the experiments with Nyx-Net, it could be inferred that sequence mutation plays a significant role in improving code coverage. With sufficient cycles of tests, it can significantly improve code coverage. However, the performance of AFLNet indicates that with limited cycles of tests, it is challenging to improve code coverage. It suggests that the sequence mutation is likely to generate message sequences that meet complex conditions. Yet, SOTA sequence mutation methods have high uncertainties, leaving room to improve toward a more stable and optimal direction.

Finding 2: 👍 Sequence mutation can effectively improve branch coverage, but existing SOTA techniques are intuitive and nondeterministic. ★ It is worthwhile to optimize the sequence mutation techniques.

4.2 RQ2. Effectiveness of State Machine Coverage

Apart from code coverage, for stateful protocols, it is intuitive to evaluate state machine coverage during the testing. However, the ways to model and calculate the states vary from one work to another. Yet, without standard and unified evaluation criteria, the comparison is meaningless.

Table 3. The Evaluation Results on State Transition Coverage. The symbol "–" denotes that the corresponding fuzzer is unable to perform testing on the corresponding benchmark.

Benchmark	Seed	Nyx-Net	AFLNet	StateAFL	AFLNetLegion	SnapFuzz	AFLNWE
Bftpd	1	2	2	2	2	–	2
LightFTP	5	**18**	**18**	10	**18**	10	1
ProFTPD	8	**58**	37	37	33	–	14
Pure-FTPd	1	1	1	1	1	–	1
Forked-Daapd	5	–	**7**	5	**7**	–	5
Live555	23	**35**	**35**	32	28	16	9
OpenSSH	5	5	5	5	5	–	5
OpenSSL	12	**20**	**20**	17	**20**	–	15
TinyDTLS	1	12	**18**	12	12	6	4
Dcmtk	7	9	**10**	**10**	**10**	**10**	9
Kamailio	5	**6**	5	5	5	–	0

We extended the state machine coverage method used in StateFuzz [32] to eliminate discrepancies. The principles for identifying state variables from programs are: (1) longer lifecycles than local variables, (2) updated by user input, and (3) impact on control flow across multiple modules. Using these extended principles, we identify state variables from the program source code and pipeline the state machine coverage for all fuzzers.

After identifying state variables, we calculate the total number of covered states and state transitions in each experimental round, focusing on the number of covered state transitions for better display. The table of covered states is placed in online website [15]. We also calculate the average state path length (APL), which represents the average length of the path from the initial state to the covered state. Higher APL indicates that fuzzers test more states far from the initial state and deeper path code. Note that we do not report state machine coverage for DNS and SMTP, as they are not typical stateful protocols.

Table 3 shows the evaluation result on state transition coverage. We can see that AFLNet and Nyx-Net cover the most state transitions in general. StateAFL and AFLNetLegion are in the second tier, and they perform worse than AFLNet and Nyx-Net on some benchmarks. Expect Dcmtk, SnapFuzz's performance is worse than StateAFL and AFLNetLegion.

On benchmarks LightFTP, Forked-Daapd, Live555, TinyDTLS and Kamailio, AFLNWE covers fewer states and state transitions than the seed already covered. The reason is that AFLNWE sends all the messages in one test case. But these benchmarks require fuzzers to send messages one by one. If one fuzzer sends multiple messages in one network packet to these benchmarks, it may drop the network packet and refuse to deal with it.

Furthermore, we analyze the statistics in detail from two aspects. **First, Quantity of covered states and state transition.** Table 4 presents the evaluation results of Nyx-Net, Nyx-Net-NS (Nyx-Net with sequence mutation disabled), AFLNet, and AFLNet-NS (AFLNet with sequence mutation disabled). It is evident that even without state coverage guidance, Nyx-Net consistently performs on par with state-guided fuzzers such as AFLNet across most benchmarks. It only underperforms on TinyDTLS and Dcmtk compared to AFLNet, and outperforms other fuzzers on ProFTPD.

Table 4. The Evaluation Results on State Transition Coverage with Disabling Sequence Mutation. The columns "Nyx-Net-NS" and "AFLNet-NS" show the number of covered state transitions when the sequence mutation is disabled. The blue-box and orange-box highlight the results where the number of covered state transitions increases or decreases with sequence mutation disabled, respectively. The data in the brackets are the reduction or increase. Because Nyx-Net is unable to perform testing on Forked-Daapd, we remove them from this table.

Benchmark	Nyx-Net	Nyx-Net-NS	AFLNet	AFLNet-NS
Bftpd	2	2	2	2
LightFTP	18	9 (-9)	18	18
ProFTPD	58	14 (-44)	37	37
Pure-FTPd	1	1	1	1
Live555	35	25 (-10)	35	32 (-3)
OpenSSH	5	5	5	5
OpenSSL	20	18 (-2)	20	17 (-3)
TinyDTLS	12	4 (-8)	18	12 (-6)
Dcmtk	9	9	10	10
Kamailio	6	5 (-1)	5	6 (+1)

Nyx-Net's state transition coverage decreases more than AFLNet's on most benchmarks. This suggests that without state coverage guidance and sequence mutation, it is challenging for fuzzers to cover more state transitions. AFLNet, guided by state coverage, also shows decreased coverage on some benchmarks when sequence mutation is disabled, highlighting the crucial role of sequence mutation in increasing state machine coverage. There is an overlap between state coverage guidance and sequence mutation in their effectiveness on state machine coverage. To cover specific states and transitions, fuzzers need to generate specific message types and combine them into sequences in a specific order, which is difficult without sequence mutation.

Finding 3: 👍 Sequence mutation plays an essential role in increasing state machine coverage.

Second, the Average Path Length of Covered States. Table 5 shows the evaluation result of APL. Exclude AFLNWE, Nyx-Net has the lowest APL, performing the worst on most benchmarks, while AFLNet and StateAFL perform the best on different benchmarks, and AFLNetLegion lies in the middle. Compared with Nyx-Net and AFLNet, AFLNet outperforms Nyx-Net on APL by 5.2% to 67.3% in six benchmarks (including Bftpd, LightFTP, Live555, OpenSSH, OpenSSL, and Dcmtk).

Table 5. The Average State Path Length (APL). The APL is that the average length of path form initial state to covered state. High APL means fuzzers test more states which far from initial state. The symbol "–" denotes that the corresponding fuzzer is unable to perform testing on the corresponding benchmark.

Benchmark	Nyx-Net	AFLNet	StateAFL	AFLNetLegion	SnapFuzz	AFLNWE
Bftpd	1.01	**1.69**	1.2	1.61	–	1.32
LightFTP	1.12	**1.35**	1.07	1.21	1.3	1
ProFTPD	**1.44**	1.14	1.28	1.34	–	1.28
Pure-FTPd	1	1	1	1	–	1
Forked-Daapd	–	**1.12**	1.07	1.08	–	1.03
Live555	1.14	**1.21**	1.18	1.19	1.2	1.2
OpenSSH	1.68	**1.86**	1.85	1.71	–	1.85
OpenSSL	1.35	**1.68**	1.49	1.56	–	1.1
TinyDTLS	**1.46**	1.2	1.17	1.12	1.24	1.01
Dcmtk	2.89	3.2	3.64	3,89	**5.46**	2.92
Kamailio	**2.98**	1.81	2.02	2.5	–	0

But Nyx-Net has the highest APL on ProFTPD, TinyDTLS, and Kamailio. For ProFTPD, the direct reason is that Nyx-Net covers more state transitions. FTP's definition is simple while ProFTPD implements many complex features. ProFTPD has an LoC that is at least 7.8 times larger than other FTP programs in the benchmark. So Nyx-Net with high test throughput covers more state transitions in a limited time (24h). For TinyDTLS and Kamailio, we find that it is due to the feature of DTLS and SIP protocol. They are all based on unreliable UDP protocol. This leads to a large number of test cases being discarded during the initial stages when tested by other fuzzers. It ultimately causes these fuzzers to focus on the initial and the final states. In contrast, Nyx-Net replaces the asynchronous unreliable UDP protocol with the synchronous shared memory (i.e., hooking the read function and using shared memory to put test case), making TinyDTLS and Kamailio more capable of correctly handling test cases.

Finding 4: ★ It is essential to replace the asynchronous network socket with synchronous share memory when fuzzing stateful network programs.

Based on the above observations, the fuzzers with the state coverage guidance lead to more covered states and transitions than those without. As a result, more protocol codes could be covered and tested, increasing the possibility of hidden bugs being revealed.

Finding 5: 👍 ★ State coverage guidance enables the fuzzers to reach deep states, which are hard to reach if guided by code coverage only.

4.3 RQ3. Bug Revealing Capability

After evaluating the test adequacy in terms of code coverage (*i.e.*, branch coverage) and state machine coverage (*i.e.*, state and transition coverage), we further study the bug revealing capability of fuzzing techniques. In particular, we use ASAN and GDB to record all bugs' backtrace and conduct a manual analysis of all bugs. We deduplicate bugs with the same root cause by recognizing different bugs' backtrace. About detailed experiment data like time-to-bug is avaiable on the online website [15]. And the total number of bugs revealed in the experiment is shown in the Table 6. Nyx-Net and AFLNet perform the best, with respective strengths and weaknesses. AFLNetLegion and StateAFL perform at a second-tier level with similar results, while SnapFuzz performs at the third-tier level. AFLNWE performs the worst on bug revealing. AFLNet achieved better results on TinyDTLS and Live555, while Nyx-Net individually revealed bugs on ProFTPD. Both revealed the same number of bugs on Dcmtk and Dnsmasq. Compared with the baseline fuzzer AFLNWE, SnapFuzz revealed the same number of bugs on TinyDTLS.

Table 6. Number of Bugs Revealed by Fuzzers. The symbol "–" denotes that the corresponding fuzzer is unable to perform testing on the corresponding benchmark. The benchmarks where no fuzzers can reveal bugs are excluded.

Benchmark	Nyx-Net	AFLNet	StateAFL	AFLNetLegion	SnapFuzz	AFLNWE	Total
ProFTPD	**1**	0	0	0	–	0	1
Dcmtk	**1**	**1**	**1**	**1**	1	1	1
Dnsmasq	**1**	**1**	**1**	**1**	**1**	0	1
Live555	**4**	**4**	3	3	3	1	5
TinyDTLS	3	**7**	4	4	2	2	7

Furthermore, we carefully analyze the bugs that were revealed and categorize them into three types according to the locations of the root causes.

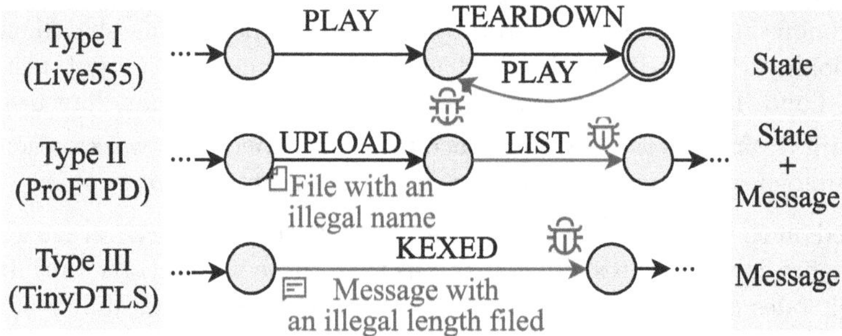

Fig. 3. Different Types Bug in Stateful Protocol Implementations. The destinations of red arrows are the states where bugs are revealed.

TYPE I. State-Related Bugs. Type I bugs, pertaining solely to protocol state, manifest during state transition handling within the protocol implementation. To trigger these bugs, it is necessary to construct a specific message sequence. In Fig. 3, we use a bug revealed in Live555 by AFLNet as an example. The bug, revealed only by AFLNet, is triggered by sending a TEARDOWN message to stop the video stream, followed by a PLAY message to resume the previously stopped video stream. Other revealed bugs are UAF bugs.

As shown in Table 7, AFLNet performs better in revealing this type of bug compared to Nyx-Net. The reason for Nyx-Net's poor performance in this aspect is its lack of state coverage guidance. State-related bugs need to be covered not only to specific code, but also to specific states and state transitions. Therefore, state coverage is necessary as an independent dimension for test effectiveness evaluation. Although state coverage guidance cannot bring significant improvement to code coverage, it can improve the bug discovery ability for stateful protocol programs. Currently, compared with code coverage guidance scheduling algorithms, state coverage guidance scheduling algorithms are still simple, which is a worthwhile research direction.

Table 7. Number of Different Types Bugs Revealed by Fuzzers.

Bug Type	Nyx-Net	AFLNet	StateAFL	AFLNetLegion	SnapFuzz	AFLNWE	Total
I	3	**4**	3	3	2	0	4
II	**1**	0	0	0	0	0	1
III	6	**9**	6	6	5	4	10

Finding 6: ★ State coverage is another evaluation metric of test effectiveness that is different from code coverage. State coverage guidance can help fuzzers find more bugs in situations where it is difficult to improve code coverage.

Type II. State and Message Related Bugs. As shown in Type II of Fig. 3, the cause of these bugs is related to both the protocol state and message. To reveal such a bug, it is necessary to first construct and send a specific message, and then make the program under test reach a specific state. We will use a bug revealed by Nyx-Net in ProFTPD as an example. This bug is revealed when a file with a non-printable character name is stored in the FTP server, followed by sending a message to make the FTP server list all the file names it stores. The root cause of the bug is an incorrect calculation of the buffer length when processing non-printable characters, resulting in a buffer overflow. Revealing this type of bug requires both constructing specific messages and specific message sequences. As shown in Table 7, only Nyx-Net could reveal this type of bug.

Type III. Bugs that Relate to Protocol Messages. As shown in Type III of Fig. 3, the cause of these bugs is unrelated to the protocol state, and revealing them only requires constructing specific types of messages. We use a bug revealed by the fuzzers in TinyDTLS as an example. This bug occurs in the message parsing logic of TinyDTLS. TinyDTLS directly uses the content from message as size of one area of memory, this makes TinyDTLS crash when the size is wrong. As shown in Table 7, all bugs revealed by ALFNWE are this type. It indicates that fuzzers without sequence mutation and state coverage guidance is difficult to reveal bugs related states.

Upon synthesizing the analysis above, traditional fuzzers can be effective in discovering bugs that can be triggered by the construction of specific messages. Also, state coverage guidance can help fuzzers to better discover bugs that can be triggered by covering specific states. But for bugs that can be triggered by the construction of specific messages and covering special states, current fuzzers lack an effective method to discover them. It is meaningful to develop new methods to discover bugs more effectively by generating specific messages in specific states. One possible direction is to find the correspondence between states and messages.

Finding 7: 👎 Current fuzzers lack effective algorithms for discovering bugs that need to be triggered by a specific message while covering a specific state.

4.4 RQ4. Evaluation on Test Throughput

Table 8 shows the evaluation results of fuzzers on test throughput, with the "Nyx-Net-NR" column showing Nyx-Net's throughput when state recovery is disabled. Nyx-Net significantly outperforms other fuzzers in test throughput, with the method of replacing asynchronous network sockets with synchronous shared memory contributing the most to the increase, often leading to a several-fold improvement. In contrast, state recovery improves test throughput by no more than four times. In most cases, it does not exceed a one-fold improvement.

Table 8. The Evaluation Results on Test Throughput. The column "Nyx-Net-NR" shows the test throughput when Nyx-Net's state recovery is disabled. The symbol "–" denotes that the corresponding fuzzer is incapable of performing testing on the corresponding benchmark. Nyx-Net's data on Forked-daapd is taken from [29].

Benchmark	Nyx-Net	Nyx-Net-NR	AFLNet	StateAFL	AFLNetLegion	SnapFuzz	AFLNWE
Bftpd	**1,009.8**	438.8	3.4	2	4.4	–	4.1
LightFTP	**1,439.1**	1,115.2	4.9	1.3	1.5	264.9	19.3
ProFTPD	**458.9**	354.5	1.9	1.6	0.5	–	1.7
Pure-FTPd	**968.3**	751.8	6	5.2	5.3	–	3.7
Dnsmasq	**2,463**	1,690.7	5.8	7	6.3	376.7	36.4
Exim	298.7	**315**	1.8	2.4	4.3	–	3.1
Forked-Daapd	**19.5**	–	0.8	0.7	0.5	–	0.8
Live555	**89.7**	68.9	4.5	2.2	3.6	29.4	44.1
OpenSSH	**618.7**	155.3	21.3	16	21	–	2.2
OpenSSL	319.4	**446.7**	5.6	3.3	6.2	–	14.7
TinyDTLS	924	**1,750.5**	2.3	1.6	1.3	253.5	14.8
Dcmtk	**2,028.5**	1,021.9	25.5	3.1	54.6	82.3	6
Kamailio	**575.9**	176.7	4.5	0.1	4.2	–	0.8

Fuzzers wait a specific period after sending each message, as they cannot know when the program has completed processing it. This waiting time is usually the longest processing time the program takes, leading to longer waiting times for test cases with more messages. This is the primary reason for the loss of throughput. Consequently, the method of replacing the asynchronous network socket with synchronous share memory can substantially improve test throughput. Nyx-Net hooks the library function like read and uses the shared memory to put the test case.

Finding 8: 👍 Replacing the asynchronous network socket with synchronous share memory is the most useful method to improve test throughput.

4.5 Summary and Analyze

In the following, we summarize and analyze the findings found in stateful protocol fuzzer experiments based on three stateful protocol fuzzing methods.

For **state coverage guidance**, we conclude the following:

Effectiveness in Reaching Deep States: Findings 5 and 6 highlight that state coverage guidance significantly contributes to reaching deeper states. This is crucial for finding bugs that are not detectable through traditional code coverage metrics alone. It emphasizes that state coverage is a distinct and valuable metric for assessing test effectiveness, particularly in complex stateful programs where certain bugs only manifest in specific states.

Limitations in Code Coverage Improvement: According to Finding 1, state coverage guidance is effective for deep state exploration, it might not contribute to a broader code base exploration.

For **sequence mutation**, we conclude the following:

Impact on Code and State Coverage: Findings 2 and 3 emphasize the role of sequence mutation in effectively improving both code and state coverage. This suggests that optimizing sequence mutation methods could be a valuable area for future work, as current methods are noted to be overly simplistic and random.

For **replacement of asynchronous network socket with synchronous shared memory**, we conclude the following:

Improvement in Test Throughput: Finding 8 indicates that this replacement is the most effective method for improving test throughput. This is a critical consideration for the efficiency and speed of fuzzing processes, especially when dealing with complex stateful network programs.

Essential for Fuzzing Stateful Network Programs: Finding 4 highlights the necessity of this replacement for fuzzing stateful network programs. It implies that synchronous shared memory facilitates a more controlled and efficient testing environment, which is essential for the intricate environment of stateful fuzzing.

5 Threats to Validity

There are three major validity threats. First, the choice of subjects may lead to potential biases in the experimental results. In our study, we selected 13 subjects that have widespread usage in real-world scenarios, encompassing both simplistic and intricate protocol implementations. Second, the randomness inherent in the fuzzing process also poses a threat. To mitigate this factor, we executed multiple iterations of experiments and computed the mean and aggregate of the experimental outcomes. Third, concerning RQ2, determining state variables can affect the results. In prior research, disparate fuzzers opted for state variables to calculate state machine coverage based on their individual algorithms. In contrast, our study ensures that all fuzzers employ an identical set of state variables for state machine coverage computation.

6 Related Work

Template-Based Fuzzers. Early fuzzing work [6,9,13,25,26] on stateful protocols mostly relied on templates. Banks et al. proposed SNOOZE [6], a framework that uses an XML-based descriptive language to allow users to specify message grammar. BooFuzz [26] provided users with APIs that facilitate the specification of rules for fuzzing stateful protocols. SGPFuzzer [31] and PAVFuzz [33] were respectively based on Boofuzz and Peach. They added code coverage guidance.

Mutation-Based Fuzzers. Mutation-based fuzzers do not require manually crafted templates and have been widely researched and used in recent years. In addition to the ones mentioned earlier, there are the following works. SNPSFuzzer [16] used process-level snapshots to improve test throughput. PNFUZZ [14] adopted a clustering-based approach to identify protocol states.

FitM [20] used man-in-the-middle and qemu snapshots to test stateful protocol implementations. Bleem [19] also used man-in-the-middle to test stateful protocol implementations. NSFuzz [28] found state variants by program analysis. IoTInfer [30] used L* algorithm to construct the state machine. ChatAFL [22] uses a large languae model to predict the state transition. LABRADOR [18] obtains state from response for fuzzing black-box IoT devices.

7 Conclusion

In this paper, we conducted a systematic and fair study on the effectiveness of six state-of-the-art fuzzers for stateful protocol fuzzing using the benchmark ProFuzzBench. We compared these techniques based on code coverage, state machine coverage, bug revealing, and test throughput. Our findings suggest that (i) state coverage guidance effectively navigates complex states, despite limitations in directly improving code coverage; (ii) sequence mutation is crucial but need refinement; (iii) replacing asynchronous network sockets with synchronous shared memory improves both test throughput and efficiency. Our research provides insight into improving existing techniques and developing new ones.

Acknowledgment. The authors would like to thank the anonymous reviewers for their valuable feedback. This work is partly supported by the National Key R&D Program of China under Grant #2022YFB3103900, Strategic Priority Research Program of the CAS under Grant #XDCO2030200, Chinese National Natural Science Foundation (Grants #62032010, #62202462), and Hong Kong RGC/GRF #16205821.

References

1. Alrahem, T., et al.: Interstate: a stateful protocol fuzzer for sip. Defcon **15**, 1–5 (2007)
2. Andronidis, A., Cadar, C.: Snapfuzz: high-throughput fuzzing of network applications. In: Ryu, S., Smaragdakis, Y. (eds.) ISSTA '22: 31st ACM SIGSOFT International Symposium on Software Testing and Analysis, 18–22 July 2022, pp. 340–351. ACM, Virtual Event, South Korea (2022)
3. Aschermann, C., Schumilo, S., Abbasi, A., Holz, T.: IJON: exploring deep state spaces via fuzzing. In: 2020 IEEE Symposium on Security and Privacy, SP 2020, 18–21 May 2020, pp. 1597–1612. IEEE, San Francisco, CA, USA (2020)
4. Atlidakis, V., Godefroid, P., Polishchuk, M.: Restler: stateful REST API fuzzing. In: Proceedings of the 41st International Conference on Software Engineering, ICSE 2019, 25–31 May 2019, pp. 748–758. IEEE/ACM, Montreal, QC, Canada (2019)
5. Ba, J., Böhme, M., Mirzamomen, Z., Roychoudhury, A.: Stateful greybox fuzzing. In: 31st USENIX Security Symposium (USENIX Security 22), pp. 3255–3272. USENIX Association, Boston, MA, August 2022
6. Banks, G., Cova, M., Felmetsger, V., Almeroth, K., Kemmerer, R., Vigna, G.: SNOOZE: toward a stateful network protocol fuzzer. In: Katsikas, S.K., López, J., Backes, M., Gritzalis, S., Preneel, B. (eds.) ISC 2006. LNCS, vol. 4176, pp. 343–358. Springer, Heidelberg (2006). https://doi.org/10.1007/11836810_25

7. beyondsecurity: beSTORM (2022). https://www.beyondsecurity.com/bestorm-and-the-sdl
8. Ferreira, G.M.: SPIKE (2022). https://github.com/guilhermeferreira/spikepp
9. GitLab: peach-fuzzer-community (2022). https://gitlab.com/peachtech/peach-fuzzer-community
10. Goodin, D.: NSA-leaking Shadow Brokers just dumped its most damaging release yet (2022). https://arstechnica.com/security/2017/04/nsa-leaking-shadow-brokers-just-dumped-its-most-damaging-release-yet/
11. Google: AFL (2021). https://github.com/google/AFL
12. Google: AFLNWE (2021). https://github.com/thuanpv/aflnwe
13. Gorbunov, S., Rosenbloom, A.: Autofuzz: automated network protocol fuzzing framework. Ijcsns **10**(8), 239 (2010)
14. He, H., Wang, Y.: Pnfuzz: a stateful network protocol fuzzing approach based on packet clustering. Comput. Sci. Inf. Technol. (CS & IT) **10**, 61–69 (2020)
15. Jian, K., et al.: Fuzzing for stateful protocol implementations: are we there yet? Evaluation's data (2024). https://sites.google.com/view/stateprotocolfuzzevaluation
16. Li, J., Li, S., Sun, G., Chen, T., Yu, H.: Snpsfuzzer: a fast greybox fuzzer for stateful network protocols using snapshots. IEEE Trans. Inf. Forensics Secur. **17**, 2673–2687 (2022)
17. Liu, D., Pham, V., Ernst, G., Murray, T., Rubinstein, B.I.P.: State selection algorithms and their impact on the performance of stateful network protocol fuzzing. In: IEEE International Conference on Software Analysis, Evolution and Reengineering, SANER 2022, 15–18 March 2022, pp. 720–730. IEEE, Honolulu, HI, USA (2022)
18. Liu, H., et al.: Labrador: response guided directed fuzzing for black-box IoT devices. In: 2024 IEEE Symposium on Security and Privacy (SP), p. 126. IEEE Computer Society, Los Alamitos, CA, USA (2024)
19. Luo, Z., et al.: Bleem: packet sequence oriented fuzzing for protocol implementations. In: 32st USENIX Security Symposium, USENIX Security 2023, 9–11 AUGUST 2023. p. Accepted. USENIX Association, ANAHEIM, CA, USA (2023)
20. Maier, D., Bittner, O., Munier, M., Beier, J.: FiTM: binary-only coverage-guided fuzzing for stateful network protocols. In: Workshop on Binary Analysis Research (BAR), 2022 (2022)
21. McKnight, P.E., Najab, J.: Mann-whitney u test. The Corsini encyclopedia of psychology (2010)
22. Meng, R., Mirchev, M., Böhme, M., Roychoudhury, A.: Large language model guided protocol fuzzing. In: Proceedings of the 31st Annual Network and Distributed System Security Symposium (NDSS) (2024)
23. Natella, R.: Stateafl: greybox fuzzing for stateful network servers. Empir. Softw. Eng. **27**(7), 191 (2022)
24. Natella, R., Pham, V.: Profuzzbench: a benchmark for stateful protocol fuzzing. In: Cadar, C., Zhang, X. (eds.) ISSTA '21: 30th ACM SIGSOFT International Symposium on Software Testing and Analysis, 11–17 July 2021, pp. 662–665. ACM, Virtual Event, Denmark (2021)
25. OpenRCE: Sulley (2019). https://github.com/llvm/llvm-project
26. Pereyda, J.: boofuzz (2022). https://github.com/jtpereyda/boofuzz
27. Pham, V., Böhme, M., Roychoudhury, A.: AFLNET: a greybox fuzzer for network protocols. In: 13th IEEE International Conference on Software Testing, Validation and Verification, ICST 2020, 24–28 October 2020, pp. 460–465. IEEE, Porto, Portugal (2020)

28. Qin, S., Hu, F., Zhao, B., Yin, T., Zhang, C.: Registered report: nsfuzz: towards efficient and state-aware network service fuzzing. In: International Fuzzing Workshop (FUZZING) 2022. San Diego, CA, USA (2022)
29. Schumilo, S., Aschermann, C., Jemmett, A., Abbasi, A., Holz, T.: Nyx-net: network fuzzing with incremental snapshots. In: Bromberg, Y., Kermarrec, A., Kozyrakis, C. (eds.) EuroSys '22: Seventeenth European Conference on Computer Systems, April 5–8, 2022, pp. 166–180. ACM, Rennes, France (2022)
30. Shu, Z., Yan, G.: Iotinfer: automated blackbox fuzz testing of iot network protocols guided by finite state machine inference. IEEE Internet Things J. **9**(22), 22737–22751 (2022)
31. Yu, Y., Chen, Z., Gan, S., Wang, X.: Sgpfuzzer: a state-driven smart graybox protocol fuzzer for network protocol implementations. IEEE Access **8**, 198668–198678 (2020)
32. Zhao, B., et al.: StateFuzz: system call-based state-aware linux driver fuzzing. In: 31st USENIX Security Symposium (USENIX Security 22), pp. 3273–3289. USENIX Association, Boston, MA (2022)
33. Zuo, F., Luo, Z., Yu, J., Liu, Z., Jiang, Y.: Pavfuzz: state-sensitive fuzz testing of protocols in autonomous vehicles. In: 58th ACM/IEEE Design Automation Conference, DAC 2021, 5–9 December 2021, pp. 823–828. IEEE, San Francisco, CA, USA (2021)

CtxFuzz: Discovering Heap-Based Memory Vulnerabilities Through Context Heap Operation Sequence Guided Fuzzing

Jiacheng Jiang[1], Cheng Wen[2(✉)], and Shengchao Qin[2(✉)]

[1] College of Computer Science and Software Engineering, Shenzhen University, Shenzhen, China

[2] Guangzhou Institute of Technology, Xidian University, Xi'an, China

wencheng@xidian.edu.cn, shengchao.qin@gmail.com

Abstract. Heap-based memory vulnerabilities are significant contributors to software security and reliability. The presence of these vulnerabilities is influenced by factors such as code coverage, the frequency of heap operations, and the specific execution order. Current fuzzing solutions aim to efficiently detect these vulnerabilities by utilizing static analysis or incorporating feedback on the sequence of heap operations. However, these solutions have limited practical applicability and do not comprehensively address the temporal and spatial aspects of heap operations. In this paper, we propose a dedicated fuzzing technique called CtxFuzz to efficiently discover heap-based temporal and spatial memory vulnerabilities without requiring any domain knowledge. CtxFuzz utilizes context heap operation sequences (the sequences of heap operations such as allocation, deallocation, read, and write that are associated with corresponding heap memory addresses) as a new feedback mechanism to guide the fuzzing process. By doing so, CtxFuzz can explore more heap states and trigger more heap-based memory vulnerabilities, both temporal and spatial. We evaluate CtxFuzz on 9 real-world open-source programs and compare their performance with 5 state-of-the-art fuzzers. The results demonstrate that CtxFuzz outperforms most fuzzers in terms of discovering heap-based memory vulnerabilities. Moreover, Our experiments led to the identification of 10 zero-day vulnerabilities (10 CVEs).

1 Introduction

Heap-based temporal vulnerabilities (*e.g.*, null-pointer dereference, use-after-free and double-free) and spatial memory vulnerabilities (*e.g.*, buffer-overflow and allocation failure) pose serious threats to software security and reliability [6,20,31]. These vulnerabilities occur when a program performs incorrect or unsafe operations on heap memory, such as using freed memory, accessing invalid memory addresses, or consuming a large amount of memory. Such operations can result in memory corruption, which can cause the program to crash, behave unpredictably, or execute arbitrary code injected by an attacker.

W.-N. Chin and Z. Xu (Eds.): TASE 2024, LNCS 14777, pp. 205–223, 2024.
https://doi.org/10.1007/978-3-031-64626-3_12

Problem and Challenges. Detecting heap-based memory vulnerabilities is challenging, as they depend on various factors such as the frequency of heap operations, the specific execution order, and code coverage [14,16,24]. Moreover, these vulnerabilities can manifest themselves in different ways, such as temporal errors [4,11,22] and spatial errors [5,26,27]. Hence, it is essential to have a testing technique that can efficiently and comprehensively detect these vulnerabilities without necessitating prior knowledge of the program or the heap structure.

In recent years, fuzzing has emerged as a popular and effective testing technique for detecting and mitigating memory vulnerabilities. This technique involves supplying random or semi-random inputs to a program and observing its behavior for any irregularities. However, most fuzzing techniques do not adequately address heap-based memory vulnerabilities, particularly those that are temporal in nature. These vulnerabilities are not solely determined by code coverage, but also depend on the specific order of heap operations. Instead of being solely influenced by the amount of code exercised, these vulnerabilities arise from the sequence of heap operations. Consequently, fuzzing techniques that solely rely on code coverage as feedback may overlook a significant number of temporal errors. On the other hand, certain fuzzing techniques have been proposed to tackle heap-based memory vulnerabilities by utilizing various types of feedback, such as operation sequence coverage [28], typestate analysis [23], taint inference [30], memory usage [26], or user-defined properties [12,15]. However, these techniques often have limitations, such as focusing on a specific type of heap operation (*e.g.*, allocation or deallocation) [28], requiring expert knowledge [12], relying on imprecise static analysis [23], and thus limiting their practical applicability and effectiveness. Furthermore, these techniques frequently disregard the holistic nature of memory vulnerabilities, impeding a comprehensive approach to identifying and mitigating both temporal and spatial issues simultaneously.

Approach. We propose a novel fuzzing technique called CtxFuzz that aims to overcome the limitations of existing fuzzing solutions and efficiently discover both heap-based temporal and spatial memory vulnerabilities. CtxFuzz is a greybox fuzzing technique that does not require any domain knowledge. Instead, it utilizes Context Heap Operation S equences (CHOS) as a feedback mechanism to guide the fuzzing process and input generation. CHOS refers to the sequences of heap operations (*e.g.*, allocation, deallocation, read, and write) associated with the corresponding heap memory addresses. CtxFuzz monitors the program's heap state and heap memory addresses accessed through instrumentation. Modifying the seed selection strategy by counting the number of generated CHOS can facilitate the generation of inputs that trigger more potential vulnerabilities. CtxFuzz is capable of detecting both temporal and spatial errors by manipulating the heap memory addresses and CHOS in various ways.

Evaluation. We evaluated the effectiveness and efficiency of CtxFuzz on 9 widely used real-world open-source programs that have undergone extensive testing by other fuzzers. In our comparison, we assessed CtxFuzz against 5 state-of-the-art fuzzers, namely AFL [29], AFL++ [7], HTFuzz [28], Memlock [26], and TortoiseFuzz [25]. The results demonstrate that CtxFuzz outperforms most fuzzers in terms of discovering heap-based memory vulnerabilities. Specifically, CtxFuzz found 1.3x, 1.3x, 1.4x, 4.1x, and 1.7x more vulnerabilities than AFL, AFL++, HTFuzz, Memlock, and TortoiseFuzz, respectively. Furthermore, CtxFuzz identified 10 new zero-day vulnerabilities (10 CVEs) that had not been reported by any other studies. We promptly reported these vulnerabilities to the respective developers and vendors, receiving positive feedback and acknowledgments.

In summary, this paper makes the following contributions.

- ***Originality.*** We propose a dedicated fuzzing solution CtxFuzz to efficiently discover both heap-based temporal and spatial memory vulnerabilities without requiring any domain knowledge.
- ***Technique.*** Our approach leverages context heap operation sequences (CHOS) as a feedback mechanism to guide the fuzzing process and input generation. CtxFuzz monitors the program's heap state and heap memory addresses accessed through instrumentation. Modifying the seed selection strategy by counting the number of generated CHOS can facilitate the generation of inputs that trigger more potential vulnerabilities.
- ***Evaluation.*** We have implemented CtxFuzz and evaluated its effectiveness on 9 real-world open-source programs. We demonstrate that CtxFuzz outperforms 5 state-of-the-art fuzzers in terms of discovering heap-based memory vulnerabilities.
- ***Practical Impact.*** We discover 10 zero-day vulnerabilities (10 CVEs) that have not been previously reported, and report them to the corresponding developers and vendors.

2 Motivation

This section highlights the limitations of existing grey-box fuzzing techniques in detecting heap-based memory vulnerabilities. We also provide an informal description of how CtxFuzz works, exemplified by a zero-day vulnerability CVE-2023-49554 that was discovered by CtxFuzz.

Listing 1.1 shows a use-after-free (UAF) vulnerability in the real-world code processing tool *Yasm*. The vulnerability is triggered by a specific order of code execution in the function `do_directive`, which is repeatedly called by the function `nasm_parser_parse` (line 33) along with the function `pp_getline` (line 27). The function `do_directive` has a switch statement that can execute two cases: `PP_REP` (line 7) and `PP_ENDREP` (line 9). In the first case, it creates a heap memory object for a variable named `defining` (line 8) and stores its address in another variable named `istk→mstk` (line 10). In the second case, it uses the same address to access the memory object (line 10). However, before going back to `do_directive`, the function `pp_getline` may free the memory object (line 19). This leads to a UAF when `do_directive` tries to use the freed memory object again (line 3).

Existing mainstream grey-box fuzzers, such as AFL [29] mainly use code coverage as feedback to guide the fuzzing. In this case, the UAF can be triggered

```
1 // from modules/preprocs/nasm/nasm-pp.c
2 static int do_directive(Token *tline){
3     if (... && !istk->mstk->in_progress){ // Crash
4         return NO_DIRECTIVE_FOUND;
5     }
6     switch (i) {
7         case PP_REP:
8             defining = nasm_malloc(sizeof(MMacro)); // Memory allocation
9         case PP_ENDREP:
10            istk->mstk = defining; // Memory access
11    }
12 }
13
14 static char *pp_getline(void){
15    while (...){
16        ...
17        MMacro *m = istk->mstk; // Memory access
18        if (...) {
19            free_mmacro(m); // Memory deallocation
20        }
21    }
22    if (do_directive(tline) == DIRECTIVE_FOUND) {...}
23 }
24
25 // modules/preprocs/nasm/nasm-preproc.c
26 static char *nasm_preproc_get_line(yasm_preproc *preproc){
27    line = nasmpp.getline(); // a function pointer of pp_getline
28 }
29
30 // modules/parsers/nasm/nasm-parse.c
31 void nasm_parser_parse(yasm_parser_nasm *parser_nasm){
32    unsigned char *line;
33    while ((line=(unsigned char*)yasm_preproc_get_line(parser_nasm->preproc))!=NULL){
34        ...
35    }
36 }
37
38 void main(int argc, char *argv[]){
39    ...
40    nasm_parser_parse(...);
41 }
```

Listing 1.1. A UAF example simplified from CVE-2023-49554

if lines 8→10→17→19→3 are executed temporally. However, code coverage is not enough to capture the order and amount of heap operation, which is essential for triggering such heap-based memory vulnerabilities. Some fuzzing techniques also use heap operation sequences to detect heap-based memory vulnerabilities. For example, UAFL [23] uses static analysis to identify potential heap operation sequences and then directs fuzzing to cover them gradually. However, static analysis can miss some sequences, such as the aliasing between `defining` (line 8) and `istk→mstk` (line 10), or the pointees of the function pointer `getline` (line 27). HTFuzz [28] improves the diversity of heap operation sequences but does not take the corresponding memory objects into account. For example, both memory allocation (line 8) and deallocation (line 19) impact the variable `istk→mstk`. Additionally, HTFuzz overlooks memory read and write operations, exemplified by lines 10 and 17, that are critical in this context, thereby hindering efficient bug detection. Note that in our experiment, CtxFuzz was able to detect this bug in 10 h. HTFuzz and AFL took at least an additional 10 h compared to CtxFuzz. However, TortoiseFuzz [25] and MemLock [26] were unable to detect this vulnerability.

Our key insight is that tracking how heap operations manipulate different memory objects is crucial for delving into the intricate effects of memory management in the program and identifying vulnerabilities related to heap-based mem-

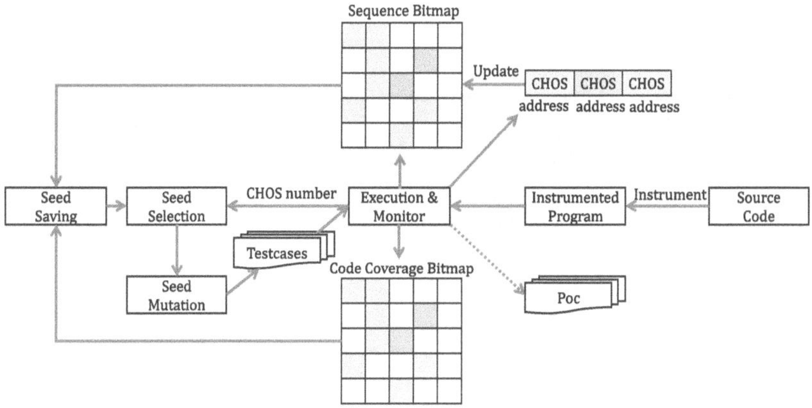

Fig. 1. The workflow of CtxFuzz

ory. Therefore, triggering various sequences of heap operations can be deemed as interesting behaviors similar to code coverage. CtxFuzz adheres to this concept by focusing on distinct heap memory addresses and the corresponding heap operations. Let us now explore the motivating example mentioned above. Assuming that we tracked each heap operation using a two-digit binary number representation: `00` for allocation, `01` for reading, `10` for writing, and `11` for deallocation. A set of heap operations can be represented as a sequence, and each sequence may be viewed as a distinct behavior of the programs. For instance, if the `do_directive` function allocates the heap memory address `0x1234` using `malloc` at line 8, we utilize the lower 16 bits of the address (`0x1234`) as the array index and record the operation `00` in the corresponding element. Subsequently, if a read operation to the address `0x1234` occurs, we append `01` to the respective element, resulting in `0001`. Finally, upon the function releasing the address `0x1234` with `free`, we add `11` to the allocated index, resulting in `000111`. This representation helps in identifying new behaviors in the sequence, similar to tracking code coverage. Our approach aids in maintaining a record of heap operation sequences for each memory address.

3 Methodology

3.1 Overview of CtxFuzz

The workflow of CtxFuzz is illustrated in Fig. 1. CtxFuzz follows the general workflow of grey-box fuzzers but introduces improvements in three areas, namely *feedback mechanism*, *instrumentation*, and *seed selection*. Specifically, CtxFuzz leverages the new context heap operation sequence (CHOS) feedback by recording a set of recently accessed heap memory addresses and their corresponding last heap operation sequences (*i.e.*, a new sequence bitmap in Fig. 1) at the entry of each basic block. To keep track of the CHOS information, CtxFuzz performs an

```
Algorithm 1: Tracking CHOS Feedback with Instrumentation
Input: A program P
Output: An instrumented program P'
Function SeqUpdate(SeqArray, RecentObj, Address, Code):
    SeqArray[Address] = SeqArray[Address] ≪ 2 | Code // Update operation sequence
    RecentObjUpdate(RecentObj, Address, K) // Update the last K accessed addresses
Function SeqFeedback(SeqCov, cur_loc, prev_loc, SeqArray, RecentObj):
    Hash = 0
    for each Address in RecentObj do
        Hash = Hash ⊕ (SeqArray[Address]&(1 ≪ (L × 2)) − 1))
    end
    SeqCov[cur_loc ⊕ prev_loc ⊕ Hash] + + // non-zero integer
INITIALIZE(BranchCov, SeqCov, SeqCount, SeqArray, RecentObj, LastOperation)
HeapInstMap = getHeapRelatedInstMap(P)
for each BB in each Func do
    cur_loc = RandomInt() // Get a basic block ID as AFL++
    Insert(BranchCov[cur_loc ⊕ prev_loc] + +) // Coverage feedback as AFL++
    for each Inst in each BB do
        if Inst in HeapInstMap and HeapInstMap[Inst] ≠ -1 then
            LastOperationUpdate(LastOperation, Inst, HeapInstMap[Inst])
    end
    for each Inst, Code in LastOperation do
        Insert(SeqUpdate(SeqArray, RecentObj, Inst, Code))
        Insert(SeqCount + +)
    end
    Insert(SeqFeedback(SeqCov, cur_loc, prev_loc, SeqArray, RecentObj)) // CHOS feedback
    prev_loc = cur_loc ≫ 1
end
```

LLVM-instrumentation pass to collect the heap-related operations and their corresponding addresses. Additionally, CTXFUZZ preserves testcases that actively contribute to either code coverage or context heap operation sequence coverage. And the seed selection strategy is refined to prioritize seeds based on the quantity of context heap operation sequences generated after their execution, thus enhancing the likelihood of uncovering potential vulnerabilities.

3.2 Context Heap Operation Sequence Feedback

Context Heap Operation Sequence (CHOS) feedback is a novel feedback mechanism that we propose for fuzzing. CHOS tracks the sequences of heap operations (*e.g.*, allocation, deallocation, read, and write) associated with corresponding heap memory addresses, and uses them to guide the generation and selection of testcases. CHOS differs from other feedback mechanisms, such as code coverage, in that it captures the dynamic behavior and state of the heap memory, which is often the source of memory vulnerabilities. CHOS also addresses the challenge of sequence record explosion, which occurs when the number of heap operation sequences grows exponentially with the number of heap memory addresses and operations. Sequence record explosion can cause significant memory and time overhead for fuzzing, and reduce the diversity and quality of testcases.

Generally, a simply way to track CHOS is to utilize all the heap operation sequences for all the heap memory addresses. However, this would be inefficient and redundant. Instead, we only utilize the last K accessed heap memory addresses, and their corresponding sequences formed by the last L heap operations. This is based on the principle of program locality, which states that programs tend to access the same or nearby memory locations repeatedly. By

Algorithm 2: Heap-related Instruction Analysis

```
Input: A program P
Output: Heap-Related Instruction Map HeapInstMap
Function getHeapRelatedInstMap(P):
    HeapInstMap ← {}
    for each Func in each Module do
        for each Arg in Func do
            if isPointerType(Arg) then
                HeapInstMap[Arg] = −1
        end
        for each BB in Func do
            for each Inst in each BB do
                if isCallInst(Inst) then
                    if isAllocFunc(Inst → getCalledFunction()) then
                        HeapInstMap[Inst] = ALLOC
                    else if isDeallocFunc(Inst → getCalledFunction()) then
                        HeapInstMap[Inst] = DEALLOC
                else if isLoadInst(Inst) and Inst → getOperand(0) in HeapInstMap then
                    HeapInstMap[Inst] = LOAD
                else if isStoreInst(Inst) then
                    if Inst → getOperand(0) in HeapInstMap then
                        HeapInstMap[Inst → getOperand(1)] = −1
                        HeapInstMap[Inst] = STORE
                    else if Inst → getOperand(1) in HeapInstMap then
                        HeapInstMap[Inst] = STORE
                else if isGetElementPtrInst(Inst) and Inst → getOperand(0) in
                 HeapInstMap then
                    HeapInstMap[Inst] = −1
                else if isBitCastInst(Inst) and Inst → getOperand(0) in HeapInstMap
                 then
                    HeapInstMap[Inst] = −1
            end
        end
    end
    return HeapInstMap
```

doing so, we can reduce the memory and time overhead of CHOS feedback, and focus on the most relevant and interesting heap operation sequences for fuzzing. This is similar to how AFL, a popular fuzzing system, saves edges to the code coverage bitmap at the entry of each basic block.

To use the heap operation sequences for fuzzing, we need a way to measure the difference or novelty of the sequences generated by different testcases. To do this, we represent each heap operation as a two-digit binary (*e.g.*, 00 for allocation, 01 for reading, 10 for writing, and 11 for deallocation) and use a simple but effective operation $\oplus$ (*a.k.a.*, XOR) to concatenate sequences for different addresses. Specifically, we select K heap memory addresses that are accessed by the testcase, and XOR the elements of the sequence array corresponding to those addresses (line 7 of function `SeqFeedback` in Algorithm 1). The result number can be considered as a representation for the heap operation sequences of the testcase. We then use this number as the index for updating the new sequence bitmap at the beginning of each basic block (line 9 of function `SeqFeedback`). The new sequence bitmap records whether a testcase has generated a new or different heap operation sequence compared to the previous testcases. If a testcase has generated a new sequence, we save the testcase as a seed for further fuzzing. Otherwise, we discard the testcase.

3.3 Instrumentation

To keep track of the CHOS information, we perform an instrumentation to collect the heap-related operations and their corresponding addresses. Algorithm 1 presents the details of our instrumentation. Our approach follows the general workflow of AFL++. Given that AFL++ already includes an LLVM-instrumentation pass [18], we have made direct modifications to it to instrument the target application while preserving the original instrumentation implemented by AFL++.

Code coverage information is collected by instrumenting the entry of each basic block using a bitmap named *BranchCov* (line 14). Prior to the instrumentation for the CHOS feedback, we perform a heap-related instruction analysis to collect the heap operations (line 11). In order to optimize fuzzing efficiency, we strategically preserve the last operation for each pointer within each basic block (lines 15–18) and instrument the preserved operations correspondingly (line 20). Additionally, we also instrument the target program to track the number of generated CHOS (line 21), which influences seed selection during fuzzing. Finally, we instrument the code to update the generated CHOS into an additional bitmap named *SeqCov* (line 23).

Our heap-related instruction analysis is presented in Algorithm 2, which takes a program as input and returns a map recording the heap-related instructions and their corresponding codes. To collect as many heap operations as possible, we record the pointer arguments in the map *HeapInstMap* with an uninteresting code –1 for each function (lines 4–7). The analysis proceeds instruction by instruction. If the instruction is involved a memory allocation function, such as `malloc()` and `realloc()`, it is recorded with the interesting code *ALLOC* (lines 11–12). Similarly, if the instruction is involved a memory deallocation function, such as `free`, it is recorded with the interesting code *DEALLOC* (lines 13–14). If the instruction is a *load* one (*i.e.*, memory reading operation) and the corresponding address is in the map (*i.e.*, interesting address), it is recorded with the interesting code *LOAD* (lines 15–16). The *store* instruction (*i.e.*, memory writing operations) is similar, but with two cases (lines 17–22). Finally, to avoid an excessive number of distinct memory addresses, we consider operations on arrays as operations on their corresponding base addresses (lines 23–24) and ignore the cast operations (lines 25–26). Note that, this analysis can be merged into the LLVM-instrumentation pass to optimize instrumentation efficiency. For better understanding, we keep them separately.

3.4 Fuzzing Loop and Seed Selection

The fuzzing loop of CtxFuzz is presented in Algorithm 3, which takes the instrumented program P' (obtained by Algorithm 1) and a set of initial seeds S as inputs and returns a set of crashes *crashSet*. The algorithm initialize the seed pool *Queue* as the initial seeds S (line 2). Then the algorithm performs the following process until interruption: it selects a seed from the seed pool *Queue* as the input (line 4) and assigns the input a *energy* value (line 5), which

Algorithm 3: Fuzzing Loop of CTXFUZZ

```
   Input: Instrumented program P', Initial seed inputs S
   Output: Set of crashes crashSet
1  crashSet ← ∅
2  Queue ← S
3  while not interruption do
4  |  input ← SelectSeed(Queue)
5  |  energy ← AssignEnergy(input)
6  |  for i = 0 to energy do
7  |  |  testcase ← Mutate(input)
8  |  |  BranchCov, SeqCov, SeqCount ← Execute(P', testcase)
9  |  |  if testcase triggers crash then
10 |  |  |  crashSet ← crashSet ⋃ {testcase }
11 |  |  else if isInteresting(BranchCov, SeqCov) then
12 |  |  |  Queue ← Queue ⋃ {testcase } // Interesting seed
13 |  |  |  update_bitmap_score(testcase, SeqCount) // Adjustment of seed order
14 |  end
15 end
16 return crashSet
```

determines the number of children (*i.e.*, testcases) to be generated from that input, following the same heuristics as AFL++ [7]. After that, for each mutated testcase, it monitors the execution of the instrumented program P' (line 8). If the program crashes or triggers alarms set by sanitizers (line 9), the testcase is recorded as a Proof of Concept (PoC) (line 10). Otherwise, if the testcase is interesting (*e.g.*, new code coverage or CHOS coverage) (line 11), the testcase is added into the seed pool for further testing (line 12) and the score, used to guide the seed selection, is updated correspondingly (line 13).

As mentioned in Sect. 3.1, CTXFUZZ follows the workflow of AFL++, but introduces new seed selection strategies (lines 12–13). First, a testcase is considered interesting if and only if it introduces either new code coverage or new CHOS coverage, as shown in Eq. (1).

$$isInteresting = \begin{cases} True, & hasNew(BranchCov) \lor hasNew(SeqCov) \\ False, & otherwise \end{cases} \tag{1}$$

Moreover, we also improve the score-updating API *update_bitmap_score()* of AFL++ (line 13), which allows for the adjustment of the seed queue's order and the designation of certain seeds as favored. These favored seeds are then given priority for mutation in subsequent iterations (line 4). Initially, AFL++ prioritizes seeds based on shorter execution times and smaller file sizes. However, we enhance this strategy by also favoring seeds that exhibit a greater number of CHOS during testing. Formally, a favored testcase is defined by Eq. (2).

$$isFavored = \begin{cases} True, & isMin(Time \times FileSize) \lor isMax(SeqCount) \\ False, & otherwise \end{cases} \tag{2}$$

4 Evaluation

We have implemented a prototype of CTXFUZZ based on AFL++ [7] version 4.08c. Our main focus is on modifying the influencing factors in the instrumentation, feedback mechanism, and seed selection. By making these modifications

Table 1. Objective real-world programs evaluated in our experiment.

Program	Version	SLoC	Input Format	Test instruction
Bento4	v1.6.0-639	104K	mp4	mp42hls @@
cflow	1.6	80K	c	cflow @@
cxxfilt	2.41	5.03M	text	cxxfilt -t
Exiv2	v0.26	386K	jpg	exiv2 -pX @@
giflib	5.2.1	14K	gif	gif2rgb @@
mJS	2.20.0	43K	js	mjs -f @@
OpenH264	8684722	141K	text	h264dec @@ ./tmp
YARA	v3.5.0	62K	text	yara @@ strings
Yasm	9defefa	173K	asm	yasm @@

without changing other components, we have successfully improved the overall performance of heap-based memory vulnerability detection. To foster further research, more information (*e.g.*, benchmark dataset, initial seed) is available at https://sites.google.com/view/ctxfuzz.

We conducted comprehensive experiments to evaluate CtxFuzz using a set of real-world programs, and compare CtxFuzz with state-of-the-art fuzzers, following Klees's suggestions [8]. In the experiments, we aim to answer the following questions:

RQ1. How effective is CtxFuzz in discovering heap-based memory vulnerabilities in real-world programs?
RQ2. How does CtxFuzz compare to other state-of-the-art fuzzers?
RQ3. Does the improvements made by CtxFuzz contribute to the efficiency of fuzzing towards heap-based memory vulnerabilities?

4.1 Experiment Setup

Benchmark Programs. We curated a collection of benchmark applications from fuzzing papers that focus on heap-based memory vulnerabilities, as shown in Table 1. The selection process took various factors into consideration, such as popularity, frequency of testing, and the presence of memory vulnerabilities. In total, we used 9 widely used real-world programs for our evaluation, all of which contain memory vulnerabilities. These programs include renowned code analysis tools (*e.g.*, cxxfilt, cflow), code processing tools (*e.g.*, mJS, Yasm), graphics processing libraries (*e.g.*, Exiv2, giflib), video processing tools (*e.g.*, Bento4, OpenH264), and a data processing library (*e.g.*, YARA), among others.

Baseline Fuzzers. We evaluated CtxFuzz by comparing it against 5 state-of-the-art fuzzers: AFL, AFL++, HTFuzz, Memlock, and TortoiseFuzz. These fuzzers were selected based on several considerations. AFL++ [7] is an enhanced version of AFL, and our work is built upon it. Memlock [26] and TortoiseFuzz [25]

Table 2. The number of heap-based memory vulnerabilities found in 48 h.

Program	CTXFUZZ		AFL		AFL++		HTFuzz		MemLock		TortoiseFuzz	
	Unique	Average	Unique	Average	Unique	Average	Unique	Average	Unique	Average	Unique	Average
Bento4	3	3.00	2	1.88	3	3.00	3	2.88	2	2.00	1	1.00
cflow	2	2.00	2	1.12	3	2.12	3	1.75	1	0.62	1	0.38
cxxfilt	1	0.12	0	0.00	0	0.00	0	0.00	0	0.00	0	0.00
Exiv2	2	2.00	1	1.00	1	1.00	2	2.00	1	1.00	1	1.00
giflib	1	0.88	1	0.12	1	0.62	1	0.38	1	0.12	1	0.25
mJS	11	3.25	10	5.25	4	1.50	4	1.75	0	0.00	4	3.38
OpenH264	5	2.38	2	1.00	3	2.25	2	2.00	0	0.00	1	0.62
YARA	5	3.88	4	2.88	5	3.88	5	4.12	3	1.00	5	3.25
Yasm	11	6.88	9	7.88	11	8.50	9	8.50	2	0.88	9	7.00
Sum/Sum	41	24.39	31	21.13	31	22.87	29	23.38	10	5.62	23	16.88

specifically focus on memory operations, including memory allocation, deallocation, and usage. HTFuzz [28] targets memory vulnerabilities through candidate heap operation sequences. All of these fuzzers are partially related to CTXFUZZ, and we ran them with their default parameters.

Performance Metrics. Instead of considering unique crash numbers reported by the fuzzers, We evaluate the performance of the fuzzers based on the number of heap-based memory vulnerabilities. To compare the vulnerability findings of different fuzzers, we also conduct the Mann-Whitney U-test for statistical evaluation.

Configuration. To ensure accurate results, we implemented two measures to mitigate performance jitter during the fuzzing process. Firstly, we conducted extensive testing by running each program for a duration of 48 h, allowing the fuzzer to reach a relatively stable state. Secondly, we repeated each experiment 8 times to minimize random noises that may occur during fuzzing. The applications were compiled using clang and AddressSanitizer [19,32], and we executed them in various fuzzers using the command options outlined in Table 1.

Experiment Infrastructure. All our experiments are performed on machines with an Intel(R) Xeon(R) Gold 6132 CPU @ 2.60 GHz and 252 GB of RAM under 64-bit Ubuntu LTS 20.04.

4.2 RQ1. Vulnerability Detection Capability

Table 2 presents the statistical results of CTXFUZZ in detecting heap-based memory vulnerabilities. As shown in the column labeled CTXFUZZ, CTXFUZZ successfully detected 41 heap-based memory vulnerabilities in our eight 48-hour experiments, out of a total of 46 vulnerabilities. We manually reviewed these 41 bugs to assess their authenticity and severity. These vulnerabilities, classified by bug type, include stack buffer overflow, heap buffer overflow, use-after-free, and double-free vulnerabilities, many of which are critical and can have severe consequences. Among the vulnerable programs, mJS and Yasm stand out with

Table 3. The zero-day vulnerabilities found by CtxFuzz.

Bug ID	Program	Version	Type
CVE-2023-49554	Yasm	9defefa	use-after-free
CVE-2023-49551	mJS	2.20.0	null-pointer dereference
CVE-2023-49555	Yasm	9defefa	null-pointer dereference
CVE-2023-49557	Yasm	9defefa	null-pointer dereference
CVE-2023-49558	Yasm	9defefa	null-pointer dereference
CVE-2023-49549	mJS	2.20.0	null-pointer dereference
CVE-2023-49550	mJS	2.20.0	null-pointer dereference
CVE-2023-49553	mJS	2.20.0	null-pointer dereference
CVE-2023-49556	Yasm	9defefa	heap-buffer-overflow
CVE-2023-49552	mJS	2.20.0	stack-overflow

11 and 11 identified bugs, respectively. We promptly reported these previously unknown bugs to the respective maintainers.

Security Impact of Newly Found Vulnerabilities. CtxFuzz showcases its effectiveness and efficiency in discovering heap-based vulnerabilities by employing guided fuzzing of CHOS. At the time of writing, 10 zero-day vulnerabilities have already been identified, resulting in the assignment of 10 CVEs by Mitre, as shown in Table 3. Out of these 10 CVEs, 9 are heap-based memory vulnerabilities, while one is a stack overflow. These heap-based memory vulnerabilities discovered by CtxFuzz pose serious threats to the security and reliability of the affected applications. These include 7 null-pointer dereferences, one use-after-free vulnerability, and one heap-buffer-overflow vulnerability, which may result in memory corruption, denial-of-service, or arbitrary code execution [10,21]. Furthermore, some of these vulnerabilities are challenging to detect and exploit, with 5 of them requiring more than 48 h for successful exploitation, particularly if they involve complex heap operations or meta-operations. Consequently, it is crucial for software developers and security researchers to identify and address these vulnerabilities promptly.

4.3 RQ2. Compare with Other SOTA Fuzzers

Table 2 also presents the number of heap-based memory vulnerabilities detected by each baseline fuzzer (*e.g.*, AFL, AFL++, HTFuzz, MemLock, TortoiseFuzz) during a period of 48 h. CtxFuzz identified a total of 41 unique vulnerabilities, surpassing the second-best performers AFL++ which only uncovered 31 unique

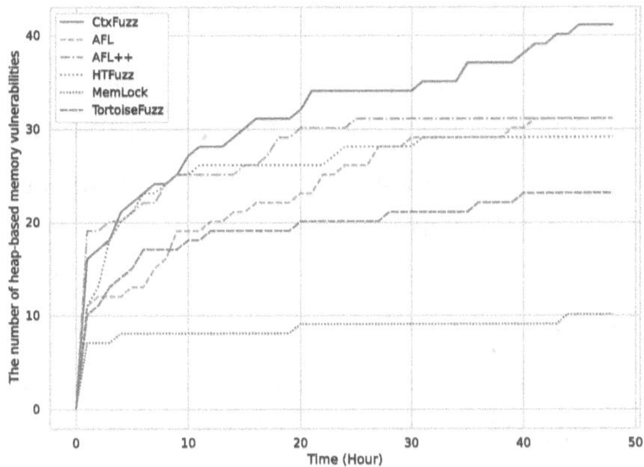

Fig. 2. Unique heap-based memory vulnerabilities accumulated over time

vulnerabilities. This represents a significant improvement, as CtxFuzz demonstrates a 32.26% enhancement over AFL++ in terms of detecting heap-based memory vulnerabilities. It is worth noting that, in some programs with frequent heap memory operations like OpenH264, CtxFuzz has a particularly significant impact, discovering over 100% more vulnerabilities than most baseline fuzzers. In terms of the average number of detected vulnerabilities, CtxFuzz slightly surpasses AFL++ and HTFuzz, while still significantly outperforming MemLock and TortoiseFuzz. In addition, although CtxFuzz detect a lower average number of vulnerabilities for some programs (*e.g.*, Yasm) than some baseline fuzzers (*e.g.*, AFL++ and HTFuzz), CtxFuzz is able to detect more or not less than the number of unique vulnerabilities. This could be partly attributed to the fact that CtxFuzz explores diverse CHOS across different runs, which highlights the necessity of exploring CHOS.

Discovered Vulnerabilities Over Time. To facilitate the comparison of different fuzzers, we also use a plot to illustrate the number of identified vulnerabilities in all 9 evaluated programs. This representation is depicted in Fig. 2. Within the initial 10-hour timeframe, CtxFuzz promptly identified nearly 27 vulnerabilities, showcasing its superior efficiency in vulnerability detection compared to other competitors. However, as the duration exceeds 30 h, the performance of the competing fuzzers gradually stagnates, with new vulnerabilities being uncovered at a slow pace. In contrast, CtxFuzz continues to discover new vulnerabilities. In summary, the plot clearly shows a consistent and robust growth trend in the discovery of vulnerabilities by CtxFuzz, surpassing other fuzzers and maintaining a leading position.

Statistical Test. According to the p-value of the Mann-Whitney U-test using CtxFuzz as the basis in Table 4, CtxFuzz outperforms the 5 compared fuzzers in 23 out of the 45 comparisons with a significant difference (*i.e.*, p-value is smaller than 0.05 [2]).

Table 4. P-values of Table 2. P-values below 0.05 are in bold.

Program	AFL	AFL++	HTFuzz	MemLock	TortoiseFuzz
Bento4	**1.03e-04**	1.00e+00	1.91e-01	**6.88e-05**	**6.88e-05**
cflow	**3.97e-04**	7.56e-01	8.50e-02	**1.55e-04**	**1.55e-04**
cxxfilt	1.91e-01	1.91e-01	1.91e-01	1.91e-01	1.91e-01
Exiv2	**6.88e-05**	**6.88e-05**	1.00e+00	**6.88e-05**	**6.88e-05**
giflib	**2.23e-03**	1.47e-01	**2.63e-02**	**2.23e-03**	**8.69e-03**
mJS	9.98e-01	**3.29e-03**	**1.01e-02**	**1.87e-04**	6.10e-01
OpenH264	**4.45e-03**	4.72e-01	8.55e-02	**1.35e-04**	**2.68e-04**
YARA	**2.29e-03**	5.00e-01	9.28e-01	**2.44e-04**	6.43e-02
Yasm	9.42e-01	9.86e-01	9.87e-01	**2.60e-04**	6.09e-01

Table 5. Results of tests with different hyperparameter settings.

Program	AFL++		K = 2, L = 3		K = 2, L = 8		K = 5, L = 3		K = 5, L = 8		CTXFUZZ-wo	
	CHOS	Bug	CHOS	Bug	CHOS	Bug	CHOS	Bug	CHOS	Bug	CHOS	Bug
Bento4	19675	3	22235	3	21005	3	20883	3	19914	3	21586	3
cflow	19607	3	23129	2	23363	2	21619	2	21323	2	24062	2
cxxfilt	16091	0	20638	1	19702	0	19333	0	16795	0	21680	0
Exiv2	2170	1	3176	2	3300	2	2851	2	2576	2	3271	2
giflib	1719	1	3524	1	3698	1	3103	1	3088	1	3738	1
mJS	21381	4	27246	11	26256	8	25676	6	24749	2	26823	7
OpenH264	37423	3	40809	5	39707	3	38061	3	38855	2	42066	6
YARA	19611	5	22108	5	21493	5	20992	4	19940	5	23284	5
Yasm	45485	11	44088	11	41176	7	41917	9	37267	8	45665	9
Avg/Sum	20351	31	22995	41	22189	31	21604	30	20501	25	23575	35

4.4 RQ3. Ablation Studies

Hyperparameter Settings. As described in Sect. 3, the number K of the last accessed heap memory addresses and the number L of the last heap operations are configurable. To determine suitable values for K and L, we conducted experiments with different settings. As our testing goal is to explore more context heap operation sequences and discover more heap-based memory vulnerabilities, we naturally consider these two metrics. The results of tests conducted with different hyperparameter settings can be found in Table 5, where"CHOS" denotes the number of different CHOS found during runtime. We collect CHOS with afl-showmap [29] and map the CHOS found by other settings into the ones found by the setting of $K = 2$ and $L = 3$ for better comparasion. According to Table 5, we set the default configuration for CTXFUZZ as $K = 2$ and $L = 3$ since it gives the best results.

Effectiveness of CHOS Feedback Mechanism. In the evaluation of CHOS feedback mechanism, we compared the performance of AFL++ and CtxFuzz without seed selection strategy (denoted as CtxFuzz-wo) in Table 5. The results show that CtxFuzz-wo explores over 15% more CHOS and discovering over 12% more vulnerabilities. In particular, it is able to detect more than nearly twice as many heap-based vulnerabilities as AFL++ on mJS and OpenH264. This indicates that the incorporation of CHOS feedback mechanism leads to more effective and targeted fuzzing, resulting in the discovery of additional heap-based vulnerabilities as compared to the baseline AFL++.

Effectiveness of Seed Selection. In evaluating the effectiveness of seed selection strategies, we compared the performance of CtxFuzz and CtxFuzz-wo in Table 5. The results indicate that CtxFuzz explores slightly fewer CHOS than CtxFuzz-wo. This difference can be attributed to the fact that CtxFuzz focuses on specific seeds that exhibit a greater number of CHOS to trigger potential vulnerabilities, which may sacrifice some diversity in CHOS generation. However, CtxFuzz is able to detect 6 more vulnerabilities. This suggests that the seed selection strategy contributes positively to the effectiveness of CtxFuzz in discovering heap-based vulnerabilities in real-world programs.

4.5 Discussion

Additional Experiments. The three aforementioned research questions illustrate the effectiveness and efficiency of CtxFuzz in detecting heap-based memory vulnerabilities. Additionally, we evaluated other secondary indicators, including code coverage, runtime overhead, and vulnerabilities beyond heap-based memory vulnerabilities. In the following, we provide a succinct and comprehensive explanation of the experimental findings. To estimate code coverage, we utilized `gcov` to obtain line coverage. The results showed that the coverage of CtxFuzz is comparable to that of baseline fuzzers. With respect to runtime overhead, we compared the total number of each baseline fuzzer's executions. CtxFuzz is slower in 32 out of 45 comparisons, ranging from 1.12 to 4.34 times. Although CtxFuzz does introduce some runtime overhead, we consider it worthwhile as it has been successful in discovering more vulnerabilities, even in resource-intensive scenarios. Furthermore, CtxFuzz primarily emphasizes the analysis of the heap operation sequence, which may limit its ability to detect other types of vulnerabilities (*e.g.*, the stack-overflow in Table 3 is a stack-based memory vulnerability). For readers interested in more detailed information, additional experimental results can be found on CtxFuzz's website.

Threat to Validity. We discuss the potential threats to the validity and generalizability of our study, as well as the measures we have taken to mitigate or control them. One potential threat is the selection bias that may arise from using only 9 open-source programs, which could limit the diversity of our dataset. To address this concern, we made sure to select diverse programs from various domains and with different characteristics. We are continuously working on improving and evaluating CtxFuzz. Another potential concern entails the sampling error that may arise when utilizing a restricted number of seeds and inputs for each program and fuzzer. This limitation has the potential to impact the comprehensive nature of our testing process and introduce factors that create noise or variance in our findings. To address this, we employed an identical set of seeds for each fuzzer and conducted a 48-hour runtime. We repeated each experiment 8 times and reported the average and standard deviation to account for any potential variations. A third threat to consider is the possibility of statistical errors. In order to compare CtxFuzz with other testers, we utilized statistical tests and significance levels. However, it is important to acknowledge that these tests have certain assumptions and limitations. To address this concern, we thoroughly checked the assumptions and conditions before applying the tests, ensuring that we used the appropriate test for each specific scenario.

5 Related Work

Existing fuzzing solutions that aim to detect heap-based memory vulnerabilities can be broadly categorized into two groups: temporal memory vulnerabilities and spatial memory vulnerabilities. Use-after-free is a common temporal memory vulnerability, and there exist dedicated fuzzing techniques designed to detect Use-after-free vulnerabilities. UAFL [23] employs typestate analysis to detect operation sequences that may violate typestate properties. It utilizes operation sequence coverage as feedback to direct test generation and gradually cover the operation sequences. UAFuzz [15] relies on user-defined UAF sites to guide the fuzzer during exploration. However, these approaches rely on expert knowledge or imprecise static analysis, which presents challenges for their widespread adoption and effectiveness in practical scenarios. There are also some fuzzing techniques that can test for a wider range of temporal memory vulnerabilities. For example, HTFuzz [28] introduces heap operation sequences as new feedback, in addition to code coverage, to increase the diversity of heap operation sequences. However, these tools primarily concentrate on memory allocation and deallocation, neglecting the significant aspects of memory read and write operations. Many techniques primarily focus on identifying spatial memory vulnerabilities. Memlock [26] identifies statements and operations that are relevant to memory consumption and is guided by memory usage. Concolic execution-based smart fuzzing [13] only focuses on detecting heap-based buffer overflows as spatial memory vulnerabilities. However, it is important to note that CtxFuzz is capable of efficiently discovering both spatial and temporal memory vulnerabilities.

While there are other fuzzing techniques that target temporal and spatial vulnerabilities, they mainly focus on algorithm complexity vulnerability rather than memory vulnerability [1,3,9,17]. For instance, HotFuzz [3] is a framework that utilizes a genetic algorithm to generate inputs that lead to the worst-case performance of Java methods. In contrast, CtxFuzz specifically focuses on memory safety vulnerabilities, distinguishing it from HotFuzz's primary focus on algorithmic complexity vulnerabilities.

6 Conclusion

We proposed CtxFuzz, a fuzzing technique that leverages context heap operation sequences as a new feedback mechanism to efficiently discover heap-based temporal and spatial memory vulnerabilities. We evaluated CtxFuzz on 9 real-world programs and showed that it outperformed 5 state-of-the-art fuzzers in terms of discovering heap-based memory vulnerabilities. We also reported 10 new zero-day vulnerabilities (10 CVEs) to the corresponding vendors. CtxFuzz demonstrates its utility for testing real-world programs that are susceptible to heap-based memory vulnerabilities.

Acknowledgements. The authors would like to thank the anonymous reviewers for their constructive comments. This work was supported in part by the National Natural Science Foundation of China (Nos. 62372304, 62302375, 62192734), the China Postdoctoral Science Foundation funded project (No. 2023M723736), and the Fundamental Research Funds for the Central Universities.

References

1. Alsaeed, Z., Young, M.: Finding short slow inputs faster with grammar-based search. In: Proceedings of the 32nd ACM SIGSOFT International Symposium on Software Testing and Analysis, pp. 1068–1079 (2023)
2. Arcuri, A., Briand, L.: A practical guide for using statistical tests to assess randomized algorithms in software engineering. In: Proceedings of the 33rd International Conference on Software Engineering, pp. 1–10 (2011)
3. Blair, W., et al.: Hotfuzz: discovering temporal and spatial denial-of-service vulnerabilities through guided micro-fuzzing. ACM Trans. Priv. Secur. **25**(4), 1–35 (2022)
4. Chen, Z., Liu, D., Xiao, J., Wang, H.: All use-after-free vulnerabilities are not created equal: an empirical study on their characteristics and detectability. In: Proceedings of the 26th International Symposium on Research in Attacks, Intrusions and Defenses, pp. 623–638 (2023)
5. Du, C., Cui, Z., Guo, Y., Xu, G., Wang, Z.: Memconfuzz: memory consumption guided fuzzing with data flow analysis. Mathematics **11**(5), 1222 (2023)
6. Farkhani, R.M., Ahmadi, M., Lu, L.: {PTAuth}: temporal memory safety via robust points-to authentication. In: 30th USENIX Security Symposium (USENIX Security 21), pp. 1037–1054 (2021)
7. Fioraldi, A., Maier, D., Eißfeldt, H., Heuse, M.: AFL++: combining incremental steps of fuzzing research. In: 14th USENIX Workshop on Offensive Technologies (WOOT 20). USENIX Association, August 2020
8. Klees, G., Ruef, A., Cooper, B., Wei, S., Hicks, M.: Evaluating fuzz testing. In: Proceedings of the 2018 ACM SIGSAC Conference on Computer and Communications Security, pp. 2123–2138 (2018)
9. Lemieux, C., Padhye, R., Sen, K., Song, D.: Perffuzz: automatically generating pathological inputs. In: Proceedings of the 27th ACM SIGSOFT International Symposium on Software Testing and Analysis, pp. 254–265 (2018)
10. Liu, J., An, H., Li, J., Liang, H.: Detecting exploit primitives automatically for heap vulnerabilities on binary programs. arXiv preprint arXiv:2212.13990 (2022)

11. Lu, F., Tang, M., Bao, Y., Wang, X.: A survey of detection methods for software use-after-free vulnerability. In: Wang, Y., Zhu, G., Han, Q., Zhang, L., Song, X., Lu, Z. (eds.) Data Science. ICPCSEE 2022. CCIS, vol. 1629, pp. 272–297. Springer, Singapore (2022). https://doi.org/10.1007/978-981-19-5209-8_19
12. Meng, R., Dong, Z., Li, J., Beschastnikh, I., Roychoudhury, A.: Linear-time temporal logic guided greybox fuzzing. In: Proceedings of the 44th International Conference on Software Engineering, pp. 1343–1355. ICSE '22, Association for Computing Machinery, New York, NY, USA (2022)
13. Mouzarani, M., Sadeghiyan, B., Zolfaghari, M.: A smart fuzzing method for detecting heap-based buffer overflow in executable codes. In: 2015 IEEE 21st Pacific Rim International Symposium on Dependable Computing (PRDC), pp. 42–49. IEEE (2015)
14. Mouzarani, M., Sadeghiyan, B., Zolfaghari, M.: A smart fuzzing method for detecting heap-based vulnerabilities in executable codes. Secur. Commun. Netw. **9**(18), 5098–5115 (2016)
15. Nguyen, M.D., Bardin, S., Bonichon, R., Groz, R., Lemerre, M.: Binary-level directed fuzzing for Use-After-Free vulnerabilities. In: 23rd International Symposium on Research in Attacks. Intrusions and Defenses (RAID 2020), pp. 47–62. USENIX Association, San Sebastian, October 2020
16. Novark, G., Berger, E.D.: Dieharder: securing the heap. In: Proceedings of the 17th ACM Conference on Computer and Communications Security, pp. 573–584 (2010)
17. Petsios, T., Zhao, J., Keromytis, A.D., Jana, S.: Slowfuzz: automated domain-independent detection of algorithmic complexity vulnerabilities. In: Proceedings of the 2017 ACM SIGSAC Conference on Computer and Communications Security, pp. 2155–2168 (2017)
18. Sarda, S., Pandey, M.: LLVM Essentials. Packt Publishing Ltd., Birmingham (2015)
19. Serebryany, K., Bruening, D., Potapenko, A., Vyukov, D.: Addresssanitizer: a fast address sanity checker. In: 2012 USENIX Annual Technical Conference (USENIX ATC 12), pp. 309–318 (2012)
20. Simpson, M.S., Barua, R.K.: Memsafe: ensuring the spatial and temporal memory safety of c at runtime. Softw. Pract. Exp. **43**(1), 93–128 (2013)
21. Tu, H.: Boosting symbolic execution for heap-based vulnerability detection and exploit generation. In: 2023 IEEE/ACM 45th International Conference on Software Engineering: Companion Proceedings (ICSE-Companion), pp. 218–220. IEEE (2023)
22. Van Der Kouwe, E., Nigade, V., Giuffrida, C.: Dangsan: scalable use-after-free detection. In: Proceedings of the Twelfth European Conference on Computer Systems, pp. 405–419 (2017)
23. Wang, H., et al.: Typestate-guided fuzzer for discovering use-after-free vulnerabilities. In: Proceedings of the ACM/IEEE 42nd International Conference on Software Engineering, pp. 999–1010. ICSE '20, Association for Computing Machinery, New York, NY, USA (2020)
24. Wang, W., Fan, M., Yu, A., Meng, D.: Towards heap-based memory corruption discovery. In: 2021 17th International Conference on Mobility, Sensing and Networking (MSN), pp. 502–511. IEEE (2021)
25. Wang, Y., et al.: Not all coverage measurements are equal: fuzzing by coverage accounting for input prioritization. In: NDSS (2020)
26. Wen, C., et al.: Memlock: memory usage guided fuzzing. In: Proceedings of the ACM/IEEE 42nd International Conference on Software Engineering, pp. 765–777. ICSE '20, Association for Computing Machinery, New York, NY, USA (2020)

27. Younan, Y., Joosen, W., Piessens, F.: Efficient protection against heap-based buffer overflows without resorting to magic. In: Ning, P., Qing, S., Li, N. (eds.) ICICS 2006. LNCS, vol. 4307, pp. 379–398. Springer, Heidelberg (2006). https://doi.org/10.1007/11935308_27
28. Yu, Y., et al.: HTFuzz: heap operation sequence sensitive fuzzing. In: Proceedings of the 37th IEEE/ACM International Conference on Automated Software Engineering. ASE '22, Association for Computing Machinery, New York, NY, USA (2023)
29. Zalewski, M.: American fuzzy lop (afl) fuzzer (2013). http://lcamtuf.coredump.cx/afl/
30. Zhang, G., Wang, P.F., Yue, T., Kong, X.D., Zhou, X., Lu, K.: Ovaflow: detecting memory corruption bugs with fuzzing-based taint inference. J. Comput. Sci. Technol. **37**(2), 405–422 (2022)
31. Zhang, T., Lee, D., Jung, C.: Bogo: buy spatial memory safety, get temporal memory safety (almost) free. In: Proceedings of the Twenty-Fourth International Conference on Architectural Support for Programming Languages and Operating Systems, pp. 631–644 (2019)
32. Zhang, Y., Pang, C., Portokalidis, G., Triandopoulos, N., Xu, J.: Debloating address sanitizer. In: 31st USENIX Security Symposium (USENIX Security 22), pp. 4345–4363 (2022)

An Adaptive Real-Time Garbage Collection Method Based on File Write Prediction

Jingjing Jiang[1(✉)], Mengfei Yang[2], Lei Qiao[1], Tingyu Wang[3], Zhi Ma[3], Shaofeng Li[3], and Shenghui Zhu[3]

[1] Beijing Institute of Control Engineering, Beijing, China
jiangjiang05252023@126.com
[2] China Academy of Space Technology, Beijing, China
[3] Xidian University, Xian, China

Abstract. Garbage collection is a significant way to ensure free space for the flash file system. In real-time embedded systems, the system response time is significant for tasks. Motivated by the need to optimize the system response time and the garbage collection overhead in the embedded flash file system, we propose an adaptive trigger garbage collection based on write periodicity prediction (called PWAgc) to efficiently optimize the worst-case response time and average response time. We also propose an optimal block partition selection method to reduce valid page copy overhead and victim block selection time. We implement our method based on yaffs2 and compare PWAgc with several classical real-time garbage collection methods based on benchmark traces. The results show that for the worst write response time, PWAgc can reduce 35%–70% by the hybrid method, 7%–56% by the on-demand partial method, and 25.47%–72% by the on-demand concentrate method in three workloads. The average response time of PWAgc is similar to other methods. The average page copy and block erase count per write are similar. We also conducted experiments using a real-world application, and the results showed that PWAgc can reduce 14.95%–31.4% for file write worst response time, improve 1.32%–5.36% for write bandwidth, reduce 5.87%–8.5% for average page copy count and reduce 1.59%–2.1% for average block erase count compared with the other three methods. Our method can be used in some real-time embedded systems that have periodic and regular file write operations.

Keywords: Garbage collection · Adaptive trigger · Block partition selection · Flash file system

1 Introduction

As a reliable storage medium, NAND flash is widely used in embedded systems. The capacity of the NAND flash becomes more and more large, and data volume

Supported by the National Natural Science Foundation of China under Grant No. 62032004.

W.-N. Chin and Z. Xu (Eds.): TASE 2024, LNCS 14777, pp. 224–241, 2024.
https://doi.org/10.1007/978-3-031-64626-3_13

also grows rapidly. As the amount of data increases, the free available space of flash memory decreases gradually, and invalid space in flash memory needs to be reclaimed and managed. Garbage collection is a useful way to recycle invalid flash blocks in flash file systems.

Garbage collection is a time-consuming process, it includes four steps [26]: garbage collection trigger, selecting victim blocks, migrating valid data in victim blocks, and erasing victim blocks. When there is enough flash space, garbage collection may not be necessary. However, garbage collection is required immediately when there is not enough free space.

At present, there are several kinds of research on garbage collection of flash file systems: victim block selection [14], trigger time, and garbage collection execution step division [12]. The victim block selection algorithm is used to find the optimal victim block. However, few studies have taken into account the time overhead of the garbage block selection process. Current studies pay more attention to the mechanisms of victim block selection and adopt the global search method by default. In that case, the victim selection process will take a long time because it needs to calculate the all-flash block to obtain the optimal block. Besides, the garbage collection execution time is indeterminate because the number of valid pages is not fixed and the data copy time is uncertain. The time of garbage collection triggers affects system performance. Triggering garbage collection too early will result in too many data-valid page copies and block wear. But triggering too late will increase the response time of file write tasks. At present, there are two trigger methods in flash file systems: on-demand trigger and hybrid trigger based on two trigger methods: the on-demand trigger and idle time trigger. It only triggers garbage collection when there is not enough space left for file write in the on-demand trigger method, and the hybrid trigger method uses idle time to trigger garbage collection based on the on-demand trigger method. The on-demand trigger method will result in excessively long write response latency. The hybrid trigger method can avoid long response latency problem but whether it needs to trigger garbage collection in every idle task is noteworthy. In the garbage collection process, step division also affects system response time. It includes partial and concentrated garbage collection. The partial garbage collection [10] has a lower response latency than the concentrated garbage collection method.

In embedded real-time systems, the deadline requirement for the period task is strict, and the execution of one task should not affect the execution of the next task. The garbage collection process must satisfy the real-time requirement. Besides, in some embedded systems such as satellite systems, file writing operations may follow some periodic rules. The garbage collection mechanism can be designed by taking full advantage of file operation behavior.

In this paper, we focus on the long latency of garbage collection, we propose a file-write task prediction model to predict the space required for the next write task and trigger early garbage collection to reduce the response time effect of garbage collection on the write task. We call our work PWAgc. The main contributions of this paper are as follows:

- **Write task prediction.** We propose a write task prediction modular to predict the page count that the next write task needs. By this method, it can reduce the latency of the writing task.
- **Adaptive trigger garbage collection.** We propose an adaptive garbage collection trigger method that decides whether to trigger garbage collection and use which victim block selection mechanism. By this method, it can avoid producing too much unnecessary garbage collection overhead.
- **Multi-condition victim block selection.** We use the greedy algorithm and the oldest block-first recycling method as the garbage selection algorithms. According to the different conditions, it needs to select different algorithms.
- **Partition record of victim blocks.** We introduce a flash partition victim block record which uses an array to record the best garbage block of the partition. The whole flash will be divided into several partitions and the block of every partition with the least valid page needs to be added to the array.

The structure of this article is as follows: Sect. 2 presents the background and related work of garbage collection in the flash file system. Section 3 introduces our proposed new garbage collection scheme for the flash file system. Section 4 introduces the experiments and summarizes the evaluation results of the proposed scheme. Section 5 gives the conclusions and future work.

2 Background and Motivation

2.1 Flash Devices and Flash File Systems

Many embedded devices use NAND chips to store data which is organized by a series of blocks, and each block is organized by multiple pages. The special characteristics of NAND flash make its management challenging [5]. First of all, NAND flash does not support updates in place, the entire block corresponding to the page must be erased before the data can be written. However, the erase count of blocks has a limited number. For example, single-level cells (SLC) [2] usually sustain as many as one hundred thousand cycles, while multi-level (MLC) and triple-level (TLC) [3] can only sustain less than ten thousand cycles. Since the character of the out-of-place updates, when the free blocks are not enough, garbage collection is needed. In existing typical flash file systems [6,11,18,22,24], garbage collection is fully designed.

2.2 Garbage Collection

Garbage Collection Problems. In flash memory, new data cannot be overwritten in place, each data needs to be written to a new location, and original location data is set as invalid data. As the number of file writes increases, the location of invalid data needs to be recycled, and garbage collection needs to be performed to obtain free space during system running process.

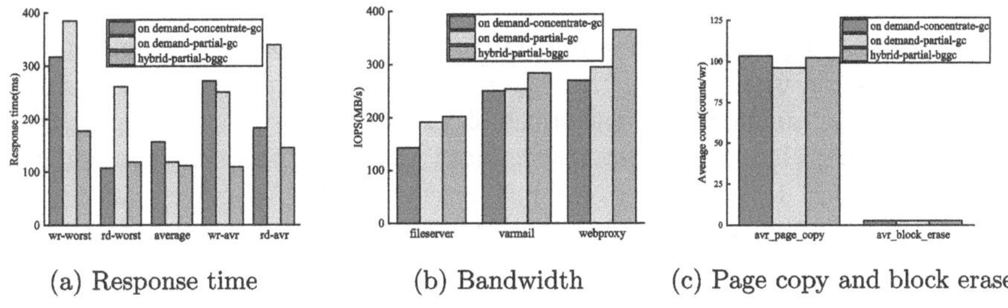

(a) Response time (b) Bandwidth (c) Page copy and block erase

Fig. 1. Performance comparison in different workloads

For file write operation, when flash memory space is insufficient, garbage collection will cause a mismatch between data written by the user and the actual data written, resulting in the problem of write amplification. When a writing task needs flash memory space to store data but the left space is not enough, then the garbage collection must be triggered and this will cause long tail latency for file write tasks. Besides, too much garbage collection will also increase the system response time. The balance of average response time and worst-case response time is one problem that garbage collection trigger time and garbage collection process division caused.

On the other hand, frequently updated blocks will soon be worn out when in-place-update is used. Flash wear-leveling is another problem that garbage collection will reduce the average lifespan of flash devices.

Existing Solutions for Garbage Collection Problems. The purpose of garbage collection is to recycle garbage blocks to get free blocks. To achieve better performance of garbage collection, it is mainly studied in several aspects: victim block selection algorithm, trigger time, and collection process.

Victim Block Selection Algorithm. The greedy algorithm [27] is the earliest victim block selection algorithm which selects the block with the smallest number of valid pages as a candidate for garbage collection. The greedy algorithm can minimize the copy overhead of valid pages during the procedure of garbage collection. The d-choice [4] algorithm is developed based on the greedy algorithm which selects the victim block from d blocks. The cost-benefit (CB) [21] algorithm evaluates the cost-benefit value of each block and selects the block with the largest value as a victim. Cost Age Time (CAT) [9] algorithm is a method that considers the cost of selecting each block by evaluating valid page copy overhead, erase count of a block, and the age of the latest invalidated page when block recycling. However, the procedure of CAT is time-consuming and the weight of each term is not balanced. The hot-cold swapping (HC) [16] algorithm selects a candidate for garbage collection by considering both the cleaning cost and the erase count of each block. The turn-based (TB) [11,18] selection algorithm consists of two phases. It selects a victim block using the greedy algorithm during the first phase to minimize the overhead and selects a victim block according to some wear-leveling rules to extend the lifetime of flash memory during the second phase. The Static-Dynamic (SD) [1] algorithm consists of dynamic and static phases for wear-leveling. In the dynamic phase, it selects a block from the round-robin queue, and in the static phase, hot-cold swapping is performed. Dual-Pool (DP) [7] algorithm performs data swapping between a young block and an old block. It also takes too much overhead. The Adaptive Garbage Collection (AGC) [12] algorithm selects the block that has the largest number of log blocks as a victim to minimize the effect of garbage collection on the system performance. However, if the I/O workload becomes heavy, AGC selects the block that has the smallest number of log blocks to minimize the garbage collection time. FeGC [19] algorithm divided free blocks into young and old to balance the wear leveling. Scoring [28] algorithm focuses on improving the lifetime of flash and reducing the search overhead of victim block selection by using a priority block queue. This method can achieve wear-leveling, but the memory overhead of the priority queue is very high. From the above introduction, we know the greedy algorithm has the lowest garbage collection time because it can ensure the fewest valid page copy operations. However, the global search process used to select victim blocks takes a long time and needs to be improved in the search process.

Trigger Time and Collection Process. The garbage collection trigger time has a significant effect on system performance [12]. When there is no space to satisfy the write request, it is needed to start garbage collection. This condition can be called on-demand garbage collection [15] method. This method can only affect the current write task and can not affect other tasks before the current task. However, such a method may repeatedly trigger garbage collection to release free space which will result in cascade garbage collection, and might seriously worsen the response time of write requests. Triggering garbage collection [13] during system idle time is introduced to solve this problem. This method can amortize the garbage collection overheads to system idle time to reduce the response time of writing tasks. It might worsen the live page copying overheads and increase the frequency of garbage collection which will degrade the lifetime of flash memory.

In the real-time system, to achieve garbage collection, the garbage collection process will be designed to one or several procedures. According to the different procedures of garbage collection, the garbage collection process can be divided into 2 types: concentrate garbage collection and partial garbage collection [23]. The concentrate garbage collection algorithm centrally manages all the blocks to be collected in the flash memory chip. The collection of each block is an atomic operation and cannot be split. The partial garbage collection algorithm divides the garbage collection process into multiple steps. The partial garbage collection algorithm can amortize the time cost of a collection block to multiple I/O operations and reduce the waiting time of each IO operation. Li-Pin Chang [8] proposed the real-time garbage collection mechanism for the first time, providing a garbage collection guarantee through the idle page supplement mechanism and ensuring the real-time performance of the garbage collection task through the non-preemption. GFTL algorithm [10] and RFTL algorithm [20] both adopt local garbage recovery algorithms to provide a guarantee for a real-time system. Lazy-RTGC [29] divides the garbage collection process into several steps, each step corresponds to a task execution process, and optimizes the average response time and worst response time of the system.

Figure 1 gives an experiment result between the on-demand trigger with concentrate garbage collection [8], on-demand trigger with partial garbage collection [29], and hybrid condition trigger garbage collection [18] using three benchmarks: fileserver, varmail, and webproxy benchmarks. Figure 1(a) shows the worst write, worst read, average, average write, and average read response time results under the fileserver workload. The worst write response time of the hybrid method is lower than the other methods because the garbage collection time of the hybrid method is lower than others. Figure 1(b) shows the bandwidth in 3 different workloads. The results show the hybrid method has a higher bandwidth than the other two methods. Figure 1(c) shows the valid page copy and block erase count per write results under the fileserver workload. The valid page copy and block erase count per write are similar to the other two methods. These experiment results show that the hybrid method has better performance than others. Making full use of idle time for garbage collection can effectively reduce system response time. Based on the hybrid method, our method adds additional mechanisms.

2.3 Real-Time Requirement and Task Periodicity in Embedded Systems

The worst-case response time and average response time of the system are two significant performances. For writing tasks, it needs to execute garbage collection when there is not enough flash space, and garbage collection will increase the response time of writing tasks. For system average response time, the frequency of garbage collection has an impact on the average system response time. The more frequent garbage collection, the longer the average system response time.

In many embedded systems, file data tasks usually have a certain regularity and periodicity. For example, on the satellite, there are many kinds of payload devices, but each payload device will perform data acquisition tasks at fixed intervals and write data to flash memory. The data generated by payload devices on the satellite is periodically written into the system. This periodic character can be fully utilized in the design of garbage collection mechanisms. From the above introduction, there are two challenges:

- How to design the trigger time to balance the worst-case and the average response time?
- How to design the victim select algorithm to balance the time overhead and space overhead?

3 Real-Time Garbage Collection

In this section, we introduce the details of our work PWAgc. We first introduce the system architecture of the real-time flash file system. Then we introduce the specific garbage collection methods: periodic write behavior prediction, adaptive trigger time, multi-condition victim block selection, and partition record of victim block.

3.1 Design Overview

In this section, we give the system architecture of the real-time flash file system corresponding to this paper. The architecture is shown in Fig. 2. In the architecture, the modular of conventional architecture is included and a real-time task modular is included.

We take full advantage of the periodic behavior of file writing to predict the page count that the next file writing task needs. By predicting the page count of the next file write task, we design an adaptive trigger method to reduce the worst response time and average response time. We use an optimal victim block record structure to record blocks containing the fewest valid pages by partitioning flash memory.

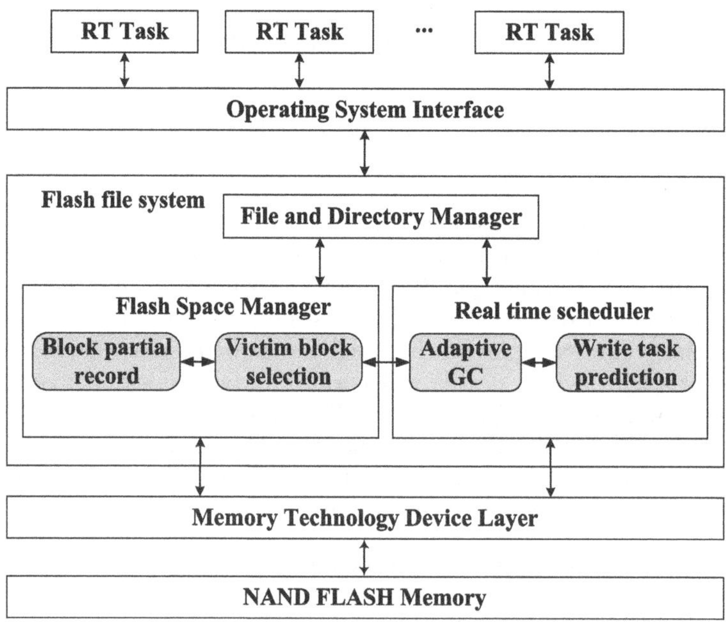

Fig. 2. Garbage collection architecture

3.2 Periodic Write Behavior Prediction

In the satellite, periodic sensor acquisition tasks make write operations regular. We can use the periodicity of the write operation to predict the count of physical pages required for the write operation at the next moment. There are two conditions of the writing task according to the period of each task. One condition is that all different writing tasks have the same period. The other condition is that different writing task has a different period. Figure 3 shows the task model of the first condition. In the model, task1, task2, and task3 have different execution time but their order remains the same.

In this paper, we only consider the first condition. In the first condition, we only need to calculate the minimum period of these series tasks using the classical minimum string matching algorithm called Knuth-Morris-Pratt (KMP) [17]. After we get the minimum period, we record the period, pages required by all tasks in the full period, and the current write task type. When the physical flash memory space is insufficient, we can use idle time to predict the next write task and decide whether to start garbage collection before the next write task arrives. By this method, it can reduce the response latency of the write task caused by garbage collection.

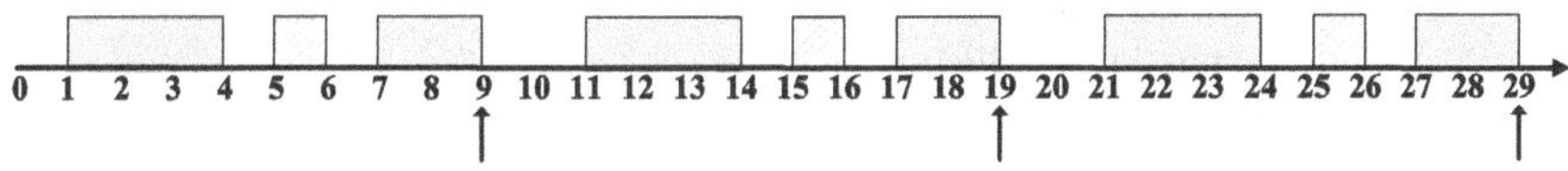

Fig. 3. Period task model

In the satellite system, the data obtained by the payload device is periodic and the size of each payload data is fixed, so the data written into the payload file in the system has a certain periodic rule. It has periodicity in the file write interval and file write size. Therefore, by recording the order and size of each file written in the system, periodic prediction is performed each time the file is written, and the cycle of file write data is obtained to predict the number of free pages required for the next file write operation. According to the conditions of file write, it can be divided into two conditions: file first-time write and file update. Owing to the uncertainty of file update operation and the regular characters of the file first-time write, we only use the file first-time write as the recording element. By using this record, it can calculate the period of file write operation and predict the free space of the next file write need. File update operation will not affect the reliability of the file write prediction. In the satellite system, the stable period of file write in every payload data guarantees the prediction.

In the system, we use the linear table to record the size of each file written for the first time according to the order of file writing. Every time a record is added to the record table, the minimum string matching algorithm is used to calculate whether the file size in these records has a periodic rule. After a record is written and the minimum period is calculated, the subsequent file writes do not need to be periodically calculated, and only the record entries within the minimum period are updated to predict the size of the next file to be written. Each time the minimum string matching algorithm is used, the number of flash pages required for each file recorded in the table is used as the string for analysis and each time the shortest string is found from the first position of the table as the minimum period.

Algorithm 1. Garbage Collection

Require: first threshold $Th1$; second threshold $Th2$; free page count Fp; block partial record Arr; select victim block Blk; function file write Fwr; idle task It; page count of the next write Np; oldest block flush counts Fc; oldest block number Min_seq.

```
function GC
    if Fp < Th1 && Fwr then
        Blk = select(Arr);
        concentrate_gc(Blk);
    else
        if It then
            Np = predict();
            if Np < Fp − Th1 then
                if Fc > Th2 && Min_seq then
                    Blk=Min_seq;
                    partial_gc(Blk);
                else
                    no gc;
                end if
            else
                Blk=select(Arr);
                partial_gc(Blk);
            end if
        end if
    end if
end function
```

3.3 Adaptive Trigger Garbage Collection

Similar to usual flash garbage collection schemes, we use the on-demand method that triggers garbage collection when the free space is up to a threshold. Besides, we also make full use of idle time to perform garbage collection operations. During idle time, we divide garbage collection into several conditions: advanced garbage collection based on write operation prediction, garbage collection based on a stable threshold, and garbage collection based on the allocation sequence of blocks. In the worst case, when a file task arrives and there is not enough free flash memory space, it must trigger garbage collection. Owing to the urgent need to use flash memory space for the writing task, the concentrated garbage collection method with the greedy algorithm as the victim block selection is used. If it is idle time and the free space is not enough for the next writing task, it will trigger the advanced garbage collection. In advanced garbage collection, we use the greedy algorithm to select the victim block and generate part of the garbage collection steps. Similar to the previous work, we take the block erase time as the max time of the partial step. If the system is idle and there is enough free space, then decide whether to carry out garbage collection that considers the order in which blocks are allocated.

Algorithm 1 shows the garbage collection mechanism based on the multi-condition trigger. It can be divided into three conditions. When the file write is coming and there are not enough flash pages, then trigger garbage collection and use greedy as the victim block selection algorithm. The process takes the concentrate method. When it is in idle time, it first predicts the next write behavior, if it can be predicted, then judge whether the left space is enough for the next write operation. If it is enough then select the block that has the min sequence number in the suitable time. This time is decided by a threshold whether the sequence number of blocks is satisfied. If it is not enough, then take greedy and partial garbage collection methods to recycle the block with the least valid page.

3.4 Multi-condition Victim Block Selection Algorithm

In this section, we propose a new victim block algorithm that abandons the conventional method based on the stable threshold. According to the system state and garbage collection trigger condition, we use the adaptive victim block selection method which provides several types of algorithms for selection. When the file write task arrives and the free page counts are not enough, the greedy algorithm and non-preemptive garbage collection mechanism are used. In the idle time, it needs to identify the state of the flash memory and decide to use which block selection algorithm. It first predicts the next write task and compares the free space with the page counts that the next write task needs. If the free space is not enough then use the greedy algorithm as the victim block algorithm and use the distribute collection process. If the free space is enough then use the block selection algorithm that considers the block allocation sequence. The algorithms can be described with one formula:

$$val = \alpha \times (tol - inv) + (1 - \alpha) \times seq \tag{1}$$

In this formula, α represents the weight of the valid page count. The tol, inv, and seq represent the total chunk count in a block, the invalid page count in a block, and the block allocation sequence number. In different conditions, the parameters are different. For example, when α is 1 the algorithm becomes greedy algorithm.

3.5 Partition Record of Victim Blocks

To reduce the time of the victim block selection procedure, we adopted a structure to record the blocks that contain the least valid pages and partitioned the blocks, with one record structure for each partition. This structure consists of an array. The array is used to indicate the partition position and record the block numbers which has the most invalid pages in a block. Assume we partition records in units of 100 blocks, for a total of 10 partitions. The elements in the array are the number of blocks that have the least valid pages and the valid page count of the blocks. The structure is shown in Fig. 4. This figure shows that in the first partition, the 65th block is recorded in the array and this block has 2 valid pages. Similarly, block 110 is selected as the victim block and it has 1 valid page in the second partition.

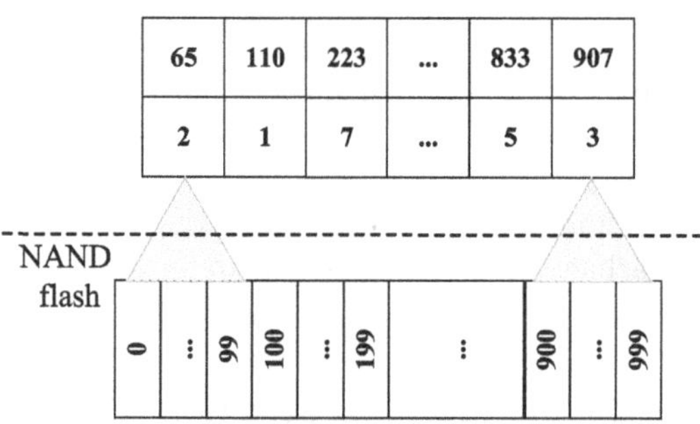

Fig. 4. Partition record structure

The record structure is used to accelerate the victim block selection process when using the greedy algorithm. When the position of a selected block has no record, then a search process in this partition must start to get the victim block. If a physical page becomes invalid because of file deletion or file data update, it needs to check whether the number of valid pages in this block is smaller than the optimal reclaim block in the partition corresponding to the block. If the valid page count is smaller than the victim block of this partition, then update the optimal victim block in the record. If a block recorded in the array is collected, a new optimal garbage block needs to be found from the corresponding partition of that block.

Using the victim block partition record method can effectively reduce the search time of the block selection process in garbage collection. Assuming that the number of partitions is n, the garbage block selection time can be reduced by $(n-1)/n$ compared with the global search method. In addition, since the victim blocks selected each time are the blocks containing the smallest number of invalid pages, the victim block partition record method can effectively reduce the garbage collection time compared with the random interval garbage block selection method. In terms of memory overhead, the partition victim block recording method only needs to record the optimal victim block physical number and the number of valid pages in the garbage block in each partition. The tuple of garbage blocks in each partition occupies 8 bytes, assuming that it is divided into n partitions, the memory overhead occupies only $8 \times n$ bytes.

3.6 Correctness of Prediction Algorithm

When we make a prediction, we record the number of free pages required for the first write operation of each file and perform periodic acquisition after each record by using the classical minimum string matching algorithm. If these records are periodic, the minimum period can be obtained by this method. Because of the periodicity of the data collected by various payload devices in the system, the periodicity of the data can be fully utilized. File data written in the system can be classified into initial file write and file update operations. File update operations may be unpredictable, so this article only records the number of free pages required for the first write of a file to ensure that the next file that writes data to the file for the first time can obtain the required free pages in advance. Therefore, the file update operation does not affect the reliability of the prediction. Secondly, in the satellite system, the payload data write operation has a fixed periodicity so that the prediction can be guaranteed in this system. The system prediction is affected if some write operations of other tasks are suddenly added to the system. Usually, this condition rarely appears in satellite systems.

In our application scenario, the file write operation generated by the payload system on the satellite is periodic and does not contain burst file write, so the minimum cycle can be correctly used. We apply the existing classical minimum string matching algorithm to calculate the minimum period to ensure the correct calculation.

4 Evaluation

4.1 Experimental Setup

We implemented our garbage collection method based on the typical flash file system yaffs2 in Linux via MTD interfaces. We use the NANDSim [4] to simulate a 128 MB NAND flash in kernel 5.4.0. The time of page write and read are set to 200 μs and 25 μs, respectively. Table 1 shows the parameters of the NAND flash in the NANDSim.

We compare our proposed method with several typical real-time garbage collection methods: on-demand garbage collection with concentrate process [8], on-demand garbage collection with partial process [29], and the hybrid garbage collection method based on the on-demand and periodic [18]. We use a test tool called Filebench [25] to collect the IO workload. The comparison items include the worst-case write response time, average write response time, bandwidth, valid page copy counts per write, and block erase counts per write.

To test the performance of our method on different file operations, we use fileserver as the base version of multiple test sets. That is, we make changes to the test set on the fileserver. Fileserver is a workload that includes create, write, append, and delete operations supported by the filebench tool. We design three modes to simulate file behaviors as shown in Table 2. In this paper, we give 3 different attributes in the fileserver. In the first mode, it creates, writes, reads,

Table 1. Parameters of the NAND Flash Memory

Parameter	Value
Total bytes per page	2 KB
The number of pages per block	64
Total bytes per block	128 KB
Page read latency	25 µs
Page write latency	200 µs
Block erase latency	2 ms
Total Capacity	128 MB

Table 2. Workloads characters

Workloads	flow of operations	Runtime
Fileserver_1	create, write, read, delete, get status	3 s
Fileserver_2	create, write, delete, get status	3 s
Fileserver_3	create, write, delete	3 s

deletes, and obtains file status in turn. We called this workload fileserver_1. In fileserver_1, we set 1000 files and the file size follows a gamma distribution. The file size in each file is a multiple of 4 KB and the average file size of all files is 128 KB. The test time is set to 3 s. In the second mode (called fileserver_2), it creates, writes, deletes, and obtains file status in turn. In this mode, we set 1000 files and each file size is 100 KB. The test time is set to 3 s. In the third mode (called fileserver_3), it creates, writes, and deletes files. In this mode, we set 100 files and each file size is 100 KB. We set 3 s as the test time.

4.2 Experimental Results

Figure 5 shows the result of the four methods by using three different workloads. Figure 5(a) shows the worst-case write response time and Fig. 5(b) shows the average write response time of four methods in these three different modes. Figure 5(c) shows the bandwidth of four methods. For worst-case write response time, PWAgc can reduce 35%–70% than the hybrid method, 7%–56% than the on-demand partial method, and 25.47%–72% than the on-demand concentrate method in three workloads. This is because our method can reduce response time in the victim block select process and garbage collection process. For system average response time, these four methods are similar in three workloads. This is because the garbage collection in idle time will affect file write, so the average write response time is similar in these four methods. For the bandwidth, PWAgc can improve by 1.13%–7.13% to the hybrid method and 1.17%–9.7% than the on-

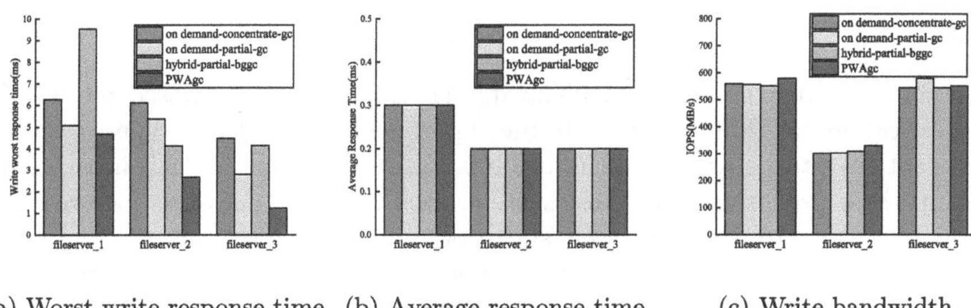

(a) Worst write response time (b) Average response time (c) Write bandwidth

Fig. 5. Response and bandwidth results

demand concentrate method in three workloads. But the bandwidth of PWAgc is lower than the on-demand partial method in fileserver_3. This is because our method has a higher garbage collection trigger frequency than the on-demand partial method and this behavior makes the results.

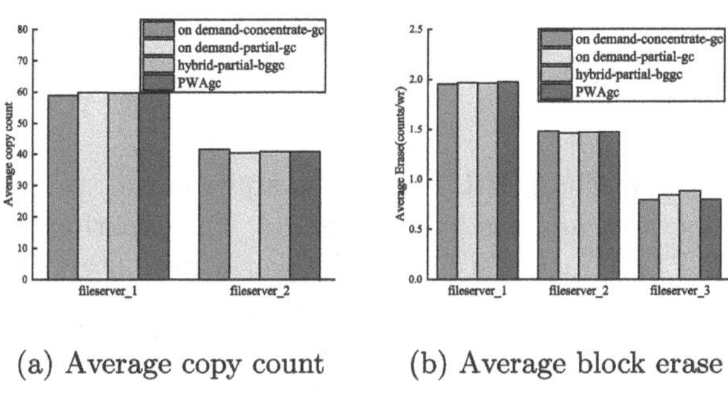

(a) Average copy count (b) Average block erase

Fig. 6. Garbage collection overhead results

Figure 6 shows the garbage collection overhead results of the four methods. Figure 6(a) shows the number of valid page copies and Fig. 6(b) shows the number of blocks erases per write operation. For the valid page copy and block erase, the valid page copy and erase copy per write is similar to the other 3 methods. As the write and delete operations increase, the free space of the system is similar. Our method uses the greedy algorithm as the main selection method and selects the block with min valid page in the whole space, so the average page copy count and the average block erase count can remain similar to the other three methods.

4.3 Real-World Applications Experimental Results

We conduct an experiment to illustrate the value of our proposed method in real-world application scenarios. In the experiment, we set three types of files of different sizes to be written including 100 KB, 200 KB, and 300 KB in turn. We set up three processes in the test system, each of which performs file creation, write, close, delete, and obtain file status operations for files, and set the system to perform 300 s. Through the simulation of such regular file write operations, the performance and overhead in real application scenarios are compared. Figure 7 shows the results.

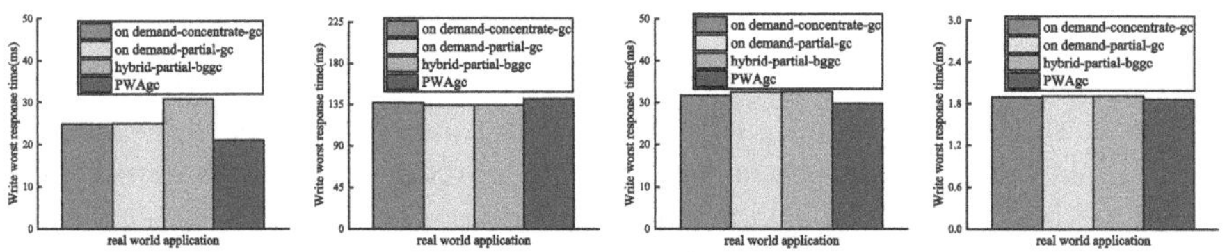

(a) Worst write time (b) Write bandwidth (c) Avr page copy (d) Avr block erase

Fig. 7. Real-world application results

We compare our method with the on-demand concentrate method, the on-demand partial method, and the hybrid method. The experimental results show that in the actual application scenario, the worst response time of PWAgc is reduced by 14.98%, 15.6%, and 31.4%, the write bandwidth is increased by 1.32%, 5.27% and 5.36%, and the average copy time of valid pages of write operation is reduced by 5.87%, 8.45% and 8.5%, respectively compared with the other three methods. The average erase block time for write operations decreased by 1.59%, 2.1%, and 2.1% respectively. Our method fully exploits the characteristics of periodic execution tasks, the worst response time of write operations can be reduced by predicting the number of free pages required for the next write operation in advance in idle tasks while avoiding excessive garbage collection. By recording the data block containing the least number of valid pages in each partition as a garbage block, a large amount of time due to data copy time in valid pages is reduced and more free page space is generated. In addition, similar to the previous experiment, the average response time of operations for all four methods is similar.

According to the above results, our method PWAgc can achieve a shorter worst write response time with the same average response time in the system when there are frequent file data writes and deletes, and the file has periodic and regular characters. In other words, our method is suitable for some real-time systems with periodic and regular write tasks.

5 Conclusion and Future Work

In this paper, we propose a real-time garbage collection method that makes full use of the periodic characteristics of file writing in embedded systems. By recording the file write behavior to get the write operation period and predict the page count needs of the next write, it can decide whether to perform advanced garbage collection in the idle time to reduce the worst response time of the write operation. Besides, using the garbage collection partition records structure can reduce the garbage block selection time. We propose the multi-condition trigger method to balance the overhead of garbage collection and system response time. We evaluate our method using several benchmarks with three representative works. The experimental results show that our method can significantly improve the worst system performance with the same average system performance. The block erase count and valid page copy of the garbage collection are similar.

In the future, we will conduct research on garbage collection in other scenarios without fixed cycle write behavior, using artificial intelligence to predict the next write behavior and decide new garbage collection method. Besides, we will make full use of the characteristics of file update frequency and divide files into several categories according to update frequency. When valid pages are migrated in the garbage collection process, the valid data of files whose update frequency belongs to the same interval will be written together. In this way, the migration times of low-frequency file data are reduced. Besides, we will use the formal verification method to prove the correctness of the prediction algorithm theoretically.

References

1. Trueffs wear-leveling mechanism. M-Systems (2002)
2. Samsung k9f8g08uxm SLC flash memory datasheet. Samsung Electronics (2007)
3. Micron mt29fxxg08cxxxx asynchronous MLC flash memory datasheet. Micron Technology (2009)
4. Linux memory technology device website (2019). http://www.linux-mtd.infradead.org
5. Agrawal, N., Prabhakaran, V., Wobber, T., Davis, J.D., Manasse, M., Panigrahy, R.: Design tradeoffs for SSD performance. In: USENIX 2008 Annual Technical Conference, pp. 57–70. USENIX Association (2008)
6. Lee, C., Sim, D., Hwang, J., Cho, S.: F2FS: a new file system for flash storage. In: 13th USENIX Conference on File and Storage Technologies (FAST), pp. 273–286 (2015)
7. Chang, L.P.: On efficient wear leveling for large-scale flash-memory storage systems. In: Proceedings of the 2007 ACM Symposium on Applied Computing, pp. 1126—1130. Association for Computing Machinery (2007)
8. Chang, L.P., Kuo, T.W., Lo, S.W.: Real-time garbage collection for flash-memory storage systems of real-time embedded systems. ACM Trans. Embed. Comput. Syst. **3**(4), 837–863 (2004)
9. Chiang, M.L., Chang, R.C.: Cleaning policies in mobile computers using flash memory. J. Syst. Softw. **48**(3), 213–231 (1999)

10. Choudhuri, S., Givargis, T.: Deterministic service guarantees for NAND flash using partial block cleaning. In: Proceedings of the 6th IEEE/ACM/IFIP International Conference on Hardware/Software Codesign and System Synthesis, pp. 19–24. Association for Computing Machinery (2008)
11. David, W.: JFFS: the journaling flash file system. In: Ottawa Linux Symposium (2001)
12. Du, Y., Cai, M., Dong, J.: Adaptive garbage collection mechanism for N-log block flash memory storage systems. In: 16th International Conference on Artificial Reality and Telexistence–Workshops (ICAT 2006) (2006)
13. Jo, H., Kang, J.U., Park, S.Y., Kim, J.S., Lee, J.: FAB: flash-aware buffer management policy for portable media players. IEEE Trans. Consumer Electron. **52**(2), 485–493 (2006)
14. Kawaguchi, A., Nishioka, S., Motoda, H.: A flash-memory based file system. In: Proceedings of the USENIX 1995 Technical Conference Proceedings, pp. 155–164. USENIX Association (1995)
15. Khanbadr, A., Binesh Marvasti, M., Asghari, S.A., Khanbadr, S., Rahmani, A.M.: A novel method for victim block selection for NAND flash-based solid state drives based on scoring. J. Supercomput. **76**(12), 10186–10211 (2020)
16. Kim, H.J., Sang-Goo, L.: A new flash memory management for flash storage system. In: Twenty-Third Annual International Computer Software and Applications Conference, pp. 284–289. IEEE (1999)
17. Knuth, D.E., Morris Jr, J.H., Pratt, V.R.: Fast pattern matching in strings. SIAM J. Comput. **6**(2), 323–350 (1977)
18. Manning, C.: How YAFFS works, vol. 48, p. 2011 (2010)
19. Ohhoon, K., Kern, K., Jaewoo, L., Hyokyung, B.: FeGC: an efficient garbage collection scheme for flash memory based storage systems. J. Syst. Softw. **84**(9), 1507–1523 (2011)
20. Qin, Z., Wang, Y., Liu, D., Shao, Z.: Real-time flash translation layer for NAND flash memory storage systems. In: Proceedings of the 2012 IEEE 18th Real Time and Embedded Technology and Applications Symposium, pp. 35–44. IEEE Computer Society (2012)
21. Rosenblum, M., Ousterhout, J.K.: The design and implementation of a log-structured file system. ACM Trans. Comput. Syst. (TOCS) **10**(1), 26–52 (1992)
22. Schierl, A., Schellhorn, G., Haneberg, D., Reif, W.: Abstract specification of the UBIFS file system for flash memory. In: Cavalcanti, A., Dams, D.R. (eds.) FM 2009. LNCS, vol. 5850, pp. 190–206. Springer, Heidelberg (2009). https://doi.org/10.1007/978-3-642-05089-3_13
23. Shen, Z., Li, X., Ju, L., Jia, Z.: A real-time flash translation layer via adaptive partial garbage collection. Int. J. Embed. Syst. **6**(2/3), 167–175 (2014)
24. Sun, D., Song, Y., Chai, Y., Peng, B., Lu, F., Deng, X.: Light-GC: a lightweight and efficient garbage collection scheme for embedded file systems. In: Proceedings of the 23rd ACM/IFIP International Middleware Conference, pp. 216–227. Association for Computing Machinery (2022)
25. Vasily, T., Erez, Z., Spencer, S.: Filebench: a flexible framework for file system benchmarking. USENIX Mag. **41**, 6 (2016)
26. Wang, S., Zhou, Y., Zhou, J., Wu, F., Xie, C.: An efficient data migration scheme to optimize garbage collection in SSDs. IEEE Trans. Comput.-Aided Des. Integr. Circ. Syst. **40**(3), 430–443 (2021)
27. Wu, M., Zwaenepoel, W.: eNVy: a nonvolatile main memory storage system. In: Proceedings of IEEE 4th Workshop on Workstation Operating Systems, WWOS-III, pp. 116–118. IEEE (1993)

28. Yang, M.C., Chang, Y.M., Tsao, C.W., Huang, P.C., Chang, Y.H., Kuo, T.W.: Garbage collection and wear leveling for flash memory: past and future. In: 2014 International Conference on Smart Computing, pp. 66–73. IEEE (2014)
29. Zhang, Q., Li, X., Wang, L., Zhang, T., Wang, Y., Shao, Z.: Lazy-RTGC: A real-time lazy garbage collection mechanism with jointly optimizing average and worst performance for NAND flash memory storage systems. ACM Trans. Des. Autom. Electron. Syst. **20**(3), 1–32 (2015)

Tree-Based Synthesis of Web Test Sequences from Manual Actions

Pengkun Jiang[1,2], Sinan Wang[1], and Yepang Liu[1,2(✉)]

[1] Research Institute of Trustworthy Autonomous Systems, Southern University of Science and Technology, Shenzhen, China
{12132334,wangsn}@mail.sustech.edu.cn

[2] Department of Computer Science and Engineering, Southern University of Science and Technology, Shenzhen, China
liuyp1@sustech.edu.cn

Abstract. The thrive of web technologies and applications demands effective testing methods for quality assurance. For this purpose, researchers have proposed various testing techniques to automate the interaction with web applications in recent years. While such techniques help save human testers from repetitive and tedious manual testing tasks, they often only explore limited usage scenarios due to the lack of domain knowledge. In practice, constructing test sequences that align with application business logic still requires substantial manual efforts. In this work, we explore a new paradigm that leverages the synergy between humans and machines. Our key observation is that in many web applications, interactive elements within or across web pages often exhibit similarities in functionality and interaction style. Leveraging this observation, we propose a novel testing method, FRET, which combines manual recording of an example test sequence with automated synthesis of multiple new test sequences that have similar intentions through action mutation. To detect similar elements to the example, FRET employs a programming-by-example technique, in which similar elements are described as the intersection within a well-defined version space. To avoid redundant mutations, FRET builds a tree representation of the mutation process, which helps preserve the logical dependence between actions and monitor the progress of test generation. The experiment results on 32 top-ranking websites show that, given an example sequence, FRET can effectively generate an average of 138 new sequences to interact with the web application under test with a false positive rate of only 0.69% on similar element searching, significantly outperforming the baseline method in terms of covered elements and generated valid test sequences. Additionally, FRET has also led to the discovery of 86 real errors in 19 web applications, which demonstrates its practical usefulness.

Keywords: Web Testing · Sequence Generation · Record and Replay

1 Introduction

To cope with the growing number of end-users and minimize losses caused by errors, many web applications require thorough testing before being launched

W.-N. Chin and Z. Xu (Eds.): TASE 2024, LNCS 14777, pp. 242–260, 2024.
https://doi.org/10.1007/978-3-031-64626-3_14

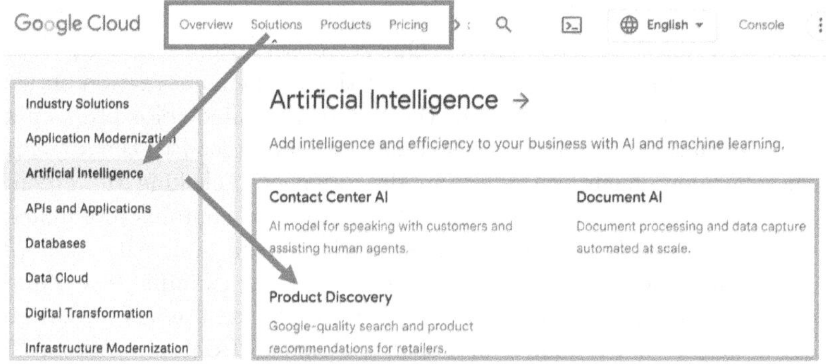

Fig. 1. Example test sequence on Google Cloud (Color figure online)

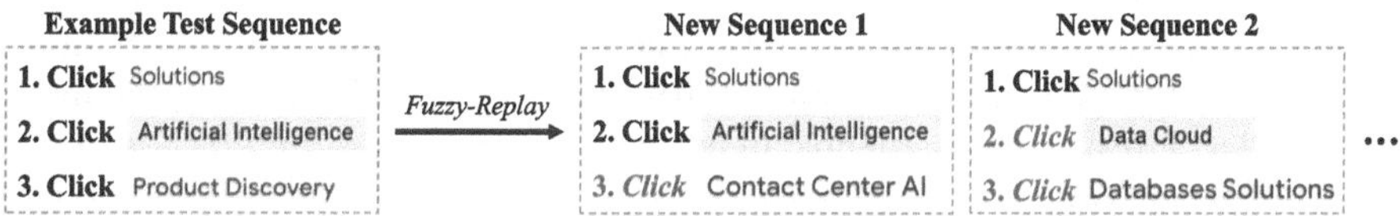

Fig. 2. Test generation via fuzzy-replay (Color figure online)

online. In practice, *automatic end-to-end testing* [8,39] is often adopted, whose testing objective is maximizing the functional coverage. However, such techniques do not involve domain knowledge of the web under testing (WUT). This limitation can easily trap the testing agents in a local optimal state, preventing them from exploring deeper functionalities of the WUTs.

Many test automation frameworks support recording user actions on a web browser and replaying the recorded actions. Such a *record-and-replay* technique is widely used [20], especially for regression testing purposes. In existing practices of record-and-replay, a recorded user action sequence is usually saved as a definite test script that can be played back later. Compared with automatic testing, record-and-replay allows testers to use their domain knowledge during recording to test some important but hard-to-reach features, so as to improve the effectiveness of regression testing.

In order to thoroughly test a webpage, testers should manually record many action sequences, which can be labor-intensive. Take the Google Cloud homepage in Fig. 1 as an example. Testers may record the sequence of click actions as shown in Fig. 2 (see Example Test Sequence) and replay the sequence when needed. While this facilitates regression testing, it is not efficient. For instance, to test whether users can still visit the "Contact Center AI" page or pages related to "Data Cloud" after the website evolves, the testers need to record all corresponding action sequences in advance. Due to combinatorial explosion, testers will need to record hundreds of similar sequences to the example one (Fig. 2) to ensure complete functional coverage.

Recognizing this limitation, our work aims to enhance the efficiency of conventional record-and-replay techniques. Our key observation is that UI elements within or across web pages may have similarities in their interaction style. For example, in Fig. 1, the UI elements in the box of the same color are similar to each other: clicking the elements in the blue box will all lead to the appearance of a dropdown menu such as the one in the green box; clicking the green box elements will all lead to the appearance of a frame that contains more clickable elements (i.e., the red box). By leveraging such element similarity, it is possible to create many new diverse sequences based on one example test sequence. Consider the example test sequence in Fig. 2. By replacing the last action "Click 'Product Discovery"' with a click on a similar element "Contact Center AI", we can obtain a new test sequence. By replacing the second action "Click 'Artificial Intelligence"' with a click on a similar element "Data Cloud", we can create more test sequences to explore the pages related to "Data Cloud". We call this process *fuzzy-replay*, in which we obtain new test sequences from an example test sequence by replacing user actions with similar ones while keeping the interaction order. Fuzzy-replay expands an existing manually recorded test sequence into multiple logically-consistent ones, thus significantly improving web test efficiency with the least human effort.

In this paper, we propose a web test generation framework FRET, which stands for Fuzzy-REply for web Testing. FRET formulates the web element selector with *version space algebra* (VSA) [13], which has been adopted in various *programming by example* (PBE) tasks [10,28]. This formulation describes the selection of similar elements as the intersection operation of directed graphs in a well-defined space. To address the challenge of dynamic content loading in web applications, FRET replays the actions with the selected similar elements (called mutation) in an online manner. In addition, FRET maintains a tree-structure of the mutation process during test generation, which helps preserve the logical relationships between generated actions and monitor the progress of fuzzy-replay. With little manual effort in the recording stage, FRET can quickly learn the interaction logic with domain knowledge, generate new test sequences similar to the example, and thus comprehensively test a web page.

We evaluated FRET on 32 top-ranking websites under different categories. Based on the experimental results, **Fret can generate an average of 138 new test sequences and detect 86 web errors**, with a false positive rate of only 0.69% on similar element searching, which significantly outperforms other baseline methods. In summary, this paper makes the following contributions:

- We propose FRET, which employs PBE-based similar element selection and tree-coloring based action sequencing to generate new test sequences from a manually-recorded web action sequence.
- We have evaluated FRET on 32 top-ranking web applications of different kinds, demonstrating its effectiveness in boosting functional coverage and exposing real web errors based on the manually-recorded examples.

```
{ "url": "https://cloud.google.com",
  "tests": [{
    "commands": [
      { "command": "open" },
      { "command": "click", "target": "xpath=//body/tab[2]/a" },
      { "command": "click", "target": "xpath=//tab[2]/div/div/ul/li[3]/a" },
      { "command": "click", "target": "xpath=//div[3]/ul[4]/li/a/div" },
      { "command": "input", "target": "xpath=//header[1]//input", "value": "AI solution"}
    ]
}]}
```

Listing 1: An snippet of Selenium IDE test script

2 Background and Challenges

Selenium IDE [33] enables human testers to record their web test sequences and replay them as unit test cases using Selenium's WebDriver API, thereby achieving record-and-replay tasks. Listing 1 is a snippet of the Selenium IDE test script for a test sequence in Fig. 2. Typically, a test script (or test sequence) consists of a series of test actions:

$$Seq_{\text{example}} := \{act^{(1)}, act^{(2)}, ..., \ act^{(n)}\} \tag{1}$$

There are two types of actions: browser actions and element actions. Browser actions configure the state of the web driver, including opening a URL, resizing the window, and running some JavaScript program, etc. An element action consists of three key components: the action type, the targeting DOM element, and an (optional) interaction value. They correspond to the `command`, `target` and `value` attributes in Listing 1:

$$act^{(i)} := \langle action\_type^{(i)},\ target\_element^{(i)},\ interaction\_value^{(i)} \rangle \tag{2}$$

Here, the *interaction_value* provides the necessary message for executing the given *action_type*. For example, for an input action, this attribute stores the textual input value. As for a selection action, it can be the selected option in the particular `<select>` menu.

A web application usually contains elements that are similar in functionality and interaction pattern. Usually, an element action can also be applied to interact with other similar elements. Such similarity in human-computer interaction patterns provides the opportunity to reuse manual tests to generate new test sequences. Also, we can obtain new test actions by altering the original *interaction_value*. We call this process as **mutation**. As such, the similar actions generated by mutation are called **mutated actions**, as shown below:

$$act\langle typ_0, tgt_0, val_0\rangle \xrightarrow{\text{mutate}} \begin{cases} \hat{act}\langle typ_0, tgt_1, val_0\rangle, \\ \hat{act}\langle typ_0, tgt_2, val_0\rangle, \\ \hat{act}\langle typ_0, tgt_2, val_1\rangle, \\ ... \end{cases} \tag{3}$$

For each element action in the example test sequence, we can obtain multiple mutated actions. By recombining mutated actions in the order of the example test sequence, we can generate new test sequences, which we call **mutation sequences**. Ideally, the mutation sequences will retain the domain knowledge in the example test sequence, thus achieving higher functional coverage for WUT:

$$Seq_{\text{mutation}} := \{\hat{act}^{(1)}, \hat{act}^{(2)}, \dots \hat{act}^{(n)}\} \tag{4}$$

Technically, fuzzy-replay generates new test sequences by mutating and recombining the example test sequence. However, it faces two major challenges:

1. **How to find similar elements?** Due to the diverse implementation styles, we cannot directly obtain the interaction types and functionalities of web elements. Determining the similarity of web elements is hard.
2. **How to recombine mutated actions?** The logical relation between actions in the example test sequence requires recombining the mutated actions in a meaningful order. Otherwise, the mutation sequences can be invalid.

In this paper, we propose FRET, the first framework that generates web GUI test sequences with fuzzy-replay. It explicitly addresses the above challenges with two techniques: PBE-based searching and coloring-based action sequencing. We will illustrate them in the next section.

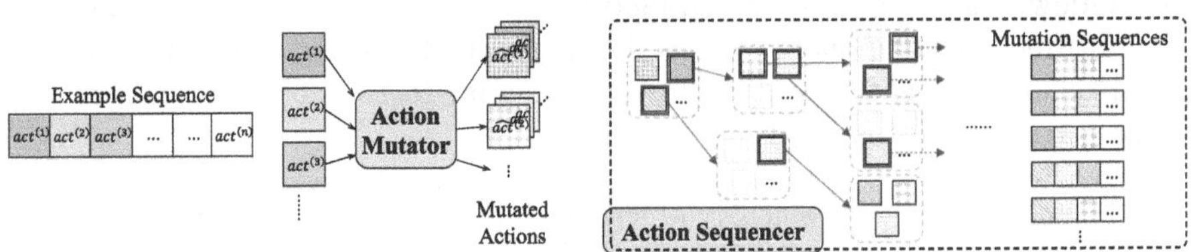

Fig. 3. The overview of FRET

3 The FRET Test Generation Framework

3.1 Overview

Figure 3 shows the overview of our proposed web GUI test generation framework, FRET. Similar to traditional record-and-replay techniques, FRET also accepts a manually recorded test sequence as input. Then, it tries to generate new test sequences that experience other functionalities of WUT. This is accomplished by two core components: an *Action Mutator* that mutates each action in the example test sequence to generate mutated actions, and an *Action Sequencer* that combines mutated actions with respect to their original ordering in the example. They will be illustrated in detail in the following parts.

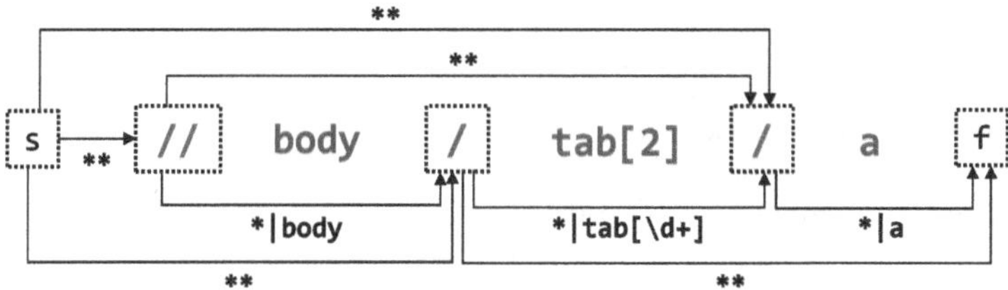

Fig. 4. The version space of XPath "//body/tab[2]/a" (self-loops hidden)

3.2 The Action Mutator

Programming by Example. At high-level, the Action Mutator mutates an action by replacing its target element with similar elements. Technically, this is accomplished by selecting elements whose XPaths share common patterns with the original one. Similar elements usually exhibit spatial locality in the webpage (Fig. 1), which enables a wildcard element selector to assign common visual property or page layout to all of them. Such intuition makes it possible to formulate our task as a *programming by example* (PBE) problem [28]: given a single element selector (XPath in our task), construct all possible selectors that maximize the similarity criterion on the current web state. We define the syntax of the element selector as follows:

XPath	xp	$\longrightarrow$	$/lvl \mid xp/lvl$
Level	lvl	$\longrightarrow$	$cond \mid * \mid **$
Condition	$cond$	$\longrightarrow$	regular expression

This syntax can be converted from the original XPaths [21] via simple text processing. Each selector has multiple levels separated by slash symbols (/), while each level has a condition represented by a regular expression or wildcard symbol. Here, a single asterisk (*) matches exactly one level, while a double asterisk symbol (**) matches zero or more levels. To simplify representation, we transform a double slash (//) into a wildcard condition (/**), which preserves its semantics [21]. The level condition *cond* is stored as a regular expression, which is usually a constant string of the node's tag name (see Listing 1). In particular, we convert the indexing operator (e.g., `[1]`) into a regular expression `[\d+]`, which can match all elements at the same DOM level.

Version Space Algebra of Element Selector. The XPath selector syntax above allows a powerful tool *version space algebra* (VSA) to encode an even more general representation of our desired web elements. VSA has been successfully applied in commercial text processing products [10,28], demonstrating its viability in related tasks. Our version space definition of XPath selectors follows

Algorithm 1: PBE-based similar element selection

Input: target element ω, all elements E
Output: set of similar elements E_{similar}
1 $G_\Omega \longleftarrow$ `version_space`(ω)
2 **while** $\exists e \in E.\neg trivial(G_\Omega \sqcap G_e)$ **do**
3 $\quad e^* \longleftarrow \arg\max_{e \in E \setminus \{\omega\}} \sum_{x \in \mathcal{X}(G_\Omega \sqcap G_e)}$ `match_score`(G_Ω, x)
4 $\quad E \longleftarrow E \setminus \{e^*\}$
5 $\quad E_{\text{similar}} \longleftarrow E_{\text{similar}} \bigcup \{e^*\}$
6 $\quad G_\Omega \longleftarrow G_\Omega \sqcap$ `version_space`(e^*)

the widget path VSA employed by JIGSAW [17]. However, our XPath selector is more general, as JIGSAW only supports `id` selector as the level condition. As an example, Fig. 4 shows the version space representation of an XPath in Listing 1. Given the XPath of an element from the example sequence, we first transform it into a directed graph by creating edges:

$$\begin{aligned} E \;=\; & \{(v_i, v_j, **) \mid 1 \leq i \leq j < n\} \cup \\ & \{(v_i, v_{i+1}, *) \mid 1 \leq i < n\} \cup \\ & \{(v_i, v_{i+1}, cond_i) \mid 1 \leq i < n\} \end{aligned}$$

Here, $cond_i$ is the condition of the i-th level of the XPath, represented by a regular expression mentioned above. Each node v_i is a slash (/) in the XPath. There are also two special nodes, s and f, the source and sink nodes. As such, an XPath can be accepted by this directed graph, if each of its level conditions matches regular expressions along a path from the source node s to the sink node f.

Given two VSA directed graphs $G = (V, E)$ and $G' = (V', E')$, an important operation is their *intersection* $G \sqcap G' = (V_\sqcap, E_\sqcap)$, which selects common XPaths accepted by both graphs. Their definitions are:

$$V_\sqcap = \{\langle v, v' \rangle | \; v \in V, v' \in V'\}$$
$$E_\sqcap = \{(\langle u, u' \rangle, \langle v, v' \rangle, l \sqcap l') | \; (u, v, l) \in E, (u', v', l') \in E'\}$$

where the intersection of level conditions is: $l \sqcap l' = l$, if l and l' are identical; or $l \sqcap * = l$; the remaining intersections result in an invalid condition. It has been proven by Li et al. [17] that, this VSA intersection is well-defined and can soundly capture all XPaths acceptable to both G and G'.

Similar Element Selection. Algorithm 1 describes how the Action Mutator finds similar elements. All available elements E can be obtained via trivial element selectors on the current web page, while Action Mutator will select those similar to the target element w among them. G_Ω is the directed graph that accepts all desired similar elements. It is initialized with the version space of the target element ω in the example sequence (line 1), and will grow by taking

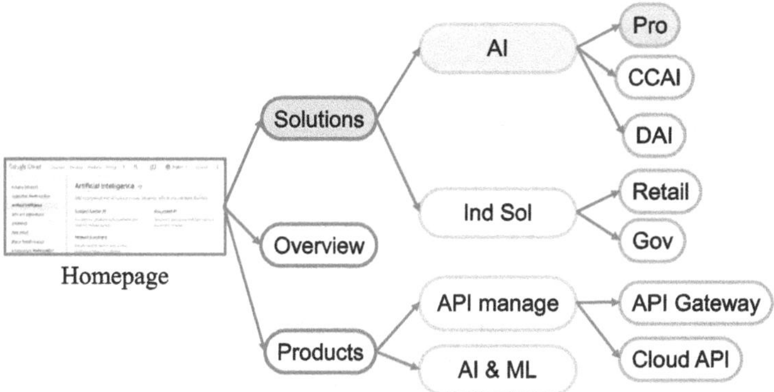

Fig. 5. A mutation tree of the example on Google Cloud

its intersection with the selected similar elements (line 6). Similar to the widget selector synthesis of JIGSAW [17], the Action Mutator also employs an iterative process, until the remaining elements only match a trivial selector (line 2). Here, "trivial" means the resultant graph is equivalent to a wildcard selector "`/**/*`". Each time, an element is selected based on the evaluation of a *match score*. It adopts the idea of `FlashFill`'s compatibility score [10], such that matching elements should be selected earlier to avoid computational cost. For an element e, $\mathcal{X}(G_\Omega \sqcap G_e)$ denotes all XPaths selected by its intersection with G_Ω. Intuitively, these XPaths should evaluate to a higher match score with the original element selector G_Ω. Therefore, we prefer the one that achieves the maximum sum of match scores (line 3). Here, `match_score` counts the number of *exact matching* of level conditions in an XPath.

3.3 The Action Sequencer

With the mutated actions, the next step is to combine them into new sequences. FRET employs *online action sequencing*, which is executed during the interaction with WUT. Online sequencing validates the mutated actions in real-time. As a result, all the generated test sequences will be valid.

Mutation Tree. In a manually recorded sequence, the execution order of actions describes the use case scenario from the testers. This logical dependence encodes domain knowledge such that subsequent actions could be executed after the preceding action, while the preceding action should be executed before its succeeding actions. We model such logical dependence as a tree structure, which we call a *mutation tree*.

In a mutation tree (Fig. 5), each node saves an action from the example test sequence, or its mutated actions discovered by the Action Mutator. The descendants of each node compose all possible subsequent actions that can be executed afterwards. In particular, the root node indicates the test entry and

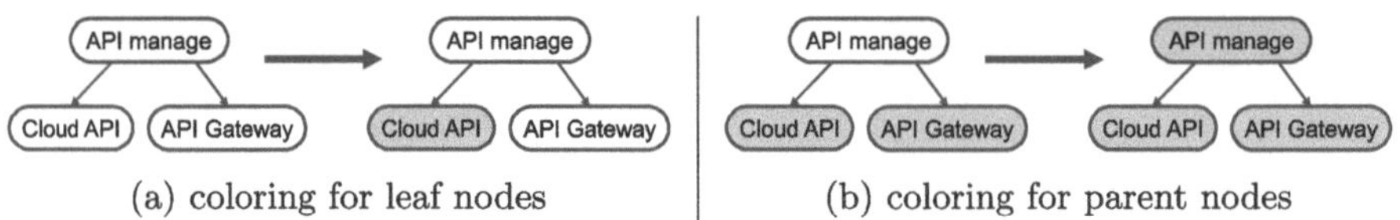

(a) coloring for leaf nodes (b) coloring for parent nodes

Fig. 6. Tree-coloring based action sequencing

does not save any action. The mutation tree has two characteristics: first, the target elements between each layer of the mutation tree are similar to each other; second, a path from the root node to any leaf node is a legal test sequence. During test generation, the mutation tree is expanded from the current web state, such that all similar elements of the current action's target element will become the children nodes of the current node. To avoid repeating elements or loops, each node and its incoming edge will be added to the tree by exactly once. This constraint ensures maintaining the mutation tree property. Once all actions from the example sequence are mutated and the mutation tree along this path is fully expanded, the Action Sequencer will start from the root node and continue to visit other paths, until the mutation tree can no longer grow. Therefore, the mutation tree provides a cache for mutated actions and quantifies the test sufficiency criterion.

Tree-Coloring Based Sequencing. As action sequencing progresses, the proportion of unselected mutated actions decreases. To eliminate the potential of generating duplicate sequences, Action Sequencer adopts *tree-coloring based action sequencing* to expand the mutation tree. The key idea is that, each path from the root node to a leaf node in the mutation tree can form a valid test sequence. Since each leaf node is unique, there is only one path from the root node to a specific leaf node. When a leaf node is selected to generate a test sequence, it is colored to indicate that this node should not be selected again in the future. There are two coloring strategies:

- Figure 6a: for a leaf node, it will be colored every time it is executed, to indicate it should not be selected again.
- Figure 6b: for a non-leaf node, once its children nodes have all been colored, selecting it again will produce duplicate test sequences. Therefore, we color this node to avoid such cases.

When selecting the next mutated action to execute, an uncolored node in the mutation tree shall be selected to avoid duplicate sequences. When the root node is colored, it indicates a corresponding test sequence has been generated for each functional point in WUT, and the test generation shall terminate. All newly generated sequences will be output as test sequences.

Theoretically, the Action Sequencer performs a *post-order depth-first search* (DFS) on the mutation tree, in which visiting the web state corresponds to the coloring operation on the tree node. Meanwhile, a backtrack operation should be implemented to ensure the proper execution of DFS. To achieve this goal, the Action Sequencer will store the current web state, which will be loaded back once all its child nodes are colored. Nevertheless, the store and reload operations will not be recorded in the generated test sequences.

An important objective of testing is to discover errors. Action Sequencer will record errors captured by the web browser during the online sequencing process. These recorded errors indicate the ability of FRET to expose real web bugs. What's more, they can form the test oracles [27] in the generated test cases. However, there is one type of error that should not be regarded as a real bug, that is, the target element is not found. We will drop such errors and consider the corresponding test sequences invalid.

4 Evaluation

4.1 Research Questions

To evaluate the performance of FRET, we investigated three research questions:

- **RQ1 (Similar Element Detection)**: Can the Action Mutator effectively identify similar elements?
- **RQ2 (Mutation Sequence Legality)**: How many valid mutation sequences can be generated by the Action Sequencer?
- **RQ3 (Mutation Sequence Redundancy)**: To what extent can FRET avoid generating redundant test sequences?
- **RQ4 (Tool Usefulness)**: Can FRET outperform the baseline methods in generating unique valid tests and triggering real web errors?

4.2 Subject Websites

To select subject WUTs, we referred to Semrush[1]. The website provides traffic rankings for global public websites under 32 different categories. Within its indexed websites, we selected our subjects based on the following criteria:

- The website should not have an anti-robot system like reCAPTCHA. FRET generates test sequences and automatically replays them with Selenium. It, however, cannot automatically pass the anti-robot system.
- The website's core functionality should not rely on specific text input. For example, the Google homepage does not contain too many interactive elements. Most of its functionalities should be accessed through inputs on the search bar. However, currently FRET cannot purposefully mutate text inputs.

Finally, we selected 32 top-ranking websites for our experiment.

[1] https://www.semrush.com/website/top/global/all/.

4.3 Experimental Setup

FRET was implemented on top of Selenium and Selenium IDE [33]. It supports the mutation of element click actions and input texts (random modification). We recorded one example test sequence for each of the 32 WUTs. We ensure all recorded sequences can effectively experience the WUTs' core functionalities. All experiments were run with a Chromium browser and corresponding Webdriver, on a Macbook with a 2 GHz i5 processor and 16 GB RAM.

4.4 RQ1: Similar Element Detection

Metric. We evaluated the performance of the Action Mutator using *false positive rate* (FPR). During test generation, once the Action Mutator generates invalid actions (or dissimilar actions), the subsequent example actions will not be able to playback. Therefore, its precision is crucial for preserving the legality of the generated sequences. We saved the results of similar element selection and manually determined whether they were valid similar elements. In other words, we shall manually check whether the mutated actions can experience similar functionalities to their original example actions.

Result. We manually identified 6,275 similar elements selected by Action Mutator, which correspond to 116 elements across 32 example test sequences. Among them, 43 elements from four WUTs (Advertising, Airlines, Entertainment, and Restaurants) were determined to be dissimilar to their corresponding original elements, resulting in an FPR of 0.69% for the similar element searching algorithm. By investigating the misjudging elements, we found that 34 of them were due to regular expression simplification of the element indexes, while the remaining were selected due to the same special tag names.

Comparison. For comparison, we also implemented a naive similar element selection algorithm, that is, **only selecting the elements in the same DOM level that acquire identical tag names and class names**. This simple rule only reveals 5,034 valid similar elements being selected (FPR = 19.8%), which is a significant performance downgrade. Moreover, this simple rule could not identify similar elements in eight example sequences. Compared to the PBE-based similar element selection, the naive algorithm fails to capture the inter-relationship between similar elements. Nevertheless, we still found that the simple algorithm discovers non-overlap valid similar elements compared to the PBE-based approach. The main reason is that similar elements may have same class yet different tag names. In the future, we will improve the precision of the Action Mutator by cooperating with the DOM attributes in the algorithm.

4.5 RQ2: Mutation Sequence Legality

Baseline. To compare with FRET's Action Sequencer, we implemented a baseline method, called *offline action sequencer.* This baseline simply takes a Cartesian product over all mutated actions with respect to their parents' ordering in the example sequence. That is, for the sequence in (1), and the mutated actions for each of its actions $A^{(i)} = \{\hat{act}_k^{(i)} \mid 1 \leq k \leq |E_s^{(i)}|\}$, the offline action sequencer will output all sequences produced by $A^{(1)} \times A^{(2)} \cdots \times A^{(n)}$. It is realized by performing Algorithm 1 during the manual recording stage, thus no Internet connection is needed during offline action sequencing.

Table 1. Experiment result of RQ2

WUT	example seq. length	#seq. (offline)	#sample seq. (offline)	#legal seq. (offline)	#seq. (FRET)
Agoda	5	74,030	382	0	63
Doubleclick	4	35,420	380	0	372
Ryanair	6	2,826,252	384	0	109
Chase	3	168,480	384	0	102
Sephora	3	55,680	381	0	138
Openai	4	58,562	381	2	289
Stackoverflow	4	23,440	377	1	93
Onliner	3	3,386,812	384	0	89
Youtube	4	1,695,200	384	0	162
Archive.	4	162,150	383	0	341
Shein	4	1,617,000	384	0	197
Paypal	3	37,352	380	1	213
All Recipes	4	74,700	382	0	289
Steam	3	603,720	383	0	52
NIH	3	90,896	382	0	74
Wordpress	3	617,760	383	0	20
Robobank	4	169,664	383	0	292
Upstox	3	304,128	383	0	55
ADP	4	44,649	380	0	119
Qualtrics	3	26,895	378	1	161
Genius	3	41,040	380	0	81
Wikipedia	4	509,184	383	0	236
Google Cloud	3	31,140	379	1	84
Redfin	4	58,590	381	0	123
Uber eats	3	110,700	382	1	125
Sciencedirect	4	536,130	383	0	42
Marca	4	55,440	381	0	96
Samsung	4	57,456	381	0	59
Usps	3	32,480	379	1	105
Bahn	3	54,272	381	0	121
Av.by	4	78,064	382	0	85
Mayoclinic	5	25,984	378	0	52

Metric. We evaluate the effectiveness of the Action Sequencer using *legality rate of action sequences*. To be specific, if a generated test sequence produces errors like "fail to locate the target element", we consider it illegal. Since the number of sequences generated by the offline action sequencer is exponentially large, validating all of them is impossible. Therefore, we randomly sampled the results using a 95% confidence interval and a 5% margin of error [37], and ran them to compute the legality rate under statistical significance.

Result. Table 1 shows the results. For all WUTs, the offline action sequencer generated more than 20,000 action sequences. Among our randomly-sampled sequences, most of them cannot be exactly replayed. Moreover, in 25 WUTs, the offline action sequencer did not output any legal sequences, indicating that its legality rate is extremely low. On the other hand, FRET's Action Sequencer produced only legal action sequences, as they were generated in an online manner. Online sequencing ensures that only interactable web elements are selected as target elements in the mutation sequences. In conclusion, FRET's online action sequencing algorithm, compared to the offline version, can produce significantly more legal test sequences.

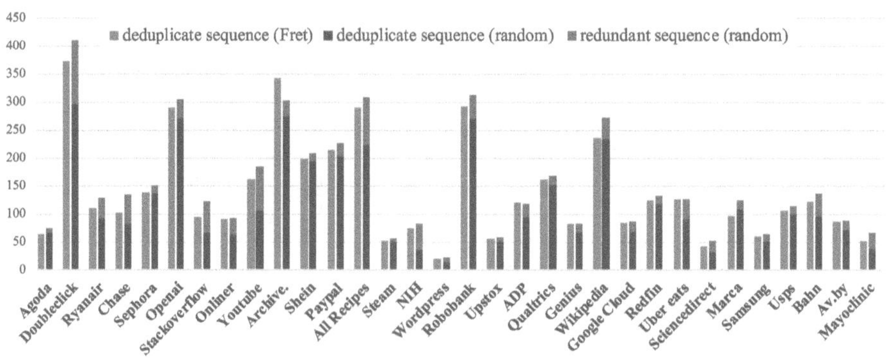

Fig. 7. Experiment result of RQ3

4.6 RQ3: Mutation Sequence Redundancy

Baseline. We introduce a *random online action sequencer* as the baseline to compare with FRET's Action Sequencer in their generated redundant sequences. The random sequencer will randomly pick a mutated action from all available ones during the online replay stage. Unlike FRET, it cannot determine whether the replay is finished; thus, it will endlessly (and repeatedly) mutate all available actions from the example sequence.

Metric. We count identical sequences as the *number of redundant sequences* generated by the random sequencer to investigate redundancy in test generation. The coloring-based sequencer can determine whether the replay is complete, while the random sequencer cannot. Hence, for each WUT, we record the duration spent by FRET's Action Sequencer, and run the random sequencer for the same duration for fair comparison. In RQ2, we have already shown that the offline sequencer can only produce a few legal sequences. Therefore, in RQ3, we will not evaluate it due to its poor performance.

Result. Figure 7 shows the total number of sequences and redundant sequences generated by the random sequencer. The random sequencer generated a certain amount of redundant sequences for all 32 WUTs. Among them, in NIH, it generated the highest proportion of redundant sequences, which accounts for 55%. An analysis of the WUTs with a high redundancy rate revealed that some of their elements may result in states with no subsequent actions. Due to the lack of memorization, the random sequencer will repeatedly select such elements and produce a large amount of redundancy (e.g., repeated short sequences). False positive elements in "Archive." caused unhandled exceptions. Handling these web errors consumes time. Without a coloring mechanism, the random sequencer will trigger these errors repeatedly, thus wasting more time but generating fewer new sequences. Except for "Archive.", the total number of randomly generated sequences is greater than that of tree-coloring based sequencing.

Figure 7 also shows the number of generated action sequences by two strategies after deduplication. Among the four out of 32 WUTs, FRET generated more than 300 action sequences, while in Doubleclick, it generated the most unique sequences, with a number of 372. In 13 WUTs, FRET generated less than 100 action sequences, and Wordpress had the fewest unique sequences. There are mainly two reasons for its poor performance: 1) the slow loading speed of web pages reduces the number of interactive elements; 2) the functionalities involved in the example test sequence are limited and there are no sufficient similar elements to produce more action sequences. It indicates that the number of action sequences generated by FRET is greatly influenced by the subject websites and the example test sequences provided by the human testers. Nevertheless, FRET still generated a considerable amount of valid and unique test sequences.

A deep analysis of the number of generated action sequences by the two strategies shows that, within 2 h, the coloring-based online sequencer successfully traversed the mutation tree of three WUTs (NIH, Sciencedirect, and Mayoclinic) and generated all possible test sequences based on the example test sequences. In the three WUTs, the number of action sequences generated by the random online sequencer is significantly lower. This indicates that while FRET's tree-coloring based action sequencer generates all possible test sequences, the random sequencer has a significant disadvantage. Among 12 WUTs, the differences in the number of generated action sequences between the two strategies did not exceed 10, indicating there is no significant performance difference between them.

Among 30 WUTs, the coloring-based online sequencer generated more new test sequences than the random online sequencer. Due to the redundancy of random online sequencing, the coloring mechanism has better performance, even though it has overhead of maintaining the mutation tree.

4.7 RQ4: Tool Usefulness

Following previous web testing work [34,39], we also count the *number of web errors* triggered by different strategies to measure their ability to detect bugs. There were a total of 86 unique web errors found by FRET on 19 different WUTs during our experiment, while the random sequencer only triggered 73 web errors. Since the offline sequencer is poor at producing valid test sequences, we cannot further count the number of web errors it can trigger.

5 Threats to Validity

There are several potential threats to the validity of our experiments. Firstly, we conducted our experiments on 32 WUTs; however, our selection process focused on high-traffic webs without anti-robot systems within each web category. This means that FRET may not be directly applicable to all web applications. In such cases, it could potentially introduce unknown errors or lead to an increased false positive rate when identifying similar elements. Secondly, Action Mutator extends the example element's XPath selector to other syntactically similar elements within the same web state. However, due to their inherent complexity and diversity, it is unlikely that the generated tests can cover all elements. This makes it challenging to achieve full functional coverage. Moreover, FRET currently can only handle limited types of web actions (clicking, mouseover, and random text input). In order to improve the logical coherence of the generated mutation actions, it is essential to purposefully mutate the interaction value.

6 Related Work

- **Record-and-replay.** Record-and-replay method has shown its practical uses on diverse platforms, including web applications [1,33] and mobile apps on Android [18,26] or iOS [29]. However, most GUI tests are prone to break [22,31], and many techniques were proposed to improve the robustness of GUI element locators [14–16,25]. There were also techniques leveraging machine learning methods to fix the broken recorded test cases [6,11,20,35]. FRET directly utilizes the recorded test script and generates new tests with PBE-based similar element selection and tree-coloring based action sequencing.
- **Test generation.** The techniques generate web test scripts based on the DOM structure of WUT. To measure the sufficiency of test generation, a common approach is to utilize state flow graphs (SFGs) of WUTs. An SFG

abstracts web pages into different states, and uses user events that trigger state transition as edges. Based on SFG, search-based algorithms generate test paths as unit test cases [2–5,7,23,36]. However, it is difficult to determine whether different generated paths have logical dependencies. FRET also generates new tests, from which the business logic (domain knowledge about WUT) is represented by the human-recorded examples.

- **Similar element detection.** Web GUI testing techniques use varying criteria to determine the similarity between web elements. For example, [3,7] compare the similarity between web states and select states with significant differences in similarity to achieve higher coverage. [6,20,24,30] find elements corresponding to the target element in the WUT's new version. They rely on the elements' attributes to determine element correspondence. FRET involves Action Mutator, which detects similar GUI elements in the current web page using a PBE-based element selection algorithm.
- **Test reuse.** Test reuse is a technique that uses existing test scripts to generate new tests. One application scenario is to extend tests of a web application to another WUT with similar functionality [12,30,32]. Test reuse can also enhance automated testing. It often builds an initial SFG based on the example tests, and then uses a web crawler to extend the SFG. When searching for new test paths, the web page state is abstracted and the similarity between the newly selected state and the corresponding state of the example test will be compared. The new test path will be constructed based on the most similar state [19,24]. Test reuse is similar to FRET's approach. However, test reuse relies on human-written scripts, while FRET does not require explicit test scripting.

7 Conclusions and Future Work

We proposed FRET, a fuzzy-replay framework to facilitate web testing by synthesizing test sequences from a human-recorded example. With such an example, FRET expands the test actions to similar target elements through PBE-based element selection, and connects these selected elements with a tree-coloring based sequencing algorithm, thus generating new test sequences similar to the example one. Our experiments show that FRET , compared to two baseline methods, can generate a considerable number of valid test sequences for 32 top websites under different categories. FRET also successfully improves the number of covered elements during testing and identifies many real web errors.

In the future, we will further improve FRET's similar element searching algorithm. We plan to add visual attributes [38] or use large language models (LLMs) to assist in determining similar elements [9] and find more similar elements that the current Action Mutator may miss. Additionally, FRET can be combined with other test generation techniques [3,7,23] to access hard-to-reach web states, thus increasing the overall functional coverage.

Acknowledgements. We thank all reviewers for their valuable comments, which have helped improve this paper. This work is supported by the National Natural Science Foundation of China (Grant Nos. 61932021 and 62372219).

References

1. Andrica, S., Candea, G.: WaRR: a tool for high-fidelity web application record and replay. In: 2011 IEEE/IFIP 41st International Conference on Dependable Systems & Networks (DSN), pp. 403–410. IEEE (2011)
2. Artzi, S., et al.: Finding bugs in dynamic web applications. In: Proceedings of the 2008 International Symposium on Software Testing and Analysis, pp. 261–272 (2008)
3. Biagiola, M., Ricca, F., Tonella, P.: Search based path and input data generation for web application testing. In: Menzies, T., Petke, J. (eds.) SSBSE 2017. LNCS, vol. 10452, pp. 18–32. Springer, Cham (2017). https://doi.org/10.1007/978-3-319-66299-2_2
4. Biagiola, M., Stocco, A., Ricca, F., Tonella, P.: Diversity-based web test generation. In: Proceedings of the 2019 27th ACM Joint Meeting on European Software Engineering Conference and Symposium on the Foundations of Software Engineering, pp. 142–153 (2019)
5. Choudhary, S.R., Prasad, M.R., Orso, A.: CrossCheck: combining crawling and differencing to better detect cross-browser incompatibilities in web applications. In: ICST 2012, pp. 171–180 (2012)
6. Choudhary, S.R., Zhao, D., Versee, H., Orso, A.: Water: web application test repair. In: Proceedings of the First International Workshop on End-to-End Test Script Engineering, pp. 24–29 (2011)
7. Dincturk, M.E., Jourdan, G.V., Bochmann, G.V., Onut, I.V.: A model-based approach for crawling rich internet applications. ACM Trans. Web (TWEB) **8**(3), 1–39 (2014)
8. Fan, Y., Wang, S., Wang, S., Liu, Y., Wen, G., Rong, Q.: A comprehensive evaluation of Q-learning based automatic web GUI testing. In: Tenth International Conference on Dependable Systems and Their Applications (2023)
9. Gilardi, F., Alizadeh, M., Kubli, M.: ChatGPT outperforms crowd workers for text-annotation tasks. Proc. Natl. Acad. Sci. **120**(30), e2305016120 (2023)
10. Gulwani, S.: Automating string processing in spreadsheets using input-output examples. ACM Sigplan Not. **46**(1), 317–330 (2011)
11. Hammoudi, M., Rothermel, G., Stocco, A.: Waterfall: an incremental approach for repairing record-replay tests of web applications. In: Proceedings of the 2016 24th ACM SIGSOFT International Symposium on Foundations of Software Engineering, pp. 751–762 (2016)
12. Hu, G., Zhu, L., Yang, J.: AppFlow: using machine learning to synthesize robust, reusable UI tests. In: Proceedings of the 2018 26th ACM Joint Meeting on European Software Engineering Conference and Symposium on the Foundations of Software Engineering, pp. 269–282 (2018)
13. Lau, T.A., Domingos, P.M., Weld, D.S.: Version space algebra and its application to programming by demonstration. In: ICML, pp. 527–534 (2000)
14. Leotta, M., Ricca, F., Tonella, P.: Sidereal: statistical adaptive generation of robust locators for web testing. Softw. Test. Verification Reliab. **31**(3), e1767 (2021)

15. Leotta, M., Stocco, A., Ricca, F., Tonella, P.: Using multi-locators to increase the robustness of web test cases. In: 2015 IEEE 8th International Conference on Software Testing, Verification and Validation (ICST), pp. 1–10. IEEE (2015)
16. Leotta, M., Stocco, A., Ricca, F., Tonella, P.: Robula+: an algorithm for generating robust XPath locators for web testing. J. Softw. Evol. Process **28**(3), 177–204 (2016)
17. Li, C., Jiang, Y., Xu, C.: Push-button synthesis of watch companions for Android apps. In: 2022 International Conference on Software Engineering (ICSE). IEEE (2022)
18. Li, X., Jiang, Y., Liu, Y., Xu, C., Ma, X., Lu, J.: User guided automation for testing mobile apps. In: 2014 21st Asia-Pacific Software Engineering Conference, vol. 1, pp. 27–34. IEEE (2014)
19. Lin, J.W.: Advancing Automated Software Testing Through Test Reuse. University of California, Irvine (2021)
20. Long, Z., Wu, G., Chen, X., Chen, W., Wei, J.: Webrr: self-replay enhanced robust record/replay for web application testing. In: Proceedings of the 28th ACM Joint Meeting on European Software Engineering Conference and Symposium on the Foundations of Software Engineering, pp. 1498–1508 (2020)
21. MDN: XPath - MDN - developer.mozilla.org (2023). https://developer.mozilla.org/en-US/docs/Web/XPath
22. Memon, A.M., Soffa, M.L.: Regression testing of GUIs. ACM SIGSOFT Softw. Eng. Notes **28**(5), 118–127 (2003)
23. Mesbah, A., Van Deursen, A., Roest, D.: Invariant-based automatic testing of modern web applications. IEEE Trans. Softw. Eng. **38**(1), 35–53 (2011)
24. Milani Fard, A., Mirzaaghaei, M., Mesbah, A.: Leveraging existing tests in automated test generation for web applications. In: Proceedings of the 29th ACM/IEEE International Conference on Automated Software Engineering, pp. 67–78 (2014)
25. Montoto, P., Pan, A., Raposo, J., Bellas, F., López, J.: Automated browsing in AJAX websites. Data Knowl. Eng. **70**(3), 269–283 (2011)
26. Nguyen, B.N., Robbins, B., Banerjee, I., Memon, A.: Guitar: an innovative tool for automated testing of GUI-driven software. Autom. Softw. Eng. **21**, 65–105 (2014)
27. Pezze, M., Zhang, C.: Automated test oracles: a survey. In: Advances in Computers, vol. 95, pp. 1–48. Elsevier (2014)
28. Polozov, O., Gulwani, S.: Flashmeta: a framework for inductive program synthesis. In: Proceedings of the 2015 ACM SIGPLAN International Conference on Object-Oriented Programming, Systems, Languages, and Applications, pp. 107–126 (2015)
29. Qin, Z., Tang, Y., Novak, E., Li, Q.: Mobiplay: a remote execution based record-and-replay tool for mobile applications. In: Proceedings of the 38th International Conference on Software Engineering, pp. 571–582 (2016)
30. Rau, A., Hotzkow, J., Zeller, A.: Transferring tests across web applications. In: Mikkonen, T., Klamma, R., Hernández, J. (eds.) ICWE 2018. LNCS, vol. 10845, pp. 50–64. Springer, Cham (2018). https://doi.org/10.1007/978-3-319-91662-0_4
31. Ricca, F., Leotta, M., Stocco, A.: Three open problems in the context of E2E web testing and a vision: neonate. In: Advances in Computers, vol. 113, pp. 89–133. Elsevier (2019)
32. Roy Choudhary, S., Prasad, M.R., Orso, A.: Cross-platform feature matching for web applications. In: Proceedings of the 2014 International Symposium on Software Testing and Analysis, pp. 82–92 (2014)
33. SeleniumHQ: Selenium: a browser automation framework and ecosystem (2004). https://github.com/SeleniumHQ/selenium/

34. Sherin, S., Muqeet, A., Khan, M.U., Iqbal, M.Z.: QExplore: an exploration strategy for dynamic web applications using guided search. J. Syst. Softw. **195**, 111512 (2023)
35. Stocco, A., Yandrapally, R., Mesbah, A.: Visual web test repair. In: Proceedings of the 2018 26th ACM Joint Meeting on European Software Engineering Conference and Symposium on the Foundations of Software Engineering, pp. 503–514 (2018)
36. Thummalapenta, S., Lakshmi, K.V., Sinha, S., Sinha, N., Chandra, S.: Guided test generation for web applications. In: 2013 35th International Conference on Software Engineering (ICSE), pp. 162–171. IEEE (2013)
37. Wang, S., Wen, M., Liu, Y., Wang, Y., Wu, R.: Understanding and facilitating the co-evolution of production and test code. In: 2021 IEEE International Conference on Software Analysis, Evolution and Reengineering (SANER), pp. 272–283. IEEE (2021)
38. Yu, S., Fang, C., Yun, Y., Feng, Y.: Layout and image recognition driving cross-platform automated mobile testing. In: 2021 IEEE/ACM 43rd International Conference on Software Engineering (ICSE), pp. 1561–1571. IEEE (2021)
39. Zheng, Y., et al.: Automatic web testing using curiosity-driven reinforcement learning. In: 2021 IEEE/ACM 43rd International Conference on Software Engineering (ICSE), pp. 423–435. IEEE (2021)

Gradual Typing Performance, Micro Configurations and Macro Perspectives

Mohammad Wahiduzzaman Khan and Sheng Chen(✉)

UL Lafayette, Lafayette, LA 70503, USA
{mohammad-wahiduzzaman.khan1,chen}@louisiana.edu

Abstract. Static typing and dynamic typing have respective strengths and weaknesses, and a language often commits to one typing discipline and inherits the qualities, good or bad. Gradual typing has been developed to reconcile these typing disciplines, allowing a single program to mix both static and dynamic typing. It protects soundness of typed regions with runtime checks when values flown into them do not have required static types. One issue with gradual typing is that such checks can incur significant performance overhead. Previous work on performance has focused on coarse-grained gradual typing where each module (file) has to be fully typed or untyped. In contrast, the performance of fine-grained gradual typing where each single parameter can be partially-typed (such as specifying the parameter as a list without giving element type) has not been investigated.

Motivated by this situation, this paper systematically investigates performance of fine-grained gradual typing by studying the performance of more than 1 million programs. These programs are drawn from seven commonly-used benchmarks with different types for parameters: some parameters are untyped, some are statically typed, and others are partially statically typed. The paper observes many interesting phenomena that were previously unknown to the research community. They provide insights into future research directions of understanding, predicting, and optimizing gradual typing performance as well as migrating gradual programs towards more static.

1 Introduction

In static typing, compilers use types to catch programming errors, provide documentation, and optimize program performance. Static type systems are considered as one of the most successful formal methods. Static typing also has several shortcomings. For example, it requires the program to be complete and free of type errors before it can be run, even though the region that causes the type error may not be covered in a certain execution. It also prevents some commonly used programming idioms for fast prototyping, such as heterogeneous data structures and reflection.

Dynamic typing provides the flexibility that not supported by static typing but offer little static error detection. Overall, these two typing disciplines are complementary, offering different strengthens and having different weaknesses. In early years, a language chose one typing discipline and committed to it. It is impossible to have the advantage of a typing discipline that the language did not choose to follow. For example, it is impossible to have the flexibility of dynamic typing in C, which uses static typing and to have static error detection in Python, which uses dynamic typing.

W.-N. Chin and Z. Xu (Eds.): TASE 2024, LNCS 14777, pp. 261–278, 2024.
https://doi.org/10.1007/978-3-031-64626-3_15

In real-world development, it is often desirable for a single language to support both static and dynamic typing. There have been two different typing disciplines developed for this purpose, *optional typing* and *gradual typing*. In both disciplines, type annotations can optionally be added to variables, parameters, and return values to specify their types, allowing for static type checking. However, unannotated code retains the flexibility of dynamic typing, enabling rapid prototyping and exploration without the burden of explicit type declarations. Both have attracted enormous attention, from both industry and academia.

The main difference between optional typing and gradual typing is that the latter performs runtime type checks while the former does not. There are many advantages of performing runtime type checks, including ensuring the soundness of typed code, early detection of runtime type errors, and precise blaming of code that violates runtime errors. The main issue with runtime type checks is, however, such checks can significantly slowdown program performance.

The performance problem has been well known. Several studies have conducted in-depth investigations of gradual typing performance [13,29]. These studies have observed that sound gradual typing incurs significant performance overhead, in some case the slowdown could be more than 100 times. However, such studies have focused on gradual typing where type additions are supported only at the granularity level of modules. Specifically, if developers wanted to add type annotations to their codebase, then they have to add type annotations to all functions in a module or they have to leave the module completely untyped. For a codebase with n modules, 2^n different *configurations* may be created, where each configuration adds type annotations to a certain subset of all n modules. Such a gradual typing system has been added to Racket to create Typed Racket.

However, no studies have investigated the performance characteristics of *micro* gradual type systems, where type annotations may be added to any individual function of a module or even a single parameter. Moreover, in practice, the type for each parameter may be a mix of static and dynamic types, rather than fully dynamic (denoting that the parameter is untyped) or fully static (denoting that the full type information for the parameter can be completely decided at compile time). To illustrate, consider the function `reduce` in Fig. 1. This function takes three parameters and reduces the list (`lst`) into a single value using the function `f` with the initial value `init`. In this example, the parameter `f` has a dynamic type, written as `Dyn`. This type indicates that the type of `f` can not be known at compile time, and its usage should not be type checked statically. The type for `init` is `Int`, which is fully static. The type for `lst`, `List(Dyn)`, is a partially static type. This type specifies that the parameter `lst` will be used as a list without any restrictions on the element type of the list.

Without a clear understanding of the performance landscape of micro gradual typing, a few questions remain unanswered. First, how to evaluate the performance of micro gradual typing and specific benchmarks? The full configuration space of using micro gradual typing is very huge. For a program with n parameters, we are able to generate 2^n configurations, where the type for each parameter is a `Dyn` or a fully static type. We refer to such configurations as *outlying configurations*. In addition, we are able to generate more configurations where the type for some parameter is a mix of `Dyns` and

```
def reduce(f:Dyn, lst:List(Dyn), init:Int):
  result = init
  for i in range(len(lst)):
    result = f(result,lst[i])
  return result
```

Fig. 1. A gradual program in Python type hint syntax that mixes different kinds of type annotations.

static types. We refer to such configurations as *intermediate configurations*. For example, `reduce` in Fig. 1 is an intermediate configuration because the type for `lst` contains both static type information (`List`) and a `Dyn`. However, had we changed the type of `lst` to `Dyn` or `List(List(Int))`, then `reduce` is an outlying configuration. The number of intermediate configurations quickly doubles the number of outlying configurations, depending on the type structure of each parameter. For example, if the static type for a parameter is `Tuple(Int,Float,List(Int))`, then in an outlying configuration, the parameter may be assigned eleven different types, with two possibilities for the first component of the tuple, two for the second component, and three (`Dyn`, `List(Dyn)`, `List(Int)`) for the third component[1].

Given this sheer number of possible configurations, how to measure the performance of gradual programs? It is obviously infeasible to measure all configurations. Sampling is therefore necessary. The question is, what sampling strategy should be used? Should the samples include both outlying configurations and intermediate configurations or outlying configurations are sufficiently representative? Early work on micro gradual typing performance [4,5,32–34] considered only outlying configurations. Should future work on micro gradual typing also sample intermediate configurations for evaluation?

The second question remains unanswered is, what are desirable type annotations for parameters? This question is closely intertwined with the problem of gradual type migration, which studies the challenges and solutions of adding static type annotations to gradual programs. While manually adding type annotations is one possible way for small programs, it does not scale to large programs. Several approaches based on type inference [2,3,6,7,14,16,22,24,27], dynamic approaches [9,18], and machine learning based approaches [1,17,21,23], have been developed. Such approaches often fail to infer most static types for parameters. It is very likely that the user will start from the types added by such type migration tools and make the types more static. The questions are then, how diverse are the run times of the configurations when a single parameter is assigned different types, do the performance keep on increasing when the type for a parameter becomes more static, does the most static type lead to the best performance?

This paper aims to answer these questions through a systematic evaluation of around 1.25 million configurations drawn from six commonly-used benchmarks for gradual typing research. This paper makes the following contributions:

[1] $2 \times 2 \times 3 = 12$, but we need to minus one combination whose all components are static.

```
def reduce1(f:Function([Int,Dyn],Int),
            lst:[Dyn], init:Int):
    result = init
    for i in range(len(lst)):
        result = f(result,lst[i])
    return result

def wider(cw:Int, ci:Dyn) -> Int:
    return max(cw, len(ci))

cont = [[1],[2,3],[4,5,6]]
reduce1(wider,cont,0)
```

(a) reduce1, with lst type being [Dyn]

```
def reduce1(f, lst, init):

    result = init
    for i in range(len(lst)):
        result = f(result, lst[i])
    return result : Int => Dyn

def wider(cw, ci):
    return max(cw, len(ci)) : Dyn => Int

cont = [[1],[2,3],[4,5,6]]
reduce1(wider, cont : Dyn => [Dyn], 0)
```

(b) Cast inserted version of reduce1

```
def reduce2(f:Function([Int,Dyn],Int),
           lst:[[Dyn]], init:Int):
    result = init
    for i in range(len(lst)):
        result = f(result,lst[i])
    return result

reduce2(wider,cont,0)
```

(c) reduce2, with lst type being [[Dyn]]

```
def reduce2(f, lst, init):

    result = init
    for i in range(len(lst)):
        result = f(result, lst[i] : [Dyn] => Dyn)
    return result : Int => Dyn

reduce2(wider, cont : Dyn => [[Dyn]], 0)
```

(d) Cast inserted version of reduce2

Fig. 2. Two different versions of `reduce` (left) that differ by only one parameter type and their corresponding cast-inserted programs (right). The function type with two parameters whose types are `t1` and `t2` and with return type `t3` is written as `Function([t1,t2],t3)`.

1. It creates a benchmark with around 1.25 million configurations. Such configurations have fine-grained types. With precise type information and corresponding execution times, it facilitates future research in gradual typing.
2. It studies three research questions concerning the representativeness of outlying configurations and performance change as parameter types undergo minor changes.
3. Based on the evaluation results, it makes affirmative answers to the studied research questions. Specifically, the result reveals that outlying configurations are not always representative, the performance can change radically even with small changes in type annotations, and counter-intuitively, the performance often decreases as parameter types become more precise. These answers suggest a better performance evaluation method for future work on gradual typing performance. They also indicate where further research attention is needed to make gradual typing practical.

2 Background

The purpose of gradual typing is to strike a balance between the safety and performance guarantees of static typing and the flexibility and expressiveness of dynamic typing. As such, in gradual typing, a parameter or variable may be assigned a static type if the type expectation of the parameter or variable can be statically determined and the uses of it need to be statically checked. In contrast, if the type can not be determined statically, then the type should remain dynamic. The absence of a type annotation or a `Dyn` for a parameter denotes that the parameter has dynamic type. It is also possible that a parameter is annotated with a partially static type, as `[Dyn]` for `lst` in Fig. 2(a).

A static type annotation for a parameter is a protocol for both the internal and external of the function. For the internal of the function, the type specifies the *guarantee* of the type of the parameter to the rest of the function definition. For example, the type for `f` indicates that the return type is `Int`. As a result, inside the function, every call will always return a value of type `Int`. For the external of the function, the type specifies the *expectation* of the corresponding argument to the function. For example, when `reduce1` is called, the first argument must be a function type and the first parameter type and the return type of it must be `Int`.

The argument may be statically typed and matches the expectation of the parameter type. In this case, no runtime checks are needed. Otherwise, runtime checks will be inserted to protect the type annotations, a notion known as enforcing *type soundness*. To illustrate, consider the execution of the program in Fig. 2(a). When a gradually-typed program is executed, it is often translated to a program in the underlying language with runtime checks inserted. For example, the gradually-typed language Reticulated Python [32,34] is translated to Python. The translated program for Fig. 2(a) is given in Fig. 2(b).

In translating the call of `reduce1` (the last line of Fig. 2(a)), the type expectation of `f` (`Function([Int,Dyn],Int)`) matches the type of the argument since the type of `wider` is also `Function([Int,Dyn],Int)` (see the caption of Fig. 2 for an explanation of type syntax for function types). As a result, no runtime checks will be inserted for `wider`. However, for `lst`, the expectation is `[Dyn]` (based on the type annotation for `lst` in the definition of `reduce1`), and the argument has type `Dyn` (many gradual type systems do not assign a static type to a list because lists can be heterogeneous). As a result, a runtime check, often called a *cast*, is inserted to make sure that `cont` has the expected type for calling `reduce1`. The cast is written as `cont: Dyn => [Dyn]`, expressing that the statically known type of `cont` is `Dyn` but it is used in a context that requires it to have the type `[Dyn]`. A general form of a cast is written as `expr : source_type => target_type`.

Casts may have very different runtime overheads. Basic casts involving primitive types (such as `Int`, `Bool`, and `Float`) and `Dyn` are very lightweight. For example, the cast `e: Dyn => Int` induces very little runtime overhead because a single runtime type check (such as `isinstance(e,int)` in Python) suffices to check if the cast will be successful. However, casts involving other types, such as lists and functions, can be very expensive. The reason is that such casts can not be verified at where they appear. To illustrate, consider a cast `f:Dyn => Int -> Bool`. This cast means that `f` should return a `Bool` value whenever it is called with an `Int` value. It is impossible to measure whether `f` satisfies the cast at its occurrence location because in dynamic languages a function may return values of different types for values of the same type.

Instead, for such a cast, a proxy needs to be created to make sure that it has expected type at each call site. Continuing the example from the previous paragraph, when `f` is called, the proxy for `f` checks whether the argument has the type `Int` and the return type of `f` has the type `Bool`. Creating proxies and checking the argument and return types for each call involves more significant overheads.

Such casts are the main reason that sound gradual typing radically slows down program performance. Earlier work [29] observed this phenomenon when types are added to a single module (file). This work investigates the impact of changing the type annotation of a single parameter on program performance. To illustrate how performance may be affected due to a type change, consider the program in Fig. 2(c). The only difference (with a gray background) compared to Fig. 2(a) is that the type annotation for `lst` is changed to `[[Dyn]]`. The single type change, however, led to the changes of two inserted casts, shown in Fig. 2(d) with a gray background. One of these casts is inside a `for` loop, and it in fact induces high overhead for this program. We measured the performance of these programs and observed that the performance for program in Fig. 2(c) doubles that in Fig. 2(a).

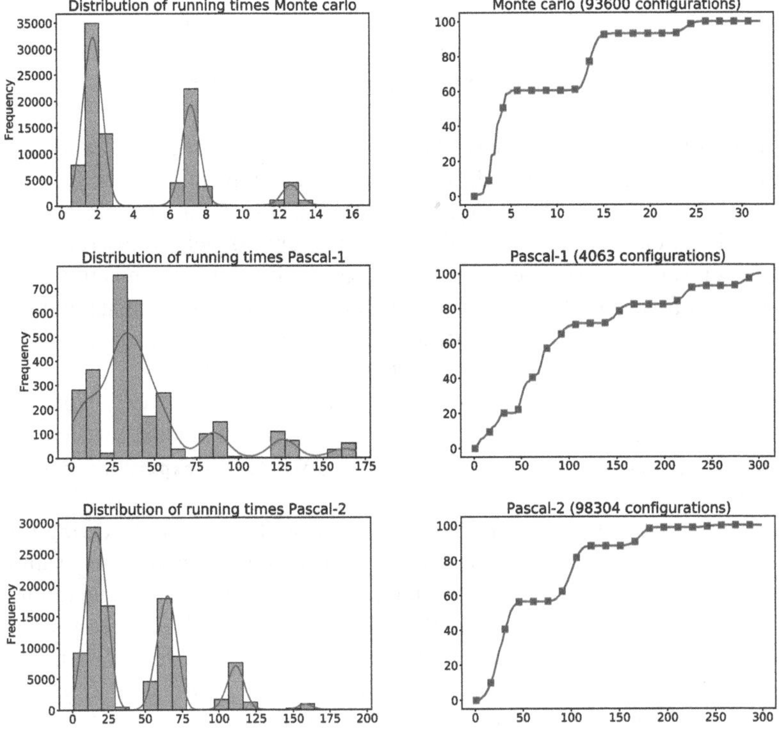

Fig. 3. The execution time distribution for each benchmark.

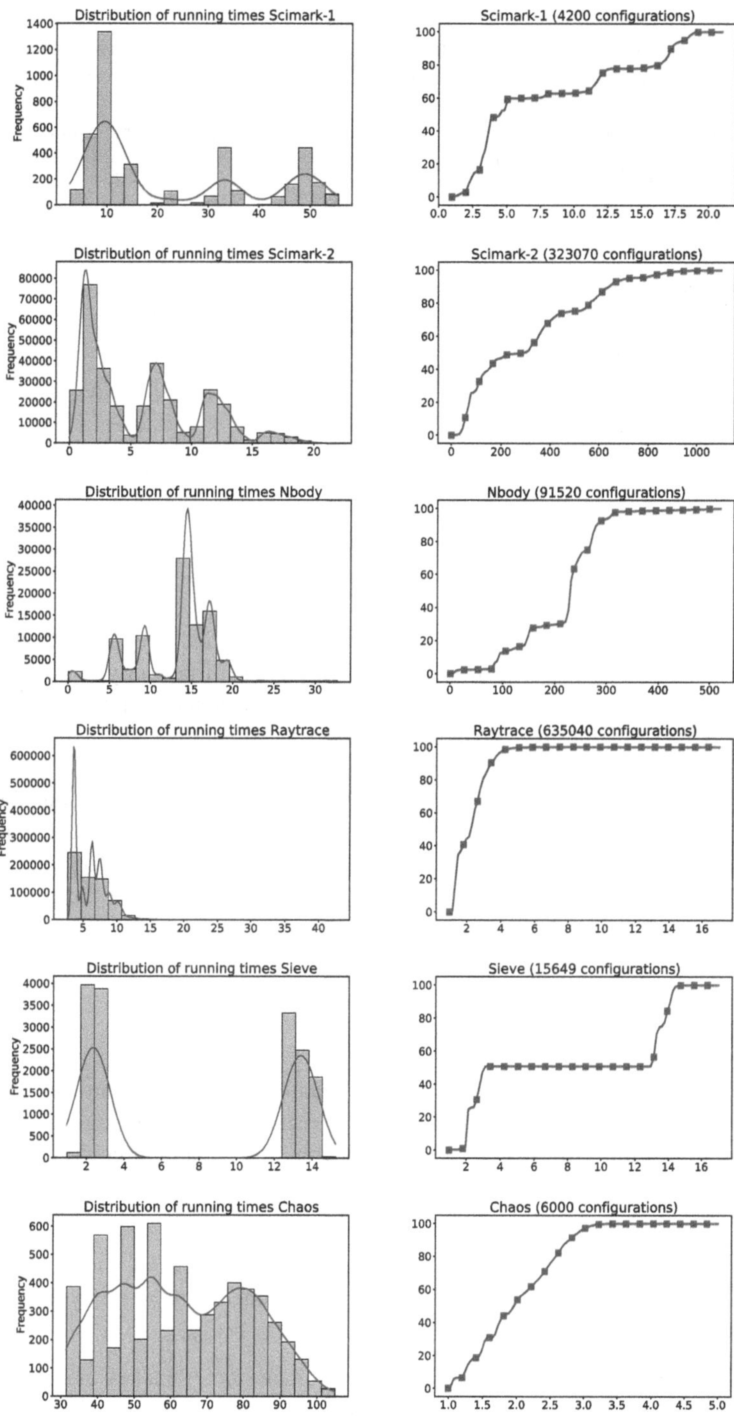

Fig. 4. The execution time distribution for each benchmark (continued)

Table 1. Python benchmarks used for performance evaluation. The last column gives the number of configurations generated for the corresponding benchmark. We generated two datasets for Pascal and Scimark to investigate how the size of dataset affects evaluation results.

Benchmark	LOC	# of functions	# of pars	# of typed pars	# of configurations
Monte Carlo	90	4	9	9	93600
Pascal-1	70	7	19	15	4062
Pascal-2	70	7	19	15	98304
Scimark-1	65	5	22	17	4602
Scimark-2	65	5	22	17	323070
Nbody	195	4	21	18	91525
Raytrace	455	21	94	67	635040
Sieve	56	9	22	21	15361
Chaos	271	22	42	29	6000

3 Benchmarks and Evaluation Protocol

For the purpose of evaluation, we consider seven benchmarks. They are mainly adapted from Python performance benchmark suits and have been frequently in gradual typing research [4,5,32,34]. Table 1 lists some basic metrics of each benchmark, such as number of lines of code, number of functions, etc. Note, the number of typed parameters may be fewer than the number of parameters in a program because not all parameters can receive static types. For a parameter that can be statically typed, we consider different possible types for the parameter, from `Dyn` to most static. To generate a manageable number of configurations for each benchmark, we set a single type for some parameter if the parameter does not have much interaction with the rest of the program. For example, for Nbody benchmark, it has one function defined as follows.

```
def bench_nbody(loops, reference, iterations):
        for _ in xrange(loops):
                ...
```

Here `loops` can be given two possible types: `Dyn` or `Int`. Since `loops` does not interact with the rest of the code except for being used in `xrange`, we consider only assigning `Int` to `loops`. To test the validity this idea, we generate many pairs of configurations such that in each pair `loops` receive different types. We observed that the execution times are almost exactly the same within each pair. We briefly describe each benchmark below.

Monte Carlo. This benchmark is to predict possible outcomes of uncertain events by generating random numbers. It contains complex parameter and return types for several functions. One such type is `Tuple([Float],[Float],[Int])`.

Pascal. The purpose of this benchmark is to evaluate the efficiency and performance of algorithms and functions related to generating Pascal's triangle and permutations in Python. One of the parameter in this benchmark is `matrix`, which is essentially a 2-D array. In our generated configurations, we assigned four different types to this parameter: `Dyn`, `[Dyn]`, `[[Dyn]]`, and `[[Float]]`.

Scimark. It has six functions which contains a parameter `arr`. The most static type of `arr` is `Tuple(Int,Int,Int)`. This parameter can be typed in 8 different ways.

Sieve. This benchmark implements the search of prime numbers using the idea of a "Steam". A main parameter in this benchmark is `st`, which represents the current state of the stream. Its most static type is class `Stream`.

Nbody. This benchmark simulates the movement of celestial bodies under gravity. It has several complex parameter types. For example, one of them is `[Tuple(Tuple([Float], [Float], Float), Tuple([Float], [Float], Float))]` There can be multiple ways with `Dyn` combinations to type this parameter.

Raytrace. This benchmark is for simulating lighting for games. Its type structure is similar to that of `Scimark`.

Figures 3 and 4 depict the runtime distribution of generated configurations for each benchmark. For the left column in each figure, the x-axis is the execution time in seconds and the y-axis is the number of configurations. Each image in the right column presents the performance slowdowns compared to the fastest configuration in each benchmark. The x-axis is the slowdown and the y-axis is the percentage of all configurations. A point of (x, y) on the curve means that x% of all configurations have a slowdown of smaller than y compared to the fastest configuration.

From these figures, we can observe that the execution times are very different within and across benchmarks. The distributions are also very different, some have more spread-out times while others are clustered. The number of clusters and the distances between them are also quite different. These factors encourage the validity of the observations we make in this paper.

Evaluation Protocol. We use Reticulated Python [32,34], a gradual typing implementation for Python, to measure the execution time. The experiments are run on a system equipped with Intel(R) 533 Core(TM) i9-9900K CPU @ 3.60 GHz, 8 Core(s), and 32 GB RAM. Each measured time is an average of 10 runs.

4 Representativeness of Outlying Configurations

While previous work [4,33,34] on gradual typing performance has largely focused on outlying configurations, it is an interesting question to know if such configurations are indeed representative of the whole benchmark.

For this investigation, we first separate all configurations into outlying configurations and intermediate configurations. A configuration is outlying if the type for each parameter in the configuration is a `Dyn` or a fully static type. Otherwise, a configuration is intermediate.

We depict the temporal distribution of runtimes for outlying and intermediate configurations. The kernel density (KD) plots (the left column of the figures) illustrate the divergence in runtime characteristics between outlying and intermediate configurations.

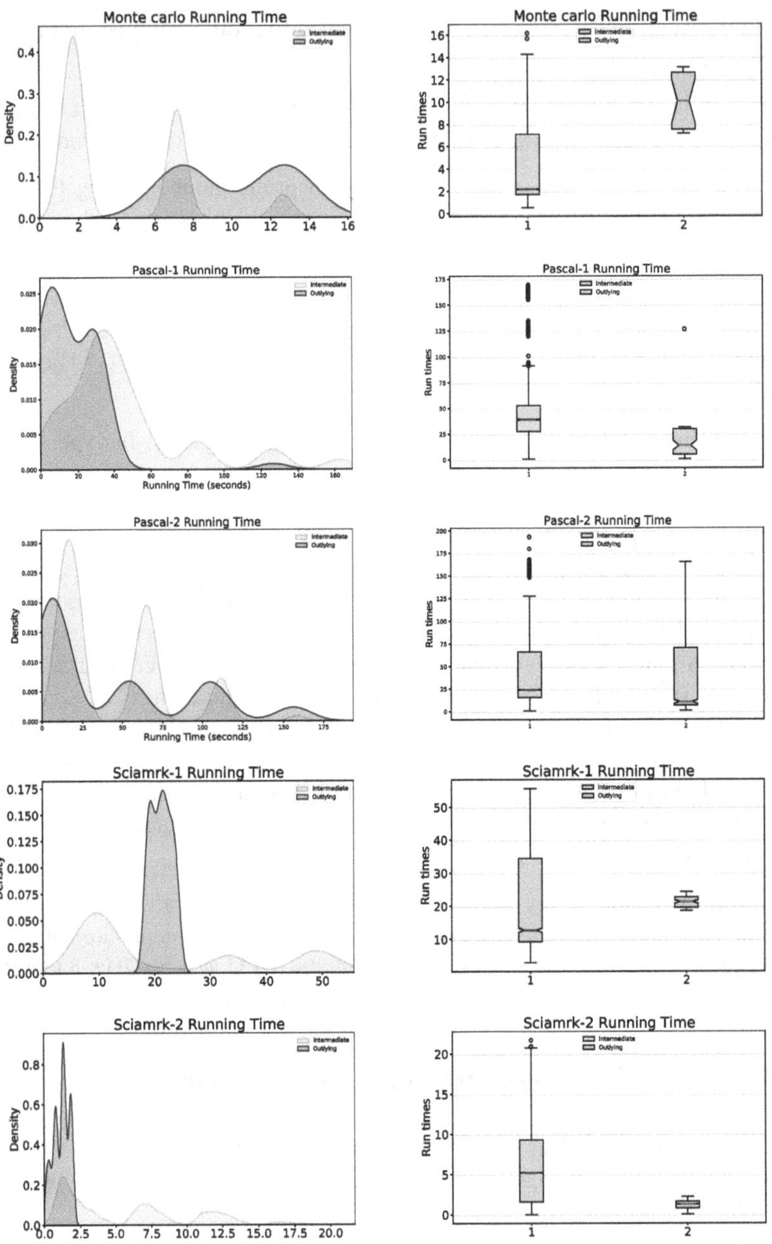

Fig. 5. Execution time distribution of outlying and intermediate configurations

An inspection of the KD plots reveals that the multimodal nature of both outlying and intermediate configurations is characterized by the presence of multiple peaks. The box plots (the right column of these figures) provide insights into the central tendency of

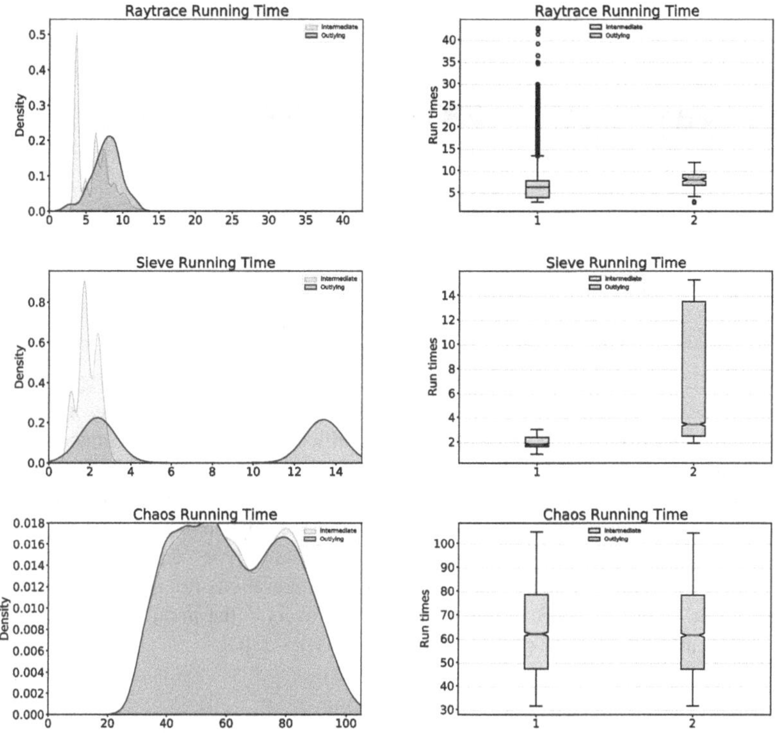

Fig. 6. Execution time distribution of outlying and intermediate configurations (continued)

each distribution. Notably, outlying configurations exhibit a tendency to clusters closer to their mean, while intermediate configurations display numerous outliers distributed far from the mean (Figs. 5 and 6).

Based on these figures, we can observe that, except for Pascal-2, Raytrace, and Chaos, the outlying configurations do not represent the whole benchmark well. Moreover, the reason why they are not representative vary across benchmarks. For example, for Monte Carlo, outlying configurations represent configurations with large execution times only while for Pascal-1 they represent only those with small execution times.

Overall, these figures suggest that future work on gradual typing performance should sample from outlying as well as intermediate configurations to make sure the result is representative.

5 Time Variations of Intermediate Configurations

This section investigates how diverse are execution times of intermediate configurations that differ by type annotations for a few parameters. Understanding the diversity is an important problem that has both practical and theoretical implications.

In practice, type migrations are often done in small steps or with the help of type migration tools. It is often common that such tools infer only part of the type informa-

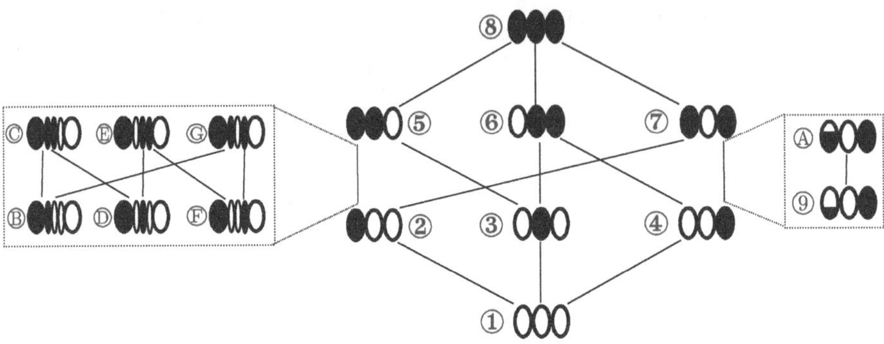

Fig. 7. The lattice, which has 8 outlying configurations (① through ⑧), for a program with three parameters. Each configuration is represented as three ovals, which each oval indicates if the corresponding parameter is typed (filled) or not (unfilled). Each solid line connects a less precise configuration (lower in the lattice) to a more precise one (higher in the lattice). Assume the fully static type of the first parameter is `[[Float]]`, two intermediate configurations, one with the type of first parameter being `[Dyn]` (⑨) and the other being `[[Dyn]]` (Ⓐ), may be added between ④ and ⑦. Likewise, assuming the full static type of the second parameter is `Tuple(Int,Float,Bool)`, then eight intermediate configurations (Ⓑ through Ⓖ) can be generated between ② and ⑤. In Ⓑ through Ⓖ, the three ovals in the middle indicate whether the three components of the second parameter have static types or not.

tion, infer too specific type, or contain incorrect types, particularly when the static type is complex. In this case, it is likely that the developer will fix the type annotations, make them more specific, or change them to new types. From the performance perspective, there are several related questions. First, how such changes will affect the performance of the program? Will the performance largely stay the same because the change of the type is relatively minor compared to the type annotations for the whole program or will such a small change already lead to significant performance swings?

Second, if the performance indeed changes radically due to such small type changes, is the performance getting better or worse? The answer to this question provides useful guidance for type migration. For example, if slightly making the type of a parameter more specific decreases the performance, should the user make it even more specific or reverse the type addition to restore the performance?

The answers to these questions can help both the users and researchers of gradual typing. For the former, these answers will help develop useful guidance with program migration, making programs more static while aware of the performance landscape. For the latter, these answers reveal the real challenges of harmonizing program migration and performance issues, indicating where the research is needed to make gradual typing practical.

To answer these questions, we need to first find out groups that have different type annotations for a specific number of parameters. To illustrate, consider the lattice in Fig. 7. From this lattice, we can extract two groups. The first group contains four configurations (④, ⑦, ⑨, and Ⓐ), differing types in the first parameter. The second group

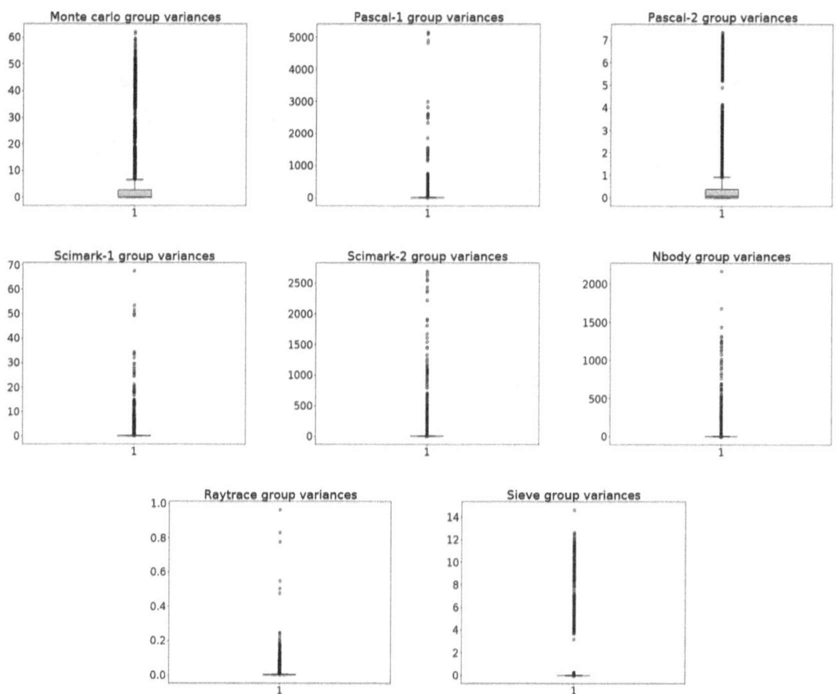

Fig. 8. Benchmark's group variance distribution

contains 8 configurations (②, ⑤, and Ⓑ through Ⓖ), differing types in the second parameter.

Given a group, we want to measure how diverse are the execution times of the configurations in that group. We use *variance* to measure the variability of execution times. Variance gives us an idea of how much the execution times deviate from the average or mean runtime for that group. We calculate variance for each group in the following steps. First, we compute the mean runtime for each group of programs. This is achieved by summing up all the execution times within a group and dividing the total by the number of configurations in that group. Second, for each individual runtime in the group, the squared difference between it and the mean runtime is determined. Squaring these differences ensures that negative and positive deviations do not cancel each other out, providing a more accurate representation of dispersion. Third, the average of all the squared differences calculated in the previous step is determined. This average value represents the variance of the runtimes within the group.

Based on the calculation, a larger variance indicates greater spread or variability of runtimes from the mean, suggesting a less consistent or stable performance across the programs within the group. Conversely, a smaller variance signifies that the runtimes are closer to the mean, indicating less variability and potentially more consistent performance.

Table 2. Benchmarks groups variance information

Benchmark	# of Groups	Avg group size	min variance	average variance	max variance
Monte Carlo	57120	8	0.0	2.58	61.976
Pascal-1	4096	4	0.0	30.97	5153.21
Pascal-2	110376	7	0	0.27	7.33
Scimark-1	8226	3	0.0	0.83	67.57
Scimark-2	446875	5	0.0	3.56	2700.23
Nbody	43969	8	0.0	2.87	2170.60
Raytrace	10061	6	0.0	0.06	0.96
Sieve	71888	3	0.0	0.82	14.62

Table 3. Benchmarks group ordering information

Benchmark	# of Groups	Avg group size	% of increasing	% of decreasing	% of neutral
Monte Carlo	57120	8	34.69%	21.26%	44.04%
Pascal-1	4096	4	36.54%	16.62%	46.82%
Pascal-2	110376	7	12.15%	16.28%	71.56%
Scimark-1	8226	3	66.44%	21.34%	12.20%
Scimark-2	446875	5	11.29%	41.89%	46.81%
Nbody	43969	8	67.18%	4.55%	28.26%
Raytrace	10061	6	32.85%	14.34%	52.79%
Sieve	71888	3	88.37%	11.45%	0.16%

Table 2 gives the information about the number of groups for each benchmark, average group size, the minimum, average, and maximum variance for all the groups within a benchmark. Figure 8 depicts the variances of all groups within each benchmark. Based on this figure, it becomes evident that certain benchmark groups exhibit notably higher variances compared to others. For instance, despite having similar code structures, Pascal-1 and Pascal-2 demonstrate significantly different variances, with Pascal-1 displaying a notably higher variance. Conversely, in the case of Scimark-1 and Scimark-2, which also share similar code structures, Scimark-1 exhibits considerably higher runtime than Scimark-2.

Based on these results, we can conclude that, with a small change of type annotation for a single parameter, the performance can be very different. This indicates the importance of finding the right type for each parameter to achieve good performance.

Given that each groups has a lot of variance, it is interesting to study if the performance is increasing, decreasing, or a mix of them. For such a study, we first order all configurations within a group based on the precision of the type. For example, as the type for the first parameter in ④ (Fig. 7) is `Dyn` while that for ⑨ is `[Dyn]`, we say ⑨ is more precise than ④. After ordering, ⑦ is the most precise, followed by Ⓐ, ⑨, and ④. It is possible that not all configurations in a group can be ordered, such as Ⓑ and Ⓔ. For such groups, we consider only the path that configurations can be fully ordered along the path.

After ordering each group, we can easily decide if the execution time is decreasing, increasing, or a mix. Table 3 summarizes the result for this study. In the table, the last three columns calculate the percentage of all groups whose execution times are increasing, decreasing, or neutral. Note, if a group has an increasing execution time, the performance degrades as configurations become more precise. Based on the results, we can conclude that the performance often decreases as programs become more precise. Fortunately, there are exist groups whose performance increases as program become more precise. This indicates that future research is needed that takes into consideration both performance and program migration. In particular, it is critical to find parameters such that making them more precise also increases the performance.

6 Related Work

This paper studies the performance of micro gradual typing, where a partial or full static type annotation may be given to a parameter, return value, or variable. Micro gradual typing has been used in Reticulated Python [32,34], Grift [15], and many others [25,26]. There is another kind of gradual typing, adopted by Typed Racket [30], where the decision of whether adding type annotation or not is made at the granularity of a module. Several studies [13,29] have investigated the performance of this kind of gradual typing. A benchmark for this kind of gradual typing research has also been developed [12]. The goal of these papers are thus quite different from ours. Moreover, this paper also investigates representativeness of outlying configurations and how performance changes as the type for a single parameter experiences changes, which are unique to micro gradual typing.

The overhead of gradual typing is due to the checks inserted for protecting typed regions. Such checks are performed at runtime. In contrast, *optional typing* uses type annotations for performing static type checking to catch more programming mistakes before program are run. TypeScript [10], Flow [8], and type hints for Python[2] fall in this approach. To illustrate the difference between optional and gradual typing, consider the expression `reduce1(add,['c','d'],0)` where `add` is defined as follows and `reduce1` is defined in Fig. 2(a).

```
def add(a:Int, b:Int) -> Int:
    return a+b
```

In both optional typing and gradual typing, no static type errors are detected in the expression `reduce1(add,['a','b'],0)`. However, the behavior of runtime error reporting is very different. In optional typing, the runtime error is reported inside the definition of `add`, when `a` receives the value 0 and `b` receives the value `'c'`. In gradual typing, the type error is reported at `lst[i]` within `reduce1` because `lst[i]` has the type `String` while the parameter type of `add` is `Int`. An important design principle of gradual typing is that well-typed programs should not be blamed [28,35] for causing runtime type errors. Since `add` is fully typed, its body should never be blamed for causing dynamic type errors.

[2] https://docs.python.org/3/library/typing.html.

A recent user study [31] with programmers has revealed that in practice programmers anticipate type systems to behave like gradual typing. When a runtime error happens, they prefer the error to not be reported within a typed function.

Program migration, which aims to add static type annotations to a dynamic program, and performance understanding and optimization have been two important aspects of gradual typing. Many approaches have been proposed for program migration [2,3,6,7,14,16,22,24,27] and performance optimization [5,11,15,19,20,33]. While these approaches have focused on a single aspect, this work tries to bridge these two by investigating how the small change of a type annotation may affect performance. This work also suggests that performance evaluation should focus on intermediate configurations as well as outlying configurations while most previous work have largely focused on outlying configurations.

7 Conclusion

Gradual typing has received a lot of attention in the past decade thanks to its promises of harmonizing static and dynamic typing. However, a systematic study of the performance landscape for gradual typing that supports fine-grained type annotations was still missing. This work solves this issue through a systematic study of around 1.25 million micro configurations that covers all type variations across the untyped-typed spectrum of parameter types.

Based on this study, we extract several major perspectives regarding gradual typing performance. First, a small change of the type annotation for a certain parameter may significantly change the performance, sometimes larger than 10 times. Second, making types more static is strongly correlated to degrading program performance. These observations indicate that, while currently treated separately, program migration and program performance should be considered in unison in future research in gradual typing. Also, better tooling support is needed for understanding, predicting, and optimizing fine-grained gradual typing to make it more practical.

Due to space limitation, several questions are left out for future investigation, such as under what context the type change for a parameter leads to more abrupt performance swings.

References

1. Allamanis, M., Barr, E.T., Ducousso, S., Gao, Z.: Typilus: neural type hints. In: Proceedings of the 41st ACM SIGPLAN Conference on Programming Language Design and Implementation. ACM (2020). https://doi.org/10.1145/3385412.3385997
2. Campora, J., Chen, S., Erwig, M., Walkingshaw, E.: Migrating gradual types. In: Proceedings of the 45th ACM SIGPLAN Symposium on Principles of Programming Languages, POPL 2018. ACM, New York (2018)
3. Campora, J.P., Chen, S.: Taming type annotations in gradual typing. Proc. ACM Program. Lang. **4**(OOPSLA) (2020). https://doi.org/10.1145/3428259
4. Campora, J.P., Chen, S., Walkingshaw, E.: Casts and costs: harmonizing safety and performance in gradual typing. Proc. ACM Program. Lang. **2**(ICFP), 98:1–98:30 (2018). https://doi.org/10.1145/3236793

5. Campora, J.P., Khan, M.W., Chen, S.: Type-based gradual typing performance optimization. Proc. ACM Program. Lang. **8**(POPL) (2024). https://doi.org/10.1145/3632931
6. Castagna, G., Lanvin, V., Petrucciani, T., Siek, J.G.: Gradual typing: a new perspective. Proc. ACM Program. Lang. **3**(POPL) (2019). https://doi.org/10.1145/3290329
7. Chandra, S., et al.: Type inference for static compilation of JavaScript. In: Proceedings of the 2016 ACM SIGPLAN International Conference on Object-Oriented Programming, Systems, Languages, and Applications, OOPSLA 2016, pp. 410–429. ACM, New York (2016). https://doi.org/10.1145/2983990.2984017
8. Chaudhuri, A., Vekris, P., Goldman, S., Roch, M., Levi, G.: Fast and precise type checking for JavaScript. Proc. ACM Program. Lang. **1**(OOPSLA), 48:1–48:30 (2017). https://doi.org/10.1145/3133872
9. Cristiani, F., Thiemann, P.: Generation of typescript declaration files from JavaScript code. In: Proceedings of the 18th ACM SIGPLAN International Conference on Managed Programming Languages and Runtimes, MPLR 2021, pp. 97–112. Association for Computing Machinery, New York (2021). https://doi.org/10.1145/3475738.3480941
10. Feldthaus, A., Møller, A.: Checking correctness of typescript interfaces for JavaScript libraries. SIGPLAN Not. **49**(10), 1–16 (2014). https://doi.org/10.1145/2714064.2660215
11. Feltey, D., Greenman, B., Scholliers, C., Findler, R.B., St-Amour, V.: Collapsible contracts: fixing a pathology of gradual typing. Proc. ACM Program. Lang. **2**(OOPSLA) (2018). https://doi.org/10.1145/3276503
12. Greenman, B.: GTP benchmarks for gradual typing performance. In: Proceedings of the 2023 ACM Conference on Reproducibility and Replicability, ACM REP 2023, pp. 102–114. Association for Computing Machinery, New York (2023). https://doi.org/10.1145/3589806.3600034
13. Greenman, B., et al.: How to evaluate the performance of gradual type systems. J. Funct. Program. **29**, e4 (2019). https://doi.org/10.1017/S0956796818000217
14. Kristensen, E.K., Møller, A.: Type test scripts for typescript testing. Proc. ACM Program. Lang. **1**(OOPSLA), 90:1–90:25 (2017). https://doi.org/10.1145/3133914
15. Kuhlenschmidt, A., Almahallawi, D., Siek, J.G.: Toward efficient gradual typing for structural types via coercions. In: Proceedings of the 40th ACM SIGPLAN Conference on Programming Language Design and Implementation, PLDI 2019, pp. 517–532. Association for Computing Machinery, New York (2019). https://doi.org/10.1145/3314221.3314627
16. Migeed, Z., Palsberg, J.: What is decidable about gradual types? Proc. ACM Program. Lang. **4**(POPL) (2019). https://doi.org/10.1145/3371097
17. Mir, A.M., Latoškinas, E., Proksch, S., Gousios, G.: Type4Py: practical deep similarity learning-based type inference for python. In: Proceedings of the 44th International Conference on Software Engineering, pp. 2241–2252 (2022)
18. Miyazaki, Y., Sekiyama, T., Igarashi, A.: Dynamic type inference for gradual Hindley–Milner typing. Proc. ACM Program. Lang. **3**(POPL), 18:1–18:29 (2019). https://doi.org/10.1145/3290331
19. Moy, C., Nguy∼ên, P.C., Tobin-Hochstadt, S., Van Horn, D.: Corpse reviver: sound and efficient gradual typing via contract verification. Proc. ACM Program. Lang. **5**(POPL) (2021). https://doi.org/10.1145/3434334
20. Ortin, F., Garcia, M., McSweeney, S.: Rule-based program specialization to optimize gradually typed code. Knowl.-Based Syst. **179**, 145–173 (2019). https://doi.org/10.1016/j.knosys.2019.05.013
21. Peng, Y., et al.: Static inference meets deep learning: a hybrid type inference approach for python. In: Proceedings of the 44th International Conference on Software Engineering, ICSE 2022, pp. 2019–2030. Association for Computing Machinery, New York (2022). https://doi.org/10.1145/3510003.3510038

22. Phipps-Costin, L., Anderson, C.J., Greenberg, M., Guha, A.: Solver-based gradual type migration. Proc. ACM Program. Lang. **5**(OOPSLA) (2021). https://doi.org/10.1145/3485488
23. Pradel, M., Gousios, G., Liu, J., Chandra, S.: Typewriter: neural type prediction with search-based validation (2020)
24. Rastogi, A., Chaudhuri, A., Hosmer, B.: The ins and outs of gradual type inference. In: POPL 2012, pp. 481–494. ACM, New York (2012). https://doi.org/10.1145/2103656.2103714
25. Rastogi, A., Swamy, N., Fournet, C., Bierman, G.M., Vekris, P.: Safe & efficient gradual typing for TypeScript. In: POPL (2015)
26. Siek, J.G., Vitousek, M.M., Cimini, M., Tobin-Hochstadt, S., Garcia, R.: Monotonic references for efficient gradual typing. In: Vitek, J. (ed.) ESOP 2015. LNCS, vol. 9032, pp. 432–456. Springer, Heidelberg (2015). https://doi.org/10.1007/978-3-662-46669-8_18
27. Siek, J.G., Vachharajani, M.: Gradual typing with unification-based inference. In: Proceedings of the 2008 Symposium on Dynamic Languages, DLS 2008, pp. 7:1–7:12. ACM, New York (2008). https://doi.org/10.1145/1408681.1408688
28. Siek, J.G., Vitousek, M.M., Cimini, M., Boyland, J.T.: Refined criteria for gradual typing. In: LIPIcs-Leibniz International Proceedings in Informatics, vol. 32. Schloss Dagstuhl-Leibniz-Zentrum fuer Informatik (2015)
29. Takikawa, A., Feltey, D., Greenman, B., New, M.S., Vitek, J., Felleisen, M.: Is sound gradual typing dead? In: Proceedings of the 43rd Annual ACM SIGPLAN-SIGACT Symposium on Principles of Programming Languages, POPL 2016, pp. 456–468. ACM, New York (2016). https://doi.org/10.1145/2837614.2837630
30. Tobin-Hochstadt, S., Felleisen, M.: Interlanguage migration: from scripts to programs. In: Companion to the 21st ACM SIGPLAN Symposium on Object-Oriented Programming Systems, Languages, and Applications, OOPSLA 2006, pp. 964–974. ACM, New York (2006). https://doi.org/10.1145/1176617.1176755
31. Tunnell Wilson, P., Greenman, B., Pombrio, J., Krishnamurthi, S.: The behavior of gradual types: a user study. In: Proceedings of the 14th ACM SIGPLAN International Symposium on Dynamic Languages, DLS 2018, pp. 1–12. Association for Computing Machinery, New York (2018). https://doi.org/10.1145/3276945.3276947
32. Vitousek, M.M., Kent, A.M., Siek, J.G., Baker, J.: Design and evaluation of gradual typing for python. In: Proceedings of the 10th ACM Symposium on Dynamic Languages, DLS 2014, pp. 45–56. ACM, New York (2014). https://doi.org/10.1145/2661088.2661101
33. Vitousek, M.M., Siek, J.G., Chaudhuri, A.: Optimizing and evaluating transient gradual typing. In: DLS 2019, pp. 28–41. ACM, New York (2019). https://doi.org/10.1145/3359619.3359742
34. Vitousek, M.M., Swords, C., Siek, J.G.: Big types in little runtime: open-world soundness and collaborative blame for gradual type systems. In: Proceedings of the 44th ACM SIGPLAN Symposium on Principles of Programming Languages, POPL 2017, pp. 762–774. ACM, New York (2017). https://doi.org/10.1145/3009837.3009849
35. Wadler, P., Findler, R.B.: Well-typed programs can't be blamed. In: Castagna, G. (ed.) ESOP 2009. LNCS, vol. 5502, pp. 1–16. Springer, Heidelberg (2009). https://doi.org/10.1007/978-3-642-00590-9_1

ISS-Scenario: Scenario-Based Testing in CARLA

Renjue Li[1,2], Tianhang Qin[1,2], and Cas Widdershoven[1,3(✉)]

[1] Institute of Software, Chinese Academy of Sciences, Beijing, China
[2] University of Chinese Academy of Sciences, Beijing, China
[3] Institute of Intelligent Software, Guangzhou, P.R. China
cas.widdershoven@ios.ac.cn

Abstract. The rapidly evolving field of autonomous driving systems (ADSs) is full of promise. However, in order to fulfil these promises, ADSs need to be safe in all circumstances. This paper introduces ISS-Scenario, an autonomous driving testing framework in the paradigm of scenario-based testing. ISS-Scenario is designed for batch testing, exploration of test cases (e.g., potentially dangerous scenarios), and performance evaluation of autonomous vehicles (AVs). ISS-Scenario includes a diverse simulation scenario library with parametrized design. Furthermore, ISS-Scenario integrates two testing methods within the framework: random sampling and optimized search by means of a genetic algorithm. Finally, ISS-Scenario provides an accident replay feature, saving a log file for each test case which allows developers to replay and dissect scenarios where the ADS showed problematic behavior.

Keywords: Autonomous Driving Systems · Scenario-based Testing · CARLA Simulator

1 Introduction

Recent years have seen big improvements in the area of autonomous driving systems (ADSs). Advances in machine learning and computer vision have enabled higher and higher degrees of autonomy to ADSs, and businesses such as Tesla and BYD show that ADSs have reached a high enough state of maturity that they can be an important basis for commercial success. ADSs have the potential to transform society, but before that is the case there are still significant hurdles to be overcome.

One of the biggest hurdles is the question of safety. Modern traffic has to be safe in a variety of challenging situations, which is why drivers have to train and take an exam before being allowed on the road. Wide-spread adoption of ADSs would be contingent on them being at least as safe as human drivers, and ideally even safer. Hence, safety for ADSs is paramount.

In classical settings, safety of a system is shown either through model-based analysis, or through experimentation. However, for autonomous driving systems,

---

The original version of the chapter has been revised. Chapter 16 was inadvertently published with incorrect author affiliation for Renjue Li, Tianhang Qin and Cas Widdershoven. A correction to this chapter can be found at https://doi.org/10.1007/978-3-031-64626-3_28

W.-N. Chin and Z. Xu (Eds.): TASE 2024, LNCS 14777, pp. 279–286, 2024.
https://doi.org/10.1007/978-3-031-64626-3_16

models are inaccurate and too large to prove safety through model-based analysis. Moreover, real-world experimentation requires ADSs to drive millions if not billions of miles through many real-world scenarios, making this approach prohibitively expensive as well. For this reason, an important part in proving safety of ADSs is virtual, scenario-based testing. This type of scenario-based testing employs driving simulators such as CARLA to test an ADS in various different driving scenarios.

In this paper we introduce ISS-Scenarios. ISS-Scenarios is a testing framework for scenario-based testing of ADSs in the open-source CARLA simulator. It is designed for batch testing, exploration of test cases, and performance evaluation of autonomous vehicles. Unlike other testing frameworks, ISS-Scenarios includes a diverse simulation scenario library with parameterized design. Users can easily select suitable scenarios, configure parameter ranges (e.g., adjust weather or other traffic participants' positions and speeds), and automate testing to explore numerous test cases based on their needs.

Furthermore, ISS-Scenarios integrates two testing methods within the framework: random sampling and optimized search by means of a genetic algorithm. Due to its modular design, other sampling or search algorithms can be easily integrated into the framework.

Finally, ISS-Scenarios provides an accident replay feature, saving a log file for each test case. Users can use the provided interface to replay the entire accident process in the simulator, enabling analysis of accidents using all simulator data.

The main contributions of this paper are as follows:

1. Development and design of a parameterized scenario library based on the CARLA simulator.
2. Design and implementation of a batch simulation scenario testing framework based on the parameterized scenario library. The goal is to create a simple and user-friendly simulation testing tool for testing, evaluating, and improving autonomous driving systems.
3. Using ISS-Scenarios, we select four scenarios from the scenario library, apply random sampling and optimized search within the testing framework, and test the response capabilities of the TCP and InterFuser autonomous driving systems in scenarios such as intersection encounters and pedestrian crossings. Experimental results indicate that despite the good performance of TCP and InterFuser in CARLA's benchmark tests, ISS-Scenarios can still effectively and automatically find a series of settings that ead to dangerous behavior.

The paper has the following structure: in Sect. 2 we will discuss related literature. In Sect. 3 we will give an overview of the different types of scenarios provided by ISS-Scenario. In Section 4 we will discuss the batch testing capabilities of ISS-Scenario, and in Sect. 5 we will discuss some case studies done using ISS-Scenario. Finally we conclude in Sect. 6.

ISS-Scenario is available at https://github.com/CAS-LRJ/ISS_Scenario.

2 Related Works

Autonomous Driving Systems (ADS) [8–10,17,24,27,28] demonstrate promising potential for efficient and safe driving pipelines. The modular ADS pipeline [17] comprises individual modules with distinct functionalities, such as perception, prediction, localization, planning, and control. Conversely, modern end-to-end pipelines [8–10,24,28] are presented as single comprehensive models that directly generate control signals from sensor inputs. In our case study, we selected two state-of-the-art ADS, namely Interfuser [24] and TCP [28], to evaluate our testing framework. Real-world testing of ADS is prohibitively expensive, thus autonomous driving simulators [5,11] have been developed to facilitate large-scale testing before implementation on the road. We implemented our framework using the most popular simulator, CARLA [11]. Previous works such as Scenic [13], CommonRoad [3], and GeoScenario [23] describe autonomous driving scenarios using domain-specific languages (DSLs) and utilize generated scenarios to test ADS. In our framework, we construct common corner-case scenarios using the CARLA ScenarioRunner, which streamlines the complex DSL definition process and enhances framework usability. Search-based testing approaches [1,2,4,6,7,12,14–16,18–22,25,26,29] play a crucial role in testing ADS and identifying dangerous corner cases. We have adopted commonly used genetic algorithms to search for corner cases within our framework.

3 ISS-Scenario Scenario Library

Central to ISS-Scenario is the scenario library. This extensive library contains many different scenarios an ADS may encounter, all of which can be adjusted through different parameters such as the speed of vehicles, or the positions of different actors on the road. This highly configurable approach allows for batch testing of ADSs in many different settings. There are five main categories of scenarios in ISS-Scenario:

- **Obstacle recognition:** these are scenarios in which the ADS encounters static obstacles in the road. Examples of these include general static obstacles on a straight road, stationary vehicles, and obstacles after a turn at an intersection.
- **Intersection encounters:** these are scenarios in which the ADS has to deal with traffic at an intersection. Examples are oncoming traffic at a crossroads or traffic coming from the side streets at a crossroads.
- **Pedestrian and non-motorized vehicle interactions:** in these scenarios the ADS has to deal with pedestrians and non-motorized vehicles participating in traffic. Examples include pedestrians crossing at a crosswalk, bicycles traveling along the road, and bicycles crossing diagonally at an intersection.
- **Surrounding vehicle interactions:** these scenarios deal with vehicles traveling in the same direction as the ADS. Examples of this are vehicles merging in the lane ahead, vehicles in front slowing down to a halt before accelerating again, and vehicles joining the lane from an access ramp.

- **Emergency evasion:** these are emergency scenarios in which the ADS needs to take urgent action. Examples are emergency braking after a vehicle merges in front, sudden pedestrians crossing, and adjacent vehicles losing control.

Four examples of scenarios in ISS-Scenario can be seen in Fig. 1. Consider *Scenario(1)*, where the ADS encounters a pedestrian crossing in front of the vehicle. Two possible parameters of this scenario are v, the velocity of the pedestrian, and d_{trigger}, the distance between the car and the pedestrian when the pedestrian starts crossing the road.

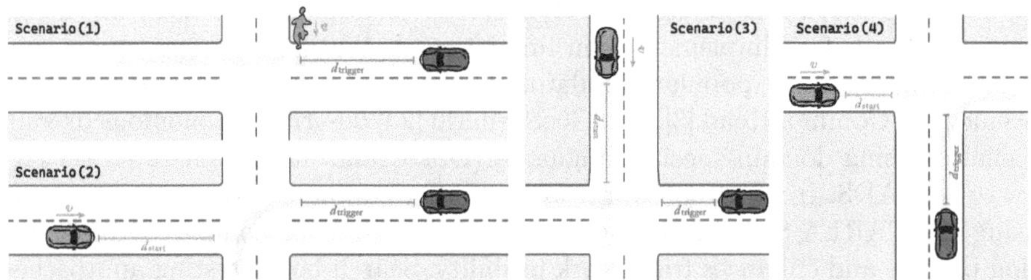

Fig. 1. Example scenario: a pedestrian crossing in front of the ADS.

4 Batch Scenario Testing

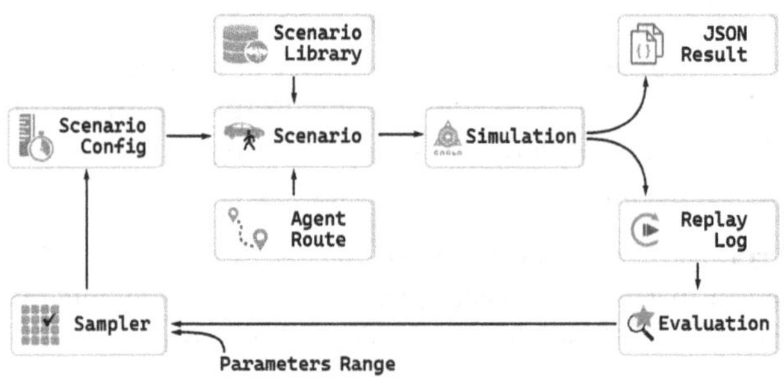

Fig. 2. The batch testing pipeline.

In addition to the scenario library, ISS-Scenario contains a batch testing framework. The basic pipeline for the batch testing procedure is given in Fig. 2. The basic procedure has six steps:

1. **Scenario configuration:** batch testing starts by delineating the circumstances in which the ADS will be tested. Different parameters such as "cloudiness" and "pedestrian velocity" are given a range of possible values with which the ADS will be tested.

2. **Sampling:** the sampling module is responsible for generating specific scenario configurations by fixing parameter values within their possible ranges. There are two different sampling methods: *uniform sampling,* where the values are picked uniformly at random within the range, and *optimization-based sampling,* which uses a genetic algorithm to search for parameter values that lead to interesting scenarios.
3. **Scenario generation:** once the parameter values are sampled, a specific scenario configuration file is generated using the sampled parameter values.
4. **Simulation:** the ADS is then tested against this specific scenario in CARLA.
5. **Evaluation:** after completion of the scenario, a log file and a JSON file are stored containing the outcomes of the simulation. The evaluation module assesses the performance of the ADS using the log file. Evaluation criteria include the minimum distance between the ADS and other traffic participants, with a higher score being assigned for a smaller distance, indicating a close encounter or potential collision.
6. **Iteration:** the process restarts at the sampling step, with the sampler's decisions potentially being guided by the previous evaluation.

The replay log coming out of the simulation step can be used to deterministically rerun specific simulations, allowing for comprehensive analysis of accidents using all of the simulator data.

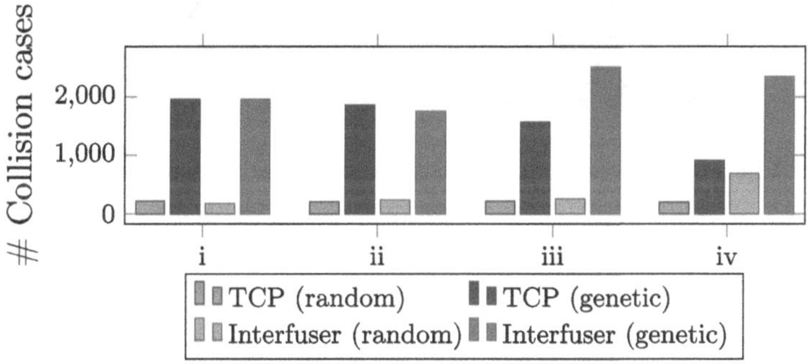

Fig. 3. Number of collision cases found in 4 scenarios. Compared to random search, the genetic algorithm was able to find many more collisions.

5 Case Studies

We evaluate the testing framework by examining two end-to-end autonomous driving systems, namely TCP and Interfuser. For this case study, we employ four distinct scenarios to investigate potential collision cases using both random sampling and genetic algorithms. The selected scenarios are depicted in Fig. 1. The scenario parameters are the start distance, the trigger distance and the actor velocity. All other parameters are kept constant. All experiments are conducted on two servers equipped with AMD EPYC 7543 CPUs, 128 GB of RAM, and 4 Nvidia RTX 3090 GPUs.

Experimental Results: We present the experimental results in Fig. 3, indicating the total number of generated testing cases and the identified collision cases. Regarding testing efficiency, a notable improvement is observed in the genetic algorithm approach, resulting in the discovery of more collision cases. The significant proportion of collision cases underscores the challenge that even end-to-end ADSs with robust deep learning algorithms may struggle to handle complex traffic corner cases effectively.

Collision Cases Analysis: We further investigate the collision cases. The accident replay feature enables us to deterministically rerun the simulations that lead to these collision cases. We illustrate some examples of these in Fig. 4. We found that the ADSs are more prone to be unsafe during the night time.

Fig. 4. Replay of collision cases. Above: TCP Below: Interfuser

6 Conclusion

In this paper we introduced ISS-Scenario. ISS-Scenario provides an extensive, parametrized scenario library for the evaluation of autonomous driving systems. Moreover, it contains a framework for the automated testing of an ADS against many different settings including a genetic algorithm to search intelligently for potentially dangerous settings. We evaluated ISS-Scenario by testing the ADSs TCP and InterFuser against four different scenarios, showing that these ADSs are more prone to unsafe behavior during the simulated night time. ISS-Scenario is available at https://github.com/CAS-LRJ/ISS_Scenario.

Acknowledgements. This study is part of the CAS Project for young Scientists in Basic Research (YSBR-40) and ISCAS New cultivation Project (ISCAS-PYFX-202201). We are grateful to the National Natural Science Foundation of China (62172217) and the Chinese Academy of Sciences for funding this work.

This work is part of the European Union's Horizon 2020 research and innovation programme under the Marie Skłodowska-Curie grant no. 101008233.

References

1. Abdessalem, R.B., Nejati, S., Briand, L.C., Stifter, T.: Testing vision-based control systems using learnable evolutionary algorithms. In: ICSE, pp. 1016–1026. ACM (2018)
2. Abdessalem, R.B., Panichella, A., Nejati, S., Briand, L.C., Stifter, T.: Testing autonomous cars for feature interaction failures using many-objective search. In: Huchard, M., Kästner, C., Fraser, G. (eds.) Proceedings of the 33rd ACM/IEEE International Conference on Automated Software Engineering, ASE 2018, Montpellier, France, 3–7 September 2018, pp. 143–154. ACM (2018)
3. Althoff, M., Koschi, M., Manzinger, S.: Commonroad: composable benchmarks for motion planning on roads. In: IEEE Intelligent Vehicles Symposium, IV 2017, pp. 719–726. IEEE (2017)
4. Arcaini, P., Zhang, X., Ishikawa, F.: Targeting patterns of driving characteristics in testing autonomous driving systems. In: 14th IEEE Conference on Software Testing, Verification and Validation, ICST 2021, Porto de Galinhas, Brazil, 12-16 April 2021, pp. 295–305. IEEE (2021)
5. BeamNG GmbH: BeamNG.tech (2022). https://www.beamng.tech/
6. Borg, M., Abdessalem, R.B., Nejati, S., Jegeden, F.X., Shin, D.: Digital twins are not monozygotic–cross-replicating ADAS testing in two industry-grade automotive simulators. In: ICST, IEEE (2021)
7. Calò, A., Arcaini, P., Ali, S., Hauer, F., Ishikawa, F.: Generating avoidable collision scenarios for testing autonomous driving systems. In: ICST, pp. 375–386. IEEE (2020)
8. Chen, D., Krähenbühl, P.: Learning from all vehicles. In: CVPR, pp. 17222–17231 (2022)
9. Chen, D., Zhou, B., Koltun, V., Krähenbühl, P.: Learning by cheating. In: Kaelbling, L.P., Kragic, D., Sugiura, K. (eds.) CoRL. Proceedings of Machine Learning Research, vol. 100, pp. 66–75. PMLR (2019)
10. Chitta, K., Prakash, A., Jaeger, B., Yu, Z., Renz, K., Geiger, A.: Transfuser: imitation with transformer-based sensor fusion for autonomous driving. In: PAMI (2022)
11. Dosovitskiy, A., Ros, G., Codevilla, F., Lopez, A., Koltun, V.: CARLA: an open urban driving simulator. In: CoRL (2017)
12. Dreossi, T., et al.: VerifAI: a toolkit for the formal design and analysis of artificial intelligence-based systems. In: Dillig, I., Tasiran, S. (eds.) CAV 2019. LNCS, vol. 11561, pp. 432–442. Springer, Cham (2019). https://doi.org/10.1007/978-3-030-25540-4_25
13. Fremont, D.J., Dreossi, T., Ghosh, S., Yue, X., Sangiovanni-Vincentelli, A.L., Seshia, S.A.: Scenic: a language for scenario specification and scene generation. In: PLDI, pp. 63–78. ACM (2019)
14. Gambi, A., Mueller, M., Fraser, G.: Automatically testing self-driving cars with search-based procedural content generation. In: ISSTA (2019)
15. Gambi, A., Müller, M., Fraser, G.: Asfault: testing self-driving car software using search-based procedural content generation. In: ICSE-Companion, pp. 27–30. IEEE (2019)
16. Gladisch, C., Heinz, T., Heinzemann, C., Oehlerking, J., von Vietinghoff, A., Pfitzer, T.: Experience paper: search-based testing in automated driving control applications. In: 34th IEEE/ACM International Conference on Automated Software Engineering, ASE 2019, San Diego, CA, USA, 11–15 November 2019, pp. 26–37. IEEE (2019)

17. Gog, I., Kalra, S., Schafhalter, P., Wright, M.A., Gonzalez, J.E., Stoica, I.: Pylot: a modular platform for exploring latency-accuracy tradeoffs in autonomous vehicles. In: ICRA, pp. 8806–8813. IEEE (2021)
18. Haq, F.U., Shin, D., Briand, L.: Efficient online testing for DNN-enabled systems using surrogate-assisted and many-objective optimization. In: ICSE, pp. 811–822 (2022)
19. Ishikawa, F.: Testing and debugging autonomous driving: experiences with path planner and future challenges. In: 2020 IEEE International Symposium on Software Reliability Engineering Workshops, ISSRE Workshops, Coimbra, Portugal, 12–15 October 2020, pp. xxxiii–xxxiv. IEEE (2020)
20. Klück, F., Zimmermann, M., Wotawa, F., Nica, M.: Genetic algorithm-based test parameter optimization for ADAS system testing. In: 19th IEEE International Conference on Software Quality, Reliability and Security, QRS 2019, Sofia, Bulgaria, 22–26 July 2019, pp. 418–425. IEEE (2019)
21. Li, G., et al.: AV-FUZZER: finding safety violations in autonomous driving systems. In: Vieira, M., Madeira, H., Antunes, N., Zheng, Z. (eds.) 31st IEEE International Symposium on Software Reliability Engineering, ISSRE 2020, Coimbra, Portugal, 12-15 October 2020, pp. 25–36. IEEE (2020)
22. Luo, Y., et al.: Targeting requirements violations of autonomous driving systems by dynamic evolutionary search (HOP at gecco 2022). In: Fieldsend, J.E., Wagner, M. (eds.) GECCO 2022: Genetic and Evolutionary Computation Conference, Companion Volume, Boston, Massachusetts, USA, 9–13 July 2022, pp. 33–34. ACM (2022)
23. Queiroz, R., Berger, T., Czarnecki, K.: Geoscenario: an open DSL for autonomous driving scenario representation. In: 2019 IEEE Intelligent Vehicles Symposium, IV 2019, pp. 287–294. IEEE (2019)
24. Shao, H., Wang, L., Chen, R., Li, H., Liu, Y.: Safety-enhanced autonomous driving using interpretable sensor fusion transformer. In: Conference on Robot Learning, pp. 726–737. PMLR (2023)
25. Sun, Y., Poskitt, C.M., Sun, J., Chen, Y., Yang, Z.: Lawbreaker: an approach for specifying traffic laws and fuzzing autonomous vehicles. In: 37th IEEE/ACM International Conference on Automated Software Engineering, ASE 2022, Rochester, MI, USA, 10–14 October 2022, pp. 62:1–62:12. ACM (2022)
26. Tian, H., et al.: Mosat: finding safety violations of autonomous driving systems using multi-objective genetic algorithm. In: ESEC/FSE, pp. 94–106 (2022)
27. Toromanoff, M., Wirbel, É., Moutarde, F.: End-to-end model-free reinforcement learning for urban driving using implicit affordances. In: CVPR, pp. 7151–7160. Computer Vision Foundation/IEEE (2020)
28. Wu, P., Jia, X., Chen, L., Yan, J., Li, H., Qiao, Y.: Trajectory-guided control prediction for end-to-end autonomous driving: a simple yet strong baseline. In: NeurIPS
29. Zhong, Z., Kaiser, G.E., Ray, B.: Neural network guided evolutionary fuzzing for finding traffic violations of autonomous vehicles. IEEE Trans. Software Eng. **49**(4), 1860–1875 (2023)

Verified Validation for Affine Scheduling in Polyhedral Compilation

Xuyang Li, Hongjin Liang, and Xinyu Feng(✉)

State Key Laboratory for Novel Software Technology, Nanjing University, Nanjing 210023, Jiangsu, China
xuyang.li@smail.nju.edu.cn, {hongjin,xyfeng}@nju.edu.cn

Abstract. Structural nested loops can be abstracted into polyhedral models, based on which one can perform aggressive loop optimizations; however, the optimizations are often heuristic and complex, and therefore error-prone. Meanwhile, verified compilers, though rigorously correct, still miss powerful optimizing transformations and therefore produce less efficient code than industrial ones. To bridge this gap, this work provides a general verified validation framework based on Bernstein's conditions for affine scheduling, the core component of polyhedral optimization techniques. It is parameterized over the concrete definitions and proofs of the instruction language to be reusable. As shown in our evaluation, the framework is flexible enough to support both existing verified compilers like CompCert and existing polyhedral compilers like Pluto. The result is fully mechanized in the Coq proof assistant.

1 Introduction

Nested loops are heavily used in scientific computing, operating over multidimensional arrays. People have tried to analyze and transform such code fragments, seeking better memory locality or parallelization. Such efforts lead to compilation and optimization based on *polyhedral models* [14]. Common industrial compilers have integrated polyhedral optimizers to empower generated code, like LLVM [16] and GCC [25]. Some domain-specific areas also resort to polyhedral optimizations, like image processing [27], and tensor compilation in AI systems [6,34].

Though powerful, polyhedral optimizations are error-prone just like other loop-specific optimizations [21], which is partly due to its complex and heuristic algorithms (e.g., the Pluto algorithm [4]) based on integer programming. We aim to equip the powerful polyhedral techniques with formal guarantees to achieve verified and optimizing compilation.

This work reports the *verified validation* for the core component of the polyhedral compilation. Verified validation is a kind of compiler verification technique. The validation algorithm takes the source and target programs as its inputs and checks that the target always behaves the same as the source. The validation algorithm itself should be verified for a more rigorous correctness guarantee. Several passes of CompCert are verified this way, including the parser [17],

W.-N. Chin and Z. Xu (Eds.): TASE 2024, LNCS 14777, pp. 287–305, 2024.
https://doi.org/10.1007/978-3-031-64626-3_17

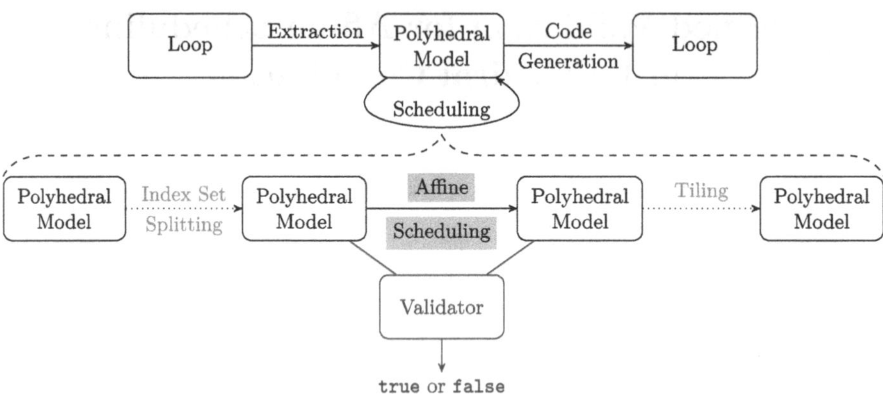

Fig. 1. The pipeline of polyhedral compilation. The blue part is our focus. (Color figure online)

register allocation [28], loop-invariant code motion [22], superblock scheduling [29], lazy code motion and strength reduction [15].

We focus on the validation for the *affine scheduling* pass in polyhedral compilation. As Fig. 1 shows, polyhedral compilation comprises three passes, namely *extraction*, *scheduling* and *code generation*. Extraction and code generation are responsible for the conversions between the structural nested loops and the mathematical polyhedral model. The scheduling pass does semantic-preserving transformation of polyhedral models. It can be further decomposed into several steps. Affine scheduling [11,12] is the main step. It reorders iterations of the loop for better locality and parallelization. Correctness of the reordering is known as *Bernstein's conditions* [13], which requires the preservation of write-after-write (WAW), write-after-read (WAR) and read-after-write (RAW) dependencies.

This work develops a general verified validation framework for affine scheduling in polyhedral compilation. It makes the following new contributions:

- We implement and verify a general validation framework in the Coq proof assistant, partly reusing previous mechanizations in Verified Polyhedron Library (VPL) [5] and the verified polyhedral code generator PolyGen [8]. Its algorithm checks Bernstein's conditions and is apt for affine scheduling. Further, as nested loops prevail in different programming languages, the framework is parameterized over instruction-level languages for reusability.
- We instantiate the framework with a variant of CompCert's instruction language, called CInstr, to show the practicality of the framework and the possibility towards an extension of CompCert with polyhedral optimization to complement CompCert's current loop optimizations.
- We evaluate the validation algorithm's *efficiency* and *completeness* with the Pluto compiler and its test suite. Shown in the result, the implementation is able to prove the equivalence between the polyhedral models before and after Pluto's affine scheduling of all the 62 test cases with reasonable overhead.

```
for (j1 = 1; j1 <= M; j1++) {
    for (j2 = j1; j2 <= M; j2++) {
        for (i = 1; i <= N; i++) {
            I0: symmat[j1][j2] += data[i][j1] * data[i][j2];
        }
        I1: symmat[j2][j1] = symmat[j1][j2];
}}
```

Fig. 2. Sample code π_{cov} for covariance matrix calculation.

In the following parts of the paper, we give an overview of polyhedral compilation in Sect. 2, and present the basic technical settings for our polyhedral model in Sect. 3. In Sect. 4, we outline the validation algorithm for affine transformations together with its proofs. In Sect. 5, we show how our framework can be applied to existing verified compiler CompCert and the polyhedral compiler Pluto. Finally, we discuss related work in Sect. 6, and conclude in Sect. 7. The complete artifact in Coq is available at https://github.com/verif-scop/PolCert.

2 Background

In this section, we give an overview of polyhedral models and show the key ideas to validate model transformations *w.r.t.* Bernstein's conditions.

2.1 Overview of Polyhedral Models

The polyhedral model is an expressive representation of a subclass of *nested loops* described by the following grammar:

$$s ::= \texttt{for (}i\texttt{ = }\varepsilon_1\texttt{; }i\texttt{ <= }\varepsilon_2\texttt{; }i\texttt{++) \{ }s\texttt{ \}} \mid s\texttt{;}s \mid \texttt{if (}\varepsilon\texttt{ <= 0) \{ }s\texttt{ \}} \mid \texttt{I}$$

where the variable i is called *loop iterators*, and ε stands for *affine* expressions in the form of $a_1 * x_1 + \cdots + a_n * x_n + c$. Here we use $a_1, \ldots, a_n$ and c to represent integer literals, and $x_1, \ldots, x_n$ for surrounding loop iterators (like i) or parameters (normally symbolic constants representing the problem size). I stands for primitive instructions such as assignments, which may contain array access expressions $\texttt{arr[}\varepsilon_1\texttt{]}\ldots\texttt{[}\varepsilon_n\texttt{]}$ and never modify loop iterators.

Such code fragments can be effectively analyzed and transformed into polyhedral models, with the assumption that all variables are non-aliased. Figure 2 shows sample fragment π_{cov} of covariance matrix calculation from PolyBench [26]. It has instructions $\texttt{I}_0$ and $\texttt{I}_1$, arrays `symmat` and `data`, loop iterators `j1`, `j2` and `i`, and parameters `M` and `N`.

Since instructions can be executed multiple times in the iterations, we use *iteration vector* p to identify individual execution *instances* of each instruction, like $[\texttt{M},\texttt{N};\texttt{j1},\texttt{j2},\texttt{i}]$ for $\texttt{I}_0$ and $[\texttt{M},\texttt{N};\texttt{j1},\texttt{j2}]$ for $\texttt{I}_1$. Concrete values of `j1`, `j2` and

$\mathtt{i}$ specify the specific iteration where the instruction is executed. We use $\mathtt{I}(p)$ to locate the instance of the instruction $\mathtt{I}$ with the iteration vector p.

In the polyhedral model, we use a *domain* $\mathcal{D}$ to represent the set of iteration vectors for each instruction. Back to our example, domains $\mathcal{D}_0, \mathcal{D}_1$ of $\mathtt{I}_0$ and $\mathtt{I}_1$ respectively are shown below. With the affine bound constraints of each iterator, we can see each $\mathcal{D}_i$ is essentially a polyhedron.

$$\begin{aligned}\mathcal{D}_0 &= \{[\mathtt{M},\mathtt{N};\mathtt{j1},\mathtt{j2},\mathtt{i}] \mid 1 \le \mathtt{j1} \le \mathtt{M} \wedge \mathtt{j1} \le \mathtt{j2} \le \mathtt{M} \wedge 1 \le \mathtt{i} \le \mathtt{N}\}\\ \mathcal{D}_1 &= \{[\mathtt{M},\mathtt{N};\mathtt{j1},\mathtt{j2}] \mid 1 \le \mathtt{j1} \le \mathtt{M} \wedge \mathtt{j1} \le \mathtt{j2} \le \mathtt{M}\}\end{aligned}$$

The execution order of all instances is specified with an affine function θ, namely *schedule*, mapping iteration vectors to *timestamps.* A timestamp is also a vector that can be lexicographically ordered, with each dimension broadly corresponding to a layer of nested loop. For identity transformations that do not reorder instruction instances, the schedules are simply identity functions, as shown by the schedules θ_0 and θ_1 below for $\mathtt{I}_0$ and $\mathtt{I}_1$ respectively.

$$\begin{aligned}\theta_0([\mathtt{M},\mathtt{N};\mathtt{j1},\mathtt{j2},\mathtt{i}]) &= (\mathtt{j1},\mathtt{j2},\mathtt{i})\\ \theta_1([\mathtt{M},\mathtt{N};\mathtt{j1},\mathtt{j2}]) &= (\mathtt{j1},\mathtt{j2})\end{aligned}$$

Polyhedral models also need information about instructions' memory access patterns to reason about their execution. We use a pair of an identifier and a vector to represent the location of a memory access, where the identifier is the name of a multidimensional array, and the vector represents the array indices.

$$(\mathit{MemCell})\ c\ \in\ \mathsf{Id} \times \mathit{List}(\mathbb{Z})$$

For each instruction, we use two *access functions* to describe the write-set and read-set of each instance. Each access function maps an iteration vector p to the corresponding set of memory cells. For our sample, read and write access functions $\mathcal{W}_0, \mathcal{R}_0, \mathcal{W}_1$ and $\mathcal{R}_1$ for $\mathtt{I}_0$ and $\mathtt{I}_1$ are given below.

$$\begin{aligned}\mathcal{W}_0([\mathtt{M},\mathtt{N};\mathtt{j1},\mathtt{j2},\mathtt{i}]) &= \{(\mathtt{symmat},[\mathtt{j1},\mathtt{j2}])\}\\ \mathcal{R}_0([\mathtt{M},\mathtt{N};\mathtt{j1},\mathtt{j2},\mathtt{i}]) &= \{(\mathtt{symmat},[\mathtt{j1},\mathtt{j2}]),(\mathtt{data},[\mathtt{i},\mathtt{j1}]),(\mathtt{data},[\mathtt{i},\mathtt{j2}])\}\\ \mathcal{W}_1([\mathtt{M},\mathtt{N};\mathtt{j1},\mathtt{j2}]) &= \{(\mathtt{symmat},[\mathtt{j2},\mathtt{j1}])\}\\ \mathcal{R}_1([\mathtt{M},\mathtt{N};\mathtt{j1},\mathtt{j2}]) &= \{(\mathtt{symmat},[\mathtt{j1},\mathtt{j2}])\}\end{aligned}$$

Then the whole polyhedral model $\mathcal{P}_{cov}$ of π_{cov} is defined as a set of tuples, each tuple consisting of an instruction, the corresponding domain, schedule, and access functions.

$$\mathcal{P}_{cov} = \{(\mathtt{I}_0,\mathcal{D}_0,\theta_0,\mathcal{W}_0,\mathcal{R}_0),(\mathtt{I}_1,\mathcal{D}_1,\theta_1,\mathcal{W}_1,\mathcal{R}_1)\}$$

Normally, as in Fig. 1, after we calculate the polyhedral model $\mathcal{P}_{cov}$ of π_{cov}, a *scheduling* algorithm is applied to transform $\mathcal{P}_{cov}$ to a new polyhedral model $\mathcal{P}'_{cov}$. Here we focus on the key *affine scheduling* sub-pass, which tries to find new schedules θ'_0, θ'_1 for $\mathtt{I}_0, \mathtt{I}_1$.

$$\begin{aligned}&\mathcal{P}'_{cov} = \mathit{Schedule}(\mathcal{P}_{cov}) = \{(\mathtt{I}_0,\mathcal{D}_0,\theta'_0,\mathcal{W}_0,\mathcal{R}_0),(\mathtt{I}_1,\mathcal{D}_1,\theta'_1,\mathcal{W}_1,\mathcal{R}_1)\}\\ &\quad\textbf{where } \theta'_0([\mathtt{M},\mathtt{N};\mathtt{j1},\mathtt{j2},\mathtt{i}]) = (\mathtt{0},\mathtt{i},\mathtt{j1},\mathtt{j2}),\theta'_1([\mathtt{M},\mathtt{N};\mathtt{j1},\mathtt{j2}]) = (\mathtt{1},\mathtt{j1},\mathtt{j2})\end{aligned}$$

```
for (i = 1; i <= N; i++) {
    for (j1 = 1; j1 <= M; j1++) {
        for (j2 = j1; j2 <= M; j2++) {
            I0: symmat[j1][j2] += data[i][j1] * data[i][j2];
}}}
for (j1 = 1; j1 <= M; j1++) {
    for (j2 = j1; j2 <= M; j2++) {
        I1: symmat[j2][j1] = symmat[j1][j2];
}}
```

Fig. 3. Optimized code π'_{cov} for covariance matrix calculation.

This specific transformation applies a combination of loop fission (see the extra dimension with values `0, 1`) and loop interchange (see the fronted iterator `i`) to the old schedule. It will be intuitive after the final code generation, recovering the structural loop structure, say π'_{cov} in Fig. 3.

The above compilation pipeline from π_{cov} to π'_{cov} is producible by Pluto compiler [4]. It achieves about 4 times speed-up on our machine with `M=N=1500`.

2.2 Validation via Bernstein's Conditions

A compilation validation algorithm takes in source and target programs, and reports `true` if it can establish refinement relation, `false` otherwise. To design a validation algorithm for a specific compilation pass, a decidable correctness criterion of that pass is needed. Intuitively, affine scheduling is a *reordering* transformation of instances. Such transformation's correctness is well-studied as *Bernstein's conditions* [3,13].

Bernstein's conditions describe when it is correct to reorder two operations. Let $\mathsf{W}(u)$ and $\mathsf{R}(u)$ be the write-set and read-set of an operation u respectively. Bernstein's conditions require $\mathsf{W}(u) \cap \mathsf{W}(v) = \mathsf{W}(u) \cap \mathsf{R}(v) = \mathsf{R}(u) \cap \mathsf{W}(v) = \emptyset$. That is, Bernstein's conditions require the preservation of write-after-write (WAW), write-after-read (WAR) and read-after-write (RAW) dependencies.

In summary, to validate the polyhedral affine scheduling pass, we need to implement a validation algorithm based on Bernstein's conditions. Further, to achieve formal correctness guarantees, the algorithm should be itself formally verified by showing its sufficiency to guarantee an affine scheduling's correctness, that is the refinement relation between the target and the source.

3 Language Setting

In this section, we present the formalization of the polyhedral model, and the instruction language interface for our parameterized framework.

3.1 Polyhedral Models

We give the formal definition of polyhedral models *PolyProg* in Fig. 4. We use $\mathcal{P} = (\mathcal{I}, \mathcal{V}, \Gamma)$ to denote a polyhedral program, which contains a polyhedral instruction list $\mathcal{I}$, a parameter list $\mathcal{V}$ and a typing context Γ (which is explained in Sect. 3.2). For each list, say $\mathcal{I}$, we use $|\mathcal{I}|$ to represent its length, and $\mathcal{I}[n]$ for its n-th element (from zero).

PolyProg is parameterized over the instruction language (see Sect. 3.2), borrowing its definitions such as identifiers (of type Id), instructions (denoted by $\mathtt{I}$), states (denoted by σ), semantics of instruction instances (in the form of $p \vdash \mathtt{I}, \sigma \xrightarrow{\Delta_r, \Delta_w} \sigma'$) . We refer readers to Sect. 3.2 for their details.

$$
\begin{array}{rcll rcll}
\textit{(Vec)} & p, t, v, x, \mathcal{E} & \in & \textit{List}(\mathbb{Z}) & \textit{(MemCells)} & \Delta_w, \Delta_r & \in & \textit{Set(MemCell)} \\
\textit{(Poly)} & \mathcal{D} & \in & \textit{Set(Vec)} & \textit{(AcsFunc)} & \mathcal{R}, \mathcal{W} & \in & \textit{Vec} \to \textit{MemCells} \\
\textit{(AffFunc)} & \theta & \in & \textit{Vec} \to \textit{Vec} & \textit{(PolyInstr)} & I & ::= & (\mathtt{I}, \mathcal{D}, \theta, \mathcal{R}, \mathcal{W}) \\
\textit{(Params)} & \mathcal{V} & \in & \textit{List}(\mathsf{Id}) & \textit{(PolyInstrs)} & \mathcal{I} & \in & \textit{List(PolyInstr)} \\
\textit{(MemCell)} & c & \in & \mathsf{Id} \times \textit{Vec} & \textit{(PolyProg)} & \mathcal{P} & ::= & (\mathcal{I}, \mathcal{V}, \Gamma)
\end{array}
$$

Fig. 4. Syntax of *PolyProg*.

$$
\begin{array}{rcl}
\textit{(Index)}\ n & \in & \mathbb{N} \\
\textit{(Instance)}\ \iota & ::= & (\mathtt{I}, n, p, t) \\
\textit{(Instances)}\ \mathcal{L} & ::= & \textit{List(Instance)}
\end{array}
$$

Fig. 5. Auxiliary definitions of *PolyProg*'s semantics.

A polyhedral instruction I is a tuple $(\mathtt{I}, \mathcal{D}, \theta, \mathcal{R}, \mathcal{W})$. The instruction $\mathtt{I}$ is the base instruction. The polyhedron $\mathcal{D}$ is the domain of the instruction; we call every vector $p \in \mathcal{D}$ the *iteration vector.* θ is the affine schedule which maps each p in $\mathcal{D}$ to a timestamp t (also a vector, as explained in Sect. 2.1). $\mathcal{R}, \mathcal{W}$ denotes the instruction's read access function and write access function, respectively. Note that we omit the linear algebra representations and implementations of the notions for presentation simplicity, and use their more intuitive mathematical notions instead (e.g., sets and functions).

The polyhedral program's semantics judgment is of the form $\vdash \mathcal{P}, \sigma \longrightarrow \sigma'$ in Fig. 6, saying that, starting from an initial state σ, the polyhedral program $\mathcal{P}$ executes and terminates at the final state σ'. The semantics first flattens the polyhedral instruction list $\mathcal{I}$ into instances $\mathcal{L}$ (defined in Fig. 5) and sorts it (rule Init), then iteratively executes the instance with the least timestamp (rule Progress), until there are no remaining instances (rule Done).

Below we give explanations of the semantic components occurring in Fig. 6.

- An instance ι is a four-tuple $(\mathtt{I}, n, p, t)$ (see Fig. 5), recording its instruction $\mathtt{I}$, its n in list $\mathcal{I}$, its iteration vector p and its timestamp t. We order instances with their timestamps lexicographically, with notations like $\prec, \preccurlyeq, \succcurlyeq$.
- Propositions Compat, $\mathsf{Retrieve}$ and $\mathsf{NonAlias}$ together describe valid initial states and are defined within the instruction language (see Sect. 3.2).

$$\frac{\begin{array}{c}\mathcal{P} = (\mathcal{I}, \mathcal{V}, \Gamma) \\ \mathsf{Compat}(\Gamma, \sigma) \quad \mathsf{Retrieve}(\mathcal{V}, \mathcal{E}, \sigma) \quad \mathsf{NonAlias}(\sigma) \\ \mathsf{flatten}(\mathcal{I}, \mathcal{E}, \mathcal{L}) \quad \mathsf{Permut}(\mathcal{L}, \mathcal{L}') \quad \mathsf{Sorted}(\mathcal{L}', \preccurlyeq) \\ \vdash \mathcal{L}', \sigma \longrightarrow \sigma'\end{array}}{\vdash \mathcal{P}, \sigma \longrightarrow \sigma'} \text{ (INIT)}$$

$$\frac{\begin{array}{c}\mathcal{L} = \iota :: \mathcal{L}' \quad \iota = (\mathtt{I}, n, p, t) \\ p \vdash \mathtt{I}, \sigma \xrightarrow{\Delta_r, \Delta_w} \sigma' \quad \vdash \mathcal{L}', \sigma' \longrightarrow \sigma''\end{array}}{\vdash \mathcal{L}, \sigma \longrightarrow \sigma''} \text{ (PROGRESS)} \qquad \frac{}{\vdash \mathsf{nil}, \sigma \longrightarrow \sigma} \text{ (DONE)}$$

Fig. 6. Semantics of *PolyProg*.

- The proposition $\mathsf{flatten}(\mathcal{I}, \mathcal{E}, \mathcal{L})$ defines how a list of polyhedral instructions $\mathcal{I}$ is expanded into a set of instances $\mathcal{L}$, with the parameters $\mathcal{E}$ (e.g., $[\mathtt{M}, \mathtt{N}]$ in the example in Sect. 2.1). It holds if and only if:
  1. Elements in $\mathcal{L}$ have unique (n, p) pairs.
  2. For any instance $\iota = (\mathtt{I}, n, p, t) \in \mathcal{L}$, we have $\mathcal{I}[n] = (\mathtt{I}, \mathcal{D}, \theta, \mathcal{R}, \mathcal{W})$, and
     (a) $p \in \mathcal{D}$ and p's prefix of length $|\mathcal{E}|$ is equal to $\mathcal{E}$,
     (b) $\theta(p) = t$.
- $\mathsf{Permut}(\mathcal{L}, \mathcal{L}')$ says $\mathcal{L}$ and $\mathcal{L}'$ are permutations of each other (they contain the same set of instances), and $\mathsf{Sorted}(\mathcal{L}, \preccurlyeq)$ says $\mathcal{L}$ is sorted by relation $\preccurlyeq$.

We define the refinement relation $\mathcal{P}_t \sqsubseteq \mathcal{P}_s$ between two polyhedral programs $\mathcal{P}_s$ and $\mathcal{P}_t$ in Definition 1, to which the validation's correctness refers. It says, starting from any valid state σ, if the target program $\mathcal{P}_t$ terminates at state σ', the source $\mathcal{P}_s$ also terminates at σ'.

Definition 1 (Refinement Relation between Polyhedral Programs).

$$\mathcal{P}_t \sqsubseteq \mathcal{P}_s \triangleq \forall \sigma, \sigma'.\ \vdash \mathcal{P}_t, \sigma \longrightarrow \sigma' \implies \vdash \mathcal{P}_s, \sigma \longrightarrow \sigma'.$$

3.2 Instruction Language Interface

The polyhedral compilation does high-level structural transformations, not relying on the concrete definition of the underlying instruction language. However, the underlying language must expose its memory access patterns and guarantee some properties. We modularize these essential definitions as the module type $\mathbb{I}$ (see Fig. 7). Our polyhedral model is parameterized over instances of the type $\mathbb{I}$.

An instruction language must define its identifier Id, its variable type T (normally multi-dimensional arrays), its base instruction's syntax I, and its state S. We use notations $\mathtt{I}$, τ and σ for concrete instruction, type, and state.

We use Γ to denote a typing context, which is a list of variable-type pairs that contains all live variables and their corresponding types for the code fragment.

$$\textit{(TypCtxt)}\ \Gamma \in \textit{List}(\mathsf{Id} \times \mathsf{T})$$

The semantics is defined in the form of $p \vdash \mathtt{I}, \sigma \xrightarrow{\Delta_r, \Delta_w} \sigma'$. It says that, the instance of the base instruction $\mathtt{I}$ under the iteration vector p executes from the initial state σ and terminates at the final state σ', reading and writing memory cells Δ_r and Δ_w (see Fig. 4 for the definitions). The iteration vector p contains the exact values for parameters $\mathcal{V}$ and all the iterators. That is, $p[i-1]$ is the value of the i-th parameter (if $i \leq |\mathcal{V}|$), and $p[|\mathcal{V}|+j-1]$ is the value of the j-depth iterator.

$$
\begin{array}{l}
\textsf{Module Type } \mathbb{I} \triangleq \\
\left\{
\begin{array}{l}
\textsf{Id}, \textsf{T}, \textsf{I}, \textsf{S} : \mathit{Type} \\
\vdash\ : \textsf{I} \to \mathit{List}(\mathbb{Z}) \to \mathit{MemCells} \to \mathit{MemCells} \to \textsf{S} \to \textsf{S} \to \mathit{Prop} \\
\textsf{Compat} : \mathit{TypCtxt} \to \textsf{S} \to \mathit{Prop} \\
\textsf{Retrieve} : \mathit{List}(\textsf{Id}) \to \mathit{List}(\mathbb{Z}) \to \textsf{S} \to \mathit{Prop} \\
\textsf{NonAlias} : \textsf{S} \to \mathit{Prop} \\
\textsf{NonAliasPsrv} : \\
\quad \forall \mathtt{I}, \sigma, \sigma'.\ \textsf{NonAlias}(\sigma) \wedge p \vdash \mathtt{I}, \sigma \xrightarrow{\ \_,\_\ } \sigma' \implies \textsf{NonAlias}(\sigma'). \\
\textsf{Check} : \textsf{I} \to \mathit{AcsFuncs} \to \mathit{AcsFuncs} \to \mathit{Bool} \\
\textsf{Correct}(\textsf{Check}) : \\
\quad \forall \mathtt{I}, \mathcal{W}, \mathcal{R}.\ \textsf{Check}(\mathtt{I}, \mathcal{W}, \mathcal{R}) = \textsf{true} \\
\qquad \implies (\forall \sigma, \sigma', p, \Delta_r, \Delta_w.\ p \vdash \mathtt{I}, \sigma \xrightarrow{\Delta_r, \Delta_w} \sigma' \implies \Delta_r \subseteq \mathcal{R}(p) \wedge \Delta_w \subseteq \mathcal{W}(p)). \\
\textsf{BCPermut} : \\
\quad \forall \mathtt{I}_1, \mathtt{I}_2, p_1, p_2, \sigma, \sigma', \sigma'', \Delta_r, \Delta_w, \Delta_r', \Delta_w'. \\
\quad (p_1 \vdash \mathtt{I}_1, \sigma \xrightarrow{\Delta_r, \Delta_w} \sigma' \wedge p_2 \vdash \mathtt{I}_2, \sigma' \xrightarrow{\Delta_r', \Delta_w'} \sigma'' \\
\qquad\qquad \wedge \Delta_r \cap \Delta_w' = \emptyset \wedge \Delta_w \cap \Delta_r' = \emptyset \wedge \Delta_w \cap \Delta_w' = \emptyset) \wedge \textsf{NonAlias}(\sigma) \\
\qquad \implies \exists \sigma^*.\ p_2 \vdash \mathtt{I}_2, \sigma \xrightarrow{\Delta_r', \Delta_w'} \sigma^* \wedge p_1 \vdash \mathtt{I}_1, \sigma^* \xrightarrow{\Delta_r, \Delta_w} \sigma''.
\end{array}
\right.
\end{array}
$$

Fig. 7. Definition of instruction language module $\mathbb{I}$.

The proposition Compat describes the validity of the initial states *w.r.t.* the program's typing context, e.g. correct allocations. The proposition Retrieve collects the parameters $\mathcal{V}$'s values $\mathcal{E}$ from the initial state σ, which will be the constant prefix of every iteration vector. The proposition NonAlias describes non-aliasing states; the preservation of the state's non-aliasing property *w.r.t.* instruction's semantics is captured by lemma NonAliasPsrv.

Polyhedral models summarize access patterns with read and write access functions. A procedure Check should be defined to validate the consistency between every instruction's semantics and its access functions. It should satisfy the correctness property Correct(Check), which says: if Check returns `true` for instruction $\mathtt{I}$ and its read and write access functions $\mathcal{R}$ and $\mathcal{W}$, then the read and write memory footprints Δ_r, Δ_w of $\mathtt{I}$'s any execution under iteration vector p are over-approximated by $\mathcal{R}(p)$ and $\mathcal{W}(p)$, respectively.

Finally, the instruction language should respect Bernstein's conditions, specified with lemma BCPermut. It says that, from a non-aliasing state, if two instructions $\mathtt{I}_1$ and $\mathtt{I}_2$ are executed in sequence under some iteration vectors and their footprints satisfy Bernstein's conditions, then the permutation of their executions does not affect the final state.

4 Validation Algorithm and Its Proofs

In this section, we outline our validation algorithm and its correctness proofs.

4.1 Validation Algorithm

Preprocessing. We first simplify the inputs with the function $\mathsf{Compose}$, as defined below. The validator assumes the two input polyhedral programs only differ in each instruction's schedule functions and tries to compose them into an extended program $\hat{\mathcal{P}}$. If the two inputs are not composable, the validator returns `false` directly. Note that the function seq transforms a list of optional values into an optional list, returning `Some` if all elements are not `None`, and `None` otherwise.

$$\begin{aligned}\textit{(ExtPolyInstr)}\ \hat{I} &::= (\mathtt{I}, \mathcal{D}, \theta_s, \theta_t, \mathcal{R}, \mathcal{W})\\ \textit{(ExtPolyInstrs)}\ \hat{\mathcal{I}} &::= \textit{List(ExtPolyInstr)}\\ \textit{(ExtPolyProg)}\ \hat{\mathcal{P}} &::= (\hat{\mathcal{I}}, \mathcal{V}, \Gamma)\end{aligned}$$

$$\mathsf{Compose}((\mathcal{I}_s, \mathcal{V}_s, \Gamma_s), (\mathcal{I}_t, \mathcal{V}_t, \Gamma_t)) ::=$$
$$\begin{cases}\mathtt{Some}\ (\hat{\mathcal{I}}, \mathcal{V}_s, \Gamma_s) & \text{if } \mathsf{seq}\ (\mathsf{map}\ \mathsf{Compose}'\ (\mathsf{zip}\ \mathcal{I}_s\ \mathcal{I}_t)) = \mathtt{Some}\ \hat{\mathcal{I}} \wedge \mathcal{V}_s = \mathcal{V}_t \wedge \Gamma_s = \Gamma_t\\ \mathtt{None} & \text{otherwise}\end{cases}$$
$$\mathsf{Compose}'((\mathtt{I}_s, \mathcal{D}_s, \theta_s, \mathcal{R}_s, \mathcal{W}_s), (\mathtt{I}_t, \mathcal{D}_t, \theta_t, \mathcal{R}_t, \mathcal{W}_t)) ::=$$
$$\begin{cases}\mathtt{Some}\ (\mathtt{I}_s, \mathcal{D}_s, \theta_s, \theta_t, \mathcal{R}_s, \mathcal{W}_s) & \text{if } \mathtt{I}_s = \mathtt{I}_t \wedge \mathcal{D}_s = \mathcal{D}_t \wedge \mathcal{R}_s = \mathcal{R}_t \wedge \mathcal{W}_s = \mathcal{W}_t\\ \mathtt{None} & \text{otherwise}\end{cases}$$

The composability suggests instances of the two input polyhedral programs are of one-to-one correspondence. We also compose two corresponding instances into one extended instance $\hat{\iota}$, carrying both the old and new timestamps. It can be ordered either by its old timestamp using $\prec_s, \preccurlyeq_s, \succcurlyeq_s$ or its new timestamp using $\prec_t, \preccurlyeq_t, \succcurlyeq_t$. Similarly, lists of extended instances exist. We introduce operators $\langle\cdot\rangle_s$ and $\langle\cdot\rangle_t$ to split the extended definitions to the originals.

$$\begin{aligned}\textit{(ExtInstance)}\ \hat{\iota} &::= (\mathtt{I}, n, p, t_s, t_t)\\ \textit{(ExtInstances)}\ \hat{\mathcal{L}} &::= \textit{List(ExtInstance)}\end{aligned}$$

Further, the proposition $\mathsf{flatten}$ is lifted, so that $\mathsf{flatten}(\hat{\mathcal{I}}, \mathcal{E}, \hat{\mathcal{L}})$ expands an extended polyhedral instruction list into an extended instance list. The extended instance list is just a compact representation for the non-extended, and we have $\langle\hat{\mathcal{L}}\rangle_s = \mathcal{L}_s$ and $\langle\hat{\mathcal{L}}\rangle_t = \mathcal{L}_t$ if $\mathsf{flatten}(\langle\hat{\mathcal{I}}\rangle_s, \mathcal{E}, \mathcal{L}_s)$ and $\mathsf{flatten}(\langle\hat{\mathcal{I}}\rangle_t, \mathcal{E}, \mathcal{L}_t)$.

Instruction-Level Validation. The function V_{instr} checks if Bernstein's conditions (*w.r.t.* access functions) are satisfied by every two permuted instances of instructions $\hat{I}$ and $\hat{I}'$, i.e., no violation of WAW, WAR or RAW dependencies. It invokes dependency preservation checkers *WAWPrsv*, *RAWPrsv*, *WARPrsv* on input instructions. Given that each program comprises multiple instructions, and potential dependencies could exist between any two of them, V_{instr} must be applied to all instruction pairs.

$$V_{instr}(\hat{I},\hat{I}',m) = WAWPrsv(\hat{I},\hat{I}',m) \wedge RAWPrsv(\hat{I},\hat{I}',m) \wedge WARPrsv(\hat{I},\hat{I}',m)$$

Taking *WAWPrsv* as an example, it constructs emptiness tests to find permuted instances accessing overlapped memory cells for writes. Its additional argument m will be the length $|\mathcal{V}|$ of parameters, used to enforce the same value assumption of parameters in every iteration vector. The notation $p[:m]$ slices the iteration vector p to its first m elements, i.e., the values of parameters. *RAWPrsv* and *WARPrsv* are defined in similar ways.

$$\begin{aligned}
&WAWPrsv(\hat{I},\hat{I}',m) = \\
&\quad \textbf{let } \hat{I} \ = (\mathtt{I},\mathcal{D},\theta_s,\theta_t,\mathcal{R},\mathcal{W}) \textbf{ in} \\
&\quad \textbf{let } \hat{I}' = (\mathtt{I}',\mathcal{D}',\theta'_s,\theta'_t,\mathcal{R}',\mathcal{W}') \textbf{ in} \\
&\quad \begin{cases} \mathtt{true} & \text{if } \{(p,p') \mid p \in \mathcal{D} \wedge p' \in \mathcal{D}' \wedge p[:m] = p'[:m] \\ & \qquad \wedge\ \theta_s(p) \prec \theta_s(p') \wedge \theta_t(p) \succcurlyeq \theta_t(p') \wedge \mathcal{W}(p) \cap \mathcal{W}'(p') \neq \emptyset\} = \emptyset \\ \mathtt{false} & \text{otherwise} \end{cases}
\end{aligned}$$

Validation of Access Functions. However, the function V_{instr} directly uses access functions of each instruction for granted, not checking its consistency with the instruction's semantics. To achieve formal correctness guarantees, the user should provide a checking procedure Check and prove its correctness Correct(Check) for her language (see Sect. 3.2). Procedure Check is invoked on every instruction.

Only when the procedure Check reports `true` for every instruction, the results of V_{instr} are valid *w.r.t.* the language's semantics, and the premise of lemma BCPermut, which describes Bernstein's condition with the semantics, is fulfillable.

Overall Validation Algorithm. So far, we have all the ingredients to define the overall validation algorithm *Validate*. It first composes the two input polyhedral programs into one and invokes V_{instr} for every two extended instructions. Finally, it invokes user-defined access function checker Check for every instruction. If all checks pass, the algorithm returns `true`; otherwise, it cannot establish the refinement relation and returns `false`.

Definition 2 (Definition of the Validation Algorithm).

$$Validate(\mathcal{P}_s,\mathcal{P}_t) = \begin{cases} \forall \hat{I},\hat{I}' \in \hat{\mathcal{I}}.\ V_{instr}(\hat{I},\hat{I}',|\mathcal{V}|) = \mathtt{true} \\ \quad \wedge \forall \hat{I} \in \hat{\mathcal{I}}.\ \mathsf{Check}(\hat{I}.\mathtt{I},\hat{I}.\mathcal{W},\hat{I}.\mathcal{R}) = \mathtt{true} \\ \qquad\qquad \text{if } \mathsf{Compose}(\mathcal{P}_s,\mathcal{P}_t) = \mathtt{Some}\ (\hat{\mathcal{I}},\mathcal{V},\Gamma) \\ \mathtt{false} \qquad \text{if } \mathsf{Compose}(\mathcal{P}_s,\mathcal{P}_t) = \mathtt{None} \end{cases}$$

4.2 Proof Goal and Its Sketch

The correctness of the validator *Validate*, which is our proof goal, is given in Theorem 1. It says that whenever it reports `true` on input programs $\mathcal{P}_s$ and $\mathcal{P}_t$, it guarantees the establishment of their refinement relation $\mathcal{P}_t \sqsubseteq \mathcal{P}_s$.

Theorem 1 (Correctness of the Validator).

$$\forall \mathcal{P}_s, \mathcal{P}_t.\ \textit{Validate}(\mathcal{P}_s, \mathcal{P}_t) = \texttt{true} \implies \mathcal{P}_t \sqsubseteq \mathcal{P}_s.$$

Now we outline the proof of Theorem 1.

Proof. Unfold the goal. We have an extended instance list $\hat{\mathcal{L}}$ for the composed program $\hat{\mathcal{P}}$. Now for every possible permutation $\hat{\mathcal{L}}_t$ of $\hat{\mathcal{L}}$ where $\mathsf{Sorted}(\hat{\mathcal{L}}_t, \preccurlyeq_t)$, which determines a possible iteration $\langle \hat{\mathcal{L}}_t \rangle_t$ for the target program, we need to find a semantic equivalent instance list $\hat{\mathcal{L}}_s$ where $\mathsf{Sorted}(\hat{\mathcal{L}}_s, \preccurlyeq_s)$ that determines the iteration $\langle \hat{\mathcal{L}}_s \rangle_s$ for the source program.

$$\frac{\hat{\mathcal{L}}_1 = \hat{\iota}_1 :: \hat{\iota}_2 :: \hat{\mathcal{L}}' \quad \hat{\mathcal{L}}_2 = \hat{\iota}_2 :: \hat{\iota}_1 :: \hat{\mathcal{L}}' \quad \hat{\iota}_1 \sim \hat{\iota}_2}{\mathsf{StablePermut}'(\hat{\mathcal{L}}_1, \hat{\mathcal{L}}_2, \sim)}\ (\text{SPMTSWAP}) \qquad \frac{\hat{\mathcal{L}}_1 = \hat{\iota} :: \hat{\mathcal{L}}_1' \quad \hat{\mathcal{L}}_2 = \hat{\iota} :: \hat{\mathcal{L}}_2' \quad \mathsf{StablePermut}'(\hat{\mathcal{L}}_1', \hat{\mathcal{L}}_2', \sim)}{\mathsf{StablePermut}'(\hat{\mathcal{L}}_1, \hat{\mathcal{L}}_2, \sim)}\ (\text{SPMTSKIP})$$

$$\frac{\hat{\mathcal{L}}_1 = \hat{\mathcal{L}}_2 = \mathsf{nil}}{\mathsf{StablePermut}(\hat{\mathcal{L}}_1, \hat{\mathcal{L}}_2, \sim, 0)}\ (\text{SPMTNIL}) \qquad \frac{\mathsf{StablePermut}'(\hat{\mathcal{L}}_1, \hat{\mathcal{L}}_2, \sim) \quad \mathsf{StablePermut}(\hat{\mathcal{L}}_2, \hat{\mathcal{L}}_3, \sim, n)}{\mathsf{StablePermut}(\hat{\mathcal{L}}_1, \hat{\mathcal{L}}_3, \sim, n+1)}\ (\text{SPMT})$$

Fig. 8. Definition of stable permutation.

First we define the relation $\sim$ to $\lambda \hat{\iota}, \hat{\iota}'.\ \hat{\iota} \succ_s \hat{\iota}' \wedge \hat{\iota} \preccurlyeq_t \hat{\iota}'$, which establishes if two extended instances are permuted.

Now we sort $\hat{\mathcal{L}}_t$ and let $\hat{\mathcal{L}}_s = \mathsf{sort}(\hat{\mathcal{L}}_t, \preccurlyeq_s)$. The sorting algorithm sort establishes $\mathsf{Sorted}(\hat{\mathcal{L}}_s, \preccurlyeq_s) \wedge \mathsf{Permut}(\hat{\mathcal{L}}_t, \hat{\mathcal{L}}_s)$ and the additional property:

$$\exists n.\ \mathsf{StablePermut}(\hat{\mathcal{L}}_t, \hat{\mathcal{L}}_s, \sim, n)$$

where $\mathsf{StablePermut}$ is defined in Fig. 8. $\mathsf{StablePermut}(\hat{\mathcal{L}}_t, \hat{\mathcal{L}}_s, \sim, n)$ says there exists a permuting sequence of length n that transforms $\hat{\mathcal{L}}_t$ to $\hat{\mathcal{L}}_s$, and each permutation always swaps adjacent instances satisfying relation $\sim$ (i.e., only do *necessary* swaps); this fact is obvious as $\hat{\mathcal{L}}_t$ is sorted by $\preccurlyeq_t$ and if sort is designed efficiently (so that it never increases inversion number during its operation *w.r.t.* $\preccurlyeq_s$, i.e., only swaps two instances satisfying $\succ_s$).

Now we move on to prove two list's equivalence, by induction on StablePermut. The rule SPMTSWAP is the only rule that enables the permutation, swapping two adjacent instances; other rules are correct trivially or by induction hypothesis.

The `true` result of the validation guarantees that any two necessarily swapped instances (i.e., satisfy relation $\sim$) have no WAW, WAR, or RAW dependencies *w.r.t.* access functions. From Correct(Check), we know the access functions over-approximate every instruction's real memory access pattern. Then whenever we swap two adjacent instances $\hat{\iota}_1, \hat{\iota}_2$ with the rule SPMTSWAP, we know that they have no real WAW, RAW, or WAR dependencies.

Recall that all variables in the initial state are non-aliased. This property is preserved during execution thanks to the language's property NonAliasPsrv.

By the provided property BCPermut of the instruction language (see Sect. 3.2), saying that two instances are permutable if they have no real WAW, WAR, or RAW dependencies and all variables are non-aliased, we finish the proof. □

5 Evaluation

In this section, we show how the framework can be applied to existing verified compilers and polyhedral compilers, and discuss our engineering efforts.

5.1 Support Existing Verified Compiler

To demonstrate the practicality of our approach, we instantiate the validator with a variant of CompCert's instruction language (called CInstr), making the proof complete. Several manual-written tests, like $\mathcal{P}_{cov}$ and $\mathcal{P}'_{cov}$ in Sect. 2, are successfully validated.

Now we explain the main components of CInstr's formalization.

- The syntax `I` of CInstr is a subset of CompCert's instruction language[1], including only assignments with multi-dimensional array accesses. We reuse CompCert's unary and binary operators while defining expressions. Id is defined as positive integers as in CompCert. Type T is defined as k-dimensional array types of the base type (CompCert's signed 32-bit integer).
- The state S is directly inherited from CompCert's formalization, which contains an environment that records definitions of global and local variables, and the CompCert memory model [18,19]. In such formalization, each variable is associated with a block identifier in the memory model.
- The semantics of CInstr reuses most CompCert's semantics, like its evaluation of normal expressions. The exception is that CInstr evaluates array subscripts in $\mathbb{Z}$, rather than fixed-width integer arithmetic. The CompCert memory model is one-dimensional, so multi-dimensional array accesses should be correctly mapped. Without loss of generality, loop iterators are considered ghost variables in $\mathbb{Z}$ that do not write to the state during iteration; their values are converted to fixed-width integers when necessary.
- The proposition Compat(Γ, σ) is defined as the appropriate allocation of typing context Γ in state σ, similar to how CompCert initializes variables. The proposition Retrieve$(\mathcal{V}, \mathcal{E}, \sigma)$ asserts how each parameter's value is retrieved

[1] https://compcert.org/doc/html/compcert.cfrontend.Csyntax.html.

from the state; it involves casting fix-width integers to $\mathbb{Z}$. The proposition $\mathsf{NonAlias}(\sigma)$ signifies that each variable's reference (i.e., the assigned block identifier) is not equivalent to any other.
- The procedure $\mathsf{Check}(\mathtt{I}, \mathcal{W}, \mathcal{R})$ is defined to symbolically evaluate every array-access expression of instruction I to get its access functions and check if it is contained by input access functions $\mathcal{W}$ and $\mathcal{R}$. For example, the instruction `I: res += arr[i][(j+i)+(j-i)]` has write and read access functions $\mathcal{W}_{\checkmark}([\mathtt{i},\mathtt{j}]) = \{(\mathtt{res}, [])\}$ and $\mathcal{R}_{\checkmark}([\mathtt{i},\mathtt{j}]) = \{(\mathtt{res}, []), (\mathtt{arr}, [\mathtt{i}, 2*\mathtt{j}])\}$; if the inputs are $\mathcal{W} = \mathcal{W}_{\checkmark}$ and $\mathcal{R}([\mathtt{i},\mathtt{j}]) = \{(\mathtt{res}, []), (\mathtt{arr}, [\mathtt{i}, 2*\mathtt{j}]), (\mathtt{redundant}, [])\}$, the procedure returns `true`.
- Finally, with tedious yet straightforward proofs, we establish properties NonAliasPsrv, Correct(Check), and BCPermut for the above definitions.

5.2 Support Existing Polyhedral Compiler

Polyhedral compilers like Pluto use similar polyhedral representations as *PolyProg*, like the OpenScop format [2]. After developing the converter for OpenScop and *PolyProg*, we can validate the Pluto's affine scheduling pass.

However, we have to give up some formal guarantees because Pluto underspecifies its inputs. To be concrete, Pluto's validator is instantiated with empty instruction language, and the procedure Check always returns `true`. This is because Pluto has no formal specification of its inputs, which only contain textual code fragments without sufficient contexts like typing to fully describe a nested loop. Consequently, as instructions have no formal semantics, we cannot define a verified checker for their semantics and access functions.

Nevertheless, it still makes sense to adopt our framework to Pluto. Like other polyhedral compilers, Pluto implicitly presumes its input programs agree on some properties like non-aliasing states and in-bound array accesses [10], which we believe are well-summarized by our instruction interface $\mathbb{I}$ in Sect. 3.2. Though we have to suspend the definition of the instruction language and give up checking the input access functions, we can still utilize the verified validation algorithm.

We collect all relevant tests and examples from Pluto's repository[2] as our test suite, counting to 62. We configure Pluto so that it only does affine scheduling, but still does its best:

```
pluto --smartfuse --rar \
      --notile --noparallel --noprevector --nounrolljam [.c]
```

Let's say Pluto compiles $\mathcal{P}_s$ to $\mathcal{P}_t$. Table 1 gives Pluto affine scheduler's running time (P-Time) and validator's running time (V-Time, for both *Validate*$(\mathcal{P}_s, \mathcal{P}_t)$ and *Validate*$(\mathcal{P}_t, \mathcal{P}_s)$) for each test[3]. The validator successfully validates every test's compilation, guaranteeing $\mathcal{P}_s \sqsubseteq \mathcal{P}_t \wedge \mathcal{P}_t \sqsubseteq \mathcal{P}_s$. Measurements are performed on an Intel i7-11700 processor with 64 GB memory, running in Windows Subsystem for Linux (WSL2) of Ubuntu 18.04 on Windows

[2] https://github.com/bondhugula/pluto.

[3] Please note that P-Time and V-Time for each test are not comparable, as they pertain to implementations of different algorithms in different programming languages.

10.0.19045. The result shows the validation algorithm runs in a reasonable time. As examples, the test case `tce` (Tensor Contraction Engine for four indexes) with the largest runtime (around 4.5 s) has 4 instructions operating over four-dimensional arrays, nested within loops at a depth of 5; for the corner test `noloop`, which contains no loops but one trivial assignment, the validation spends zero time.

Discussion on Validation's Completeness. We already mechanize formal proofs for the validator's *soundness*, which guarantees that the validator never

Table 1. Evaluation results on Pluto's test suite.

Test	P-Time (ms)	V-Time (ms,ms)	Test	P-Time (ms)	V-time (ms,ms)
covcol	3.5	434.6, 320.7	dsyr2k	2.6	106.0, 83.4
fdtd-2d	46.4	1615.5, 1296.3	gemver	7.0	247.9, 240.4
lu	6.1	410.6, 331.2	mvt	2.2	70.2, 56.3
ssymm	40.7	726.0, 551.2	tce	568.6	4442.0, 4422.5
adi	77.5	2531.7, 2377.8	corcol	5.5	442.5, 362.1
dct	21.8	879.4, 739.4	dsyrk	1.8	96.8, 78.9
floyd	12.1	502.6, 421.7	jacobi-1d-	3.8	184.0, 167.8
matmul-init	2.9	257.8, 192.4	pca	202.5	2923.6, 2679.5
strmm	1.9	141.4, 110.8	tmm	1.6	109.7, 89.6
advect3d	1023.1	579.1, 498.1	corcol3	13.6	851.3, 733.4
doitgen	10.4	1069.2, 837.4	fdtd-1d	6.0	268.7, 229.9
jacobi-2d-...	17.7	619.5, 543.5	matmul	3.2	157.1, 125.5
seidel	24.5	818.1, 725.5	strsm	6.4	209.3, 161.2
trisolv	5.1	338.9, 248.8	1dloop-invar	0.3	6.7, 6.0
costfunc	0.8	47.4, 35.0	fusion1	0.9	15.3, 13.9
fusion2	4.7	36.8, 31.6	fusion3	3.3	33.6, 33.8
fusion4	4.3	26.2, 23.4	fusion5	1.3	41.3, 38.9
fusion6	0.5	24.2, 25.4	fusion7	0.4	14.3, 13.8
fusion8	0.6	4.6, 3.8	fusion9	4.3	111.5, 110.2
fusion10	4.6	32.4, 25.7	intratileopt1	0.4	11.0, 7.8
intratileopt2	0.3	28.7, 21.3	intratileopt3	0.7	40.8, 35.9
intratileopt4	0.8	40.6, 33.3	matmul-seq	7.9	329.8, 275.7
matmul-seq3	19.8	531.4, 502.4	multi-loop-	1.2	46.3, 45.6
multi-stmt-...	14.7	57.4, 53.6	mxv	1.2	73.9, 61.8
mxv-seq	2.6	102.4, 96.2	mxv-seq3	6.3	200.4, 194.5
negparam	1.5	128.4, 118.4	nodep	0.4	26.5, 18.1
noloop	0.0	0.2, 0.0	polynomial	1.4	100.8, 90.0
seq	1.1	54.2, 50.5	shift	1.9	101.6, 88.2
spatial	0.3	29.9, 21.0	tricky1	5.7	105.6, 93.7
tricky2	0.5	19.3, 16.2	tricky3	3.7	105.1, 107.0
tricky4	0.2	6.1, 4.8	wavefront	0.7	39.0, 32.3

gives false positive results. Now we discuss its *completeness*: does the validator try its best to prove the correctness, validating valid transformations as much as possible? This matters because a validator always returning `false` is useless.

We argue that the validator is complete enough in practice, as shown in the evaluation. The completeness of the validation algorithm relies on the completeness of VPL's emptiness check isEmpty(), which only gives one-way implication $\forall \mathcal{P}.\ \mathsf{isEmpty}(\mathcal{P}) \implies \mathcal{P} = \emptyset$. If we assume VPL's implementation is complete enough, then the validation algorithm should be equally complete. That's because the well-studied Bernstein's conditions basing the validation, should be the very correctness criterion of all reordering transformations like affine scheduling. Polyhedral scheduling algorithms were designed with this in mind, such as the *legality constraints* in Pluto's core algorithm that allow permutations of instances only when Bernstein's conditions are established [4].

5.3 Engineering Efforts

This work is fully mechanized in Coq, based on the Verified Polyhedron Library (VPL) [5] and the basic libraries and formalizations of PolyGen [8].

We've written around 17000 lines of Coq and 1000 lines of OCaml not counting blanks, comments and original proofs. In Coq, our proof efforts mainly involve additions to existing linear algebra and polyhedron libraries, formalization of *PolyProg*'s properties based on the instruction interface $\mathbb{I}$, implementation and verification of the validator and CInstr. In OCaml code, we provide basic functionalities like parser and printer for OpenScop format, compiler driver, building and testing scripts, etc.

6 Related Work

In this section, we discuss verification of polyhedral compilation and tensor compilation, as well as verified validation for other compiler optimizations.

6.1 Verification of Polyhedral Compilation

Courant and Leroy [8] provide basic formalizations of the polyhedral model and the first verified polyhedral code generator based on VPL [5]. Pilkiewicz [24] provides a prototypical verified validator (called s2sloop) of polyhedral scheduling ten years ago, sharing the idea to base the validation algorithm on Bernstein's conditions. In our hindsight, its abeyance is attributed to its excessive use of dependent type (making its proof engineering harder) and the lack of supported libraries, such as VPL. As emphasis, we do not merely reimplement his work. We go a step further, giving stronger proof and a well-designed framework with extensive evaluation. To be more specific with the first point, s2sloop's final theorem demands determinism (say, Det()) of its first input program as an additional assumption, which makes it weaker than ours (see Sect. 4.2):

$$\mathsf{Correct}(\mathit{Validate}) \triangleq \forall \mathcal{P}_s, \mathcal{P}_t.\ \mathit{Validate}(\mathcal{P}_s, \mathcal{P}_t) = \mathtt{true} \land \mathsf{Det}(\mathcal{P}_s) \Rightarrow \mathcal{P}_t \sqsubseteq \mathcal{P}_s$$

This matters as a polyhedral compiler may make use of non-determinism to express parallelism [33], and the validator should be able to handle two parallelized inputs.

Similarly, Namjoshi and Singhania [23] provides a validator based on dependency violation (i.e., Bernstein's condition) for their semi-automatic polyhedral scheduling framework. However, the validator is itself unverified and only supports sequential programs. Our work can equip it with stronger correctness guarantees.

Polyhedral models assume arbitrary precision arithmetic for expressions in specific positions, which is not compatible with real-world fixed-width integer arithmetic that possibly overflows. Cuervo Parrino et al. [9] attempt to bridge such semantics gap using an optimistic approach [10].

6.2 Verification of Tensor Compilation

Tensor compilations allow users to model complex matrix computations with high-level mathematical representations and help to compile them to efficient low-level codes (involving nested loop), and validation in such domain also attracts attention. Clément and Cohen [7] design an end-to-end validation method between affine Halide algorithm [27] and its low-level imperative generated code. Liu et al. [20] design a Halide-like system within Coq, enabling developers to design and verify optimized schedules at the same time with the provided tactics, semi-automatically. Bang et al. [1] supports validating tensor-related dialects of `mlir` with appropriate SMT encoding; it does not support aggressive optimizations like the polyhedral-based yet.

6.3 Verified Validation for Compiler Optimization

Only a few validation algorithms for compiler optimization are formally verified. Tristan and Leroy [30–32] provides verified validators for instruction scheduling, software pipelining, and lazy code motion within CompCert; Gourdin et al. [22],Monniaux and Six [29],Six et al. [15] use block-level simulation to support verified validation of loop unrolling, loop invariant code motion, superblock scheduling, strength reduction and others within CompCert. All of these works focus on low-level RTL code, which is conceptually a control flow graph. These validation algorithms must synchronize two graphs correctly. To validate reordered instructions, they compare the summaries of subgraphs (such as basic blocks) obtained through symbolic execution, rather than directly checking Bernstein's conditions, which may require heavy dependence analysis.

7 Conclusions and Future Work

In this paper, we provide a well-designed verified validation framework for affine scheduling in polyhedral compilation, fully mechanized in Coq proof assistant. It is highly extensible, as we demonstrate by instantiating it with CInstr, a variant of CompCert's instruction language. Its core algorithm checks Bernstein's conditions for two input polyhedral models, which is complete and efficient enough to validate all 62 Pluto's tests as shown in our evaluation. We believe this work makes solid progress towards verified optimizing compilation.

As future work, it would be interesting to support advanced polyhedral techniques like tiling. Moreover, to seamlessly integrate polyhedral compilation into CompCert, we still need efficient extraction and its verification, which requires bridging the semantics gaps between C and polyhedral model [9,10].

Acknowledgments. We thank anonymous referees for their suggestions and comments on earlier versions of this paper. This work is supported in part by National Natural Science Foundation of China (NSFC) under Grant No. 62232015.

References

1. Bang, S., Nam, S., Chun, I., Jhoo, H.Y., Lee, J.: Smt-based translation validation for machine learning compiler. In: Computer Aided Verification: 34th International Conference, CAV 2022, Haifa, Israel, 7–10 August 2022, Proceedings, Part II, p. 386-407, Springer, Berlin (2022). https://doi.org/10.1007/978-3-031-13188-2_19
2. Bastoul, C.: Openscop: A specification and a library for data exchange in polyhedral compilation tools. Paris-Sud University, France (September, Technical Report (2011)
3. Bernstein, A.J.: Analysis of programs for parallel processing. IEEE Trans. Electron. Comput. **15**, 757–763 (1966). https://doi.org/10.1109/PGEC.1966.264565
4. Bondhugula, U., Hartono, A., Ramanujam, J., Sadayappan, P.: A practical automatic polyhedral parallelizer and locality optimizer. SIGPLAN Not. **43**(6), 101–113 (2008). https://doi.org/10.1145/1379022.1375595
5. Boulmé, S., Maréchaly, A., Monniaux, D., Périn, M., Yu, H.: The verified polyhedron library: an overview. In: 2018 20th International Symposium on Symbolic and Numeric Algorithms for Scientific Computing (SYNASC), pp. 9–17, September 2018. https://doi.org/10.1109/SYNASC.2018.00014
6. Chen, T., et al.: Tvm: an automated end-to-end optimizing compiler for deep learning. In: Proceedings of the 13th USENIX Conference on Operating Systems Design and Implementation, OSDI 2018, pp. 579–594, USENIX Association, USA (2018)
7. Clément, B., Cohen, A.: End-to-end translation validation for the halide language. Proc. ACM Program. Lang. **6**(OOPSLA1) (2022). https://doi.org/10.1145/3527328
8. Courant, N., Leroy, X.: Verified code generation for the polyhedral model. Proc. ACM Program. Lang. **5**(POPL) (2021). https://doi.org/10.1145/3434321
9. Cuervo Parrino, B., Narboux, J., Violard, E., Magaud, N.: Dealing with arithmetic overflows in the polyhedral model. In: Bondhugula, U., Loechner, V. (eds.) IMPACT 2012–2nd International Workshop on Polyhedral Compilation Techniques. Louis-Noel Pouchet, Paris, France, January 2012
10. Doerfert, J., Grosser, T., Hack, S.: Optimistic loop optimization. In: Proceedings of the 2017 International Symposium on Code Generation and Optimization, CGO 2017, pp. 292-304, IEEE Press (2017). https://doi.org/10.1109/CGO.2017.7863748
11. Feautrier, P.: Some efficient solutions to the affine scheduling problem: Part i. one-dimensional time. Int. J. Parall. Program. **21**(5), 313–348 (1992a). https://doi.org/10.1007/BF01407835

12. Feautrier, P.: Some efficient solutions to the affine scheduling problem. part ii. multidimensional time. Int. J. Parall. Program. **21**, 389–420 (1992b). https://doi.org/10.1007/BF01379404
13. Feautrier, P.: Bernstein's Conditions, pp. 130–134. Springer US, Boston, MA (2011).https://doi.org/10.1007/978-0-387-09766-4_521
14. Feautrier, P., Lengauer, C.: Polyhedron model. In: Padua, D. (ed.) Encyclopedia of Parallel Computing, pp. 1581–1592, Springer, Boston (2011). https://doi.org/10.1007/978-0-387-09766-4_502
15. Gourdin, L., Bonneau, B., Boulmé, S., Monniaux, D., Bérard, A.: Formally verifying optimizations with block simulations. Proc. ACM Program. Lang. **7**(OOPSLA2) (2023). https://doi.org/10.1145/3622799
16. Grosser, T., Zheng, H., Aloor, R., Simbürger, A., Größlinger, A., Pouchet, L.N.: Polly - polyhedral optimization in LLVM. In: Alias, C., Bastoul, C. (eds.) 1st International Workshop on Polyhedral Compilation Techniques (IMPACT). Chamonix, France (2011)
17. Jourdan, J.-H., Pottier, F., Leroy, X.: Validating $LR(1)$ parsers. In: Seidl, H. (ed.) ESOP 2012. LNCS, vol. 7211, pp. 397–416. Springer, Heidelberg (2012). https://doi.org/10.1007/978-3-642-28869-2_20
18. Leroy, X., Appel, A.W., Blazy, S., Stewart, G.: The CompCert memory model, version 2. Research report RR-7987, INRIA (Jun 2012)
19. Leroy, X., Blazy, S.: Formal verification of a C-like memory model and its uses for verifying program transformations. J. Autom. Reasoning **41**(1), 1–31 (2008). https://doi.org/10.1007/s10817-008-9099-0
20. Liu, A., Bernstein, G.L., Chlipala, A., Ragan-Kelley, J.: Verified tensor-program optimization via high-level scheduling rewrites. Proc. ACM Program. Lang. **6**(POPL) (2022). https://doi.org/10.1145/3498717
21. Livinskii, V., Babokin, D., Regehr, J.: Fuzzing loop optimizations in compilers for c++ and data-parallel languages. Proc. ACM Program. Lang. **7**(PLDI) (2023). https://doi.org/10.1145/3591295
22. Monniaux, D., Six, C.: Formally verified loop-invariant code motion and assorted optimizations. ACM Trans. Embed. Comput. Syst. **22**(1) (2022). https://doi.org/10.1145/3529507
23. Namjoshi, K.S., Singhania, N.: Loopy: programmable and formally verified loop transformations. In: Rival, X. (ed.) SAS 2016. LNCS, vol. 9837, pp. 383–402. Springer, Heidelberg (2016). https://doi.org/10.1007/978-3-662-53413-7_19
24. Pilkiewicz, A.: s2sloop: a validator for polyhedral transformations. https://github.com/pilki/s2sLoop (2010-2013)
25. Pop, S., Cohen, A., Bastoul, C., Girbal, S., Silber, G.A., Vasilache, N.: Graphite: polyhedral analyses and optimizations for GCC. In: Proceedings of the 2006 GCC Developers Summit, p. 2006 (2006)
26. Pouchet, L.N., Bondhugula, U., et al.: The polybench benchmarks. https://www.cs.colostate.edu/~pouchet/software/polybench/ (2010-2015)
27. Ragan-Kelley, J., et al.: Halide: decoupling algorithms from schedules for high-performance image processing. Commun. ACM **61**(1), 106–115 (2017). https://doi.org/10.1145/3150211
28. Rideau, S., Leroy, X.: Validating register allocation and spilling. In: Gupta, R. (ed.) CC 2010. LNCS, vol. 6011, pp. 224–243. Springer, Heidelberg (2010). https://doi.org/10.1007/978-3-642-11970-5_13
29. Six, C., Gourdin, L., Boulmé, S., Monniaux, D., Fasse, J., Nardino, N.: Formally verified superblock scheduling. In: Proceedings of the 11th ACM SIGPLAN Inter-

national Conference on Certified Programs and Proofs, CPP 2022, pp. 40–54, Association for Computing Machinery, New York, NY, USA (2022). https://doi.org/10.1145/3497775.3503679

30. Tristan, J.B., Leroy, X.: Formal verification of translation validators: a case study on instruction scheduling optimizations. SIGPLAN Not. **43**(1), 17–27 (2008). https://doi.org/10.1145/1328897.1328444
31. Tristan, J.B., Leroy, X.: Verified validation of lazy code motion. SIGPLAN Not. **44**(6), 316–326 (2009). https://doi.org/10.1145/1543135.1542512
32. Tristan, J.B., Leroy, X.: A simple, verified validator for software pipelining. In: Proceedings of the 37th Annual ACM SIGPLAN-SIGACT Symposium on Principles of Programming Languages, POPL 2010, pp. 83–92, Association for Computing Machinery, New York, NY, USA (2010). https://doi.org/10.1145/1706299.1706311
33. Verdoolaege, S., Guelton, S., Grosser, T., Cohen, A.: Schedule trees. In: Rajopadhye, S., Verdoolaege, S. (eds.) Proceedings of the 4th International Workshop on Polyhedral Compilation Techniques (IMPACT), Vienna, Austria, January 2014
34. Zhao, J., et al.: Akg: automatic kernel generation for neural processing units using polyhedral transformations. In: Proceedings of the 42nd ACM SIGPLAN International Conference on Programming Language Design and Implementation, PLDI 2021, pp. 1233–1248, Association for Computing Machinery, New York, NY, USA (2021). https://doi.org/10.1145/3453483.3454106

A Formally Verified Scheme for Security Protocols with the Operational Semantics of Strand Space

Yongjian Li[1], Hongjian Jiang[2], and Yongxin Zhao[3(✉)]

[1] Key Laboratory of System Software (Chinese Academy of Sciences) and State Key Laboratory of Computer Science, Institute of Software, Chinese Academy of Sciences, Beijing, China

[2] Max Planck Institute for Informatics, University of Kaiserslautern, Kaiserslautern, Germany

[3] Shanghai Key Laboratory of Trustworthy Computing, East China Normal University, Shanghai, China

yxzhao@sei.ecnu.edu.cn

Abstract. Security protocols are essential to ensure privacy, integrity, and authentication. However, to guarantee the security objectives of a protocol, formal tools are necessary. Currently, existing formal tools employ specific input languages to model protocols. Typically, protocols are presented in strand space specification format in textbooks, which depict the messages shared among trusted communication participants during a correct protocol operation. Strand space specifications prioritize conciseness and readability over formal preciseness, and their formal semantics are only considered and clarified in specific contexts. Therefore, a gap exists between strand space specifications and the modelling languages of formal tools. To address this issue, we propose a verified security scheme with the operational semantics of strand space. We successfully tested our framework on several typical protocol benchmarks using the model checker Murphi and identified potential attacks on them. In summary, our framework offers an innovative and comprehensible scheme for model checking security protocols.

1 Introduction

Security protocols are created to ensure security properties such as privacy, integrity, and authentication. These protocols typically consist of encrypted messages exchanged between two or more agents, often utilizing symmetric or asymmetric encryption. Nonetheless, designing these protocols is prone to errors, particularly in safety-critical areas. Notably, design flaws have been identified in established protocols such as 5G [1], WiFi WPA2 [2], and TLS [3]. Poorly designed protocols may be vulnerable to various malicious attacks.

The Alice&Bob [4] notation used in textbooks is an intuitive and readable way to specify a security protocol. This notation explicitly describes the protocol through a series of messages exchanged among the involved principals. For

W.-N. Chin and Z. Xu (Eds.): TASE 2024, LNCS 14777, pp. 306–323, 2024.
https://doi.org/10.1007/978-3-031-64626-3_18

example, the following notation expresses Alice's intention to send a message to Bob:

$$Alice \longrightarrow Bob : message$$

Strand space [5] offers a powerful and intuitive framework for analyzing the correctness of security protocols. Initially, security protocols were analyzed manually using this framework, but later, automatic tools such as Athena and the Isabelle theorem prover were adopted to assist with the analysis. However, the current strand space framework lacks an operational semantics for simulation or model checking.

Although a high-level notation like Alice&Bob provides helpful context and explanations for understanding the protocol's meaning, the specification of a security protocol is inherently complex and ambiguous. Thus, it is unsuitable for direct use in formal verification or code implementation. While the modelling language used in formal verification tools such as Murphi provides a detailed characterization of the protocol process, it is also low-level and challenging to use. Consequently, the formal modeling or manual implementation of security protocols is often a cumbersome and time-consuming process.

In this work, we introduce a formal verification framework to verify security protocols based on the operational semantics of strand space. Initially, we develop a parse towards strand space specifications which draws inspiration from Alice&Bob notation while being more concrete and closer to operational semantics. Subsequently, we propose the operational semantics of strand space to formally describe the behaviors of regular agents and intruders. To compile the intermediate format into a Murphi formal model, we present several novel strategies, including forward messaging, pattern matching, and reduction schemes. Finally, we successfully complete experiments on typical protocol benchmarks such as Needham-Schroeder [6], Otway-Rees [7], and Diffie Hellman protocols [8]. Overall, our framework provides an innovative and understandable approach to verify security protocols.

This paper contributes in the following ways:

- **Operational Semantics**: The paper proposes the first operational semantics of strand space, which provides a formal definition of the behavior of participants and ensures semantic consistency of the compilation between intermediate format and Murphi formal model. The paper also introduces a pattern matching procedure for formalizing the behavior of receiving message actions, which assists in formal reasoning within the operational semantics context.
- **Formal Model**: A formally verified scheme is developed to perform model checking on security protocols in Murphi based on the proposed operational semantics. This scheme includes the encoding of recursively defined messages and the modeling of the behavior of regular agents and the intruder in the Delvo-Yao security model [9]. Specifically, the operational semantics of strand space semantics is implemented in Murphi form to enable verification by Murphi.

- **Reduction Scheme**: When model checking a security protocol instance, the model constraints are solved for the concatenation and encryption strands, which construct only compound messages that are accepted by regular agents. The paper introduces two novel messages: X, representing an unknown message, and NULL, representing a null message, for formal reasoning in operational semantics. The reduction scheme helps avoid unnecessary state-space exploration, ensuring the state enumeration of large-scale instances such as the 5G EAP-TLS authentication protocol.

The paper is structured as follows: Sect. 2 reviews related works, while Sect. 3 provides a brief introduction to formal strand specification and strand space specification. Section 4 presents the operational semantics of strand space, and Sect. 5 reports the formal verification framework and demonstrates basic algorithms of the proposed theory. It is followed by experiments and evaluation in Sect. 6. Finally, Sect. 7 concludes the paper and discusses future work.

2 Related Work

There has been a lot of discussion on the formal verification of security protocols, and strand space is an important branch of this field due to its intuitiveness and conciseness. Authentication tests, introduced in [10] and [11] provide a formalization of the basic challenge-response style primitive, which is a building block for many protocols. Authentication tests offer a generally powerful technique to prove the correctness of authentication protocols, formalized in Isabelle in [12]. Automatic verification techniques based on strand space model have also been developed. Athena [13], an automatic tool for security protocol analysis, has incorporated the authentication tests. In [14], authentication tests are employed for automatic security protocol design. Works relating strand space theory to other semantics for security, such as multiset rewriting [15], distributed logics [16], process algebra [17], and multi-agent systems [18], have also been conducted. However, there is almost no research about associating strand space with a version of operational semantics. Our work fills this gap by providing an operational semantics that is close to the implementation of programming languages.

Recently, the research of Alice&Bob notation, which adopts a high-level of protocol specification, has received considerable attention. In [19], the authors generalized formal protocol specification languages and gave the formal semantics for a language based on algebraic reasoning. However, it does not adequately address the challenges of synchronizing message communication and expressing diverse perspectives within an encrypted message. In [20] the authors proposed a formal protocol specification language based on the popular Alice&Bob notation, i.e., AnBx. This specification language extends the formal semantics of Alice&Bob notation with a novel notation of forwarding channels, which inspires us to use a specific term to represent forwarded specific messages in the implementation process. In [21], Omar et al. formalized the language SPS and an automatic translation from real-world implementations and corresponding formal models. In [22], JC et al. proposed the computational primitive of XOR theory in strand space, which can be verified using formal methods. Considering the above, we propose a formal protocol specification, i.e., strand space specification.

Several developments have been made to convert Alice&Bob specifications into detailed implementations. For instance, Basin et al. [23] translated Alice&Bob protocol specifications into the input language of Tamarin. However, Tamarin [24] is a theorem prover that uses multiset rewriting to verify the correctness of the protocol, which requires the user to have a precise understanding of the protocol and provide auxiliary lemmas using heuristics. More recently, Yan et al. [25] integrated reinforcement learning techniques into Tamarin to verify security protocols dynamically. Another automatic symbolic protocol verifier, ProVerif [26], has been used to formally analyze the 5G protocol by hand in [27]. In this paper, we present a general modeling scheme for security protocols in Murphi that allows high-level strand space specifications to be compiled into a Murphi formal model based on the semantics of the strand space.

3 Preliminaries

3.1 Formal Strand Specification

Message Terms. To formally define security protocols, we must first specify the formalization of agents and messages. We identify three types of agents: *Server*, *Friend*, and *Spy*. Formally, the type of *Agent* is defined as follows:

$$\mathsf{Agent} ::= \mathsf{Server}(N) \mid \mathsf{Friend}(N) \mid \mathsf{Spy}$$

where the variable N ranges over natural numbers. In an asymmetric key protocol, an agent A possesses a public key denoted as $\mathsf{Pk}(A)$, which is known to all agents, and a private key denoted as $\mathsf{Sk}(A)$. The inverse key of $\mathsf{Sk}(A)$ is $\mathsf{Pk}(A)$, and vice versa. In a symmetric key protocol, each agent A has a long-term symmetric key denoted as $\mathsf{shrK}(A)$, and the inverse key of $\mathsf{shrK}(A)$ is itself. For convenience, we denote k^{-1} as the inverse key of k. We assume that (1) asymmetric keys and symmetric keys are distinct; (2) the functions shrK, Pk, and Sk are injective, meaning if $\mathsf{shrK}\ A = \mathsf{shrK}\ A'$, then $A = A'$. The set bad denotes the group of intruders, which includes at least the agent Spy. If an agent A is not in bad, then A is either Server or Friend.

The set of messages msg is defined using the following BNF notation:

$$\begin{array}{lll}
\mathsf{M} ::= \mathsf{Agent}(A) & \mid \mathsf{Nonce}(N) & \mid \mathsf{Key}(k) \\
\quad \mid \mathsf{MPair}(m_1, m_2) & \mid \mathsf{Crypt}(m, k) & \mid \mathsf{Hash}(m) \\
\quad \mid \mathsf{Exp}(m_1, m_2) & \mid \mathsf{Mod}(m_1, m_2) & \mid \mathsf{Sign}(m, k) \\
\quad \mid \mathsf{Number}(N) & \mid \mathsf{Tmp}(\mathsf{X}) & \mid \mathsf{NULL}
\end{array}$$

$$\begin{array}{lll}
\mathsf{K} ::= \mathsf{Pk}(A) & \mid \mathsf{Sk}(A) & \mid \mathsf{K}(A, B) \\
\quad \mid \mathsf{M} & &
\end{array}$$

In this notation, A and B are elements of the set Agent, while N and k are natural numbers, and K is a key. The message $\mathsf{MPair}(m_1, m_2)$ is a composite message consisting of m_1 and m_2, while $\mathsf{Crypt}(m, k)$ represents the encryption of message m with key k. For brevity, we use $\{\!|m|\!\}_k$ to denote $\mathsf{Crypt}(m, k)$, and $\{\!|m_1, \ldots, m_{n-1}, m_n|\!\}$ to denote $\mathsf{MPair}(m_1 \ldots \mathsf{MPair}(m_{n-1}, m_n))$. Additionally, $\mathsf{Hash}(m)$ and $\mathsf{Sign}(m, k)$ denote the hash and signature of message m using private key k. The messages $\mathsf{Mod}(m_1, m_2)$ and $\mathsf{Exp}(m_1, m_2)$ represent the messages $\{\!|m1, m2|\!\}_m$ and $\{\!|m1, m2|\!\}_e$, respectively, and support XOR theory. For formal reasoning, we introduce $\mathsf{Tmp(X)}$ to represent an unknown message that can match any message, and NULL to represent an empty message.

Extended Alice&Bob Specification. The Alice&Bob notation for the Otway-Rees protocol, which involves the distribution of a shared symmetric key by a trusted server, is shown below:

1. $\mathsf{A \rightarrow B : M, A, B, \{Na, M, A, B\}_{K(A,S)}}$
2. $\mathsf{B \rightarrow S : M, A, B, \{Na, M, A, B\}_{K(A,S)}, \{Nb, M, A, B\}_{K(B,S)}}$
3. $\mathsf{S \rightarrow B : \{Na, Nab\}_{K(A,S)}, \{Nb, Nab\}_{K(B,S)}}$
4. $\mathsf{B \rightarrow A : M, \{Na, Nab\}_{K(A,S)}}$

Subsequently, the overall structure of a formal extended alice&bob specification is shown in Fig. 1.

- **Knowledge** part defines the initial knowledge of the roles, which an agent must possess to start running a role. For the role *Init*, we introduce the function $\mathsf{initKnRole}(r)$ to represent its initial knowledge.
- **Agents** block gives the actions and freshness terms of Agents, and the form of the agent is a triples (agent, message list, actionlist), send action of agents is as follows:

$$[seq] + \ B\ (m_1, \cdots, m_n) : msg$$

  where agent A generates a composed message msg with (usually) atomic messages m_1, $\cdots$, m_n, then intends msg to agent B. Here m in message list means that m originating from agent A. The send actions denotes the agent sends message msg on the channel seq. And receive action is as follow:

$$[seq] - : msg$$

  which denotes the agent receives the message msg from the channel seq.
- **Goals** block specifies the security properties that a protocol must ensure. Our study concentrates on establishing secrecy and (non-) injective agreement. Secrecy implies that the adversary cannot obtain any information from the protocol execution, while (non-) injective agreement necessitates that agents share identical parameter values of the protocols.
- **Environment** block specifies a protocol instance and defines a strand or configuration of a session for an agent acting as the role *Init*. It provides the actual parameters to instantiate the formal atomic parameters defined in the Knowledge block.

```
Protocol OTWAY-REES:
Knowledge:(* Intitial Knowledge*)
Init : A, B, S, Na, M
Resp : B, S, Nb
Server : S, Nab

Agents: (* Play the Role*)
Init(A,B,M,Na,S)
[1]+ : B, (Na, M, A, B) : M, A, B, {|Na, M, A, B|}_K(A,S)
[4]- : {|Na, Nab|}_K(A,S)

Resp(B,S,Nb)
[1]- : M, A, B, H
[2]+ : S, (Nb) : M, A, B, H, {|Nb, M, A, B|}_K(B,S)
[3]- : H', {|Nb, Nab|}_K(B,S)
[4]+ : A, ( ) : H'

Server(S,Nab)
[2]- : M, A, B, {|Na, M, A, B|}_K(A,S), {|Nb, M, A, B|}_K(B,S)
[3]+ : B, (Nab) : {|Na, Nab|}_K(A,S), {|Nb, Nab|}_K(B,S)

Goals: (*Security Goals*)
[secrecy] Nab secret of < A, B, S >
[weakB] B non-injectively agrees with A on Na

Environments: (*Protocol instance*)
[str1]Init[1] :< Alice, Intruder, Server, Na, M >
[str2]Resp[1] :< Intruder, Server, Nb >
[str3]Server[1] :< Server, Nab >
end
```

Fig. 1. The Otway-rees Protocol in extended alice&bob specification

Subterms, Message Pattern, Substitutions. $m_1 \sqsubset m_2$ denotes that m_1 is a sub-term of m_2. We define $\mathsf{subterms}(S) = \{m | \exists m'.m' \in S \wedge m \sqsubset m'\}$. For two messages m_1 and m_2, $\mathsf{match}(m_1, m_2)$ is used to inductively determine whether they have the same pattern.

- If both agents exchange the same atomic messages, such as keys, nonces, or agent identities;
- If both are of concatented messages $\{\!|m_1; m_2|\!\}$ and $\{\!|m'_1; m'_2|\!\}$, then $\mathsf{match}(m_1, m'_1)$, and $\mathsf{match}(m_2, m'_2)$;
- if both are of encrypted messages $\{\!|m|\!\}_k$ and $\{\!|m'|\!\}_{k'}$, then $\mathsf{match}(k_1, k'_1)$, and $\mathsf{match}(m_1, m'_1)$.

Let $[x_i \mapsto y_i]_{i=1}^n$ denote a list of substitutions, where x_i and y_i are the same kind of atomic messages, we define $\mathsf{actSub}(m)[x_i \mapsto y_i]_{i=1}^n$ substitutes each occurrence of x_i in m by y_i. For instance, the substitutes towards the concatenated message $\mathsf{actSub}(\{\!|M, A, B, \{\!|Na, M, A, B|\!\}_{K(A,S)}|\!\})[Na \mapsto Na, A \mapsto Alice, B \mapsto Bob, M \mapsto M, S \mapsto Bob] \equiv \{\!|M, Alice, Bob, \{\!|Na, M, Alice, Bob|\!\}_{K(Alice,Bob)}|\!\}$.

3.2 Strand Space

A security protocol specifies a sequence of message-exchanged events among agents. In strand space theory, an agent's action during a protocol execution comprises sending or receiving messages. The set of signs $\mathsf{Sign} = \{+, -\}$ represents sending and receiving actions, respectively. An event is a pair (τ, m), where $\tau \in \mathsf{Sign}$. Regular and intruder strands are two types of standard strands.

Definition 1. *A strand represents a sequence of an agent's actions in a particular protocol run, and is an instance of a role. A strand space is a mapping from a strand set Σ to a trace $SP : \Sigma \Longrightarrow (Sign \times Msg)$ list, where Msg is the type of all messages. For a strand (list) str, we define $\mathsf{hd}(str)$ and $\mathsf{tl}(str)$ to be the head and tail of str.*

A strand space Σ represents a collection of strands that correspond to the principals taking part in the protocol.

- The relation $n \Longrightarrow n'$ represents the inner-strand communication. It holds between nodes n and n' if $n = (s, i)$ and $n' = (s, i + 1)$.
- The relation $n \longrightarrow n'$ represents the inter-strand communication. The inter-strand communication $(s_{Init}, 1) \longrightarrow (s_{Resp}, 1)$ represents that role $Init$ is sending a message $\{\!|M, A, B, \{\!|Na, M, A, B|\!\}_{K(A,S)}|\!\}$ out, and role $Resp$ will finally receive a message like this.

3.3 Murphi

Murphi is an explicit state model checker that employs its own input language and supports the *guard* $\longrightarrow$ *action* notation. It has been successfully applied to various industrial protocols, particularly in cache coherence protocols and multiprocessor memory models [28], such as the German and Flash protocols. The tool can abstract a system's behavior and simulate its running rules. The Murphi model checker includes a formal verifier that uses explicit state enumeration, whose performance is directly related to the number of states. During the enumeration, encountered states are saved in a global hash table, and already existing states in the table are not expanded. The symmetric reduction protocol algorithm [29] has effectively reduced the number of states of verified protocols.

The Murphi input language includes declarations of constants, data types, global variables, initialization part, transition rule part, and property part. The transition rule part is the most crucial and complicated component, defining the transition from one state to another. A transition rule comprises two parts: guard and action. The action part executes only if the predicates in the guard are satisfiable. Murphi model checker explores the entire state space explicitly until no new reachable state can be discovered or the properties fail to hold on to the protocol. The set of all possible reachable states is known as the reachable state set. Murphi starts from the initial state specified in the initialization part and randomly selects a transition rule whose guard is satisfied and executes the corresponding action. Desired protocol properties are specified as invariants in Murphi, which must hold in every reachable state. The verification process involves the verifier reading the state variables in each new state, halting and providing an error message in case of false results, and halting without an error message if a state has no successor other than itself.

4 Operational Semantics of Strand Space

A protocol session is a concurrent execution of several regular strands $(i_1, str_1) \mid \cdots \mid (i_n, str_n)$ representing an agent, along with implicit intruder strands representing the Spy. Note that the intruder strands are not explicitly included in a session. Instead, the Spy controls all network traffic, intercepts all protocol messages m generated by a regular strand, and adds them to its knowledge. The Spy utilizes this knowledge to make deductions and send fake messages to regular agents. Each agent possesses local storage to maintain the values of all protocol variables. The Spy's local variable Kn stores its knowledge, i.e., the set of currently known messages. The protocol's state is defined by the terms *Init* and *Run*.

Init. For all instances i of a strand, any variable v with type $\mathcal{T}_v$, the function σ is a state mapping between strand i and variable v to a specific value.

$$\sigma(i)(v) = \begin{cases} [v/i] & \text{if} \, v \text{is in} \, \mathsf{initKnRole(ofAgent(i))} \\ \mathsf{NULL} & \text{otherwise} \end{cases}$$

where variable v substitutes on strand i, and NULL represents the absence of a value.

Run. Prior to introducing the operational semantics, it is necessary to have a preliminary function $\mathsf{update}(s, i, m, M)$ that uses pattern matching to define the semantics of the Recv action.

Function $\mathsf{update}(s, i, m, M)$ is defined recursively to update the local copies of the variables of a strand i by pattern matching m and M at some state s, as shown in the following equation. Here, m is a message pattern composed of atomic variables, while M is a message composed of atomic values. If m and M do not belong to the same pattern, the matching will fail, and the function will return $\perp$, indicating a deadlock state. We omit similar cases for random nonce message, encrypted message, concatenation message and so on here.

$$\mathsf{update}(s, i, m, M) = \begin{cases} \mathsf{actSub}(i)[m \mapsto M] & \text{if} \, \sigma_m^i = \mathsf{X} \\ s & \text{if} \, \sigma_m^i = M \\ \perp & \text{otherwise} \end{cases}$$

In this context, we use the notation $[\![v]\!]_s^i$ to represent the value of local variable v in state s as seen by agent i. Similarly, we use $[\![m]\!]_s^i$ to denote the value of message m in state s as seen by agent i. We can also define a function $\mathsf{curRecvs}(s, i, act)$to represent a message that agent i is currently waiting to receive, given that it is performing action act in state s.

$$\mathsf{curRecvs}(s, i, act) = \begin{cases} \mathsf{NULL} \text{ if} act = (+, m) \\ [\![m]\!]_s^i \text{ if} act = (-, m) \end{cases}$$

Semantics. In our theory, agents communicate with each other through a public channel, which can be intercepted by an intruder. We formalize the configuration of a running session using a quadruple $<p, s, m, L>$. The parallel composition of pairs p is expressed as (i, str), where i is a strand identifier and str is a strand. State s maps each variable to its value from the point of view of all agents. The variable m can be a message put in the public channel or NULL, indicating that the channel is empty. Finally, L is a list (or multiset) of messages that are currently available for some regular agents i to receive.

Table 1. The Strand Transition Rules Standard Agent

$$\textbf{(Send)}\ \frac{s \neq \bot; \mathsf{hd}(str) = (+, m)}{< (i, str), s, \mathsf{NULL}, L > \rightarrow < (i, \mathsf{tl}(str)), s, [\![m]\!]_s^i, add(L, \mathsf{cur}(s, i, \mathsf{hd}(\mathsf{tl}(str)))) >}$$

$$\textbf{(Recv)}\ \frac{s \neq \bot; hd(str) = (-, m)}{< (i, str), s, M, L > \rightarrow < (i, \mathsf{tl}(str)), \mathsf{update}(s, i, m, M), \mathsf{NULL}, L' >}$$

$$\textbf{(Parl)}\ \frac{(p_1, str_1), s, M_1, L \rightarrow (p_1, str_1'), s', M_1', L'}{< (p_1 \| p_2, str_1 \| str_2), s, M_1, L > \rightarrow < (p_1 \| p_2, str_1' \| str_2), s', M_1', L' >}$$

The proof rules governing the transition system for standard strands are illustrated in Table 1. In the initial row of *Send*, the process of transmitting a message via the public channel is delineated. The *Recv* rule serves to gather the anticipated message from the channel and subsequently update the local knowledge. Consequently, the channel becomes clear following the execution of the Recv action. Additionally, the *Parl* rule facilitates the introduction of multiple instances of strands, enabling them to operate concurrently within the system.

Table 2 delineates the transition calculus governing the intruder's specialized strand instance. The *Emit* rule, akin to the *Send* rule, injects message m into the communication channel within Kn, albeit with the intention of espionage, as the recipient becomes the intruder. The *Flush* rule, on the other hand, is employed to monitor messages on the public channel and update the intruder's local knowledge accordingly. The subsequent four rules address actions such as splitting concatenated messages, handling connectionist atomic messages, decrypting encrypted messages, and managing encrypted messages. Additionally,

Table 2. The Strand Transition Rules for Penerator

$$\textbf{(Emit)}\ \frac{s \neq \bot; \exists m.M \in [\![\mathsf{Kn}]\!]_s^{spy} \wedge M \in L \wedge match(m, M)}{<(i', str), s, \mathsf{NULL}, L> \rightarrow <(i', str), s, m, L>}$$

$$\textbf{(Flush)}\ \frac{s \neq \bot}{<(i', str), s, M, L> \rightarrow <(i', str), s(i)[\mathsf{Kn} \rightsquigarrow [\![\mathsf{Kn}]\!]_s^{spy} \cup \{M\}], \mathsf{NULL}, L>}$$

$$\textbf{(Sep)}\ \frac{s \neq \bot, \{\!|m_1; m_2|\!\} \in [\![\mathsf{Kn}]\!]_s^{spy}, m_1 \notin [\![\mathsf{Kn}]\!]_s^{spy} \vee m_2 \notin [\![\mathsf{Kn}]\!]_s^{spy}}{<(i', str), st, \mathsf{NULL}, L> \rightarrow <(i', str), s(i)[\mathsf{Kn} \rightsquigarrow [\![\mathsf{Kn}]\!]_s^{spy} \cup \{m_1, m_2\}], \mathsf{NULL}, L>}$$

$$\textbf{(Cat)}\ \frac{s \neq \bot, m_1, m_2 \in [\![\mathsf{Kn}]\!]_s^{spy}, \{\!|m_1; m_2|\!\} \notin [\![\mathsf{Kn}]\!]_s^{spy}, \{\!|m_1; m_2|\!\} \in \mathsf{sub}(\mathsf{cur}(L))}{<(i', str), s, \mathsf{NULL}, L> \rightarrow <(i', str), s(i)[\mathsf{Kn} \rightsquigarrow [\![\mathsf{Kn}]\!]_s^{spy} \cup \{\{\!|m_1; m_2|\!\}\}], \mathsf{NULL}, L>}$$

$$\textbf{(Dec)}\ \frac{s \neq \bot, \{\!|m|\!\}_k \in [\![\mathsf{Kn}]\!]_s^{spy}, m \notin [\![\mathsf{Kn}]\!]_s^{spy}, k^{-1} \in [\![\mathsf{Kn}]\!]_s^{spy}}{<(i', str), s, \mathsf{NULL}, L> \rightarrow <(i', str), s(i)[\mathsf{Kn} \rightsquigarrow [\![\mathsf{Kn}]\!]_s^{spy} \cup \{m\}], \mathsf{NULL}, L} >$$

$$\textbf{(Enc)}\ \frac{s \neq \bot, m \in s(spy)(\mathsf{Kn}), k \in [\![\mathsf{Kn}]\!]_s^{spy}, \{\!|m|\!\}_k \notin [\![\mathsf{Kn}]\!]_s^{spy}, \{\!|m|\!\}_k \in \mathsf{sub}(\mathsf{cur}(L))}{<(i', str), s, \mathsf{NULL}, L> \rightarrow <(i', str), s(spy)[\mathsf{Kn} \rightsquigarrow [\![\mathsf{Kn}]\!]_s^{spy} \cup \{\{\!|m|\!\}_k\}], \mathsf{NULL}, L>}$$

$$\textbf{(Mod)}\ \frac{s \neq \bot, m_1, m_2 \in [\![\mathsf{Kn}]\!]_s^{spy}, \{\!|m1, m2|\!\}_m \notin [\![\mathsf{Kn}]\!]_s^{spy}, \{\!|m1, m2|\!\}_m \in \mathsf{sub}(\mathsf{cur}(L))}{<(i', str), s, \mathsf{NULL}, L> \rightarrow <(i', str), s(spy)[\mathsf{Kn} \rightsquigarrow [\![\mathsf{Kn}]\!]_s^{spy} \cup \{\!|m1, m2|\!\}_m], \mathsf{NULL}, L>}$$

$$\textbf{(Exp)}\ \frac{s \neq \bot, m_1, m_2 \in [\![\mathsf{Kn}]\!]_s^{spy}, \{\!|m1, m2|\!\}_e \notin [\![\mathsf{Kn}]\!]_s^{spy}, \{\!|m1, m2|\!\}_e \in \mathsf{sub}(\mathsf{cur}(L))}{<(i', str), s, \mathsf{NULL}, L> \rightarrow <(i', str), s(spy)[\mathsf{Kn} \rightsquigarrow [\![\mathsf{Kn}]\!]_s^{spy} \cup \{\!|m1, m2|\!\}_e], \mathsf{NULL}, L>}$$

to mitigate the production of redundant messages, it is stipulated that m_k must be a constituent of a message receivable by a regular agent. The Mod and Exp rules empower the intruder to execute exponentiation operations and generate a message m_1, m_{2_e}, where m_1 signifies the exponentiation group's generator. Subsequently, the intruder assimilates this newly formed message into Kn.

5 The Verification Framework

In this section, we delve into a comprehensive explanation of the formally verified security scheme. Illustrated in Fig. 2, our verification tool comprises two intuitive components: a front-end and a back-end. The front-end is tasked with receiving the formalization of the Alice& Bob specification and the security property. Within this component, a parser is employed to translate the input into an intermediate strand space format.

Meanwhile, the back-end serves as an oracle, employing the Murphi model checker for verification purposes. It fulfills two critical functions: (a) validating whether the generated model during the compilation procedure adheres to the specified property, and (b) in cases where the security property is not satisfied, generating a counter-example for the front-end. Subsequently, the protocol designer can review the protocol details and adjust the specification to ensure compliance with the security property.

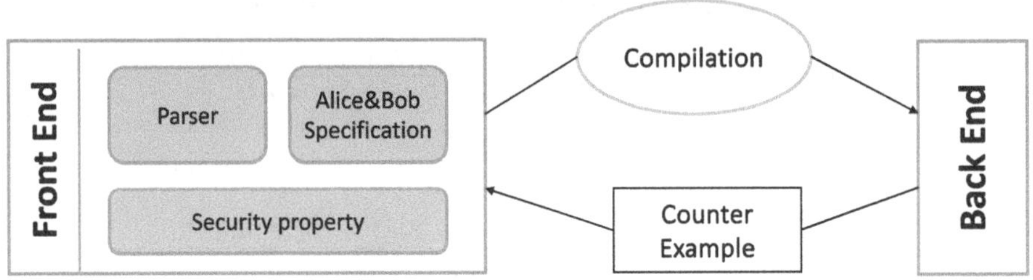

Fig. 2. The Workflow of Formal Verification Framework

The operational semantics provided in last section enable the linkage between the strand space format and the Murphi formal model, facilitating the compilation of the behaviors of regular and intruder strands into the Murphi formal model. Also, Li et al. [30] has already proved the correctness of operational semantics using Isabelle, which as the theoretical cornerstone of our verification tool. Subsequently, the Murphi model checker leverages this formal model to verify the security protocol. Interested readers may refer to our previous work [31], where we introduced a valuable translator that converts each segment of the Alice & Bob specification into Murphi Mode. However, when dealing with large and practical security protocols, the resulting model lacks guarantees of correctness and verification efficiency. Therefore, We optimize the efficiency of model based on the operational semantics and below algorithms. Now we elaborate two algorithms among the parse phase and compilation phase.

Parse Phase: Extended Alice&Bob specifications explicitly define the message-exchanged communication among regular agents, and can also simulate the protocols' real-world environment. We developed an Ocaml parser for the extended Alice&Bob specification language used in security protocols, which translates the specification into the strand space format. The extended Alice&Bob specification employs concepts from the Alice&Bob notation for modeling messages, and is closely related to operational semantics.

Algorithm 1 delineates the straightforward parsing procedure, serving as the algorithm's entry point with a single parameter: the strand space specification context c. Within the while loop of the PARSING_PROCEDURE, the computation iterative gathers basic terminologies t (such as messages, agents, and channels), standard regular strands s, generator strands ps, and security properties p from the context c.

Implemented in Ocaml utilizing ocamllex and ocamlyacc, the algorithm proceeds as follows:

1. Initialization of variables t, s, ps, and p to empty sets, denoting variables refined by preceding loops.
2. Update of the basic message term from the context's knowledge when the context is non-empty. Subsequently, the remaining variables are updated. For agents in the context, instantiation of their names from the environment of c

to regular strands occurs when agents exist and do not belong to the spy set, with the addition of action lists from the agent block. Similarly, for generator strands, when agents belong to the spy set, the intruder's action lists are appended to the *ps*(*spy*) set.

3. Handling of specified security properties in the goals block, treating secrecy and agreement properties differently. The presence of the "secret" keyword in the clause of *c.goal* indicates a secrecy property, added to the *p.secrecy* set; otherwise, it is included in the *p.agreement* set.
4. Conclusion of the loop body updates the sets t, s, ps, and p, refining them for use as input in the compilation procedure.

This algorithm facilitates the parsing of key components necessary for subsequent compilation, streamlining the process for verification purposes.

Algorithm 1. The algorithm of parsing

```
procedure PARSING_PROCEDURE(Context c)
    t = ∅; s = ∅; ps = ∅; p = ∅
    while c ≠ ∅ do
        t ← t ∪ c.knowledge
        while c.agent ≠ ∅ and c.agent ≠ spy do
            s(env[agent]).action_list ← c.agent.action_list
        end while
        while c.agent ≠ ∅ and c.agent = spy do
            ps(spy).als ← c.agent.action_list
        end while
        while c.goal ≠ ∅ do
            if secret ∈ c.goal then
                p.secrecy ← p.secrecy ∪ c.goal
            else if agreement ∈ g then
                p.agreement ← p.agreement ∪ c.goal
            end if
        end while
    end while
    return (t, s, ps, p)
end procedure
```

Certainly, Algorithm 1 leverages the extended context of the Alice& Bob specification, establishing a crucial link between the specification and the formal model. This linkage ensures semantic consistency, allowing for a seamless transition from the extended specification to the formal model.

In the pursuit of automatically discovering protocol flaws, the generator strands operate within the framework of the Dolev-Yao attacker model. Within this model, intruders interact with regular strands through a sequence of cryptographic operations. By incorporating this model into the parsing algorithm, potential vulnerabilities can be systematically identified and addressed.

Compilation: Consider a strand space $\Sigma = (\mathcal{A}, \mathcal{C}, \mathcal{P})$, where $\mathcal{A}$ contains the possible messages that can be exchanged between principals in a protocol, and $\mathcal{C}$ is a finite subgraph made up of edges to express the causal dependencies of the nodes and $\mathcal{P}$ represents the security properties that the model should satisfy. The goal of the compilation process is to convert a strand space Σ into a Murphi model M. As previously mentioned, the Murphi model consists of four parts: $\mathcal{A}$ for declarations, R for transition rules, I for initial states, and ϕ for invariants. Before compiling the strands into a Murphi formal model, extended Alice&Bob specifications are parsed into a strand space format.

Algorithm 2. The algorithm of compilation

procedure ENCODE_MURPHI_MODEL(σ, t, s, ps, p)
    while $\sigma \neq \emptyset$ **do**
        while $t \neq \emptyset$ **do**
            Transform t into Murphi declaration part, role, channel, message, emit flag, states et cl.
        end while
        while $s \neq \emptyset$ or $ps \neq \emptyset$ **do**
            Transform agent stand s and penerator starnd ps action list into guard-command rules
        end while
        while $p.secrecy \neq \emptyset$ or $p.agreement \neq \emptyset$ **do**
            Collect and rewrite security properties into invariant formalization.
        end while
        Encode builtin part of model(construct, destruct and match et cl) into procedure formalization.
    end while
end procedure

To encode the corresponding Murphi model, Algorithm 2 is proposed. It begins by analyzing whether the context σ is empty. If σ is indeed empty, indicating the presence of syntax errors within the strand space specification, the model generation process is unnecessary. Otherwise, the algorithm proceeds as follows:

1. Encoding of basic terms t in strand space format into elaborated datatypes, such as message, agent, and nonce, which are pivotal for defining transition rules.
2. Specification of the behavior of regular agents and intruders based on the operational semantics of strand space. Guards represent premises, while actions denote conclusions, collected from strands s and ps.
3. Transformation of the security property p into predicates. If p is not empty, secrecy properties ($p.secrecy$) and agreement properties ($p.agreement$) are converted into predicates that evaluate the state variables across all generated states.

6 Verification Towards 5G EAP-TLS Protocol

In this section, we assessed the performance of our verified security protocol scheme by examining the Extensible Authentication Protocol (EAP) protocols developed by the 3rd Generation Partnership Project (3GPP) group [32]. Our focus was particularly on the EAP-TLS protocol, designed to authenticate subscribers in constrained environments such as private networks or Internet of Things (IoT) deployments.

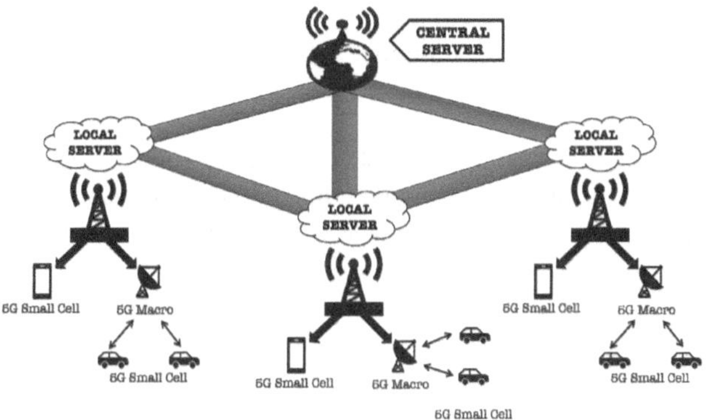

Fig. 3. 5G Network Architecture

In Fig. 3, we model the EAP-TLS protocol using the extended Alice& Bob specification, involving up to 18 message exchanges among four participants, and generate the model using our verification framework. There are four roles among the protocol: User Equipment (UE), Security Anchor Function (SEAF), Authentication Server Function (AUSF) and Unified Data Management (UDM). Our focus lies in verifying two critical security properties: ensuring the secrecy of the pre-master key (*prekey*) among the four participants and guaranteeing non-injective agreement between AUSF and UE for nonce ausf. Interesting readers could refer to link https://github.com/StrandSpace2Murphi/StrandSpace2Murphi/blob/main/image/EAP-TLS.png.

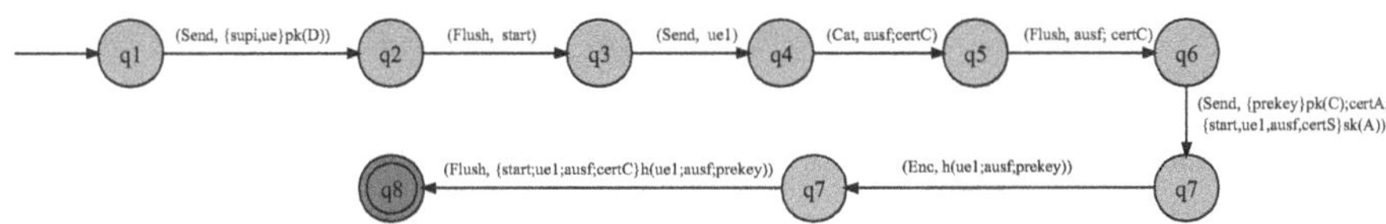

Fig. 4. The Counter Example Strands of Weak-agreement

Running with the model, we succeed to find two vulnerabilities. A counter example to the weak-agreement property is depicted in Fig. 4 in automaton formalization. Firstly, A signature message containing the adversary's hash key was transmitted to the UE. Consequently, determining the message's origin - whether it originated from the adversary or the SEAF. This scenario ultimately enabled the adversary to intercept the UE's secrecy in the final state.

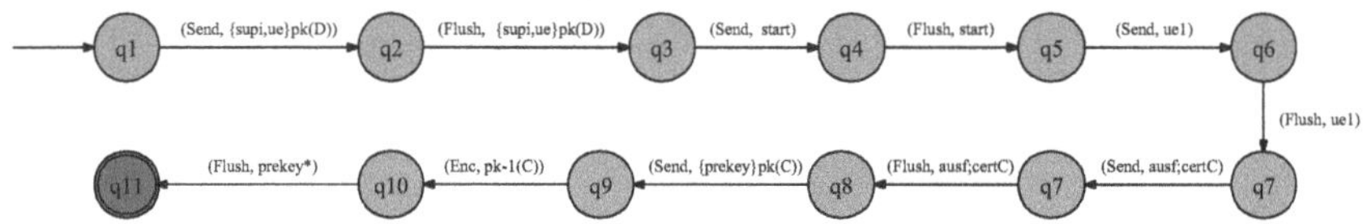

Fig. 5. The Counter Example Strands of Privace of Prekey

Figure 5 illustrates a privacy attack exploiting the adversary's inability to decrypt the pre-master key *prekey*. The counter example path is almost identical to that of man-in-the-middle attack, where the attack ecrypts using known keys from Key K to obtain the pre-master key *prekey*.

The evaluations were conducted on an Intel Core i7-10510U CPU at 1.8 GHz with 32 GB of RAM running on Windows 10. And the results are presented in Table 3.

Table 3. Verification Evaluation

Protocols	Security Property	Verified	Time(s)
Needham-Schroder	secrecy(Nb)	False	0.10
	weakB(Na)	False	
Lowe's Needham-Schroder	secrecy(Nb)	True	0.10
	weakB(Na)	True	
Diffie-Hellman key exchange	secrecy(Na)	False	0.10
Otway – Rees	secrecy(Kab)	True	2.13
CCITT X.509(1)	secrecy(Ya)	False	0.21
	weakB(Xa)	False	0.84
	weakA(Ya)	False	
CCITT X.509(1c)	weakB(Xa)	True	0.45
	weakA(Ya)	True	
Woo and Lam Pi	secrecy(Nb)	False	0.10
Andrew Secure RPC	secrecy(Kab)	False	2.77
EAP-TLS authentication	secrecy(prekey)	False	1.21
	weakC	False	51.50
EAP-AKA authentication	secrecy(snn)	True	1.50

7 Conclusion and Future Work

In this paper, we propose a novel operational semantics to ensure semantic consistency between the strand space specification and the generated formal model. The strand space specification, which uses uninterpreted messages and mathematical operations in combination with Alice&Bob notation, can handle complex protocols. We compile the strand space specification into the Murϕ formal model, with operational semantics serving as the cornerstone of the formal model. Our framework has been successfully applied to both classical security benchmarks and real-world examples.

Our future work involves extending the framework to prove the correctness of unbound sessions in strand space theory and compiling high-level strand space specifications into Isabelle. We plan to use the general results of authentication tests to prove authentication and secrecy properties of the protocol and enhance the intruder's inference efficiency within our framework, based on the mechanical formalization of strand space in Isabelle. Additionally, we aim to develop techniques or heuristics to improve the intruder's inference efficiency. Finally, a good operational semantics of a security protocol language is the first step towards a verified implementation in C++/Java [33]. Therefore, we will implement a verified strand space in C++/Java.

Acknowledgements. Yongjian Li is supported by the Strategic Priority Research Program of the Chinese Academy of Sciences, Grant No. XDA0320000 and XDA0320300. Yongxin Zhao is supported by National Natural Science Foundation of China Projects (No. 92370201), the "Digital Silk Road" Shanghai International Joint Lab of Trustworthy Intelligent Software (Grant No. 22510750100), and Shanghai Trusted Industry Internet Software Collaborative Innovation Center.

References

1. Basin, D., Dreier, J., Hirschi, L., Radomirovic, S., Sasse, R., Stettler, V.: A formal analysis of 5g authentication. In: Proceedings of the 2018 ACM SIGSAC Conference on Computer and Communications Security, pp. 1383–1396 (2018)
2. Vanhoef, M., Piessens, F.: Key reinstallation attacks: Forcing nonce reuse in wpa2. In: Proceedings of the 2017 ACM SIGSAC Conference on Computer and Communications Security, pp. 1313–1328 (2017)
3. Cremers, C., Horvat, M., Scott, S., van der Merwe, T.: Automated analysis and verification of TLS 1.3: 0-RTT, resumption and delayed authentication. IEEE Symp. Secur. Priv. (SP) **2016**, 470–485 (2016)
4. Rivest, R., Shamir, A., Adleman, L.: A method for obtaining digital signatures and public-key cryptosystems. Commun. ACM **21**, 120–126 (1978)
5. Thayer, F.J., Herzog, J.C., Guttman, J.D.: Strand spaces: why is a security protocol correct? In: Proceedings of 19th IEEE Symposium on Security and Privacy, pp. 96–109. IEEE CS (1998)
6. Needham, R.M., Schroeder, M.D.: Using encryption for authentication in large networks of computers. Commun. ACM **21**(12), 993–999 (1978)
7. Otway, D., Rees, O.: Efficient and timely mutual authentication. ACM SIGOPS Oper. Syst. Rev. **21**(1), 8–10 (1987)

8. Merkle, R.C.: Secure communications over insecure channels. Commun. ACM **21**(4), 294–299 (1978)
9. Dolev, D., Yao, A.: On the security of public key protocols. IEEE Trans. Inf. Theory **29**(2), 198–208 (1983)
10. Guttman, J.D., Thayer, F.J.: Authentication tests. In: Proceedings of 12th IEEE Symposium on Security and Privacy, pp. 96–109. IEEE CS (2001)
11. Guttman, J.D., Javier Thayer, F.: Authentication tests and the structure of bundles. Theor. Comput. Sci. **283**(2), 333–380 (2002)
12. Li, Y., Pang, J.: An inductive approach to strand spaces. Formal Aspects Comput. **25**(4), 465–501 (2013). https://doi.org/10.1007/s00165-011-0187-2
13. Song, D.X.: Athena: a new efficient automated checker for security protocol analysis. In: Proceedings of 12th IEEE Computer Security Foundations Workshop, pp. 192–202. IEEE CS (1999)
14. Perrig, A., Song, D.X. Looking for diamonds in the desert: extending automatic protocol generation to three-party authentication and key agreement protocols. In Proceedings of 13th IEEE Computer Security Foundations Workshop, pp. 64–76. IEEE CS (2000)
15. Cervesato, I., Durgin, N., Lincoln, P., Mitchell, J., Scedrov, A.: A comparison between strand spaces and multiset rewriting for security protocol analysis. In: Okada, M., Pierce, B.C., Scedrov, A., Tokuda, H., Yonezawa, A. (eds.) ISSS 2002. LNCS, vol. 2609, pp. 356–383. Springer, Heidelberg (2003). https://doi.org/10.1007/3-540-36532-X_22
16. Caleiro, C., Viganó, L., Basin, D.: Relating strand spaces and distributed temporal logic for security protocol analysis. Logic J. IGPL **13**(6), 637–663 (2005). https://doi.org/10.1093/jigpal/jzi048
17. Yang, F., Escobar, S., Meadows, C., Meseguer, J., Santiago, S.: Strand spaces with choice via a process algebra semantics. In: Proceedings of the 18th International Symposium on Principles and Practice of Declarative Programming, ser. PPDP 2016. New York, NY, USA, Association for Computing Machinery, pp. 76–89 (2016). https://doi.org/10.1145/2967973.2968609
18. Halpern, J.Y., Pucella, R.: On the relationship between strand spaces and multi-agent systems. ACM Trans. Inf. Syst. Secur. **6**(1), 43–70 (2003). https://doi.org/10.1145/605434.605436
19. Mödersheim, S.: Algebraic properties in alice and bob notation. In: 2009 International Conference on Availability, Reliability and Security, pp. 433–440. IEEE (2009)
20. Bugliesi, M., Calzavara, S., Mödersheim, S., Modesti, P.: Security protocol specification and verification with ANBX. J. Inf. Secur. Appl. **30**, 46–63 (2016)
21. Almousa, O., Mödersheim, S., Viganò, L.: Alice and bob: reconciling formal models and implementation. In: Bodei, C., Ferrari, G.-L., Priami, C. (eds.) Programming Languages with Applications to Biology and Security. LNCS, vol. 9465, pp. 66–85. Springer, Cham (2015). https://doi.org/10.1007/978-3-319-25527-9_7
22. Herzog, J.C.: The diffie-hellman key-agreement scheme in the strand-space model. In: 16th IEEE Computer Security Foundations Workshop, Proceedings. IEEE vol. **2003**, pp. 234–247 (2003)
23. Keller, M., Basin, P.D.D.: Converting alice&bob protocol specifications to tamarin, Ph.D. dissertation, Bachelor's thesis, ETH Zurich 2014. https://infsec.ethz.ch/research/software/anb.html (2014)

24. Meier, S., Schmidt, B., Cremers, C., Basin, D.: The TAMARIN prover for the symbolic analysis of security protocols. In: Sharygina, N., Veith, H. (eds.) CAV 2013. LNCS, vol. 8044, pp. 696–701. Springer, Heidelberg (2013). https://doi.org/10.1007/978-3-642-39799-8_48
25. Xiong, Y., Su, C., Huang, W., Miao, F., Wang, W., Ouyang, H.: Smartverif: push the limit of automation capability of verifying security protocols by dynamic strategies. In: 29th USENIX Security Symposium (USENIX Security 20). USENIX Association, pp. 253–270, August 2020. https://www.usenix.org/conference/usenixsecurity20/presentation/xiong
26. Blanchet, B.: Proverif automatic cryptographic protocol verifier user manual. CNRS, Departement dInformatique, Ecole Normale Superieure, Paris (2005)
27. Zhang, J., Yang, L., Cao, W., Wang, Q.: Formal analysis of 5g EAP-TLS authentication protocol using proverif. IEEE Access **8**(23) 674–23 688 (2020)
28. Dill, D.L., Park, S., Nowatzyk, A.G.: Formal specification of abstract memory models. In: Proceedings of the 1993 Symposium on Research on Integrated Systems, pp. 38–52 (1993)
29. Gibson-Robinson, T., Lowe, G.: Symmetry reduction in CSP model checking. Int. J. Softw. Tools Technol. Transfer **21**, 567–605 (2019)
30. Li, Y., Pang, J.: An inductive approach to strand spaces. Formal Aspects Comput. **25**, 465–501 (2013)
31. Zhao, Y., Jiang, H., Lv, J., Tan, S., Li, Y.: Anb2murphi: a translator for converting alicebob specifications to murphi. In: The 33rd International Conference on Software Engineering and Knowledge Engineering, SEKE 2021, KSIR Virtual Conference Center, USA, July 1 - July 10, 2021, S. Chang, Ed. KSI Research Inc., pp. 108–113 (2021). https://doi.org/10.18293/SEKE2021-028
32. 3GPP.2018, Security architecture and procedures for 5g system, TS 33.501,v15.1.0
33. Bella, G.: Verified security protocol modelling and implementation with ANBX, Ph.D. dissertation, Teeside University (2011)

Empirically Scalable Invariant Generation Leveraging Divide-and-Conquer with Pruning

Hongming Liu and Guoqiang Li(✉)

Shanghai Jiao Tong University, Shanghai, China
{hm-liu,li.g}@sjtu.edu.cn

Abstract. Invariant generation is a critical task in program verification. Literature highlights Farkas' Lemma as a principal sound and complete framework for proactively generating tight invariants in constraint-solving. Recent advances have identified the conversion from CNF to DNF as a major bottleneck, leading to a combinatorial explosion. In this study, we introduce an optimized algorithm to address the combinatorial explosion by trading off space for time-efficiency. Our approach employs two key strategies to boost speed. First, we apply a divide-and-conquer strategy to decompose a complex problem into smaller, more manageable subproblems that can be solved quickly and in parallel. Second, we intelligently apply a pruning strategy in two ways, navigating the depth-first search process to avoid unnecessary checks. These improvements maintain the accuracy and speed up the analysis. The experiments indicate that our approach outperforms the state-of-the-art, demonstrating significant speed improvements. With this solution, we bring a significant advance in accelerating invariant generation with Farkas' Lemma.

Keywords: Program verification · Invariant generation · Constraint-solving · Divide and conquer · Pruning strategy

1 Introduction

An assertion at a program location is termed an *invariant* if it consistently holds true for the values taken by program variables whenever that location is reached during execution. Invariants play a pivotal role in program analysis and verification by providing an over-approximation of reachable program states. They are crucial for proving properties such as safety [24], reachability [2] and time-complexity analysis [4] among others. The quality of the invariants is measured by their accuracy, i.e., the amount of over-approximation against the actual set of reachable program states. Generating high-quality invariants has been a significant challenge for decades. Traditionally, invariants are derived through *inductive invariants* [7]. In this work, we focus on automatically generating linear inductive invariants with Farkas' Lemma, which is important for both academic research and practical applications.

W.-N. Chin and Z. Xu (Eds.): TASE 2024, LNCS 14777, pp. 324–342, 2024.
https://doi.org/10.1007/978-3-031-64626-3_19

Literature indicates that the principal sound and complete method for invariant generation is through Farkas' Lemma in constraint solving method, which plays an essential role in proactively generating tight invariants to aid formal analysis. To solve the invariant generation problem, constraint-solving-based approaches usually consider the following workflow: initially establish a template with unknown coefficients for the invariant, then collect constraints from the inductive conditions for invariants, and finally resolve the unknown coefficients in the template to obtain the preset invariants. In constraint-solving-based approaches for linear invariant generation, Farkas' Lemma provides a complete characterization of the inductive condition [7], which was further improved by quantifier elimination [7] and heuristics [28]. The completeness of constraint solving follows from the fact that any inductive invariant can theoretically be derived from the relevant constraints in constraint solving.

Notably, compared with other methods, constraint solving has the advantage of a theoretical guarantee on the accuracy of the generated invariants but typically requires higher runtime complexity. Furthermore, recent advance [21] has highlighted the challenge: the conversion from CNF to DNF leads to a combinatorial explosion, especially when generating invariants with Farkas' Lemma in constraint solving.

We propose an optimized approach aimed at addressing the bottleneck arising from the combinatorial explosion by trading off space for time-efficiency. The approach is developed on the abstract model of linear transition systems that capture general affine updates with affine guards between program locations, so that it is applicable to general affine programs. The strategies we contribute are as follows:

- First, a divide-and-conquer technique is introduced, which decomposes a complex problem into smaller, more manageable subproblems that can be solved quickly and in parallel, greatly cutting down on the time needed for the entire process.
- Second, the pruning strategy is utilized within two intelligent ways to navigate through the depth-first search process that helps avoid unnecessary checks, named path-recording multi-step-backtracking pruning and full-scope-predictive forward-checking pruning.

Paper Organization: The rest of the paper is organized as follows: Sect. 2 introduces some preliminaries. Section 3 provides a detailed overview of our approach, illustrated with some examples. Section 4 describes the implementation of the divide-and-conquer strategy, while Sect. 5 details the pruning strategy. Section 6 presents the experimental results. Section 7 reviews works related to our approach. Section 8 concludes the paper and suggests future work.

2 Preliminaries

Our approach builds upon and enhances the methodology presented in the previous work [21], sharing a common foundation in terms of background and theoretical underpinnings.

Linear Transition System (LinTS) is described by a tuple $\langle X, X', L, \ell^*, \mathcal{T}, \theta \rangle$, where X denotes a finite set of real-valued variables representing the current value, X' represents the values in the next step, L is a finite set of locations including the initial location ℓ^*, $\mathcal{T}$ is a finite set of transitions, with each transition τ specifying the current and next locations ℓ and ℓ' along with a guard condition ρ, and θ represents the initial condition at ℓ^*.

Example 1. Consider a scenario of a vagrant robot from [7]. The control of the robot works in two alternating modes ℓ_0, ℓ_1. In ℓ_0, the robot moves forward in the positive direction of both x and y through ρ_1, and in ℓ_1, it moves forward in the positive direction of x and the negative direction of y through ρ_2.

$$X = \{x, y, t\},\ L = \{\ell_0^*, \ell_1\},\ \mathcal{T} = \{\tau_1, \tau_2\},\ \tau_1 : \langle \ell_0, \ell_1, \rho_1 \rangle,\ \tau_2 : \langle \ell_1, \ell_0, \rho_2 \rangle,$$
$$\theta : x = 0 \wedge y = 0 \wedge t = 0,$$
$$\rho_1 : \begin{bmatrix} t' - t \leq x' - x \leq 2(t' - t) \wedge \\ t' - t \leq y' - y \leq 2(t' - t) \wedge \\ 1 \leq t' - t \leq 2 \end{bmatrix}, \rho_2 : \begin{bmatrix} t' - t \leq x' - x \leq 2(t' - t) \wedge \\ -2(t' - t) \leq y' - y \leq -(t' - t) \wedge \\ 1 \leq t' - t \leq 2 \end{bmatrix}$$

Fig. 1. The LinTS for a Vagrant Robot [21]

Figure 1 shows the LinTS of a vagrant robot that consists of three variables x, y, t and two locations ℓ_0, ℓ_1. The variable t records the amount of the elapsed time. θ specifies the initial condition at ℓ^*. A path under this LinTS is $(\ell_0, (x, y, t) = (0, 0, 0))$, $(\ell_1, (x, y, t) = (2, 2, 1))$, $(\ell_0, (x, y, t) = (3, 1, 2))$. □

Theorem 1 (Farkas' Lemma). *Consider an affine assertion φ over $X = \{x_1, \ldots, x_n\}$, where $\bowtie \in \{=, \geq\}$. When φ is satisfiable, $\varphi \models \psi$ if and only if there exists $\lambda \geq 0$ such that (i) $c_j = \sum_{i=1}^m \lambda_i a_{ij}$ for $1 \leq j \leq n$ and (ii) $d = \lambda_0 + \sum_{i=1}^m \lambda_i b_i$ as in Fig. 2. Moreover, φ is unsatisfiable if and only if the inequality $\psi : -1 \geq 0$ can be derived.*

$$\begin{array}{c|rcl} \lambda_0 & & 1 \geq 0 & \\ \lambda_1 & a_{11}x_1 + \cdots + a_{1n}x_n + b_1 \bowtie_1 0 & & \\ \vdots & \vdots & & \varphi \\ \lambda_m & a_{m1}x_1 + \cdots + a_{mn}x_n + b_m \bowtie_m 0 & & \\ \hline & c_1x_1 + \cdots + c_nx_n + d \geq 0 \leftarrow \psi, \text{or} & & \\ & -1 \geq 0 \leftarrow \mathit{false} & & \end{array} \Rightarrow \begin{array}{r} \lambda_1 a_{11} + \cdots + \lambda_m a_{m1} = c_1 \\ \vdots \\ \lambda_1 a_{1n} + \cdots + \lambda_m a_{mn} = c_n \\ \lambda_0 + \lambda_1 b_1 + \cdots + \lambda_m b_m = d \\ \vdots \end{array}$$

Fig. 2. The Tabular Form and Application for Farkas' Lemma [7,28]

Polyhedra, Polyhedral Cones and Projection. A subset P of $\mathbb{R}^n$ is a *polyhedron* if $P = \{\mathbf{x} \in \mathbb{R}^n \mid \mathbf{A} \cdot \mathbf{x} \leq \mathbf{b}\}$ for some real matrix $A \in \mathbb{R}^{m \times n}$ and real vector $\mathbf{b} \in \mathbb{R}^m$. A polyhedron P is a *polyhedral cone* if $P = \{\mathbf{x} \in \mathbb{R}^n \mid \mathbf{A} \cdot \mathbf{x} \leq \mathbf{0}\}$ for some real matrix $A \in \mathbb{R}^{m \times n}$, where $\mathbf{0}$ is the m-dimensional zero column vector. For a polyhedron $P = \{(\mathbf{x}^{\mathrm{T}}, \mathbf{u}^{\mathrm{T}})^{\mathrm{T}} \in \mathbb{R}^{p+q} \mid \mathbf{A} \cdot \mathbf{x} + \mathbf{B} \cdot \mathbf{u} \leq \mathbf{c}\}$ where $\mathbf{A} \in \mathbb{R}^{m \times p}, \mathbf{B} \in \mathbb{R}^{m \times q}$ are real matrices and $c \in \mathbb{R}^m$ is a real vector, the projection of P onto the dimensions $\mathbf{x}$ is defined as the polyhedron $P[\mathbf{x}] := \{\mathbf{x} \in \mathbb{R}^p \mid \exists \mathbf{u} \in \mathbb{R}^q . (\mathbf{x}^{\mathrm{T}}, \mathbf{u}^{\mathrm{T}})^{\mathrm{T}} \in P\}$. It is guaranteed by Fourier-Motzkin Elimination [29, Chapter 12.2] that $P[\mathbf{x}]$ will always be a polyhedron.

3 An Overview of Our Approach

In this section, we first review the original approaches. Then, we discuss their potential challenges. Finally, aiming at the challenges, we outline our key strategy: divide-and-conquer and pruning.

3.1 The Original Approaches [7,21,28]

The basic approach [7,28] pioneers a sound and complete framework to generate invariants via Farkas' Lemma with some techniques like quantifier elimination and reasonable heuristics method. The latest approach [21] improves the scalability of the basic approach with location-by-location strategy and segment subsumption testing strategy, which is the state-of-the-art improvement.

The Basic Approach via Farkas' Lemma. [7,28] Within this approach, the Farkas' Lemma initially transforms the inductive condition for linear invariants into an equivalent system of quadratic constraints in the conjunctive normal form (CNF). After converting CNF to the disjunctive normal form (DNF), we could obtain concrete invariants by solving DNF. To grasp the fundamental ideas of these techniques, we recall its workflow of the basic approach in the following example.

Example 2. Consider the LinTS in Example 1. The basic approach first establishes a template $\eta(\ell_i) := c_{\ell_i,1}x + c_{\ell_i,2}y + c_{\ell_i,3}t + d_{\ell_i} \geq 0$ for $i \in \{0, 1\}$. After applying the tabular form of Farkas' Lemma in Fig. 2 and eliminating the λ_i's, we obtain $\Phi_\theta := [d_{\ell_0} \geq 0]$, $\Phi_{\rho,1}$ by setting μ to 1 and $\Phi_{\rho,2}$ by setting μ to 0 as shown in Fig. 3 (here substitutes μ for λ in the specific row of the template), where each atomic proposition is a polyhedral cone over the unknown coefficients c_{ℓ_i} and d_{ℓ_i} in the CNF formula $\Phi_\theta \wedge \Phi_{\rho_2} \wedge \Phi_{\rho_1}$. The approach further equivalently expands the CNF formula into the DNF formula. Deriving from the polyhedral cone of one disjunctive clause $\Psi_1 = \Phi_\theta \wedge \Phi_{\rho_2,1} \wedge \Phi_{\rho_1,1}$, we obtain their corresponding invariants $\eta(\ell_0)$ $[-x+2t \geq 0, -y+t \geq 0, x-t \geq 0, y+t \geq 0]$ and $\eta(\ell_1)$ $[-x+2t \geq 0, -y+t+2 \geq 0, -y+2t \geq 0, t-1 \geq 0, y+t-2 \geq 0, x-t \geq 0]$. It happens that the invariants obtained from Ψ_1 above coincide with the ones from the whole DNF formula $\Psi_1 \vee \Psi_2 \vee \Psi_3 \vee \Psi_4$ because the polyhedral cone of $\Psi_2 \vee \Psi_3 \vee \Psi_4$ were subsumed by Ψ_1, i.e., $\Psi_1 \supseteq \Psi_2 \vee \Psi_3 \vee \Psi_4$. □

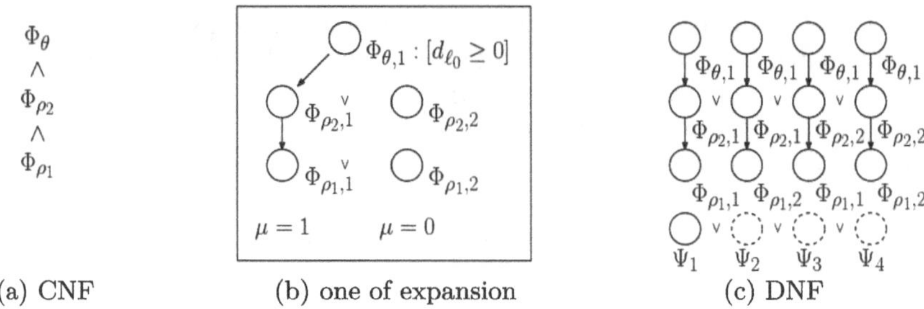

Fig. 3. The expansion of CNF-to-DNF following a DFS order

As depicted in Fig. 3, guessing the μ value leads to a combinatorial explosion in the CNF-to-DNF expansion. The latest approach introduces two main techniques to address, including (i) a location-by-location strategy and (ii) a segmented subsumption testing.

The Latest Approach via Farkas' Lemma. [21] Within the latest approach, the location-by-location strategy was employed to split the computation for all locations into separate computation for single location, and the segmented subsumption testing further decomposes the original CNF-to-DNF converting into a smaller one. These methods still maintain original correctness and accuracy, which is also proved by the latest approach. Since it is the most closely related and recent work to our approach, we revisit its workflow from the perspective of the depth-first search (DFS) in the following examples.

Example 3. Follow the basic approach in Example 2 and obtain the CNF formula $\Phi_\theta \wedge \Phi_{\rho_2} \wedge \Phi_{\rho_1}$. Recall that the location-by-location strategy focuses on one target location in one invariant generation process by employing two key ideas: (i) reordering and (ii) projection.

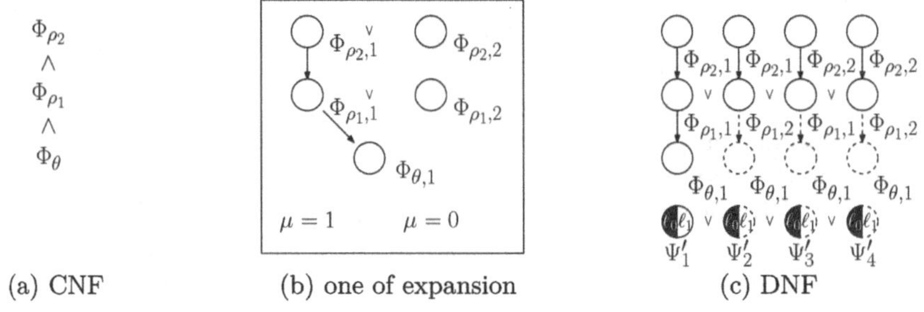

Fig. 4. The expansion of CNF-to-DNF reordered by ℓ_1

Suppose that we focus on the target location ℓ_1. (i) Reordering: Based on that the basic approach employs a subsumption testing to detect the redundant disjunctive clauses Ψ_2, Ψ_3, Ψ_4 earlier to mitigate the combinatorial explosion, we can reorder the expansion process then obtain $\Phi_{\rho_2} \wedge \Phi_{\rho_1} \wedge \Phi_\theta$ by prioritizing the expansion related to ℓ_1 as shown in Fig. 4a. Notably, Φ_θ only involves ℓ_0, which leads to its de-prioritization. This approach enables the earlier detection of subsumption for redundant disjunctive clauses $\Psi_2' = \Phi_{\rho_2,1} \wedge \Phi_{\rho_1,2}$ than $\Psi_2 = \Phi_{\rho_2,1} \wedge \Phi_{\rho_1,2} \wedge \Phi_{\theta,1}$, resulting in $\Psi_1' \supseteq \Psi_2'$ as shown in Fig. 4c. (ii) Projection: For the polyhedral cone Ψ_1 in Fig. 3c, we project the polyhedral cone onto the dimensions of coefficients c_{1j}'s $(1 \leq j \leq 3)$ and d_1 that are related to the location ℓ_1, to obtain the polyhedral cone Ψ_1' as shown in Fig. 4c, where the white right-hand-side represents the reserved dimensions related to ℓ_1. The final resultant invariants derived from Ψ_1' coincide with the invariants $\eta(\ell_1)$ in Example 2. Treat the target location ℓ_0 in a similar way.

Suppose that under the segmented subsumption testing strategy. Consider the scenario that the CNF formula to be expanded is $\Phi = \Phi_1 \wedge \cdots \wedge \Phi_i \wedge \cdots \wedge \Phi_m$ $(1 \leq i \leq m)$ where each Φ_i is a disjunction $\Phi_{i,1} \vee \cdots \vee \Phi_{i,j} \vee \cdots \vee \Phi_{i,n}$ $(1 \leq j \leq n)$. This strategy divides the CNF into small segments without overlap such as $\Phi_p \wedge \cdots \wedge \Phi_q$ $(1 \leq p \leq q \leq m)$ and then performs the local subsumption testing in each segment. The potential advantage of applying segmented subsumption testing is that small segments may detect local subsumption and get simplified, so that the combinatorial explosion could be mitigated. □

Challenge for the Original Approaches. The basic approach uses reasonable heuristics and subsumption testing to avoid the high runtime complexity in quantifier elimination, however, leading to a rapid and massive combinatorial explosion. The latest approach leverages two main improvements to mitigate the combinatorial explosion but still leaves two challenges: (i) how to enable the parallel processing for segmented subsumption testing and (ii) there are redundant and unnecessary checking in the expansion of CNF-to-DNF.

To further reduce the complexity of problems, we improve the approach with two main strategies: (i) a divide-and-conquer strategy to decompose the tasks into mutually independent minimal units to enable parallel processing and (ii) a pruning strategy to reduce the complexity in CNF-to-DNF expansion. In the following, we will outline two key improvements of our approach.

3.2 Divide-and-Conquer Strategy

This strategy targets the CNF-to-DNF expansion process. Segmented subsumption testing divides the CNF formula into segments for local checks but leaves one issue: the scalability of the segmented subsumption testing, which serves as a pre-processing step. We address this issue by introducing a framework that extends the segmented subsumption testing method into a divide-and-conquer strategy. This framework is designed to enhance scalability and further enable parallel processing of CNF-to-DNF expansion.

Example 4. Continuing with Example 3, we first obtain the CNF $\Phi_{\rho_2} \wedge \Phi_{\rho_1} \wedge \Phi_\theta$ equivalent to Fig. 4a. The divide-and-conquer strategy comprises two processes:

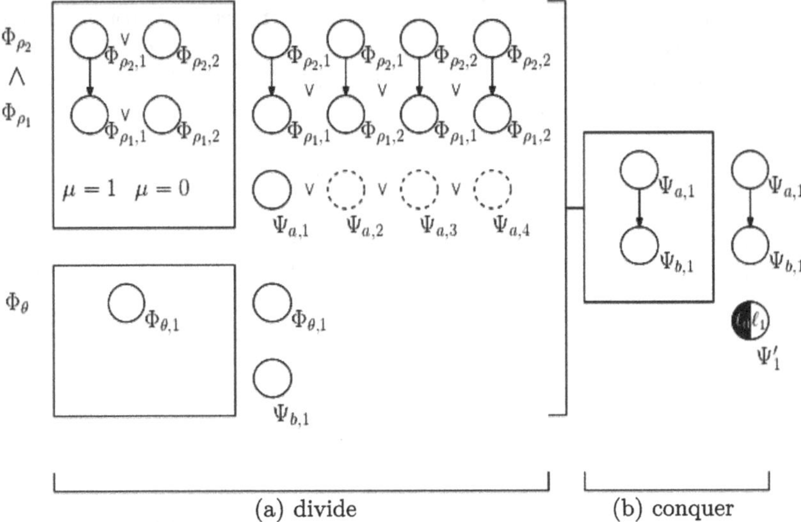

Fig. 5. The divide-and-conquer strategy for Example 4

(i) divide and (ii) conquer. In the divide process illustrated in Fig. 5a, we divide the CNF into sub-CNFs, i.e., $\Phi_{\rho_2} \wedge \Phi_{\rho_1}$ and Φ_θ, which are then transformed into sub-DNFs, i.e., $\Psi_{a,1}, \Psi_{a,2}, \Psi_{a,3}, \Psi_{a,4}$ and $\Psi_{b,1}$. These sub-DNFs can be operated in parallel. This allows for local checks-determining if $\Psi_{a,1} \supseteq \Psi_{a,2}$ or $\Psi_{a,1} \subseteq \Psi_{a,2}$, for instance-to be operated in parallel. Operating n sub-DNFs costs $n(n-1)$ unit-processes and $n(n-1)$ unit-time within a single processing framework. However, leveraging parallel processing significantly reduces the computation time among $\Psi_{a,1}$, $\Psi_{a,2}$, $\Psi_{a,3}$, and $\Psi_{a,4}$ from $4 \times (4-1)$ unit-time to just one unit-time. It is worth mentioning that, reducing the number of conjunctions within the sub-CNFs, such as limiting to at most two components like $\Phi_1 \wedge \Phi_2$ and Φ_3, effectively decreases the computational load during polyhedral computations. Finally, the divide process results in two distinct formulas, $\Psi_{a,1}$ and $\Psi_{b,1}$. In the conquer process illustrated in Fig. 5b, following the divide process, we combine two formulas $\Psi_{a,1}$ and $\Psi_{b,1}$ into one. The conquer process iteratively merges pairs of sub-DNFs until a complete disjunctive clause is formed, for example, $\Phi_{\rho_2,i} \wedge \Phi_{\rho_1,j} \wedge \Phi_\theta$. This process involves continuously conjuncting sub-DNFs until no further sub-DNFs exist. Overall, after obtaining $\Psi_{a,1}$ and $\Psi_{b,1}$ by the divide process, we merge these to form the final complete disjunctive clause Ψ'_1, which is achieved by projecting $\Psi_{a,1} \wedge \Psi_{b,1}$ onto the target location ℓ_1. □

3.3 Pruning Strategy

This strategy focuses on enhancing the pruning capabilities during subsumption checking. We observed that the original approaches rely heavily on the conventional pruning technique limited to a single-step backtrack each time, which unfortunately leads to redundant and unnecessary checks. To address this inefficiency and significantly improve the pruning capabilities for the CNF-to-DNF expansion, we introduce two distinct and innovative pruning strategies.

Path-Recording Multi-step-Backtracking Pruning (PMP). The PMP strategy tackles the limitations inherent in traditional backtracking pruning by comparing recorded formulas against existing invariants, thus eliminating multiple unnecessary subsumption checks.

Example 5. Continuing with Example 3, we first obtain $\Phi_{\rho_2} \wedge \Phi_{\rho_1} \wedge \Phi_{\theta}$ equivalent to Fig. 4a. The PMP strategy reveals subsumptions starting with the most comprehensive combination and narrowing down, identifying the earliest subsumption point, which is achieved through the comparison between recorded invariants η and current formulas Φ of disjunctive clauses. Suppose that under this strategy, we focus on target ℓ_1. Upon updating the invariants $\eta(\ell_1)$ to include Ψ_1', i.e., $\eta(\ell_1) \leftarrow \eta(\ell_1) \cup inv(\Psi_1')$, we locate the earliest point of subsumption at $\Phi_{\rho_2,1}$. To identify this point, we sequentially perform subsumption checks by comparing $\eta(\ell_1)$ against progressively smaller sets of formulas within the clause $\Phi_{\rho_2,1} \wedge \Phi_{\rho_1,1} \wedge \Phi_{\theta,1}$. The process begins with a comparison involving the entire clause $\Phi_{\rho_2,1} \wedge \Phi_{\rho_1,1} \wedge \Phi_{\theta,1}$, then narrows down to $\Phi_{\rho_2,1} \wedge \Phi_{\rho_1,1}$, and ultimately focuses on $\Phi_{\rho_2,1}$ alone, which determines that the earliest point of subsumption is $\Phi_{\rho_2,1}$. The detection of subsumption at $\Phi_{\rho_2,1}$ prompts us to prune disjunctive clauses originating from $\Phi_{\rho_2,1}$, such as $\Psi_2' = \Phi_{\rho_2,1} \wedge \Phi_{\rho_1,2} \wedge \Phi_{\theta}$, as demonstrated in Fig. 6a. Here, clauses like Ψ_2', indicated by dashed lines, are exempt from further subsumption checks. Through this strategy, we efficiently eliminate redundant subsumption checks. □

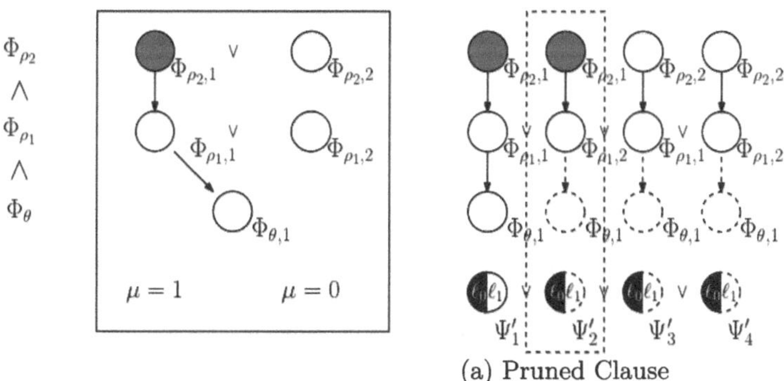

Fig. 6. The PMP strategy for Example 5

Full-Scope-Predictive Forward-Checking Pruning (FFP). The FFP strategy proactively eliminates unnecessary nodes-those already subsumed by newly updated invariants-through subsumption checks between the single formula and recorded invariants, immediately following an invariant update. This strategy ensures that only necessary formulas are processed, significantly reducing the exploration of unnecessary formulas.

Example 6. Continuing with Example 5, we first obtain $\Phi_{\rho_2} \wedge \Phi_{\rho_1} \wedge \Phi_\theta$ equivalent to Fig. 4a. The FFP strategy could prune unnecessary formulas, which is achieved through the comparison between recorded invariants η and the single formula Φ of disjunctive clauses, such as the polyhedral cones $\Phi_{\rho_i,j}$ and $\Phi_{\theta,1}$ as shown in Fig. 7. Suppose that under this strategy, we focus on ℓ_1. Upon updating the invariants $\eta(\ell_1)$ to include Ψ_1', i.e., $\eta(\ell_1) \leftarrow \eta(\ell_1) \cup inv(\Psi_1')$, we locate the point of subsumption at $\Phi_{\rho_1,1}$, i.e., $\eta(\ell_1) \supseteq \Phi_{\rho_1,1}$. This point is identified by comparing $\eta(\ell_1)$ against each formula $\Phi_{\rho_i,j}$ or $\Phi_{\theta,1}$. The subsumption happens at $\Phi_{\rho_1,1}$ and thus we prune these disjunctive clauses traversing through $\Phi_{\rho_1,1}$ such as $\Psi_3' = \Phi_{\rho_2,2} \wedge \Phi_{\rho_1,1}$ as shown in Fig. 7a, where the disjunctive clause Ψ_3' in dashed line do not need subsumption checking. This pruning strategy will remove the unnecessary polyhedral cone. □

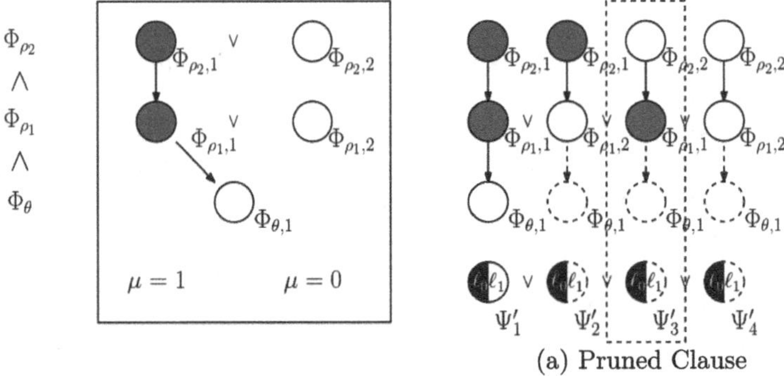

Fig. 7. The FFP strategy for Example 6

4 Divide-and-Conquer Strategy

This section presents the implementation for divide-and-conquer strategy (illustrated in Fig. 8). An intuition is that we initially decompose the CNF formula $\Phi_1 \wedge \cdots \wedge \Phi_i \wedge \cdots \wedge \Phi_m$ into independent conjunctive clauses $\Phi_1, \cdots, \Phi_i, \cdots, \Phi_m$ where $\Phi_i = \Phi_{i,1} \vee \cdots \vee \Phi_{i,N_i}$, and we conjunct two neighboring conjunctive clauses into sub-DNF clauses as the segmented subsumption testing to obtain the segmented disjunctive clauses Ψ_j's, then we repeat the merging process until all the neighboring segmented disjunctive clauses were conjuncted together into a set of disjunctive clauses $\Psi := \{\Phi_{1,k_1} \wedge \cdots \wedge \Phi_{i,k_i} \wedge \cdots \wedge \Phi_{m,k_m} | 1 \leq k_i \leq N_i\}$, finally we generate invariants from these disjunctive clauses. With this framework, the combinatorial explosion could be solved by enabling parallel-processing.

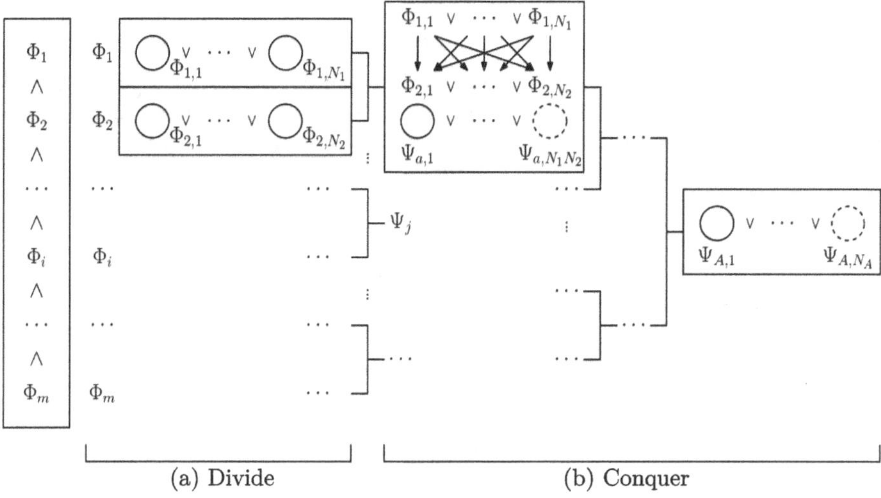

Fig. 8. The workflow of Divide-and-Conquer strategy

Divide. For the divide process, we decompose the original CNF formula into the conjunctive clauses by simply breaking the conjunction linking the two neighboring conjunctive clauses, for instance, as shown in Fig. 8a. We obtain the CNF formula $\Phi_1 \wedge \cdots \wedge \Phi_i \wedge \cdots \wedge \Phi_m$ where $\Phi_i = \Phi_{i,1} \vee \cdots \vee \Phi_{i,N_i}$ and $1 \leq i \leq m$. Next, we break the conjunction which is connecting every two neighboring conjunctive clauses and obtain these conjunctions $\Phi_1, \cdots, \Phi_i, \cdots, \Phi_m$. Notably, each disjunctive clause Φ_{i,k_i} for $1 \leq k_i \leq N_i$ in Φ_i has been checked their subsumption, and thus, there is no subsumption from each other. □

Conquer. For the conquer process, we repeat the merging process until all the decomposed conjunctive clauses are conjuncted together into the DNF formula, which the DNF formula we obtained is carried without redundant disjunctive clauses. As shown in Fig. 8, we assume that m and $i + 1$ are even for the sake of simple illustration. After we obtain the unlinked conjunctions $\Phi_1, \cdots, \Phi_i, \cdots, \Phi_m$ followed by the process of divide, we conquer the CNF-to-DNF process with every two neighboring unit. Below we present the main technical details in following the steps (**Step B1** – **Step B2**).

Step B1. As shown in Fig. 8b, we merge each adjacency clause Φ_i and Φ_{i+1} and conjunct every pairwise Φ_{i,k_i} and $\Phi_{i+1,k_{i+1}}$ where there will be $N_i N_{i+1}$ pair of segmented disjunctive clauses. For instance, we merge Φ_1 and Φ_2 by conjuncting Φ_{1,k_1} and Φ_{2,k_2} resulting $N_1 N_2$ pair of disjunctive clauses $(\Phi_{1,1} \wedge \Phi_{2,1}) \vee \cdots \vee (\Phi_{1,1} \wedge \Phi_{2,N_2}) \vee \cdots \vee (\Phi_{1,N_1} \wedge \Phi_{2,1}) \vee \cdots \vee (\Phi_{1,N_1} \wedge \Phi_{2,N_2})$, and we apply subsumption testing to check whether one of them is subsumed by others. Then, the redundant Ψ_{a,k_a} is removed where $\Psi_{a,1} = \Phi_{1,1} \wedge \Phi_{2,1}, \cdots, \Psi_{a,N_1 N_2} = \Phi_{1,N_1} \wedge \Phi_{2,N_2}$ and $1 \leq k_a \leq N_1 N_2$, and suppose that the resultant $\Psi_a = \Psi_{a,1} \vee \cdots \vee \Psi_{a,N_a}$. Then we repeat the merging process until every pair in $\Phi_1, \cdots, \Phi_i, \cdots, \Phi_m$ was conjuncted into a disjunctive clause such as $\Psi_a, \cdots, \Psi_j, \cdots$.

Step B2. After collecting $\Psi_a, \cdots, \Psi_j, \cdots$, we apply the method in **Step B1** again on these disjunctive clauses. And then we repeat the process in **Step B2** until all the decomposed conjunctive clauses were conjuncted together into a set of disjunctive clauses $\Psi_A = \Psi_{A,1} \vee \cdots \vee \Psi_{A,N_A}$ which is denoted by $\{\Phi_{1,k_1} \wedge \cdots \wedge \Phi_{i,k_i} \wedge \cdots \wedge \Phi_{m,k_m} | 1 \leq k_i \leq N_i\}$.

Finally, we generate invariants from these disjunctive clauses of their polyhedral cones, which the DNF formula we obtained has removing redundant disjunctive clauses. □

5 Pruning Strategy

This section presents the pruning strategy. Consider the original subsumption checking strategy as shown in Example 2 and Example 3, the original approaches are burdened with redundant and unnecessary subsumption checking through the DFS search. Our pruning strategy aims at the pruning process and escape the redundant and unnecessary subsumption checking by employing two pruning ideas: (i) Path-Recording Multi-Step-Backtracking Pruning and (ii) Full-Scope-Predictive Forward-Checking Pruning.

5.1 Path-Recording Multi-step-Backtracking Pruning (PMP)

This section demonstrates the PMP strategy (illustrated in Fig. 9). Recall that the invariants will be updated after adding new invariants generated by the

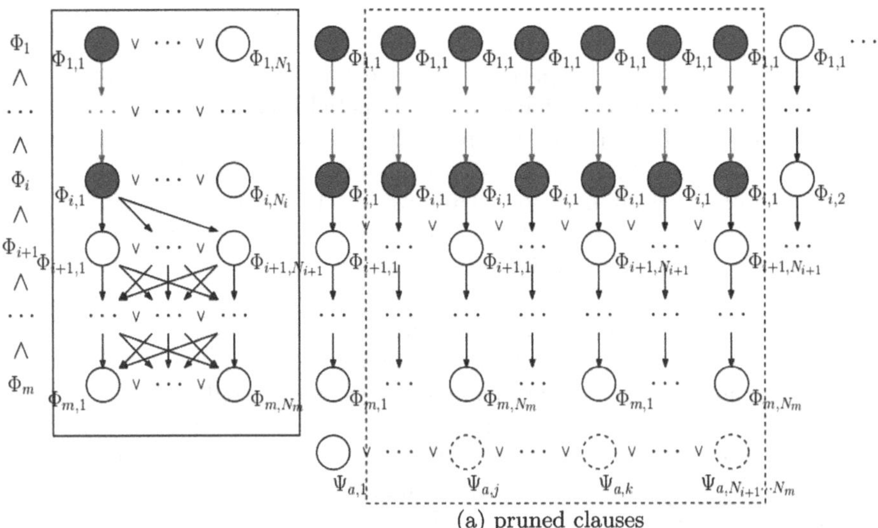

Fig. 9. The PMP strategy

polyhedral cones of a complete disjunctive clause $\Psi := \{\Phi_{1,k_1} \wedge \cdots \wedge \Phi_{i,k_i} \wedge \cdots \wedge \Phi_{m,k_m} | 1 \leq k_i \leq N_i\}$, which happens that we do not find successful subsumption along with the current disjunctive clauses. For instance, after we update invariants obtained from the disjunctive clause $\Psi_{a,1} = \Phi_{1,1} \wedge \cdots \wedge \Phi_{i,1} \wedge \Phi_{i+1,1} \wedge \cdots \wedge \Phi_{m,1}$ which is the first disjunctive clause in DFS-searching. Then, we check the subsumption between the current invariants with each polyhedral cone of current disjunctive clauses $\Psi_{a,1}$ step-by-step in a reversing forward. We check whether the polyhedral cones of $\Phi_{1,1} \wedge \cdots \wedge \Phi_{k,1}$ for $1 \leq k \leq m$ were subsumed by current invariants where the k starts at m and ends at 1. As shown in Fig. 9, the earlier subsumption is detected at the disjunctive clauses $\Phi_{1,1} \wedge \cdots \wedge \Phi_{i,1}$. Consider this scenario, all the redundant disjunctive clauses originating from these clauses $\Phi_{1,1} \wedge \cdots \wedge \Phi_{i,1}$ will certainly be subsumed by current invariants and hence should be removed. With this pruning strategy, the redundant disjunctive clauses will be removed without wasting much running time, as shown in Fig. 9. The pseudo-code is given in Algorithm 1.

Algorithm 1: Path-Recording Multi-Step-Backtracking Pruning

Input: $\bigwedge_{i=1}^{m} \Phi_i$: the CNF formula; **Gen**(*poly*) : a procedure that generates the invariants given a polyhedron *poly* over the unknown coefficients

Output: a collection *inv* of linear invariants

$\bigwedge_{i=1}^{m} \Phi_i$; $//\Phi_i = \bigvee_{j=1}^{N_i} \Phi_{i,j}$

$inv \leftarrow \emptyset$; $i \leftarrow 1$; $n_i \leftarrow 1$ (for $1 \leq i \leq m$);

while $i > 0$ **do**

    if $n_i \leq N_i$ **then**

        $d_i \leftarrow \Phi_{i,n_i}$; $n_i \leftarrow n_i + 1$;

        if $\bigwedge_{s=1}^{i} d_s \not\subseteq inv$ **then**

            if $i = m$ **then**

                $inv \leftarrow inv \cup$ **Gen**$(\bigwedge_{s=1}^{m} d_s)$;

                /*Path-Recording Pruning*/

                while $\bigwedge_{s=1}^{i-1} d_s \subseteq inv$ **do**

                    $n_i \leftarrow 1$; $i \leftarrow i - 1$;

            else

                $i \leftarrow i + 1$;

    else

        $n_i \leftarrow 1$; $i \leftarrow i - 1$;

return *inv*;

5.2 Full-Scope-Predictive Forward-Checking Pruning (FFP)

This section demonstrates the FFP strategy (illustrated in Fig. 10). Recall the same happening in Sect. 5.1 that the invariants updates arisen from $\Psi := \{\Phi_{1,k_1} \wedge \cdots \wedge \Phi_{i,k_i} \wedge \cdots \wedge \Phi_{m,k_m} | 1 \leq k_i \leq N_i\}$. For instance, we update invariants obtained from the disjunctive clause $\Psi_{a,1} = \Phi_{1,1} \wedge \cdots \wedge \Phi_{i,1} \wedge \Phi_{i+1,1} \wedge \cdots \wedge \Phi_{m,1}$ which is the first disjunctive clause in DFS-searching. By predictively detecting the subsumption between the current invariants with each polyhedral cone

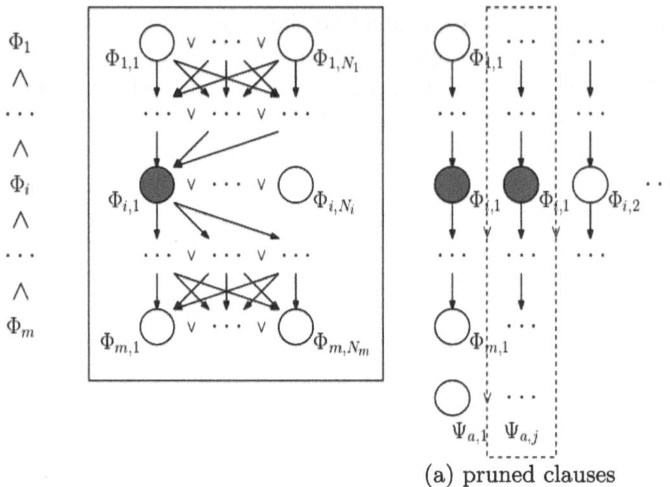

Fig. 10. The FFP strategy

of corresponding disjunctive clauses, we locate that the polyhedral cone $\Phi_{i,1}$ is subsumed. As shown in Fig. 10, every disjunctive clause traversing through the $\Phi_{i,1}$ will certainly be subsumed by current invariants so that all the disjunctive clauses carried with $\Phi_{i,1}$ are removed, i.e., the disjunctive clauses $\Psi_{a,j} = \Phi_{1,k_1} \wedge \cdots \wedge \Phi_{i,1} \wedge \cdots \wedge \Phi_{m,k_m}$ for $1 \leq k_i \leq N_i$ except $\Psi_{a,1}$. With this pruning strategy, the disjunctive clauses traversing through the unnecessary polyhedral cones will be removed. The algorithm could be achieved by detecting the unnecessary polyhedral cone (i.e., DFS vertex in Fig. 10) and removing it.

6 Evaluation

We summarize experimental results in the following tables. Notably, we obtain the same invariants as the original approaches [7,21,28] so that we mainly focus on the comparison of runtime, successful subsumption count and pruning count. Then, we describe the tables and discuss the details of our experimental results. Experiments were conducted on a system with an Intel Core i7-7700 CPU (3.6 GHz) and 16 GiB RAM, running Ubuntu 22.04.4 LTS.

Benchmarks. We consider benchmarks from a variety of application domains [16,20,28,30]. ***SVCOMP*** [30]. The C programming language benchmarks selected from the category of loop-invgen in Competition on Software Verification [30]. ***Scheduler*** [16,28]. The invariant analysis for cooperative multitask scheduling activated by interrupts and pre-emptive programming can be used to ensure the liveness of scheduling. The category "Scheduler*" contains original benchmarks from [28] that follow a non-standard setting and "Scheduler" considers these benchmarks with the standard setting [16]. ***Fischer*** [20]. The Fischer mutual exclusion protocol is a real-time mutual exclusion algorithm for a distributed system with timing skew. ***Cars*** [28]. A scenario of car systems is illustrated as a dynamic decision problem in which invariant analysis can be used to ensure the safety of autopilot.

Table Description. In all tables, "Lines of Code" means the number of lines of C code used to measure the scale, "Our Approach" means the experimental results obtained by our approach, "StInG" means the experimental results obtained by basic approach in StInG [28], "OOPSLA22" means the experimental results obtained by latest approach in OOPSLA22 [21], "Time (s)" means the runtime for DNF transformation following preliminary preparations measured in seconds, "SS" means the number of successful subsumption in the process of CNF-to-DNF expansion, "Speedup" shows the ratio of the runtime consumed by OOPSLA22 against our corresponding approach specified in the table (i.e., OOPSLA22/Ours), "D-and-C" means the experimental results obtained by divide-and-conquer strategy, "P-Pruning" means the experimental results obtained by path-recording multi-step-backtracking pruning strategy, "F-Pruning" means the experimental results obtained by full-scope-predictive forward-checking pruning strategy, "P" means the number of pruning in the process of P-Pruning, "F" means the number of pruning in the process of F-Pruning, the symbol "-" means not applicable due to either the absence of code representation or time-out or out-of-memory. We set a time-out of 10 min for all the tables.

Table 1. Experimental Results for Pruning Strategy

Benchmarks			StInG		OOPSLA22		Our Approach							
Name		Lines of Code	Time (s)	SS	Time (s)	SS	Only P-Pruning Strategy				Only F-Pruning Strategy			
							Time (s)	SS	P	Speedup	Time (s)	SS	F	Speedup
SVCOMP	down	-	0	9	0.01	15	0.01	6	5	1.00x	0.01	7	3	1.00x
	frag	-	0	109	0.05	102	0.03	71	15	1.67x	0.05	91	2	1.00x
	half	-	0	32	0.02	49	0.01	26	30	2.00x	0.02	35	3	1.00x
	large	-	0	123	0.03	146	0.03	110	22	1.00x	0.03	133	2	1.00x
	seq	-	0	39	0.01	48	0.02	25	15	0.50x	0.01	29	4	1.00x
	upb	-	0	9	0.01	15	0.01	6	5	1.00x	0.01	7	3	1.00x
	up	-	0	60	0.02	52	0.01	32	20	2.00x	0.01	52	0	2.00x
Scheduler*	2p	-	0.01	26	0.01	26	0	13	8	-	0.01	19	4	1.00x
	3p	-	0.17	380	0.06	207	0.05	102	23	1.20x	0.05	176	7	1.20x
	4p	-	60.81	26,629	0.48	1,348	0.46	1,043	51	1.04x	0.47	1,347	9	1.02x
	5p	-	7,436.34	2,548,704	6.88	15,172	6.28	14,454	86	1.10x	7.84	15,076	13	0.88x
	6p	-	-	-	299.77	54,862	295.21	52,348	151	1.02x	298.89	54,692	29	1.00x
Scheduler	3p	336	0.17	279	0.05	234	0.07	112	22	0.71x	0.08	169	9	0.63x
	4p	609	4.16	2,895	0.36	1,318	0.73	933	44	0.49x	0.66	1,210	14	0.55x
	5p	1017	135.8	39,150	3.8	6,728	3.84	5,677	85	0.99x	5.08	6,419	20	0.75x
	6p	1587	7,541.53	906,454	68.46	51,342	66.35	49,206	122	1.03x	68.43	50,988	27	1.00x
	7p	2352	-	-	742.25	299,471	730.70	295,661	187	1.02x	747.35	298,531	35	0.99x
Fischer	6p	710	9.18	8,423	0.67	2,808	0.82	1,496	100	0.82x	0.82	2,808	0	0.82x
	7p	987	59.16	32,668	2.62	6,188	3.83	3,936	121	0.68x	3.21	6,188	0	0.82x
	8p	1327	373.62	127,918	10.69	14,231	5.28	10,290	205	2.02x	13.63	14,231	0	0.78x
	9p	1736	2,345.96	503,369	43.14	34,033	36.78	28,117	236	1.17x	47.47	34,033	0	0.91x
	10p	2218	14,664.68	1,985,857	186.40	90,362	161.33	81,102	366	1.16x	195.32	90,362	0	0.95x
	11p	2780	-	-	766.24	235,812	720.10	222,982	409	1.06x	783.37	235,812	0	0.98x
Cars	2p	216	0.01	28	0.01	61	0.02	51	3	0.50x	0.01	57	1	1.00x
	3p	616	560.7	788,508	0.94	2,279	1	2,245	5	0.94x	1.53	2,275	1	0.61x
	4p	1283	-	-	83.87	37,525	89.4	37,454	10	0.94x	85.4	37,519	1	0.98x

In Table 1, we compare the runtime, successful subsumption count and pruning count with the tool of StInG and OOPSLA22 under the setting that our approach only employs P-Pruning strategy or only employs F-Pruning strategy without divide-and-conquer strategy. We can observe that the P-Pruning strategy could reduce the successful subsumption count, which means that successful subsumption could be detected earlier so that leading to a less subsumption count. The pruning count also represents that the P-Pruning strategy could work and the speedup also indicates that less runtime is needed if the redundant and unnecessary checking is removed.

Table 2. Experimental Results for Divide-and-Conquer Strategy

Benchmarks			StInG		OOPSLA22		Our Approach							
Name		Lines of Code	Time (s)	SS	Time (s)	SS	Only D-and-C Strategy			D-and-C + P + F				
							Time (s)	SS	Speedup	Time (s)	SS	P	F	Speedup
SVCOMP	down	-	0	9	0.01	15	0.01	27	1.00x	<0.01	22	2	3	-
	frag	-	0	109	0.05	102	0.05	234	1.00x	0.03	224	13	2	1.67x
	half	-	0	32	0.02	49	0.01	123	2.00x	0.01	116	27	3	2.00x
	large	-	0	123	0.03	146	0.02	503	1.50x	0.03	496	20	2	1.00x
	seq	-	0	39	0.01	48	0.01	108	1.00x	0.01	99	11	4	1.00x
	upb	-	0	9	0.01	15	0.01	27	1.00x	0.01	22	2	3	1.00x
	up	-	0	60	0.02	52	0.01	113	2.00x	0.01	106	20	0	2.00x
Scheduler*	2p	-	0.01	26	0.01	26	0.01	46	1.00x	<0.01	47	3	2	-
	3p	-	0.17	380	0.06	207	0.04	407	1.50x	0.05	410	13	3	1.20x
	4p	-	60.81	26,629	0.48	1,348	0.19	2,010	2.53x	0.26	2,013	33	4	1.85x
	5p	-	7,436.34	2,548,704	6.88	15,172	0.82	10,177	8.39x	0.73	10,178	65	5	9.42x
Scheduler	3p	336	0.17	279	0.05	234	0.03	517	1.67x	0.05	519	10	3	1.00x
	4p	609	4.16	2,895	0.36	1,318	0.21	3,110	1.71x	0.23	3,111	23	5	1.57x
	5p	1017	135.8	39,150	3.8	6,728	0.83	17,095	4.58x	0.98	17,099	55	6	3.88x
	6p	1587	7,541.53	906,454	68.46	51,342	4.53	57,661	15.11x	4.05	57,668	82	7	16.90x
Fischer	6p	710	9.18	8,423	0.67	2,808	0.33	8,559	2.03x	0.32	8,553	100	0	2.09x
	7p	987	59.16	32,668	2.62	6,188	0.72	39,345	3.64x	0.73	39,338	121	0	3.59x
	8p	1327	373.62	127,918	10.69	14,231	1.17	148,044	9.14x	1.33	148,036	205	0	8.04x
Cars	2p	216	0.01	28	0.01	61	0.01	130	1.00x	0.01	131	2	1	1.00x
	3p	616	560.7	788,508	0.94	2,279	0.07	1,912	13.43x	0.06	1,913	4	1	15.67x
	4p	1283	-	-	83.87	37,525	0.48	43,931	174.73x	0.70	43,931	7	1	119.81x

In Table 2, we compare the runtime, successful subsumption count and pruning count with StInG and OOPSLA22 under the setting that our approach employs P-Pruning and F-Pruning strategy with divide-and-conquer strategy, where requires a trading off between using more memory and processing more local subsumption in parallel. We can observe that the D-and-C strategy could reduce the runtime. The successful subsumption count for D-and-C strategy is more than StInG and OOPSLA22 because the subsumption was solved in segment. The pruning count also represents that the pruning strategy works and the speedup shows that the D-and-C strategy actually has a positive effect.

7 Related Work

Compared to related works, we focus on the invariant generation problem.

Constraint Solving. Our invariant generation approach falls in the category of constraint solving. Most relevantly, we compare our approach with the template-based linear invariant generation which is based on Farkas' Lemma. The approach proposed in [7] pioneers the framework of linear invariant generation using Farkas' Lemma, which is based on the template. It generates linear invariants through quantifier elimination and several heuristics but suffers from high run-time complexity. After that, the approach proposed in [21] focuses on improving the scalability of the approaches [28] by employing the location-by-location strategy with the segmented subsumption testing. Furthermore, our approach employs two strategies to mitigate the combinatorial explosion caused by using heuristics, hence enhancing the scalability of the latest approach [21]. The approach proposed in [13] introduces a method for reducing the second-order constraints (derived from Farkas' Lemma) to SAT formulate which is then solved by the SAT solver, focusing on the field of inter-procedural program verification, weakest precondition and strongest postcondition inference. However, their approach aims to present new techniques and applications in program analysis, but our approach aims to boost up the process of program analysis. Thus, their approach is orthogonal to ours. The approach proposed in [14] and the tool InvGen [15] introduce a method for integrating abstract interpretation and constraint solving, while our approach aims at speeding up and enhancing the scalability in constraint solving. Thus, their approaches are orthogonal to ours. The approach proposed in [19] suggests a matrix-algebra method with Farkas' Lemma to synthesize linear invariant only over the single unnested while-loop, but our approach considers the general transition system for arbitrary program structure. Thus, its approach is orthogonal to ours. Other relevant approaches proposed in [1,5,6,18,23,26] describe the method that handles the polynomial invariant generation problems, which focuses on a different aspect to linear invariant generation and thus is orthogonal to ours.

Other Methods. Invariant generation method also includes logical inference [10,31], machine learning [11,17,32], dynamic analysis [8,22] and abstract interpretation [25,27]. However, these methods could not ensure accuracy on the generated invariants due to the specialized inference rules or the principles of data fitting, except for rare cases [12] in abstract interpretation. The recurrence analysis [3,9] is only applicable to the scenarios where the recurrence relation can be solved with a closed form solution. In contrast, constraint solving offers a more generally applicable approach, capable of addressing a wider range of problems even when a closed form solution does not exist.

8 Conclusion

We propose an optimized algorithm to address the combinatorial explosion issue by trading off space for time-efficiency. Our approach employs two key strategies to boost speed. First, we apply a divide-and-conquer strategy to decompose a complex problem into smaller, more manageable subproblems that can be solved quickly and in parallel. Second, we utilize the pruning strategy within two intelligent ways to navigate through the depth-first search process to avoid redundant and unnecessary checks. These improvements maintain the accuracy and speed up the analysis. Our experiments indicate that our approach outperforms the state-of-the-art, demonstrating significant speed improvements. With this solution, we make a significant advance in speeding up the invariant generation with Farkas' Lemma. Future work could consider more powerful pruning strategies to reduce redundant and unnecessary checks.

Acknowledgement. This work is supported by the National Natural Science Foundation of China Grant No. 61872232.

References

1. Adjé, A., Garoche, P.-L., Magron, V.: Property-based polynomial invariant generation using sums-of-squares optimization. In: Blazy, S., Jensen, T. (eds.) SAS 2015. LNCS, vol. 9291, pp. 235–251. Springer, Heidelberg (2015). https://doi.org/10.1007/978-3-662-48288-9_14
2. Asadi, A., Chatterjee, K., Fu, H., Goharshady, A.K., Mahdavi, M.: Polynomial reachability witnesses via stellensätze. In: PLDI, pp. 772–787. ACM (2021). https://doi.org/10.1145/3453483.3454076
3. Breck, J., Cyphert, J., Kincaid, Z., Reps, T.W.: Templates and recurrences: better together. In: PLDI, pp. 688–702. ACM (2020).https://doi.org/10.1145/3385412.3386035
4. Chatterjee, K., Fu, H., Goharshady, A.K.: Non-polynomial worst-case analysis of recursive programs. ACM Trans. Program. Lang. Syst. **41**(4), 20:1–20:52 (2019). https://doi.org/10.1145/3339984
5. Chatterjee, K., Fu, H., Goharshady, A.K., Goharshady, E.K.: Polynomial invariant generation for non-deterministic recursive programs. In: PLDI, pp. 672–687. ACM (2020). https://doi.org/10.1145/3385412.3385969
6. Chen, Y.-F., Hong, C.-D., Wang, B.-Y., Zhang, L.: Counterexample-guided polynomial loop invariant generation by lagrange interpolation. In: Kroening, D., Păsăreanu, C.S. (eds.) CAV 2015. LNCS, vol. 9206, pp. 658–674. Springer, Cham (2015). https://doi.org/10.1007/978-3-319-21690-4_44
7. Colón, M.A., Sankaranarayanan, S., Sipma, H.B.: Linear invariant generation using non-linear constraint solving. In: Hunt, W.A., Somenzi, F. (eds.) CAV 2003. LNCS, vol. 2725, pp. 420–432. Springer, Heidelberg (2003). https://doi.org/10.1007/978-3-540-45069-6_39
8. Csallner, C., Tillmann, N., Smaragdakis, Y.: Dysy: dynamic symbolic execution for invariant inference. In: ICSE, pp. 281–290. ACM (2008).https://doi.org/10.1145/1368088.1368127
9. Farzan, A., Kincaid, Z.: Compositional recurrence analysis. In: FMCAD, pp. 57–64. IEEE (2015)
10. Garg, P., Löding, C., Madhusudan, P., Neider, D.: ICE: a robust framework for learning invariants. In: Biere, A., Bloem, R. (eds.) CAV 2014. LNCS, vol. 8559, pp. 69–87. Springer, Cham (2014). https://doi.org/10.1007/978-3-319-08867-9_5

11. Garg, P., Neider, D., Madhusudan, P., Roth, D.: Learning invariants using decision trees and implication counterexamples. In: POPL, pp. 499–512. ACM (2016https://doi.org/10.1145/2837614.2837664
12. Giacobazzi, R., Ranzato, F.: Completeness in abstract interpretation: a domain perspective. In: Johnson, M. (ed.) AMAST 1997. LNCS, vol. 1349, pp. 231–245. Springer, Heidelberg (1997). https://doi.org/10.1007/BFb0000474
13. Gulwani, S., Srivastava, S., Venkatesan, R.: Program analysis as constraint solving. In: PLDI, pp. 281–292. ACM (2008).https://doi.org/10.1145/1375581.1375616
14. Gupta, A., Majumdar, R., Rybalchenko, A.: From tests to proofs. In: Kowalewski, S., Philippou, A. (eds.) TACAS 2009. LNCS, vol. 5505, pp. 262–276. Springer, Heidelberg (2009). https://doi.org/10.1007/978-3-642-00768-2_24
15. Gupta, A., Rybalchenko, A.: InvGen: an efficient invariant generator. In: Bouajjani, A., Maler, O. (eds.) CAV 2009. LNCS, vol. 5643, pp. 634–640. Springer, Heidelberg (2009). https://doi.org/10.1007/978-3-642-02658-4_48
16. Halbwachs, N., Proy, Y., Roumanoff, P.: Verification of real-time systems using linear relation analysis. Formal Methods Syst. Des. **11**(2), 157–185 (1997). https://doi.org/10.1023/A:1008678014487
17. He, J., Singh, G., Püschel, M., Vechev, M.T.: Learning fast and precise numerical analysis. In: PLDI, pp. 1112–1127. ACM (2020). https://doi.org/10.1145/3385412.3386016
18. Hrushovski, E., Ouaknine, J., Pouly, A., Worrell, J.: Polynomial invariants for affine programs. In: LICS, pp. 530–539. ACM (2018). https://doi.org/10.1145/3209108.3209142
19. Ji, Y., Fu, H., Fang, B., Chen, H.: Affine loop invariant generation via matrix algebra. In: Shoham, S., Vizel, Y. (eds.) Computer Aided Verification - 34th International Conference, CAV 2022, Haifa, Israel, 7-10 August 2022, Proceedings, Part I, LNCS, vol. 13371, pp. 257–281. Springer, Cham (2022). https://doi.org/10.1007/978-3-031-13185-1_13
20. Lamport, L.: A fast mutual exclusion algorithm. ACM Trans. Comput. Syst. **5**(1), 1–11 (1987). https://doi.org/10.1145/7351.7352
21. Liu, H., Fu, H., Yu, Z., Song, J., Li, G.: Scalable linear invariant generation with farkas' lemma. Proc. ACM Program. Lang. **6**(OOPSLA2), 204–232 (2022). https://doi.org/10.1145/3563295
22. Nguyen, T., Kapur, D., Weimer, W., Forrest, S.: Using dynamic analysis to discover polynomial and array invariants. In: ICSE, pp. 683–693. IEEE Computer Society (2012). https://doi.org/10.1109/ICSE.2012.6227149
23. de Oliveira, S., Bensalem, S., Prevosto, V.: Polynomial invariants by linear algebra. In: Artho, C., Legay, A., Peled, D. (eds.) ATVA 2016. LNCS, vol. 9938, pp. 479–494. Springer, Cham (2016). https://doi.org/10.1007/978-3-319-46520-3_30
24. Padon, O., McMillan, K.L., Panda, A., Sagiv, M., Shoham, S.: Ivy: safety verification by interactive generalization. In: PLDI, pp. 614–630. ACM (2016). https://doi.org/10.1145/2908080.2908118
25. Rodríguez-Carbonell, E., Kapur, D.: An abstract interpretation approach for automatic generation of polynomial invariants. In: Giacobazzi, R. (ed.) SAS 2004. LNCS, vol. 3148, pp. 280–295. Springer, Heidelberg (2004). https://doi.org/10.1007/978-3-540-27864-1_21
26. Rodríguez-Carbonell, E., Kapur, D.: Automatic generation of polynomial loop invariants: algebraic foundations. In: ISSAC, pp. 266–273. ACM (2004). https://doi.org/10.1145/1005285.1005324

27. Rodríguez-Carbonell, E., Kapur, D.: Automatic generation of polynomial invariants of bounded degree using abstract interpretation. Sci. Comput. Program. **64**(1), 54–75 (2007). https://doi.org/10.1016/j.scico.2006.03.003
28. Sankaranarayanan, S., Sipma, H.B., Manna, Z.: Constraint-based linear-relations analysis. In: Giacobazzi, R. (ed.) SAS 2004. LNCS, vol. 3148, pp. 53–68. Springer, Heidelberg (2004). https://doi.org/10.1007/978-3-540-27864-1_7
29. Schrijver, A.: Theory of linear and integer programming. Wiley-Interscience series in discrete mathematics and optimization, Wiley (1999)
30. Software verification competition. https://sv-comp.sosy-lab.org (2023)
31. Xu, R., He, F., Wang, B.: Interval counterexamples for loop invariant learning. In: ESEC/FSE, pp. 111–122. ACM (2020). https://doi.org/10.1145/3368089.3409752
32. Yao, J., Ryan, G., Wong, J., Jana, S., Gu, R.: Learning nonlinear loop invariants with gated continuous logic networks. In: PLDI, pp. 106–120. ACM (2020). https://doi.org/10.1145/3385412.3385986

DeepCDCL: A CDCL-based Neural Network Verification Framework

Zongxin Liu[1,2], Pengfei Yang[1], Lijun Zhang[1,2(✉)], and Xiaowei Huang[3]

[1] Key Laboratory of System Software (Chinese Academy of Sciences) and State Key Laboratory of Computer Science, Institute of Software, Chinese Academy of Sciences, Beijing, China
{liuzx,yangpf,zhanglj}@ios.ac.cn

[2] University of Chinese Academy of Sciences, Beijing, China

[3] The University of Liverpool, Liverpool, UK
xiaowei.huang@liverpool.ac.uk

Abstract. Neural networks in safety-critical applications face increasing security and safety concerns due to their susceptibility to little disturbance. In this paper, we propose DeepCDCL, a novel neural network verification framework based on the Conflict-Driven Clause Learning (CDCL) algorithm. We introduce an asynchronous clause learning and management structure, reducing redundant time consumption compared to the direct application of the CDCL framework. Furthermore, we also provide a detailed evaluation of the performance of our approach on the ACAS Xu and MNIST datasets, showing a significant speed-up in most verification problems.

1 Introduction

With the widespread application of deep neural networks (DNNs) in safety-critical areas such as flight control [16] and autonomous driving [37], any mistake in their decision-making process can lead to catastrophic consequences. Ensuring the safety of neural networks has become increasingly important. Formal verification is a technique to prove the correctness of hardware or software systems. However, formal verification of neural networks can be time-consuming, which limits its practical application. To promote its broader application, it is necessary to explore more efficient verification frameworks.

Most state-of-the-art DNN verification tools are based on the basic branch-and-bound framework. These tools primarily focus on accelerating and improving the accuracy of computing the bounds for each neuron, as well as selecting the branching order. For instance, α, β-CROWN [40,43,47] employs GPU acceleration to compute neuron bounds and uses Lagrange multipliers to encode the constraints of branching decisions, thus enhancing the accuracy of the bounds. MN-BaB [10] utilizes Lagrange multipliers to encode multi-neuron constraints and improve the accuracy of the bound. Marabou [19] uses SOI local search to determine a suitable branching order, with the decision based on the neuron that has the most significant impact on the output layer. LayerSAR [45] and PeregriNN [21] select the neuron closest to the input layer for branching, as it may have the most significant impact on the whole network.

W.-N. Chin and Z. Xu (Eds.): TASE 2024, LNCS 14777, pp. 343–355, 2024.
https://doi.org/10.1007/978-3-031-64626-3_20

However, these methods do not fully utilize the infeasible search paths generated during verification, which could be used to prune the search space. To address this limitation, some verification frameworks have been introduced. For example, Planet [9] incorporated the SAT framework into neural network verification. However, Planet did not fully exploit the impact of node branching on boundaries. Additionally, the selection of split nodes in Planet is determined by the SAT solver at the SAT problem level, without fully leveraging neural network characteristics. Moreover, the traditional SAT framework is not well suited for parallel solving and asynchronous learning of conflict clauses, leading to additional time consumption in the solving process. This highlights the need for further research and development of verification tools that can effectively leverage infeasible paths and optimize the verification process for neural networks.

Based on the aforementioned circumstances, we propose the DEEPCDCL framework. This framework is built upon the Conflict-Driven Clause Learning (CDCL) algorithm, which uses conflict clauses to prune the search space and accelerate the solution process. In order to further enhance the efficiency of the CDCL framework, we introduce an asynchronous clause learning and management structure that mitigates additional time consumption during the solving process. The contributions of this work can be succinctly outlined as follows.

1. We propose DEEPCDCL, a novel neural network verification framework integrating state-of-the-art neural network verification tools with the CDCL framework.
2. Based on the characteristics of neural network verification problems, we introduce an asynchronous clause learning and management structure, reducing redundant time consumption compared to the direct application of the CDCL framework.
3. We demonstrate specific speed-ups of DEEPCDCL on two datasets and provide an illustration of the acceleration of DEEPCDCL in branch cutting.

2 Background

In this section, we provide an overview of the neural network verification problem and traditional verification techniques.

2.1 Neural Network Verification Problem

Consider a feedforward neural network $f : \mathbb{R}^{n_0} \rightarrow \mathbb{R}^{n_L}$ with L layers and n_i neurons in each layer. Pre-activation and post-activation functions are defined as $z^{(i)}(\boldsymbol{x}) = \mathbf{W}^{(i)}\hat{z}^{(i-1)}(\boldsymbol{x}) + \boldsymbol{b}_i$ and $\hat{z}^{(i)}(\boldsymbol{x}) = \sigma(z^{(i)}(\boldsymbol{x}))$, where σ denotes an activation function, $\hat{z}^{(0)}(\boldsymbol{x}) = \boldsymbol{x}$, $\mathbf{W}^{(i)} \in \mathbb{R}^{n_i \times n_{i-1}}$, $\boldsymbol{b}^{(i)} \in \mathbb{R}^{n_i}$ and $i \in [L]$, here $[L]$ denote the set $\{1, 2, \ldots, L\}$. The neural network function is then defined as $f(\boldsymbol{x}) = z^{(L)}(\boldsymbol{x})$. In this paper, we focus on neural networks with the ReLU activation function, which is defined as $\mathrm{ReLU}(x) = \max(0, x)$ for $x \in \mathbb{R}$.

Formally, the neural network verification problem can be defined as follows.

Definition 1 (Neural Network Verification Problem). *Neural Network Verification Problem is a tuple* $\langle f, \mathcal{C}, \mathcal{P} \rangle$, *to determine whether* $\forall \boldsymbol{x} \in \mathcal{C}, f(\boldsymbol{x}) \in \mathcal{P}$ *holds, where:*

– $f : \mathbb{R}^{n_0} \rightarrow \mathbb{R}^{n_L}$ *is a neural network,*

- $\mathcal{C} = \{\boldsymbol{x} \in \mathbb{R}^{n_0} \mid \bigwedge_{i\in[n_0]} \boldsymbol{l}_i \le \boldsymbol{x}_i \le \boldsymbol{u}_i\}$ *is the input constraint, and* $\boldsymbol{l}_i$ *and* $\boldsymbol{u}_i$ *are the lower and upper bounds of the input* $\boldsymbol{x}_i$,
- $\mathcal{P} = \{\boldsymbol{y} \in \mathbb{R}^{n_L} \mid \bigwedge_j {\boldsymbol{a}^j}^{\mathrm{T}} \boldsymbol{y} \le b^j\}$ *is the property constraint, where* $\boldsymbol{a}^j$ *and* b^j *are the coefficients and the constant term of the* j*-th constraint.*

If an input $\boldsymbol{x}^* \in \mathcal{C}$ *satisfies* $f(\boldsymbol{x}^*) \notin \mathcal{P}$, *we call* $\boldsymbol{x}^*$ *a counterexample.*

We focus on the local robustness verification problem, where input constraints are defined as $\mathcal{C} = \{\boldsymbol{x} \in \mathbb{R}^{n_0} \mid \bigwedge_{i\in[n_L]} |\boldsymbol{x}_i - \boldsymbol{x}_i^0| \le \varepsilon\}$ and the property constraint is defined as $\mathcal{P} = \{\boldsymbol{y} \in \mathbb{R}^{n_L} \mid \bigwedge_{j\in[n_L], j\ne c} \boldsymbol{y}_j - \boldsymbol{y}_c \le 0\}$, where $\boldsymbol{x}^0$ is the original input, ε is the robustness radius, and $c = \arg\max_j f(\boldsymbol{x}^0)_j$ is the original classification result.

2.2 Traditional Verification Techniques

A neural network verification procedure typically involves three components: constraint solving, bound computation, and branch selection, where the latter two are known as the Branch-and-Bound (BaB) process. It begins with abstracting each neuron using linear relaxations [34] and calculating its upper/lower bound. If property verification cannot be achieved through the bound computation, more accurate constraint solving method like linear programming (LP) is employed. If constraint solving still cannot determine the property validity, the process proceeds to branch selection on ReLU activations, where a ReLU relation with uncertain activation patterns is split into the activated branch and the deactivated one. The process continues recursively until the property is verified or a counterexample is found.

Conflict-Driven Clause Learning (CDCL) [24] is a vital technique widely used in contemporary SAT and SMT solvers. The CDCL framework integrates conflict clause learning, unit propagation and other techniques to improve efficiency, showing its effectiveness in many branch-and-bound problems like SAT and linear SMT [28,30], but it has not been well suited for neural network verification.

3 DEEPCDCL Verification Framework

This section introduces DEEPCDCL, a CDCL-based neural network verification framework. We provide an overview of the DEEPCDCL before detailing its Solver Module and Clause Manager, followed by implementation and optimization strategies.

3.1 Overview of DEEPCDCL

The comprehensive workflow of the DEEPCDCL framework is illustrated in Fig. 1 , which outlines two key modules: the Solver module and the Clause Manager. The Solver module undertakes the task of solving verification problems through n Solver threads. Each thread employs an SAT solver to apply conflict clauses generated earlier and call a neural network verifier to solve subproblems. Subproblems can be represented as search paths, which are generated by branch selection or partitioning the input space.

In contrast, the Clause Manager module generates, collects, and manages conflict clauses. In the verification context, conflict clauses can be seen as a sub-UNSAT path

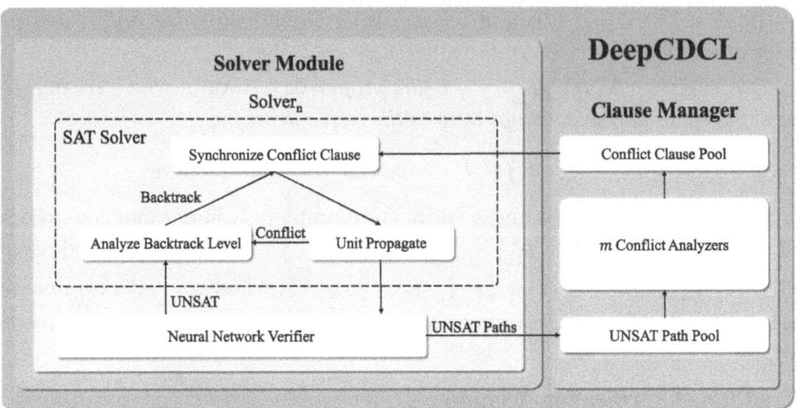

Fig. 1. DEEPCDCL Framework

Algorithm 1. DEEPCDCL Framework

Input:

A verification problem $\langle f, \mathcal{C}, \mathcal{P}\rangle$, number of solver threads n, number of conflict analyzer threads m

Output:

UNSAT ($\forall \boldsymbol{x} \in \mathcal{C}, f(\boldsymbol{x}) \in \mathcal{P}$) or **SAT** ($\exists \boldsymbol{x}^* \in \mathcal{C}, f(\boldsymbol{x}^*) \notin \mathcal{P}$) of $\langle f, \mathcal{C}, \mathcal{P}\rangle$

function DEEPCDCL($f, \mathcal{C}, \mathcal{P}, n, m$)
  $\mathcal{P}ool_c \leftarrow \emptyset, \mathcal{P}ool_u \leftarrow \emptyset$ ▷ $\mathcal{P}ool_c, \mathcal{P}ool_u$ are shared with different threads
  $\mathcal{S} \leftarrow$ GENERATE_SUBPROBLEMS($f, \mathcal{C}, \mathcal{P}$) ▷ $\mathcal{S}$ is a set of search paths $p_1, p_2, ..., p_k$
  CLAUSE_MANAGER($f, \mathcal{C}, \mathcal{P}, \mathcal{P}ool_c, \mathcal{P}ool_u, m$) ▷ Runs asynchronously (Alg 4)
  $res \leftarrow$ SOLVER_MODULE($f, \mathcal{C}, \mathcal{P}, \mathcal{S}, \mathcal{P}ool_c, \mathcal{P}ool_u, n$) ▷ Runs asynchronously (Alg 2)
  return res

of the original UNSAT path. This module involves a collection of m Conflict Analyzer threads specifically designed to analyze UNSAT paths during the verification process and maintains two distinct pools: the Conflict Clause Pool and the UNSAT Path Pool. These pools serve as repositories for conflict clauses generated by the m conflict analyzers and UNSAT paths generated by the n solvers, respectively.

As illustrated in Algorithm 1, the DEEPCDCL framework first initializes the Conflict Clause Pool and the UNSAT Path Pool, which are shared among all threads. It then generates a set of search paths $\mathcal{S}$ as subproblems and initiates the Clause Manager and Solver Module. The Solver Module and Clause Manager run asynchronously. Once the Solver Module completes the verification, the DEEPCDCL framework stops all additional threads and returns the verification result.

3.2 Solver Module

Algorithm 2 shows the Solver Module, which solves the verification problem. The Solver Module initializes n Solver Threads and assigns each free thread a subproblem

Algorithm 2. Solver Module

Input:
Verification Problem $\langle f, \mathcal{C}, \mathcal{P} \rangle$, subproblems $\mathcal{S}$, conflict clause pool $\mathcal{P}ool_c$, UNSAT path pool $\mathcal{P}ool_u$, number of solver threads n

Output:
UNSAT ($\forall \boldsymbol{x} \in \mathcal{C}, f(\boldsymbol{x}) \in \mathcal{P}$) or **SAT** ($\exists \boldsymbol{x}^* \in \mathcal{C}, f(\boldsymbol{x}^*) \notin \mathcal{P}$) of $\langle f, \mathcal{C}, \mathcal{P} \rangle$

function SOLVER_MODULE($f, \mathcal{C}, \mathcal{P}, \mathcal{S}, \mathcal{P}ool_c, \mathcal{P}ool_u, n$)
    $\mathcal{T}_s \leftarrow$ Initialize n Solver Threads
    for $p \in \mathcal{S}$ **do** ▷ Runs in parallel
        $t_s \leftarrow$ FREE_THREAD($\mathcal{T}_s$)
        $res = t_s$.SOLVE($f, \mathcal{C}, \mathcal{P}, p, \mathcal{P}ool_c, \mathcal{P}ool_u$)
        if $res =$ **SAT then**
            Stop all solver threads in $\mathcal{T}_s$
            return SAT
    Wait for all solver threads in $\mathcal{T}_s$ to finish
    return UNSAT

from $\mathcal{S}$. When creating subproblems, it is crucial to ensure that solving all subproblems equals solving the original problem. Each Solver Thread then calls the SOLVE function to solve its assigned subproblem. If any Solver Thread returns **SAT**, indicating that a counterexample has been found, the Solver Module returns **SAT**, indicating a property violation. Conversely, if all subproblems are resolved without finding a counterexample, the Solver Module returns **UNSAT**, confirming that the property holds.

The algorithm 3 details the function SOLVE. It begins by initializing an SAT solver and a neural network verifier. Then, it adds the subproblem, represented as a search path p, to the SAT solver as a clause. The search path p is a conjunction of literals, with each literal representing a branching decision. We use a literal to represent the activation state of a neuron, where the positive literal means the activated state and the negative literal signifies the deactivated state. For example, to deactivate the j-th neuron in the i-th layer, we add the literal $\neg z_j^{(i)}$ to the search path. In the neural network verifier, each literal in the path is translated into a set of constraints and incorporated into the verifier. For example, the literal $\neg z_j^{(i)}$ can be translated into the constraint $z_j^{(i)}(\boldsymbol{x}) \leq 0$.

After initializing the current search path p_{cur} as an empty set, the function enters a verification loop. First, it synchronizes the conflict clauses from the conflict clause pool and adds them to the SAT solver. If a conflict arises during unit propagation, the function analyzes the backtracking level, a common SAT solver technique, to identify the appropriate level to backtrack to. Typically, this process backtracks at least one level to resolve the conflict. The SAT solver then backtracks to the specified level, and the function returns to the beginning of the loop to repeat unit propagation. As backtracking involves adding certain literals to the current search path p_{cur}, this process may result in new conflicts. If the backtracking level is less than zero, indicating that the subproblem is unsatisfiable, the function returns **UNSAT**. Otherwise, the SAT solver backtracks and the function continues the loop. If the unit propagation process finishes without conflict, the function calls the neural network verifier to verify the current search path $p \wedge p_{\text{cur}}$ under the constraints of the original problem. If the verifier returns **SAT**,

Algorithm 3. Solve Function

Input:

Verification Problem $\langle f, \mathcal{C}, \mathcal{P} \rangle$, search path (subproblem) p, conflict clause pool $\mathcal{P}ool_c$, UNSAT path pool $\mathcal{P}ool_u$

Output:

UNSAT or **SAT** of the subproblem with search path p

```
function SOLVE(f, C, P, p, Pool_c, Pool_u)
    solver_SAT ← Initialize an SAT Solver, solver_NN ← Initialize a Neural Network Verifier
    solver_SAT.ADD_CLAUSE(p)
    p_cur ← ∅
    while True do
        clauses ← GET_LATEST_CLAUSES(Pool_c)        ▷ Get the new added conflict clause
        for c ∈ clauses do
            solver_SAT.ADD_CLAUSE(¬c)
        if solver_SAT.UNIT_PROPAGATION(p_cur) = CONFLICT then
            level ← solver_SAT.ANALYZE_BACKTRACK_LEVEL(p_cur)
            if level < 0 then
                break
            solver_SAT.BACKTRACK(level, p_cur)
            continue
        res ← solver_NN.VERIFY(f, C, ¬P, p ∧ p_cur)
        if res = SAT then
            return SAT
        else if res = UNKNOWN then
            p_cur ← p_cur ∧ BRANCH()
        else if res = UNSAT then
            Pool_u ← Pool_u ∪ {p ∧ p_cur}
            solver_SAT.ADD_CLAUSE(¬p_cur)
    return UNSAT
```

which means that a counterexample has been found under the current constraints, the function returns **SAT** since the counterexample also violates the original problem. If the verifier returns **UNKNOWN**, which means the constraints are satisfiable but the verifier cannot find a real counterexample due to the approximation of the network, the function extends the current search path p_{cur} by branch selection and continues the loop. If the verifier returns **UNSAT**, which means that the constraints are unsatisfiable under the current search path, the function adds the conjunction of the current search p_{cur} and the given search path p to the UNSAT path pool ($\mathcal{P}ool_u$) and adds the negation of the current search path to the SAT solver as a clause. The function then continues the loop until the subproblem is determined to be **UNSAT** or **SAT**.

3.3 Clause Manager Module

Algorithm 4 illustrates the Clause Manager, which is responsible for generating, collecting, and managing conflict clauses. The Clause Manager initializes m conflict analyzer threads and runs asynchronously with the Solver Module.

Algorithm 4. Clause Manager

Input:
Verification Problem $\langle f, \mathcal{C}, \mathcal{P} \rangle$, conflict clause pool $\mathcal{P}ool_c$, UNSAT path pool $\mathcal{P}ool_u$, number of conflict analyzer threads m

Output:
Synced conflict clause pool $\mathcal{P}ool_c$ and UNSAT path pool $\mathcal{P}ool_u$

```
function CLAUSE_MANAGER(f, C, P, Pool_c, Pool_u, m)
    T_c ← Initialize m Conflict Analyzer Threads
    while True do
        if STOP_CONDITION() then
            Stop all conflict analyzer thread in T_c
            break
        paths ← GET_LATEST_PATHS(Pool_u)          ▷ Get the new added UNSAT paths
        for p ∈ paths do
            if SHOULD_ANALYZE(p) then             ▷ Check if the path should be analyzed
                t_c ← FREE_THREAD(T_c)
                clause ← t_c.ANALYZE_CLAUSE(f, C, P, p)
                if SHOULD_ADD(cluase) then        ▷ Check if the clause should be added
                    Pool_c ← Pool_c ∪ {clause}
        MANAGE_CLAUSES(Pool_c)
```

The Clause Manager continuously checks the UNSAT Path Pool for new UNSAT paths and analyzes them. If an UNSAT path p should be analyzed, the Clause Manager assigns a free conflict analyzer thread to analyze the path by calling the function ANALYZE_CLAUSE. If the leaned clause needs to be added to the conflict clause pool, the Clause Manager adds it accordingly. The function MANAGE_CLAUSES is used to manage the conflict clauses in the conflict clause pool at intervals to ensure that the conflict clauses are up to date, do not contain redundant clauses and do not exceed the memory limit. The functions SHOULD_ANALYZE, SHOULD_ADD, and MANAGE_CLAUSES collectively manage the conflict clauses. The specific implementations of these functions could be heuristic. We use simple heuristics in our implementation. For the function SHOULD_ANALYZE, we check if the UNSAT path is the latest. As for function SHOULD_ADD, we check if the learned conflict clause is less than half of the original path, as long conflict clauses may not be helpful. In the function MANAGE_CLAUSES, we remove redundant conflict clauses and ensure that the number of conflict clauses does not exceed a certain threshold.

Drawing inspiration from [9], we use elastic filtering [7] as a basic implementation of the function ANALYZE_CLAUSE to generate conflict clauses. This method introduces slack variables to the constraints corresponding to each branching decision in an UNSAT search path. The sum of these slack variables acts as an optimization objective. Subsequently, the procedure iteratively selects the slack variable with the maximum relaxation and sets it to zero until the constraints become unsatisfiable or all slack variables are set to zero. Due to the difficulty in incorporating bound propagation and other verification methods in the elastic filtering process, its verification capabilities are weaker than those of neural network verification tools. Therefore, a search path proven to be unsatisfiable by the neural network verification tool may not be proven as such by this method. If all slack variables are zero and the constraints remain satisfied, the search for conflict clauses fails; otherwise, the constraints corresponding to slack variables set to zero are selected as conflict clauses.

Directly applying elastic filtering to neural network verification problems can be time-consuming, so we have adapted it into an asynchronous process. We use the conflict clause pool to store the learned conflict clauses so that a clause generated from one solver can be used by other solvers. We also add a timestamp to each UNSAT path and only process the latest path when learning conflict clauses. This approach reduces redundant time consumption and ensures that the learned clauses are up-to-date. Furthermore, traditional elastic filtering can be excessively time-consuming when the constraints cannot be identified as unsatisfiable after adding all constraints. To resolve this, we introduce a binary search method to discover conflict clauses based on the original algorithm. This method efficiently filters out undecidable cases by initially adding all constraints and accelerates the conflict clause learning process.

3.4 Implementation and Optimization

In our implementation, we use Z3 [26] as the SAT solver, Marabou [19], the second-place tool in VNN-COMP 23 [6], as the neural network verifier and Gurobi [14] as the LP solver to solve the constraints.

Besides the clause learning method mentioned in Sect. 3.3, we also introduce another conflict clause generation method. During the verification process(Algorithm 3 line 15), we calculate the bounds of each neuron in the neural network. If the lower bound of a neuron exceeds 0 or the upper bound falls to 0 during this process, we can determine its activation state and encode this as a learned clause.

Additionally, we also propose several optimizations. We observed that partitioning the input space a limited number of times can significantly accelerate the verification especially when the number of inputs is small. Therefore, we set a threshold to stop the input partitioning when the number of input partitions exceeds the threshold. We also streamlined the complex and redundant data structures in Marabou during backtracking, retaining only the core components necessary for verification.

4 Evaluation

In our experimental set-up, we utilized a compute server equipped with 256 AMD EPYC 7702 64-core processors, 2TB of memory, and operated on the GNU/Linux operating system. The Marabou tool served as the neural network verifier in the solver module, providing specifications to carry out our experiments.

For ACAS Xu [17], which focuses on the safety of aircraft collision avoidance systems, we used neural networks consisting of 6 layers with 50 neurons in each layer. In our analysis a total of 45 neural networks were utilized, accompanied by four specifications of the Marabou tool. To ensure efficient execution, we established a timeout of 1800 s for each verification task. In the case of the MNIST dataset [8], designed for recognizing handwritten digits, seven neural networks with varying sizes, namely 2×256,

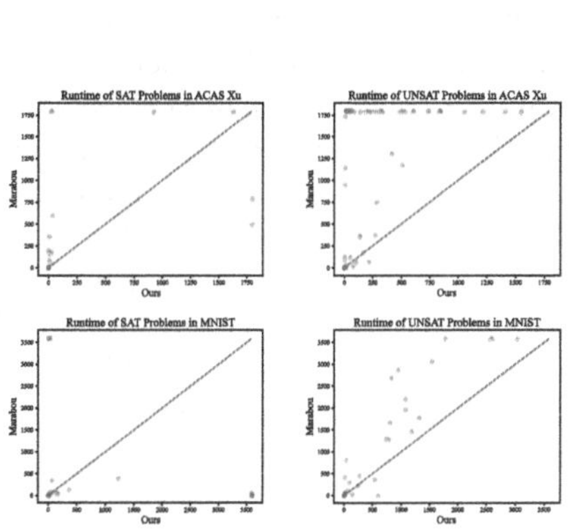

Fig. 2. Comparison of the running time

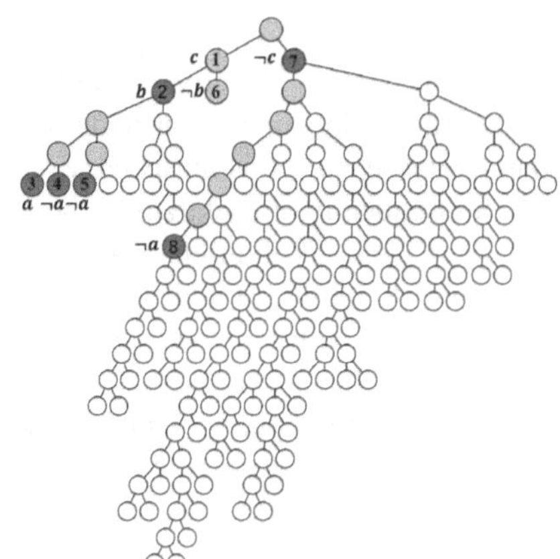

Fig. 3. Case study: search trees generated by Marabou (all the nodes) and DEEPCDCL (colored nodes)

4×256, 6×256, 10×10, 10×20, 20×20, and 20×40, were employed. Specifications were crafted by selecting three images, setting robustness radii at 0.01, 0.03, and 0.1, with classification results ranging from 0 to 9. We chose 81 specifications from the initial set of specifications, thus forming a total of 567 verification tasks. We then exclude 97 tasks that can be successfully attacked by the PGD attack [23]. A timeout of 3,600 s was imposed on each verification task. All experiments were executed with 20 concurrent threads, and we set $n = 10$ and $m = 10$ for DEEPCDCL.

Figure 2 shows the comparison of the running time of DEEPCDCL and Marabou. Overall, DEEPCDCL outperforms Marabou in most cases, solving problems faster than Marabou. In the ACAS Xu dataset, our approach successfully resolves two additional **SAT** problems and 47 more **UNSAT** problems compared to Marabou. Furthermore, our method achieves notable computational efficiency, solving one problem 205 times faster than Marabou, while 11 problems exhibit over 100 times speedup and 24 problems demonstrate more than a 10-fold acceleration relative to Marabou.

In MNIST, DEEPCDCL consistently outperforms Marabou in speed across nearly all **UNSAT** problems. Our approach solves four additional **UNSAT** problems, one instance achieving an impressive 1,478 times speedup. Furthermore, 75 problems show a minimum acceleration of 25%. However, DEEPCDCL does not perform so well in the **SAT** problems, solving 6 fewer than Marabou, but still solving 3 problems that the Marabou tool cannot solve.

To further illustrate the reasons for our acceleration on the **UNSAT** problems, we present a case study in Fig. 3. The figure shows the search trees of a neural network with 2×256 neurons, a specified image 1, target 6, and a robustness radius of 0.05 under the L_∞ norm. The whole search tree is generated by Marabou and the sub-tree of colored nodes is generated by DEEPCDCL with red indicating the conflict clause learned from the corresponding search path. For simplicity, we use the literal a to represent that a neuron is activated and the negative literal $\neg a$ to represent that a neuron is inactivated. Specifically, at node 3, a conflict clause a is identified. At node 5, the conflict clause $\neg a \wedge b$ is retrieved. Consequently, it is deduced that $\neg b$ must always be true. Subsequently, a backtrack to node 1 occurs, where the constraint $\neg b$ is added to the solver. This action renders certain constraints unsatisfiable for Marabou, implying that c cannot be true. At node 8, the conflict clause $\neg a \wedge \neg c$ is retrieved. Note that both c and a cannot be true. However, $\neg a \wedge \neg c$ is a conflict clause, which means they cannot be false either. This leads to the direct conclusion that the problem is unsatisfiable. Compared to Marabou, which explores 179 states and 90 UNSAT paths, DEEPCDCL only explores 17 states and 5 UNSAT paths. Reduced exploration signifies less time consumption, elucidating the reason for our superior speed in **UNSAT** problems.

However, for problems where the verification result is **SAT**, Marabou can utilize multiple threads to explore a broader search space. In contrast, when DEEPCDCL explores a subtree with unsatisfiable problems, it continues until the subproblem's unsatisfiability is confirmed, which can increase time consumption. In addition, although we have improved in solving efficiency, the difference in the maximum network size that DEEPCDCL can verify compared to Marabou is not significant.

5 Related Work

The neural network verification problem was first proposed in 2010 [29]. Since 2017, the field of neural networks verification has rapidly developed, with many neural network verification tools and various verification methods emerging, such as abstract interpretation [11,25,31–34], symbolic propagation [5,13,22,38,39,41,46], convex optimization [1,27], SMT [3,9,12,15,18,20], mathematical programming [4,35,36], Lipschitz constants [41,42] and counterexample-guided abstraction refinement [1,2, 44].

6 Conclusion

In this paper, we propose a novel neural network verification framework, DEEPCDCL that is based on the CDCL framework and tailored to the context of neural network verification. We show that DEEPCDCL achieves faster verification. We provide a detailed evaluation of DEEPCDCL in the ACAS Xu and MNIST datasets, showing that DEEPCDCL is more efficient than Marabou in most cases, especially for unsatisfiable verification problems. We also provide a case study to illustrate why DEEPCDCL outperforms in solving UNSAT problems. In the future, we plan to further optimize the DEEPCDCL framework by designing heuristic CDCL strategies and incorporating our framework into other advanced tools.

Acknowledgement. This work was partially supported by CAS Project for Young Scientists in Basic Research, Grant No. YSBR-040, ISCAS New Cultivation Project ISCAS-PYFX-202201, and ISCAS Basic Research ISCAS-JCZD-202302.

References

1. Anderson, G., Pailoor, S., Dillig, I., Chaudhuri, S.: Optimization and abstraction: a synergistic approach for analyzing neural network robustness. In: Proceedings of the 40th ACM SIGPLAN Conference on Programming Language Design and Implementation, pp. 731–744 (2019)
2. Ashok, P., Hashemi, V., Kretínský, J., Mohr, S.: DeepAbstract: neural network abstraction for accelerating verification. In: Hung, D.V., Sokolsky, O. (eds.) Automated Technology for Verification and Analysis - 18th International Symposium, ATVA 2020, Hanoi, Vietnam, 19–23 October 2020, Proceedings, LNCS, vol. 12302, pp. 92–107. Springer, Cham (2020). https://doi.org/10.1007/978-3-030-59152-6_5
3. Bastani, O., Ioannou, Y., Lampropoulos, L., Vytiniotis, D., Nori, A., Criminisi, A.: Measuring neural net robustness with constraints. In: Advances in Neural Information Processing Systems, vol. **29** (2016)
4. Bertsimas, D., Tsitsiklis, J.N.: Introduction to linear optimization, vol. 6. Athena scientific Belmont, MA (1997)
5. Boopathy, A., Weng, T., Chen, P., Liu, S., Daniel, L.: Cnn-cert: an efficient framework for certifying robustness of convolutional neural networks. In: The Thirty-Third AAAI Conference on Artificial Intelligence, AAAI 2019, The Thirty-First Innovative Applications of Artificial Intelligence Conference, IAAI 2019, The Ninth AAAI Symposium on Educational Advances in Artificial Intelligence, EAAI 2019, Honolulu, Hawaii, USA, January 27 - February 1, 2019. pp. 3240–3247. AAAI Press (2019).https://doi.org/10.1609/aaai.v33i01.33013240
6. Brix, C., Bak, S., Liu, C., Johnson, T.T.: The fourth international verification of neural networks competition (vnn-comp 2023): summary and results (2023)
7. Chinneck, J.W., Dravnieks, E.W.: Locating minimal infeasible constraint sets in linear programs. INFORMS J. Comput. **3**, 157–168 (1991). https://api.semanticscholar.org/CorpusID:207225476
8. Deng, L.: The MNIST database of handwritten digit images for machine learning research. IEEE Signal Process. Mag. **29**(6), 141–142 (2012)
9. Ehlers, R.: Formal verification of piece-wise linear feed-forward neural networks. In: D'Souza, D., Narayan Kumar, K. (eds.) ATVA 2017. LNCS, vol. 10482, pp. 269–286. Springer, Cham (2017). https://doi.org/10.1007/978-3-319-68167-2_19
10. Ferrari, C., Müller, M.N., Jovanovic, N., Vechev, M.T.: Complete verification via multi-neuron relaxation guided branch-and-bound. In: The Tenth International Conference on Learning Representations, ICLR 2022, Virtual Event, 25–29 April 2022. OpenReview.net (2022). https://openreview.net/forum?id=l_amHf1oaK
11. Gehr, T., Mirman, M., Drachsler-Cohen, D., Tsankov, P., Chaudhuri, S., Vechev, M.: Ai2: Safety and robustness certification of neural networks with abstract interpretation. In: 2018 IEEE Symposium on Security and Privacy (SP), pp. 3–18. IEEE (2018)
12. Gopinath, D., Katz, G., Păsăreanu, C.S., Barrett, C.: DeepSafe: a data-driven approach for assessing robustness of neural networks. In: Lahiri, S.K., Wang, C. (eds.) ATVA 2018. LNCS, vol. 11138, pp. 3–19. Springer, Cham (2018). https://doi.org/10.1007/978-3-030-01090-4_1
13. Gowal, S., et al.: Scalable verified training for provably robust image classification. In: Proceedings of the IEEE/CVF International Conference on Computer Vision, pp. 4842–4851 (2019)
14. Gurobi Optimization, L.: Gurobi optimizer reference manual (2021). http://www.gurobi.com
15. Huang, X., Kwiatkowska, M., Wang, S., Wu, M.: Safety verification of deep neural networks. In: Majumdar, R., Kunčak, V. (eds.) CAV 2017. LNCS, vol. 10426, pp. 3–29. Springer, Cham (2017). https://doi.org/10.1007/978-3-319-63387-9_1

16. Julian, K.D., Kochenderfer, M.J., Owen, M.P.: Deep neural network compression for aircraft collision avoidance systems. J. Guid. Control. Dyn. **42**(3), 598–608 (2019)
17. Julian, K.D., Lopez, J., Brush, J.S., Owen, M.P., Kochenderfer, M.J.: Policy compression for aircraft collision avoidance systems. In: 2016 IEEE/AIAA 35th Digital Avionics Systems Conference (DASC), pp. 1–10. IEEE (2016)
18. Katz, G., Barrett, C., Dill, D.L., Julian, K., Kochenderfer, M.J.: Reluplex: an efficient SMT solver for verifying deep neural networks. In: Majumdar, R., Kunčak, V. (eds.) CAV 2017. LNCS, vol. 10426, pp. 97–117. Springer, Cham (2017). https://doi.org/10.1007/978-3-319-63387-9_5
19. Katz, G., Huang, D.A., Ibeling, D., Julian, K., Lazarus, C., Lim, R., Shah, P., Thakoor, S., Wu, H., Zeljić, A., Dill, D.L., Kochenderfer, M.J., Barrett, C.: The marabou framework for verification and analysis of deep neural networks. In: Dillig, I., Tasiran, S. (eds.) CAV 2019. LNCS, vol. 11561, pp. 443–452. Springer, Cham (2019). https://doi.org/10.1007/978-3-030-25540-4_26
20. The marabou framework for verification and analysis of deep neural networks. In: CAV 2019. LNCS, vol. 11561, pp. 443–452. Springer, Cham (2019). https://doi.org/10.1007/978-3-030-25540-4_26
21. Khedr, H., Ferlez, J., Shoukry, Y.: PEREGRiNN: penalized-relaxation greedy neural network verifier. In: Silva, A., Leino, K.R.M. (eds.) CAV 2021. LNCS, vol. 12759, pp. 287–300. Springer, Cham (2021). https://doi.org/10.1007/978-3-030-81685-8_13
22. Li, J., Liu, J., Yang, P., Chen, L., Huang, X., Zhang, L.: Analyzing deep neural networks with symbolic propagation: towards higher precision and faster verification. In: Chang, B.-Y.E. (ed.) SAS 2019. LNCS, vol. 11822, pp. 296–319. Springer, Cham (2019). https://doi.org/10.1007/978-3-030-32304-2_15
23. Madry, A., Makelov, A., Schmidt, L., Tsipras, D., Vladu, A.: Towards deep learning models resistant to adversarial attacks. In: ICLR 2018. OpenReview.net, Vancouver, BC, Canada (2018)
24. Marques-Silva, J., Lynce, I., Malik, S.: Conflict-driven clause learning sat solvers. In: Handbook of Satisfiability, pp. 133–182. IOS press (2021)
25. Mirman, M., Gehr, T., Vechev, M.: Differentiable abstract interpretation for provably robust neural networks. In: International Conference on Machine Learning, pp. 3578–3586. PMLR (2018)
26. de Moura, L., Bjørner, N.: Z3: an efficient SMT solver. In: Ramakrishnan, C.R., Rehof, J. (eds.) TACAS 2008. LNCS, vol. 4963, pp. 337–340. Springer, Heidelberg (2008). https://doi.org/10.1007/978-3-540-78800-3_24
27. Müller, M.N., Makarchuk, G., Singh, G., Püschel, M., Vechev, M.: PRIMA: general and precise neural network certification via scalable convex hull approximations. Proc. ACM Program. Lang. **6**(POPL), 1–33 (2022)
28. Nieuwenhuis, R., Oliveras, A., Tinelli, C.: Solving SAT and SAT modulo theories: from an abstract davis–putnam–logemann–loveland procedure to dpll(T). J. ACM **53**(6), 937–977 (2006). https://doi.org/10.1145/1217856.1217859
29. Pulina, L., Tacchella, A.: An abstraction-refinement approach to verification of artificial neural networks. In: Touili, T., Cook, B., Jackson, P. (eds.) CAV 2010. LNCS, vol. 6174, pp. 243–257. Springer, Heidelberg (2010). https://doi.org/10.1007/978-3-642-14295-6_24
30. Sebastiani, R.: Lazy satisability modulo theories. J. Satisf. Boolean Model. Comput. **3**(3-4), 141–224 (2007). https://doi.org/10.3233/SAT190034
31. Singh, G., Ganvir, R., Püschel, M., Vechev, M.: Beyond the single neuron convex barrier for neural network certification. In: Advances in Neural Information Processing Systems, vol. **32** (2019)
32. Singh, G., Gehr, T., Mirman, M., Püschel, M., Vechev, M.: Fast and effective robustness certification. In: Advances in Neural Information Processing Systems, vol. **31** (2018)

33. Singh, G., Gehr, T., Püschel, M., Vechev, M.: Boosting robustness certification of neural networks. In: International conference on learning representations (2018)
34. Singh, G., Gehr, T., Püschel, M., Vechev, M.T.: An abstract domain for certifying neural networks. PACMPL **3**(POPL), 41:1–41:30 (2019)
35. Tjeng, V., Xiao, K.Y., Tedrake, R.: Evaluating robustness of neural networks with mixed integer programming. In: 7th International Conference on Learning Representations, ICLR 2019, New Orleans, LA, USA, 6–9 May 2019. OpenReview.net (2019). https://openreview.net/forum?id=HyGIdiRqtm
36. Tran, H.-D., Yang, X., Manzanas Lopez, D., Musau, P., Nguyen, L.V., Xiang, W., Bak, S., Johnson, T.T.: NNV: the neural network verification tool for deep neural networks and learning-enabled cyber-physical systems. In: Lahiri, S.K., Wang, C. (eds.) CAV 2020. LNCS, vol. 12224, pp. 3–17. Springer, Cham (2020). https://doi.org/10.1007/978-3-030-53288-8_1
37. Urmson, C., Whittaker, W.: Self-driving cars and the urban challenge. IEEE Intell. Syst. **23**(2), 66–68 (2008)
38. Wang, S., Pei, K., Whitehouse, J., Yang, J., Jana, S.: Efficient formal safety analysis of neural networks. In: Advances in Neural Information Processing Systems, vol. **31** (2018)
39. Wang, S., Pei, K., Whitehouse, J., Yang, J., Jana, S.: Formal security analysis of neural networks using symbolic intervals. In: 27th USENIX Security Symposium (USENIX Security 18), pp. 1599–1614 (2018)
40. Wang, S., Zhang, H., Xu, K., Lin, X., Jana, S., Hsieh, C.J., Kolter, J.Z.: Beta-CROWN: efficient bound propagation with per-neuron split constraints for neural network robustness verification. Adv. Neural. Inf. Process. Syst. **34**, 29909–29921 (2021)
41. Weng, L., et al.: Towards fast computation of certified robustness for ReLu networks. In: International Conference on Machine Learning, pp. 5276–5285. PMLR (2018)
42. Weng, T., et al.: Evaluating the robustness of neural networks: An extreme value theory approach. In: 6th International Conference on Learning Representations, ICLR 2018, Vancouver, BC, Canada, April 30–May 3, 2018, Conference Track Proceedings. OpenReview.net (2018). https://openreview.net/forum?id=BkUHlMZ0b
43. Xu, K., et al.: Fast and complete: enabling complete neural network verification with rapid and massively parallel incomplete verifiers. In: 9th International Conference on Learning Representations, ICLR 2021, Virtual Event, Austria, 3–7 May 2021. OpenReview.net (2021). https://openreview.net/forum?id=nVZtXBI6LNn
44. Yang, P., et al.: Improving neural network verification through spurious region guided refinement. In: TACAS 2021. LNCS, vol. 12651, pp. 389–408. Springer, Cham (2021). https://doi.org/10.1007/978-3-030-72016-2_21
45. Yin, B., Chen, L., Liu, J., Wang, J.: Efficient complete verification of neural networks via layerwised splitting and refinement. IEEE Trans. Comput. Aided Des. Integr. Circuits Syst. **41**(11), 3898–3909 (2022). https://doi.org/10.1109/TCAD.2022.3197534
46. Zhang, H., et al.: Towards stable and efficient training of verifiably robust neural networks. arXiv preprint arXiv:1906.06316 (2019)
47. Zhang, H., et al.: General cutting planes for bound-propagation-based neural network verification. In: NeurIPS (2022). http://papers.nips.cc/paper_files/paper/2022/hash/0b06c8673ebb453e5e468f7743d8f54e-Abstract-Conference.html

Energy-Efficient Motion Planning for Autonomous Vehicles Using UPPAAL STRATEGO

Muhammad Naeem[1,2(✉)], Rong Gu[2(✉)], Cristina Seceleanu[2(✉)], Kim Guldstrand Larsen[1], Brian Nielsen[1], and Michele Albano[1]

[1] Department of Computer Science, Aalborg University, Aalborg, Denmark
{mnaeem,kgl,bnielsen,mialb}@cs.aau.dk

[2] Division of Networked and Embedded Systems, Mälardalen University, Västerås, Sweden
{muhammad.naeem,rong.gu,cristina.seceleanu}@mdu.se

Abstract. Energy-efficient motion planning for autonomous battery-powered vehicles is crucial to increase safety and efficiency by avoiding frequent battery recharge. This paper proposes algorithms for synthesizing energy- and time-efficient motion plans for battery-powered autonomous vehicles. We use stochastic hybrid games to model an appropriate abstraction of the autonomous vehicle and the environment. Based on the model, we synthesize energy- and time-efficient motion plans using Q-learning in UPPAAL STRATEGO. Via experiments, we show that pure Q-learning is insufficient when the problem becomes complex, e.g., Motion Planning (MOP) in large environments. To address this issue, we propose Concatenated Motion Planning (CoMOP), which divides the environment into several regions, synthesizes a motion plan in each region and concatenates the local plans into an entire motion plan for the whole environment. CoMOP enhances the applicability of Q-learning to large and complex environments, reduces synthesis time, and provides efficient navigation and precise motion plans. We conduct experiments with our approaches in an industrial use case. The results show that CoMOP outperforms MOP regarding synthesis time and the ability to deal with complex models. Moreover, we compare the energy- and time-efficient strategies and visualize their differences on different terrains.

1 Introduction

Autonomous vehicles are equipped with advanced sensors, cameras, and communication devices, which enable them to perceive the environment and perform

The research was supported by the ERC Advanced Grant LASSO and Villum Investigator Grant S4OS, and the Swedish Knowledge Foundation via the synergy project ACICS - Assured Cloud Platforms for Industrial Cyber-Physical Systems, grant nr. 20190038, and the profile project DPAC - Dependable Platform for Autonomous Systems and Control, grant nr: 20150022.

W.-N. Chin and Z. Xu (Eds.): TASE 2024, LNCS 14777, pp. 356–373, 2024.
https://doi.org/10.1007/978-3-031-64626-3_21

various tasks without human intervention. In particular, using autonomous vehicles in construction sites can lead to increased productivity, safety, and reduced costs. Ensuring energy efficiency is a critical challenge in autonomous vehicle design, especially for battery-powered ones, where limited energy constrains operating range and duration. Therefore, an efficient motion-planning algorithm is crucial for real-world deployment. However, energy-efficient motion planning is not trivial. Intuitively, a time-efficient motion plan should be energy-efficient, which means a path-finding algorithm like A* [18] would suffice. However, our experiments show that these two kinds of motion plans are not necessarily the same on different terrains and that the energy efficiency of driving depends on the terrain type. For instance, on slopes, the fastest plan can be energy-consuming, while a curved path may cost less energy.

In recent years, reinforcement learning [20] gained popularity for motion planning [1,3]. Despite the simple idea of allowing the machine to learn and accumulate rewards from its actions, these algorithms are data-hungry, and tuning a reward function can be challenging and time-consuming, as our experiments show; synthesizing an energy-efficient motion plan with Q-learning [21] in a 20×20 environment with 2 obstacles takes nearly 2 hours. This motivates us to develop a new method that is able to solve real-world motion-planning problems in a reasonable time, and provide a systematic way of evaluating the learning results, such as the probability of finishing a job before the energy consumption exceeds a threshold.

In this paper, we propose a method (backed by experiments) to generate *energy-efficient motion planning* for battery-powered autonomous vehicles. First, we model the autonomous vehicles and the environment as a *Stochastic Hybrid Game* (SHG) [12]. By using this modeling language, we can construct the control logic as timed games (TG) [2], and encode the vehicle's kinematics and energy consumption as ordinary differential equations (ODE) in the TG. Next, we design *methods* for solving the SHG by using Q-learning, that is, synthesizing time- and energy-efficient motion plans of the model. We construct the model and conduct the synthesis in UPPAAL Stratego [6], which is a toolset of modeling, simulation, verification, and synthesis of timed games. As aforementioned, motion planning by Q-learning is restricted by the scale of the problem, such as the environment size and obstacle numbers. To scale the synthesis, we propose a *novel algorithm*, called *concatenation-based motion planning* (CoMOP), which splits the environment into sub-components, synthesizes a motion plan in each of the sub-components, concatenates the motion plans into a complete one, and verifies the complete plan by using statistical model checking [19]. When concatenating two motion plans, we must ensure the *validity* and *automation* of the concatenation, that is, the final set of states of a partial motion plan is equivalent to the initial set of states of its following motion plan, and the work must be done automatically by our tool, such that CoMOP does not break the autonomy of the system. To meet this ambition, we realize the concatenation via an external library that is invoked by UPPAAL STRATEGO, in which assertions are used for checking the validity of the concatenation. We evaluate CoMOP on an industrial case study, that is, an autonomous quarry. We design several groups of experiments that have different sizes of the quarry and obstacles, different numbers of obstacles, and various terrains. Via the experiments, we show the significant difference in performance between CoMOP and MOP (motion planning without concatenation), and the difference between time- and energy-efficient trajectories on various terrains. In summary, our contributions are as follows:

1. This paper proposes a novel *concatenation-based motion planning* (CoMOP) method, using reinforcement learning. We show that CoMOP is much more efficient than MOP when the scale of the problem is large.
2. We demonstrate the use of statistical model checking (SMC) in learning motion plans. Via experiments, we show the *qualitative evaluation of the synthesized motion plans* by using SMC, which exposes the correct rate of the resulting motion plan before testing it on an actual system implementation.
3. We demonstrate the difference between *time- and energy-efficient motion plans*. Our large-scale evaluation of CoMOP in an industrial case study shows the efficiency of obtaining these two kinds of motion plans.

The rest of the paper is structured as follows: We review the previous work in Sect. 2. In Sect. 3, we provide an introduction to Reinforcement Learning and UPPAAL STRATEGO. Section 4 elaborates on the case study and presents the vehicle's kinematic and energy model. In Sect. 5, we describe the modeling of the case study in UPPAAL STRATEGO and strategy synthesis. Furthermore, Sect. 6 outlines the motion planning concatenated motion planning. In Sect. 7, we conduct a thorough examination of the energy- and time-efficient strategies for the case study. Finally, we conclude our research results in Sect. 8.

2 Related Work

In recent years, there has been a growing interest in developing energy-efficient motion planning algorithms for autonomous vehicles. Energy consumption can be minimized by a parametric curve fit [14], by applying machine learning [16, 17], or by employing physics-based models of energy consumption [5,10]. The energy prediction method used by Quann et al. [16,17] abstracts from kinematic considerations such as velocity and acceleration. Physics-based modeling [10] that accounts for these assume mostly flat terrains. In Wallace et al. [5], the authors consider elevation and a detailed kinematic model. However, their model is analytical, being validated via simulation. In our work, we model both vehicle kinematics, although not as detailed as in the work of Wallace et al. [5], and we consider environments that include slopes and employ a combination of learning and model-checking techniques for the automatic synthesis of energy-efficient motion plans.

Compositional reinforcement learning is a promising approach for training policies to perform complex long-horizon tasks. Jothimurugan et al. [11] propose a novel framework based on two reinforcement learning algorithms by formulating the learning problem of choosing what tasks to perform from an existing set, as an adversarial reinforcement learning problem. Although close in spirit, our approach does not focus on robust task choices w.r.t. functionality, but rather w.r.t. optimizing time- and energy usage by combining task learning with assertion-based space decomposition within stochastic hybrid games.

As formal methods are capable of providing rigorous analysis for complex systems, a combination of formal methods and learning in the field of robotics has been a trend. Yang et al. [23] propose guided and safe reinforcement learning, and Pek et al. [15] employ Spatio-Temporal Logic in monitoring and planning complex robotic tasks. Mariano et al. [8] proposed an optimal motion planning approach by integrating cell-mapping techniques and reinforcement learning to improve trajectory generation. Xu et al. [22] present an autonomous vehicle motion planning and control system that integrates a unified behavior planner and robust trajectory generation. Our work approaches the motion planning of autonomous systems from another angle: (i) a compositional learning technique, to cope with complex environments, and (ii) quantitative evaluation of the results by using statistical model checking.

3 Preliminaries

In this section, we overview reinforcement learning, stochastic hybrid games, and UPPAAL STRATEGO, which form the paper's necessary background information.

3.1 Reinforcement Learning

Reinforcement learning (RL) [20] is a machine-learning method that trains a machine's behaviour by letting it interact with the environment, collecting scores of the machine's actions at different states, and calculating the state-action pairs' values. *Q-learning* [21] is a classic RL algorithm that uses the Bellman-optimal equation to calculate the values of state-action pairs, shown as follows.

$$q^*(s,a) = \mathbb{E}[R(s,a) + \gamma \max_{a'} q^*(s',a')], \tag{1}$$

where $q^*(s,a)$ represents the expected value of performing action a at state s, $\mathbb{E}$ denotes the expected value function, $R(s,a)$ is the reward returned from the environment by taking a at s, $\gamma \in [0,1]$ is a discounting value indicating how much the future reward is evaluated in the calculation, s' is the next state originating from s by taking a, and $\max_{a'} q^*(s',a')$ is the maximum reward that can be obtained by any possible next state-action pair (s',a').

3.2 UPPAAL STRATEGO

UPPAAL STRATEGO allows for the modeling of Stochastic Hybrid Games (SHG) and facilitates the synthesis of nearly optimal strategies through Reinforcement

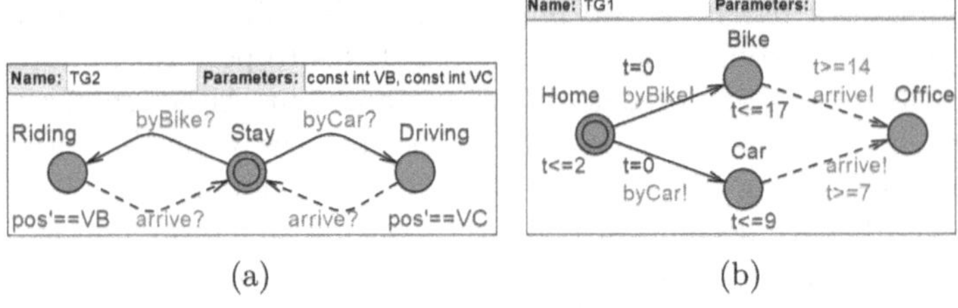

(a) (b)

Fig. 1. An example of NSHG templates in UPPAAL STRATEGO

Learning (RL). SHG are two-player games that are played on SHG [4,12]. We recall the formal definition of SHG as follows:

Definition 1. *A SHG $\mathcal{G} = \langle L, l_0, C, \Sigma, E, Inv, F_l, \mu, \gamma, l_f \rangle$ is a tuple, where L is a finite set of locations, l_0 is the initial location, C is a finite set of non-negative real-valued variables (including clocks that evolve at rate 1); $\Sigma = \Sigma_c \cup \Sigma_u$ is a finite set of actions (Σ_c denotes the set of controllable actions, and Σ_u denotes the uncontrollable ones), $E \subseteq L \times \mathcal{B}(C) \times \Sigma \times 2^C \times L$ is a finite set of edges, where $\mathcal{B}(C)$ is the set of guards over C, that is, conjunctive formulas of constraints of the form $c_1 \bowtie n$ or $c_1 - c_2 \bowtie n$, where $c_1, c_2 \in C$, $n \in \mathbb{N}$, $\bowtie \in \{<, \leq, =, \geq, >\}$, $Inv : L \rightarrow \mathcal{B}(C)$ is a partial function assigning invariants to locations, for each $l \in L$, $F_l : \mathbb{R}_{>0} \times \mathbb{R}^C \rightarrow \mathbb{R}^C$ is the flow-function that describes the evolution of the continuous variables over time, typically represented by Ordinary Differential Equations (ODE$_s$), μ is a family of delay density functions (can be uniform or exponential distributions), $\mu_l : \mathbb{R}_{\geq 0} \times L \rightarrow \mathbb{R}_{\geq 0}$ that determine the time point for the next discrete jump, for each location $l \in L$, respectively, γ is the set of probability functions $\gamma_l : L \times L \rightarrow \mathbb{R}_{\geq 0}$ determining the next location, and l_f is the set of goal locations.*

Intuitively, *controllable* actions are performed by the system, e.g., autonomous vehicles in this paper, and *uncontrollable actions* are performed by the environment. The semantics of the SHG is defined over a timed transition system, whose states are pairs $s = (l, v) \in L \times \mathbb{R}^C$, with $v \models Inv(l)$, and transitions are defined as: (i) delay transitions $(l, v) \xrightarrow{d} (l, v')$ with $d \in \mathbb{R}_{\geq 0}$ and $v' = v + d$ such that $v' \models Inv(l)$, and (ii) discrete transitions $(l, v) \xrightarrow{a} (l', v')$ if there is an edge (l, g, a, Y, l'), where $a \in \Sigma$ and $Y \subseteq C$, such that $v \models g$, $v \models Inv(l)$, $v' = v[Y]$, and $v[Y]$ is a clock valuation by assigning 0 to $x \in Y$ such that $v' \models Inv(l')$. We write $\rho = (l, v) \rightsquigarrow (l', v')$, where ρ is a finite sequence of delay and discrete transitions from (l, v) to (l', v').

A solution of an SHG is a *winning strategy*, which is a function $\pi : \rho \rightarrow \Sigma_c' \subseteq \Sigma_c$. As the strategies in this paper are *memoryless*, our winning strategy can be formulated as $\pi : s \rightarrow \Sigma_c' \subseteq \Sigma_c$, where $s = last(\rho)$ is the last state of ρ. Intuitively, strategy π indicates the "system" player what controllable actions to choose at each state, such that it can eventually reach the desired goal and avoid obstacles with the minimum cost, where cost can be time and energy consumption modelled by the ODEs in Definition 1.

UPPAAL STRATEGO [6] is a powerful tool for modeling, strategy synthesis, and (statistical) model checking of SHG, in which SHG can be composed in parallel as a *network* of SHG (NSHG) synchronized via *channels*. Figure 1 depicts SHG templates that can be instantiated into NSHG models by assigning concrete values to the parameters of the template, such as `VB` in TG2 (Fig. 1a). Blue circles are *locations* that are connected by directional *edges*. Double-circled locations are the *initial* locations (e.g. `Stay`). In UPPAAL STRATEGO, there are two special kinds of locations: *urgent* locations (i.e., encircled "u"), and *committed* locations (i.e., encircled "c"). A UPPAAL STRATEGO SHG requires that time does not elapse in those two kinds of locations, with committed locations being even stricter, that is, the next edge to be traversed must start from one of them. On the edges, there are assignments resetting clocks (e.g., `t=0`) and updating data variables, guards (e.g., `t>=14`), and synchronization channels (e.g., `arrive!` and `arrive?`). On location `Bike` in Fig. 1b, an invariant `t<=17` means that clock `t` must never exceed 17. Derivatives of clocks can be specified by Ordinary Differential Equations (ODE), such as `pos'==VB` in Fig. 1a.

In UPPAAL STRATEGO, the SHG have a stochastic interpretation based on: (i) the probabilistic choices between multiple enabled discrete transitions (that assume a uniform distribution by default), and (ii) the non-deterministic time delays that are refined based on probability distributions, either uniform distributions for time-bounded delays, or user-defined exponential distributions for unbounded delays. In this paper, we use only the default uniform distributions for discrete transitions and time-bounded delays. For instance, Fig. 1 models a driver taking different transportation tools to visit his office. In UPPAAL STRATEGO, one can synthesize a strategy that guides the system player (e.g., the driver) to reach its goal (e.g., the office) by using the following query:

$$\texttt{strategy s} = \texttt{minE(cost)}\,[\leq \texttt{T}]\,\{\texttt{ExpList1}\} \rightarrow \{\texttt{ExpList2}\} :<> \texttt{goal} \tag{2}$$

where `minE(exp)` means that strategy `s` is to minimize the value of expression `cost` within T time-units or when the goal predicate becomes true. `ExpList1` and `ExpList2` are lists of observable state expressions used in Q-learning [21]. `ExpList1` are discrete variables and `ExpList2` are continuous variables. UPPAAL STRATEGO simulates the model and samples traces for the learning algorithm, with `<> goal` specifying criteria for trace selection. The learning algorithm receives controllable actions in these traces, representing partial observation of the state space [9]. Additionally, UPPAAL STRATEGO supports calling external C-libraries, an important feature used in this work.

4 Use Case and Models

In this paper, we demonstrate the applicability of our method on an industrial case study provided by Volvo Construction Equipment, Sweden. The use case focuses on reducing the energy consumption of autonomous wheel loaders that

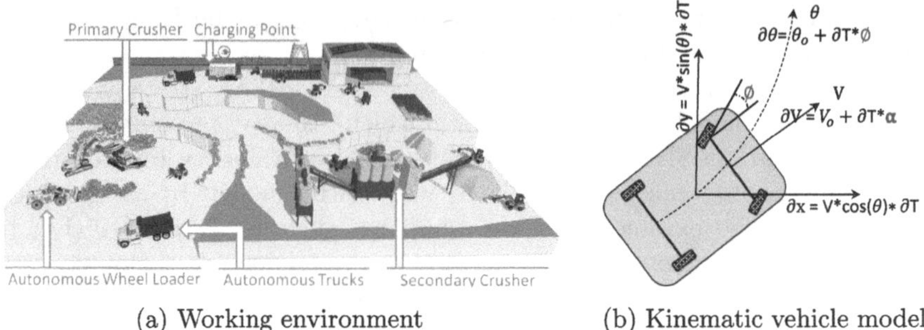

(a) Working environment (b) Kinematic vehicle model

Fig. 2. An example of an autonomous vehicle

transport materials within a construction site. An example is shown in Fig. 2a, where the autonomous wheel loader needs to transport stones to a primary crusher to crush them into smaller pieces. After that, it transports the crashed stones to the secondary crusher, which is the destination of the stones. We aim to develop time- and energy-efficient motion planning for battery-powered autonomous vehicles to extend the vehicle's operating time on a single charge.

4.1 Vehicle's Kinematic Model

In Fig. 2b, one can see a simple kinematic model that illustrates the configuration of a vehicle using seven parameters: (x, y, ϕ, α, V, θ, T), where x and y model the vehicle's current position in a 2D environment, ϕ the steering angle, α the acceleration, V the velocity, θ the vehicle's orientation, and T the time.

The vehicle's trajectory must satisfy a reach-avoid requirement, that is, eventually reaching the destination while always avoiding obstacles. It can be seen that by controlling acceleration α and steering angle ϕ, one can determine the vehicle's position, that is, the values of X and Y. Therefore, our motion planning is about controlling parameters α and ϕ. In Sect. 4.2, we introduce how energy optimization is considered in our motion planning.

4.2 Energy Model

The tractive power model described by Lascurain et al. [13] and Gao et al. [7] is widely used to calculate the power required by a vehicle powertrain. The tractive power is the amount of energy required to overcome the vehicle's resistance to motion, and it considers various factors that affect the vehicle's performance, including the environment. The following equation can be used to calculate the vehicles' tractive power:

$$W_{tract} = m \cdot V \cdot \frac{dV}{dt} + m \cdot g \cdot C_{rr} \cdot V + m \cdot g \cdot V \cdot sin(\Theta) \tag{3}$$

where W_{tract} is the tractive power, m is the vehicle's mass, V is the velocity, g is the gravitational acceleration constant, C_{rr} is a coefficient of rolling resistance,

Table 1. Energy Parameters

Name	Value	Name	Value	Name	Value	Name	Value
m	$7-22Ton$	C_{rr}	2–3%	η_{mot}	0.88	Θ	12%
W_{acc}	3.75	η_{batt}	0.98	η_{wh}	0.99	η_{fd}	0.98

Θ is the road's slope. Parameter values obtained from the Volvo project are shown in Table 1, which contains other parameters that we introduce later.

In this study, we use the energy model presented in the literature [13]. The authors propose a model for estimating the electric power output of an electric vehicle (EV), which considers the efficiencies of the electric components, such as the motor and battery, and the related drive-train components, such as the final drive and wheel efficiencies shown in Eq. 4. The equations for calculating the driving power and braking power of an EV are as follows.

$$\begin{aligned} &Driving\ Power : W_{drive} = W_{acc} + \frac{W_{tract}}{\eta_{wh} \cdot \eta_{fd} \cdot \eta_{mot} \cdot \eta_{batt}} \\ &Braking\ Power : W_{Braking} = W_{acc} \\ &TotalPower : W = W_{drive} + W_{Braking} \end{aligned} \tag{4}$$

where W_{acc} is a conventional vehicle's accessory load (kW), η_{wh} is the wheel efficiency, η_{fd} is the final drive efficiency, η_{mot} is the motor efficiency, and η_{batt} is the battery efficiency. Table 1 depicts the coefficient values used in this paper.

4.3 Abstract View of Vehicle Model

We develop a framework for simulating a vehicle's movement to find a path to the destination while avoiding obstacles, which includes a dynamic decision-making process based on the Q-learning algorithm. Specifically, we construct an SHG model of an autonomous wheel loader in UPPAAL STRATEGO, which can navigate along the x and y axes. The vehicle's movement is controlled by selecting the right steering angle (ϕ) and acceleration (α), chosen from a strategy synthesized by the Q-learning algorithm. To illustrate our SHG model in an abstract way, Fig. 3 depicts a graphical representation of the vehicle model.

The decision-making process of the vehicle is controlled by the Q-learning block, which determines the appropriateness of the chosen ϕ and α values for each time unit during the vehicle's movement, that is, the evolution of x and y. Additionally, when a large steering angle (ϕ) is chosen, and the vehicle's current velocity exceeds a predefined safety threshold or comfortableness at that specific ϕ, the model enters the `Braking` block. In this block, the vehicle can move to the `Drive` block when the velocity is reduced to a required level or return to its decision-making block to reconsider whether the destination is close. Alternatively, the model also enters the `Braking` block as it approaches the destination, where it keeps braking until the vehicle fully arrives and stops. Furthermore, if

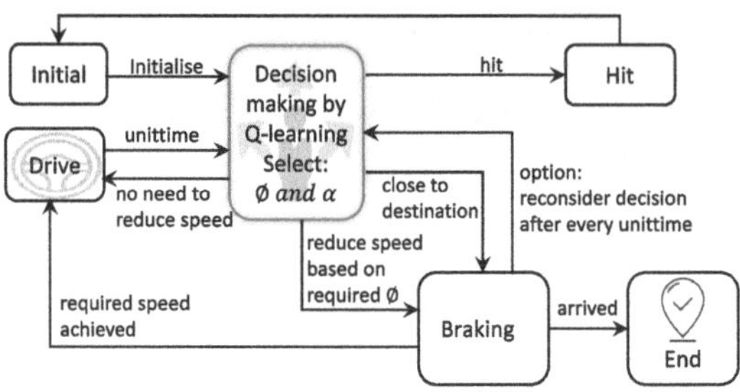

Fig. 3. Abstract View of Vehicle Model in UPPAAL STRATEGO

the vehicle hits an obstacle or crosses a boundary of the environment, it enters the `Hit` block to indicate a collision or boundary violation.

Now, we define the problem of motion planning as follows:

Definition 2 (Motion Planning). *Given an autonomous vehicle whose kinematics and energy consumption are described by ordinary differential equations, e.g., Eqs. (2b) and (4), respectively, a motion plan for the vehicle is a function* $(\theta, V) = f(x, y, t)$*, where* $\theta, v, x,$ *and* y *are the state variables of the vehicle in Eq. (2b),* $t \in [0, T]$ *is a time point within* 0 *and* T*, and* $T \in \mathbb{R}^+$ *is the time of reaching the destination. The goal of motion planning is to synthesize motion plans that are time-efficient, i.e.,* T *is minimal, or energy-efficient, i.e., total power* W *is minimal.*

5 Vehicle Model in UPPAAL STRATEGO

This section demonstrates how we use UPPAAL STRATEGO to model the vehicle's actions. Figure 4 depicts an SHG model that implements the abstract vehicle model in Fig. 3. UPPAAL STRATEGO handles this motion planning problem as an SHG. The model contains two types of elements (locations and edges), and the edges are further divided into controllable (solid line) and uncontrollable ones (dotted line). The locations of the model represent the system's processes like *Braking* and *Driving*, and edges are the actions controlling these processes. Table 2 presents some important variables used in the model.

Locations `Braking` and `Drive` are the main locations in our model. All other locations are used to help in taking different actions between or on these locations. The edge associated with the `Initial` location invokes the `Initialise()` function to initialize variables such as the initial position and angle. The edge from `T7` is controllable and includes a statement of *selections*, which allows the vehicle model to select an acceleration from a defined range from 0 to 10. Within the `Drive` location, continuous variables evolve according to the differential equations defined in the model, e.g., `agl'==ar` define the vehicle's orientation.

Now, we describe the vehicle's movement defined at the `Drive` location. First, the coordinates of the vehicle, x, and y, begin to change in the direction specified

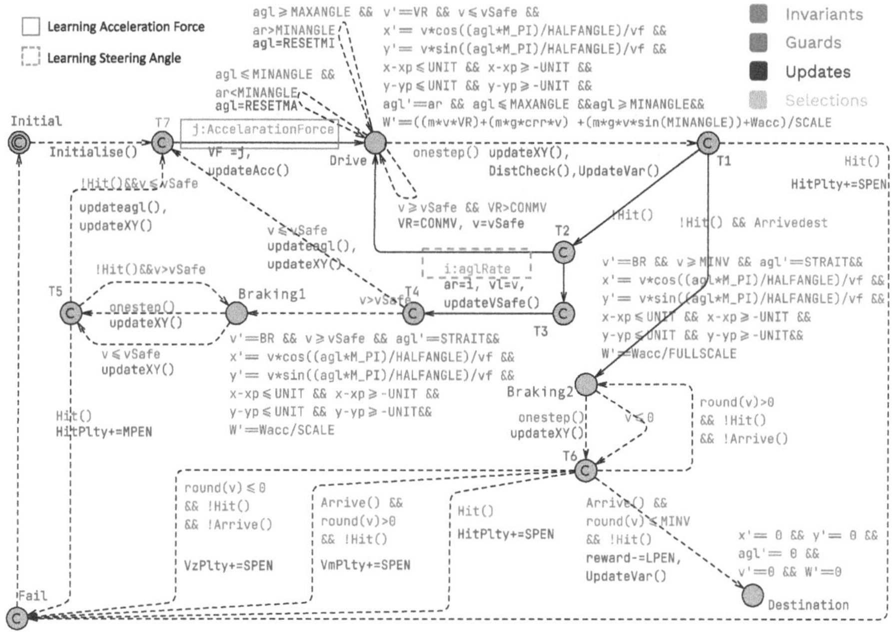

Fig. 4. Vehicle's SHG model in UPPAAL STRATEGO

by `agl` (the orientation of the vehicle) while consuming energy. Second, the loops in the `Drive` location control the value of `agl` between 0 and 360 and restrict the acceleration when it reaches the maximum safe speed (`vSafe`). Third, the model should leave the `Drive` location and move to `T1` when the `x` or `y` value evolves a step on the map. The duration spent in a location is determined by the location's invariants and the guard on the outgoing edge. Therefore, the invariants in location `Drive`, such as `x-xp≤UNIT`, and the guard `onestep()` regulate the duration in `Drive` to be *one step*. The length of the step is a constant defined in the model.

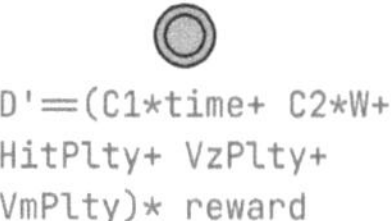

Fig. 5. Reward function

The model moves from location `T1` to `Fail`, if an obstacle or boundary is encountered. Otherwise, it offers two controllable actions: continuing to drive or moving to the `Braking2` location to check if the destination has been reached. The edge from `T1` to `Braking2` is guarded by the `Arrivedest` variable, enabling it only when the vehicle is close to the destination, thus avoiding unnecessary execution towards the final braking.

Two controllable actions towards the `Drive` location are changing the steering angle or moving to `Drive` with the same steering angle. En route to `T3`, another controllable edge involves selecting a steering angle from -45 to 45. The model assumes instantaneous steering angle changes. Updating the angle requires adjusting the maximum safe speed (`vSafe`) based on the new angle. If the cur-

Table 2. Vehicle's variables used in the model.

Variable	Type	Description
`X,Y`	Clock	Position on the x and y axes.
`V`	Clock	Velocity.
`agl`	Clock	Orientation, denoted as θ in Fig. 2b.
`W`	Clock	Energy consumption.
`ar`	Int	Steering angle, labelled as ϕ in Fig. 2b.
`VR`	Int	Acceleration, labelled as α in Fig. 2b.
`vSafe`	Real	Safety threshold of velocity.

rent velocity exceeds the new maximum safe velocity, the model transitions to `Braking1` to reduce speed before moving to `Drive`; otherwise, it directly proceeds to `Drive`.

Penalties in our model training include `HitPlty` for reaching the `hit` location, `VmPlty` for arriving with non-zero vehicle speed, and `VzPlty` for stopping without reaching the destination. Conversely, a reward is granted for the successful arrival of the destination. The model learns to minimize penalties and maximize rewards, refining strategies through these feedback mechanisms.

The automaton shown in Fig. 5 models the objective function. `D` is a continuous variable, and its derivative depends on a set of variables, that is, `Time` , `W`, `HitPlty`, `VzPlty`, `VmPlty`, and `reward`. The variable `time` is used for the time-efficient strategy, and `W` is used for the energy-efficient one. `C1` and `C2` are coefficients for balancing `time` and `W` in developing strategies. Variable `reward` is updated with a negative value when it reaches the goal and starts reducing the objective function. We run a query as Query 2 in Uppaal Stratego, which minimizes this objective function to generate an efficient strategy.

5.1 Strategy Synthesis

This section details strategy queries (shown in Eq. 5) for motion-plan synthesis, following the structure described in Sect. 3.2. Here, `D` is the objective function, and `minE` means the goal of synthesis is to minimize `D`. The query passes the set of discrete and continuous variables (described in Sect. 3.2) to the Q-learning algorithm embedded in Uppaal Stratego to develop a strategy.

$$\begin{aligned}\texttt{strategy GoFast} = \texttt{minE(D)}\,[\texttt{time} \leq \texttt{T}]\,\{\texttt{location}, \texttt{ar}, \texttt{VR}, \texttt{VzPlty}, \texttt{VmPlty},\\ \texttt{HitPlty}, \texttt{reward}\} \rightarrow \{\texttt{agl}, \texttt{x}, \texttt{y}, \texttt{v}, \texttt{W}\} : <> \texttt{shg.Destination}\,\&\&\,\texttt{time} <= \texttt{T}\end{aligned} \tag{5}$$

$$\texttt{simulate}\,[\leq \texttt{T}; 1]\{\texttt{x}, \texttt{y}\}\ \texttt{under GoFast} \tag{6}$$

After constructing the strategy, simulation queries (shown in Eq. 6), are employed to simulate the model under the synthesized strategy. The query prints the values of `x` and `y`, representing the vehicle's moving trajectory.

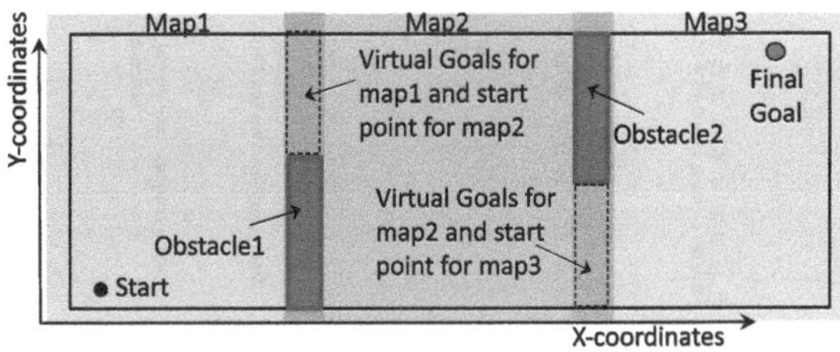

Fig. 6. Abstract view of a map and sub-maps

6 Assertion-Based Concatenated Motion Planning

This section introduces our new method *CoMOP*. First, we implement the vehicle model in UPPAAL STRATEGO. Next, we use two methods to synthesize motion plans (a.k.a., strategies in UPPAAL STRATEGO) to reach the destination.

Method 1: MOtion Planning (MOP). MOP considers the entire environment (a.k.a., map) as a single entity and learns a holistic motion plan from the starting point to the destination while taking into account time or energy consumption.

Method 2: Concatenated MOtion Planning (CoMOP). CoMOP also aims to synthesize efficient motion planning. The difference is that CoMOP divides the map into sub-maps. Each sub-map represents a distinct area of the environment. Figure 6 depicts the subdivision of a map into sub-maps. As shown in the figure, overlapped regions exist between two sub-maps, and such regions serve as virtual destinations for one sub-map, and starting regions for the next, respectively.

To synthesize a motion-planning strategy, we use a **reverse calculation** approach, starting from *Map3*, determining an efficient starting point within the overlapped region for a precise virtual goal point. We also analyze the suitable vehicle orientation for the forward path strategy in *Map3*. A similar approach is employed for *Map2*, ensuring the model concludes at the starting points determined in *Map3*. This sequential process establishes a motion-planning strategy considering both sub-maps with consistent starting points and orientations.

In each sub-map, we employ a sequential execution approach for forward motion planning. Illustrated in Fig. 7, we develop a strategy for a sub-map, followed by simulating the vehicle model and obtaining variable trajectories (x

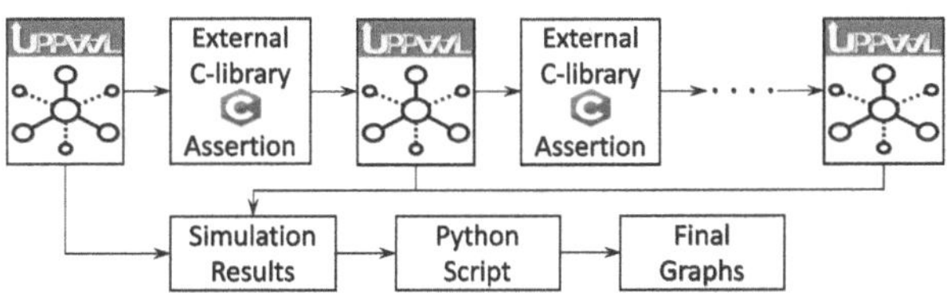

Fig. 7. Cascaded execution of model for CoMOP simulation

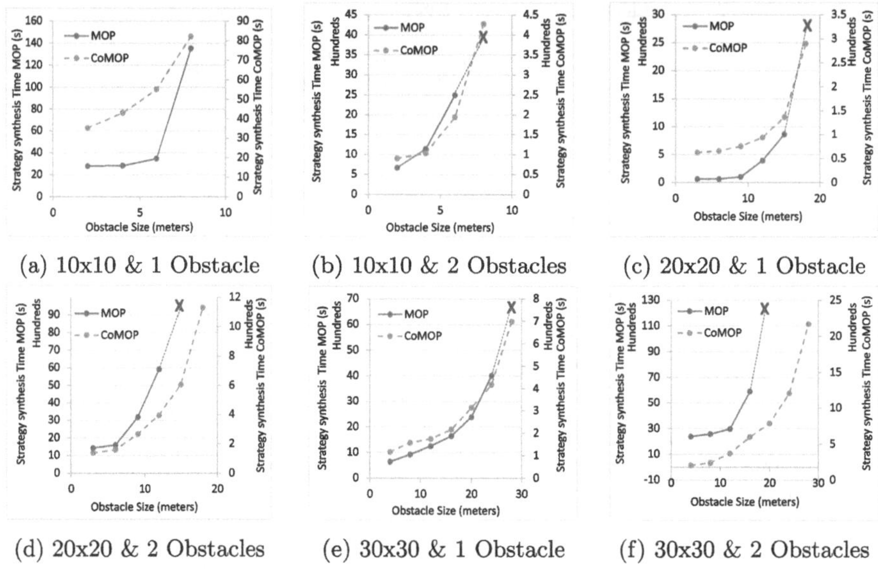

(a) 10x10 & 1 Obstacle (b) 10x10 & 2 Obstacles (c) 20x20 & 1 Obstacle

(d) 20x20 & 2 Obstacles (e) 30x30 & 1 Obstacle (f) 30x30 & 2 Obstacles

Fig. 8. Strategy Synthesis time with different map sizes, obstacle heights, and number of obstacles

`, y, agl, W, V, T`). The final values are then forwarded to the next strategy using an external C library, ensuring a continuous information flow between consecutive sub-maps. **Assertions** in the external C-library guarantee smooth transitions between the **concatenated** strategies, validating that final variable values in one sub-map are within valid regions for the subsequent sub-map.

7 Experimental Evaluation

In this section, we introduce the experiments that we have conducted to evaluate the performance of our method. Next, we explore and answer the following research questions according to the experimental results.

- **RQ1**: Considering map size, slope, obstacle size, and obstacle number, what is their impact on the performance of our synthesis methods?
- **RQ2**: Does CoMOP outperform MOP?
- **RQ3**: Is the time-efficient motion plan significantly different from the energy-efficient motion plan of the same problem?

7.1 RQ1: Impact Factors on the Synthesis Methods' Performance

Based on the industrial use case, we explore the influential factors in this series of experiments by systematically varying three key parameters: map size, number of obstacles, and obstacle size. The experimental design encompasses three different

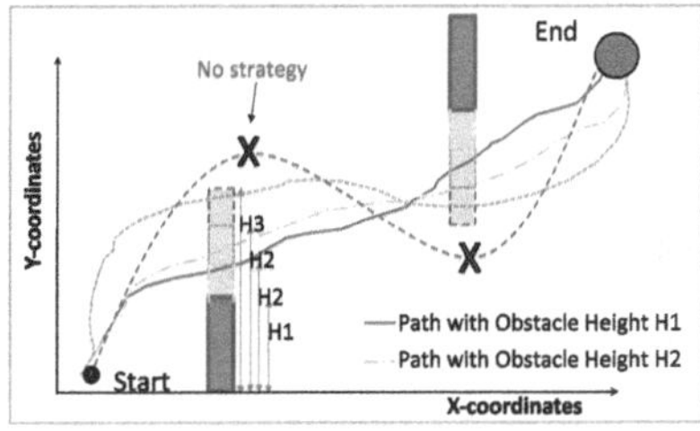

Fig. 9. Path trajectories of MOP

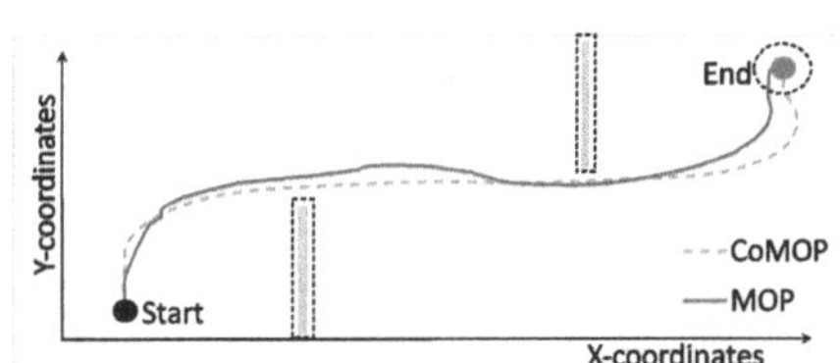

Fig. 10. Comparison of successful strategies developed by MOP and CoMOP

map sizes, namely 10, 20, and 30 units, with each map configuration simulated under two obstacle conditions: one obstacle and two obstacles. Additionally, we examine the effect of obstacle size.

Note that the unit of a map is not specified because one step in a map (i.e., the guard `onestep()` in Fig. 4) represents the granularity of decision making.

The results in Fig. 8 offer insights into dominant factors impacting learning time for motion plan synthesis. By analyzing the results, we can discern the influence of each factor on the simulation outcomes. Increasing the complexity in terms of obstacle size, map size, and the number of obstacles generally resulted in longer simulation times for both the MOP and CoMOP models. Comparatively, CoMOP needs less time to find a strategy, except in the experiment shown in Fig. 8a, having a small map with a small obstacle. However, it is essential to note that in certain experiments, the MOP algorithm encounters difficulties in finding a strategy. For example, in the experiment conducted on a 20-size map with a single obstacle of size 18, MOP fails to generate any result (see the red cross in Fig. 8c). CoMOP, on the other hand, demonstrates its ability to address complex motion-planning problems by employing the sub-map division approach.

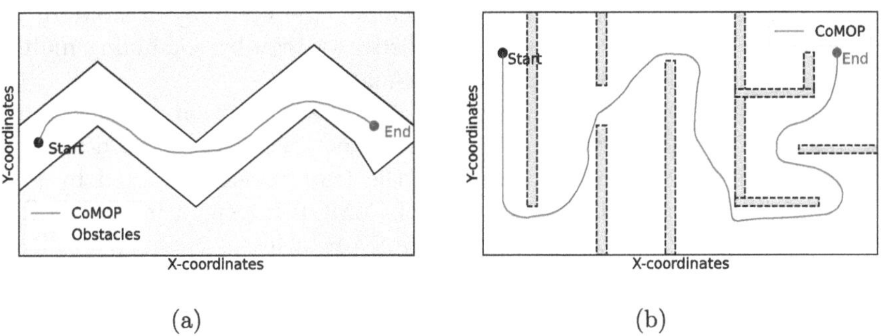

Fig. 11. Energy efficient path trajectories developed by CoMOP

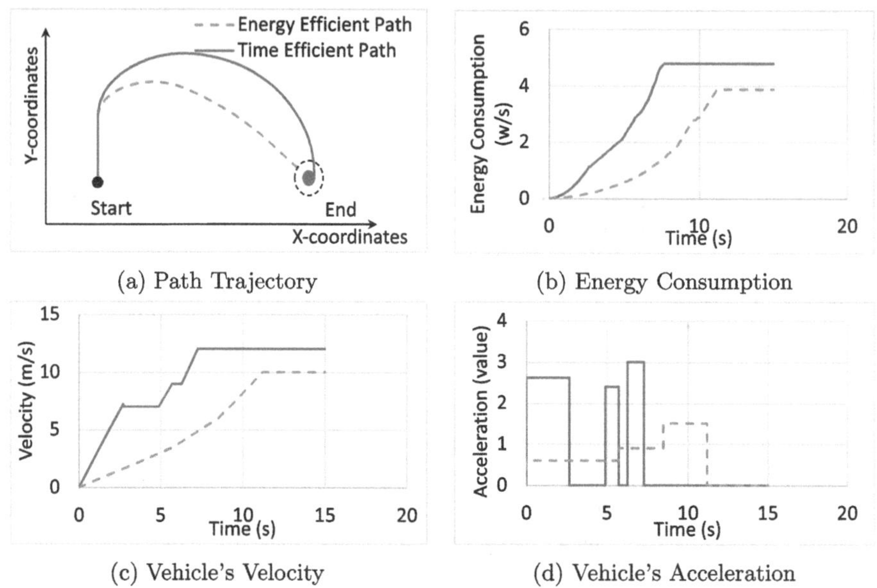

Fig. 12. Energy- and time-efficient path trajectories and behavior of velocity, Acceleration, and Energy consumption

7.2 RQ2: Performance Improvement of Learning with CoMOP

Figure 9 shows a subset of the experiments of Fig. 8, highlighting the impact of obstacle height and the number of obstacles on path trajectories. Increasing obstacle height complicates strategy synthesis, particularly for two obstacles; learning a second sharp turn to reach the goal is more challenging. Although there is a significant margin between the obstacles and the map edges, MOP failed to generate any results as shown in the figure. We conducted simulations on a 20-size map with two obstacles to compare the accuracy of CoMOP and standalone MOP. CoMOP generates a holistic strategy by combining multiple strategies generated by MOP for the entire-map.

Figure 10 depicts the path trajectories of executing motion plans. It can be observed that CoMOP produces smoother trajectories toward the destination with less dramatic turnings compared to the trajectories generated by MOP alone. Figure 11 illustrates the versatility of CoMOP in generating path trajectories for intricate environments with multiple obstacles.

In summary, CoMOP improves overall motion-planning performance. It can even solve problems that cannot be addressed by MOP alone.

7.3 RQ3: Time-Efficient and Energy-Efficient Motion Plans

We synthesize energy- and time-efficient strategies and generate path trajectories to the destination by simulating the strategies. In Fig. 12a, it can be seen

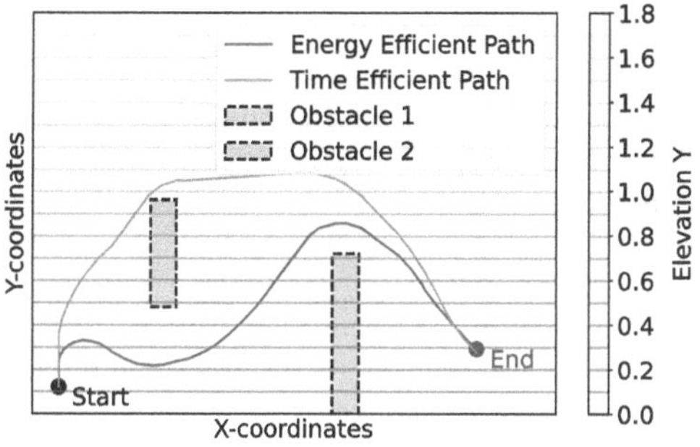

(a) Path trajectories with 12% slope on the y-axis.

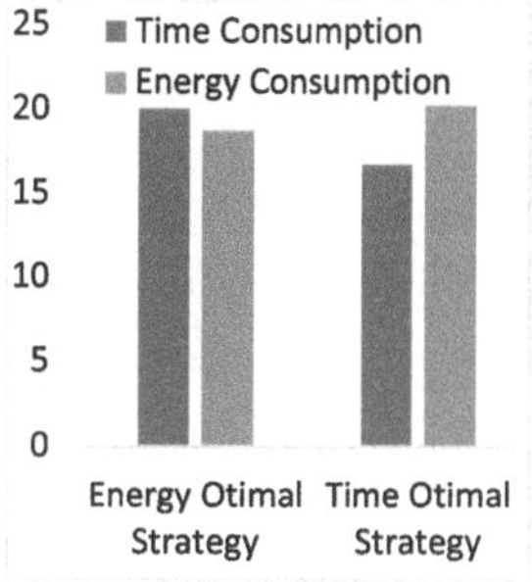

(b) Energy and time

Fig. 13. Syntheses of time- and energy-efficient strategies to reach the destination by avoiding obstacles.

that there are distinct trajectories for time and energy. Figure 12b illustrates that the time-efficient strategy is fast but consumes more energy than that of the energy-efficient strategy. Figures 12c and 12d show that the energy-efficient strategy involves choosing a lower acceleration value and driving at a low speed to conserve energy. Driving at a low speed allows the vehicle to take sharp turns for an energy-efficient strategy comparatively, which can be seen in Fig. 12a. We further run an experiment in an environment having an obstacle and a 12% slope on the x-axis. Figure 13a depicts that CoMOP develops different trajectories for time and energy, and Fig. 13b represents the cost of energy and time for both strategies.

By considering time and energy factors in strategy synthesis, we can generate balanced trajectories that optimize both time and energy usage by controlling the constant factors (`C1 and C2` shown in Fig. 5) in the optimization function.

8 Conclusions and Future Work

In this paper, we propose automatic synthesis strategies for time- and energy-efficient motion planning for autonomous vehicles, using stochastic hybrid games in UPPAAL STRATEGO. We present two techniques for motion planning based on the model: regular MOtion Planning (MOP) and Concatenated MOtion Planning (CoMOP). For CoMOP, we develop an assertion-based method to execute the UPPAAL STRATEGO model in a cascaded fashion. The results show that the CoMOP performs better than MOP for complex models. We demonstrate the method's applicability on an industrial use case: energy-efficient path planning for an autonomous vehicle provided by Volvo CE, Sweden. The results show that our method can synthesize time-efficient and energy-efficient path trajectories.

In future work, we plan to extend the model to manage multiple operational vehicles in the environment and concurrent execution of each map's sub-part.

References

1. Aradi, S.: Survey of deep reinforcement learning for motion planning of autonomous vehicles. IEEE Trans. Intell. Transp. Syst. **23**(2), 740–759 (2020)
2. Behrmann, G., Cougnard, A., David, A., Fleury, E., Larsen, K.G., Lime, D.: Uppaal-tiga: timed games for everyone. In: Nordic Workshop on Programming Theory (NWPT 2006) (2006)
3. Bouton, M., Karlsson, J., Nakhaei, A., Fujimura, K., Kochenderfer, M.J., Tumova, J.: Reinforcement learning with probabilistic guarantees for autonomous driving. arXiv preprint arXiv:1904.07189 (2019)
4. Brorholt, A.H., Jensen, P.G., Larsen, K.G., Lorber, F., Schilling, C.: Shielded reinforcement learning for hybrid systems. arXiv preprint arXiv:2308.14424 (2023)
5. D. Wallace, N., Kong, H., J. Hill, A., Sukkarieh, S.: Energy aware mission planning for WMRs on uneven terrains. IFAC-PapersOnLine **52**(30), 149–154 (2019). 6th IFAC Conference on Sensing, Control and Automation Technologies for Agriculture AGRICONTROL 2019
6. David, A., Jensen, P.G., Larsen, K.G., Mikučionis, M., Taankvist, J.H.: UPPAAL STRATEGO. In: Baier, C., Tinelli, C. (eds.) TACAS 2015. LNCS, vol. 9035, pp. 206–211. Springer, Heidelberg (2015). https://doi.org/10.1007/978-3-662-46681-0_16
7. Gao, Z., et al.: Battery capacity and recharging needs for electric buses in city transit service. Energy **122**, 588–600 (2017)
8. Gómez, M., González, R., Martínez-Marín, T., Meziat, D., Sánchez, S.: Optimal motion planning by reinforcement learning in autonomous mobile vehicles. Robotica **30**(2), 159–170 (2012)
9. Gu, R., Jensen, P.G., Seceleanu, C., Enoiu, E., Lundqvist, K.: Correctness-guaranteed strategy synthesis and compression for multi-agent autonomous systems. Sci. Comput. Program. **224**, 102894 (2022)
10. Henkel, C., Bubeck, A., Xu, W.: Energy efficient dynamic window approach for local path planning in mobile service robotics. IFAC-PapersOnLine **49**(15), 32–37 (2016). 9th IFAC Symposium on Intelligent Autonomous Vehicles IAV 2016
11. Jothimurugan, K., Hsu, S., Bastani, O., Alur, R.: Robust subtask learning for compositional generalization. In: 40th International Conference on Machine Learning (ICML 2023) (2023)
12. Kamgarpour, M., Ding, J., Summers, S., Abate, A., Lygeros, J., Tomlin, C.: Discrete time stochastic hybrid dynamical games: verification & controller synthesis. In: 2011 50th IEEE Conference on Decision and Control and European Control Conference, pp. 6122–6127. IEEE (2011)
13. Lascurain, M.B., et al.: Medium truck duty cycle data from real-world driving environments: project final report. ORNL/TM-2012/240. Oak Ridge National Laboratory, Oak Ridge, TN (2012)
14. Mei, Y., Lu, Y.H., Hu, Y., Lee, C.: Energy-efficient motion planning for mobile robots. In: IEEE International Conference on Robotics and Automation, ICRA 2004, vol. 5, pp. 4344–4349. IEEE (2004)
15. Pek, C., Schuppe, G.F., Esposito, F., Tumova, J., Kragic, D.: Spatial: monitoring and planning of robotic tasks using spatio-temporal logic specifications (2023)
16. Quann, M., Ojeda, L., Smith, W., Rizzo, D., Castanier, M., Barton, K.: Chance constrained reachability in environments with spatially varying energy costs. Robot. Auton. Syst. **119**, 1–12 (2019)

17. Quann, M., Ojeda, L., Smith, W., Rizzo, D., Castanier, M., Barton, K.: Power prediction for heterogeneous ground robots through spatial mapping and sharing of terrain data. IEEE Robot. Autom. Lett. **5**(2), 1579–1586 (2020)
18. Rabin, S.: A* aesthetic optimizations. In: Game Programming Gems. Charles River Media (2000)
19. Sen, K., Viswanathan, M., Agha, G.: Statistical model checking of black-box probabilistic systems. In: Alur, R., Peled, D.A. (eds.) CAV 2004. LNCS, vol. 3114, pp. 202–215. Springer, Heidelberg (2004). https://doi.org/10.1007/978-3-540-27813-9_16
20. Sutton, R.S., Barto, A.G.: Reinforcement Learning: An Introduction. MIT Press, Cambridge (2018)
21. Watkins, C.J.C.H.: Learning from delayed rewards. King's College, Cambridge United Kingdom (1989)
22. Xu, S., et al.: System and experiments of model-driven motion planning and control for autonomous vehicles. IEEE Trans. Syst. Man Cybern. Syst. **52**(9), 5975–5988 (2021)
23. Yang, Q., Simão, T.D., Jansen, N., Tindemans, S.H., Spaan, M.T.: Reinforcement learning by guided safe exploration. arXiv preprint arXiv:2307.14316 (2023)

CFStra: Enhancing Configurable Program Analysis Through LLM-Driven Strategy Selection Based on Code Features

Jie Su[1], Liansai Deng[1], Cheng Wen[1], Shengchao Qin[1,2](✉), and Cong Tian[1,2](✉)

[1] Guangzhou Institute of Technology, Xidian University, Xi'an, China
{sujie01,wencheng}@xidian.edu.cn, 23031212358@stu.xidian.edu.cn, shengchao.qin@gmail.com, ctian@mail.xidian.edu.cn

[2] ICTT and ISN Laboratory, Xidian University, Xi'an, China

Abstract. Configurable Program Analysis (CPA) allows users to customize program analysis based on their preferences. However, current program verification tools like CPAchecker require manual strategy selection, which can be complex and error-prone. In this paper, we present a novel approach to efficiently perform program verification tasks by harnessing the capabilities of Large Language Models (LLMs) to automatically select verification strategies based on code features and specifications. Specifically, we begin by extracting relevant code snippets and querying LLMs to identify code features. Based on the identified code features, we propose a strategy selector to automatically choose the verification strategy. Finally, we execute the CPAchecker with the selected verification strategy. We evaluated our approach using a diverse set of 600 verification tasks. The results demonstrate the effectiveness of our approach, surpassing basic strategies and SOTA combination strategies while also standing out for its simplicity and ease of understanding.

Keywords: Program Verification · Strategy Selection · Large Language Model · Code Feature

1 Introduction

Background and Problem. Program verification is a complex and tedious task as it often requires users to specify the desired properties of the program, choose the appropriate verification technique and tool, and provide the necessary strategy or other configuration parameters. Different verification tools, algorithms, abstract domains, and configurations, coexist with their different strengths in terms of approaching a verification problem.

Configurable Program Analysis (CPA) [5,31] is a technique that allows users to customize the analysis of programs based on their specific needs and preferences. The well-known framework CPAchecker simplifies configuration and

W.-N. Chin and Z. Xu (Eds.): TASE 2024, LNCS 14777, pp. 374–391, 2024.
https://doi.org/10.1007/978-3-031-64626-3_22

automates analysis and verification tasks, supporting techniques like predicate abstraction and model checking. CPAchecker also provides a rich set of configuration parameters that can be used to adjust the precision, performance, and resource consumption of the analysis. However, the default configuration often inadequate for large and complex programs, requiring manual selection of advanced verification strategies. This often necessitates a deep understanding of the target source code and the use of expert knowledge. This process can be arduous and time-consuming, especially for inexperienced users.

Existing Work. To address the usability issues of existing verification tools, numerous techniques for verification strategy selection have been proposed. For example, Dirk *et al.* [3] presented a strategy selection method that is based on a straightforward model using a succinct set of Boolean features extracted statically from source code. This approach involves focusing on simple features while excluding more intricate ones such as recursion and concurrency, thus limiting its efficacy in handling complex programs. In addition to this, various techniques utilizing machine learning have been suggested to automatically choose a promising verification strategy, as demonstrated by recent developments [14,15]. One approach involves using implicit features derived from the input program to forecast a strategy ranking, eliminating the need to explicitly define these features [14]. The learner is provided with the program dependency graph, a directed graph capable of illustrating the data, control, and concurrency dependencies within a program, enabling it to deduce the necessary characteristics. Nevertheless, this technique is overly burdensome and constrained in its scalability.

Insight. AI-powered Generative Large Language Models (LLMs) routinely make tremendous progress in software engineering tasks. Examples include program synthesis from natural language descriptions by GPT-4 [33] or Github Copilot [50], solving competitive programming problems with AlphaCode [29], generating loop invariant with ChatGPT [10,35], and generating entire proofs of theorems using fine-tuned LLMs [21], among others. Many of these tasks require strong reasoning skills over code and code understanding. This raises the question of whether we can utilize the reasoning skills of LLMs in the formal setting of software verification and complement existing automatic verifiers such as CPAchecker. Our key insight is that LLMs possess advanced program comprehension capabilities, allowing them to serve as proficient human experts in identifying code features and selecting verification strategies.

Contribution. In this paper, we propose a novel approach to effectively complete the verification task by driving the CPAchecker on selecting verification strategies based on code features, and harnessing (some of) the powers of Large Language Models (LLMs). We begin by extracting relevant code snippets from the target program and querying LLMs to identify their code features. Based on these identified code features, we propose a strategy selector to automatically choose the verification strategy that is most suitable for the program. Finally, we execute the CPAchecker with the configuration corresponding to the selected verification strategy. Our main contributions are:

```
int main() {
    struct node *list = create_list();
    struct node *low = NULL;
    struct node *high = NULL;
    // Split list into low and high
    struct node *p = list;
    while (p) {
        struct node *l = p->value >= 0 ? high : low;
        struct node *next = p->next;
        p->next = l;
        l = p;
        p = next;
    }
    // Check that low and high contain expected elements
    while (low) {
        if (!(low->expected_list == LOW))
            {reach_error();}
        low = low->next;
    }
    ...
}
```

Listing 1.1. An Motivating Example of quick_sort_split.c, from SV-COMP

- *Novelty.* We present a fast, general, and easily extensible approach to efficiently perform program verification tasks by harnessing the capabilities of LLMs to automatically select verification strategies based on code features.
- *Practical Approach.* We identify and address several practical challenges by combining code feature identification via LLMs, prompt engineering, and customized verification strategy selection.
- *Open-source Implementation.* We have developed and implemented our proposed approach as a tool named CFStra. We have made the implementation, along with all relevant publicly available data, accessible to facilitate comparison: https://sites.google.com/view/cfstra/.
- *Evaluation.* We extensively evaluate our approach using a diverse set of 600 verification tasks against 8 basic strategies and 4 SOTA combination strategies (*i.e.*, CPA-Seq, BMC-BAM$_R$-PA, VA-BAM$_R$-KI, PIChecker) to demonstrate its effectiveness, efficiency, and scalability.

2 Background and Motivation

In this section, we motivate our approach by employing a motivating example for SV-COMP, as well as providing the necessary background on LLMs.

Consider the code snippet that implements a quick sort splitting algorithm for a linked list, as shown in Listing 1.1. To verify its correctness, users need to identify the relevant code features like pointers, dynamic memory allocation, and input-dependent loops. Choosing appropriate verification strategies like predicate abstraction or k-induction significantly impacts precision and performance. However, manually identifying and selecting strategies can be challenging due to limited understanding, lack of expert knowledge, and dealing with numerous verification tasks.

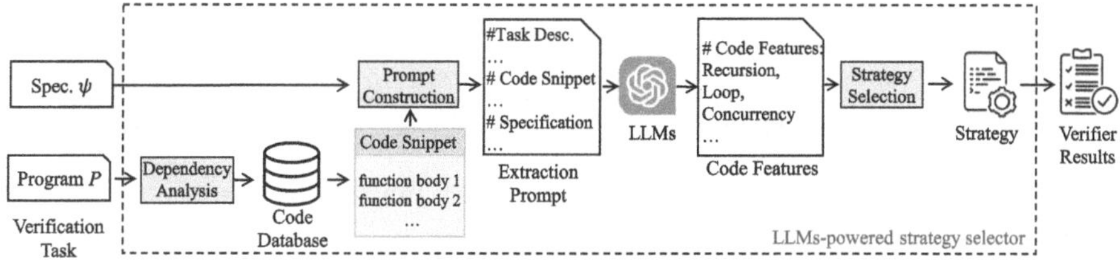

Fig. 1. The workflow of our approach

Therefore, there is a need for an automated and intelligent approach that can leverage the program comprehension capabilities of LLMs to drive the CPAchecker. LLMs are neural network models that are trained on large corpora of natural and programming languages, and can generate natural language texts or code snippets based on given inputs or queries. LLMs have shown remarkable abilities in understanding and generating programs, such as code completion, code repair, and code synthesis. We hypothesize that LLMs can also serve as proficient human experts in identifying code features for selecting verification strategies. By using LLMs, we can reduce the manual effort and the cognitive load of the users, and improve the efficiency and the effectiveness of the program verification.

3 Methodology

In this section, we describe the main components and steps of our approach to automate program verification by driving the CPAchecker based on code features. Figure 1 shows an overview of our approach, which consists of three phases: code snippets extraction, code feature identification, and strategy selection.

3.1 Code Snippet Extraction

When manually analyzing a program, it is common not to expensively analyze the entire source code. Instead, this process typically focuses on some key functions such as the main entry and the relevant functions it invokes. These functions and their intrinsic dependencies often reflect the structure, semantics, and behavioral features of the entire program. Based on this observation, CFStra derives only the key functions enriched with necessary calling contexts. To achieve this, CFStra extracts code snippets of the key functions by performing dependency analysis on the provided source program.

During the process of dependency analysis, the program dependency graph [19], denoted as $G = (N, E)$, is utilized to explicitly represent the dependencies for each operation in the program. It consists of a set of nodes N representing statements and the variables defined in the program, along with a set of directed edges $E \subseteq N \times N$ corresponding to data and control dependencies [1] between the nodes. In addition, we also augment the graph with concurrency-related dependence to extend its applicability: **Data dependence**: Each edge $e \in E$

Algorithm 1: Code Snippet Extraction through traversal on program dependency graph

Input : A program dependency graph $G = (N, E)$, and an initial key function f.

Output: A code snippet S including a set of key function bodies.

```
1  begin
2      // Search the graph node corresponding to the given function.
3      n := search_node(G, f);
4      W ← {n}, I ← ∅;
5      // Traverse the dependency graph to collect all the related key functions.
6      while W ≠ ∅ do
7          n := pop(W);
8          if ¬visited(n) then
9              // Get all the nodes that have data/control/concurrency dependence
               with n in G.
10             W := W ∪ {n′|(n, n′) ∈ E};
11             I := I ∪ {n};
12     // Collect all the key functions.
13     S ← ∅;
14     for n ∈ I do
15         // Retrieve the function containing this node.
16         s := retrieve_function(n);
17         if s ∉ S then
18             S := S ∪ {s};
19     return S;
```

is directed from one statement to the other statements that reference the same variable; **Control dependence**: Each edge $e \in E$ is directed from one statement to an if-statements; **Concurrency dependence**: Each edge $e \in E$ directed from: 1. a thread creation statement (e.g., pthread_create) to the entry node of the thread template function; 2. the return statement of thread template function to the statement (e.g., pthread_join) waiting for the thread to finish.

Algorithm 1 shows the details of extracting the code snippets. It takes two inputs: an initial key function f and a constructed program dependency graph G. The initial key function can be the entry function of the entire program or be determined based on error information such as program exception stacks and defect reports. In our algorithm, we define the extracted code snippet as S, containing key function bodies associated with input function f. To extract S, we initiate from the initial entry function node and traverse connected nodes in G using depth-first search (DFS) manner (lines 6–11) until all reachable nodes are gathered in set I (line 11). Subsequently, functions corresponding to nodes in I will be retrieved and stored in set S (lines 14–18), representing the key functions invoked or indirectly related to the initial key function f. The extracted code snippet S provides the necessary calling context and information for language models to analyze code features and mitigates the existing constraint of mainstream language models in handling lengthy texts.

Prompt

I am an expert in code analysis and verification, possessing a profound ability to comprehend and analyze program source code.

Task Description
The code snippet will be provided to me for the purpose of extracting the code features (e.g., loop, recursion, concurrency, array, pointer deference, etc.). The code features should be concluded in the format of 'Code Features: F1, F2, ...', where F1, F2 are specific program structure, complex data type, or operations.

Code Snippet
```C
<CODE_SNIPPET>
```

Fig. 2. The simplified prompt template we used

In the above algorithm, although the utilization of precise program dependency graphs can effectively improve the completeness of extracted key functions, creating precise dependency relationships for a large-scale program is typically time-consuming and not scalable. Considering the strong correlation between dependency relationships and intrinsic syntactic structure in source code, we devise a lightweight and efficient approach to improve the practicality of the code snippet extraction step. Specifically, CodeQuery [37], a pattern-based static analysis approach, is employed to construct a comprehensive code database, allowing for the retrieval of symbol references, global definitions, callee and caller functions. This enables us to efficiently analyze dependency relationships by leveraging the retrieved information.

3.2 Code Feature Identification

The second phase of our approach involves identifying the code features within the target program's source code utilizing LLMs. Code features are the characteristics or properties of the code that affect the choice of verification strategy, such as arrays, pointers, floating points, loops, concurrency, recursion, *etc.* Code features can be syntactic, semantic, or behavioral, depending on the level of abstraction and analysis.

To identify code features, we use LLMs that are trained on large corpora of natural and programming languages, such as ChatGPT [47]. LLMs have shown remarkable abilities in understanding and generating programs, such as code completion, code synthesis, and code repair. We hypothesize that LLMs can also serve as proficient human experts in identifying code features, by using their natural language and program comprehension capabilities.

To use LLMs, we formulate the code feature identification task as a natural language query and response problem. For the extracted code snippet, we generate a natural language query that asks the LLM to list the code features of the snippet. The prompts mainly comprise three key elements: role declaration, task description, and code snippet. Specifically, CFStra creates a document with contents in Markdown format to construct the prompt. As shown in Fig. 2, the

Response

- **Pointers**: The code extensively uses pointers to manipulate linked list nodes.
- **Struct Definition**: The code defines and uses a structure (struct node) to represent nodes in a linked list.
- **Loop**: The code contains two while loops for iterating through the linked list.
- **Conditional Statements**: Conditional statements are used to determine whether a node should be added to the low or high list based on the value of p->value.
- **Function Calls**: The code calls functions create_list() and reach_error().

Code Features: pointer operations, struct data type, loop, conditional statements, function calls.

Fig. 3. The response from LLMs

role declaration statement is provided in the first line, while the instructions are placed below the "Task Description" section. Besides, the extracted code snippets are presented in blue text. Furthermore, the "Task Description" section concludes with a sentence that instructs the desired output format. This output format is critical as it requires programmatic processing of the LLM's response. We then feed the query and the code snippet to the LLM, and expect the LLM to generate a natural language response that lists the code features of the snippet. For example, the response for extracting code features of the quick sort splitting algorithm is shown in Fig. 3.

We then parse the response and extract the code features from it, and store them in the database along with the code snippet. In order to balance the diversity and randomness of code features extracted from the source code, avoid the problem of insufficient consideration of the core features that affect strategy selection due to the high randomness of the output, and the problem of inadequate code feature extraction caused by low randomness output. We sample the query response multiple times by using the same prompt while applying a relatively high temperature for LLM to capture more comprehensive code features. Thereafter, we count and retain the extracted features that appear in more than half of the query instances. Intuitively, the retained code features appear frequently in the query results and are highly representative.

3.3 Strategy Selection

The third phase of our approach is to select the verification strategy for the program to be verified, based on the identified code features. A verification strategy is a combination of verification techniques and configuration parameters that are used to analyze and verify the target program.

The description of our four verification strategies will refer to the components: **VA-NoCEGAR**: value analysis without CEGAR [7]; **VA-CEGAR**: value analysis with CEGAR [7]; **PA**: predicate analysis with CEGAR [6]; **KI**: k-induction with continuously refined invariant generation [4]; **BAM$_\mathbf{R}$**: block-abstraction memorization (BAM) for a composite abstract domain of predicate analysis and value analysis [45]; **BMC**: bounded model checking (BMC) [9]; **C-Intp**: conditional interpolation empowered predicate analysis with CEGAR [39]; **PC-DPOR**: prioritized constraint-aided partial-order reduction [40]. The first six components are primarily used for verifying sequential programs, while the last two components are mainly employed for verifying concurrent programs.

The set of four verification strategies that we use in our strategy classifier are based on components from the above list: **CPA-Seq** sequentially combines VA-NoCEGAR, VA-CEGAR, PA, KI, and BAM_R. Any of the components may terminate early if it detects that it cannot handle the task. If none of the four components VA-NoCEGAR, VA-CEGAR, PA and KI can handle the task, and if KI fails due to the task requires handling of recursion, the BAM_R component runs. If either VA-NoCEGAR or VA-CEGAR find a bug, the feasibility of error path will be checked; if the check passes, the bug is reported, otherwise, the component result is disregarded and the subsequent component is executed. **BMC-BAM_R-PA** is a sequential combination of BMC, BAM_R, and PA. As above, any of the components may terminate early if it detects that it cannot handle the task. If the first component BMC fails because the task requires handling of recursion, the BAM_R component runs; if the reason why BMC fails was not recursion or if BAM_R fails to solve the task, PA runs. In this strategy, BAM_R and PA are only used as fallback components if the BMC components fails due to recursion or other unsupported features. **VA-BAM_R-KI** sequentially combines VA-NoCEGAR, VA-CEGAR, BAM_R, and KI. Any of the components may terminate early if it detects that it cannot handle the task. As in CPA-Seq, if either VA-NoCEGAR or VA-CEGAR find a bug, the feasibility of error path will be checked; if the check passes, the bug is reported. If the reason why VA-CEGAR failed was not recursion or if BAM_R also fails to solve the task, KI runs. **PIChecker** [41] is a sequential combination of PC-DPOR, C-Intp (MathSAT5 back-end [12]), C-Intp (SMTInterpol back-end [11]). If a counterexample is reported by PC-DPOR, the feasibility of this error path will be checked. If PC-DPOR fails due to some unsupported features such as array operations, the verification will continue by using the other two C-Intp based components with different back-end solvers.

To determine the verification strategy of a program, we employ a strategy classification based on the extracted code features. The strategy classifier is a function comprises the four verification strategies mentioned above:

$$Strategy = \begin{cases} \text{PIChecker}, \quad \text{if} \quad \text{hasConcurrency} \\ \text{BMC-BAM}_\text{R}\text{-PA}, \quad \text{if} \quad \text{not hasLoop} \\ \text{VA-BAM}_\text{R}\text{-KI}, \quad \text{if} \quad \text{hasLoop} \wedge \text{hasComplexType} \\ \text{CPA-Seq}, \quad \text{Otherwise} \end{cases} \tag{1}$$

It is defined to always choose the strategy PIChecker if 'Concurrency' is present in the extracted code features, since PIChecker is the only composite strategy used for verifying concurrent programs. If 'Loop' is not in the code features, the strategy BMC-BAM_R-PA will be chosen, as there is no need to perform any potentially expensive invariant-generating algorithm if no loop exists in the program. If 'Loop' is in the code features and there are complex data types (e.g., struct, union, array, and floating point type), it chooses VA-BAM_R-KI. If 'Loop' is in the code features and there are no complex data types, it chooses the CPA-Seq strategy.

4 Evaluation

We have developed a prototype tool called CFStra and conducted a comprehensive evaluation to evaluate its effectiveness. This study aims to compare CFStra with various fixed strategies, including basic strategies and sequential combination strategies. This study also highlights the implications of each proposed improvement through an ablation study.

Table 1. Detail information of Benchmark

No.	Dataset	Files	#KLOC
1	ReachSafety	366	1668.2
2	MemSafety	164	236.0
3	ConcurrencySafety	70	55.7
Total		600	1959.9

4.1 Experimental Setup

Benchmark Set. The set of verification tasks that we use in our experiments is taken from the benchmark collection that is also used in SV-COMP. We use all verification tasks from the benchmark collection for which we have identified different strategies. We conducted the experiments on the 600 verification tasks in the *ReachSafety*, *MemSafety*, *ConcurrencySafety* from SV-COMP 2023. The detailed information is presented in Table 1.

Comparation Among Existing Strategies. We first selected 8 widely used basic strategies to demonstrate their diverse performance. Subsequently, we compared CFStra with 4 existing SOTA sequential combination strategies (*i.e.*, CPA-Seq, BMC-BAM_R-PA, VA-BAM_R-KI, and PIChecker) for comparison, which incorporate various basic verification strategies. In the ablation study, we also include two simplified versions of CFStra.

Performance Metrics. We evaluate the performance of all competitors based on the verification correctness rate, time efficiency, and memory efficiency.

Configuration of LLMs. All interactions with LLMs, including sending requests and receiving responses, are conducted through ChatGPT's API. We specifically employ version *gpt-3.5-turbo* of ChatGPT. Various hyperparameters are involved in utilizing the APIs offered by ChatGPT [25]. For our configuration, we have set the values of `max_token` to 2048, `temperature` to 0.7, and query times to 7.

Experiment Infrastructure. All our experiments were conducted by version 2.3 of CPAchecker on machines equipped with 2.2GHz CPU(AMD EPYC 7773x), featuring 128 processing units and 503.7 GB of RAM, using OpenJDK 17 and

Table 2. Results for all 600 verification tasks, for 8 widely used basic strategies

Approach	VA-NoCEGAR	VA-CEGAR	PA	KI	BAM_R	BMC	CIntp	PC-DPOR
Score	75	53	143	255	−452	40	−685	58
Correct results	67	49	103	201	41	35	43	81
Correct proofs	24	20	56	150	19	21	8	41
Correct alarms	43	29	47	51	22	14	35	40
Wrong proofs	0	0	0	2	0	0	1	1
Wrong alarms	1	1	1	2	32	1	44	2
Timeouts	163	106	107	125	168	21	308	208
Out of memory	25	14	1	11	2	1	1	1
Other inconlusive	344	430	388	261	357	542	204	258
Times for correct results								
Total CPU Time(h)	1.5	1	1	1.3	1.2	0.5	2.2	2.3
Avg. CPU Time(s)	9	6	6	7.8	7.2	3	13	14
Total Wall Time(h)	1.5	1	1	1.3	1.2	0.5	2.2	2.3
Avg. Wall Time(s)	9	6	6	7.8	7.2	3	13	14

running on a 64-bit Ubuntu LTS 20.04.5. Each verification run was restricted to two CPU cores, with a maximum runtime of 15 min and a memory allocation of 15 GB. The benchmarking framework BenchExec [8] was employed to oversee the experiments, ensuring precise and dependable measurements.

4.2 Performance of Different Strategies

Table 2 shows the results of applying 8 different basic strategies to 600 verification tasks. These verification strategies are: VA-NoCEGAR, VA-CEGAR, PA, KI, BAM_R, BMC, C-Intp, and PC-DPOR. The table assesses each strategy's performance based on score, correctness, time, and memory.

The results from Table 2 demonstrate that the basic verification strategies yield different outcomes for the same verification task. For instance, KI exhibits the highest score and the highest number of correct proofs, but also the highest number of incorrect proofs. On the other hand, BMC has the fewest timeouts and out of memory, but also the lowest number of correct results. The high frequency of inaccurate outcomes produced by BAM_R and C-Intp, along with the consequent low scores, can be attributed to the absence of support for pointer alias processing. Hence, selecting the appropriate strategy is crucial to strike a balance between accuracy, efficiency, and comprehensiveness.

Figure 4 displays the quantile functions for the 8 basic strategies examined. It is evident that KI significantly outperforms the other strategies in these experiments. However, the performance of KI based combination strategy (i.e., VA-BAM_R-KI) still lags behind our proposed approach, CFStra, and other sequential combination strategies, as depicted in Fig. 5. This is why our approach focuses on selecting existing combination strategies only, as demonstrated in Formula 1. The subsequent section will delve into a detailed analysis of the results obtained with CFStra and compare them with other sequential combination strategies.

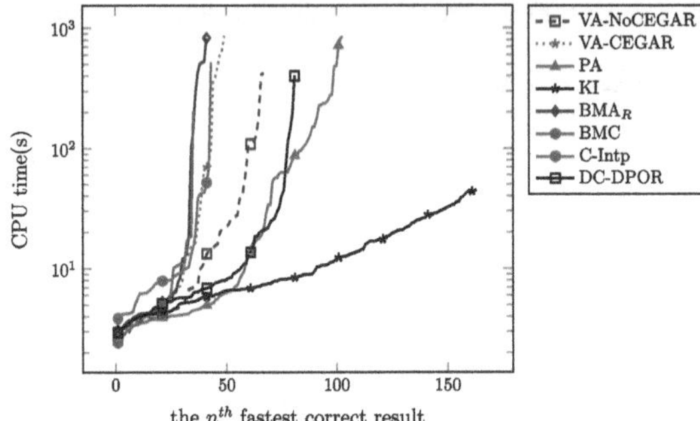

Fig. 4. The quantile plot of time consumption in logarithmic scale

Table 3. Results for all 600 verification tasks for combination strategies

Approach	CFStra	PIChecker	CPA-Seq	BMC-BAM$_R$-PA	VA-BAM$_R$-KI
Score	469	278	225	111	224
Correct results	315	228	144	103	144
Correct proofs	202	146	97	40	96
Correct alarms	113	82	47	63	48
Wrong proofs	0	1	0	0	0
Wrong alarms	3	4	1	2	1
Timeouts	224	319	187	234	186
Out of memory	13	2	24	8	25
Other inconclusive	45	47	244	253	244
Times for correct results					
Total CPU Time(h)	1.4	2.3	1.5	2	1.5
Avg. CPU Time(s)	8.4	14	9	12	9
Total Wall Time(h)	2.2	2	1.5	2	1.5
Avg. Wall Time(s)	13	14	9	12	9

4.3 Compared to Other SOTA Combination Strategies

Table 3 displays the results of CFStra, comparing it with four SOTA combination strategies (*i.e.*, PIChecker, CPA-Seq, BMC-BAM$_R$-PA, VA-BAM$_R$-KI). Even though the sequential combination strategy significantly outperformed individual basic strategies, it remains a fixed approach. CFStra achieved notably higher scores than each of the other combination strategies. The adoption of the LLM-driven strategy proved to be advantageous, resulting in a superior score compared to competitors. While this method may lead to more false alarms than other strategies, it enhances the accuracy of results significantly, effectively resolving this issue. These findings suggest that utilizing the strategy selector based on the code features identified by LLMs can lead to favorable outcomes, even when choices are limited. Furthermore, CFStra exhibits enhanced efficiency in task identification, with only 45 inconclusive tasks out of 600. The results indicate that the use of LLM-driven strategy selection is more effective than consistently selecting a fixed strategy. As a result, the strategy selector employed in *CFStra* strikes a balance between accuracy, efficiency, and comprehensiveness.

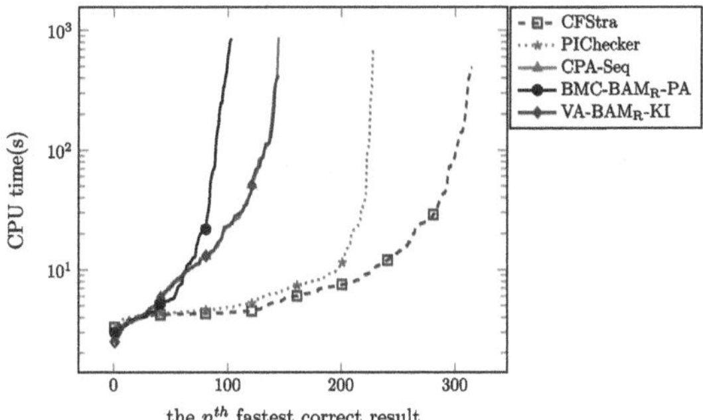

Fig. 5. The quantile plot of CFStra, compared with 4 combination strategies.

Table 4. Results for all 600 verification tasks for 3 version of CFStra

Approach	CFStra_{direct}	CFStra_{llm}	CFStra
Score	224	229	469
Correct results	143	147	315
Correct proofs	97	98	202
Correct alarms	46	49	113
Wrong proofs	0	0	0
Wrong alarms	1	1	3
Timeouts	180	183	224
Out of memory	24	25	13
Other inconlusive	252	244	45
Times for correct results			
Total CPU Time(h)	2.3	1.2	1.4
Avg. CPU Time(s)	14	7.2	8.4
Total Wall Time(h)	2.5	1.5	2.2
Avg. Wall Time(s)	15	9	13

Figure 5 depicts the quantile functions of CFStra in comparison with four combination strategies. It is clearly evident from the curves in the plot that PIChecker outperforms $\text{BMC-BAM}_\text{R}\text{-PA}$ and $\text{VA-BAM}_\text{R}\text{-KI}$ significantly, but still trails behind CFStra. Upon comparing the experimental results, it was discovered that within the 95 tasks in the *ReachSafety* dataset, PIChecker failed to achieve effective verification outcomes due to verification timeouts and other reasons. Conversely, CFStra selected more appropriate strategies based on the extracted code features, making these tasks can be effectively verified with limited resources. Therefore, the superiority of CFStra over the other combination strategies is clearly evident.

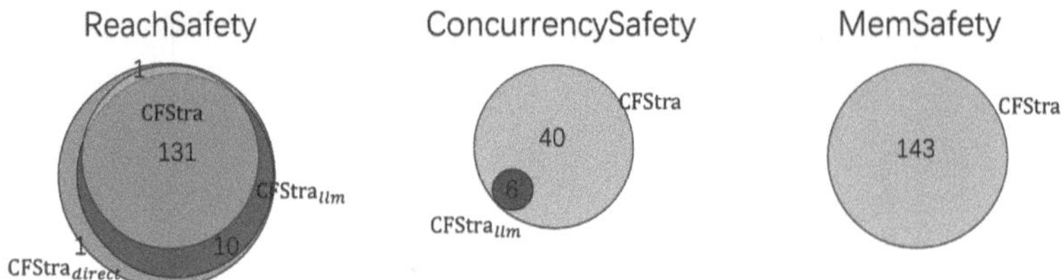

Fig. 6. The number of verification tasks successfully verified by CFStra$_{direct}$, CFStra$_{llm}$ and CFStra across different categories.

4.4 Ablation Study

To evaluate the effectiveness of our proposed approach, we performed an ablation study to compare the performance of CFStra with its two simplified versions: CFStra$_{direct}$ and CFStra$_{llm}$. CFStra$_{direct}$ directly utilizes LLM for strategy selection, without analyzing code features. CFStra$_{llm}$ decomposes the strategy selection process into two steps: first, analyzing code features using LLM, and then predicting the strategy using LLM. We used the same set of 600 verification tasks as in the previous section, where the results are shown in Table 4. We can observe that CFStra significantly outperforms both CFStra$_{direct}$ and CFStra$_{llm}$. This indicates that CFStra can effectively select the most appropriate verification strategy for each verification task, based on the code features and specifications. Moreover, CFStra achieves comparable or better CPU and wall time than CFStra$_{direct}$, demonstrating that CFStra is efficient and scalable.

Figure 6 presents the comparison of the success of the verification task among three versions of CFStra in various categories in Table 1: ReachSafety, ConcurrencySafety. The results indicate that CFStra consistently outperforms the other versions across all categories, particularly excelling in ConcurrencySafety and MemSafety by successfully verifying a notable number of tasks. This demonstrates that CFStra can effectively choose the appropriative strategy to handle complex and challenging verification tasks that involve concurrency and memory issues. On the other hand, CFStra$_{llm}$ slightly outperforms CFStra$_{direct}$ in verifying tasks within the ConcurrencySafety category, attributed to the decomposed strategy selection process into two steps. Nevertheless, the overall performance between CFStra$_{direct}$ and CFStra$_{llm}$ remains comparable. This suggests a need for integrating code features and specifications into the independent strategy selection process, as CFStra does in the formula 1.

The ablation study also reveals the limitations of CFStra$_{direct}$ and CFStra$_{llm}$. CFStra$_{direct}$ suffers from low accuracy and high inconclusiveness, as it does not take into account the code features that are crucial for strategy selection. CFStra$_{llm}$ improves slightly over CFStra$_{direct}$, as it analyzes code features using LLM, but it still fails to select the best strategy for many verification tasks, as it relies on LLM for the final prediction. This suggests that LLM alone is not sufficient for strategy selection, and that a more sophisticated strategy selector is needed. In summary, the ablation study confirms the superiority of CFStra over its two simplified versions, and validates the design choices of our approach.

4.5 Threats to Validity

There are three major validity threats. First, One potential threat is the selection bias that may arise from using only 600 verification tasks from SV-COMP, which could limit the diversity of our dataset. To address this concern, we made sure to select diverse programs from various domains with different characteristics. Second, the generalizability of different LLMs is also a concern. We have also implemented CFStrato a popular and open-source LLM called *Llama-2*. Similar results were observed in our preliminary experiments. Third, due to their inherent randomness, LLMs generate varied answers for identical programs to be verified with the same prompts. A potential threat to the validity of our study is that conclusions drawn from random results may be misleading. To address the above three potential threads, future works involve conducting multiple experiments on a substantial dataset.

5 Related Work

In this section, we review the existing literature on program verification, as well as LLMs for program analysis and verification, and explain how our work is different from or builds upon them.

Program Verification and its Strategies. Program verification is a well-studied and active research area, that aims to ensure the correctness and reliability of software systems [20,38]. There are various techniques and tools for program verification, such as static analysis [31,49], model checking [13,26], theorem proving [32,34], runtime verification [2,16], *etc.* Several studies have sought to combine various verification strategies sequentially, (*e.g.,* CPA-Seq and PeSCo) [31,36], which prove to be more effective than each strategy used alone. However, these methods are either limited in scope or scalability, or rely on external sources. Moreover, these methods do not exploit the program comprehension capabilities of LLMs, which can serve as proficient human experts in identifying code features and selecting verification strategies.

LLMs for Program Analysis and Verification. LLMs are neural network models that are trained on large corpora of natural and programming languages [30,51]. LLMs have demonstrated impressive capabilities in comprehending and producing code, leading to a surge in interest in utilizing LLMs for aiding in program analysis and verification tasks [17,22]. These tasks include static analysis [28,43], program testing [27,42], program verification [44,46], bug reproduction [23,24] and bug repair [18,48]. Recent advancements in LLMs for verification have led to the development of Baldur [21], a proof-synthesis tool that utilizes transformer-based pre-trained LLMs, fine-tuned proofs, to generate and repair complete proofs. In contrast, our approach centers on leveraging LLMs to detect code features and guide the verification tool in selecting strategies, whereas Baldur primarily automates the generation of proofs for theorems. Moreover, to the best of our knowledge, there is no comparable existing work that tries to drive program verification by using LLMs to identify code features and select verification strategies, which are the key steps of our approach.

6 Conclusions

This paper presents a novel approach for automating program verification by selecting verification strategies based on code features. Our approach leverages the program comprehension abilities of Large Language Models (LLMs) to recognize code features. Subsequently, a selection model is then developed to automatically choose appropriate verification strategies. We evaluated the effectiveness and efficiency of our approach using a substantial collection of verification tasks from SV-COMP. The outcomes indicate that our approach not only surpasses basic strategies and SOTA combination strategies but also stands out for its simplicity and ease of understanding.

Acknowledgements. The authors would like to thank the anonymous reviewers for their constructive comments. This work was supported in part by the National Natural Science Foundation of China (Nos. 62302375, 62192734, 62193273024), the China Postdoctoral Science Foundation funded project (No. 2023M723736), and the Fundamental Research Funds for the Central Universities.

References

1. Allen, J.R., Kennedy, K., Porterfield, C., Warren, J.: Conversion of control dependence to data dependence. In: Proceedings of the 10th ACM SIGACT-SIGPLAN Symposium on Principles of Programming Languages, pp. 177–189 (1983)
2. Bartocci, E., Falcone, Y., Francalanza, A., Reger, G.: Introduction to runtime verification. In: Lectures on Runtime Verification: Introductory and Advanced Topics, pp. 1–33 (2018)
3. Beyer, D., Dangl, M.: Strategy selection for software verification based on boolean features. In: Margaria, T., Steffen, B. (eds.) ISoLA 2018. LNCS, vol. 11245, pp. 144–159. Springer, Cham (2018). https://doi.org/10.1007/978-3-030-03421-4_11
4. Beyer, D., Dangl, M., Wendler, P.: Boosting k-induction with continuously-refined invariants. In: Kroening, D., Păsăreanu, C.S. (eds.) CAV 2015. LNCS, vol. 9206, pp. 622–640. Springer, Cham (2015). https://doi.org/10.1007/978-3-319-21690-4_42
5. Beyer, D., Keremoglu, M.E.: CPAchecker: a tool for configurable software verification. In: Gopalakrishnan, G., Qadeer, S. (eds.) CAV 2011. LNCS, vol. 6806, pp. 184–190. Springer, Heidelberg (2011). https://doi.org/10.1007/978-3-642-22110-1_16
6. Beyer, D., Keremoglu, M.E., Wendler, P.: Predicate abstraction with adjustable-block encoding. In: Formal Methods in Computer Aided Design, pp. 189–197. IEEE (2010)

7. Beyer, D., Löwe, S.: Explicit-state software model checking based on CEGAR and interpolation. In: Cortellessa, V., Varró, D. (eds.) FASE 2013. LNCS, vol. 7793, pp. 146–162. Springer, Heidelberg (2013). https://doi.org/10.1007/978-3-642-37057-1_11
8. Beyer, D., Löwe, S., Wendler, P.: Reliable benchmarking: requirements and solutions. Int. J. Softw. Tools Technol. Transfer **21**, 1–29 (2019)
9. Biere, A., Cimatti, A., Clarke, E.M., Strichman, O., Zhu, Y.: Bounded model checking. In: Handbook of Satisfiability, vol. 185, no. 99, pp. 457–481 (2009)
10. Chakraborty, S., et al.: Ranking LLM-generated loop invariants for program verification. arXiv preprint arXiv:2310.09342 (2023)
11. Christ, J., Hoenicke, J., Nutz, A.: SMTInterpol: an interpolating SMT solver. In: Donaldson, A., Parker, D. (eds.) SPIN 2012. LNCS, vol. 7385, pp. 248–254. Springer, Heidelberg (2012). https://doi.org/10.1007/978-3-642-31759-0_19
12. Cimatti, A., Griggio, A., Schaafsma, B.J., Sebastiani, R.: The MathSAT5 SMT solver. In: Piterman, N., Smolka, S.A. (eds.) TACAS 2013. LNCS, vol. 7795, pp. 93–107. Springer, Heidelberg (2013). https://doi.org/10.1007/978-3-642-36742-7_7
13. Clarke, E.M.: Model checking. In: Ramesh, S., Sivakumar, G. (eds.) FSTTCS 1997. LNCS, vol. 1346, pp. 54–56. Springer, Heidelberg (1997). https://doi.org/10.1007/BFb0058022
14. Czech, M., Hüllermeier, E., Jakobs, M.C., Wehrheim, H.: Predicting rankings of software verification tools. In: Proceedings of the 3rd ACM SIGSOFT International Workshop on Software Analytics, pp. 23–26 (2017)
15. Demyanova, Y., Pani, T., Veith, H., Zuleger, F.: Empirical software metrics for benchmarking of verification tools. Formal Methods Syst. Des. **50**, 289–316 (2017)
16. Falcone, Y., Havelund, K., Reger, G.: A tutorial on runtime verification. Eng. Dependable Softw. Syst. 141–175 (2013)
17. Fan, A., et al.: Large language models for software engineering: survey and open problems. arXiv preprint arXiv:2310.03533 (2023)
18. Fan, Z., Gao, X., Mirchev, M., Roychoudhury, A., Tan, S.H.: Automated repair of programs from large language models. In: 45th IEEE/ACM International Conference on Software Engineering, ICSE 2023, Melbourne, Australia, 14–20 May 2023, pp. 1469–1481. IEEE (2023)
19. Ferrante, J., Ottenstein, K.J., Warren, J.D.: The program dependence graph and its use in optimization. ACM Trans. Program. Lang. Syst. **9**(3), 319–349 (1987). https://doi.org/10.1145/24039.24041
20. Fetzer, J.H.: Program verification: the very idea. Commun. ACM **31**(9), 1048–1063 (1988)
21. First, E., Rabe, M., Ringer, T., Brun, Y.: Baldur: whole-proof generation and repair with large language models. In: Proceedings of the 31st ACM Joint European Software Engineering Conference and Symposium on the Foundations of Software Engineering, pp. 1229–1241 (2023)
22. Hou, X., et al.: Large language models for software engineering: a systematic literature review. arXiv preprint arXiv:2308.10620 (2023)
23. Kang, S., Yoon, J., Askarbekkyzy, N., Yoo, S.: Evaluating diverse large language models for automatic and general bug reproduction. arXiv preprint arXiv:2311.04532 (2023)
24. Kang, S., Yoon, J., Yoo, S.: Large language models are few-shot testers: exploring LLM-based general bug reproduction. In: 45th IEEE/ACM International Conference on Software Engineering, ICSE 2023, Melbourne, Australia, 14–20 May 2023, pp. 2312–2323. IEEE (2023)

25. Kocoń, J., et al.: Chatgpt: jack of all trades, master of none. Inf. Fusion 101861 (2023)
26. Kroening, D., Tautschnig, M.: CBMC – C bounded model checker. In: Ábrahám, E., Havelund, K. (eds.) TACAS 2014. LNCS, vol. 8413, pp. 389–391. Springer, Heidelberg (2014). https://doi.org/10.1007/978-3-642-54862-8_26
27. Lemieux, C., Inala, J.P., Lahiri, S.K., Sen, S.: Codamosa: escaping coverage plateaus in test generation with pre-trained large language models. In: 45th IEEE/ACM International Conference on Software Engineering, ICSE 2023, Melbourne, Australia, 14–20 May 2023, pp. 919–931. IEEE (2023)
28. Li, H., Hao, Y., Zhai, Y., Qian, Z.: Assisting static analysis with large language models: a chatgpt experiment. In: Proceedings of the 31st ACM Joint European Software Engineering Conference and Symposium on the Foundations of Software Engineering, pp. 2107–2111 (2023)
29. Li, Y., et al.: Competition-level code generation with alphacode. Science **378**(6624), 1092–1097 (2022)
30. Liu, Y., et al.: Summary of chatgpt-related research and perspective towards the future of large language models. Meta-Radiol. 100017 (2023)
31. Löwe, S., Mandrykin, M., Wendler, P.: CPAchecker with sequential combination of explicit-value analyses and predicate analyses. In: Ábrahám, E., Havelund, K. (eds.) TACAS 2014. LNCS, vol. 8413, pp. 392–394. Springer, Heidelberg (2014). https://doi.org/10.1007/978-3-642-54862-8_27
32. Matthews, J., Moore, J.S., Ray, S., Vroon, D.: Verification condition generation via theorem proving. In: Hermann, M., Voronkov, A. (eds.) LPAR 2006. LNCS (LNAI), vol. 4246, pp. 362–376. Springer, Heidelberg (2006). https://doi.org/10.1007/11916277_25
33. OpenAI: GPT-4 technical report. arxiv:2303.08774. View in Article, vol. 2, p. 13 (2023)
34. Ouimet, M., Lundqvist, K.: Formal software verification: model checking and theorem proving. Embedded Systems Laboratory Technical Report ESL-TIK-00214, Cambridge USA (2007)
35. Pei, K., Bieber, D., Shi, K., Sutton, C., Yin, P.: Can large language models reason about program invariants? In: International Conference on Machine Learning, pp. 27496–27520. PMLR (2023)
36. Richter, C., Wehrheim, H.: PeSCo: predicting sequential combinations of verifiers. In: Beyer, D., Huisman, M., Kordon, F., Steffen, B. (eds.) TACAS 2019. LNCS, vol. 11429, pp. 229–233. Springer, Cham (2019). https://doi.org/10.1007/978-3-030-17502-3_19
37. Ruben: A code-understanding, code-browsing or code-search tool. This is a tool to index, then query or search C, C++, java, python, ruby, go and javascript source code. https://github.com/ruben2020/codequery. Accessed 04 Mar 2024
38. Sieber, K.: The Foundations of Program Verification. Springer, Wiesbaden (2013). https://doi.org/10.1007/978-3-322-96753-4
39. Su, J., Tian, C., Duan, Z.: Conditional interpolation: making concurrent program verification more effective. In: Proceedings of the 29th ACM Joint Meeting on European Software Engineering Conference and Symposium on the Foundations of Software Engineering, pp. 144–154 (2021)
40. Su, J., Tian, C., Yang, Z., Yang, J., Yu, B., Duan, Z.: Prioritized constraint-aided dynamic partial-order reduction. In: Proceedings of the 37th IEEE/ACM International Conference on Automated Software Engineering, pp. 1–13 (2022)

41. Su, J., Yang, Z., Xing, H., Yang, J., Tian, C., Duan, Z.: PIChecker: a POR and interpolation based verifier for concurrent programs (competition contribution). In: Sankaranarayanan, S., Sharygina, N. (eds.) TACAS 2023. LNCS, vol. 13994, pp. 571–576. Springer, Cham (2023). https://doi.org/10.1007/978-3-031-30820-8_38
42. Tsigkanos, C., Rani, P., Müller, S., Kehrer, T.: Large language models: the next frontier for variable discovery within metamorphic testing? In: 2023 IEEE International Conference on Software Analysis, Evolution and Reengineering (SANER), pp. 678–682. IEEE (2023)
43. Wen, C., et al.: Automatically inspecting thousands of static bug warnings with large language model: How far are we? ACM Trans. Knowl. Discov. Data (2024)
44. Wen, C., et al.: Enchanting program specification synthesis by large language models using static analysis and program verification. In: International Conference on Computer Aided Verification. Springer, Cham (2024)
45. Wonisch, D., Wehrheim, H.: Predicate analysis with block-abstraction memoization. In: Aoki, T., Taguchi, K. (eds.) ICFEM 2012. LNCS, vol. 7635, pp. 332–347. Springer, Heidelberg (2012). https://doi.org/10.1007/978-3-642-34281-3_24
46. Wu, H., Barrett, C., Narodytska, N.: Lemur: integrating large language models in automated program verification. arXiv preprint arXiv:2310.04870 (2023)
47. Wu, T., et al.: A brief overview of ChatGPT: the history, status quo and potential future development. IEEE/CAA J. Automatica Sinica **10**(5), 1122–1136 (2023)
48. Xia, C.S., Wei, Y., Zhang, L.: Automated program repair in the era of large pre-trained language models. In: 45th IEEE/ACM International Conference on Software Engineering, ICSE 2023, Melbourne, Australia, 14–20 May 2023, pp. 1482–1494. IEEE (2023)
49. Xu, Z., Wen, C., Qin, S.: State-taint analysis for detecting resource bugs. Sci. Comput. Program. **162**, 93–109 (2018)
50. Yetistiren, B., Ozsoy, I., Tuzun, E.: Assessing the quality of github copilot's code generation. In: Proceedings of the 18th International Conference on Predictive Models and Data Analytics in Software Engineering, pp. 62–71 (2022)
51. Zhao, W.X., et al.: A survey of large language models. arXiv preprint arXiv:2303.18223 (2023)

Improved Incremental Verification for Neural Networks

Xuezhou Tang(✉)

Shenzhen University, Shenzhen, China
2110276137@email.szu.edu.cn

Abstract. The formal verification of deep neural networks (DNNs) guarantees their robustness. However, DNNs deployed in real-world applications frequently undergo adjustments due to, for instance, quantization and model repair, necessitating the repetition of computationally expensive formal verification. To efficiently verify the robustness of such adjusted DNNs, incremental techniques for DNN verification are proposed recently. These techniques use the information obtained from the verification of original networks to expedite the verification of their adjusted counterparts. In particular, the state-of-the-art incremental technique based on the Branch-and-Bound method exploits branching information from verifying original DNNs, to efficiently generate subproblems for verifying the adjusted counterparts. This paper goes beyond this idea. When verifying adjusted DNNs, we prioritize checking subproblems that falsify the robustness of the original ones, with the expectation of prompt falsification. Furthermore, we collect information from the *Bound* processes while verifying original DNNs, then utilize it for more efficient *Bound* processes when verifying the adjusted networks. We propose a DNN incremental verification framework I-IVAN and realize it for evaluation. It is compared against IVAN, the state-of-the-art DNN verification tool with incremental techniques, on networks trained by datasets MNIST and CIFAR-10. The experimental results show that I-IVAN is much more efficient than IVAN within 7.71 times faster than IVAN at most.

Keywords: Neural network verification · Incremental verification · Branch-and-Bound

1 Introduction

DNNs find widespread adoption in safety-critical domains, including automatic driving and drone piloting [17]. Ensuring the safety and robustness of these networks remains paramount. However, their vulnerability to input perturbations poses a significant challenge for practical deployment [19]. For instance, manipulated traffic signs could mislead specific autonomous driving systems, resulting in

This work is partially supported by the Natural Science Foundation of Guangdong Province (Grant No. 2022A1515011458).

W.-N. Chin and Z. Xu (Eds.): TASE 2024, LNCS 14777, pp. 392–409, 2024.
https://doi.org/10.1007/978-3-031-64626-3_23

erroneous predictions [20]. While various works focus on identifying adversarial examples using testing techniques, it's important to note that such methods do not provide formal certification of network robustness [33]. In contrast, *formal verification* offers a mathematical proof of a network's robustness to perturbed inputs, granting certification for safety-critical applications.

1.1 Neural Network Verification

Neural network verification centers around framing the verification problem as a reachability problem [13]. Specifically, we consider an input region-an infinite set resulting from perturbations applied to a specific input. The goal of verification is to compute the reachability set of the output corresponding to all inputs within this region. However, the presence of non-linear activation functions in neural networks renders the input-output relationship highly non-linear, thereby making the reachability problem NP-hard [16]. The task in neural network verification is to ascertain whether the output region satisfies certain properties [14]. The challenge lies in effectively handling these non-linear activation functions.

Existing neural network verification methods fall into two broad categories: *complete* and *sound but incomplete*. Complete methods accurately compute the precise output region, investing significant time due to the inherent complexity of the reachability problem. As a trade-off, they guarantee either a 'safe' or 'unsafe' answer for any verification query, regardless of time constraints. Among the complete verifiers, the Branch-and-Bound (BaB)-based technique is mainly composed of the branching and *Bound* process. BaB splits non-linear activation functions into linear pieces or partition of the input region of non-linear functions to ensure piecewise linearity within each sub-region [28]. However, their scalability remains limited due to computational complexities.

The sound but incomplete techniques manage complexity by approximating the non-linear input-output relationship with linear constraints. Consequently, they may yield 'UNKNOWN' results during verification, despite their high efficacy. Notably, state-of-the-art sound verifiers, such as $\alpha\beta$-CROWN [29] and FaGMR [25], incorporate strategies for tight over-approximated constraints. Although these methods achieve efficient and precise verification, the inherent over-approximation still leads to 'UNKNOWN' outputs.

1.2 Incremental Verification for Neural Network

In practical applications, neural networks undergo frequent adjustments for various reasons, including approximation [11], model repair [18], and transfer learning [30]. These adjustments perturb network weights or biases, yet the adjusted networks serve the same purposes as the originals [11,18]. When a new network emerges from adjusting the original, time-costly verification becomes essential to assess its safety properties-even for minor adjustments. Consequently, neither complete nor incomplete methods find widespread deployment in practical scenarios. Developers often rely on testing technology [9], which lacks robustness guarantees, to evaluate neural network safety.

To address the limitation in the practicality of existing complete verifiers, incremental verifies for neural networks [26,32] are proposed currently. The incremental verification problem for networks is to leverage information from the verification of the original network. Consider an original network denoted as N. Its adjusted counterpart, represented as N', closely mirrors the structure of N. Consequently, the verification process for N' can be related to that of N [26]. It is important to clarify that when we refer to 'structure', we specifically mean the weights and biases of the network, rather than its topological arrangement. Two existing incremental verifiers for neural networks, namely DeepInc [32] and IVAN [26], leverage information derived from the original networks to verify the properties of the adjusted networks efficiently. IVAN, which relies on the BaB method [7], reconstructs information generated during the *Branch* process in BaB for the original networks using heuristics. This reconstructed information is utilized to enhance the verification process for the adjusted networks. On the other hand, DeepInc relies on the SMT/SAT solver [9]. It prioritizes checking output properties based on the information resulting from the original networks' *SAT* answer, aiming to simplify the verification for the adjusted networks.

1.3 Contributions of This Paper

The current incremental verifier for BaB, IVAN, faces challenges when considering the use of unreconstructed information to further enhance efficiency due to its heuristic reconstruction. Furthermore, while the state-of-the-art incremental verification for BaB primarily emphasizes the *Branch* process, it is also viable to leverage information from the *Bound* process for incremental verification.

Our paper specifically addresses incremental verification within the context of Branch-and-Bound. Specifically, we give priority to checking subproblems that falsify the robustness of the original network N during the verification of the adjusted network N'. Additionally, we gather information from strategies related to tight over-approximated constraints during the verification of N within the *Bound* process. We then reuse this information in the *Bound* process for N', avoiding redundant strategy calculations. We propose an incremental neural network framework, referred to as I-IVAN (Improved Incremental Verification for Neural Networks), and we realize the framework and then evaluate its effectiveness. I-IVAN is compared with the state-of-the-art, IVAN, on the neural networks trained by popular datasets MNIST and CIFAR-10. Our contributions are summarized as:

- We define the *SAT* specification (as per Definition 6) to represent the specifications that challenge the robustness of the original network N. During incremental verification of the adjusted network N', we give priority to assessing whether the *SAT* specification falsifies the robustness of N'. This approach enables early termination of the BaB algorithm if the adjusted network N' is found to lack robustness, thereby enhancing the overall effectiveness of the state-of-the-art method.

- We designate the information computed during the verification of the original network N, specifically related to the strategies for tight over-approximated constraints within the *Bound* process, as the ancillary specification (according to Definition 7). Our proposal involves reusing the ancillary specification as the output of the strategies, rather than recalculating the strategies several times in incremental scenarios. As a result, the computational overhead of the *Bound* process for verifying N' is reduced.
- We realize our proposed framework I-IVAN and rigorously evaluate its effectiveness. Experimental results indicate that, using the same ReLU splitting technique [7], I-IVAN achieves a speedup of up to 7.71 times compared to IVAN on both MNIST and CIFAR-10 datasets.

Organaization. Section 2 provides the preliminaries on neural network verification and incremental verification. Our methodology is detailed in Sect. 3 and it is evaluated in Sect. 4. Section 5 discusses related works before concluding this paper in Sect. 6.

2 Preliminaries

This section provides the notions about incremental verification with a complete verifier to understand our approach.

2.1 Neural Networks

A neural network can be regarded as a $|\boldsymbol{Y}|$-dimensional vector valued function $: \boldsymbol{X} \to \mathbb{R}^{|\boldsymbol{Y}|}$. In particular, the constraint formed by $\boldsymbol{X}$, $\mathcal{X}$, is the input specification.

Definition 1 ***(Input specification).*** *The input domain* $\boldsymbol{X}$ *is defined by a p-norm ball neighborhood of the input* $\boldsymbol{x}$ *with the perturbation threshold* ε: $\boldsymbol{X} = \{\boldsymbol{x}' = \boldsymbol{x} + \boldsymbol{\delta} \mid \|\boldsymbol{\delta}\|_p \leq \varepsilon\}$. *The input specification* $\mathcal{X}$ *is the constraint formed by* $\boldsymbol{X}$: $\mathcal{X} := (\|\boldsymbol{x}' - \boldsymbol{x}\|_p \leq \varepsilon)$.

Definition 2 ***(Output specification).*** *For a neuron network* $N : \mathbb{R}^{n_0} \to \mathbb{R}^{n_l}$, *output specification* ψ *is defined as* $\psi : \mathbb{R}^{n_l} \to \{true, false\}$ *which is a predicate to the output region, and* ψ *is also called the output property of* N.

In this paper, we focus on the neural network which is a composition of affine function layers $\boldsymbol{g}_i(\boldsymbol{x}) = \boldsymbol{W}_i\boldsymbol{x} + \boldsymbol{b}_i$, with non-linear activation layers $\boldsymbol{f}_i(\boldsymbol{x})$:

$$\boldsymbol{h}(\boldsymbol{x}) = \boldsymbol{g}_L \circ \boldsymbol{f}_L \circ \boldsymbol{g}_{L-1} \circ \cdots \circ \boldsymbol{f}_1 \circ \boldsymbol{g}_0(\boldsymbol{x})$$

where L is the number of hidden layers, $\boldsymbol{f}_i(\boldsymbol{x})$ applies $ReLU(x)$ in an element-wise manner. A verifier should verify that the output of the neural networks $\mathcal{Y} = \boldsymbol{h}(\boldsymbol{x})$ satisfies the property ψ for any perturbed input in the input domain $\boldsymbol{X}$. Most neural network verifiers consider the following properties: $\psi(\mathcal{Y}) = (\boldsymbol{C}^T\mathcal{Y} \geq 0)$. The satisfied property means that the network is robust for the input and perturbation. Formally, the verification problem and verifiers can be defined as:

Definition 3 ***(Verifier).*** *Given a neural network $\mathcal{Y} = \boldsymbol{h}(\boldsymbol{x})$, an input $\boldsymbol{x} \in \boldsymbol{X}$, a perturbation threshold ε, and the output specification ψ, a verification problem is to prove whether $\forall \boldsymbol{x} \in \boldsymbol{X}, \psi(\mathcal{Y}) = true$ or $false$.*

A complete verifier $\boldsymbol{V}$ always verifies the property ψ with the results *true* or *false*, it can be formally defined as:

$$\boldsymbol{V}(\mathcal{X}, \psi, \boldsymbol{h}(\cdot)) = SAT \Leftrightarrow \exists \boldsymbol{x} \in \boldsymbol{X}, \psi(\boldsymbol{h}(\boldsymbol{x})) = false$$

$$\boldsymbol{V}(\mathcal{X}, \psi, \boldsymbol{h}(\cdot)) = UNSAT \Leftrightarrow \exists \boldsymbol{x} \in \boldsymbol{X}, \psi(\boldsymbol{h}(\boldsymbol{x})) = true$$

If $\boldsymbol{V}$ is a sound but incomplete verifier, when there exists an input $\boldsymbol{x} \in \boldsymbol{X}$ s.t. $\psi(\boldsymbol{h}(\boldsymbol{x})) = false$, it will return $UNKNOWN$ or SAT due to the over-approximation of $\boldsymbol{h}(\boldsymbol{x})$. Only when no possible input satisfies the property ψ, $\boldsymbol{V}$ returns SAT. The sound but incomplete verifiers are defined as:

$$\boldsymbol{V}(\mathcal{X}, \psi, \boldsymbol{h}(\cdot)) = \begin{cases} UNSAT, & \forall \boldsymbol{x} \in \boldsymbol{X}, \psi(\boldsymbol{h}(\boldsymbol{x})) = true \\ SAT, & \forall \boldsymbol{x} \in \boldsymbol{X}, \psi(\boldsymbol{h}(\boldsymbol{x})) = false \\ UNKNOWN, & else \end{cases}$$

If a verifier returns SAT, it indicates the existence of a counter-example that falsifies the robustness of the network $\boldsymbol{h}(\cdot)$. Conversely, if it returns $UNSAT$, the network is considered safe or robust. The $UNKNOWN$ output signifies that the verifier fails to verify the specified property ψ.

2.2 Branch-and-Bound for Verification

This section introduces the Branch-and-Bound (BaB) for the complete verification of deep neural networks (DNNs). The core concept of the BaB approach lies in employing a divide-and-conquer strategy to compute both the lower bound $LB(\boldsymbol{C}^T\mathcal{Y})$ and the upper bound $UB(\boldsymbol{C}^T\mathcal{Y})$ for the expression $\boldsymbol{C}^T\mathcal{Y}$. We verify the property ψ: $\boldsymbol{C}^T\mathcal{Y} \geq 0$. State-of-the-art verifiers certify neural networks employing ReLU activation functions. Consider a ReLU neuron $v_{i,j}$ with input $x_{i,j}$. Next, we delve into the *Branch* and *Bound* processes within the BaB framework.

Bound Process. During the *Bound* process, a sound but incomplete verifier $\boldsymbol{V}$ calculates the over-approximated bounds $LB(\boldsymbol{C}^T\mathcal{Y})$ and $UB(\boldsymbol{C}^T\mathcal{Y})$ for each subproblem generated by the *Branch* process. If the verifier determines that $UB(\boldsymbol{C}^T\mathcal{Y}) < 0$, implying $\boldsymbol{C}^T\mathcal{Y} < 0$ for all $\boldsymbol{x} \in \boldsymbol{X}$, the BaB algorithm outputs SAT, indicating that the network violates the safety specification ψ. If for all subproblems, the results from the *Bound* process are $LB(\boldsymbol{C}^T\mathcal{Y}) \geq 0$, the BaB outputs $UNSAT$ implying the safety of the network. Conversely, when $LB(\boldsymbol{C}^T\mathcal{Y}) \leq 0 \leq UB(\boldsymbol{C}^T\mathcal{Y})$ holds for some of the subproblems, it is considered that these subproblems fail to be proved by $\boldsymbol{V}$. In such cases, the subproblems should be further analyzed through the *Branch* process.

Branch Process. When the *Bound* process fails to verify the property of the problem, the *Branch* process decomposes it into several subproblems. These subproblems are more suitable for verification using the Bound process. State-of-the-art Branch-and-Bound (BAB) techniques emphasize ReLU splitting [12]-a prevalent branching strategy-to decompose and address the verification problem systematically. In ReLU verification, we refer to the ReLU activation with input $x_{i,j}$ as ambiguous neurons. These neurons exhibit lower and upper bounds such that $lb(x_{i,j}) < 0 < ub(x_{i,j})$. During the *Branch* process, ambiguous neurons are branched into two distinct subproblems. One subproblem assumes $x_{i,j} \leq 0$, while the other assumes $x_{i,j} > 0$. These distinct assumptions are referred to as split decisions. These subproblems linearize the non-linear relationship between network inputs and outputs, enhancing the precision of the *Bound* process. The ReLU splitting process can be visualized as a full-rooted binary tree, with each node corresponding to a subproblem resulting from the *Branch* process. By annotating the nodes with split decisions, input specifications, and output specifications, we create a specification tree.

Definition 4 ***(Specification Tree).*** *Given a set of neurons $\mathcal{R} = \{v_1, v_2, \cdots v_k\}$, a full-rooted binary tree T is a specification tree. If $\forall n \in Nodes(T)$, n_l,$n_r \in Children(n)$, edges (n, n_l) and (n, n_r) are labeled with split decisions. Specifically, we label edge (n, n_l) with $r_i^+ := \{x_i \geq 0\}$ and edge (n, n_r) with $r_i^- := \{x_i \leq 0\}$, $i \in [|\mathcal{R}|]$. Additionally, each node n maintains input specification $\mathcal{X}_n = \mathcal{X} \wedge \bigwedge_{r_i^{\{+,-\}} \in (n_a, n_b)} r_i^{\{+,-\}}$, where $\forall n_a, n_b \in Ancestors(n) \cup \{n\}, n_b \in Children(n_a)$. Furthermore, the node n records output specification ψ and verified network N.*

2.3 Incremental Verification

IVAN, an incremental verification technique for neural networks, represents the state-of-the-art in incremental verification within the Branch-and-Bound (BAB) framework. Specifically, IVAN leverages the specification tree created by BAB for the original network to verify the adjusted network, the process referred to as *Reuse*. Additionally, IVAN introduces a heuristic strategy called *Reorder* to reconstruct the specifications from the *Reuse* process. The underlying premise of these techniques rests on the observation that the specification tree generated by BAB for the original network should exhibit similarities to the one associated with the adjusted network.

Reuse. Consider an original network N, its final specification tree resulting from a complete end-to-end BAB process is denoted as T_f^N. The *Reuse* process gathers specifications $\boldsymbol{s}$ from the leaf nodes of T_f^N and reflects the verified network N recorded in $\boldsymbol{s}$ to the adjusted network N', generating the specification $\boldsymbol{s'}$. Rather than constructing a new tree for the adjusted network N', the *Bound* process verifies specifications $\boldsymbol{s'}$. Intuitively, the *Reuse* process uses the T_f^N as the starting tree $T_0^{N'}$ to verify adjusted network N'.

Definition 5 ***(Reuse)***. *Given a neuron network N and its adjusted network N', the specifications tree T_f^N, and a sound verifier $\boldsymbol{V}$ with the specification $\boldsymbol{s} = (\mathcal{X}_n, \psi, N')$. The Reuse process is performed by*

$$\forall n \in Leaves(T_f^N),\ (X_n, \psi, N) \rightarrow (X_n, \psi, N')$$

When the result from the verifier $\boldsymbol{V}$ for specification $\boldsymbol{s}$ is $UNKNOWN$, the specification $\boldsymbol{s}$ remains unsolved. The *Reuse* process reduces the time required to generate a specification tree, thereby enhancing the effectiveness of the Branch-and-Bound (BAB) algorithm for the adjusted network. If all specifications evaluated during the Reuse process yield $UNSAT$ results, IVAN will return $UNSAT$. As soon as any specification produces a SAT result, IVAN returns SAT. However, if there are unsolved problems arising from the specifications, IVAN will invoke BAB algorithm to regularly branch and address the problems. An undesirable scenario occurs when incremental verification degrades to the point where it must verify the network adjustment N' using the complete BaB approach.

Reorder. The *Reorder* process described in IVAN serves as a branching heuristic that evaluates the splitting for neuron v and guides the *Branch* process to create subproblems that can be readily solved by the verifier $\boldsymbol{V}$. This approach can reconstruct the specifications in T_f^N, with the belief that the specifications reconstructed by using the *Reorder* process are effective for verification.

Reorder process generates a set of bad split (n_b, v) as set $\mathcal{B}(T_f^N)$ according to a hyperparameter ϑ where $n_b \in Node(T_f^N)$ and v represents neurons. Then it selects one of the children of each n_b as $n_{k'}$. For every input specification at the leaf nodes of T_f^N, the constraints arising from the split decisions r^+, r^- represented by (n_b, v), and the split decisions within the subtree rooted at $n_{k'}$ are removed. The reconstructed input specifications are denoted as $\mathcal{X'}_n$ replacing the original $\mathcal{X}_n$ in the *Reuse* process. If $\exists n \in Node(T_f^N),\ s.t.\ \mathcal{X'}_n = \mathcal{X}$, we omit the specifications involving such $\mathcal{X'}_n$ during the *Reuse* process.

Intuitively, the *Reorder* process prunes the specification tree T_f^N with heuristics. After discarding the node n along with one of its children $n_{k'}$, and the subtree rooted at $n_{k'}$, the remaining child n_k is repositioned as a child of either n's parent node or the root node.

3 Improved Incremental Verification

The process of BAB (Sect. 2.2) reveals that once the verifier $\boldsymbol{V}$ can falsify the robustness of the network through a specific subproblem, the BAB terminates. Additionally, drawing from the observation claimed in Sect. 2.2 of IVAN's paper, the structural similarities (especially about weights and biases) between the original network N and the adjusted one N' make that: specifications obtained from verifying N yield similar results as those from verifying N'. Inspired by the approach in DEEPINC [32], we define and incorporate the SAT specification while verifying N to falsify the robustness of N' and terminate the BAB early.

Definition 6 ***(SAT specification).*** *Given the specification tree T_f^N for network N, a set of ReLU activations neurons $\mathcal{R} = \{v_1, v_2, ..., v_k\}$, a sound verifier $\boldsymbol{V}$ used in Bound process, and split decisions $r_i^{\{+,-\}}$ for each v_i, if there exists a specification that is $\boldsymbol{s}_{SAT} = (\mathcal{X} \wedge \bigwedge_{i=1, v_i \in \mathcal{R}}^{k} r_i^{\{+,-\}}, \psi, N) \in T_f^N$. It is called as a SAT specification if a verifier $\boldsymbol{V}(\boldsymbol{s}_{SAT}) = SAT$.*

Since the state-of-the-arts reconstruct the specifications from original networks, it is hard to use the SAT specification, as the situation shown by Fig. 1, the SAT specification on n_4 in T_f^N is broken in $T_0^{N'}$ by the reconstruction technique (like reuse&reorder in IVAN). The green node means the subproblem is verified as $UNSAT$, the red one means SAT, and the grey one means $UNKNOWN$ which should be dealt with in the *Branch* process.

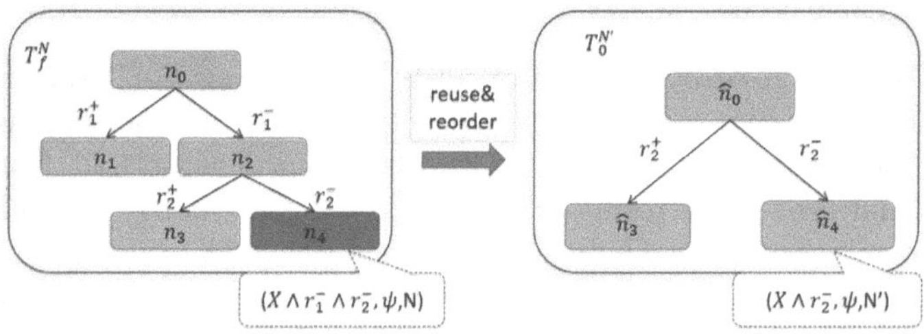

Fig. 1. the SAT specification on n_4 in T_f^N is broken in $T_0^{N'}$ by reuse&reorder in IVAN

Rather than discarding either the SAT specification or the reconstruction, our framework combines them into a queue of specifications. During the *Bound* process for N', the sound verifier $\boldsymbol{V}$ first checks the property ψ with the SAT specification, and subsequently examines the reconstructed specifications, following a similar process as described in IVAN's work. Additionally, we observe that certain information generated by the verifier $\boldsymbol{V}$ during the *Bound* process for N can also be leveraged for N'. This information primarily impacts the efficacy of the BaB. By incorporating this information, we anticipate enhancements in the verification efficacy for N'.

3.1 Overview of I-IVAN

The ideas of our framework I-IVAN involve prioritizing the verification of the SAT specification over the reconstructed specifications. Additionally, we leverage information from the *Bound* process for N to expedite the verification of N'.

1. ***Append.*** Firstly, I-IVAN generates the specification tree T_f^N through once BaB. Simultaneously, it appends certain information $\boldsymbol{a}$ to each specification. The $\boldsymbol{a}$ is computed by verifier $\boldsymbol{V}$ for tight over-approximation. In Fig. 2(1), when I-IVAN generates the specification tree, it appends the reusable information $a(n_1)$, $a(n_3)$, and $a(n_4)$ from *Bound* process for N, to the corresponding specifications on n_1, n_3, and n_4.

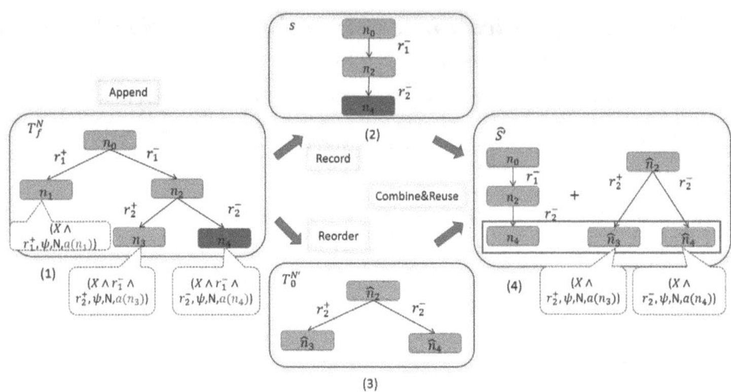

Fig. 2. Workflow of I-IVAN for incremental verification of BAB

2. ***Record and Reorder.*** I-IVAN records the existing SAT specification as $\boldsymbol{s}_{SAT}$ (shown in Fig. 2(2)) and proceeds to reconstruct specifications in T_f^N using a heuristic strategy. We utilize the *Reorder* method from IVAN. Assume that for n_4, the result of $\boldsymbol{V}(\mathcal{X} \wedge r_1^- \wedge r_2^-, \psi, N, \boldsymbol{a}(n_4))$ is SAT, for others, the results are $UNSAT$. The SAT specification $(\mathcal{X} \wedge r_1^- \wedge r_2^-, \psi, N, \boldsymbol{a}(n_1))$ is recorded as $\boldsymbol{s}_{SAT}$. If the bad splitting set is $\mathcal{B}(N_f^N) = \{(n_0, v_1)\}$ and the $n_{k'}$ is n_1, the split decisions r_1^+ and r_1^- implied by (n_0, v_1) and the split decisions on subtrees rooted at n_1 (which is $\emptyset$) are eliminated from the specifications in T_f^N. The SAT specification is not involved in the reconstruction. For instance, the specification $(\mathcal{X} \wedge r_1^- \wedge r_2^-, \psi, N, \boldsymbol{a}(n_4))$ originally associated with node n_4 in Fig. 2(1) is reconstructed as the $(\mathcal{X} \wedge r_2^-, \psi, N', \boldsymbol{a}(n_4))$ for node $\hat{n}_4$ in Fig. 2(3).
3. ***Combine and Reuse.*** Finally, we combine the reconstructed specifications with the existing $\boldsymbol{s}_{SAT}$ to form a queue of specifications denoted as $\hat{\boldsymbol{S}}$. Then *Reuse* process reflects the specifications $\boldsymbol{s} \in \hat{\boldsymbol{S}}$ to $\boldsymbol{s}'$, generating the queue $\hat{\boldsymbol{S}}'$. The verifier $\boldsymbol{V}$ prioritizes checking the formula ψ on the existing $\boldsymbol{s}'_{SAT}$. If $\boldsymbol{s}'_{SAT}$ remains unsolved or results in $UNSAT$, the verifier $\boldsymbol{V}$ checks the reconstructed specifications. Additionally, any subproblem raised from $\boldsymbol{s}'_{SAT}$ receives equal priority as other subproblems. For the unsolved specifications in $\hat{\boldsymbol{S}}'$, we perform branching and proceed with the *Bound* process per the regular BAB procedure. In Fig. 2(4), we combine the SAT specification $\boldsymbol{s}_{SAT}$ with the reconstructed specifications for nodes $\hat{n}_3$ and $\hat{n}_4$, forming the queue $\hat{\boldsymbol{S}}$. The queue $\hat{\boldsymbol{S}}$ is reflected to $\hat{\boldsymbol{S}}'$ through *Reuse* process (indicated by the red box). As the *Bound* process begins to check the specifications in $\hat{\boldsymbol{S}}'$, it first checks $\boldsymbol{s}'_{SAT}$ by regular BAB process, it then proceeds to address subproblems related to nodes $\hat{n}_3$ and $\hat{n}_4$.

3.2 Append

During the *Bound* process in the BAB, certain sound but incomplete verifiers generate information-such as parameters or heuristic decisions-that allows verifiers to compute tighter over-approximated bounds for output. While this type of information varies across different verifiers, the commonality is that these verifiers invest additional effort in determining optimal values based on the input specification $\mathcal{X}$. In our paper, we refer to this information as the ancillary specification. Notably, due to the structural similarities between the specifications generated by N and N', their input specifications also exhibit similarity. Consequently, the ancillary specifications produced by verifier $\boldsymbol{V}$ during the *Bound* process while verifying both N and N' share common characteristics.

Definition 7 ***(Ancillary specification).*** *Given a neuron network N, the input specification $\mathcal{X}$, an output specification ψ, a sound but incomplete verifier $\boldsymbol{V}$, and the strategy for generating the information $\boldsymbol{a}$: $\phi(\mathcal{X}, \psi, N, \emptyset) = \boldsymbol{a}$, the strategy ϕ can be viewed as nested within the verifier $\boldsymbol{V}$. As for information $\boldsymbol{a}$, if*

$$\boldsymbol{V}(\mathcal{X}, \psi, N, \emptyset) = \boldsymbol{a}, \{SAT, UNSAT, UNKNOWN\},$$
$$\boldsymbol{V}(\mathcal{X}, \psi, N, \boldsymbol{a}) \in \boldsymbol{V}(\mathcal{X}, \psi, N, \emptyset).$$

The $\boldsymbol{a}$ represents the ancillary specification. In the first formula, if $\boldsymbol{a} = \emptyset$ in the specification, verifier $\boldsymbol{V}$ will augment its output by including $\boldsymbol{a}$ calculated by ϕ. The second formula asserts that utilizing $\boldsymbol{a}$ as the output of phi does not compromise the soundness of the verifier $\boldsymbol{V}$.

When BaB constructs the specificaiton tree T_f^N, the verifier $\boldsymbol{V}$ generates ancillary specification $\boldsymbol{a}$ for tight over-approximated bounds. $\forall n \in Nodes(T_f^N)$, after $\boldsymbol{V}(\mathcal{X}_n, \psi, N, \emptyset)$ returns result, our framework appends ancillary specification $\boldsymbol{a}(n)$ to the specifications on n as $(\mathcal{X}_n, \psi, N, \boldsymbol{a}(n))$. Subsequently, during the *Bound* process for verification of N', our framework directly employs ancillary specification $\boldsymbol{a}(n)$ to compute bounds, bypassing the need to calculate the strategy ϕ. This optimization reduces the computation time within verifier $\boldsymbol{V}$.

As an illustrative example, in $\alpha\beta$-CROWN [29], the parameters α and β undergo iteration via strategy ϕ to generate tighter over-approximated bounds. More iterations mean better parameters and tighter over-approximation. An appropriately chosen initial parameter can reduce the number of iterations required to achieve tight bounds. We posit that the optimal parameters determined for N are also optimal for N'. Assume that the optimal parameters iterated for N are (α, β) which can be the reusable information $\boldsymbol{a}$. By initializing the iteration value as the ancillary specification, $\boldsymbol{a} = (\alpha, \beta)$, we expedite each *Bound* process that employs $\alpha\beta$-CROWN due to the reduction of the number of iterations. Notably, our framework supports to be realized based on different sound verifiers $\boldsymbol{V}$.

The ancillary specification $\boldsymbol{a}$ can not alter the soundness of verifier $\boldsymbol{V}$ during the *Bound* process, because $\boldsymbol{a}$ only affects the tightness of the over-approximated constraints from sound verifier $\boldsymbol{V}$. In the worst-case scenario, the $\boldsymbol{V}$ in *Bound* process returns $UNKNOWN$ with $\boldsymbol{a}$, and BaB would necessitate additional *Branch* processes to reserve its completeness, especially when the iterations within BaB are unrestricted.

3.3 Record and Combine

The *Record* and *Combine* processes operate on the pre-existing SAT specification within T_f^N. Before checking the reconstructed specifications, our framework verifies property ψ on the SAT specification recorded from T_f^N. Formally, there exists a SAT specification $\boldsymbol{s}_{SAT} \in T_f^N$ and a set of reconstructed specification $\boldsymbol{S}$ from the *Reorder* process. I-IVAN combines the $\boldsymbol{S}$ with $\boldsymbol{s}_{SAT}$, forming a queue denoted as $\hat{\boldsymbol{S}} = \boldsymbol{s}_{SAT} \cup \boldsymbol{S}$. After the *Reuse* process, the verifier $\boldsymbol{V}$ first checks whether the $\boldsymbol{s'}_{SAT}$ falsifies the robustness of adjusted network N'. Subsequently, it considers reconstructed specifications. The subproblems from $\boldsymbol{s'}_{SAT}$ are assigned equal priority alongside others.

Definition 8 ***(Record and Combine).*** *Given a neuron network N, its specification tree T_f^N, the Record process is defined as:*

$$\boldsymbol{s} := (X_{n_s}, \psi, N, \boldsymbol{a}(n_s)),\ n_s \in T_f^N, s.t.\boldsymbol{V}(\boldsymbol{s}) \ = SAT.$$

Given the set of reconstructed specifications $\boldsymbol{S} := \{(\boldsymbol{X'}_i, \psi, N', a_i)\}_{i\in[|\boldsymbol{S}|]}$, the Combine process can be expressed as:

$$\hat{\boldsymbol{S}} = \{\boldsymbol{s}\} \cup \boldsymbol{S} = \{(X'_i, \psi, N, a_i)\}_{i\in[|\hat{\boldsymbol{S}}|]}, \boldsymbol{s} = (X'_0, \psi, N, a_0)$$

In our framework, after the *Reuse* process, the verifier $\boldsymbol{V}$ checks the specifications in $\hat{\boldsymbol{S}}'$ in order by the index i so that the $\boldsymbol{s}_{SAT}$ will be first verified while verifying N'.

3.4 Algorithm for I-IVAN

The details of our framework are presented in Algorithm 1. It accepts input parameters, including the original network N and its adjusted counterpart N', input specifications $\mathcal{X}$ from N and $\mathcal{X}'$ from N', output specification ψ, hyper-parameter ϑ used in the *Record* process, the sound but incomplete verifier $\boldsymbol{V}$ in the *Bound* process, and the branching heuristic H used during branching. The algorithm outputs SAT when $\psi = false$, otherwise, it yields $UNSAT$.

Initially, the algorithm invokes the BaB procedure for the original network N, yielding the specification tree T_f^N, the pre-existing SAT specification $\boldsymbol{s}_{SAT}$, and ancillary specifications $\boldsymbol{a}$ for each leaf nodes in T_f^N (line 3). Subsequently, the verifier $\boldsymbol{V}$ computes the bounds using specifications $(\mathcal{X}_n, \psi, N, \emptyset)$ for $n \in Leaves(T_f^N)$. The resulting ancillary specification $\boldsymbol{a}(n)$ is collected by the algorithm and appended to the leaf node's specification as $(\mathcal{X}_n, \psi, N, \boldsymbol{a}(n))$ (line 4). Next, the specifications in T_f^N undergo reconstruction via the *Reorder* process in IVAN (line 5). The reconstructed specifications are combined with the SAT specification, forming a queue denoted as $\hat{\boldsymbol{S}}$ (line 6). Then, $\hat{\boldsymbol{S}}$ consisted of specifications are reflected by *Reuse* process to the queue $\hat{\boldsymbol{S}}'$(line 7). After that, the verifier $\boldsymbol{V}$ calculates the bounds using the specifications in $\hat{\boldsymbol{S}}'$ and the SAT specification is invoked at first. The specifications resulting in $UNSAT$

Algorithm 1. I-IVAN for incremental verification

1: **Input:** the networks N and N', input specifications $\mathcal{X}$ and $\mathcal{X}'$, output specification ψ, parameter ϑ used in *Record*, verifier $\boldsymbol{V}$ in Bound process, and branching heuristic H.
2: **Output:** if $\psi = ture$, returns $UNSAT$, otherwise, returns SAT.
3: Branch-and-Bound for N: $T_f^N, \boldsymbol{s}_{SAT}, a \leftarrow \text{BAB}(\mathcal{X}, \psi, N)$
4: Append the ancillary specification a to the specification tree T_f^N: $T_f^N \leftarrow Append(T_f^N, a)$
5: Prune the T_f^N by heuristic strategy *Reorder*: $\boldsymbol{S} \leftarrow Reorder(T_f^N, \vartheta)$
6: Combine the SAT specification and the reconstructed ones as a queue $\hat{\boldsymbol{S}}$: $\hat{\boldsymbol{S}} \leftarrow Combine(\boldsymbol{s}_{SAT}, \boldsymbol{S})$
7: Reuse the specifications in the queue $\hat{\boldsymbol{S}}$: $\hat{\boldsymbol{S}}' \leftarrow Reuse(\hat{\boldsymbol{S}})$
8: **for** $\boldsymbol{s}$ in $\hat{\boldsymbol{S}}'$ **do**
9:    **if** $\boldsymbol{V}(\boldsymbol{s})$ = UNSAT **then**
10:       Remove the solved subproblem from the queue: $\hat{\boldsymbol{S}}'$.remove($\boldsymbol{s}$)
11:    **end if**
12:    **if** $\boldsymbol{V}(\boldsymbol{s})$ = UNKNOWN **then**
13:       Remove the unsolved problem from the queue: $\hat{\boldsymbol{S}}'$.remove($\boldsymbol{s}$)
14:       Use heuristic H to select the split neuron: $r_{chosen} \leftarrow argmax_{r \in N} H(N, \boldsymbol{s})$
15:       Two specifications generated from *Branch*: $n_l,\ n_r \leftarrow Split(\boldsymbol{s},\ r_{chosen})$
16:       Insert the specifications at the end of the queue: $\hat{\boldsymbol{S}}'$.insert($n_l,\ n_r$)
17:    **end if**
18:    **if** $\boldsymbol{V}(\boldsymbol{s})$ = SAT **then**
19:       Terminates BAB immediately if there exists a subproblem resulting as SAT: Return SAT
20:    **end if**
21: **end for**
22: Return $UNSAT$

are removed (line 10). However, specifications resulting in $UNKNOW$ are split into new subproblems by the *Branch* process, these subproblems are inserted into the queue $\hat{\boldsymbol{S}}'$ (line 13 to 16). If the specification yields a result of SAT, the algorithm returns SAT (line 19). Conversely, if all specifications result in $UNSAT$, the algorithm returns $UNSAT$ (line 22).

4 Experiments

We implement our framework as an incremental verification of neural network, I-IVAN (Improved Incremental Verification of Neural Networks). Notably, both IVAN and I-IVAN are built upon the framework of OVAL [7]. IVAN realized on OVAL's framework is called IVAN-O. The verifier realized on framework I-IVAN based on $\boldsymbol{V}$ is called I-IVAN [$\boldsymbol{V}$].

In this section, we evaluate the efficacy of I-IVAN [$\boldsymbol{V}$] on common benchmarks. Specifically, we compare the speedup of I-IVAN [$\boldsymbol{V}$] against IVAN-O by verifying the robustness properties on the quantized networks in Sect. 4.2. Additionally, we analyze the contributions of individual components within I-IVAN using single-neuron relaxation verification, $\alpha\beta$-CROWN [29], as the verifier $\boldsymbol{V}$ in Sect. 4.3. Finally, we demonstrate the generalization capabilities of I-IVAN using multi-neuron relaxation verification, FaGMR [25], as $\boldsymbol{V}$ in Sect. 4.4.

4.1 Experiment Configurations

Networks and Properties. The evaluation is conducted on MNIST and CIFAR-10 datasets with standard perturbation ε. Table 1 shows the details about all the networks used in our experiments. They are benchmarks from IVAN toolbox [2] or VNN-COMP2021 [3]. In the following experiments, the input perturbation is standard for each network.

Speedup and Perturbation. We consider the speedup S_p computed by the sum time t_b from the BaB algorithm for all involved cases on adjusted network N' and the sum time of the incremental verification for adjusted networks t_i where $S_p = \frac{t_b}{t_i}$. We verify the l_∞-norm perturbation on correctly classified inputs from the datasets. All verifiers answer problems are defined by Definition 3.

Machine and Software. All experiments are conducted on a 12-core 2.20GHz Intel Xeon Silver 4212 platform with 64GB memory. I-IVAN is implemented in Python 3.8 and uses Gurobi 9.5.1 [1] for LP solving.

Table 1. Neural Networks used in the experiments. "Training" is the used robust training technique: Standrad [15], PGD [19], or Certified Robust [4].

Dataset	Model	Training	Neurons	Layers	ε
MNIST	FCN-MNIST	Standard	512	2	0.2
	CONV-MNIST-MED	PGD	3604	3	0.1
CIFAR-10	CONV-CIFAR-BASE	Certified Robust	3172	2	$\frac{2}{255}$
	CONV-CIFAR-WIDE	Certified Robust	6244	4	$\frac{4}{255}$
	CONV-CIFAR-DEEP	Certified Robust	6756	6	$\frac{4}{255}$

4.2 Comparison on Quantized Networks

We compare the speedup of I-IVAN [LP] against IVAN-O on quantized networks. Both of them use the single-neuron relaxation method based on the Linear Program(LP) [22] as the $\boldsymbol{V}$. The original networks N are all INT32 with their weights and biases. Subsequently, the weights and biases are quantized to INT16 or INT8 as the adjusted networks N'. We verify and compare with the first 100 cases in both MNIST and CIFAR-10 datasets. The time-out of the once *Bound* process in BaB is 200s for FCN-MNIST and CONV-CIFAR-BASE, otherwise, the time-out is 400s the same as IVAN. All subjects have the same number of verified cases.

Table 2. Comparisons on quantized networks between I-IVAN [LP] and IVAN-O.

Network	Approximation	IVAN-O		I-IVAN [LP]	
		S_p	*#call*	S_p	*#call*
FCN-MNIST	INT16	2.34	6	2.56	5
	INT8	1.97	23	2.91	16
CONV-MNIST-MED	INT16	1.17	62	9.02	36
	INT8	0.98	65	1.28	42
CONV-CIFAR-BASE	INT16	1.34	76	1.81	58
	INT8	0.85	85	1.37	57
CONV-CIFAR-WIDE	INT16	1.27	17	1.50	15
	INT8	1.03	27	1.08	25
CONV-CIFAR-DEEP	INT16	1.51	14	1.70	11
	INT8	1.13	22	2.03	18

In Table 2, it presents the speedup S_p of IVAN-O and I-IVAN [LP] for each benchmark. The "Approximation" Column indicates the quantized value for cases. "IVAN-O" displays results obtained by applying the *Reuse* and *Reorder* processes within OVAL framework . "I-IVAN [LP]" records results from I-IVAN. "*#call*" shows the total calls of verifier $\boldsymbol{V}$ in the *Bound* process. Table 2 shows that I-IVAN is $7.71 (\approx 9.02 \div 1.17)$ times faster than IVAN-O at most on different quantizations. Notably, the *Combine* process of I-IVAN [LP] reduces the calls for verifier $\boldsymbol{V}$ by considering *SAT* specifications, leading to improve efficacy. For example, consider the case of INT16 CONV-MNIST-MED, I-IVAN [LP] calls verifier for 36 times, yielding a speedup of 9.02 while IVAN-O calls verifier for 62 times with a speedup of 1.17. In addition, the improvement is generally more pronounced for INT16 quantization compared to INT8 due to the greater similarity in constructions between the original network N and the adjusted counterpart N'.

4.3 Contribution of *Append* and *Combine*

To analyze the impact of the *Append* and *Combine* processes on incremental verification, we use single-neural relaxation verifier $\alpha\beta$-CROWN [29] as the verifier $\boldsymbol{V}$ in the *Bound* process. Table 3 presents the comparison of the contribution of each technique involved in I-IVAN for each model with quantized networks. Column "I-IVAN (Append)" shows results only using the *Append* technique, while column "I-IVAN (Combine)" is the I-IVAN only using the *Combine* technique. Column "I-IVAN [$\alpha\beta$-CROWN]" is using both of the techniques. The timeout is 300s which is commonly configured in IVAN. All subjects have the same number of cases verified successfully.

In Table 3, although the number of verifier calls are the same between IVAN-O and I-IVAN (Append), the speedup of the latter achieves a higher speedup.

Table 3. Comparisons on quantized networks among IVAN-O, I-IVAN (Append), I-IVAN (Combine), and I-IVAN [$\alpha\beta$-CROWN].

Network	Approximation	IVAN-O		I-IVAN [$\alpha\beta$-CROWN]		I-IVAN (Combine)		I-IVAN (Append)	
		S_p	*#call*	S_p	*#call*	S_p	*#call*	S_p	*#call*
FCN-MNIST	INT16	1.03	11	1.09	6	1.07	6	1.05	11
	INT8	1.01	12	1.06	7	1.04	7	1.02	12
CONV-MNIST-MED	INT16	1.27	107	1.43	85	1.36	85	1.30	107
	INT8	1.12	99	1.20	79	1.17	79	1.15	99
CONV-CIFAR-BASE	INT16	2.52	118	6.60	61	5.57	61	3.31	118
	INT8	1.45	139	2.19	121	2.08	121	1.78	139
CONV-CIFAR-WIDE	INT16	2.82	28	4.52	11	3.89	11	3.48	28
	INT8	1.51	21	1.88	15	1.70	15	1.59	21
CONV-CIFAR-DEEP	INT16	2.71	33	4.52	11	3.85	11	2.94	33
	INT8	1.05	12	1.13	7	1.10	7	1.08	12

The reason lies in the ancillary specifications, which save the time of finding tighter over-approximated bounds in the *Bound* process. Notably, I-IVAN (Combine) is 1.68($\approx$ 5.57 $\div$ 3.31) times faster than I-IVAN (Append) at most. This indicates that *Combine* is more effective than *Append* using $\alpha\beta$-CROWN as verifier $\boldsymbol{V}$. According to Ferrar et al. [10], the *Bound* process calls increase exponentially. Therefore, reducing the number of the *Bound* process calls improves efficacy compared to the acceleration of the *Bound* process. Crucially, *Combine* enhances efficacy more effectively than *Append*, ultimately leading to the termination of the BaB by falsifying the robustness of the networks.

4.4 The Generalization of I-IVAN

To demonstrate the generalization of I-IVAN applying various verifiers in the *Bound* process, we use the multi-neural relaxation verifier FaGMR [25] as the $\boldsymbol{V}$ for evaluation. FaGMR uses a strategy ϕ to select neuron groups $\mathcal{G}$ while verifying the original network N. I-IVAN [FaGMR] reuses the $\mathcal{G}$ instead of invoking the strategy ϕ during the verification of adjusted counterpart N'. In our experiments, the timeout for cases on FCN-MNSIT and CONV-MNIST-MED is 500 s, otherwise, the timeout is 1000 s, remaining consistent with the configuration used in MN-BAB [10], which combines the BaB with multi-neuron relaxation. The experiments are conducted on quantized scenarios, consistent with those described in Sect. 4.2. "#verify" records the number of cases verified successfully.

The experiments from Tabel 4 reveal that the *Bound* process calls in I-IVAN are always fewer than those in IVAN-O, mainly due to the effectiveness of the *Combine* process. Additionally, the *Append* process expedites the *Bound* process. Consequently, I-IVAN [FaGMR] is faster than IVAN-O while using FaGMR as $\boldsymbol{V}$, achieving 1.88($\approx$ 3.44$\div$1.83) times faster than IVAN-O at most. Importantly, I-IVAN [FaGMR] effectively mitigates time-out issues compared to IVAN-O, as evidenced by the counts of "#verify". For complete verifier BaB, the only reason for failure is the time-out issue. In the case of CONV-CIFAR-BASE INT16, I-IVAN [FaGMR] successfully verifies 41 cases, whereas IVAN

Table 4. Comparison between IVAN-O and I-IVAN [FAGMR] on quantized networks.

Network	Approximation	IVAN-O			I-IVAN [FAGMR]		
		S_p	*#verify*	*#call*	S_p	*#verify*	*#call*
FCN-MNIST	INT16	1.01	2	11	1.05	2	6
	INT8	1.00	2	11	1.02	2	6
CONV-MNIST-MED	INT16	1.03	9	77	1.08	10	64
	INT8	1.07	9	74	1.13	10	61
CONV-CIFAR-BASE	INT16	1.28	39	94	1.77	41	47
	INT8	1.83	39	109	3.44	41	91
CONV-CIFAR-WIDE	INT16	4.38	56	22	6.20	58	10
	INT8	5.12	59	15	7.30	59	9
CONV-CIFAR-DEEP	INT16	1.54	43	24	1.78	43	12
	INT8	79.43	44	10	103.83	44	6

achieves 39. This difference highlights how the framework I-IVAN improves efficacy, avoiding time-out issues. In conclusion, the experiments demonstrate that I-IVAN can be effectively applied with both single-neural and multi-neural relaxation as the verifier $\boldsymbol{V}$.

5 Related Work

Incremental program verification [6,8,23] has improved its scalability to an industrial one [21,24]. They reuse partial results [31], constrains [27], and precision information [5] for the efficacy of individual commits. Currently, an incremental verification based on SAT/SMT solver for DNN, named DEEPINC [32], prioritizes checking the property of outputs based on the information, such as basic variables from simplicity for verifying the original N, to efficient the simplicity for the adjusted counterpart N'.

6 Conclusion

This paper introduces an enhanced framework for incremental verification of deep neural networks (DNNs). Our framework focuses on two central principles: prioritizing the examination of subproblems that reveal vulnerabilities in the original networks and reusing information generated by the verifier during the *Bound* process for incremental verification. Experimental results demonstrate that our incremental verifier, I-IVAN, achieves a remarkable speedup-up to 7.71 times faster than IVAN while maintaining superior verification precision.

References

1. Gurobi optimizer reference manual (2008). http://www.gurobi.com
2. Ivan (2023). https://github.com/uiuc-focal-lab/IVAN
3. Bak, S., Liu, C., Johnson, T.T.: The second international verification of neural networks competition (VNN-COMP 2021): summary and results. CoRR **abs/2109.00498** (2021). https://arxiv.org/abs/2109.00498
4. Balunovic, M., Vechev, M.: Adversarial training and provable defenses: Bridging the gap. In: International Conference on Learning Representations (2019)
5. Beyer, D., Löwe, S., Novikov, E., Stahlbauer, A., Wendler, P.: Precision reuse for efficient regression verification. In: Proceedings of the 2013 9th Joint Meeting on Foundations of Software Engineering, pp. 389–399 (2013)
6. Borgonovo, E., Buzzard, G.T., Wendell, R.E.: A global tolerance approach to sensitivity analysis in linear programming. Eur. J. Oper. Res. **267**(1), 321–337 (2018)
7. Bunel, R., Mudigonda, P., Turkaslan, I., Torr, P., Lu, J., Kohli, P.: Branch and bound for piecewise linear neural network verification. J. Mach. Learn. Res. **21**(2020), 1–39 (2020)
8. Eén, N., Sörensson, N.: Temporal induction by incremental sat solving. Electron. Notes Theor. Comput. Sci. **89**(4), 543–560 (2003)
9. Ehlers, R.: Formal verification of piece-wise linear feed-forward neural networks. In: D'Souza, D., Narayan Kumar, K. (eds.) ATVA 2017. LNCS, vol. 10482, pp. 269–286. Springer, Cham (2017). https://doi.org/10.1007/978-3-319-68167-2_19
10. Ferrari, C., Muller, M.N., Jovanovic, N., Vechev, M.: Complete verification via multi-neuron relaxation guided branch-and-bound. arXiv preprint arXiv:2205.00263 (2022)
11. Gholami, A., Kim, S., Dong, Z., Yao, Z., Mahoney, M.W., Keutzer, K.: A survey of quantization methods for efficient neural network inference. arXiv preprint arXiv:2103.13630 (2021)
12. Henriksen, P., Lomuscio, A.: Deepsplit: an efficient splitting method for neural network verification via indirect effect analysis. In: IJCAI, pp. 2549–2555 (2021)
13. Huang, X., et al.: A survey of safety and trustworthiness of deep neural networks: verification, testing, adversarial attack and defence, and interpretability. Comput. Sci. Rev. **37**, 100270 (2020). https://doi.org/10.1016/j.cosrev.2020.100270
14. Huang, X., Kwiatkowska, M., Wang, S., Wu, M.: Safety verification of deep neural networks. In: Majumdar, R., Kunčak, V. (eds.) CAV 2017. LNCS, vol. 10426, pp. 3–29. Springer, Cham (2017). https://doi.org/10.1007/978-3-319-63387-9_1
15. Julian, K.D., Kochenderfer, M.J., Owen, M.P.: Deep neural network compression for aircraft collision avoidance systems. J. Guid. Control. Dyn. **42**(3), 598–608 (2019)
16. Katz, G., Barrett, C., Dill, D.L., Julian, K., Kochenderfer, M.J.: Reluplex: an efficient SMT solver for verifying deep neural networks. In: Majumdar, R., Kunčak, V. (eds.) CAV 2017. LNCS, vol. 10426, pp. 97–117. Springer, Cham (2017). https://doi.org/10.1007/978-3-319-63387-9_5
17. Kaufmann, E., Loquercio, A., Ranftl, R., Müller, M., Koltun, V., Scaramuzza, D.: Deep drone acrobatics. arXiv preprint arXiv:2006.05768 (2020)
18. Laurel, J., Yang, R., Sehgal, A., Ugare, S., Misailovic, S.: Statheros: compiler for efficient low-precision probabilistic programming. In: 2021 58th ACM/IEEE Design Automation Conference (DAC), pp. 787–792. IEEE (2021)
19. Madry, A., Makelov, A., Schmidt, L., Tsipras, D., Vladu, A.: Towards deep learning models resistant to adversarial attacks. arXiv preprint arXiv:1706.06083 (2017)

20. Morgulis, N., Kreines, A., Mendelowitz, S., Weisglass, Y.: Fooling a real car with adversarial traffic signs. CoRR **abs/1907.00374** (2019). http://arxiv.org/abs/1907.00374
21. O'Hearn, P.W.: Continuous reasoning: scaling the impact of formal methods. In: Proceedings of the 33rd annual ACM/IEEE Symposium on Logic in Computer Science, pp. 13–25 (2018)
22. Singh, G., Gehr, T., Mirman, M., Püschel, M., Vechev, M.: Fast and effective robustness certification. In: Bengio, S., Wallach, H., Larochelle, H., Grauman, K., Cesa-Bianchi, N., Garnett, R. (eds.) Advances in Neural Information Processing Systems. vol. 31. Curran Associates, Inc. (2018). https://proceedings.neurips.cc/paper/2018/file/f2f446980d8e971ef3da97af089481c3-Paper.pdf
23. Sotoudeh, M., Thakur, A.V.: Computing linear restrictions of neural networks. In: Advances in Neural Information Processing Systems, vol. **32** (2019)
24. Stein, B., Chang, B.Y.E., Sridharan, M.: Demanded abstract interpretation. In: Proceedings of the 42nd ACM SIGPLAN International Conference on Programming Language Design and Implementation, pp. 282–295 (2021)
25. Tang, X., Zheng, Y., Liu, J.: Boosting multi-neuron convex relaxation for neural network verification. In: Hermenegildo, M.V., Morales, J.F. (eds.) Static Analysis, SAS 2023, LNCS, vol. 14284, pp. 540–563. Springer, Cham (2023). https://doi.org/10.1007/978-3-031-44245-2_23
26. Ugare, S., Banerjee, D., Misailovic, S., Singh, G.: Incremental verification of neural networks. Proc. ACM Program.Lang. **7**(PLDI), 1920–1945 (2023)
27. Visser, W., Geldenhuys, J., Dwyer, M.B.: Green: reducing, reusing and recycling constraints in program analysis. In: Proceedings of the ACM SIGSOFT 20th International Symposium on the Foundations of Software Engineering, pp. 1–11 (2012)
28. Wang, S., Pei, K., Whitehouse, J., Yang, J., Jana, S.: Formal security analysis of neural networks using symbolic intervals. In: Enck, W., Felt, A.P. (eds.) 27th USENIX Security Symposium, USENIX Security 2018, Baltimore, MD, USA, 15–17 August 2018, pp. 1599–1614. USENIX Association (2018). https://www.usenix.org/conference/usenixsecurity18/presentation/wang-shiqi
29. Wang, S., Zhang, H., Xu, K., Lin, X., Jana, S., Hsieh, C.J., Kolter, J.Z.: Beta-crown: efficient bound propagation with per-neuron split constraints for neural network robustness verification. Adv. Neural. Inf. Process. Syst. **34**, 29909–29921 (2021)
30. Weiss, K., Khoshgoftaar, T.M., Wang, D.: A survey of transfer learning. J. Big data **3**(1), 1–40 (2016)
31. Yang, G., Dwyer, M.B., Rothermel, G.: Regression model checking. In: 2009 IEEE International Conference on Software Maintenance, pp. 115–124. IEEE (2009)
32. Yang, P., Chi, Z., Liu, Z., Zhao, M., Huang, C.C., Cai, S., Zhang, L.: Incremental satisfiability modulo theory for verification of deep neural networks. arXiv preprint arXiv:2302.06455 (2023)
33. Zhang, J.M., Harman, M., Ma, L., Liu, Y.: Machine learning testing: survey, landscapes and horizons. IEEE Trans. Software Eng. **48**(2), 1–36 (2022)

Automatic Construction of HD Maps for Simulation-Based Testing of Autonomous Driving Systems

Siqi Wang[1,2], Changwen Li[1,2], Tiantian Sun[1,2], Fuqi Jia[1,2], Rongjie Yan[1,2(✉)], and Jun Yan[1,2,3]

[1] Key Laboratory of System Software (CAS) and State Key Laboratory of Computer Science, ISCAS, Beijing, China
[2] University of Chinese Academy of Sciences, Beijing, China
[3] Technology Center of Software Engineering, ISCAS, Beijing, China
yrj@ios.ac.cn

Abstract. In the development and testing of autonomous driving systems, high-definition (HD) maps play an indispensable role by providing vehicles with precise information about their surroundings, encompassing road markings, topographical features, and intricate junction layouts. Despite their importance, creating HD maps through real-world data acquisition or manual design can be laborious, time-consuming, and hard to ensure correctness and diversity. This paper introduces a model-based framework for the automated construction of HD maps. The framework considers junctions as essential components within the road network topology. It formulates the inherent constraints of junction configurations and their interconnections through a Maximum Satisfiability (MaxSAT) model. Based on the optimized configuration for the junctions, the framework defines and integrates the external and internal road connections linked to these junctions, alongside assigning corresponding traffic signal systems. In the experimental evaluation, the comparison with real-world maps and embedded maps in open-source simulation platforms demonstrates that the generated map maintains a compelling balance between diversity and structural simplicity, thus effectively replicating the complexity of real-life road networks. Moreover, the usability of the generated maps has been validated via simulation-based testing of an open-source autopilot system, uncovering several map-related issues.

Keywords: HD map · Automatic generation · Autonomous driving · Simulation-based Testing

1 Introduction

Autonomous driving systems are sophisticated systems built from heterogeneous components, thus being difficult to design and validate. Global validation through testing appears to be a viable approach to obtain evidence of the

W.-N. Chin and Z. Xu (Eds.): TASE 2024, LNCS 14777, pp. 410–427, 2024.
https://doi.org/10.1007/978-3-031-64626-3_24

trustworthiness of ADS. Road testing is desirable but costly. A recent study [14] shows that the minimal requirement to demonstrate safety for an autonomous vehicle is hundreds of millions of miles, taking possibly tens of years for a vehicle to complete. Simulation-based testing is one of the feasible solutions to reduce the cost. However, a challenging problem is how to connect simulated miles to real miles [12]. A simple simulation, even with an extremely high number of simulated miles or hours, is not sufficient. That is, the simulation should cover diverse situations in the real world, including maps and traffic conditions.

High-definition (HD) maps with various road networks [11] are essential ingredients in simulation-based testing. Existing HD maps are either owned by commercial companies that are not publicly available or open source but with limited diversity. Various efforts exist to generate HD maps. One solution is to generate HD maps from real-world data, e.g., using SLAM to extract HD maps from 3D point clouds. Another solution is manual generation, e.g., using map editors to construct an HD map. However, generating HD maps from reality may still suffer from diversity problems, for the road networks in a city area can be uniform. Manually generating HD maps can satisfy diversity requirements but suffer from high costs.

In this paper, we provide a method to automatically generate HD maps, to relieve the efforts in creating HD maps while increasing the diversity of the road networks. The framework of the method is shown in Fig. 1. Given a set of specified junctions, first, the configuration of these junctions is optimized to reduce the number of dead-end roads. Once the configuration is optimized, the junctions are fed into the instantiator. Next, based on the configuration, the instantiator establishes connections between junctions with the external roads and then concretizes the internal roads within the junctions. Finally, the map model with road data is converted into the desired format.

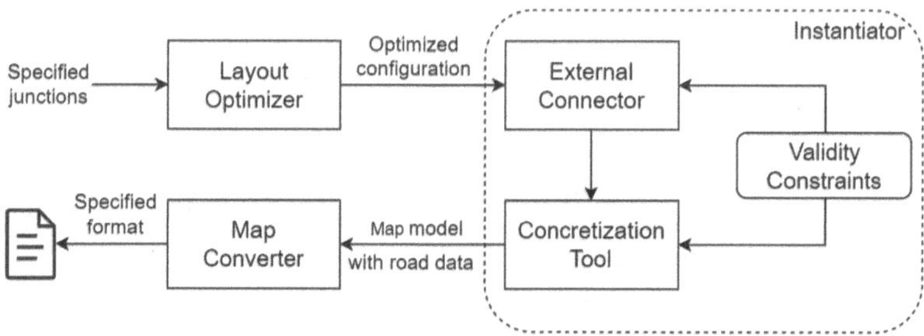

Fig. 1. Framework of automatic map generation

The contribution of the paper is multi-fold. First, we provide a framework for the automatic generation of HD maps. It takes specified or automatically generated junction topology as input, and provides HD map files in the OpenDRIVE format, with optimized configuration of junctions and diversified roads and traffic signals. Second, we formalize the constraints on junction configuration and the connections as a MaxSAT problem and obtain the optimized configuration. Finally, the comparison with existing open-source maps demonstrates the diversity of the generated Map. Moreover, we also have detected map-related defects with the generated map in the simulation-based testing of an autonomous driving system.

The rest of the paper is organized as follows. Section 2 discusses the related work. Section 3 recaps a format of HD map and presents the concept of our map model. Section 4 proposes the automatic HD-map generation method. Section 5 provides the experimental results. Finally, Sect. 6 concludes.

2 Related Work

Testing is a popular approach to ensure the safety of autonomous driving. Considering the high cost of road testing, testing is usually carried out in simulation, in particular, to validate behavior in critical situations that are both dangerous and difficult to reproduce in real life. HD maps, which can provide accurate environmental data, are essential elements in simulation-based testing. For example, Castellano et al. [7] consider various road representations in testing lane-keeping systems. They claim that curvatures and orientation can affect the behaviors of these systems. The tool ASFault can generate virtual roads in testing lane-keeping systems [13]. Experiments on BeamNG.AI [5] show that it is possible to create roads that cause vehicles to deviate from the correct lane.

Large commercial companies like HERE, NVIDIA, and TomTom have already built HD maps for different scenarios and purposes of autonomous driving. However, commercial HD maps are not open source and are only available for internal research or automotive enterprises. As commercial HD maps are not open-source, there are two ways to create HD maps for simulation. The first method is to construct maps from actual road data [21]. This method requires collecting sufficient road network information, which is labor-intensive. To facilitate the virtual testing of motion planners for automated vehicles, the work in [15] first extracts diversified road networks from OpenStreetMap. Then it uses the traffic simulator SUMO to generate traffic scenarios for these road networks. The second method involves manually creating maps through road scene editors with graphical user interfaces [18]. RoadRunner Scene Builder [18] allows for the visualization and editing of road models, adding trees, streets, road signs, and other elements to create three-dimensional scene systems, which can then be exported to various simulation environments. Such tools can create specific road networks. However, they face difficulties in automatically generating a large number of roads usable in simulation environments. JunctionArt is another tool for HD map generation [19]. It takes a series of control lines as input, generates compliant roads based on the control lines, and selects control points to connect roads, forming intersections. It also needs to specify multiple indicators, such as maximum turning curvature (maxCurvature), corner deviation (cornerDeviation), and the number of internal connecting lanes. By configuring different control lines, JunctionArt can create different intersections.

Some works provide command lines to facilitate map generation. For example, Becker et al. [6] have defined a logical road description based on the format of OpenDRIVE HD map and implemented a command-line-based tool to assist in map generation. However, the tool still requires providing XML Schema files and specifying the properties of road elements.

CROUTE is a tool that can generate an HD map based on the extracted topological features [23]. The tool takes a simulator's HD map as input and models the map as a labeled Petri net to record the topological features of intersections and route features for intersection classification are defined. Finally, it provides a reduced HD map by randomly combining the junctions of each feature.

Compared with the existing works, our method also focuses on generating maps with diversified road networks. The distinction is that our method does not rely on extracting features from real-world data or existing maps. Instead, it can automatically enumerate all the types of junction topology and build the road network without manual intervention.

3 Preliminaries

The paper focuses on how to generate an HD map supported by the OpenDRIVE framework. The key is to generate the data of the map, including the relationships and attributes between elements. In this section, we first recap the OpenDRIVE framework and provide its file structure in BNF. Then, we introduce the map model of an HD map and the associated elements.

3.1 OpenDRIVE Framework

The ASAM OpenDRIVE framework format offers a comprehensive basis for representing road networks through XML syntax with the .xodr file extension [3]. An ASAM OpenDRIVE file contains information about the geometric attributes of roads and functional elements such as lanes and signals [3]. It enables the representation of both synthetic and authentic road networks, primarily aiming to provide detailed descriptions that can be seamlessly integrated into simulations across diverse systems.

We define the syntax of OpenDRIVE in BNF as follows. To emphasize the structure of the format, we omit the XML format and only keep the main content. Items prefixed with '@' are the attributes of an element, containing type information, textual descriptions and possible values. An OpenDRIVE file organizes multiple children elements, which can be roads or junctions. In the OpenDRIVE format, every road and junction has a unique index denoted as id within the whole file. In addition to the index, a road also contains attributes such as $junctionId$, $length$, and sub-elements such as road link, road geometry, lanes, and signals. The link includes predecessor and successor elements, which can be empty, denoted as ϵ. Terminal NAT is used as an abbreviation for natural numbers, while FLOAT represents floating-point numbers.

⟨OpenDRIVE⟩ ::= ⟨member⟩
⟨member⟩ ::= ⟨element⟩ ⟨member⟩ | ⟨element⟩
⟨element⟩ ::= ⟨road⟩ | ⟨junction⟩
⟨road⟩ ::= ⟨@id⟩⟨@junctionId⟩ ⟨@length⟩⟨link⟩⟨geometry⟩⟨lanes⟩⟨signals⟩
⟨junction⟩ ::= ⟨@id⟩⟨connections⟩
⟨link⟩ ::= ⟨predecessor⟩⟨successor⟩
⟨predecessor⟩ ::= ⟨@elementType⟩⟨@id⟩⟨@contactPoint⟩ | ϵ
⟨successor⟩ ::= ⟨@elementType⟩⟨@id⟩⟨@contactPoint⟩ | ϵ
⟨geometry⟩ ::= ⟨@s⟩⟨@x⟩⟨@y⟩⟨@hdg⟩⟨@id⟩⟨@contactPoint⟩⟨curve⟩
⟨curve⟩ ::= ⟨line⟩ | ⟨arc⟩ | ⟨parametric cubic⟩
⟨lanes⟩ ::= ⟨left⟩⟨center⟩⟨right⟩ | ⟨left⟩⟨center⟩ | ⟨center⟩⟨right⟩
⟨left⟩ ::= ⟨lane⟩⟨left⟩|⟨lane⟩
⟨center⟩ ::= ⟨lane⟩
⟨right⟩ ::= ⟨lane⟩⟨right⟩|⟨lane⟩
⟨lane⟩ ::= ⟨@id⟩⟨width⟩
⟨signals⟩ ::= ⟨signal⟩⟨signals⟩ | ⟨signal⟩
⟨signal⟩ ::= ⟨@id⟩⟨@s⟩⟨@t⟩⟨@signalType⟩ | ϵ
⟨connections⟩ ::= ⟨connection⟩ | ⟨connection⟩⟨connections⟩
⟨connection⟩ ::= ⟨@id⟩⟨@id-incommingRoad⟩⟨@id-connectingRoad⟩ ⟨@contactPoint⟩⟨connection⟩
⟨@id⟩ ::= `NAT` *index of element*
⟨@s⟩ ::= `FLOAT` *s value in reference line system*
⟨@t⟩ ::= `FLOAT` *t value in reference line system*
⟨@x⟩ ::= `FLOAT` *x value in coordinate system*
⟨@y⟩ ::= `FLOAT` *y value in coordinate system*
⟨@hdg⟩ ::= `FLOAT` *hdg heading of reference line with x-axis*
⟨@junctionId⟩ ::= `NAT` | −1 *index of junction*[1]
⟨@length⟩ ::= `FLOAT` *length of road*
⟨@elementType⟩ ::= `"road"` | `"junction"`
⟨@contactPoint⟩ ::= `"start"` | `"end"`
⟨line⟩ ::= *represents a line*
⟨arc⟩ ::= *represents a arc curve*
⟨parametric cubic⟩ ::= *represents a parametric cubic curve*
⟨width⟩ ::= *represents a curve of road width change*
⟨@signalType⟩ ::= *represents the type of a signal*

[1] When a road does not belong to any junction, its index is −1.

3.2 Map Model

To simplify the generation of map data, especially considering the complexity of the OpenDRIVE framework, we have developed an abstract map model that serves as a basis for the subsequent generation steps.

Map Model. A map model is represented by a tuple $\mathcal{M} = (\mathcal{R}, \mathcal{J}, \mathcal{S})$, which consists of a finite set of roads, a finite set of junctions, and a finite set of signals. The roads can be external to junctions, or covered by some junctions. Signals are associated with roads and can be grouped by junctions with specified policies.

Road. For every road $R \in \mathcal{R}$, it is denoted by $R = (jid, ref, L, pred, succ)$, where

- jid denotes the index of the junction to which the road belongs. The default value is -1 showing that the road is not in any junction, which we call an *external road.* Otherwise, it is an *internal road.*
- ref defines the reference line of the road, showing the geometry of the road. A reference line is denoted by $(x, y, \vec{r}, geom)$, where x and y denote the start position of the road in the coordinate system, $\vec{r} = (cos(hdg), sin(hdg))$ is a unit direction vector indicating the direction of the reference line, hdg is the start orientation. The notation $geom \in \{line, arc, parampoly\}$ indicates the geometry of the road in the form of line, arc, or parametric cubic curves, respectively.
- L represents the set of lanes in the road, each is denoted by $(index, width)$ for its index in the road and the width. The right lanes align with the road reference line in terms of driving direction, while the left lanes oppose it. The lateral deviation between each lane and the reference line corresponds to the t-direction in the reference line coordinate system. To facilitate lane numbering, we consider there exists a lane number 0 with $width = 0$ at the location of the reference line as a baseline for enumeration. Other lanes are numbered starting from the center: decreasing numbers indicate right lanes towards negative t-direction (aligns with the negative t-axis in reference line system), while increasing numbers denote left lanes towards positive t-direction. The indexes of lanes in a road are unique. However, the indexes of lanes between various roads may be the same. Lane numbering is continuous without any gaps.
- $pred$ shows the index of its predecessor. The predecessor element can be a road or a junction.
- $succ$ shows the index of its successor. The successor element can be a road or a junction.

Connection Between Roads. Connections between predecessors and successors of roads are the essential elements of a map. We consider three types of connections between roads.

- Given two roads R_i and R_j, if $R_i.jid = -1 \wedge R_j.jid = -1$ and $R_i.succ = R_j \vee R_i.prec = R_j$, the two roads are connected.

- Given two roads R_i and R_j, if $R_i.jid \neq -1 \wedge R_j.jid \neq -1$ and $R_i.succ = R_j \vee R_i.prec = R_j$, the two roads belong to a roundabout.
- Given two roads R_i and R_j, if $R_i.jid \neq -1 \vee R_j.jid \neq -1$ and $R_i.succ = R_j \vee R_i.prec = R_j$, the connection builds the link between roads and junctions.

Junctions. A junction is defined as a point or area where two or more roads meet, merge, or diverge, with an attribute *branch* representing the number of branches (legs) of the junction. The number of branches and the angle between two neighboring branches decide the types of junctions. For example, a junction with three branches can be a T-junction, Y-junction, or y-junction.

Signal. A signal is denoted by $S = (pos, type)$, where pos decides its position on the reference line coordinates of the road it occupies, and $type \in \{stop\ sign, yield\ sign, speed\ limit, traffic\ light\}$ indicates the type of the signal.

4 Automatic Generation of HD Maps

Junctions play a pivotal role in the testing of autonomous driving systems, as they necessitate the navigation of intricate traffic scenarios, be it for altering course or advancing safely. Given a set of specified junction topologies, we first optimize the configuration of the junctions, to reduce the required number of roads to connect the junctions. Once the configuration of the junctions is ready, we construct the connection between roads and junctions, and instantiate the lanes, and the signals of roads with diversity considerations. To generate valid and reasonable HD maps, the instantiation process follows specific constraints.

4.1 Junction Topology

In determining the optimal configuration for junctions, we introduce the concept of *grid map*. This serves as a simplified, structured representation of HD maps, facilitating the planning and visualization of junction layouts. The grid map is essentially a lattice composed of *square grids*, with *vertices* defining the corners of these squares. Each vertex is connected to its eight immediate neighbors by *edges*. Within this structure, individual junctions are located at vertices, while the edges of the vertex indicate the potentially connected roads of the junction. Therefore, a junction may have eight associated external roads, which are called the *legs* of the junction. More complex junction structures can be obtained by the composition of junctions with their legs.

With the grid map, the topology of a junction can be described by the directions of legs in the junction, denoted as an 8-bit feature vector $\mathbf{d} = (d_0, d_1, \ldots, d_7)$ with $d_i \in \{0, 1\}$, where each d_i corresponds to one of the cardinal and inter-cardinal directions. The corresponding directions in the vector are east, northeast, north, northwest, west, southwest, south, and southeast, respectively. For example, for the junction in Fig. 2, the feature vector is $(0, 1, 1, 0, 1, 0, 1, 0)$,

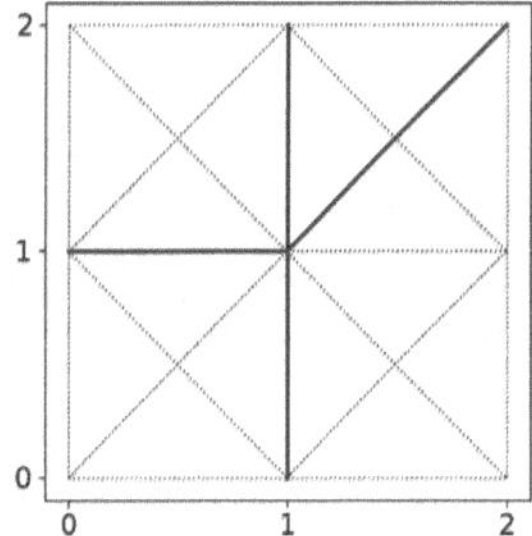

Fig. 2. A four-leg junction in the grid map

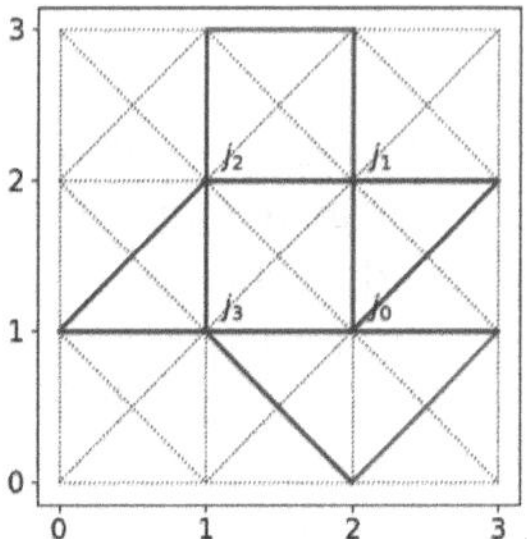

Fig. 3. An optimized configuration of four junctions

Table 1. Classification of junction topologies in the abstract form

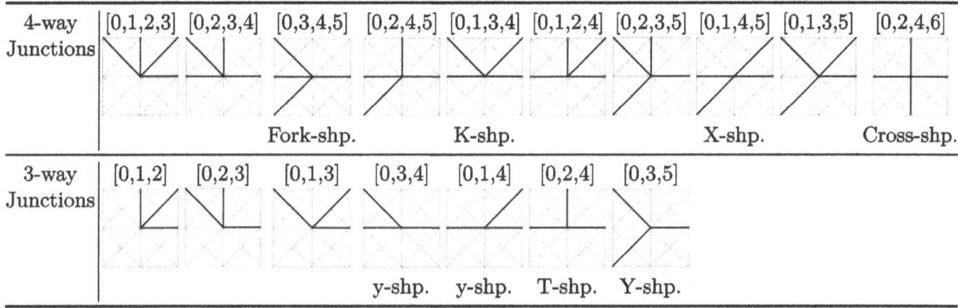

4-way Junctions	[0,1,2,3]	[0,2,3,4]	[0,3,4,5]	[0,2,4,5]	[0,1,3,4]	[0,1,2,4]	[0,2,3,5]	[0,1,4,5]	[0,1,3,5]	[0,2,4,6]
			Fork-shp.		K-shp.			X-shp.		Cross-shp.
3-way Junctions	[0,1,2]	[0,2,3]	[0,1,3]	[0,3,4]	[0,1,4]	[0,2,4]	[0,3,5]			
				y-shp.	y-shp.	T-shp.	Y-shp.			

showing the direction of its four legs and the existence of external roads to the junction.

Given a topology of a junction in feature vector $\mathbf{d} = (d_0, d_1, \ldots, d_7)$, the rotation is counter-wise by 45°C, denoted by $\rho(\mathbf{d}) = (d_1, d_2, \ldots, d_7, d_0)$. For example, after rotation once, the junction in Fig. 2 is $(1, 1, 0, 1, 0, 1, 0, 0)$.

The traffic rules and the behavior of autonomous vehicles are associated with the relative positions and independent of their absolute positions. Therefore, if the topologies of two junctions are the same by rotation, they are equivalent. Such equivalence helps to reduce the number of junctions to explore the diversity with the specified topology.

To obtain a compact representation for the feature vectors of the junction, we adopt an array to record the index of the directions whose value is true. For example, given a junction with four legs, the size of the array is four. For the junction in Fig. 2, its compact representation is $[1, 2, 4, 6]$. Table 1 enumerates respectively the types of topology for 3-way and 4-way junctions with different abstract forms. There are ten different abstract topologies for 4-way junctions and seven for three-way junctions. For some common junction shapes, we have given them aliases, like Cross-shaped, abbreviated as *Cross-shp.*

4.2 Generation of Junction Layouts

After obtaining the complete set of possible feature vectors for the junctions, we construct a grid map including those junctions connected by the minimal number of roads. The construction involves placing each junction at a specific vertex, considering their possible rotation, and mapping roads onto the edges of the grid, connecting each junction leg to another junction leg.

We formalize the construction problem as a MaxSAT model [17] whose solution corresponds to the layout of junctions in a grid map. The MaxSAT problem is an extension of the satisfiability problem, where not all constraints can be satisfied simultaneously, and the objective is to maximize the number of satisfied constraints [1]. Given a square grid with size $M \times N$ and the set of junctions with K elements, we introduce the following notations for the presentation of the model.

- We use $V = M \times N$ to represent the number of vertices in the square grid, and denote v_i as the vertex located at (x, y) with $x \times N + y = i$. We also use $\pi(i)$ to denote the set of indices for vertices that are the immediate neighbors of v_i. Note that $j \in \pi(i) \Leftrightarrow i \in \pi(j)$.
- We use the unordered set $\{i, j\}$ to denote an edge connecting vertices v_i and v_j in the grid, and $j \in \pi(i)$ should be satisfied. We denote the set of edges as $\mathbb{E}$. Some pairs of edges have a crossing that is not at their endpoints. We denote the set of such pairs as $\mathbb{E}_c^2$.
- We use J_k to represent the kth junction in the set which has a 8-bit feature vector $\mathbf{d}^{(k)}$. We define $\lambda(i, n)$ as the adjacent vertex of v_i along the direction corresponding to the nth dimension of feature vectors.
- We use $\mathbb{V} \stackrel{\text{def}}{=} [0, V)$ and $\mathbb{J} \stackrel{\text{def}}{=} [0, K)$ to denote the range of vertices and junctions, respectively.

We have the following decision boolean variables that determine the junction layout.

- a_{ki} indicates whether junction j_k is allocated to vertex v_i.
- e_{ij} indicates whether there is a road on the edge (v_i, v_j) where $(i, j) \in \mathbb{E}$.

The decision variables must be assigned to ensure that each given junction is in the layout and that the layout satisfies the constraints of road networks. The following predicates are adopted to describe the constraints.

- For a set of clauses X and a number n, $\mathsf{AtMost}(X, n)$ defines that at most n clauses in X are satisfied and $\mathsf{TrueNum}(X, n)$ defines that exactly n clauses in X are satisfied. AtMost is a common predicate used in SAT models and has the optimized encoding [17], and $\mathsf{TrueNum}(X, n) \stackrel{\text{def}}{=} \mathsf{AtMost}(X, n) \wedge \mathsf{AtMost}(\{\neg x \mid x \in X\}, |X| - n)$.
- For a feature vector $\mathbf{d}$ and a vertex v_i, $\mathsf{Match}(\mathbf{d}, v_i)$ shows that the edges connected to v_i have the roads that matches the feature vector $\mathbf{d}$, i.e., $\mathsf{Match}(\mathbf{d}, v_i) \stackrel{\text{def}}{=} (\bigwedge_{d_n=1} e_{n,\lambda(i,n)}) \wedge (\bigwedge_{d_n=0} \neg e_{n,\lambda(i,n)})$.

- For a vertex v_i, $\mathsf{HasJunction}(i)$ expresses whether there is a junction allocated to v_i, i.e., $\mathsf{HasJunction}(i) \stackrel{\text{def}}{=} \bigvee_{k \in \mathbb{J}} a_{ij}$.

Utilizing the predicates, the constraints are formulated as follows.
Constraint 1 specifies that each given junction should allocated to a vertex.

$$\forall k \in \mathbb{J}.\ \mathsf{TrueNum}(\{a_{ki}\}_{i \in \mathbb{V}}, 1) \tag{1}$$

Constraint 2 specifies that each vertex can be allocated at most one junction.

$$\forall i \in \mathbb{V}.\ \mathsf{AtMost}(\{a_{ki}\}_{k \in \mathbb{J}}, 1) \tag{2}$$

Constraint 3 specifies that two crossing edges cannot both be roads.

$$\forall \{\{i, j\}, \{k, l\}\} \in \mathbb{E}_c^2.\ (\neg e_{ij} \vee \neg e_{kl}) \tag{3}$$

Constraint 4 specifies that the roads connected to the vertex with a junction should match the shape of the junction.

$$\forall k \in \mathbb{J}.\ \forall i \in \mathbb{V}.\ a_{ki} \rightarrow \bigvee_{r \in [0,8)} (\mathsf{Match}(\rho^r(\mathbf{d}_k), v_i)) \tag{4}$$

Constraint 5 specifies that the vertex without junctions cannot have many connected roads or a terminated path.

$$\begin{aligned} \forall i \in \mathbb{V}.\ \neg\mathsf{HasJunction}(i) \rightarrow (&\mathsf{TrueNum}(\{e_{ij}\}_{j \in \pi(i)}, 0) \vee \\ &\mathsf{TrueNum}(\{e_{ij}\}_{j \in \pi(i)}, 2)) \end{aligned} \tag{5}$$

Given four 4-way junctions, we present the optimized configuration of junctions in Fig. 3. In the figure, junction J_2 and J_3 are connected with two types: one is by the direct connection between two legs of the junctions, and the other is the indirect connection with an *intermediate* vertex at $(0, 1)$.

The optimization goal is to ensure that every leg is connected to another leg, while minimizing the total number of edges on the map. Ideally, the sum of all legs of each junction would represent the desirable outcome, indicating that no additional edges are required to connect different legs.

$$\forall (i, j) \in \mathbb{E}.\ \mathsf{Min}(|\{e_{ij}|\}) \tag{6}$$

4.3 Instantiation

The instantiation process concretizes the roads and the connection with junctions according to the configuration of abstract junctions. The instantiation involves three steps. First, we transform the legs of junctions into external roads in the map model. Second, we create new external roads to connect the legs of the junctions such that the junctions are connected. Finally, we figure out the internal roads and their connection with the external roads for each junction. These steps ensure that the generated map is systematic and adheres to the realistic constraints and configurations in actual traffic scenarios.

4.3.1 Constraints To generate valid and feasible maps, the map generation is restricted by the following constraints.

- Non-crossing roads. The external roads of junctions should not intersect with each other. The rule requires that simultaneous equations of the parametric curves for any two external roads should not have a solution.
- Fairing curve. A lane should maintain a consistent curvature that aligns with the predecessor and successor lanes, ensuring seamless path planning. In scenarios with additional or fewer lanes along the traffic direction, it is necessary to employ approximate curves for the lane boundaries to keep the curve fairing.
- Number of lanes per road. A road is required to have at least one lane, either a left or a right lane.

4.3.2 Transformation of Legs After configuration optimization, the first step is to transform the legs into the roads according to its definition in the map model. For example, edges in Fig. 3 from vertex $(1, 2)$ to vertex $(2, 2)$ connect a leg of J_2 with another leg of J_1. We will instantiate these two legs and their connection separately.

For each leg of an abstract junction, the attributes of the corresponding road are as follows: the jid of the junction index is -1, and the reference line ref is set towards the junction. Predecessor *pred* will be decided once the connection between the two legs is established. Successor *succ* is the index of the junction. The number of lanes is randomly assigned within the range of $[0, n]$, where n is a positive integer, indicating that the number of lanes on the left or right side of the reference line can vary from 0 to n.

4.3.3 External Connection The next step is to establish connections of legs (external roads) in different junctions according to the optimized configuration.

The example in Fig. 3 presents two types of connections between two junctions, i.e., direction and indirect connections. For both types of connections, we need to create a new external road to connect the legs of the junctions. Different from the transformation from leg to external road, the orientation of the reference line here is randomized. The predecessor is the external road with a smaller index, and the successor refers to the road with a higher index number.

4.3.4 Concretizing Junctions The internal information of a junction involves two components: internal roads and traffic signals. Junction topology introduced in Sect. 4.1 only considers the shape of the junction. To generate valid and feasible maps, it is essential to describe the connection of each leg to the internal road network within a junction, and subsequently equip these connections with appropriate traffic signals.

Internal Roads. The role of an internal road is to connect two external roads to the junction, such that a vehicle can enter and exit the junction. Different from

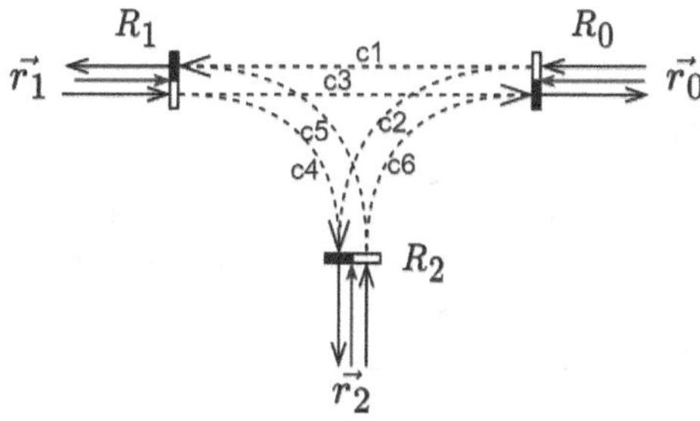

Fig. 4. Connection in a three-way junction

external roads with multiple lanes, an internal road only has one lane. Given a junction, we create its internal roads and establish the connection with the external roads to the junction. The *jid* of an internal road is the index of the located junction.

For an external road transformed from the leg of a junction, the reference line is towards the junction, and the lanes on the right side of it keep the same direction as the reference line. Therefore, an internal road takes a right lane of a connected external road as the predecessor and takes a left lane of another external road as the successor. Meantime, the reference line is calculated according to the reference lines of its predecessor and successor, while the direction is consistent with the reference line of its predecessor. For example, we provide a three-way junction in Fig. 4. Each of its legs is instantiated into a road with two lanes in opposite directions. The blue lines mark the reference lines of the three external roads. The internal roads are labeled with dash lines, with the arrows showing the direction of the reference lines. The internal road c_1 connects two external roads R_0 and R_1. It takes R_0 as the predecessor and R_1 as the successor.

To maximize connectivity, we use a fully connected mode. There are $P(3,2) = 6$ types of internal roads for a three-way junction and $P(4,2) = 12$ types of internal roads for a four-way junction. Figure 4 provides the full connection of the internal roads.

Traffic Signals. We place a set of signals at the joint of internal and external roads to control the traffic flow. We randomly add signals $s.type \in \{null, stop\ sign, traffic\ light, yield\ sign\}$ to control each external road.

For traffic lights at a junction, we need to define their policies (phase of traffic signal) based on their relative position of roads. The policies of signals located at external roads in opposite directions are the same. The opposite direction is checked with the direction of the reference lines in the two roads.

- Opposite: Given two roads R_i and R_j, and the directions of their reference lines $\vec{r_i}$ and $\vec{r_j}$, the two roads are in opposite positions, if two vectors $\vec{r_i}$ and $\vec{r_j}$ are parallel vectors and their directions are exactly opposite, i.e., $\vec{r_i} = k\vec{r_j}$ where k is a negative real number.

5 Evaluation

5.1 Implementation

The method is implemented with C++ and Python. The optimization of junction configuration adopts the Python API offered by the Z3 solver. The file generation of HD maps relies on Code Synthesis [8] with the Xerces-C++ library [2], to be consistent with the OpenDRIVE 1.7 framework. The configuration files of the tool support both Windows and Ubuntu environments.

5.2 Setup

We consider the following research questions in the experimentation.

RQ$_1$:Can the MaxSAT model achieve better layout of junctions?

RQ$_2$: Can the method generate succinct but diversified HD maps?

RQ$_3$: Is the generated HD map helpful in detecting the defects of autonomous driving systems in simulation-based testing?

To answer question **RQ**$_1$, we implement a layout optimization method using greedy strategy and compare it with the layout generated using the MaxSAT model. To answer question **RQ**$_2$, we compare the number of junctions and the types of junction topology with randomly selected OpenStreetMap(OSM) [20] and the available HD maps in the Carla simulator [10]. To answer question **RQ**$_3$, we adopt the tool ComOpT [16] to generate test cases with the generated map, run the simulation in the Carla simulator, and collect the issues in simulation-based testing.

We enumerate all the possible topologies for three-way and four-way junctions in map generation. We set $n = 2$, specifying the maximum number of lanes on the left side or the right side of a road. The width of a lane is set to 3.5 m. The size of a junction is set to 40 m, as the maximal distance between two connected external roads. With these settings, the size of the generated map is 750*700 m^2 with 17 different junctions.

We conduct experiments on a desktop equipped with GPU GeForce 1080Ti. The selected autonomous driving system are Baidu Apollo v8.0.0 system [4] and Carla 0.9.14 Traffic Manager.

5.3 Experimental Results

5.3.1 Effectiveness of the MaxSAT Model To demonstrate the benefit of using the MaxSAT model, we compare the layout with that generated by the greedy algorithm.

The greedy algorithm begins by randomly assigning the location of junctions within the grid. It then iteratively optimizes the angles of these junctions to minimize both their distance from roads and the angular deviations, thereby enhancing the smoothness of road connections within the layout.

Figure 5 provides the HD maps generated by two method. The layout generated by the greedy method contains 15 additional dead ends and one fewer

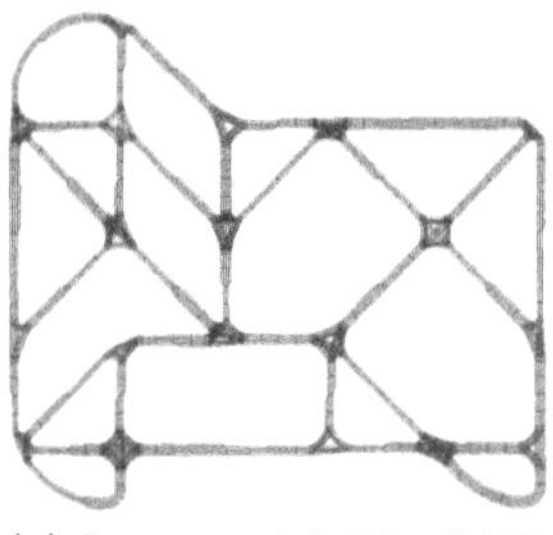

(a) Layout with MaxSAT

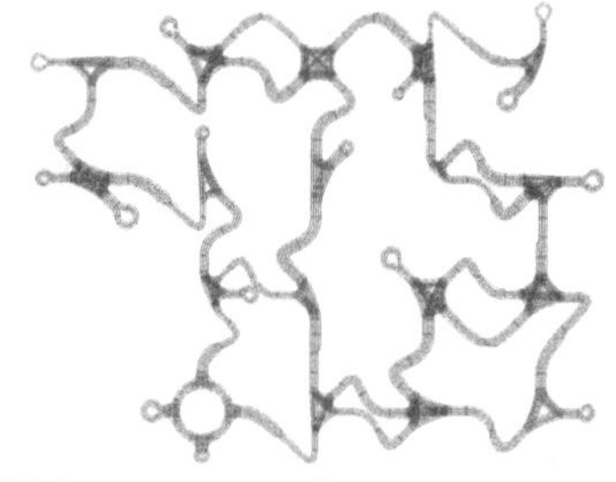

(b) Layout with Greedy algorithm

Fig. 5. Two generated HD maps with various optimization methods

junction compared to the layout produced with the MaxSAT model. The greedy strategy initially fixes the grid coordinates of junctions, leading to a higher incidence of mismatched angles with neighboring junctions and consequently resulting in an increased number of dead ends. Therefore, the generated maps with the MaxSAT model are more compact, without dead end, and with better connectivity.

5.3.2 Comparison with Existing Maps To answer RQ2, we consider both the real-world maps and the maps provided by simulators, to provide a thorough comparison with the generated map. We conduct a diversity assessment of road network information, focusing on the topology of junctions with different traffic flows. We classify the junctions with similar shapes. The classification process is automatic and manually checked.

We first select the maps from OpenStreetMap, with diversified road networks in the real world. We use random sampling to locate sub-areas within San Francisco city in latitude $(37.8071°N, 37.7081°N)$ and longitude $(-122.5153°W, -122.3578°W)$. The sampled areas have the same size as the generated map. Once the scope of the region is determined, the map of the corresponding subarea is downloaded with the API from the OpenStreetMap website and converted into OpenDRIVE format.

We have downloaded 15 sub-areas. Maps osm02, osm05, osm09, and osm10 cannot be converted to OpenDRIVE format. Though map osm03 can be converted into OpenDRIVE format, it only has one road, which is not considered in the comparison.

Table 2 provides the comparison with the sampled maps of OSM. With the same size, the number of junctions in the generated map is more than the sampled, showing a higher density. In most cases, the diversity of the generated maps is higher than the sampled. However, there are some exceptions, split/merge roads, and complex junctions, which are recorded respectively in the last row of the table. Figure 6 illustrates the constructed roundabouts in the generated map, as well as split roads and complex junctions found in OSM. We add arrows to illustrate the direction of roads. Figure 6(a) shows the topology of the round-

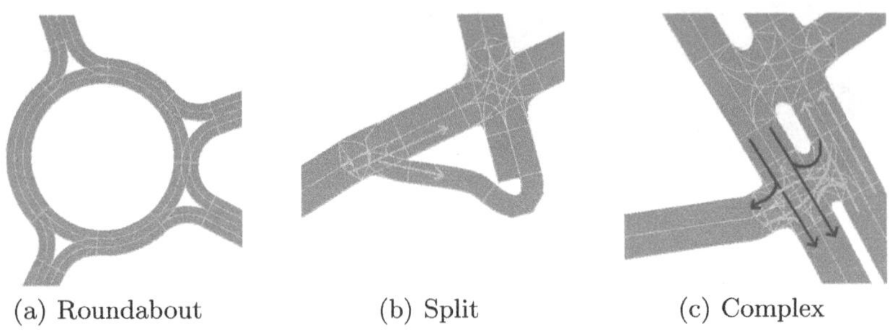

(a) Roundabout (b) Split (c) Complex

Fig. 6. Special structure in the maps

Table 2. Comparison with OpenStreetMap in San Francisco

	Ours	osm01	osm04	osm06	osm07	osm08	osm11	osm12	osm13	osm14	osm15
num of junc	19	5	6	13	10	11	12	15	7	9	11
T-shaped	✓	1	4	0	6	4	1	9	5	6	3
y-shaped	✓				1	4				2	3
Y-shaped	✓										3
Cross-shaped	✓	4	1	10	2	3	11	6		1	1
K-shaped	✓										1
special	round-about:1		split:1	complex:3	complex:1				split:1 complex:1		

about in our map, consisting of several junctions. Figure 6(b) shows the topology of a split junction in OSM. As we assume that the internal roads of junctions are fully connected, and the external roads contain lanes in opposite directions, the generated map does not contain splits and merges. However, splits and merges cases can be considered as special cases of Y-shaped (or y and T-shaped) junctions, where one leg only has one direction. Complex junctions in Fig. 6(c) can be considered as double T-shaped with split/merge roads.

There are ten HD maps in the Carla simulator, while two of the maps, i.e., Town08 and Town09, are not available. In addition to the topology considered in Table 2, we also compare the number of conflict points (CP) in a map. A conflict point refers to a point where lanes may intersect, including crossing, merging, and diverging. The larger number of conflict points indicates more frequent traffic flows. We use MathWorks RoadRunner [18] to identify the conflict points. As we cannot import maps from OSM into RoadRunner, the comparison is missing in Table 2. Table 3 provides the comparison results with eight maps in Carla. We observe that the diversity of junction topology in the generated map is richer than the maps in Carla. One exception is in Town04, with a flyover on the map. Such an exception can be supported by allowing roads at various heights.

5.3.3 Effectiveness in Simulation-Based Testing We adopt ComOpT [16] in the experiment with the generated map, which can automatically generate test cases and run the simulation to collect and evaluate the test results. The tool generates 39 test cases. The traffic participants in each test case include a vehicle controlled by Apollo and other vehicles controlled by Carla Traffic

Table 3. Comparison with maps in Carla

	Ours	Town01	Town02	Town03	Town04	Town05	Town06	Town07	Town10
num of junc	19	12	8	35	35	21	23	31	13
T-shaped	✓	✓	✓	✓	✓	✓	✓	✓	✓
y-shaped	✓		✓	✓	✓				
Y-shaped	✓		✓	✓				✓	
Cross-shaped	✓		✓	✓	✓	✓	✓	✓	✓
K-shaped	✓								
special	roundabout				flyover				
num of CP	1990	160	170	1310	1129	1684	354	508	494

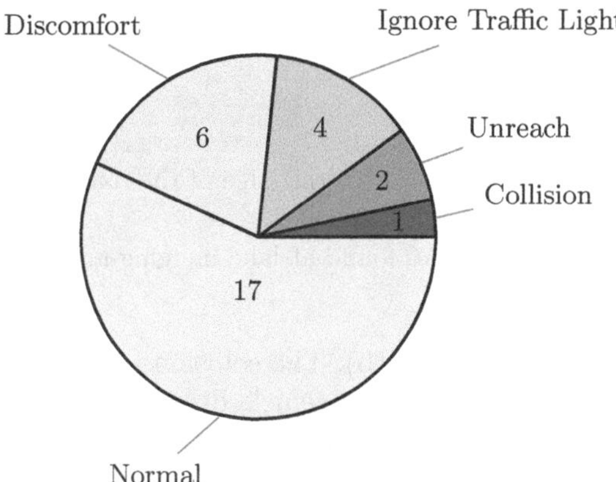

Fig. 7. Categories of detected issues for Apollo

Manager. We classify the evaluation results into various categories according to the issues. We list the issues in descending order of severity: (a) *Collision*: crash with vehicles or road infrastructures; (b) *Unreach*: fail to reach the target position in a reasonable time limit (2 min); (c) *Ignore Traffic Light*: go through a junction at a red or yellow light; and (d) *Discomfort*: proceed with discomfort deceleration, acceleration or lateral jerk.

Figure 7 shows the number of various detected issues for the vehicle controlled by Apollo. 13 test cases out of 39 trigger safety or performance issues, showing the high validity of the generated map. In addition, we found safety issues caused by the vehicle controlled by Carla Traffic Manager. We provide two of the examples in Fig. 8, which depicts a scene where two lanes merge into one. Such a topology is common in the real world but rare in maps used for simulation-based testing. For example, the structure does not exist in all the built-in and available maps in Carla and LGSVL [22], as well as GoMentum [9], a test station specifically built for automated vehicle testing. In Fig. 8(a), a vehicle (in black) controlled by Carla traffic manager collides with another vehicle (in blue) controlled by Apollo at the merging point. In another case, the collision occurs at the edge of

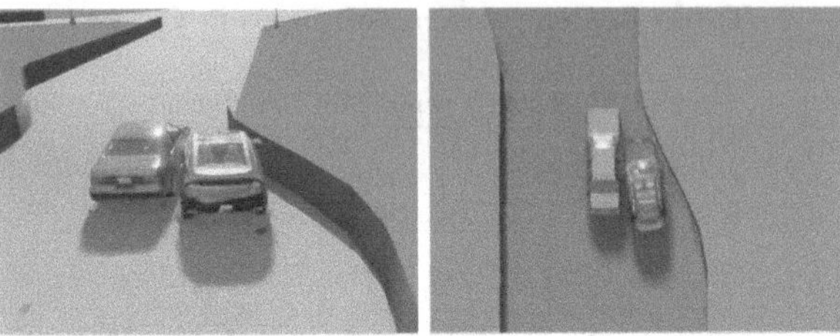

(a) Collision with another vehicle

(b) Collision with the edge of the road

Fig. 8. Issues found at lane merging area

the ending lane, as shown in Fig. 8(b). The collision is caused by the absence of road-narrowing countermeasures. The vehicle drives too fast to stop at the end of the lane, so it has to either make a lane change and collide with its neighbor vehicle or collide with the edge of the lane.

6 Conclusion

Facing the inherent complexity and labor-intensive nature of traditional HD map creation methods, the paper has introduced an automatic HD map generation framework. The comparison with real-world maps and built-in maps from popular open-source simulators underscores the effectiveness of the generated HD maps, showing their diversity and conciseness while maintaining crucial topographical details. Moreover, the application of the automatically generated HD maps in simulation-based testing not only demonstrates their viability but also highlights their capacity to uncover map-related issues that might otherwise have been overlooked.

Acknowledgments. This work has been partly funded by Major Project of ISCAS (ISCAS-ZD-202302), the Natural Science Foundation of China (Grant No.62132020), and the CAS Project for Young Scientists in Basic Research (Grant No. YSBR-040).

References

1. Ansótegui, C., Bonet, M.L., Levy, J.: Sat-based maxsat algorithms. Artif. Intell. **196**, 77–105 (2013)

2. Apache software foundation: xerces c++ parser. http://xerces.apache.org/xerces-c/ (2024)
3. ASAM: Opendrive v1.7.0 user guide (2021). https://www.asam.net/standards/detail/opendrive
4. Baidu Apollo team: Apollo: open source autonomous driving (2017). https://github.com/ApolloAuto/apollo
5. BeamNG.AI: Beamng (2022). https://documentation.beamng.com/tutorials/ai/
6. Becker, D., Ruß, F., Geller, C., Eckstein, L.: Generation of complex road networks using a simplified logical description for the validation of automated vehicles. In: IEEE ITSC, pp. 1–7 (2020)
7. Castellano, E., Cetinkaya, A., Arcaini, P.: Analysis of road representations in search-based testing of autonomous driving systems. In: IEEE QRS, pp. 167–178 (2021)
8. CODE SYNTHESIS: XSD binding. https://www.codesynthesis.com/ (2024)
9. Contra costa transportation authority: gomentum station. https://gomentumstation.net/ (2024)
10. Dosovitskiy, A., Ros, G., Codevilla, F., Lopez, A., Koltun, V.: Carla: an open urban driving simulator. In: CoRL, pp. 1–16. PMLR (2017)
11. Elghazaly, G., Frank, R., Harvey, S., Safko, S.: High-definition maps: comprehensive survey, challenges and future perspectives. IEEE Open J. ITS **4**, 527–550 (2023)
12. Fremont, D.J., et al.: Formal scenario-based testing of autonomous vehicles: from simulation to the real world. In: IEEE ITSC, pp. 1–8 (2020)
13. Gambi, A., Mueller, M., Fraser, G.: Automatically testing self-driving cars with search-based procedural content generation. In: ACM SIGSOFT ISSTA, pp. 318–328 (2019)
14. Kalra, N., Paddock, S.M.: Driving to safety: how many miles of driving would it take to demonstrate autonomous vehicle reliability? Transp. Res. Part A: Policy Pract. **94**, 182–193 (2016)
15. Klischat, M., Liu, E.I., Holtke, F., Althoff, M.: Scenario factory: creating safety-critical traffic scenarios for automated vehicles. In: IEEE ITSC, pp. 1–7 (2020)
16. Li, C., Cheng, C.H., Sun, T., Chen, Y., Yan, R.: Comopt: combination and optimization for testing autonomous driving systems. In: IEEE ICRA, pp. 7738–7744 (2022)
17. Li, C.M., Manya, F.: Maxsat, hard and soft constraints. In: Handbook of satisfiability, pp. 903–927. IOS Press (2021)
18. MathWorks: RoadRunner (2023). https://www.mathworks.com/products/roadrunner.html
19. Muktadir, G.M., Jawad, A., Paranjape, I., Whitehead, J., Shepelev, A.: Procedural generation of high-definition road networks for autonomous vehicle testing and traffic simulations. SAE Int. J. CAV **6**(12-06-01-0007), 99–120 (2022)
20. OpenStreetMap contributors: planet dump retrieved from https://planet.osm.org . https://www.openstreetmap.org (2024)
21. Richter, A., Scholz, M.: Deploying guidelines and a simplified data model to provide real world geodata in driving simulators and driving automation. Transport. Res. F: Traffic Psychol. Behav. **61**, 305–313 (2019)
22. Rong, G., et al.: Lgsvl simulator: a high fidelity simulator for autonomous driving. In: IEEE ITSC, pp. 1–6 (2020)
23. Tang, Y., et al.: Route coverage testing for autonomous vehicles via map modeling. In: IEEE ICRA, pp. 11450–11456 (2021)

Managing Traceability for Software Life Cycle Processes

Hao Wen[1,2], Jinzhao Wu[1,2(✉)], Jianmin Jiang[3], Jianqing Li[3], and Zhong Hong[4]

[1] Chengdu Institute of Computer Applications, Chinese Academy of Sciences, Chengdu, China
himrwujzh@aliyun.com

[2] University of Chinese Academy of Sciences, Beijing, China
wenhao21@mails.ucas.ac.cn

[3] Chengdu University of Information Technology, Chengdu, China
jjm@cuit.edu.cn

[4] Fujian Normal University, Fuzhou, China
fjfzhz@fjnu.edu.cn

Abstract. Various types of software artifacts are produced in the software life cycle processes. Although traceability between different artifacts is beneficial for software development, the actual practice of modeling and maintaining traceability is not always entirely successful. In this paper, we explore how to manage traceability for the software life cycle process, including a new solution for formally constructing and preserving traceability under various management operations. Such a solution allows flexibility and extensibility to define new types of traceability links (dependency relationships). Its traceability information does not pollute the inner relationships of existing artifacts. We first present a formal model called a *structure model* that is used to describe software systems, and then a traceability concept is formally defined. Based on the structure model, we investigate in theory how to preserve traceability under various management operations. Finally, a prototype tool is developed for supporting our work.

Keywords: Traceability · Management operation · Formal method

1 Introduction

Traceability is the ability to keep track between software artifacts through the dependency relationships (often called traceability links [8]). In the software life cycle, software artifacts usually refer to text-based requirements, requirements models, design models, source codes, test cases, various attached documents, etc. A traceability software system means that developers can trace from

This work is supported by National Natural Science Foundation of China (Nos. 61772006, 61772004 and 12261027), National Key R&D Program of China (No. 2022YFB3305101) and Scientific Research Foundation for Advanced Talents of Chengdu University of Information Technology (No. KYTZ202009).

W.-N. Chin and Z. Xu (Eds.): TASE 2024, LNCS 14777, pp. 428–445, 2024.
https://doi.org/10.1007/978-3-031-64626-3_25

requirements to other artifacts according to different situations. Obviously, the benefits of this ability are lower maintenance cost, clearer documentation, more focused development and more precise change impact analysis [25]. However, practitioners are poorly supported by the scientific literature when managing traceability [11]. It is necessary to explore how to build a software system that better supports the management of traceability.

Early studies fixed the types of traceability links (e.g. [9,16]) whereas recent research has supported the flexibility and extensibility of traceability links (e.g. [1,3,6]). In this paper, we propose a formal model called a *structure model* for describing software systems, which not only allows for new types of software artifacts to be introduced, but also does breaks the limit of the number of traceability link types. Then, the formal notion of traceability can be defined based on structure models. Moreover, we adopt a similar concept as in UML [13], considering various software artifacts as *model elements* named with different labels in a structure model. Such considerations facilitate the analysis and visualization representations of traceability.

The evolution of software systems is inevitable. Since evolution involves many operations that may affect traceability [11], it is a challenge to maintain traceability. Specifically, concrete change operations (activities) often contain multiple steps, and every step may delete traceable links and make software artifacts untraceable. To avoid this problem, existing studies and practices generally provide guidelines [19,21,25]. However, these guidelines are informal rules and cannot completely maintain traceability. Thus we aim to fully maintain traceability by formalizing the operations.

This paper makes the following contributions. (1) We first introduce a novel definition of traceability based on meta paths [20]. (2) Next, eight management operations are formally defined. Compared to our previous work [22], these operations focus on concrete activities in the software life cycle processes, and are more helpful for actual practice. (3) Ultimately, we illustrate that traceability is maintained as the software system evolves.

The remainder of this paper is structured as follows. Section 2 introduces the concept of traceability, Sect. 3 presents solutions to maintain traceability under 8 management operations, Sect. 4 introduces our prototype tool. Section 5 is the related work and Sect. 6 concludes this paper.

2 Traceability

In this section, we will introduce the structure model [22,23] to construct and analyze traceability. Some assistant definitions are first given. Let **VN** be the set of version numbers and ∞ be a special version number which means an *undetermined* version number and $\infty \notin \mathbf{VN}$.

Definition 1. *A* ***structure model*** *($\mathcal{SM}$) is a tuple* $\langle \mathrm{ME}, \prec, \overset{1}{\omega}, \cdots, \overset{n}{\omega}, \overset{1}{\tau}, \cdots, \overset{m}{\tau}, vs, ve \rangle$ *with*

- ME, *a finite set of the model elements,*

- $\prec \subseteq \mathrm{ME} \times \mathrm{ME}$, *the* containment relation *such that it is an (irreflexive) partial order,*
- $\forall i \in \{1, \cdots, n\}, \overset{i}{\omega} \subseteq \mathrm{ME} \times \mathrm{ME}$, *the* dependency relation,
- $\forall j \in \{1, \cdots, m\}, \overset{j}{\tau} \subseteq \mathrm{ME}$, *the* type set *of model elements such that* $\forall e \in \mathrm{ME}, \exists \tau \in \{\overset{1}{\tau}, \cdots, \overset{m}{\tau}\} : e \in \tau$.
- $vs : \mathrm{ME} \longrightarrow \mathbf{VN} \cup \{\infty\}$, *the* initial version function, *and*
- $ve : \mathrm{ME} \longrightarrow \mathbf{VN} \cup \{\infty\}$, *the* final version function.

The structure model consists of model elements, variable dependency relations between model elements (the *containment* relation is isolated as a special kind of dependency relation in order to construct the hierarchical structures), classifications and version numbers of model elements.

Next, we show how to describe a specific software system by using the structure model. A simple user account management system in Fig. 1 can be represented by $\mathcal{SM} = \langle \mathrm{ME}, \prec, \overset{trace}{\omega}, \overset{include}{\omega}, \overset{aggregation}{\omega}, \overset{requirement}{\tau}, \overset{useCase}{\tau}, \overset{class}{\tau}, \overset{code}{\tau}, vs, ve \rangle$ where $\mathrm{ME} = \{RQ, R1, R2, U1, U2, U3, C1, C2, D1\}$, $\prec = \{(R1, RQ), (R2, RQ)\}$, $\overset{trace}{\omega} = \{(U1, R1), (U2, R2), (U3, R2), (C1, U1), (C2, U1), (C2, U3), (D1, C2)\}$, $\overset{include}{\omega} = \{(U2, U3)\}$, $\overset{aggregation}{\omega} = \{(C1, C2)\}$, $\overset{requirement}{\tau} = \{RQ, R1, R2\}$, $\overset{useCase}{\tau} = \{U1, U2, U3\}$, $\overset{class}{\tau} = \{C1, C2\}$, and $\overset{code}{\tau} = \{D1\}$. Suppose the initial version number of the model elements is 1.0, thus $\forall x \in \mathrm{ME} : vs(x) = 1.0$ and $ve(x) = \infty$. Note that a model element is assigned the initial version number when it is created, whereas it is assigned the final version number when it is inactivated (the default final version number is ∞). Moreover, the version number of $\mathcal{SM}$, denoted as $\mathcal{V}(\mathcal{SM}) \in \mathbf{VN}$, is the maximum initial version number of model elements in $\mathcal{SM}$, that is, $\forall x \in \mathrm{ME} : vs(x) \leq \mathcal{V}(\mathcal{SM})$.

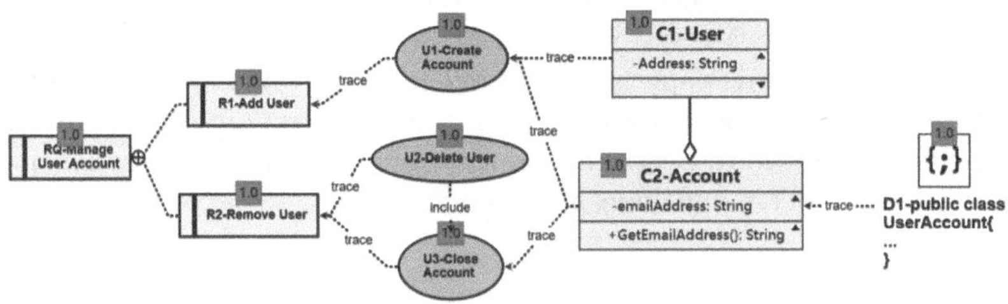

Fig. 1. A simple user account management system

Definition 2. *Let* $\mathcal{SM} = \langle \mathrm{ME}, \prec, \overset{1}{\omega}, \cdots, \overset{n}{\omega}, \overset{1}{\tau}, \cdots, \overset{m}{\tau}, vs, ve \rangle$ *be a structure model.*

(1) A sequence $\mathcal{P} = X_1 \overset{R_1}{\rightarrow} X_2 \overset{R_2}{\rightarrow} \cdots \overset{R_{l-1}}{\rightarrow} X_l$ *is called a* meta path *in* $\mathcal{SM}$ *iff* $\forall i \in \{1, \cdots, l\} : X_i \in \{\overset{1}{\tau}, \cdots, \overset{m}{\tau}\}$ *and* $\forall i \in \{1, \cdots, l-1\} : R_i \in \{\prec, \overset{1}{\omega}, \cdots, \overset{m}{\omega}\}$.

(2) The meta path $\mathcal{P}$ can also be written as $X_1 \rightarrow X_2 \rightarrow \cdots \rightarrow X_l \mid R_1 \circ R_2 \circ \cdots \circ R_{l-1}$, where $\circ$ denotes the composition operator on relations.
(3) $\mid \mathcal{P} \mid$ denotes the length of the meta path $\mathcal{P}$ (the number of relations in $\mathcal{P}$), that is, $\mid \mathcal{P} \mid = l - 1$.

A meta path is a structural path defined at the meta level, consisting of a sequence of relation between model element types [20]. Since each meta path has different semantics, we can customize it to fit the situation. For example, $\mathcal{P}_1 = \overset{code}{\tau} \overset{\overset{trace}{\omega}}{\rightarrow} \overset{class}{\tau} \overset{\overset{trace}{\omega}}{\rightarrow} \overset{useCase}{\tau} \overset{\overset{trace}{\omega}}{\rightarrow} \overset{requirement}{\tau}$ is a meta path in $\mathcal{SM}$ (see Fig. 1), implying that the model element in $\overset{code}{\tau}$ can trace the model element in $\overset{requirement}{\tau}$ via accessing $\overset{trace}{\omega}$ three times. To be convenient, we will denote the execution of k composition operations on the same relation R as R^k, i.e., the meta path $\mathcal{P}_1$ can also be written as $\overset{code}{\tau} \rightarrow \overset{class}{\tau} \rightarrow \overset{useCase}{\tau} \rightarrow \overset{requirement}{\tau} \mid \overset{trace}{\omega}{}^3$.

Inspired by the great success of meta paths in heterogeneous information networks [18,20] (a software system is essentially a heterogeneous information network), we explore how to construct traceability using meta paths.

Definition 3. *Let $\mathcal{SM} = \langle \text{ME}, \prec, \overset{1}{\omega}, \cdots, \overset{n}{\omega}, \overset{1}{\tau}, \cdots, \overset{m}{\tau}, vs, ve \rangle$ be a structure model. Assume that there exists a meta path $\mathcal{P} = X_1 \overset{R_1}{\rightarrow} X_2 \overset{R_2}{\rightarrow} \cdots \overset{R_{l-1}}{\rightarrow} X_l$ in $\mathcal{SM}$. For $x \in X_1$, the set of model elements that can be traced by x along $\mathcal{P}$ with a length h ($1 \leq h \leq \mid \mathcal{P} \mid$) is denoted as $Tr(x \overset{\mathcal{P}:h}{\rightarrow}) = \{x' \in X_{h+1} \mid (x, x') \in R_1 \circ \cdots \circ R_h\}$.*

By this definition, we can get the set of model elements that are traced under different lengths of meta paths. For example, the length of $\mathcal{P}_1$ in $\mathcal{SM}$ is 3 and $\overset{code}{\tau} = \{D1\}$, thus $Tr(D1 \overset{\mathcal{P}_1:1}{\rightarrow}) = \{C2\}$, $Tr(D1 \overset{\mathcal{P}_1:2}{\rightarrow}) = \{U1, U3\}$ and $Tr(D1 \overset{\mathcal{P}_1:3}{\rightarrow}) = \{R1, R2\}$.

Definition 4. *Let $\mathcal{SM}$ be a structure model. Assume that there exists a meta path $\mathcal{P} = X_1 \overset{R_1}{\rightarrow} X_2 \overset{R_2}{\rightarrow} \cdots \overset{R_{l-1}}{\rightarrow} X_l$ in $\mathcal{SM}$. $\mathcal{SM}$ is said to be traceable via $\mathcal{P}$, iff $\forall x \in X_1, h \in \{1, \cdots, \mid \mathcal{P} \mid\} : Tr(x \overset{\mathcal{P}:h}{\rightarrow}) \neq \emptyset$.*

Definition 4 states that the model elements of the involved types can be traced via the meta path in a traceable structure model, i.e., the structure model satisfies constraints expressed as meta paths. In Fig. 1, for each $h \in \{1, \cdots, \mid \mathcal{P}_1 \mid\}$, $Tr(D1 \overset{\mathcal{P}_1:h}{\rightarrow}) \neq \emptyset$, therefore $\mathcal{SM}$ is traceable via $\mathcal{P}_1$.

Moreover, *completeness*, as an important metric for evaluating traceability, is the number of "covered" model elements divided by the total number of model elements [10]. Hence, for each length h in a meta path $\mathcal{P} = X_1 \overset{R_1}{\rightarrow} X_2 \overset{R_2}{\rightarrow} \cdots \overset{R_{l-1}}{\rightarrow} X_l$, we can obtain the corresponding completeness.

$$Comp(\mathcal{P}:h) = \frac{\mid \bigcup_{x \in X_1} Tr(x \overset{\mathcal{P}:h}{\rightarrow}) \mid}{\mid X_{h+1} \mid} \tag{1}$$

Definition 5. *Let $\mathcal{SM}$ be a structure model. Assume that there exists a meta path $\mathcal{P} = X_1 \overset{R_1}{\to} X_2 \overset{R_2}{\to} \cdots \overset{R_{l-1}}{\to} X_l$ in $\mathcal{SM}$. $\mathcal{SM}$ is said to be fully traceable via $\mathcal{P}$, iff*

(1) $\mathcal{SM}$ is traceable via $\mathcal{P}$, and
(2) $\forall x \in X_1, h \in \{1, \cdots, | \mathcal{P} |\} : \bigcup_{x \in X_1} Tr(x \overset{\mathcal{P}:h}{\to}) = X_{h+1}$.

Full traceability is a special kind of traceability, which considers all model elements of each length in the meta path needed to be traced.

Proposition 1. *Let $\mathcal{SM}$ be a structure model. Assume that there exists a meta path $\mathcal{P}$ in $\mathcal{SM}$. If $\mathcal{SM}$ is fully traceable via $\mathcal{P}$, then $\forall h \in \{1, \cdots, | \mathcal{P} |\}$: $Comp(\mathcal{P} : h) = 1$.*

Proof. This proof is straightforward.

As the value of completeness increases, the quality of traceability continuously increases. For each length h in a meta path $\mathcal{P}$ such that $Comp(P : h) = 1$, we can consider the structure model as fully traceable via $\mathcal{P}$.

3 Management of Traceable Systems

Change has a multi-level impact for traceability from the requirements analysis down to the run-time configuration of a system [7]. We find the following 8 management operations of changing traceability, covering all possible management activities which are summarized from the literature such as [7,15]. To manage the traceability of a system, we will discuss how to preserve the traceability under these management operations. In addition, we use $\mathcal{SM} \overset{\sigma[\lambda_1;\lambda_2;\cdots]}{\Longrightarrow} \mathcal{SM}'$ to denote the evolution from the structure model $\mathcal{SM}$ to the structure model $\mathcal{SM}'$ by executing the operation σ with parameters $\lambda_1, \lambda_2, \cdots$.

3.1 Adding a Model Element

Addition is one of the basic management operations in the evolution of a software system. Adding a new model element consists of the following steps.

(1) Create a new model element, and assign a version number to the new model element. Such a version number is the initial version of the new model element, whereas final version of the new model element is not designated.
(2) Create the *trace* relations between the new model element and existing model elements. Note that the new model element must depend on existing model elements.

Definition 6. *Let $\mathcal{SM} = \langle \text{ME}, \prec, \overset{1}{\omega}, \cdots, \overset{n}{\omega}, \overset{1}{\tau}, \cdots, \overset{m}{\tau}, vs, ve \rangle$ and $\mathcal{SM}' = \langle \text{ME}', \prec', \overset{1}{\omega}', \cdots, \overset{n}{\omega}', \overset{1}{\tau}', \cdots, \overset{m}{\tau}', vs', ve' \rangle$ be two structure models.*

$\mathcal{SM}$ can evolve into $\mathcal{SM}'$ by adding a new model element e of type T, which traces all model elements in set $\mathcal{E}$, denoted $\mathcal{SM} \overset{add[e;T;\mathcal{E}]}{\Longrightarrow} \mathcal{SM}'$, if the following conditions hold:

(1) $\overset{trace}{\omega} \in \{\overset{1}{\omega}, \cdots, \overset{n}{\omega}\}$,
(2) $e \notin \mathrm{ME} \wedge \mathcal{E} \subseteq \mathrm{ME} \wedge T \in \{\overset{1}{\tau}, \cdots, \overset{m}{\tau}\}$,
(3) $\mathrm{ME}' = \mathrm{ME} \cup \{e\}$,
(4) $\prec' = \prec$,
(5) $\forall \overset{i}{\omega'} \in \{\overset{1}{\omega'}, \cdots, \overset{n}{\omega'}\} : \overset{i}{\omega'} = \begin{cases} \overset{i}{\omega} \cup \{(e, e') \mid e' \in \mathcal{E}\}, & \overset{i}{\omega} = \overset{trace}{\omega} \\ \overset{i}{\omega}, & otherwise \end{cases}$,
(6) $\forall \overset{j}{\tau'} \in \{\overset{1}{\tau'}, \cdots, \overset{m}{\tau'}\} : \overset{j}{\tau'} = \begin{cases} \overset{j}{\tau} \cup \{e\}, & \overset{j}{\tau} = T \\ \overset{j}{\tau}, & otherwise \end{cases}$, and
(7) $\forall x \in \mathrm{ME}' : vs'(x) = \begin{cases} \mathcal{V}(\mathcal{SM}), & x = e \\ vs(x), & otherwise \end{cases} \wedge ve'(x) = \begin{cases} \infty, & x = e \\ ve(x), & otherwise \end{cases}$.

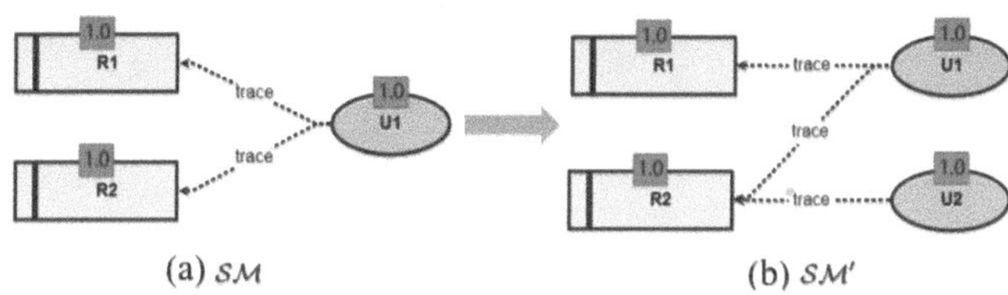

(a) $\mathcal{SM}$ (b) $\mathcal{SM}'$

Fig. 2. Adding a model element

An example of adding model elements is given in Fig. 2. The evolution from $\mathcal{SM}$ to $\mathcal{SM}'$ can be denoted as $\mathcal{SM} \overset{add[U2;\overset{useCase}{\tau};\{R2\}]}{\Longrightarrow} \mathcal{SM}'$, which means adding a new use case $U2$ and letting it trace the existing model element $R2$.

3.2 Inactivating a Model Element

When some software artifacts is outdated or redundant, a common operation is to delete them. However, we choose inactivation instead of deletion because the latter may destroy the inner structure of the software system. Inactivating a model element is to convert its final version number from undetermined to determined, which means the model element is not needed for now. The inactivation consists of only one step.

(1) Set the final version number for a given model element.

Definition 7. *Let* $\mathcal{SM} = \langle \mathrm{ME}, \prec, \overset{1}{\omega}, \cdots, \overset{n}{\omega}, \overset{1}{\tau}, \cdots, \overset{m}{\tau}, vs, ve \rangle$ *and* $\mathcal{SM}' = \langle \mathrm{ME}', \prec', \overset{1}{\omega'}, \cdots, \overset{n}{\omega'}, \overset{1}{\tau'}, \cdots, \overset{m}{\tau'}, vs', ve' \rangle$ *be two structure models.*

$\mathcal{SM}$ can evolve into $\mathcal{SM}'$ by inactivating a model element e, denoted $\mathcal{SM} \overset{ina[e]}{\Longrightarrow} \mathcal{SM}'$, if the following conditions hold:

(1) $e \in \mathrm{ME} \wedge ve(e) = \infty$,

(2) $\mathrm{ME}' = \mathrm{ME}$,
(3) $\prec' = \prec$,
(4) $\forall \overset{i}{\omega'} \in \{\overset{1}{\omega'}, \cdots, \overset{n}{\omega'}\} : \overset{i}{\omega'} = \overset{i}{\omega}$,
(5) $\forall \overset{j}{\tau'} \in \{\overset{1}{\tau'}, \cdots, \overset{m}{\tau'}\} : \overset{j}{\tau'} = \overset{j}{\tau}$, *and*
(6) $\forall x \in \mathrm{ME}' : vs'(x) = vs(x) \wedge ve'(x) = \begin{cases} vs(x), & x = e \\ ve(x), & otherwise \end{cases}$.

For example, the evolution from $\mathcal{SM}$ to $\mathcal{SM}'$ in Fig. 3 can be denoted as $\mathcal{SM} \overset{ina[U2]}{\Longrightarrow} \mathcal{SM}'$, which means the model element $U2$ is inactivated. Certainly, if $U1$ needs to be used again, then we can reactivate it. Moreover, inactive model elements are displayed as *transparent* in our tool.

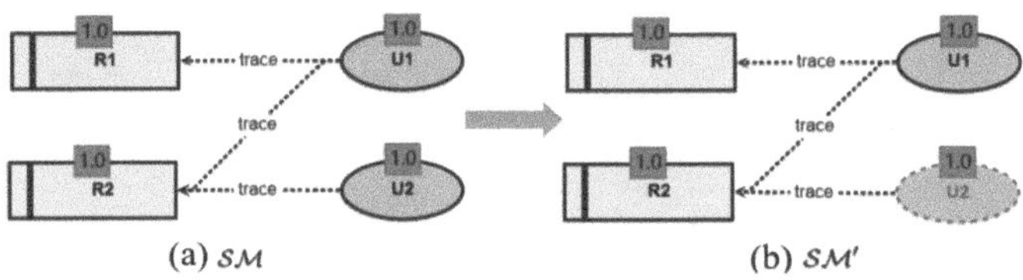

(a) $\mathcal{SM}$ (b) $\mathcal{SM}'$

Fig. 3. Inactivating a model element

3.3 Modifying a Model Element

Like the addition, the modification is also one of the important management operations. To preserve the traceability, we cannot remove the old model element. Thus, the modification operation contains the three steps:

(1) Inactivate the given (modified) model element, and make a copy of it.
(2) Modify the copy according to requirements, and assign a version number to it.
(3) Create the *modify* relation between the original model element and the newly obtained model element.
(4) Create specific relations between the newly obtained model element and the others according to the original structure.

Definition 8. *Let* $\mathcal{SM} = \langle \mathrm{ME}, \prec, \overset{1}{\omega}, \cdots, \overset{n}{\omega}, \overset{1}{\tau}, \cdots, \overset{m}{\tau}, vs, ve\rangle$ *and* $\mathcal{SM}' = \langle \mathrm{ME}', \prec', \overset{1}{\omega'}, \cdots, \overset{n}{\omega'}, \overset{1}{\tau'}, \cdots, \overset{m}{\tau'}, vs', ve'\rangle$ *be two structure models.*

$\mathcal{SM}$ can evolve into $\mathcal{SM}'$ by modifying a model element e_1 to a new model element e_2, denoted $\mathcal{SM} \overset{mod[e_1;e_2]}{\Longrightarrow} \mathcal{SM}'$, if the following conditions hold:

(1) $\overset{modify}{\omega} \in \{\overset{1}{\omega}, \cdots, \overset{n}{\omega}\}$,

(2) $e_1 \in \mathrm{ME} \wedge e_2 \notin \mathrm{ME} \wedge (\exists v \in \mathbf{VN} : vs(e_1) \leq v) \wedge ve(e_1) = \infty$,
(3) $\mathrm{ME}' = \mathrm{ME} \cup \{e_2\}$,
(4) $\prec' = \prec \cup \{(e_2, x) \mid x \in \mathrm{ME}, (e_1, x) \in \prec\}$,

$$(5)\ \forall \overset{i}{\omega'} \in \{\overset{1}{\omega'}, \cdots, \overset{n}{\omega'}\} : \overset{i}{\omega'} = \begin{cases} \overset{i}{\omega} \cup \{(e_2, e_1)\}, & \overset{i}{\omega} \overset{modify}{=} \omega \\ \overset{i}{\omega} \cup \{(e_2, x) \mid x \in \mathrm{ME}, (e_1, x) \in \overset{i}{\omega}\}, & otherwise \end{cases},$$

$$(6)\ \forall \overset{j}{\tau'} \in \{\overset{1}{\tau'}, \cdots, \overset{m}{\tau'}\} : \overset{j}{\tau'} = \begin{cases} \overset{j}{\tau} \cup \{e_2\}, & e_1 \in \overset{j}{\tau} \\ \overset{j}{\tau}, & otherwise \end{cases}, \ and$$

$$(7)\ \forall x \in \mathrm{ME}' : vs'(x) = \begin{cases} v, & x = e_2 \\ vs(x), & otherwise \end{cases} \wedge ve'(x) = \begin{cases} vs(x), & x = e_1 \\ \infty, & x = e_2 \\ ve(x), & otherwise \end{cases}.$$

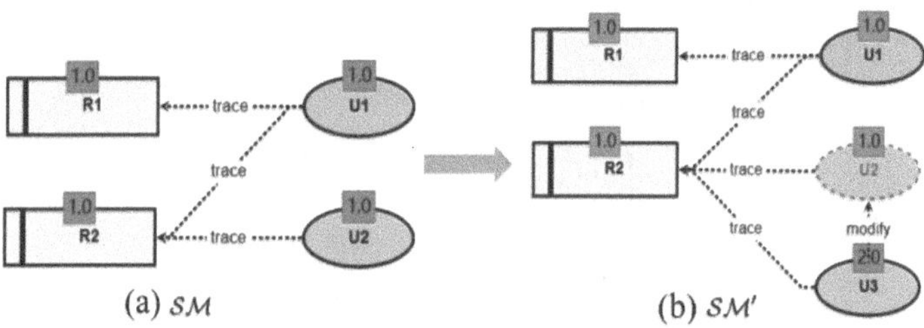

Fig. 4. Modifying a model element

In Fig. 4, the model element $U2$ is inactivated, and the new model element $U3$ is obtained from $U2$ through modification. Obviously, this evolution can be represented as $\mathcal{SM} \overset{mod[U2;U3]}{\Longrightarrow} \mathcal{SM}'$ by Definition 8.

In order to distinguish between different version numbers, once a model element is assigned a new version number, the old version number will become *grey* in our tool.

3.4 Modifying a Dependency Relation

Changing a dependency relation in fact changes the connection of two model elements. To preserve the traceability, we must store a copy of the original dependency relation. However, it is not reasonable to independently store the relation without considering related model elements. So we give the following concrete steps.

(1) Select one of the two model elements connected by the dependency relation (mostly the former in the dependency relation is preferred because the depended model element should be more stable).
(2) Inactivate the selected model element, and make a copy of it.

(3) Assign a version number to the copy, and create the *copy* relation between the copy and the selected model element.
(4) Create the specific relation between the copy and the original existing model element according to requirements.

Definition 9. *Let* $\mathcal{SM} = \langle \mathrm{ME}, \prec, \overset{1}{\omega}, \cdots, \overset{n}{\omega}, \overset{1}{\tau}, \cdots, \overset{m}{\tau}, vs, ve\rangle$ *and* $\mathcal{SM}' = \langle \mathrm{ME}', \prec', \overset{1}{\omega'}, \cdots, \overset{n}{\omega'}, \overset{1}{\tau'}, \cdots, \overset{m}{\tau'}, vs', ve'\rangle$ *be two structure models.*

$\mathcal{SM}$ can evolve into $\mathcal{SM}'$ by modifying the type of relation between model elements e_1 and e_2 to type R, denoted $\mathcal{SM} \overset{modR[(e_1,e_2);R]}{\Longrightarrow} \mathcal{SM}'$, if the following conditions hold:

(1) $\overset{copy}{\omega} \in \{\overset{1}{\omega}, \cdots, \overset{n}{\omega}\}$,
(2) $(e_1, e_2) \in ((\overset{1}{\omega} \cup \cdots \cup \overset{n}{\omega}) \setminus R) \wedge R \in (\{\prec, \overset{1}{\omega}, \cdots, \overset{n}{\omega}\} \setminus \{\overset{copy}{\omega}\}) \wedge (\exists v \in \mathbf{VN} : vs(e_1) \leq v) \wedge ve(e_1) = \infty$,
(3) $\mathrm{ME}' = \mathrm{ME} \cup \{e_1'\}$ *(e_1' is the copy of e_1),*
(4) $\prec' = \begin{cases} \prec \cup \{(e_1', e_2)\}, & \prec = R \\ \prec, & otherwise \end{cases}$,
(5) $\forall \overset{i}{\omega'} \in \{\overset{1}{\omega'}, \cdots, \overset{n}{\omega'}\} : \overset{i}{\omega'} = \begin{cases} \overset{i}{\omega} \cup \{(e_1', e_1)\}, & \overset{i}{\omega} = \overset{copy}{\omega} \\ \overset{i}{\omega} \cup \{(e_1', e_2)\}, & \overset{i}{\omega} = R \\ \overset{i}{\omega}, & otherwise \end{cases}$,
(6) $\forall \overset{j}{\tau'} \in \{\overset{1}{\tau'}, \cdots, \overset{m}{\tau'}\} : \overset{j}{\tau'} = \begin{cases} \overset{j}{\tau} \cup \{e_1'\}, & e_1 \in \overset{j}{\tau} \\ \overset{j}{\tau}, & otherwise \end{cases}$, *and*
(7) $\forall x \in \mathrm{ME}' : vs'(x) = \begin{cases} v, & x = e_1' \\ vs(x), & otherwise \end{cases} \wedge ve'(x) = \begin{cases} vs(x), & x = e_1 \\ \infty, & x = e_1' \\ ve(x), & otherwise \end{cases}$.

As shown in Fig. 5, the evolution from $\mathcal{SM}$ to $\mathcal{SM}'$ can be denoted as $\mathcal{SM} \overset{modR[(U2,U1);\overset{include}{\omega}]}{\Longrightarrow} \mathcal{SM}'$, which means that a new relation of type *include* is created according to the original relation $(U2, U1)$.

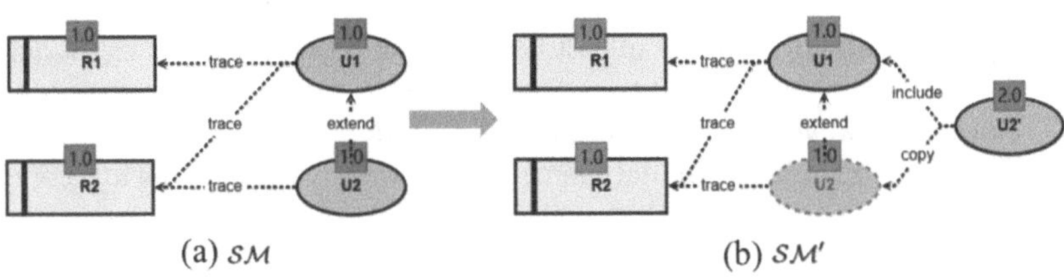

Fig. 5. Modifying a dependency relation

3.5 Relocating a Model Element

Relocation is to move a model element to a new place. The operation consists of the following steps.

(1) Inactivate the relocated model element, and make a copy of it.
(2) Assign a version number to the copy, and create the *copy* relation between the copy and the relocated model element.
(3) Create the *trace* relations between the copy and existing model elements.

Definition 10. *Let* $\mathcal{SM} = \langle \mathrm{ME}, \prec, \overset{1}{\omega}, \cdots, \overset{n}{\omega}, \overset{1}{\tau}, \cdots, \overset{m}{\tau}, vs, ve \rangle$ *and* $\mathcal{SM}' = \langle \mathrm{ME}', \prec', \overset{1}{\omega'}, \cdots, \overset{n}{\omega'}, \overset{1}{\tau'}, \cdots, \overset{m}{\tau'}, vs', ve' \rangle$ *be two structure models.*

$\mathcal{SM}$ can evolve into $\mathcal{SM}'$ by relocating a model element e which traces all model elements in set $\mathcal{E}$, denoted $\mathcal{SM} \overset{rel[e;\mathcal{E}]}{\Longrightarrow} \mathcal{SM}'$, if the following conditions hold:

(1) $\overset{copy}{\omega}, \overset{trace}{\omega} \in \{\overset{1}{\omega}, \cdots, \overset{n}{\omega}\}$,
(2) $e \in \mathrm{ME} \wedge \mathcal{E} \subseteq \mathrm{ME} \wedge (\exists v \in \mathbf{VN} : vs(e) \leq v) \wedge ve(e) = \infty$,
(3) $\mathrm{ME}' = \mathrm{ME} \cup \{e'\}$ *(e' is the copy of e),*
(4) $\prec' = \prec$,

(5) $\forall \overset{i}{\omega'} \in \{\overset{1}{\omega'}, \cdots, \overset{n}{\omega'}\} : \overset{i}{\omega'} = \begin{cases} \overset{i}{\omega} \cup \{(e', e)\}, & \overset{i}{\omega} = \overset{copy}{\omega} \\ \overset{i}{\omega} \cup \{(e', x) \mid x \in \mathcal{E}\}, & \overset{i}{\omega} = \overset{trace}{\omega} \\ \overset{i}{\omega}, & otherwise \end{cases}$,

(6) $\forall \overset{j}{\tau'} \in \{\overset{1}{\tau'}, \cdots, \overset{m}{\tau'}\} : \overset{j}{\tau'} = \begin{cases} \overset{j}{\tau} \cup \{e'\}, & e \in \overset{j}{\tau} \\ \overset{j}{\tau}, & otherwise \end{cases}$, *and*

(7) $\forall x \in \mathrm{ME}' : vs'(x) = \begin{cases} v, & x = e' \\ vs(x), & otherwise \end{cases} \wedge ve'(x) = \begin{cases} vs(x), & x = e \\ \infty, & x = e' \\ ve(x), & otherwise \end{cases}$.

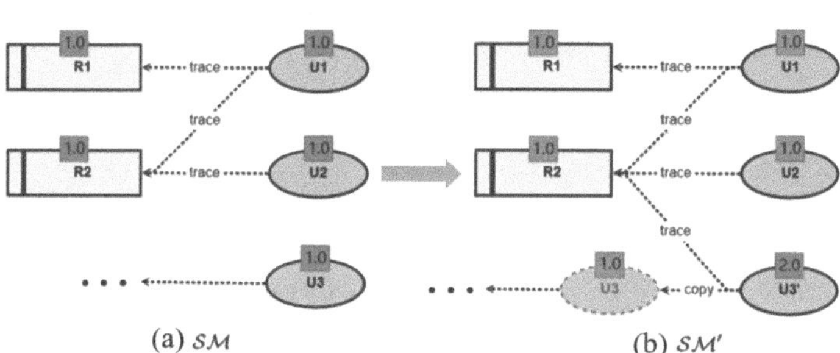

(a) $\mathcal{SM}$ (b) $\mathcal{SM}'$

Fig. 6. Relocating a model element

For example, the model element $U3$ is relocated such that the copy $U3'$ trace the existing model element $R2$ in Fig. 6. By Definition 10, this evolution can be denoted as $\mathcal{SM} \overset{rel[U3,\{R2\}]}{\Longrightarrow} \mathcal{SM}'$.

3.6 Replacing a Model Element

Replacing a model element contains the following three step.

(1) Inactivate the destination model element (used for replacement), and make a copy of it.
(2) Assign a version number to the copy, and create the *copy* relation between the copy and the destination model element.
(3) Inactivate the replaced model element, and create the *replace* relation between the copy and the replaced model element.
(4) Create specific relations between the copy and the others according to the original structure.

Definition 11. *Let* $\mathcal{SM} = \langle \mathrm{ME}, \prec, \overset{1}{\omega}, \cdots, \overset{n}{\omega}, \overset{1}{\tau}, \cdots, \overset{m}{\tau}, vs, ve \rangle$ *and* $\mathcal{SM}' = \langle \mathrm{ME}', \prec', \overset{1}{\omega'}, \cdots, \overset{n}{\omega'}, \overset{1}{\tau'}, \cdots, \overset{m}{\tau'}, vs', ve' \rangle$ *be two structure models.*

$\mathcal{SM}$ can evolve into $\mathcal{SM}'$ by replacing the model element e_1 by existing model element e_2, denoted $\mathcal{SM} \overset{rep[e_1;e_2]}{\Longrightarrow} \mathcal{SM}'$, if the following conditions hold:

(1) $\overset{copy}{\omega}, \overset{replace}{\omega} \in \{\overset{1}{\omega}, \cdots, \overset{n}{\omega}\}$,
(2) $e_1, e_2 \in \mathrm{ME} \wedge (\exists v \in \mathbf{VN} : vs(e_2) \leq v) \wedge ve(e_1) = ve(e_2) = \infty$,
(3) $\mathrm{ME}' = \mathrm{ME} \cup \{e_2'\}$ *(e_2' is the copy of e_2),*
(4) $\prec' = \prec \cup \{(e_2', x) \mid x \in \mathrm{ME}, (e_1, x) \in \prec\}$,
(5) $\forall \overset{i}{\omega'} \in \{\overset{1}{\omega'}, \cdots, \overset{n}{\omega'}\} : \overset{i}{\omega'} = \begin{cases} \overset{i}{\omega} \cup \{(e_2', e_2)\}, & \overset{i}{\omega} = \overset{copy}{\omega} \\ \overset{i}{\omega} \cup \{(e_2', e_1)\}, & \overset{i}{\omega} = \overset{replace}{\omega} \\ \overset{i}{\omega} \cup \{(e_2', x) \mid x \in \mathrm{ME}, (e_1, x) \in \overset{i}{\omega}\}, & otherwise \end{cases}$,
(6) $\forall \overset{j}{\tau'} \in \{\overset{1}{\tau'}, \cdots, \overset{m}{\tau'}\} : \overset{j}{\tau'} = \begin{cases} \overset{j}{\tau} \cup \{e_2'\}, & e_2 \in \overset{j}{\tau} \\ \overset{j}{\tau}, & otherwise \end{cases}$, *and*
(7) $\forall x \in \mathrm{ME}' : vs'(x) = \begin{cases} v, & x = e_2' \\ vs(x), & otherwise \end{cases} \wedge ve'(x) = \begin{cases} vs(x), & x = e_1 \vee x = e_2 \\ \infty, & x = e_2' \\ ve(x), & otherwise \end{cases}$.

For example, the new model element $U3'$ is a copy of the old model element $U3$ and is used to replace the old model element $U2$ in Fig. 7. By Definition 11, this evolution can be denoted as $\mathcal{SM} \overset{rep[U2,U3]}{\Longrightarrow} \mathcal{SM}'$.

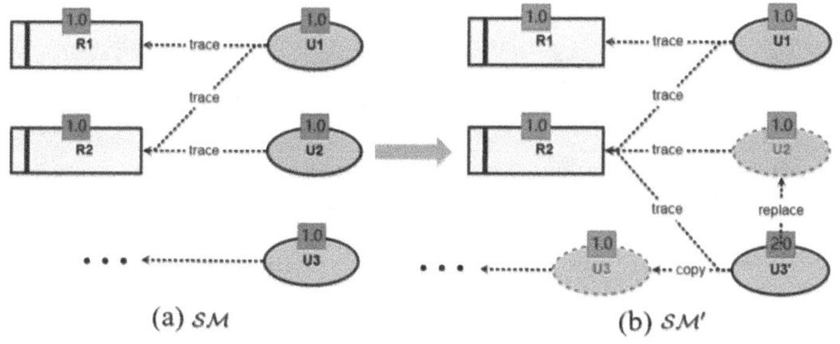

Fig. 7. Replacing a model element

3.7 Merging Two Model Elements

Unlike traditional merging methods, the merging operation has these steps.

(1) Create a new model element to store the result of the merging operation, and assign a version number to it.
(2) Inactivate all merged model elements, and create the *containment* relations between each of them and the new model element.
(3) Create specific relations between the new model element and the others according to the original structure.

Definition 12. *Let* $\mathcal{SM} = \langle \mathrm{ME}, \prec, \overset{1}{\omega}, \cdots, \overset{n}{\omega}, \overset{1}{\tau}, \cdots, \overset{m}{\tau}, vs, ve\rangle$ *and* $\mathcal{SM}' = \langle \mathrm{ME}', \prec', \overset{1}{\omega'}, \cdots, \overset{n}{\omega'}, \overset{1}{\tau'}, \cdots, \overset{m}{\tau'}, vs', ve'\rangle$ *be two structure models.*

$\mathcal{SM}$ can evolve into $\mathcal{SM}'$ by merging two model elements e_1 and e_2, denoted $\mathcal{SM} \overset{mer[e_1;e_2]}{\Longrightarrow} \mathcal{SM}'$, if the following conditions hold:

(1) $(\exists T \in \{\overset{1}{\tau}, \cdots, \overset{m}{\tau}\} : e_1 \in T \wedge e_2 \in T) \wedge ve(e_1) = ve(e_2) = \infty$,
(2) $\mathrm{ME}' = \mathrm{ME} \cup \{e_1\&e_2\}$ *($e_1\&e_2$ by merging e_1 and e_2),*
(3) $\prec' = \prec \cup\{(e_1, e_1\&e_2), (e_2, e_1\&e_2)\} \cup \{(e_1\&e_2, x) \mid x \in \mathrm{ME}, (e_1, x) \in \prec \vee (e_2, x) \in \prec\}$,
(4) $\forall \overset{i}{\omega'} \in \{\overset{1}{\omega'}, \cdots, \overset{n}{\omega'}\} : \overset{i}{\omega'} = \overset{i}{\omega} \cup \{(e_1\&e_2, x) \mid x \in \mathrm{ME}, (e_1, x) \in \overset{i}{\omega} \vee (e_2, x) \in \overset{i}{\omega}\}$,
(5) $\forall \overset{j}{\tau'} \in \{\overset{1}{\tau'}, \cdots, \overset{m}{\tau'}\} : \overset{j}{\tau'} = \overset{j}{\tau} \cup \{e_1\&e_2 \mid e_1 \in \overset{j}{\tau} \wedge e_2 \in \overset{j}{\tau}\}$, *and*
(6) $\forall x \in \mathrm{ME}' : vs'(x) = \begin{cases} \mathcal{V}(\mathcal{SM}), & x = e_1\&e_2 \\ vs(x), & otherwise \end{cases} \wedge ve'(x) = \begin{cases} vs(x), & x = e_1 \vee x = e_2 \\ \infty, & x = e_1\&e_2 \\ ve(x), & otherwise \end{cases}$.

For example, the two model elements $U1$ and $U2$ are merged into the new model element $U1\&U2$ in Fig. 8 where $U1$ and $U2$ are two children of $U1\&U2$. Obviously, this evolution can be denoted as $\mathcal{SM} \overset{mer[U1,U2]}{\Longrightarrow} \mathcal{SM}'$.

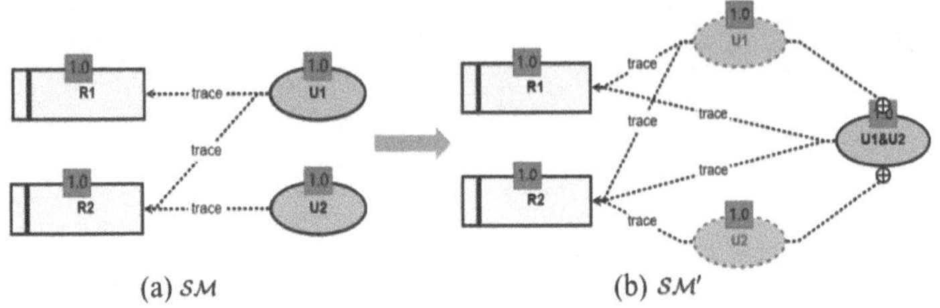

Fig. 8. Merging two model elements

3.8 Decomposing a Model Element

The decomposition operation includes the following steps.

(1) Create a given number of model elements as submodules, and assign version numbers to them.
(2) Inactivate the decomposed model element, and create the *containment* relations between them and the submodules.
(3) Create specific relations between the submodules and the others according to the original structure.

Definition 13. *Let* $\mathcal{SM} = \langle \mathrm{ME}, \prec, \overset{1}{\omega}, \cdots, \overset{n}{\omega}, \overset{1}{\tau}, \cdots, \overset{m}{\tau}, vs, ve\rangle$ *and* $\mathcal{SM}' = \langle \mathrm{ME}', \prec', \overset{1}{\omega'}, \cdots, \overset{n}{\omega'}, \overset{1}{\tau'}, \cdots, \overset{m}{\tau'}, vs', ve'\rangle$ *be two structure models.*

$\mathcal{SM}$ can evolve into $\mathcal{SM}'$ by decomposing a model element e into p submodules, denoted $\mathcal{SM} \overset{dec[e;p]}{\Longrightarrow} \mathcal{SM}'$, if the following conditions hold:

(1) $e \in \mathrm{ME} \wedge p \in \mathbb{N}^* \setminus \{1\} \wedge ve(e) = \infty$,

(2) $\mathrm{ME}' = \mathrm{ME} \cup \bigcup_{q=1}^{p} \{e.q\}$ *(e.q is the submodules of e),*

(3) $\prec' = \prec \cup \bigcup_{q=1}^{p} (\{(e.q, e)\} \cup \{(e.q, x) \mid x \in \mathrm{ME}, (e, x) \in \prec\})$,

(4) $\forall\, \overset{i}{\omega'} \in \{\overset{1}{\omega'}, \cdots, \overset{n}{\omega'}\} : \overset{i}{\omega'} = \overset{i}{\omega} \cup \bigcup_{q=1}^{p} \{(e.q, x) \mid x \in \mathrm{ME}, (e, x) \in \overset{i}{\omega}\}$,

(5) $\forall\, \overset{j}{\tau'} \in \{\overset{1}{\tau'}, \cdots, \overset{m}{\tau'}\} : \overset{j}{\tau'} = \begin{cases} \overset{j}{\tau} \cup \bigcup_{q=1}^{p} \{e.q\}, & e \in \overset{j}{\tau} \\ \overset{j}{\tau}, & otherwise \end{cases}$ *, and*

(6) $\forall x \in \mathrm{ME}' : vs'(x) = \begin{cases} \mathcal{V}(\mathcal{SM}), & \bigvee_{q=1}^{p} (x = e.q) \\ vs(x), & otherwise \end{cases} \wedge\ ve'(x) = \begin{cases} vs(x), & x = e \\ \infty, & \bigvee_{q=1}^{p} (x = e.q) \\ ve(x), & otherwise \end{cases}$.

The evolution from $\mathcal{SM}$ to $\mathcal{SM}'$ (see Fig. 9) can be denoted as $\mathcal{SM} \overset{dec[U2;2]}{\Longrightarrow} \mathcal{SM}'$, which means the model element $U1$ is decomposed into two model elements $U2.1, U2.2$.

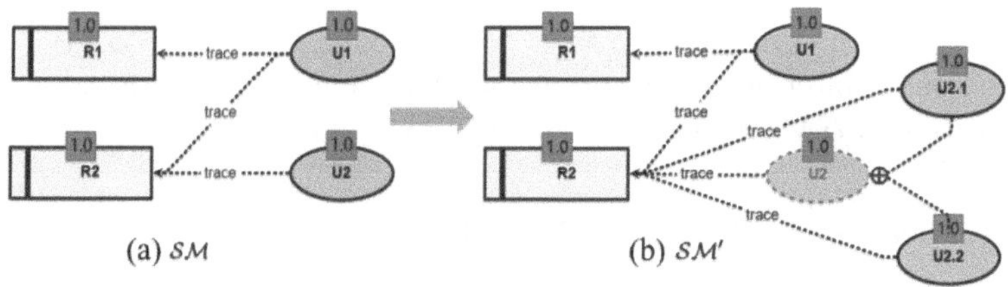

Fig. 9. Decomposing a model element

3.9 Maintenance of Traceability

In this subsection, we will discuss whether traceability is maintained after the execution of these eight management operations.

Proposition 2. *Let $\mathcal{SM}$ and $\mathcal{SM}'$ be two structure models. Assume that there exists a meta path $\mathcal{P}$ in $\mathcal{SM}$. $\mathcal{SM}'$ is traceable via $\mathcal{P}$, if the following conditions hold:*

(1) $\mathcal{SM}$ is traceable via $\mathcal{P}$, and
(2) there exists an operation $\sigma[\lambda_1; \lambda_2; \cdots]$ (one of the eight operations mentioned above) such that $\mathcal{SM} \overset{\sigma[\lambda_1;\lambda_2;\cdots]}{\Longrightarrow} \mathcal{SM}'$.

Proof. This proof is straightforward.

Essentially, we formalize these operations without polluting the original structure model [14]. An obvious benefit lies in the fact that if the original structure model was traceable, the formal operations will not break traceability.

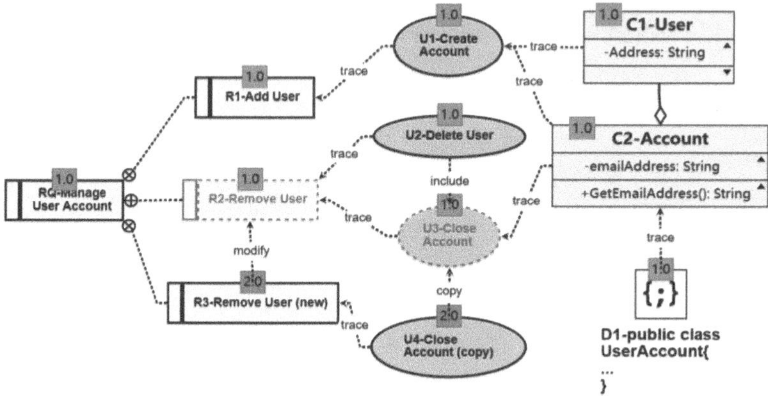

Fig. 10. A new structure model $\mathcal{SM}_1$ evolved from $\mathcal{SM}$(see Fig. 1)

For example, the structure model $\mathcal{SM}_1$ in Fig. 10 is obtained from $\mathcal{SM}$ (see Fig. 1) after two operations: modifying the model element $R2$ and relocating the model element $U3$, denoted by $\mathcal{SM} \overset{mod[R2;R3]}{\Longrightarrow} \mathcal{SM}' \overset{rel[U3;\{R3\}]}{\Longrightarrow} \mathcal{SM}_1$ ($\mathcal{SM}'$ is considered as an intermediate structure model). Since $\mathcal{SM}$ is traceable via $\mathcal{P}_1$, by Proposition 2, $\mathcal{SM}_1$ is still traceable via $\mathcal{P}_1$.

3.10 Restriction of Structure Models

As the above eight management operations do not delete any model elements or relations, the size of the system grows rapidly as it evolves. Hence, how to get proper subsystems through the restriction [22] is an issue that needs to be solved.

The implementation of version control is one of the options for improving the quality of traceability [10]. For a meta path $\mathcal{P} = X_1 \overset{R_1}{\rightarrow} X_2 \overset{R_2}{\rightarrow} \cdots \overset{R_{l-1}}{\rightarrow} X_l$, we can denote the set of model elements (along $\mathcal{P}$) that are under version control as $\varphi(\mathcal{P}) = X_1 \cup (\bigcup_{x \in X_1} \bigcup_{h \in \{1,\cdots,|\mathcal{P}|\}} \{x' \in Tr(x \overset{\mathcal{P}:h}{\rightarrow}) \mid vs(x') = vs(x)\})$, i.e., all model elements in $\varphi(\mathcal{P})$ have the same initial version number. Next, we will explore how to restrict structure models under version control.

Definition 14. *Let* $\mathcal{SM} = \langle \mathrm{ME}, \prec, \overset{1}{\omega}, \cdots, \overset{n}{\omega}, \overset{1}{\tau}, \cdots, \overset{m}{\tau}, vs, ve \rangle$ *be a structure model. Assume that there exists a meta path* $\mathcal{P}$ *in* $\mathcal{SM}$, *the restriction of* $\mathcal{SM}$ *to* $\mathcal{P}$ *is defined as a structure model* $\mathcal{SM} |_{\mathcal{P}} = \langle \mathrm{ME}', \prec', \overset{1}{\omega'}, \cdots, \overset{n}{\omega'}, \overset{1}{\tau'}, \cdots, \overset{m}{\tau'}, vs', ve' \rangle$ *with*

- $\mathrm{ME}' = \varphi(\mathcal{P})$,
- $\prec' = \{(x, y) \in \prec \mid x \in \varphi(\mathcal{P}) \wedge y \in \varphi(\mathcal{P})\}$,
- $\forall \overset{i}{\omega'} \in \{\overset{1}{\omega'}, \cdots, \overset{n}{\omega'}\} : \overset{i}{\omega'} = \{(x, y) \in \overset{i}{\omega} \mid x \in \varphi(\mathcal{P}) \wedge y \in \varphi(\mathcal{P})\}$,
- $\forall \overset{j}{\tau'} \in \{\overset{1}{\tau'}, \cdots, \overset{m}{\tau'}\} : \overset{j}{\tau'} = \overset{j}{\tau} \cap \varphi(\mathcal{P})$, *and*
- $\forall x \in \mathrm{ME}' : vs'(x) = vs(x) \wedge ve'(x) = ve(x)$.

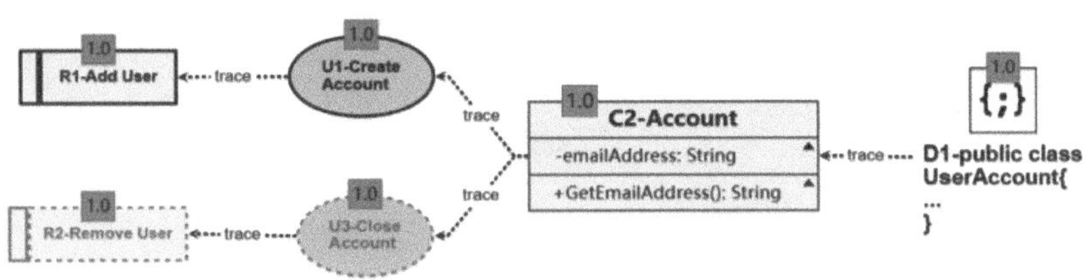

Fig. 11. The restriction of $\mathcal{SM}_1$ (see Fig. 10) to $\mathcal{P}_1$

For example, since $\varphi(\mathcal{P}_1) = \{R1, R2, U1, U3, C2, D1\}$ in Fig. 10, the restriction of $\mathcal{SM}_1$ to $\mathcal{P}_1$ can be represented by $\mathcal{SM}_1 |_{\mathcal{P}_1}$ in Fig. 11. Obviously, the developer can decompose the original system into subsystems under version control based on a given meta path.

4 Tool

To support our work, a prototype tool called Formalized Software Management System (FSMS) was developed to visualize traceability, which has been deployed on the website http://124.220.63.75/ now. Our tool not only realizes the 8 management operations mentioned above, but also implements several analysis function, such as change impact analysis and consistency checking [2,23]. More functions will be added to this tool step by step.

5 Related Work

Software traceability has been studied for many years (e.g. see [19,21,25] for surveys). In this section, we only discuss the differences between our work and the most relevant work in five aspects: extensibility, flexibility, navigability, version control and formal method (summarized from the literature [10,12,17]). Some of the evaluation results are shown in Table 1.

Lago et al. [8] give a scoped approach to identify core traceability paths and distinguish four relations in R&A: drive, depend-on, modify and influence. However, the limitation on the number of relations makes this method difficult to extend. Raţiu et al. [17] outline which properties of traceability can unleash the potential of traces, and present a framework for establishing traceability across tools. Unfortunately, their work is informal. Our work involves the formal method which helps to present rigorous semantics for software traceability in order to model, design, and reason.

Wen et al. [24] use a formal model called a behavior tree to represent functional requirements in order to ensure the integrity of change management and automatically obtain evolutionary design documents that record the change history of the designs. This work provides a semantic for traceability in terms of a logical basis for artifacts and their traces which is different from our approach.

Goknil et al. [5], the authors present an approach for generation and validation of traces between requirements and architecture with a tool support. A trace metamodel is defined with commonly used trace types between requirements and architecture. The requirements relations are captured in a model and the software architecture is expressed in the Architecture Analysis and Design Language (AADL) [4]. Model checking is used for verification and simulation of architecture models based on the available dynamic semantics of AADL. This study only focuses on the traceability between requirements and architecture, whereas our work supports the traceability in software lifecycle process.

Maro et al. [10] identify the core factors affecting the quality of traceability, and use bidirectional transformations (bx) to maintain traceability during the evolution of the software. However, bx mainly focuses on consistency between model spaces under abstract operations, while our work considers how to maintain traceability under concrete management operations.

6 Conclusion and Future Work

We have shown how to formally construct traceability, and maintain traceability under various management operations in the whole software life cycle. A prototype tool has been developed to semi-automatically establish and maintain traceability information. In the future work, since automated code generation is another research field of ours and its code templates and generation rules heavily rely on the traceability, we will investigate how to facilitate code generation in the software development process.

Table 1. Comparison of our approach with existing approaches

	Extensibility	Flexibility	Navigability	Version control	Formal method
Lago et al. [8]	○	◐	●	○	○
Wen et al. [24]	○	○	◐	●	●
Goknil et al. [5]	◐	●	◐	○	●
Raţiu et al. [17]	●	●	●	○	○
Maro et al. [10]	●	●	●	◐	◐
Our approach	●	●	●	●	●

○: Not supported; ◐: Partially supported; ●: Fully supported

References

1. Anquetil, N., et al.: A model-driven traceability framework for software product lines. Softw. Syst. Model. **9**(4), 427–451 (2010). https://doi.org/10.1007/s10270-009-0120-9
2. Demuth, A., Kretschmer, R., Egyed, A., Maes, D.: Introducing traceability and consistency checking for change impact analysis across engineering tools in an automation solution company: an experience report. In: 2016 IEEE International Conference on Software Maintenance and Evolution (ICSME), pp. 529–538. IEEE (2016)
3. Espinoza, A., Garbajosa, J.: A study to support agile methods more effectively through traceability. Innov. Syst. Softw. Eng. **7**(1), 53–69 (2011). https://doi.org/10.1007/s11334-011-0144-5
4. Feiler, P.H., Gluch, D.P.: Model-based engineering with AADL: an introduction to the SAE architecture analysis & design language. Addison-Wesley (2012)
5. Goknil, A., Kurtev, I., van den Berg, K.: Generation and validation of traces between requirements and architecture based on formal trace semantics. J. Syst. Softw. **88**, 112–137 (2014). https://doi.org/10.1016/j.jss.2013.10.006
6. Guana, V., Stroulia, E.: End-to-end model-transformation comprehension through fine-grained traceability information. Softw. Syst. Model. **18**(2), 1305–1344 (2019). https://doi.org/10.1007/s10270-017-0602-0
7. Jayatilleke, S., Lai, R., Reed, K.: A method of requirements change analysis. Requir. Eng. **23**(4), 493–508 (2018). https://doi.org/10.1007/s00766-017-0277-7
8. Lago, P., Muccini, H., van Vliet, H.: A scoped approach to traceability management. J. Syst. Softw. **82**(1), 168–182 (2009). https://doi.org/10.1016/j.jss.2008.08.026

9. Letelier, P.: A framework for requirements traceability in UML-based projects. In: Proceedings of the 1st International Workshop on Traceability in Emerging Forms of Software Engineering, pp. 30–41 (2002)
10. Maro, S., Anjorin, A., Wohlrab, R., Steghöfer, J.P.: Traceability maintenance: factors and guidelines. In: Proceedings of the 31st IEEE/ACM International Conference on Automated Software Engineering, pp. 414–425 (2016)
11. Maro, S., et al.: Managing traceability information models: not such a simple task after all? IEEE Softw. (2020)
12. Maro, S., Steghöfer, J.P., Staron, M.: Software traceability in the automotive domain: challenges and solutions. J. Syst. Softw. **141**, 85–110 (2018)
13. (OMG), O.M.G.: Omg unified modeling language tm (omg UML), version 2.5. OMG Document Number formal/2015-03-01, pp. 1–758 (2015). https://www.omg.org/spec/UML/2.5/
14. Pavalkis, S., Nemuraitė, L., Butkienė, R.: Derived properties: a user friendly approach to improving model traceability. Inf. Technol. Control **42**(1), 48–60 (2013)
15. Rahimi, M., Cleland-Huang, J.: Evolving software trace links between requirements and source code. Empir. Softw. Eng. **23**(4), 2198–2231 (2018). https://doi.org/10.1007/s10664-017-9561-x
16. Ramesh, B., Jarke, M.: Toward reference models of requirements traceability. IEEE Trans. Softw. Eng. **27**(1), 58–93 (2001). https://doi.org/10.1109/32.895989
17. Raţiu, C.C., Mayr-Dorn, C., Assunção, W.K., Egyed, A.: Taming cross-tool traceability in the wild. In: 2023 IEEE 31st International Requirements Engineering Conference (RE), pp. 233–243. IEEE (2023)
18. Shi, C., Kong, X., Yu, P.S., Xie, S., Wu, B.: Relevance search in heterogeneous networks. In: Proceedings of the 15th International Conference on Extending Database Technology, pp. 180–191 (2012)
19. Spanoudakis, G., Zisman, A.: Software traceability: a roadmap. In: Handbook of Software Engineering and Knowledge Engineering: Vol 3: Recent Advances, pp. 395–428. World Scientific (2005)
20. Sun, Y., Han, J., Yan, X., Yu, P.S., Wu, T.: PathSim: meta path-based top-k similarity search in heterogeneous information networks. Proc. VLDB Endowment **4**(11), 992–1003 (2011)
21. Torkar, R., Gorschek, T., Feldt, R., Svahnberg, M., Raja, U.A., Kamran, K.: Requirements traceability: a systematic review and industry case study. Int. J. Softw. Eng. Knowl. Eng. **22**(3), 385–434 (2012). https://doi.org/10.1142/S021819401250009X
22. Wen, H., Wu, J., Jiang, J., Li, J., Hong, Z.: A formal approach for traceability preservation in software development process. In: Cai, Z., Xiao, M., Zhang, J. (eds.) NCTCS 2023. Communications in Computer and Information Science, vol. 1944, pp. 18–35. Springer, Cham (2023). https://doi.org/10.1007/978-981-99-7743-7_2
23. Wen, H., Wu, J., Jiang, J., Tang, G., Hong, Z.: A formal approach for consistency management in UML models. Int. J. Softw. Eng. Knowl. Eng. **33**(05), 733–763 (2023)
24. Wen, L., Tuffley, D., Dromey, R.G.: Formalizing the transition from requirements' change to design change using an evolutionary traceability model. Innov. Syst. Softw. Eng. **10**(3), 181–202 (2014). https://doi.org/10.1007/s11334-014-0230-6
25. Winkler, S., von Pilgrim, J.: A survey of traceability in requirements engineering and model-driven development. Softw. Syst. Model. **9**(4), 529–565 (2010). https://doi.org/10.1007/s10270-009-0145-0

A Natural Formalized Proof Language

Lihan Xie, Zhicheng Hui, and Qinxiang Cao(✉)

Shanghai Jiao Tong University, Shanghai, China
{sheringham,laplace_demon}@sjtu.edu.cn, caoqinxiang@gmail.com

Abstract. Artificial intelligence assisted mathematical proof has become a highly focused area nowadays. One key problem in this field is to generate formal mathematical proofs from natural language proofs. Due to historical reasons, the formal proof languages adopted by traditional theorem provers were not intended to represent natural language proofs. Therefore, they are not well-suited for the aforementioned tasks and proof-checking work for educational purposes. In this paper, we design a proof language and its corresponding abstract syntax tree and implement a proof checking tool for it. This language can be easily converted from natural language, thus providing a rich corpus of formal proof. Additionally, it supports the handling of issues in informal proofs through static analysis, and enhances the expressive power of the language by introducing the structure of partial proofs. This design combines the expressiveness of natural language and the accuracy of formal language, resulting in an improved mathematical proof language.

Keywords: Formal proof language · Theorem proving · Static analysis

1 Introduction

Formal mathematical proofs are based on rigorous reasoning in formal logic, providing a completely accurate proof process that can be automatically verified by computers. Formalizing informal proofs can make them more convincing, as seen in the formal proof of the Four-Color Theorem [1,11]. Additionally, automated theorem proving relies on formal proof languages to generate rigorous proofs. The rise of large language models in recent years has spurred research in AI-assisted mathematical proof, particularly in the fields of automated theorem proving and transforming informal proofs into formal proofs [14,20]. This means that large language models can directly generate formal proofs or indirectly transform natural language proofs into formal proofs. These formal proofs can then be verified by theorem provers, ensuring their correctness.

Due to historical reasons, early versions of theorem provers were primarily focused on ensuring the correctness of proofs, rather than directly modelling natural language proofs. Subsequent developments, such as the Ltac [9] tactic language in Coq [2] and Isar [19] proof language in Isabelle [16], aimed to

L. Xie and Z. Hui—contributed equally to this work.

W.-N. Chin and Z. Xu (Eds.): TASE 2024, LNCS 14777, pp. 446–464, 2024.
https://doi.org/10.1007/978-3-031-64626-3_26

help with proof constructions. Commands in these languages can be seen as transformations that modify the current proof goal, where each proof goal comprises named premises and the conclusion that needs to be proved. However, it is still difficult to translate natural language proofs word-for-word into such formal proof languages. Consequently, for current applications like AI-assisted mathematical proofs or automated proof grading for educational purposes, these formal languages seem to be insufficient.

In the following example shown in Fig. 1 about the proof of the monotone convergence theorem through the supremum theorem, we can observe several characteristics of natural language proofs and the difficulties consequent upon the task of formalization using existing formal proof languages like Coq. We will also demonstrate how our work circumvents these difficulties.

Monotone Convergence Theorem: For every sequence of real numbers $(a_n)_{n\in\mathrm{N}}$, $(a_n)_{n\in\mathrm{N}}$ converges if it is monotonically increasing and bounded above.

Proof. (1) Assume $(a_n)_{n\in\mathrm{N}}$ is monotonically increasing and bounded above.
(2) By supremum theorem, there exists A such that $A = \sup\{a_n\}$.
(3) We use the definition of limit to show that $\lim_{n\to+\infty} a_n = A$.
(4) For every $\varepsilon > 0$, by the definition of least upper bound, there exists an integer N such that $a_N > A - \varepsilon$.
(5) Since $\{a_n\}$ increases, for every n, $n > N$ implies $a_n > a_N$.
(6) Since A is an upper bound of $(a_n)_{n\in\mathrm{N}}$, for every n, $n > N$ implies $a_n < A$.
(7) Consequently, for every n, $n > N$ implies $A - \varepsilon < a_n < A + \varepsilon$.
(8) By the definition of convergence, we have $\lim_{n\to+\infty} a_n = A$,
(9) which proves the theorem. □

Fig. 1. Proof of monotone convergence theorem.

Partial Transformation of Proof Goal. The concept of proof goal models the task of a mathematical proof, i.e. deriving the conclusion from premises and proven results. Following the steps of a proof, we implicitly transform the proof goal by introducing new variables, proving intermediate results, or posing subgoals. For example, we pose a subgoal in line 3, thereby transforming the proof goal into two subsequent proof goals: (1) proving $\lim_{n\to+\infty} a_n = A$, (2) and proving the conclusion with the intermediate result $\lim_{n\to+\infty} a_n = A$ proven. However, there are circumstances where the subsequent proof goal cannot be found directly: We pose an assumption $\epsilon > 0$ in line 4 and derive the result $\forall n > N, A-\epsilon < a_n < A+\epsilon$ in line 7 under the assumption. The overall process proves the result $\forall \epsilon > 0, \exists N \in \mathbf{N}, \forall n > N, A - \epsilon < a_n < A + \epsilon$, which is not explicitly stated in line 4. Consequently, the transformation of the proof goal in line 4 is partial. Since each tactic in tactic languages should represent a clearly defined, complete transformation of the current proof goal, formalizing the proof using tactic languages would involve the extra task of determining the subsequent proof goal. For example, by inferring the proposition to be filled in a Coq "assert" tactic. *In our work, a structure of partial proof is included in the design of proof language to model this pattern of proof, it eliminates the need for additional inferences or structural modifications on the proof during the task of formalization.*

Context-dependent Semantics. Depending on the context, the same natural language statement could have multiple interpretations, of which the semantic differences may be subtle. For example, when we write "there exists" in the proof, at least three interpretations are possible. (1) In the context of proving an existential statement, a satisfying value has been found for one of the existential quantifiers in the conclusion to be proved, (2) or a proposition beginning with an existential quantifier is stated, (3) or similar to the second case, except that the qualified variable becomes a free variable and can be used later, as in line 2 and line 4 of the example, where variables A and N are used in line 3 and line 5, respectively. In order to use the tactic language of Coq, all those semantic variances must be explicitly formulated. Namely by an "exists" tactic for the case (1), an existentially quantified variable in the proposition for the case (2) and a free variable in the proposition for the case (3). Determining the correct semantic interpretation would require analysing the context during the process of formalization. Not only is such an hidden task of analysis generally harder to perform on an unstructured natural language proof, but it is also indirect on a tactic proof, as tactics do not explicitly contain information on proof goals. That explains the difficulties faced by the tactic languages as object languages of automatic formalization. *In our work, the proof language is designed to resemble natural language in order to streamline the formalization. Moreover, the resemblance allows the proof language to temporarily preserve the context-dependent semantics, thus allowing the resolution to be postponed until we can perform static analysis on the formalized version of the proof.*

Overloading of Notation. Sometimes a notational convention may be employed though not being mathematically rigorous. For example, the appearance of $\{a_n\}$ in line 2 and line 5 does not represent a singleton but rather the set containing all elements of the sequence a. Another typical example is the extensive usage of $f(x)$ for representing the function f itself. Similar to context-dependent semantics, all mathematical formulas should be written rigorously in Coq. *By performing static analysis on the entire formal proof, the precise meaning of each expression can also be inferred.*

In summary, to address the problems mentioned above, we design a natural-language-like formal proof language for modeling mathematical proofs. We add partial proof structures to make them more similar to the natural language proofs. Furthermore, after transforming the natural formal proof into an abstract syntax tree by a parser, we can perform static analysis on it to resolve context-dependent semantics and overloading of notation.

Accordingly, we implement a framework called ProofGrader for checking mathematical proofs automatically. For each step of reasoning, corresponding solvers are chosen heuristically in order to check its correctness. Apart from the proof checking kernel, the rest of the system is designed to be highly modular so that our system may fit into different usage scenarios: It is possible to alter the mathematical objects and the usable theorems involved in the proof, the acceptable forms of proof steps, or the solvers used for checking. For example, to serve educational purposes, mild solvers fitting the level of human intuition can be plugged in instead of powerful ones, and advanced theorems can be temporarily disabled until they are proved or taught later.

In the rest of this paper, we will first present the design of our proof language in Sect. 2, with elaborations on several important elements. After that, we give the formal semantics of our proof language in Sect. 3. We then show the schema of the workflow of our checker in Sect. 4. A detailed description of our solvers is developed in Sect. 5. Section 6 gives an evaluation of the proof checker. And then we will introduce some related works in Sect. 7. Finally, Sect. 8 is devoted to a conclusion.

2 Proof Language Design

We focus on defining a natural-language-like proof language, whose structure faithfully reflects that of natural language. Thus, our natural formal proof language is provided with the hierarchy of natural language proof. At the top level are proof steps, what follows are propositions and terms. A certain amount of investigations of natural language proofs are done to incorporate common proof patterns within our proof language. Such a proof language follows predefined grammar rules but can be read directly as natural language, an explanation of its grammar can be found in the long version of this paper [21].

To perform proof checking, the natural formal proof language is further translated into an abstract syntax tree via a parser. Below shows a subset of its definitions. The definitions related to `term` and `prop` can be found in the long version of this paper [21].

⟨*proof*⟩ ::= '`ProofAction`' ⟨*action*⟩ ⟨*proof*⟩
  | '`PoseWithoutProof`' ⟨*fwd*⟩ ⟨*prop*⟩ ⟨*proof*⟩
  | '`PoseAndProve`' ⟨*fwd*⟩ ⟨*prop*⟩ ⟨*proof*⟩ ⟨*proof*⟩
  | '`ClaimSuffice`' ⟨*bwd*⟩ ⟨*prop*⟩ ⟨*proof*⟩
  | '`ProveSuffice`' ⟨*bwd*⟩ ⟨*prop*⟩ ⟨*proof*⟩ ⟨*proof*⟩
  | '`ConclWithoutProof`' ⟨*fwd*⟩
  | '`ConclAndProve`' ⟨*fwd*⟩ ⟨*proof*⟩
  | '`PosePartialProof`' ⟨*poseAction*⟩ ⟨*proof*⟩ ⟨*proof*⟩
  | '`EndPartialProof`'

⟨*fwd*⟩ ::= '`FNoHint`'
  | '`FDefinition`' ⟨*definition*⟩
  | '`FTheorem`' ⟨*theorem*⟩
  | '`FAddEqn`' {*identifier*}*
  | '`FDeriBothTerms`' ⟨*identifier*⟩
  | ...

⟨*bwd*⟩ ::= 'BNoHint'
| 'BContra'
| ...

⟨*action*⟩ ::= 'AIntros' ⟨*identifier*⟩
| 'AExists' ⟨*term*⟩
| 'ASuppose' ⟨*prop*⟩
| 'ASet' ⟨*identifier*⟩ ⟨*term*⟩
| 'ASetProp' ⟨*prop*⟩
| 'AExistVar' ⟨*identifier*⟩

⟨*poseAction*⟩ ::= 'APoseVar' ⟨*identifier*⟩ {*prop*}*
| 'APoseProp' ⟨*prop*⟩

In the following, we will explain the meaning of each proof structure. We will refer to the names of abstract syntax tree nodes because these names correspond to components of the proof language. Some of our proof structures have similar functionalities to those of certain tactic language, while others have no counterpart, which enables us to better express natural language proof.

ProofAction. The field `action` constitutes an operation on the proof goal, and the field `proof` refers to subsequent proof steps.

The design of `ProofAction` refers to some tactic languages, such as the tactic *intro* and *exists* of Coq [4], which deal with the quantifiers in the proposition to be proved. That corresponds to our proof action `AIntros` and `AExists`. However, the variety of proof actions is richer than that of tactic language. For example, `ASuppose` introduces a premise in the conclusion rather than a variable, which is also expressed by the tactic *intro* in Coq. Such a difference is due to the fact that the proof language models the natural language directly, and thus is more in line with human intuition.

`ASet` binds a name to a term, to which the proof can refer later, and the existence of the term will be verified by the checker to ensure mathematical rigor.

`ASetProp` is a generalization of `ASet`. Instead of introducing a new variable through an equation, `ASetProp` introduces new variables through a proposition. Figure 2 below contrasts the usage of these two proof actions, the one-to-one correspondence between natural language and our proof language is marked in background color.

Finally, `AExistVar` indicates the action of instantiating the variable mentioned by an existential quantifier in the last premise in the proof goal. The usage of `AExistVar` is further demonstrated in Sect. 4.3 when we perform static analysis.
In the upper part of Fig. 2, the variable A is set equal to the limit of a sequence, the checker then verifies whether the limit exists. In the lower part, a variable k is introduced implicitly due to the introduction of a subsequence, the checker then verifies whether $(a_n)_{n\in\mathbb{N}}$ admits a convergent subsequence. Both of the two proof steps will add corresponding assumptions to the proof goal.

PoseWithoutProof & PoseAndProve. These two components correspond to forward reasoning. The field `fwd` indicates the method involved in forward reasoning. The field `prop` denotes the proposition that the step proves. The last field `proof` still refers to subsequent proof steps.

Natural formal proof:
We note A as the limit of the sequence $(a_n)_{n\in\mathbb{N}}$.
... subsequent proof

Abstract syntax tree:
```
ProofAction (ASet "A" (TBinOp RLim (TInfty PositiveInfty) (TBinder LambdaB "n"
(TApply (TVar "a") (TVar "n")))) ) (... subsequent proof)
```

Natural formal proof:
We note $(a_{n_k})_{k\in\mathbb{N}}$ as the convergent subsequence of $(a_n)_{n\in\mathbb{N}}$.
... subsequent proof

Abstract syntax tree:
```
ProofAction (ASetProp (PBinOp CAnd (PBinPred IsSubseq (TBinder LambdaB "k"
(TApply (TVar "a") (TApply (TVar "seq_n") (TVar "k")))) (TVar "a"))
(PUnPred Convergent (TBinder LambdaB "k" (TApply (TVar "a") (TApply (TVar
"seq_n") (TVar "k")))))) ) (... subsequent proof)
```

Fig. 2. Example of ProofAction.

Depending on the complexity of the reasoning, one may choose to provide a proof as a justification of the reasoning or just let the checker figure it out. This makes the difference of `PoseWithoutProof` and `PoseAndProve`. `PoseAndProve` carries an extra field `prop`, which is a complete proof showing how to derive its result. This design is also widespread in tactic languages. An example is the tactic *assert* in Coq, which poses a subgoal to be proved. Figure 3 shows its usage scenario, which corresponds to the line 3 of Fig. 1.

Natural formal proof:
We use the definition of limit to show that: $\lim_{n\to+\infty} a_n = A$.
... subgoal proof
... subsequent proof
Abstract syntax tree:
```
PoseAndProve (FDefinition SeqLimit) (PBinPred REq (TBinOp RLim
(TInfty PositiveInfty) (TBinder LambdaB "n" (TApply (TVar "a") (TVar "n"))))
(TVar "A")) (... subgoal proof) (... subsequent proof)
```

Fig. 3. Example of PoseAndProve.

Since the hint of using the definition of limit is far from sufficient to prove the result, an additional proof is provided to complete this task. The proven subgoal is then available in the subsequent proof.

The set of possible methods `fwd` is rather rich. To name a few, `FTheorem` denotes applying a theorem, `FAddEqn` denotes adding several equations together to get a new one, and `FDeriBothTerms` denotes taking a derivative from both sides of an equation. If no method is indicated, `FNoHint` is filled in. It is quite easy to incorporate new methods so this set is highly expandable.

ClaimSuffice & ProveSuffice. These two components correspond to backward reasoning. The first field `bwd` indicates the method involved in backward reasoning, the second field `prop` denotes the proposition the step proves and the last field `proof` refers to subsequent proofs. The distinction between `ClaimSuffice` and `ProveSuffice` follows that between `PoseWithoutProof` and `PoseAndProve`.

Backward reasoning signifies that they start from the conclusion to be proved. The result provided is supposed to imply goal, which will then become the new goal.

ConclWithoutProof & ConclAndProve. These two components correspond to the step of deriving the conclusion and terminating the proof, only a field `fwd` is presented to indicate the method involved. `ConclAndProve` allows the choice of presenting an extra explanatory proof when the derivation of the conclusion is not immediate.

Basically, `ConclWithoutProof` corresponds to the last step of the proof, such as the line 9 "which proves the theorem" in Fig. 1, and does not carry much information. But such a concluding remark imitates natural language proof, and the similarity to natural language characterizes our proof language.

PosePartialProof & EndPartialProof. In theorem provers, we always need to explicitly keep a record of the current proof goal. In most cases, this is the overall proposition to be proved. We can also pose a subgoal and prove it subsequently, a process represented by the `PoseAndProve` component in our proof language.

As discussed in Sect. 1, natural language proofs may also involve partial transformations of the proof goal, in the sense that subgoals are not explicitly stated in advance. Instead, We simply pose certain assumptions and proceed to derive the subgoals. Refer to Fig. 4 for an illustration of how the different forms of proof goal are in the example Fig. 1. The dark gray part of the proof denotes what we term as a "partial proof", aligning with the `PosePartialProof` and `EndPartialProof` components in our proof language.

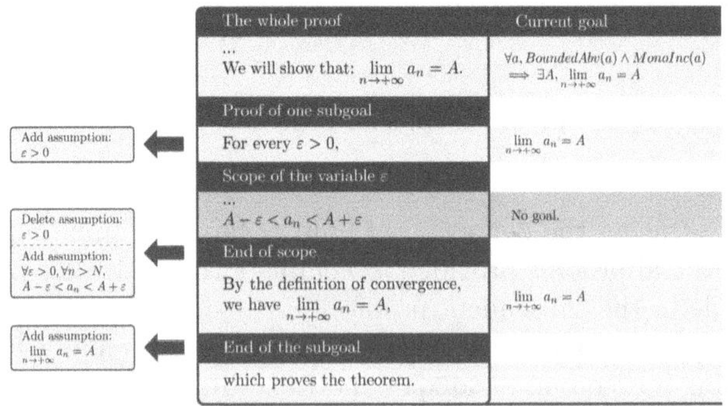

Fig. 4. Illustration of how the proof goal changes.

The notion of partial proof can be considered as one innovation of our proof language. Compared with tactic languages, it offers us extra convenience in modelling natural language proofs.
A partial proof starts with a list of variables and propositions, which then become the temporary assumptions. This information is carried by the first field `poseAction` is the grammar. `APoseVar` poses a new temporary variable along with related assumptions, while `APoseProp` poses a proposition. The former field `proof` carries the partial proof, which shall be terminated by `EndPartialProof`. After the termination of partial proof, all proven propositions will be altered to its proper form - without free variables. These altered propositions will become henceforth available in the subsequent proof - the latter field `proof`.

In Fig. 4, the variable ε and the proposition $\varepsilon > 0$ are posed to start a partial proof. When reaching the result $\forall n > N, A - \varepsilon < a_n < A + \varepsilon$ at the end of the partial proof, it is expanded to $\forall \varepsilon > 0, \forall n > N, A - \varepsilon < a_n < A + \varepsilon$, which is subsequently used to prove convergence. Figure 5 shows the how a partial proof looks like, which corresponds to line 4 of Fig. 1.

Natural formal proof:
For every $\varepsilon > 0$,
. . . partial proof in the scope of ε
. . . subsequent proof
Abstract syntax tree:
```
PosePartialProof (APoseVar "epsilon" ((PBinPred RGt (TVar "epsilon")
(TNum 0)) :: nil)) (... partial proof in the scope of ε ... EndPartialProof)
(... subsequent proof)
```

Fig. 5. Example of PosePartialProof.

3 The Formal Semantics of Proof Language

In this section, we demonstrate a selected set of the formal semantics of our proof language. Some semantics of the proof language not covered here can be found in the extended version of the paper [21]. Since each proof step defines a transformation of the proof goal, we use the notation $(pr, pg) \rightarrow (pr', pg')$ to denote that the proof goal pg' results from the proof goal pg after one or more proof steps in pr, with pr' continuing the proof. A proof goal is defined as a pair (A, C), where A is a list of premises and C a conclusion that needs to be proved. In the case of partial proof, the conclusion C does not exist and we note it as $\square$.

For convenience, we represent a list of premises as a set of propositions, and we write the triple (pr, A, C) to represent the pair $(pr, (A, C))$. We use the notation $FV(A)$ to denote the set of free variables in the set of propositions A, the same notation $FV(t)$ is also used to denote the set of free variables in the term t. We also define a constant QED such that the proof is successfully completed when $(pr, A, C) = QED$.

Proof Action.

$$\frac{v \notin FV(A \cup \{\forall x.C\})}{(\textbf{ProofAction}\ (\textbf{AIntros}\ v)\ pr, A, \forall x.C) \rightarrow (pr, A, C[v/x])}\ \text{INTROS}$$

Proof actions are proof steps that directly manipulates the proof goal, usually when some conditions are met. The behavior of **AIntros** v is to remove the universal quantifier in the conclusion $\forall x.C$ and replace the variable x in C by the variable v, when the variable v does not occur freely in the proof goal. The behavior of other **ProofAction** statements is similar. Detailed semantics and descriptions are available in the long version of the paper [21].

Partial Proof.

$$\frac{\begin{array}{c}(pr, A \cup sP, \square) \rightarrow (\textbf{EndPartialProof}, A', \square) \\ FV(sP) \subset FV(A \cup \{C\}) \cup \{s\}\end{array}}{\begin{array}{c}(\textbf{PosePartialProof}\ (\textbf{APoseVar}\ s\ sP)\ pr\ pr', A, C) \\ \rightarrow (pr', A \cup (\text{AddVarDep}\ (A' \setminus (A \cup lP))\ s\ sP), C)\end{array}}\ \text{POSEVAR}$$

$$\frac{\begin{array}{c}(pr, A \cup \{P\}, \square) \rightarrow (\textbf{EndPartialProof}, A', \square) \\ FV(P) \subset FV(A \cup \{C\})\end{array}}{\begin{array}{c}(\textbf{PosePartialProof}\ (\textbf{APoseProp}\ P)\ pr\ pr', A, C) \\ \rightarrow (pr', A \cup (\text{AddPropDep}\ (A' \setminus (A \cup \{P\}))\ P), C)\end{array}}\ \text{POSEPROP}$$

A partial proof first makes one or more assumptions and then deduces a series of results. After the partial proof terminates, these results are added with dependencies on the assumptions, by prefixing them with universal quantifiers and prerequisite conditions. The assumptions can be either (1) posing a new variable satisfying certain conditions, (2) or posing a hypothesis on the existing variables of the proof goal. These two cases correspond to the constructs **APoseVar** $s\ sP$ and **APoseProp** P defined above, where s refers to the name of the posed variable, sP a set of assumptions on the posed variable and P an assumption on existing variables. The two operators AddVarDep and AddPropDep add dependencies on the assumptions to the results derived during the partial proof. Similar to the subgoal proof, a **PosePartialProof** statement causes the checker to first check the partial proof. After reaching **EndPartialProof**, which marks the end of the partial proof, the checker integrates the proof goal back to the main proof by modifying all the derived premises.

The Table 1 shows how the proof goal gets transformed between lines 4–7 in Fig. 1, which represents a partial proof structure. It first makes an assumption $\epsilon > 0$ and then deduces several results. After that, these results are added with a prefix $\forall \epsilon > 0$ to indicate their dependency on the assumption $\epsilon > 0$.

Table 1. Transformation of proof goal between lines 4–7 in Fig. 1. The upper part of the table shows the proof goal before reaching line 4 of the proof. The middle part of the table shows the deduction of intermediate results during the partial proof. The lower part of the table shows the proof goal after terminating the partial proof in line 7 of the proof.

Premises	Conclusion
$\{a_n\}$ has an upper bound $\{a_n\}$ is monotonically increasing there exists A such that $A = \sup\{a_n\}$ $A = \sup\{a_n\}$	$A = \lim_{n \to +\infty} a_n$
+ $\epsilon > 0$ **(partial proof start)** + there exists N such that $a_N > A - \epsilon$ + for all n, if $n > N$ then $a_n > a_N$ + for all n, if $n > N$ then $a_n < A$ + for all n, if $n > N$ then $A - \epsilon < a_n < A + \epsilon$ **(partial proof end)**	$\square$
- Remove all the premises added above + for all $\epsilon > 0$, there exists N such that $a_N > A - \epsilon$ + for all $\epsilon > 0$, there exists N such that for all n, if $n > N$ then $a_n > a_N$ + for all n, there exists N such that if $n > N$ then $a_n < A$ + for all n, there exists N such that if $n > N$ then $A - \epsilon < a_n < A + \epsilon$	$A = \lim_{n \to +\infty} a_n$

4 The Workflow of ProofGrader

4.1 Overall Architecture

In this subsection, we will primarily introduce the overall working framework of ProofGrader. Figure 6 illustrates how the natural formal proof is processed step by step in our proof checking system to obtain the final result. A larger figure can be found in the long version of this paper [21] for greater clarity.

The modules described in the squares of the diagram are the main components of ProofGrader, which include the parser, static analyser, and proof checker. These three parts will be discussed in detail in the following. The other process boxes represent different forms of mathematical proof during the whole workflow. We utilize a parser to convert the natural formalized proof into an abstract syntax tree, and then perform static analysis on the abstract syntax tree to eliminate ambiguities and add omitted steps. The checker takes in the proof goal generated by the static analyser along with the complete abstract syntax tree, and checks the proof step by step by predefined rules. Finally, it confirms whether the proof goal has been proven and generates the final result.

4.2 Proof Parsing

Proof parsing is the first step of the entire workflow of ProofGrader. Since the design of our proof language also takes a large part into account readability factors, it may not be the most convenient for the subsequent checking process. Therefore, we will first convert the natural formal proof into an abstract syntax tree described in Sect. 2. In our implementation, the lexer and parser are realized by flex and bison [10,15].

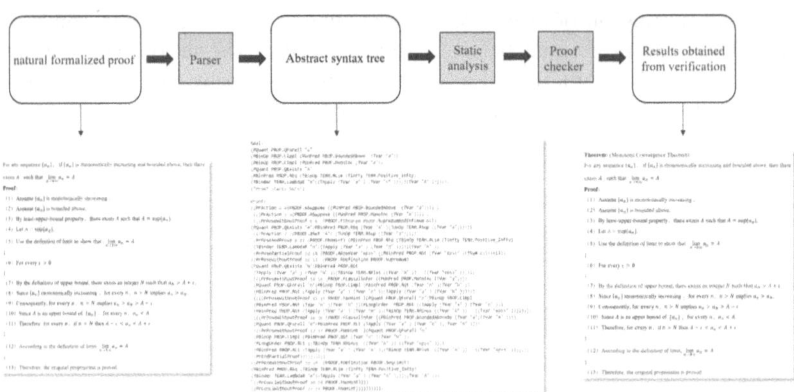

Fig. 6. Overall workflow of ProofGrader.

The parser simply performs a plain translation based on the grammar rules, without making any further modification on the proof structure or the formulation of proposition. These are the subjects of the next section where we will discuss the static analysis on the proof.

4.3 Static Analysis

As discussed in Sect. 1, natural language proofs exhibit complexities such as context-dependent semantics and overloading of notation. Given the close resemblance of our proof language to natural language and the direct translation performed by the parser, these properties will be carried into the natural formal proof, and then the abstract syntax tree. Performing static analysis on the abstract syntax tree allows us to eliminate these problems by reorganizing the proof into a more rigorous form, ready to be checked by the proof checker.

The static analyser tackles each kind of problem separately with ad hoc method. For one problematic proof step, proposition or expression, the task is to choose the right semantic between all the possible interpretations. The static analyser works by first inferring how the current proof step transforms the proof goal, based on the previous and subsequent proof goals. It then selects the semantic corresponding to this transformation, by elaborating the proof step, proposition or expression into a proper form. Judging from the problems we are currently solving by static analysis, most of them are accompanied by the appearance of free variables. So it is often the case to perform a lexical scope analysis.

Handling Context-dependent Semantics. The context-dependent semantics we currently address are stated in the descriptions of Fig. 1. In this example, the static analyser infers the correct semantic from the context, as shown in the inference steps below. As a reminder, the three possible interpretations of "there exists A such that $A = \sup\{a_n\}$" are respectively: (1) a value $\sup\{a_n\}$ has been found for an existential quantifier in the conclusion to be proved, (2) an intermediate result $\exists A = \sup\{a_n\}$ is stated, where A is qualified by a quantifier, (3) a variable A is given the value $\sup\{a_n\}$ after proving the existence of this supremum.

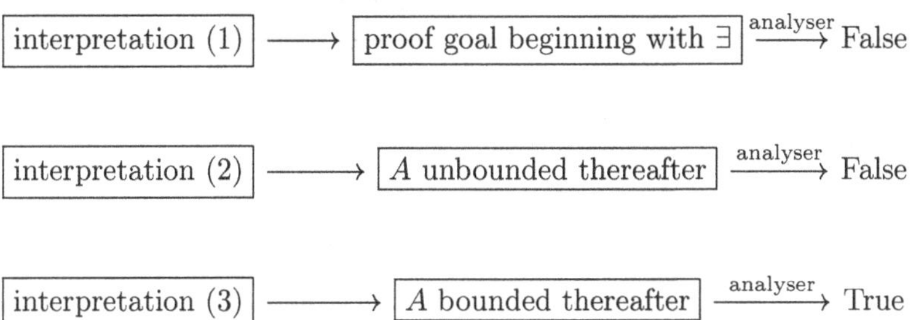

The three potential semantic interpretations appear syntactically identical in the proof. Therefore, the static analyser takes the responsibility for reflecting the result of the above analysis on the abstract syntax tree through modification. This is where the proof action `AExistVar` comes into play. Placed immediately after a proposition starting with an existential quantifier, it indicates the instantiation of the variable mentioned by the quantifier, thus bringing about the semantics corresponding to case (3), namely binding variable A of the value.

Algorithm 1 illustrates the procedure of handling context-dependent semantics in the cases of **PoseWithoutProof** and **PoseAndProve**, the processing of other cases follows a similar approach.

Algorithm 1 HCDS: Handling Context-dependent Semantics

Input: the original proof Pr before static analysis
Output: the modified proof with ontext-dependent Semantics eliminated
When Pr = PoseWithoutProof fwd $P0$ $Pr0$
$P0$ = PQuant exists "x" $P1$
"x" occur freely in $Pr0$
Then HCDS(Pr) = PoseWithoutProof fwd $P0$ (ProofAction (AExistVar "x") HCDS($Pr0$))

When Pr = PoseAndProve fwd $P0$ $Pr0$ $Pr1$
$P0$ = PQuant exists "x" $P1$
"x" occur freely in $Pr1$
Then HCDS(Pr) = PoseAndProve fwd $P0$ (HCDS($Pr0$) (ProofAction (AExistVar "x") HCDS($Pr1$))
...

Handling Overloading of Notation. If there is only one possible interpretation for notation overloading, there is no need for analysis and the static analyser simply restores its rigorous form. So far, the cases we have encountered with multiple possible interpretations for notation overloading all involve the use of formal variables. In such cases, the static analyser examines the appearance of free variables. As an example, the $\{a_n\}$ in line 2 of Fig. 1 admits two possible interpretations: (1) the singleton $\{a_n\}$, (2) or a set containing all elements of the sequence a. The correct interpretation depends on whether the variable n is bound to a value in the current proof goal. Similarly, if x is identified as a free variable in the proof goal, $f(x)$ will be transformed into either f or $\lambda x.f(x)$, rather than the value of x applied to the function f.

Algorithm 2 illustrates the procedure for handling the notation overloading of $f(x)$ in the cases of **PoseWithoutProof** and **ProofAction** (**ASet** x t), the processing of other cases follows a similar approach.

Algorithm 2 HON: Handling Overloading of Notation

Input: the original proof *pr* before static analysis
list of binded variables *binded_varlist* from the beginning to the current point of the proof
Output: the modified proof with overloading of notation eliminated
When *Pr* = PoseWithoutProof *fwd P0 Pr0*
P0 = Eq (TApply ("*f*") ("*x*")) *t1*
if "*x*" is not in *binded_varlist*
Then HON(*Pr*, *binded_varlist*) = PoseWithoutProof *fwd* (Eq ("*f*") (TBinder Lambda "*x*" *t1*))
HON(*Pr0*, *binded_varlist*)

When *pr* = ProofAction (ASet "*x*" *t*) *Pr0*
Then HON(*Pr*, *binded_varlist*) = ProofAction (ASet "*x*" *t*) HON(*Pr0*, "*x*" :: *binded_varlist*)
...

4.4 Proof Checking

Proof checking is the final step of the entire workflow of ProofGrader. The checker takes the proof and the proof goal elaborated by the static analyser as input. For each proof step, the checker takes the current proof goal and checks the step according to the formal semantics presented in Sect. 3, it computes the subsequent proof goal along with a boolean value indicating whether the step is accepted. By iteratively repeating this process, the proof checker finally generates a list of boolean values indicating the correctness of each proof step. In order to help with proposition checking, we also develop several solvers and a solver manager system. We will introduce them in Sect. 5. The entire proof checking process is detailed in Fig. 7.

5 Solver Manager

The solver manager is an important component of the proof checker, and therefore, we will introduce it separately here. It is primarily used to verify the correctness of mathematical propositions under certain conditions. When it comes to proving and simplifying mathematical expressions, we combine different solvers to check if the current proposition can be derived from known results using specific rules.

Each solver corresponds to a deduction rule based on specific mathematical concepts, and implements the corresponding algorithm internally in the proof checker. Different solvers are responsible for handling different types of mathematical expressions. For example, when dealing with expressions involving algebraic operators, ProofGrader utilizes algebra-related solvers for simplification. Similarly, solvers for trigonometric functions, exponential and logarithm, sequential limit, and other mathematical concepts are employed to handle corresponding cases.

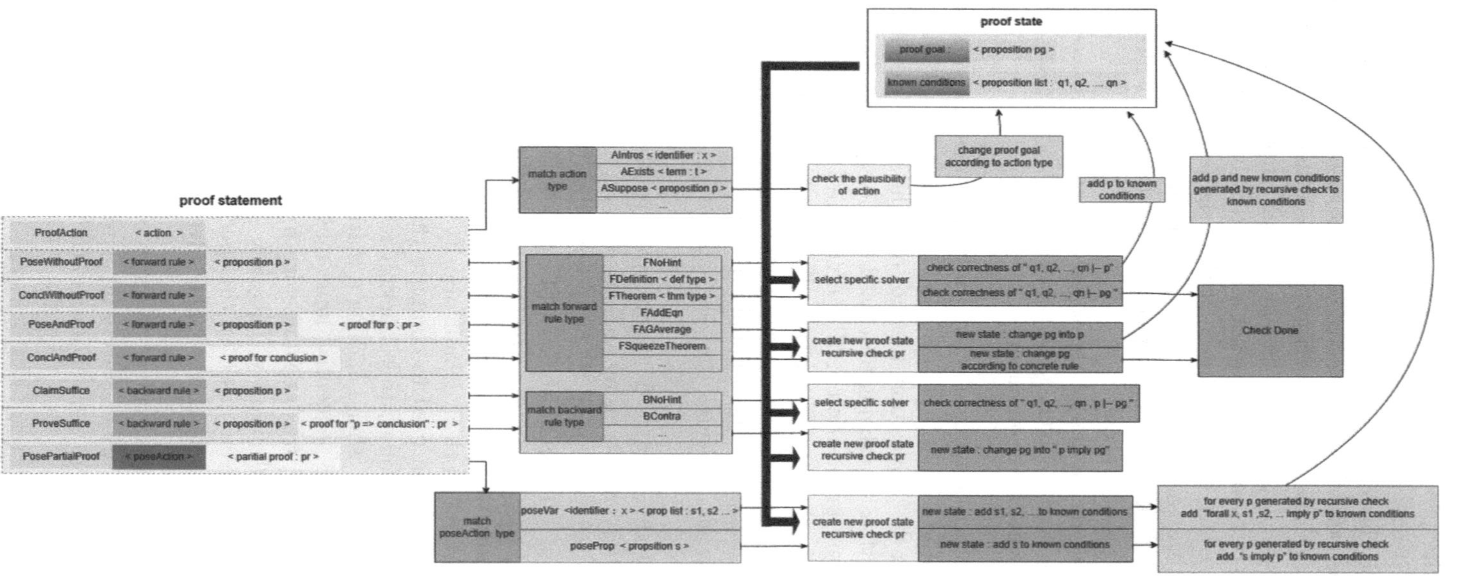

Fig. 7. Process of proof checking.

When users write proofs, they must adhere to the steps supported by the solvers. In Sect. 1, it was noted that AI-generated formal proofs sometimes use solvers like Z3 [8] to check propositions. However, Z3 possesses strong reasoning capabilities and can sometimes prove the correctness of conclusions even if the original deduction process contains error. On the other hand, our solver does not engage in excessively powerful reasoning. It only supports relatively obvious deduction methods in proofs and does not allow excessive omission of steps. This approach aims to reflect the correctness of the original proof more accurately. Additionally, since we can provide explicit deduction rules supported by each solver, users can clearly know which steps can be omitted and which steps cannot be omitted in their proof process.

Before presenting the design of the solver manager, it is necessary to first define the structure of the solver, as these two are closely related. Each solver consists of the following four components:

- *solve(s,p)* : the function used to verify the correctness of a proposition takes two parameters: the current proof goal and the proposition itself. It can either return false when the proposition does not pass the solver, or a list of propositions, indicating that after being processed by the current solver, the correctness of the original proposition can be determined by individually checking the propositions in the list. This design allows us to combine multiple solvers to simplify a proposition. The list can contain only one proposition, which means the solver simplifies the original proposition and passes it to the next solver. An empty list indicates that the current proposition is accepted by the solver.
- *fee* : the cost of this solver. While we want to combine multiple solvers, we cannot endlessly repeat using various solvers, as it may result in non-termination. Therefore, we need to set an upper limit on the total cost within the solver manager and define the cost of each solver.
- *default-priority* : the default priority of solvers. When dealing with mathematical propositions that do not exhibit any prominent characteristics, solvers can be selected based on their default priority levels.
- *priority(p)* : the function used to compute the dynamic priority. Given the current proposition as input, this function returns the dynamic priority of the solver. For example, when handling a mathematical proposition without limits, solvers related to sequential limit may have a low priority or even be unavailable. However, when dealing with limit-related propositions, these solvers would have a high priority. Therefore, it is necessary to dynamically adjust the priority of solvers based on the specific proposition. This prepares us for the subsequent development of the solver manager.

Based on the structure of the solver, we implemente a solver manager capable of dynamically scheduling various solvers by combining dynamic priorities. The specific algorithms and design can be found in the long version of this paper [21].

6 Evaluation

In this section, we give an evaluation of our proof checking system as well as our proof language. We first run our system on a set of sample mathematical proofs, covering the topic of arithmetic, trigonometric functions, exponential and logarithm, inequality, derivative, sequential limit and function continuity. The source code of our system and the dataset are available at: https://github.com/Laplace-Demon/ProofGrader. We then compare the features of our proof language with other proof languages and proof checking tools.

6.1 Performance

We test our system on a dataset of 52 mathematical proofs, Table 2 shows the average time and memory overhead of the proof parser and the checker on each of the topics, along with the average file size of the proof. We can observe that our proof parser and checker perform their task in a reasonable amount of time.

Table 2. Runtime and memory usage of the parser and checker on different topics.

Examples			Parser		Checker	
Topic	Number	File size (bytes)	Time (ms)	Memory (kb)	Time (ms)	Memory (kb)
arithmetic	6	271	34	3584	477	3456
trigonometric functions	8	599	53	3712	1409	3456
exponential and logarithm	3	371	40	3840	506	3456
inequality	10	395	58	3712	528	3456
derivative	3	385	75	3328	760	3328
sequential limit evaluation	10	550	58	3840	701	3328
sequential limit proof	10	1027	78	3968	670	3328
function continuity proof	2	923	68	3712	7758	3456

6.2 Comparison of Features

In the Table3 below, we compare the features of our proof language with some other proof languages and proof checking tools. The term "transformation chain" refers to the ability to handle and perform automated reasoning on a series of consecutive transformation derivations, such as:

$$\lim_{x\to 0}\frac{\sqrt[3]{x+1}-1}{\sqrt{x+1}-1}=\lim_{x\to 0}\frac{x}{(\sqrt[3]{x+1})^2+\sqrt[3]{x+1}+1}\cdot\frac{\sqrt{x+1}+1}{x}=\frac{2}{3}$$

Our proof checker aims to provide automated deduction capabilities that align with human judgment, while excessive step omissions are not allowed.

In terms of readability, our natural formal proof can be read with the same effort of reading a natural language mathematical proof. Even the abstract syntax tree generated by the parser remains readable since the components bear a mnemonic name.

In terms of static analysis, most theorem provers like Coq and Isabelle primarily support propositional-level static analysis. They utilize type inference to fill in missing information in user-written proofs. However, they do not perform static analysis on the entire proof. Regarding partial proofs, while it is sometimes possible to reorganize a proof to avoid partial proofs, we aim to preserve the characteristics of natural language proofs. Users should be able to write mathematical proofs without additional effort.

The work of Waterproof [18] aims to help students understand mathematical proofs. Therefore, its language readability falls between natural language and theorem provers. The proof checking functionality of Waterproof relies on Coq implementation, so it inherits some limitations of Coq as well. Diproche [6] utilizes natural language fragments as its input language. Due to its lack of support for static analysis and partial proofs, it imposes stricter requirements on the types and structure of proofs being written. Lurch [7] is limited to checking proofs in propositional logic and naive set theory. It does not have automatic reasoning capabilities and relies on users to provide detailed proofs for checking.

Table 3. Comparison of features of different mathematical proof checking tools.

Feature	ProofGrader	WaterProof	Diproche	Lurch	Isabelle [16]	Coq [2]
Natural language fragment	✓	×	✓	✓	×	×
Static analysis	proof-level	×	×	×	prop-level	prop-level
Partial proof	✓	×	×	×	×	×
Transformation chains	✓	×	✓	×	✓ [3]	×

7 Related Work

Proof assistants and other proof checkers. Recent decades have seen the emergence of various proof languages. A well-known work is Ltac [9] for the theorem prover Coq, which provides convenience for constructing proofs and facilitates better proof automation. Another famous one is that of Isar [19] for the system Isabelle. One objective of Isar is to provide a more human-readable proof language than before. Despite their efforts to improve readability, the learning curve for using these tools remains high. Wemmenhove et al. developed an educational software called Waterproof [18] based on this to assist students in practicing proofs. Since they still choose to rely on the tactic library extended with the Ltac2 tactic language, Waterproof has not actually gained stronger expressive power than these tactic-based proof language. Additionally, the proof assistant Agda [5] also employs some proof notations that resemble natural language, such as using equation chain instead of the "rewrite" tactic used in Coq. However, despite these advancements, they still struggle to effectively support the structure of partial proofs. While they can perform static analysis at the propositional level, such as type inference, they are unable to perform static analysis on the entire proof. In addition, tools mentioned in Sect. 6.2, such as Diproche and Lurch, although they support controlled natural language input, have stricter requirements on the notation and structure of proofs being written.

Machine learning for formalization. Machine learning techniques have been used in the formalization of informal proofs. The work of Yuhuai Wu et al. [20] based on large language models can correctly transform 25.3% of the solution for mathematical competition problems in MATH dataset [12] into formal specifications in Isabelle/HOL. In the work of Jiang et al. [13], they introduce Draft, Sketch, and Prove (DSP), a method that maps informal proofs to formal proof sketches, The accuracy was improved to 39.3% on the same dataset [12]. And the automatic theorem prover implemented by GPT-f [17] achieved a completion rate of 56.22% on their test set. The purpose of formalizing proofs with AI-based methods is to ensure that the proven proposition is correct, especially when proving previously unproven propositions in mathematical research. Since the target language of the transformation is often tactic-based proof languages that differ greatly from natural language, these works mainly use the original proof to guide theorem provers to complete the proof, rather than truly transforming the original proof into a formalized proof. In this case, because the language we designed combines formal rigor with similarity to natural language, if AI automatic translation is set to use our language as the target, it will complement our work well and lead to better results.

8 Conclusion

In this paper, we present our design of a natural-formalized proof language and the implementation of a mathematical proof checker. Compared to existing tactic-based proof language, our proof language has more expressive power thanks to the incorporation of partial proof. To cope with the characteristics of natural language proof, such as context-dependent semantics and overloading of notation, tactic language provides a fine-grained but cumbersome formal specification in the hope that someone can correctly reproduce the proof, while our proof language can automatically fix these problems through static analysis. All these factors result in better readability and an easier formalization process.

Regarding the process of proof checking, we implement a solver manager responsible for managing various automated proof checking strategies. It selects the most suitable strategies based on the form and contextual environment of the proposition to assess its correctness. Building upon this, the proof checker takes the proof and the proof goal provided by the static analyser, applies the appropriate checking methods, updates the proof goal iteratively, and ultimately completes the checking process.

Acknowledgements. This material is based upon work supported by NSF China 92370201.

References

1. Appel, K.I., Haken, W.: Every Planar Map is Four Colorable, vol. 98. American Mathematical Soc. (1989)
2. Barras, B., et al.: The coq proof assistant reference manual. INRIA, version 6(11) (1999)
3. Bauer, G., Wenzel, M.: Calculational reasoning revisited an Isabelle/Isar experience. In: Boulton, R.J., Jackson, P.B. (eds.) TPHOLs 2001. LNCS, vol. 2152, pp. 75–90. Springer, Heidelberg (2001). https://doi.org/10.1007/3-540-44755-5_7
4. Bertot, Y., Castran, P.: Interactive Theorem Proving and Program Development: Coq'Art The Calculus of Inductive Constructions, 1st (edn.) Springer, Incorporated (2010)
5. Bove, A., Dybjer, P., Norell, U.: A brief overview of Agda – a functional language with dependent types. In: Berghofer, S., Nipkow, T., Urban, C., Wenzel, M. (eds.) TPHOLs 2009. LNCS, vol. 5674, pp. 73–78. Springer, Heidelberg (2009). https://doi.org/10.1007/978-3-642-03359-9_6
6. Carl, M., Krapf, R.: Diproche–ein automatisierter tutor für den einstieg ins beweisen. Digitale Kompetenzen und Curriculare Konsequenzen, p. 43 (2020)
7. Carter, N.C., Monks, K.G.: Using the proof-checking word processor lurch to teach proof-writing (2014)
8. de Moura, L., Bjørner, N.: Z3: an efficient SMT solver. In: Ramakrishnan, C.R., Rehof, J. (eds.) TACAS 2008. LNCS, vol. 4963, pp. 337–340. Springer, Heidelberg (2008). https://doi.org/10.1007/978-3-540-78800-3_24
9. Delahaye, D.: A tactic language for the system Coq. In: Parigot, M., Voronkov, A. (eds.) LPAR 2000. LNAI, vol. 1955, pp. 85–95. Springer, Heidelberg (2000). https://doi.org/10.1007/3-540-44404-1_7
10. Donnelly, C.: Bison the YACC-compatible parser generator. Technical report, Free Software Foundation (1988)
11. Gonthier, G., et al.: Formal proof-the four-color theorem. Notices AMS **55**(11), 1382–1393 (2008)
12. Hendrycks, D., et al.: Measuring mathematical problem solving with the math dataset (2021)
13. Jiang, A.Q., et al.: Draft, sketch, and prove: Guiding formal theorem provers with informal proofs. arXiv preprint arXiv:2210.12283 (2022)
14. Lample, G., et al.: Hypertree proof search for neural theorem proving. In: Advances in Neural Information Processing Systems, vol. 35, pp. 26337–26349 (2022)
15. Levine, J.: Flex & Bison: Text Processing Tools. O'Reilly Media, Inc. (2009)
16. Paulson, L.C.: Isabelle: A Generic Theorem Prover. Springer, Berlin (1994)
17. Polu, S., Sutskever, I.: Generative language modeling for automated theorem proving. arXiv preprint arXiv:2009.03393 (2020)
18. Wemmenhove, J., Beurskens, T., McCarren, S., Moraal, J., Tuin, D., Portegies, J.: Waterproof: educational software for learning how to write mathematical proofs. arXiv preprint arXiv:2211.13513 (2022)
19. Wenzel, M.: Isar - a generic interpretative approach to readable formal proof documents. In: International Conference on Theorem Proving in Higher Order Logics (1999)
20. Wu, Y., et al.: Autoformalization with large language models. Advances in Neural Information Processing Systems, vol. 35, pp. 32353–32368 (2022)
21. Xie, L., Hui, Z., Cao, Q.: A natural formalized proof language (long version). arXiv preprint arXiv:2405.07973 (2024)

Strong Forgetting in Hennessy-Milner Logic

Xin Zhou[1,2], Yisong Wang[1(✉)], Renyan Feng[3], and Songhang Xu[1]

[1] Guizhou University, Guiyang, Guizhou, China 550025
yswang@gzu.edu.cn
[2] College of Computer Science, Guiyang University, Guiyang, Guizhou, China 550005
[3] School of Information, Guizhou University of Finance and Economics, Guiyang, China

Abstract. This paper concerns the problem of how to revise reactive systems for new specification in inertial principle. It proposes a notion of the weakest sufficient condition (WSC) for Hennessy-Milner logic and sets up a close connection with knowledge forgetting by generalizing the notion of strong bisimulation to restricted actions in Milner's calculus of communicating system. In principle, it suffices to revise a given system to meet the WSC of new specification.

Keywords: Reactive systems · Changes · Strong forgetting · The weakest sufficient condition · Hennessy-Milner logic

1 Introduction

Milner's Calculus of Communicating Systems (CCS), which is a kind of verification technique, and Hennessy-Milner Logic (HML) are important formal modeling and specification for reactive systems [1]. They have been widely deployed in crucial control domains and usually suffer from changes due to various reasons. It is a challenging task to revise or update a reactive system according to new specifications in an inertial principle manner such that its components keep unchanged unless they have to be changed.

As far as we know, the notion of the Weakest Sufficient Conditions (WSC) [3, 6] or the weakest preconditions plays a crucial role in characterizing changes of formal systems. For instance, suppose that a given system P which enjoys a specification T needs to be revised (limiting some signature) in order to satisfy a property φ. Under the inertial principle, it suffices to revise P such that it enjoys the weakest sufficient condition (over the limited signature) of φ under T. For this purpose, we generalized the notion of strong bisimulation of CCS on restricted actions, proposed the notion of strong forgetting for HML and presented the notion of WSC.

In fact, the notion of forgetting had been widely investigated from the perspective knowledge evolving in classical logic [6, 9, 11], nonmonotonic logic [5]

W.-N. Chin and Z. Xu (Eds.): TASE 2024, LNCS 14777, pp. 465–472, 2024.
https://doi.org/10.1007/978-3-031-64626-3_27

and various modal logic [2,10]. It was also employed to study the notion of the weakest sufficient conditions [3,4]. Different from the previous knowledge forgetting which discards proposition (or predicate) symbols, we consider forgetting actions in basic HML, which contains no proposition symbols.

2 Preliminaries

In this section, we briefly recall CCS [7] and HML [8], including their syntax and transitional semantics in particular.

We assume a underlying set $\mathcal{A}$ of *channels* and a special name τ. The *co-name* of $a \in \mathcal{A}$ is written $\overline{a}$ and $\overline{\overline{a}} = a$. We denote $\overline{\mathcal{A}} = \{\overline{a} \mid a \in \mathcal{A}\}$, $\mathcal{L} = \mathcal{A} \cup \overline{\mathcal{A}}$ is the set of *labels*, $Act = \mathcal{L} \cup \{\tau\}$ is the set of *actions*. A function $f : Act \to Act$ is a *labelling function* if $f(\bar{l}) = \overline{f(l)}$ and $f(\tau) = \tau$. We also assume a set $\mathcal{K}$ of process constants. For convenience, a singleton set $\{e\}$ is shorten as e when there is no ambiguous from its context.

2.1 Calculus of Communicating Systems

An *agent* or a *(concurrent) process* P is defined as[1]:

$$P ::= A \mid a.P \mid \sum_{i \in I} P_i \mid P|P \mid P\backslash L \mid P[f] \tag{1}$$

where $A \in \mathcal{K}$, $a \in Act$, I is an indexing set, P_i $(i \in I)$ is an agent, $|$ is a binary composition operator, $+$ is a binary choice operator which $P_1 + P_2 = \sum_{i \in \{1,2\}} P_i$ for a summation of two processes and I represents an index set, $\backslash$ is a unary restriction operator, $L \subseteq \mathcal{L}$, and f is a relabelling function. In particular, we denote $\mathbf{0}$ the agent $\sum_{i \in \emptyset} P_i$, which is the *inactive agent* and capable of no action whatever.

The set of agents is denoted by $\mathcal{P}$. For each agent constant A, it is assumed that there is a defining equation of the form $A \stackrel{def}{=} P$ where $P \in \mathcal{P}$.

The meaning of the above CCS is given by transitional semantics.

Definition 1 (Labelled Transition System).
A labelled transition system *(LTS) is of the form* $(S, T, \{\xrightarrow{t} : t \in T\})$, *where*

- S *is a set of states (or processes),*
- T *is a set of* transition labels *(or* actions*),*
- $\xrightarrow{t}$ *is a* transition relation *for each* $t \in T$*, which is a subset of* $S \times S$*.*

The semantics of the CCS is given by a LTS $(\mathcal{P}, Act, \{\xrightarrow{t} : t \in Act\})$*. The meaning of* $\mathcal{P}$ *consists in the definition of each transition relation* $\xrightarrow{t}$ *over* $\mathcal{P}$*.*

[1] Please note that agent variables are excluded here for simplicity.

2.2 Hennessy-Milner Logic

HML is developed to specify properties in a LTS and to capture logical equivalence of processes in CCS.

A *formula* φ of a (basic) HML $\mathcal{H}$ is defined as

$$\varphi ::= \bot \mid \top \mid \varphi \wedge \varphi \mid \varphi \vee \varphi \mid \langle M \rangle \varphi \mid [M]\varphi \tag{2}$$

where $M \subseteq Act$. We use $\bot$ and $\top$ denote $false$ and $true$. A *theory* of $\mathcal{H}$ is a finite set of formulas of $\mathcal{H}$. By abusing notations, we identify a theory Π as the formula $\bigwedge \Pi$ when it is clear for its context. By $Actions(e)$ we denote the set of actions occurring in e except for τ, where e is a formula or a theory of $\mathcal{H}$.

Definition 2 (Satisfaction). *Let $\mathcal{T} = (\mathcal{P}, Act, \{\xrightarrow{\alpha}: \alpha \in Act\})$ be a LTS. The* satisfaction *between a process $P \in \mathcal{P}$ (of the LTS $\mathcal{T}$) and a formula φ of $\mathcal{H}$, written $P \models_{\mathcal{T}} \varphi$ (or simply $P \models \varphi$), is defined as below:*

- $P \models \top$, $P \not\models \bot$;
- $P \models \varphi \wedge \psi$ *if* $P \models \varphi$ *and* $P \models \psi$;
- $P \models \varphi \vee \psi$ *if* $P \models \varphi$ *or* $P \models \psi$;
- $P \models \langle M \rangle \varphi$ *if* $\exists Q \in \mathcal{P}$ *such that* $P \xrightarrow{\alpha} Q$ *and* $Q \models \varphi$ *for some* $\alpha \in M$;
- $P \models [M]\varphi$ *if* $\forall \alpha \in M$ *and* $\forall Q \in \mathcal{P}$ *with* $P \xrightarrow{\alpha} Q$, $Q \models \varphi$.

In this case, φ is *satisfiable* and we call P (of $\mathcal{T}$) a *model* of φ. By $\mathsf{Mod}(\varphi)$ we denote the set of models of φ. A formula φ is *valid* if every $P \in \mathcal{P}$ is a model of φ, it is *unsatisfiable* if there is no $P \in \mathcal{P}$ satisfying $P \models \varphi$. A formula φ is a *logical consequence* of a formula ψ, written $\psi \models \varphi$, whenever $\mathsf{Mod}(\psi) \subseteq \mathsf{Mod}(\varphi)$. Two formulas (or theories) are *(logically) equivalent*, written $\psi \equiv \varphi$, if they have the same models, viz., they are logical consequence of each other. These notions can be extended for theories as usual.

3 Strong Forgetting on Actions

In this section we present the notion of strong bisimulation on given actions at first, the notion of strong forgetting for HML, and the notion of WSC.

3.1 Strong Bisimulation Discarding Actions

We firstly present a generalized notion of strong bisimulation.

Definition 3 (Strong V-bisimulation). *Let $V \subseteq Act$. A binary relation $\mathcal{S} \subseteq \mathcal{P} \times \mathcal{P}$ is a* strong V-bisimulation *if $(P, Q) \in \mathcal{S}$ implies, for all $\alpha \in Act - V$,*

(i) whenever $P \xrightarrow{\alpha} P'$ then, for some Q', $Q \xrightarrow{\alpha} Q'$ and $(P', Q') \in \mathcal{S}$;
(ii) whenever $Q \xrightarrow{\alpha} Q'$ then, for some P', $P \xrightarrow{\alpha} P'$ and $(P', Q') \in \mathcal{S}$;

Two P and Q are *strongly V-equivalent* or *strongly V-bisimilar*, written $P \sim_V Q$, if $(P, Q) \in \mathcal{S}$ for some strong V-bisimulation $\mathcal{S}$. Equivalently, it is expressed as

$$\sim_V = \bigcup\{\mathcal{S} : \mathcal{S} \text{ is a strong } V\text{-bisimulation}\}.$$

Intuitively, $P \sim_V Q$ says that, if discarding these actions in V, P and Q have the same behaviors. For instance, when discarding the action τ, the two processes $a.\overline{b}.0|\overline{a}.b.0$ and $a.\overline{b}.0 + \overline{a}.b.0$ are strong $\{\tau\}$-bisimular. However, they are clearly not strong bisimular since $a.\overline{b}.0|\overline{a}.b.0 \xrightarrow{\tau} \overline{b}.0|b.0$ but the action τ is not possible for $a.\overline{b}.0 + \overline{a}.b.0$. For the same reason, they are neither $\{a\}$-bisimular, nor $\{\overline{a}\}$-bisimular.

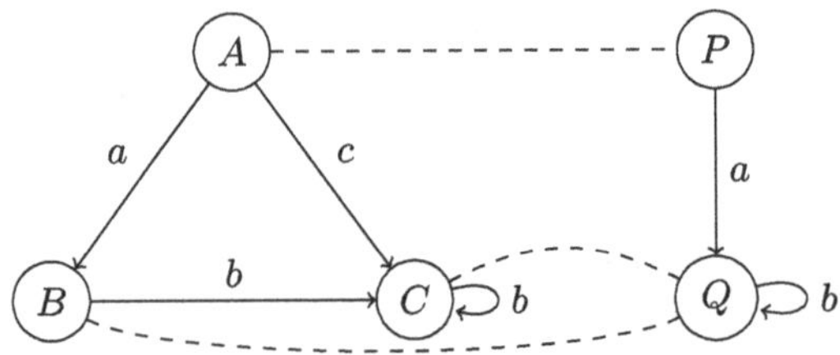

Fig. 1. A strong $\{c\}$-bisimulation of two agents A and P

Example 1. Let us consider a LTS $(\mathcal{P}, Act, \{\xrightarrow{\alpha}: \alpha \in Act\})$ shown in Fig. 1. Let $V = \{c\}$ and $\mathcal{S} = \{(A, P), (C, Q), (B, Q), (A, A), (B, B), (C, C), (P, P), (Q, Q)\}$. It is evident that P and A are not strong bisimilar since $A \xrightarrow{c} C$ but there is no P' with $P \xrightarrow{c} P'$. However, A and P are strongly bisimilar if the action c is discarded, i.e., $A \sim_{\{c\}} P$, and $\mathcal{S}$ is indeed a strong $\{c\}$-bisimulation.

3.2 Strong Forgetting on Actions

In the following we present the notion of strong forgetting from the perspective of semantics and then show its properties.

Definition 4 (Strong Forgetting). *Let $\varphi \in \mathcal{H}$, $V \subseteq \mathcal{A}$, and $L = V \cup \overline{V}$. A formula $\psi \in \mathcal{H}$ is a* result of strong forgetting *V from φ if*

$$\mathit{Mod}(\psi) = \{P \in \mathcal{P} \mid \exists Q \in \mathcal{P} : Q \models \varphi \text{ and } Q \sim_L P\}. \quad (3)$$

Intuitively, if ψ is a result of strong forgetting V from φ then its models consist of exactly the ones that are "indistinguishable" from (or strongly bisimular with) those of φ when discarding the forgetting actions in V.

It is evident that if both ψ and ψ' are results of strong forgetting V from $\varphi \in \mathcal{H}$ then $\mathsf{Mod}(\psi) = \mathsf{Mod}(\psi')$, *i.e.*, ψ and ψ' are equivalent. In this sense that the forgetting result is unique under logical equivalence (if it exists), we denote $\mathrm{F}^{\sim}(\varphi, V)$ the result of strong forgetting V from φ[2].

In the following we consider some instances of strong forgetting.

[2] It does not mean such a forgetting result always exists in $\mathcal{H}$.

Example 2. Let us consider the following formulas.

- $\varphi_1 = \langle a \rangle \top$. Clearly, $b.0 \not\models \langle a \rangle \top$ and $a.0 \models \langle a \rangle \top$. Note that $a.0 + Q \models \langle a \rangle \top$ for any $Q \in \mathcal{P}$ and $a.0 + Q \sim_{\{a,\overline{a}\}} Q$. Thus, $Q \models \mathrm{F}^{\sim}(\langle a \rangle \top, \{a\})$ for any $Q \in \mathcal{P}$, which implies $\mathrm{F}^{\sim}(\langle a \rangle \top, \{a\}) \equiv \top$.
- $\varphi_2 = \langle a \rangle \bot$. One can check that $\langle a \rangle \bot \equiv \bot$ since there is no $P, P' \in \mathcal{P}$ satisfying $P \xrightarrow{a} P'$ and $P' \models \bot$. Thus, $\mathrm{F}^{\sim}(\langle a \rangle \bot, \{a\}) \equiv \bot$.

Note that, these three agents $a.P$, $a.P + P'$ and $a.P|P'$ are models of $\langle a \rangle \top$ for any $P, P' \in \mathcal{P}$. What's more, any agent $Q \in \mathcal{P}$ that are strong $Act - \{a, \overline{a}\}$-bisimilar with any of the three agents is also a model of $\langle a \rangle \top$. Thus, any of these agents are models of $\mathrm{F}^{\sim}(\langle a \rangle \top, \{a\})$. There are infinite number of such models of $\langle a \rangle \top$.

Definition 5 (Irrelevance). *Let $V \subseteq \mathcal{A}$. A formula $\varphi \in \mathcal{H}$ is V-irrelevant, written $\mathsf{IR}(\varphi, V)$, whenever, for any $P \in \mathcal{P}$ with $P \models \varphi$, $Q \models \varphi$ holds for any $Q \sim_{(V \cup \overline{V})} P$.*

The next proposition shows some properties on strong forgetting for HML formulas.

Proposition 1. *Let $L \subseteq \mathcal{A}$, $\varphi, \varphi_i \in \mathcal{H}$ $(i = 1, 2)$.*

(i) $\mathrm{F}^{\sim}(\varphi_1 \vee \varphi_2, L) \equiv \mathrm{F}^{\sim}(\varphi_1, L) \vee \mathrm{F}^{\sim}(\varphi_2, L)$.
(ii) $\mathrm{F}^{\sim}(\varphi_1 \wedge \varphi_2, L) \models \mathrm{F}^{\sim}(\varphi_1, L) \wedge \mathrm{F}^{\sim}(\varphi_2, L)$.
(iii) $\mathrm{F}^{\sim}(\varphi_1 \wedge \varphi_2, L) \equiv \mathrm{F}^{\sim}(\varphi_1, L) \wedge \varphi_2$ *if* $\mathsf{IR}(\varphi_2, L)$.
(iv) $\varphi_1 \models \mathrm{F}^{\sim}(\varphi_1, L)$.
(v) $\varphi_1 \models \varphi_2$ *implies* $\mathrm{F}^{\sim}(\varphi_1, L) \models \mathrm{F}^{\sim}(\varphi_2, L)$.
(vi) *If* $\varphi \models \varphi \backslash L$ *then* $\mathrm{F}^{\sim}(\varphi, L) \equiv \varphi \backslash L$.
(vii) $\mathrm{F}^{\sim}(\langle \alpha \rangle \varphi, \{a\}) \equiv \top$ *if* $\alpha \in \{a, \overline{a}\}$ *and* $\varphi \not\equiv \bot$.
(viii) $\mathrm{F}^{\sim}([\alpha] \varphi, \{a\}) \equiv \top$ *if* $\alpha \in \{a, \overline{a}\}$.
(ix) $\mathrm{F}^{\sim}(\langle M \rangle \varphi, L) \equiv \top$ *if* $M \cap (L \cup \overline{L}) \neq \emptyset$ *and* $\varphi \not\equiv \bot$.

Similar to the knowledge forgetting in modal logic S5 [10], the strong forgetting should enjoy the following properties (**W**), (**PP**), (**NP**) and (**IR**). Let $\varphi, \psi \in \mathcal{H}$ and $L \subseteq \mathcal{A}$. If ψ is a result of strong forgetting L from φ, then φ and ψ should satisfy the following conditions.

(**W**) Weakening: $\varphi \models \psi$.
(**PP**) Positive Persistence: If $\mathsf{IR}(\phi, L)$ and $\varphi \models \phi$ then $\psi \models \phi$.
(**NP**) Negative Persistence: If $\mathsf{IR}(\phi, L)$ and $\varphi \not\models \phi$ then $\psi \not\models \phi$.
(**IR**) Irrelevance: $\mathsf{IR}(\psi, L)$.

Intuitively, the property weakening says that the forgetting result ψ should be weaker than the formula before forgetting φ; the property (**IR**) means the forgetting result ψ should irrelevant to the forgotten actions; the property (**PP**) requires that the logical consequence ϕ of φ which is irrelevant to the forgotten actions should be logical consequence of the forgetting result as well; while (**NP**) restricts that the nonlogical consequence ϕ of φ which is irrelevant to the forgotten actions should not be logical consequence of the forgetting result. The two properties (**PP**) and (**NP**) assert that the forgetting result does not loss any "knowledge"[3] of φ that are irrelevant to forgotten actions and, it does not introduce any "knowledge" which is not a "knowledge" of φ that are irrelevant to forgotten actions.

Theorem 1 (Representation Theorem). *Let $\varphi, \psi \in \mathcal{H}$ and $V \subseteq \mathcal{A}$. The following conditions are equivalent to each other:*

(i) ψ is a result of strong forgetting V from φ.
(ii) $\psi \equiv \{\psi' \in \mathcal{H} \mid \varphi \models \psi'$ and $\mathsf{IR}(\psi', V)\}$.
*(iii) The postulates (**W**), (**PP**), (**NP**) and (**IR**) hold for φ, ψ and L.*

3.3 Sufficient and Necessary Conditions

We are now in the position to present the notion of sufficient and necessary conditions and connect it with strong forgetting.

For a given process, a formula or a theory e, by $var(e)$ we denote the set of channels occurring in e. For instance, $var([a, \overline{b}]\top) = \{a, b\}$, $var(a.\overline{b}.0) = \{a, b\}$. A formula (or theory) e of $\mathcal{H}$ is *on* $V \subseteq \mathcal{A}$ if it is irrelevant to the channels not in V, *i.e.*, $\mathsf{IR}(e, \mathcal{A} - V)$. In this case we say e is of $V \subseteq \mathcal{A}$ if $var(e) \subseteq V$.

Definition 6 (Sufficient Condition and Necessary Condition). *Let $\varphi, \psi \in \mathcal{H}$, $T \subseteq \mathcal{H}$, $V \subseteq var(T) \cup var(\varphi)$ and $var(\psi) \subseteq V$.*

- *ψ is a* sufficient condition *of φ on V under T if $T \models \psi \rightarrow \varphi$. It is a* weakest sufficient condition *(WSC in short) of φ on V under T if it is a sufficient condition of φ on V under T and, for any sufficient condition ψ' of φ on V under T, $\psi' \models \psi$.*
- *ψ is a* necessary condition *of φ on V under T if $T \models \varphi \rightarrow \psi$. It is a* strongest necessary condition *(SNC in short) of φ on V under T if it is a necessary condition of φ on V under T and, for any necessary condition ψ' of φ on V under T, $\psi \models \psi'$.*

The following theorem establishes the close connection between strong forgetting and the weakest sufficient condition and strongest necessary condition.

Theorem 2. *Let $\varphi, \psi \in \mathcal{H}$, $T \subseteq \mathcal{H}$, $V \subseteq var(T) \cup var(\varphi)$ and $L = (var(T) \cup var(\varphi)) - V$.*

(i) $\mathrm{F}^{\sim}(\{\varphi\} \cup T, L)$ is a strongest necessary condition of φ on V under T.
(ii) $\neg\mathrm{F}^{\sim}(\{\neg\varphi\} \cup T, L)$ is a weakest sufficient condition of φ on V under T.

Example 3. Let $T = \{[a](\langle b\rangle\top \wedge [a]\bot)\}$, $\psi = \langle a\rangle\langle b\rangle\top$ and $V = \{a\}$. Suppose that the originally implemented agent $b.0$ for the specification T needs to satisfy the new specification ψ due to some new requirement. It is clear that $b.0 \models T$, $b.0 \not\models \psi$ and $T \not\models \psi$.

[3] Here the knowledge means "logical consequence".

Assume further that one is required, based on the original implementation $b.0$, to implement a new agent satisfying the new specification and the new one is restricted to use actions $a, \overline{a}$ only. We can show that, $\neg\mathrm{F}^{\sim}(T \cup \{\neg\psi\}, V) \equiv \neg[a]\bot \equiv \langle a\rangle\top$ is a WSC on $\{a\}$ of ψ under T. Consequently, the revision on the original implementation $b.0$ is possible by simply "composing" the agent $a.b.0$, which satisfies T, ψ and $\langle a\rangle\top$.

4 Concluding Remarks

In this short paper, we have presented a potential principle for revision reactive systems from the perspective of the weakest sufficient condition. It is obtained from the logical knowledge forgetting in terms of strong bisimulation over restricted signatures. These results are very preliminary and will be deeply and widely investigated, including existence, algorithms and complexities relating to the forgetting.

Acknowledgement. This work is partially supported by NSFC under grants 62376066 and 61976065 and Guizhou Science Support Project (2022-259).

References

1. Aceto, L., Ingólfsdóttir, A., Larsen, K.G., Srba, J.: Reactive Systems: Modelling, Specification and Verification. Cambridge University Press, Cambridge (2007). https://doi.org/10.1017/CBO9780511814105
2. Fang, L., Liu, Y., van Ditmarsch, H.: Forgetting in multi-agent modal logics. Artif. Intell. **266**, 51–80 (2019). https://doi.org/10.1016/j.artint.2018.08.003
3. Feng, R., Acar, E., Wang, Y., Liu, W., Schlobach, S., Ding, W.: Computing sufficient and necessary conditions in CTL: a forgetting approach. Inf. Sci. **616**, 474–504 (2022). https://doi.org/10.1016/j.ins.2022.10.124
4. Feng, R., Wang, Y., Qian, R., Yang, L., Chen, P.: Knowledge forgetting in propositional μ-calculus. Ann. Math. Artif. Intell. **91**(1), 1–43 (2023). https://doi.org/10.1007/s10472-022-09803-4
5. Gonçalves, R., Knorr, M., Leite, J.: Forgetting in answer set programming - a survey. Theory Pract. Log. Program. **23**(1), 111–156 (2023). https://doi.org/10.1017/S1471068421000570
6. Lin, F.: On strongest necessary and weakest sufficient conditions. Artif. Intell. **128**(1-2), 143–159 (2001). https://doi.org/10.1016/S0004-3702(01)00070-4
7. Milner, R.: Communication and Concurrency. Prentice Hall International Series in computer science, Prentice Hall (1989)
8. Stirling, C.: Modal and Temporal Properties of Processes, Texts in Computer Science. Springer, Berlin (2001). https://doi.org/10.1007/978-1-4757-3550-5
9. Wang, Y., Liu, H., Zhang, Y., Zhang, M., Li, D., Yang, J.: What's new is the evolution of propositional knowledge bases? J. Guizhou Univ. (Nat. Sci.) **41**(01), 1–19 (2024). https://doi.org/10.15958/j.cnki.gdxbzrb.2024.01.01

10. Zhang, Y., Zhou, Y.: Knowledge forgetting: properties and applications. Artif. Intell. **173**(16-17), 1525–1537 (2009). https://doi.org/10.1016/j.artint.2009.07.005
11. Zhao, Y., et al.: Tracking logical difference in large-scale ontologies: a forgetting-based approach. In: The Thirty-Third AAAI Conference on Artificial Intelligence, AAAI 2019, The Thirty-First Innovative Applications of Artificial Intelligence Conference, IAAI 2019, The Ninth AAAI Symposium on Educational Advances in Artificial Intelligence, EAAI 2019, Honolulu, Hawaii, USA, 27 January – 1 February 2019, pp. 3116–3124. AAAI Press (2019). https://doi.org/10.1609/aaai.v33i01.33013116

Correction to: ISS-Scenario: Scenario-Based Testing in CARLA

Renjue Li, Tianhang Qin, and Cas Widdershoven

Correction to:
Chapter 16 in: W.-N. Chin and Z. Xu (Eds.): *Theoretical Aspects of Software Engineering*, LNCS 14777,
https://doi.org/10.1007/978-3-031-64626-3_16

The original version of the chapter has been revised. Chapter 16 was inadvertently published with incorrect author affiliation for Renjue Li, Tianhang Qin and Cas Widdershoven.

The updated version of this chapter can be found at
https://doi.org/10.1007/978-3-031-64626-3_16

W.-N. Chin and Z. Xu (Eds.): TASE 2024, LNCS 14777, p. C1, 2025.
https://doi.org/10.1007/978-3-031-64626-3_28

Correction to: [illegible]SS-Scenario: Scenario-Bas[illegible] Testing in CARLA

Author Index

W.-N. Chin and Z. Xu (Eds.): TASE 2024, LNCS 14777, pp. 473–474, 2024.
https://doi.org/10.1007/978-3-031-64626-3

Zeitfracht Medien GmbH
Ferdinand-Jühlke-Straße 7
99095 Erfurt, Deutschland
produktsicherheit@kolibri360.de